INSIDE THE OVAL OFFICE

---

*The White House Tapes
from FDR to Clinton*

WILLIAM DOYLE

KODANSHA INTERNATIONAL
New York • Tokyo • London

To Naomi
and Marilou, Bill, Kate, and Joe

Kodansha America, Inc.
575 Lexington Ave., New York, New York 10022, U.S.A.

Kodansha International Ltd.
17-14 Otowa 1-chome, Bunkyo-ku, Tokyo 112-8652, Japan

Published in hardcover in 1999 by Kodansha America, Inc.
First paperback edition 2002

Library of Congress Cataloging-in-Publication Data
Doyle, William, 1957–
    Inside the Oval Office : the White House tapes from FDR to
Clinton / William Doyle.
        p. cm.
    Includes bibliographical references and index.
    ISBN 1-56836-285-4
        1-56836-316-8 (pbk.)
    1. Presidents—United States—History—20th century—Sources.
2. Presidents—United States—Biography. 3. Executive power—United
States—History—20th century—Sources. 4. United States—Politics
and government—1945–1989—Sources. 5. United States—Politics and
government—1989—Sources. 6. Audiotapes. 7. White House
(Washington, D.C.) I. Title.
E176.1.D73 1999
973.91'092'2—dc21   98-47389
[B]

Designed by Tina Thompson

Manufactured in the United States of America

02 03 04 05 06   10 9 8 7 6 5 4 3 2 1

Contents

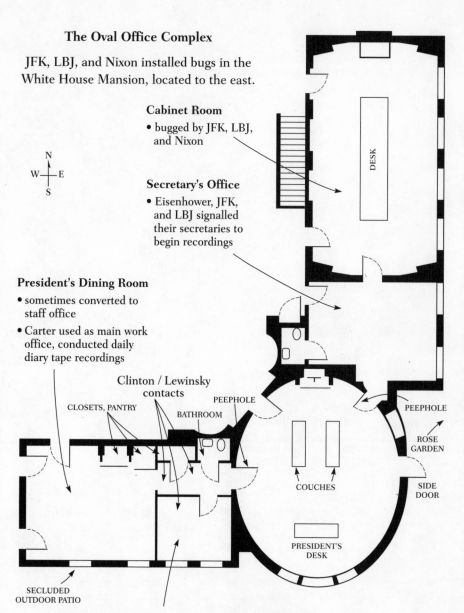

The Oval Office Complex

JFK, LBJ, and Nixon installed bugs in the White House Mansion, located to the east.

Cabinet Room
- bugged by JFK, LBJ, and Nixon

Secretary's Office
- Eisenhower, JFK, and LBJ signalled their secretaries to begin recordings

N
W—E
S

President's Dining Room
- sometimes converted to staff office
- Carter used as main work office, conducted daily diary tape recordings

Clinton / Lewinsky contacts

CLOSETS, PANTRY

BATHROOM

PEEPHOLE

PEEPHOLE

ROSE GARDEN

SIDE DOOR

COUCHES

PRESIDENT'S DESK

DESK

SECLUDED OUTDOOR PATIO

President's Private Study
- built by Eisenhower for post-heart attack naps
- JFK's "prayer room" for private calls
- LBJ's "Little Study," bugged for intimate meetings

Illustration: National Archives

The Oval Office
- William Howard Taft built office in 1909
- destroyed in 1929 fire
- FDR remodeled in 1934, moved from center-south West Wing to sunnier SE corner
- room bugged by FDR, Truman (briefly), Eisenhower, JFK, LBJ (phones only), and Nixon
- Reagan head-of-state phone calls recorded through basement Situation Room

America's Chief Executives Caught on Tape

On a late summer day in 1940, an inventor named J. Ripley Kiel was marched through a side door into the White House, and, closely flanked by a team of Secret Service men, was secretly ushered into the Oval Office, where he took up position behind Franklin Roosevelt's cluttered desk.

The president was on a working vacation hundreds of miles away, savoring sun-drenched waters off the coast of New England, enjoying long country drives and roadside picnics in his shirt-sleeves, nestled among carpets of tall grass, laughing in the summer haze. World War II was erupting across Europe and Asia, but in FDR's neutral America it was an invincible summer bright with hope and promise.

Inside the Oval Office, as Secret Service men looked on from a few feet away, J. Ripley Kiel plugged in a power tool and drilled a hole in Roosevelt's desk drawer, then the bottom of the desk, then another in the Oval Office floor itself, until it opened up to reveal the storage area below. He planted a microphone in a lamp on FDR's desk, ran a line through the holes down into the room below, and connected it to his invention, an experimental sound-recording machine.

The device was a predecessor of the tape recorder and was very high-tech by 1930s standards. It used a recording needle to feed sound signals onto ribbons of motion-picture sound film, and had a sound-activation feature that enabled it to record or idle unattended for up to twenty-four hours. Kiel proudly noted that it was the first audio recorder to feature instant playback, which eliminated the need for time-consuming processing. He split the Oval Office phone line into the machine, and installed a concealed control panel right in FDR's desk drawer, with buttons for RECORD, PAUSE, REWIND, IDLE, and PLAYBACK, plus a switch to record phone calls.

After three straight days of work and sound tests, J. Ripley Kiel pronounced the installation was complete. He placed a year's supply of recording film next to the machine in its basement chamber and was escorted out of the building. For the first time in history, the Oval Office was wired for sound.

Over the next six decades, Roosevelt and many of his successors periodically used the Oval Office as a private recording studio. They drilled microphones into White House walls, drawers, and light fixtures, wired the microphones into recording devices in secret chambers near the Oval Office, rigged secret switches into tables, desks, and lamps, and tapped presidential phone lines with Dictaphone machines stashed away in closets. Other times, they ordered stenographers, note-takers, and even video cameras to openly record White House business.

In most cases, the recorders were installed by the presidents as executive tools, as backup record-keeping devices to protect themselves in the world's most hazardous job. The tapes and transcripts left behind from this sixty-year recording experiment are a cockpit voice recorder of the presidency, a "black box" of American history that reveals the fly-on-the-wall drama of the presidents as executives in action behind closed doors, providing glimpses of the flesh-and-blood humanity of the executives who sat behind the Oval Office desk.

The moment a president is sworn into office he becomes not only America's national leader and chief politician, but the chief executive of what Harry Truman called "the largest going concern in the world," an organization with 3.5 million employees, a $2 trillion budget, and an arsenal of over 25,000 nuclear warheads. The authors of the U.S. Constitution of 1787 defined the job in a brief description: "The executive Power shall be vested in a President of the United States of America."

Presidents are often analyzed as leaders and politicians, but rarely as executives, since that side of the presidency is sealed shut as soon as the Oval Office door closes and the real work of the White House begins. The Oval Office tapes change that.

This book explores how history is shaped by the presidents' closed-door executive strengths and weaknesses, as illustrated by tapes, transcripts, and other Oval Office raw materials, as well as the testimony of Oval Office insiders back to the days of Franklin Roosevelt.

Years after his disgrace and resignation, Richard Nixon ruminated on the injustice of being so completely manacled to the Oval Office tapes by history, knowing full well that several other presidents conducted Oval Office recordings without their guests' knowledge. Nixon recalled, "I remember the headlines: NIXON BUGGED HIMSELF. Well, as a matter of fact, what really, I must say, at first amused me, and then it angered me, was to see the hypocritical, sanctimonious statements by people representing the Kennedy camp and the Johnson camp saying, oh, they had never had a taping system, they were horrified that there ever could have been a taping system in the White House. Now come on, who are they kidding?"

Historian Robert Dallek observed that "it is exceedingly difficult to get an accurate and precise record of what goes on in the White House." Many of the modern presidents actively discouraged the taking of verbatim notes, to encourage candid discussions. "There is noble talk in the Oval Office to be sure, high-minded and disinterested," Richard Nixon wrote in his memoirs. "But there are also frustration, worry, anxiety, profanity, and, above all, raw pragmatism when it comes to politics and political survival." His chief of staff, Alexander Haig, reported, "I've served seven presidents, four at very close range. Let me tell you that they are all different in character, but they all have said things that they never want repeated in the Oval Office," and there are remarkably few verbatim records of White House business.

Oval Office recordings are far from a perfect record. With the exception of hard-core tapers like JFK, LBJ, and Nixon, only microscopic portions of White House presidential business were recorded. By definition, when a president knows hidden microphones or visible video cameras are rolling and a record is being made, he behaves differently from how he would otherwise (Nixon being a colossal exception to this logic). The quality of the Roosevelt recordings is generally poor, the Eisenhower Dictabelts are worse, and the fragmentary Truman recordings are atrocious. Also, Truman was extremely soft spoken, so the distant voice patterns that are faintly, briefly audible through the riot of noise damage are little more than acoustical ghosts and shadows.

The Oval Office tapes also suffer from the fact that they take forever to transcribe, and no matter who does the transcribing, errors are guaranteed. "Every journey into the past is complicated by delusions, false memories, false namings of real events," wrote the poet Adrienne Rich, and the Oval Office tapes are a perfect example. During the Watergate trials, Nixon aides read through transcripts while tapes were played in court and said to one another: "You didn't say that, I did." Years later, former Nixon Chief of Staff H. R. Haldeman warned: "If you want to use the tapes, you have got to listen to them, you have got to draw your conclusions from what is said rather than letting someone else tell you . . . the best transcripts that could be produced for the trial were grossly inaccurate and misleading." Transcripts are an extremely inexact exercise and can miss shadings, nuances, and ambiguities of conversation. Henry Kissinger, who said it was "wrong for presidents to tape visitors in their office without their knowledge," predicted "it's very likely to be a misleading historical record," since conversations would be taken out of context.

Even with all their limitations, the Oval Office tapes do offer something no other source can: a real-time record of the presidents as executives in action as they manage the business of American history. Lyndon Johnson once showed historian Doris Kearns Goodwin a set of transcripts, presumably created from telephone recordings, and declared that from them she "could learn more about the way the government really works than from a hundred political science textbooks." The Oval Office tapes demonstrate, in the words of historian Geoffrey C. Ward, "that politics is not a science. You can hear real people wrestling with real problems and making mistakes and changing their minds and blowing off steam. I don't think presidents should record their conversations, but since some of them have, they are absolutely priceless records of what went on in that room, which is the most important room in the United States."

The Oval Office on Fire

DECEMBER 24, 1929, 5:30 P.M.

The White House glittered in the twilight snow with a thousand colored lights as the sounds of a Christmas Eve children's party drifted through the mansion and the president of the United States sat in his office putting the finishing touches on a radio speech to the nation, oblivious to the disasters hurtling toward him.

The oval-shaped office was a dreary, desolate cavern, whose green burlap walls were naked except for a small pen-and-ink portrait of Lincoln. It was one of the worst ventilated rooms in Washington, and contained no furniture other than the presidential desk, two squat bookcases, and a couple of cane-backed chairs.

The room's unusual elliptical design traced back to the first presidential offices in Philadelphia, where George Washington installed bow windows and curved walls to create oval staterooms. This was to continue the British tradition of the levee, when Washington, resplendent in powdered hair and silver buckles, slowly greeted dignitaries surrounding him in a circle. Every president from John Adams to William McKinley worked in offices on the second floor of the White House mansion, until 1902, when Theodore Roosevelt built the West Wing office extension and 1909, when William Howard Taft built and moved into the Oval Office. (The term "Oval Office" didn't come into widespread use until the 1970s.) Author Theodore White found the thirty-five-foot-long, twenty-eight-foot-wide space "almost too peaceful and luminous a place to echo to the ominous concerns that weigh upon the man who occupies it. Its great French windows, eleven and a half feet high, flood it with light, so that even on somber days it is never dark. From the south windows the president can, in leafless winter, see through the trees all the way to the Washington Monument and beyond; he can, by craning, see west to the Memorial where Lincoln broods."

The man at the desk, Herbert Hoover, was known as "The Great Engineer," and by some estimates he was the greatest humanitarian of the century, when measured in lives saved by his postwar relief efforts. He was a crushingly dour personality, but tonight he had reason to celebrate. The country was cruising through the final days of a decade of prosperity, during which he, first as secretary of commerce and now as president, joined with the titans of industry to promote scientific management and mass production. The nation blossomed with investment, factories, automobiles, radio networks, and even the first experimental TV broadcast, starring Hoover himself. Golden horizons of progress seemed to stretch out before him in the winter night. Eight weeks earlier, Wall Street had been shocked by a sudden collapse in share prices, with industrials losing 30 percent of their value, but a substantial recovery was under way and the latest economic figures indicated an overall normal year, with the crash appearing to be a sizable but aberrant fluke.

Just after 5:30 P.M., Hoover left his office for the annual Christmas tree lighting and to broadcast holiday greetings to the nation via a network radio hookup. At about the same time, in a secretary's office down the hall, a spark from an overheated fireplace landed on a wooden beam and began a smoldering fire that slowly crept up through the ceiling joist and into the attic.

As Hoover sat down to dinner in the mansion with the children and families of White House staff, the fire was spreading across the attic and burning through to the roof. Just after 8:00 P.M., White House switchboard operator W. W. Rice, on duty in the West Wing basement, noticed wisps of smoke curling into his room. On the floor above, White House police sergeant T. R. Trice was patrolling in the main reception hall, and walked into a stream of smoke curling from a basement stairway. Rice and Trice ran into each other, rushed to the firebox, and triggered the alarm at 8:09 P.M. Within minutes, fire trucks were racing to the scene from all directions.

In the state dining room of the White House mansion, while pudding was being served, news of the fire was whispered to Hoover so as not to cause a panic. Hoover pulled a heavy brown overcoat tightly over his dinner jacket, donned a gray fedora, grabbed his cigar, and hurried to the portico overlooking the West Wing to see the roof ablaze and smoke billowing over the lawn. "Look at that smoke pouring out of those windows!" he exclaimed. As the fire ate into the White House phone system and press room, firemen clambered up and chopped holes near the roof and sprayed tons of water into the building. The president called down, "Save my files!"

The White House was soon besieged by sixteen engine companies, five truck companies, five fuel wagons, a water tower, the district fire chief and all battalion chiefs, along with 150 reserve policemen, 100 soldiers, and a crowd of thousands of spectators surging around the tall iron gates. The night was so cold that the spray from the fire trucks froze as it fell, glazing the rungs of the scaling ladders. Firemen slipped and skidded on ice as they hauled at a maze of hoses crisscrossing the White House grounds.

Hoover rushed back to the rear of the building past snow-covered lawns first sculpted by Thomas Jefferson, peered through thick smoke, and was horrified to see flames dancing up the walls and the collapsing ceiling of the Oval Office. On his orders, Secret Service men began charging into the blaze to rescue his confidential files and anything else they could carry—rugs, draperies, drawers, chairs. A fireman named Fred Stine ran through carpets of smoke and water and brought out the presidential flag. Hoover's desk was too heavy to be moved, so the drawers were ripped out and it was left to the flames. White House physician Joel T. Boone saw Hoover himself struggling to carry out furniture through the smashed windows of the office.

Meanwhile, thick iron-grilled windows on the top floor blocked the fire-fighters as they tried to break into the attic where the fire was centered, so they chopped their way through an outside wall and layers of hard yellow pine partitions. At 9:52 a team of firemen scrambled onto the sagging roof and shot a hose down into the west end of the offices, but at that moment a huge flame burst through the roof, forcing the firemen to swing around to protect themselves. Fearing a total collapse, their chief soon ordered them off the roof.

By 11:00 that night the White House West Wing was a smoldering ruin, and before long, so was Hoover's presidency.

The White House Christmas Eve fire of 1929 coincided with the beginning of Hoover's end as America's last non-nuclear, pre-superpower president, the last in a long line of manager-presidents who administered the job but could not lead the nation as strong chief executives. After George Washington's epochal two terms, the office was populated often by gentle mediocrities who deferred to Congress and withdrew to the White House in cocoons of impotence, lethargy, and hesitation, a string broken periodically by forceful executives such as Jefferson, Jackson, Polk, Lincoln, Teddy Roosevelt, Woodrow Wilson, and, on his good days, Grover Cleveland.

By 1930, Hoover's America was lurching into an economic collapse of near-medieval proportions. From 1930 to 1933, national income dove from $81 billion to $39 billion. In 1932, 273,000 families were evicted from their homes. Hoover urged caution, supported private relief efforts, and even experimented with reforms that later would be expanded into FDR's New

Deal, but he proved incapable of solving the crisis, and became the most hated man in America. In the last days of his presidency, 13 million people were unemployed, 1 million roamed the country in boxcars, food riots were breaking out as relief stations ran out of cash, banks were closed or suspended in twenty-three states, and the New York Stock Exchange shut down.

Into the smashed rubble of the presidency there now appeared the dazzling figure of Franklin D. Roosevelt, governor of the most populous state in the country and a man with a radically new conception of the office. "The presidency is not merely an administrative office," he declared. "That's the least of it. It is more than an engineering job, efficient or inefficient. It is preeminently a place of moral leadership." To no one's surprise he buried Hoover in the election, and as the transition period started, Hoover began pleading with Roosevelt to join him in a joint plan of action to stabilize the economy and the nation's confidence.

On November 17, 1932, nine days after the election, Roosevelt responded to Hoover's suggestion that they meet at the White House to discuss the foreign debt by phoning Hoover to set up the meeting. Hoover hated FDR, calling him "a gibbering idiot" and "a chameleon on plaid." "Hoover and Roosevelt prepared for the conference with mutual suspicion as dark as though they were heads of two great rival states near the brink of war," reported historian Frank Freidel.

"The president doesn't want to see him alone," wrote Hoover's secretary of state, Henry L. Stimson. "He has been warned by so many people that Roosevelt will shift his words, that he wants some witnesses. So he is proposing to call some congressional leaders to meet Roosevelt at that time. Roosevelt doesn't want to meet them." Hoover now faced the dilemma of how to pin down what the notoriously fickle Roosevelt said during the phone call, so he resorted to a technique used by diplomats, politicians, and executives ever since the dawn of the telephone: having a stenographer sit in on an extension, or "dead key," listen to the conversation, and write down every word—a "manual bugging."

When Roosevelt's call came in from New York, a White House stenographer came on the line and the two bitter enemies began talking. At the end of the call, Hoover tried to pin FDR to an agreement to include congressmen in their meeting to act as witnesses. FDR seemed to agree to the plan, but soon pulled the rug out from under the tormented Hoover, providing a preview of the improvisational, volatile executive style that would dominate the country for the next twelve years.

After hanging up, Hoover quickly fired off a telegram to Roosevelt to confirm their telephone agreement, but it was too late. FDR had already changed his mind and wired back that he'd rather not include congressmen in the meeting. "Let's concentrate on one thing," FDR told a friend during the transition. "Save the people and save the nation and, if we have to change our minds twice a day to accomplish that end, we should do it." When Roosevelt got to the White House for their meeting on November 22, Hoover was seething with contempt. As the meeting ended, when the wheelchair-bound Roosevelt motioned for his aides to leave the room, Hoover snapped out, "Nobody leaves before the president."

Through the transition period, Roosevelt tortured Hoover by refusing to commit to any joint efforts to rescue the economy. He knew that job was his alone, starting on Inauguration Day. On his last day as president, Hoover looked out the Oval Office window toward the Washington Monument with reddened eyes and said the country was in "a hell of a fix." On the ride to the Capitol for the swearing-in, Hoover refused to speak to FDR.

After Roosevelt's inaugural address, spectators seated at the base of the Capitol building were witness to an astonishing sight. FDR, in top hat and formal clothes, leaned heavily on his son's arm and began lurching down a long ramp from the Capitol steps to his car, in a slow and highly precarious simulation of walking, in full view of the spectators. Roosevelt shifted and pivoted his powerful upper body in semicircular motions, rotating his hips to propel his paralyzed legs, locked straight in a pair of metal braces, out in front of him, one after another. During the ordeal, Roosevelt looked down to check if his legs were hitting their marks as he shuffled forward, then raised his head to project an illuminating, reassuring smile.

Later that day, when Roosevelt was wheeled into the Oval Office for the first time as president, he hoisted himself into the presidential chair and surveyed the room from behind the grand mahogany desk presented to Hoover by furniture makers in Grand Rapids to replace the one ruined in the 1929 fire.

He sat in the office, totally alone, with nothing to be heard or seen. The place was empty. He opened the desk drawers, but they were bare. He couldn't even write a note. He knew there were buttons to push, but he didn't know where. The control room of the American government was dead in the water.

For a couple of minutes he sat there, wondering where everybody was and what he should do next. He hadn't a clue.

So finally, he leaned back in his swivel chair and shouted at the barren Oval Office walls.

CHAPTER I

Franklin D. Roosevelt
The Creative Executive

*"The country needs, and unless I mistake,
the country demands, bold persistent experimentation."*

FRANKLIN ROOSEVELT, 1932

THE OVAL OFFICE
SEPTEMBER 27, 1940, 11:30 A.M.

A delegation of civil rights leaders was filing into the Oval Office to push Franklin Roosevelt to embrace a radical, explosive concept: integrate the armed forces of the United States. Privately, Roosevelt thought it might be a good idea some day in the future. Today it was the last thing he wanted to do. It was the dawn of World War II, a national election was weeks away, he had many other battles to wage, and he had to buy time.

What Roosevelt's guests did not know was that the president was secretly recording them through a microphone hidden in his desk lamp, which connected to an experimental sound machine hidden in a padlocked chamber right under their feet. Roosevelt had just recorded a press conference, and the machine was still running.

Taking their positions on one side of the Oval Office were the two most powerful black civil rights leaders of the day: A. Philip Randolph, president of the Brotherhood of Sleeping Car Porters and one of the most orotund, forceful speakers of his time, and lawyer Walter White, secretary of the National Association for the Advancement of Colored People and an anti-lynching crusader, whose fractional ethnic connection to African Americans—he was 1/64th black—only magnified his passion for equal justice. White's fair-skinned father died in excruciating pain when surgeons at the white wing of an Atlanta hospital, where he had been mistakenly taken for an emergency operation, refused to treat him.

On the other side of the office were Secretary of the Navy Frank Knox, a former Rough Rider and a Republican appointed by FDR in a spirit of bipartisanship, and Robert Patterson, assistant secretary of war, both of whom flatly opposed the concept of integrating the military. Patterson's boss, Secretary of War Henry Stimson, thought the whole idea was ridiculous, and boycotted the meeting altogether. Stimson found any meeting with the president to be an ordeal of exasperation, and wrote in his diary: "His mind does not follow easily a consecutive chain of thought but he is full of stories and incidents and hops about in his discussions from suggestion to suggestion and it is very much like chasing a vagrant beam of sunshine around a vacant room."

Between the two camps sat Roosevelt, a striking, blue-eyed man of fifty-eight with a huge chest and shoulders and thinning gray hair atop a large, fleshy head that projected an incandescent smile and a booming voice that were the essence of supreme confidence and command. The public believed he had largely conquered the polio that struck him in 1921, and he promoted the deception through an elaborate shell game of ramps, staged photos, black painted braces worn with dark shoes and socks, and concealed entrances and exits. The mass illusion was aided and abetted by a sympathetic White House press corps, who, at the 1936 Democratic Convention, physically blocked other photographers from snapping Roosevelt as he tumbled and nearly fell on his way to the podium just before his keynote address. Roosevelt said publicly he was a "recovered cripple" and just "a bit lame." The truth was that he was totally paralyzed from the waist down, a prisoner behind his desk all day, who went to the bathroom by calling for a valet and water bottle.

The desk he sat behind was usually cluttered with dispatches and reports spilling out of wire in-baskets and a forest of over 100 knickknacks: lighters, paperweights, stuffed elephants and toy donkeys, a "Snooty the Love Dog" doll, salt and pepper shakers, a can of Camel cigarettes, Uncle Sam hats, and during the war years, a matching pair of comic figurines, "Benito" and "Adolf." The clutter was so thick, some papers piled on the table behind his desk waited for President Roosevelt's signature for as long as six months.

The writer John Gunther, observing Roosevelt at close range in an Oval Office press conference, observed: "He has a big head, very tanned; he cocks the whole head continually, snapping his eyes this way and that as it finishes an arc; talks with a cigarette holder clenched between his teeth, at the extreme corner of the mouth; blinks to get smoke out of his eyes. . . . In twenty minutes Mr. Roosevelt's features had expressed amazement, curiosity, mock alarm, genuine interest, worry, rhetorical playing for suspense, sympathy, decision, playfulness, dignity, and surpassing charm. Yet he *said* almost nothing. Questions were deflected, diverted, diluted. Answers—when they did come—were concise and clear. But I never met anyone who showed greater capacity for avoiding a direct answer while giving the questioner a feeling he *had* been answered."

In a 1934 renovation, Roosevelt moved the Oval Office from the center rear of the West Wing to the sunnier southeast corner, which allowed him to be rolled in his special wheeled chair (not a conventional wheelchair, but an armless kitchen chair adapted with small wheels and an ashtray) from the mansion in comfort and privacy through Thomas Jefferson's covered colonnade, past the Cabinet Room windows, down the porch, and through a side door into the office. According to White House historian William Peale, the new office was "furnished somewhat more elaborately than its predecessor," and "had rather theatrical neocolonial trimmings, somewhat in the Moderne vein. The most important doors had heavy pediments, while doors of secondary status had shell-shaped niches over them." Earlier presidents had kept the Oval Office walls almost bare, but FDR blanketed them with prints of navy ships and Hudson River landscapes where he could look at them through the workday.

It was on the banks of the Hudson that FDR was born and bred on a diet of smothering love and attention, the pampered son of an elderly millionaire and his indomitable wife, who lived in a grand mansion overlooking vistas of sylvan beauty. "FDR was supremely confident," said historian Geoffrey C. Ward. "His mother taught him that he was the center of the universe and that he was the sun around which everything revolved. He never lost that attitude."

Roosevelt prepared for the presidency with a two-track career in business and government split between New York State and Washington, D.C. After starting out as a law clerk at a Wall Street firm (and occasional White House guest of his cousin and hero President Theodore Roosevelt), he became a state senator in Albany, then spent 1913 through 1920 as assistant secretary of the navy. World War I, wrote historian James MacGregor Burns, "had a maturing effect on Roosevelt. Long hours, tough decisions, endless conferences, exhausting trips, hard bargaining with powerful officials in Washington and abroad turned him into a seasoned politician-administrator." After running for vice president on Democrat Al Smith's failed 1920 ticket, he spent most of the next decade in multiple business ventures, as a lawyer, insurance man, and investor, all the while helping to manage his family's estate in Hyde Park.

Sharper outlines of Roosevelt's creative and improvisational executive style emerged during his career as a budding venture capitalist during the Roaring Twenties. He speculated in a dizzying portfolio of schemes: transatlantic dirigibles, Maine lobster futures, oil wildcatting in Wyoming, resort hotels, taxicab advertising, and vending machines. He was rarely successful. "As war administrator, as businessman, as president," wrote Burns, "he liked to try new things, to take a dare, to bring something off with a flourish." His 1921 attack of polio and years of attempted rehabilitation resulted in what his longtime aide Frances Perkins called "a spiritual transformation" that "purged the slightly arrogant attitude he had displayed on occasion before he was stricken. The man emerged completely warmhearted, with humility of spirit."

After two terms as a generally effective, progressive governor of New York, the second biggest job in the United States, Roosevelt entered the White House with a near mystical self-assurance. FDR's formula for effectiveness in the job was simple: "What is needed is a wide previous experience in government problems generally and a versatility of mind that can take up one subject after another during the day and find itself at home in all of them."

On September 27, 1940, Roosevelt was at a crossroads between the two great crises of his presidency: the Depression and the outbreak of World War II. For seven years he had navigated the country through the lingering misery of the Depression with a public leadership style of charisma and compassion, and a closed-door executive style of insouciant charm, creative tension, chaos, delay, and improvisation. Vice President Henry Wallace asserted that FDR "could keep all the balls in the air without losing his own."

Now, as the summer of 1940 turned to fall, the world was going up in flames.

In Berlin, Hitler was issuing plans for a cross-channel invasion of Britain, after incinerating London with raids by up to 1,500 aircraft per day since early August in the Battle of Britain. German troops had already surged into Czechoslovakia, Poland, Denmark, Norway, Holland, Belgium, and France. In Asia, Japanese forces were consolidating their conquests in China and Manchuria and were now invading Indochina—15,000 Japanese had just occupied Hanoi. In September, FDR had evaded Congress and granted fifty warships to Britain, but he was still performing a geopolitical high-wire act he hoped might keep the United States out of the war. He commanded a banana-republic military: his army ranked as only the eighteenth in the world, behind Germany, Japan, England, France, Spain, Switzerland—behind even Portugal, Holland, and Belgium.

At the same time, Roosevelt was in the midst of campaigning for an unprecedented third term, against the strongest contender the Republicans ever threw against him, businessman Wendell Willkie. In these final weeks, the campaign had descended into a bitter death struggle, as Willkie was dodging eggs, rotten vegetables, and lightbulbs thrown at him by panicking Democrats in cities across the United States, and pounding away at FDR as a war-mongering near-dictator. Willkie was pulling even with FDR in key states like New York as Democratic and labor bosses and even the *New York Times* deserted Roosevelt's crusade.

In this supercharged atmosphere, FDR worried that a single misquoted word—particularly in his twice-a-week, off-the-record press conferences—might trigger an unexpected disaster. The previous year, in fact, a controversy erupted when, after a closed-door White House meeting with a group of senators, he was misquoted as saying that America's defense frontier was the Rhine River in Europe, an error that could have committed the United States to going to war in the event that German troops crossed over their western border.

In the wake of this controversy, one of FDR's White House stenographers, Henry Kannee, came up with an idea—to create an exact record of FDR's comments, why not secretly rig the Oval Office for sound? Roosevelt approved, and after a failed experiment with a Dictaphone machine wired up to a microphone in Roosevelt's office, the stenographer took the problem to the RCA Corporation, which coincidentally was working on an experimental prototype of a three-and-a-half-foot-high contraption called a "Continuous-film Recording Machine," an ancestor of the tape recorder. The machine was also called a "Kiel Sound Recorder and Reporter," after J. Ripley Kiel, the Chicago inventor who invented it and licensed it to RCA. It used a recording needle to feed sound signals onto ribbons of motion-picture film. Kiel proudly described it as "the very first recording device that could record for as long as twenty-four hours unattended and could immediately have the recording played back without any time consuming processing."

RCA founder David Sarnoff donated the machine, one of only seven ever built, as a gift to FDR during a White House visit in June 1940, and the installation was performed by Kiel in August. The tall lamp on his desk was not suitable for hiding a microphone, so Kiel bought another one and hid the microphone in it. When switched on, the machine was noise activated, and began recording as soon as someone spoke or made a loud noise. Kannee, who held the key to the closet, could also activate the system by flipping a switch on the machine itself.

From August to November 1940, Roosevelt used the machine to record press conferences as a backup to his stenographer's notes. In addition to fourteen press conferences, some private Oval Office conversations and meetings were also recorded by the machine, probably absentmindedly when FDR or a staffer forgot to turn the machine off. The recordings were not found until 1978, when historian Robert J. C. Butow discovered them by accident while performing research at the FDR Library in Hyde Park, New York.

The FDR recordings reveal an intimate inside view of his patrician, gossipy, and supremely confident executive style, as he uses charm, vagueness, gossip, and occasional deviousness as tools for managing his presidency. After listening to the recordings, historian Arthur M. Schlesinger, Jr., wrote, "With all their technical imperfections, the tapes add a fascinating dimension to our sense of the Roosevelt presidency. They offer the historian the excitement of immediacy: FDR in casual, unbuttoned exchange with his staff. One is struck by how little the private voice differs from the public voice we know so well from the speeches. The tone is a rich and resonant tenor. The enunciation is clear, the timing is impeccable. The voice's range is remarkable, from high to low in register and from insinuatingly soft to emphatically loud in decibel level."

In the fall of 1940, the last thing Roosevent wanted was a fight over civil rights. He had transformed the government into an agent of social action and economic recovery, but he was not ready to commit the presidency to racial equality. His relationship with black America was complex: he was torn between his sense of decency and fair play, evidenced by his 1935 executive order banning discrimination in New Deal programs, and his pragmatic, political side, which feared those powerful Southern Democrats who prevented him even from supporting a federal anti-lynching campaign. By the mid-1930s, his juggling act was succeeding, as the party held together in the South while his wife spoke out for civil rights and convinced blacks moving onto voter rolls of northern cities that they had friends in the White House. A historic shift occurred in 1936, when blacks bolted from their traditional home in the Republican Party and joined the FDR coalition. By 1940, New Deal programs supported 1 million black families.

As America's military buildup accelerated that year, segregation in the armed forces became the "hot button" issue for African Americans, who were locked out of the military or relegated to service jobs in all branches of the service. There were only two black combat officers in the half-million-man army and none in the navy. There was not a single black soldier in the Marine Corps, Tank Corps, or Army Air Corps. Congress passed a draft law that summer pledging to increase Negro army enlistment to 10 percent, adding that "there shall be no discrimination against any person on account of race or color" anywhere in the military. The bill contained a major loophole, though, which seemed to make everything conditional on the availability of segregated military facilities, few of which existed.

A. Philip Randolph and Walter White, joined by T. Arnold Hill of the Urban League, asked for a meeting with the president to clarify his view of the bill. White House staffers ignored their request. The group then appealed to Mrs. Roosevelt, who booked the meeting directly with FDR.

THE OVAL OFFICE
SEPTEMBER 27, 1940, 11:30 A.M.

President Franklin Roosevelt with Civil Rights Leaders
RE: *Integration of U.S. Military Forces*
audio recording on 35mm motion-picture film (RCA/Kiel machine)

On the eve of both World War II and a presidential election, a delegation of black leaders lobbied FDR to desegregate the U.S. military. On the other side of the Oval Office were FDR's own government officials, dead-set against integration. Roosevelt decided to skate down a middle path of charming, almost condescending ambiguity, leading both sides to feel he agreed with them.

The meeting is a case study in miscommunication, highlights the dangers of FDR's improvisational executive style, and provoked a wave of controversy that threatened FDR's grip on the black vote as the election approached.

RANDOLPH: Mr. President, it would mean a great deal to the morale of the Negro people if you could make some announcement on the role Negroes will play in the armed forces of the nation, in the whole national defense set-up.

FDR: I did the other day! We did it the other day, when my staff told me of this thing [meeting]!

RANDOLPH: If you did it yourself, if you were to make such an announcement, it would have a tremendous effect upon the morale of the Negro people all over the country.

FDR: Yeah, yeah, yeah, yeah, yeah (*interrupting and talking over Randolph*). Now, I'm making a national defense speech around the twentieth of this month, about the draft as a whole, and the reserves, and so forth. I'll bring that in.

RANDOLPH: (*politely but firmly cutting Roosevelt off to get his point across*) It would have a tremendous effect, because I must say, it is an irritating spot for the Negro people. They feel that they are not wanted in the various armed forces of the country, and they feel they have earned their right to participate in every phase of the government by virtue of their record in past wars for the nation. And consequently, without regard to political complexion, without regard to any sort of idea whatever, the Negroes as a unit, they are feeling that they are being shunted aside, that they are being discriminated against, and that they are not wanted now.

"It was remarkable enough for anybody to interrupt FDR and to talk as much as Randolph did in a meeting," noted historian Geoffrey C. Ward, "but for a black man in that time, it's truly extraordinary." The recording soon caught FDR in a misstatement, when he claimed to be putting blacks "right in, proportionately, into the combat services," a policy that didn't begin to be implemented until late in World War II. "The trouble with the president," Harry Truman once charged, "is that he lies."

VOICE: The Negro is trying to get *in* the army!

FDR: Of course, the main point to get across in building up this draft army, the selective draft, is that we are not as we did before so much in the World War, confining the Negro in to the non-combat services. We're putting him *right in*, proportionately, into the *combat services*.

RANDOLPH: We feel that's something.

FDR: Which is, something. It's a step ahead. It's a step ahead.

WHITE: Mr. President, may I suggest another step ahead?

This has been commented on by many Negro Americans, and that is that we realize the practical reality that in Georgia and Mississippi (FDR: Yeah.) it would be impossible to have units where people's standard of admission would be ability. . . .

I'd like to suggest this idea, even though it may sound fantastic at this time, that in the states where there isn't a tradition of segregation, that we might start to experiment with organizing a division or a regiment and let them be all Americans and not black Americans or white Americans—working together.

Now, there are a number of reasons why I think that would be sound, among them that I think it would be a practical work for democracy and I think it would be less expensive and less troublesome in the long run.

FDR: Well, you see now Walter, my general report on it is this.

The thing is, we've got to *work into* this. Now, for instance, you take the divisional organization—about 12,000 men. 12, 14,000 men. Now, suppose in there that you have, one, what do they call those gun units? What?

One battery, with Negro troops, and officers, in there in that battery, like for instance New York, and another regiment, or battalion, that's a half of a regiment, of Negro troops.

They go into a division, a whole division of 12,000. And you may have a Negro regiment at work here, and right over here on my right in line would be a white regiment, in the same division. Maintain the divisional organization. Now what happens? After a while, in case of war, those people get shifted from one to the other. The thing gets backed into. We'd have one battery out of a regiment of artillery that would be a Negro battery, with the white battery here and another Negro battery, and gradually working in the field, together, you may back into what you're talking about.

RANDOLPH: I think, Mr. President, to supplement, if I may, the position of Mr. White, that idea is working in the field of organized labor. Now, for instance, there are unions where you have Negro business agents (FDR: Sure!) whereas 90 percent of the members are white. And you also even have Negroes who are parts of unions in Birmingham, Alabama, in the same union with the whites. If it can work out on the basis of democracy in the trade unions, it can in the army.

FDR: Yes. You take up on the Hudson River where Judge Patterson and I come from, we have a lot of brickworks.

RANDOLPH: Oh, yes?

FDR: Up around Fishkill, the old brickworks. Heavens, they have the same union (Randolph: Exactly.) for all the white workers and the Negro workers *in those brickworks*. (Randolph: Quite so.) And they get along, no trouble at all!

RANDOLPH: Quite so, and when they come out of their union and into the army, well, now, there isn't much justification for separating them, don't you know.

Colonel Knox, as to the navy, what is the position of the navy on the integration of the Negro in the various parts?

KNOX: You have a factor in the navy that is not present in the army, and that is that these men live aboard ships. And if I said to you that I was going to take Negroes into a ship's company [several very faint unintelligible words] this sort of thing won't do. And you can't have separate ships with a Negro crew, because everything in the navy now has to be interchangeable.

FDR: If you could have a Northern ship and a Southern ship it'd be different! (*laughs*) But you can't *do* that.

KNOX: I agree with, however, with the President's suggestion on some way of providing, in the words of the message of the Negro patriotic leaders to serve the nation without raising the question that comes from putting white men and black men living together in the same ship.

FDR: I think the proportion is going up, and one very good reason is that in the old days, ah, up to a few years ago, up to the time of the Philippine independence, practically, oh, I'd say 75 or 80 percent of the mess people on board ship, ah, were Filipinos. And, of course, we've taken in no Filipinos now for the last, what is it, four years ago, two years ago, taken in no Filipinos whatsoever.

And what we're doing, we're replacing them with colored boys— mess captain, so forth and so on.

And in that field, they can get up to the highest rating of a chief petty officer. The head mess attendant on a cruiser or a battleship is a chief petty officer.

RANDOLPH: Is there at this time a single Negro in the navy of officer status?

KNOX: There are 4,007 Negroes out of a total force at the beginning of 1940 of 139,000. They are all messmen's rank. (*chatter*)

FDR: I think, another thing, Frank [Knox], that I forgot to mention, I thought of it about a month ago, and that is this.

We are training a certain number of musicians on board ship. The ship's *band*. There's no reason why we shouldn't have a colored band on some of these ships, because they're *darn good at it*. That's something we should look into. You know, if it'll increase the *opportunity*, that's what we're after. They may develop a *leader* of the band. . . .

In the face of this unintentional insult, the civil rights leaders held their tongues. Walter White steered the discussion back to the reality of epidemic racism in the military.

WHITE: There is discrimination in the army and in the navy, and in the Air Corps, in labor in the navy yards, and particularly in industry which has contracts for the national defense program. I've just completed an article, I hope it's the last draft, for the *Saturday Evening Post,* which I gather you know about.

FDR: Yeah, yeah.

WHITE: But in Pensacola, for example, there is an apprentice school, which gives a very fine course, a four-year course, for free. But there are no Negroes allowed to go into it. And apprenticeship is tremendously important.

FDR: For flying? Ground work?

PATTERSON: Ground crews.

FDR: I think we can work on that. Get something done on that. (*chatter*)

WHITE: In Charleston, South Carolina, they practically ousted all skilled and semi-skilled Negroes.

FDR: In Charleston?

WHITE: In Charleston, yes.

FDR: Of course, on the development of this work, you've got to have somebody, for instance in the navy, you've got to have somebody [black] in the office who will look after it.

In the last Navy Department, in the old days, I had a boy who was out here by the name of Pryor. Do you know Pryor? He used to be my colored messenger in the Navy Department. He was only a kid. I gave him to Louis Howe,* who was terribly fond of him. Then when he came back here in 1933, Louis Howe said to me, "The one man I want in the office is Pryor."

Well, Pryor now is one of the best fellas we've got in the office. . . .

I think you can do that in the army and the navy. Get somebody, a boy who will act as the clearinghouse.

WHITE: An assistant, responsible to the Secretary. (*To Knox*) I want to see you about that.

FDR: (*To White, after Knox apparently gives him a stone-faced non-reply*) He's giving you what you call the silent treatment! Ha, ha, ha!

WHITE: We took the liberty of putting this out. We finished that just in time to get one set (*giving statement to FDR, apologizing for the lack of copies to give to Knox and Patterson, a likely waste of paper*), in

---

*Louis Howe, a top aide to FDR as governor of New York and as president, who died in 1936.

which we tried to give you the benefit of the comments which are most important you should be most aware about. These are—I'm not going to leave them there, you've got enough reading matter—petitions from eighty-five American Legion and Veterans of Foreign Wars posts from California to Maine protesting against discrimination.

FDR: Yup, yup, yup, yup, yup. (*Meeting breaks up amid side conversations*)

(*one-on-one with White*) Of course, what we're all after is to give some more opportunity. I used that boy as an example, Walter. I had entirely forgotten about the possibility of a Negro band, to increase the opportunity. The more of those we can get, a little opportunity here, a little opportunity there.

WHITE: Here we've been loyal in the last war—remember when they were worried about protecting Woodrow Wilson? They ordered Negroes to protect the White House. I've been trying to get—(*FDR cuts him off*)

FDR: I know it, I know it. Yeah. Well, of course, my letters are increased a bit from twenty threatening letters a day to nearly forty. But I feel all right! Ha! Ha! Goodbye!

RANDOLPH: You're looking fine, Mr. President, and I'm happy to see you again. Well, I'm proud to say that people don't like me, too. Even in Congress!

FDR: Bye!

VOICES: Goodbye, Mr. President.

Here was the president of the United States with the most influential black leaders of his time, referring to "colored" men as "boys," suggesting that mess attendant was a good career track, and that there ought to be more colored bands, "because they're darned good at it." Much of this can be explained by the fact that 1940 was a prehistoric time in race relations, and FDR had no special sensitivity to black issues beyond a patrician sense of fairness and noblesse oblige. Roosevelt treated many people with such easy, aristocratic familiarity. Dean Acheson, then assistant secretary of state, was repelled by it: "He could charm an individual or a nation. But he condescended . . . it was patronizing and humiliating. To accord the president the greatest deference and respect should be a gratification to any citizen. It is not gratifying to receive the easy greeting which milord might give a promising stable boy and pull one's forelock in return."

Like many of FDR's visitors, the civil rights delegation stepped out of the Oval Office thinking that FDR's nodding gestures and charming reassurances meant he agreed with them. But Roosevelt was not integrating combat forces and had no immediate intention of doing so. Days after the meeting, he approved a White House press release dated October 9, 1940, that announced that after the meeting with the black leaders, "the policy of the War Department is not to intermingle colored and white enlisted personnel in the same regimental organizations. This policy has proven satisfactory over a long period of years and to make changes would produce situations destructive to morale and detrimental to the preparations for national defense . . . no experiments should be tried with the organizational set-up of these units at this critical time."

Randolph and White were stunned when they read the release. The NAACP issued a furious press release on October 11: "White House Charged with Trickery in Announcing Jim Crow Policy of Army: We are inexpressibly shocked that a president of the United States at a time of national peril should surrender so completely to enemies of Democracy who would destroy national unity by advocating segregation. Official approval by the Commander-in-Chief of the Army and Navy of such discrimination is a stab in the back of Democracy and a blow at the patriotism of twelve million Negro citizens." Randolph wrote angrily to FDR: "I was shocked and amazed when I saw the newspaper reports that the Negro committee had sanctioned segregation of Negroes in the armed forces of our country because I am sure that the committee made it definitely clear that it was opposed to segregation of the armed forces of the nation." The black press launched a chorus of outrage, thousands attended a protest meeting in Harlem, and black voters began flocking to Willkie.

FDR rushed to repair the damage by issuing a statement promising steps to "ensure fair treatment on a non-discriminatory basis," and appointed several blacks to senior positions in the military. The gestures worked. The African-American press applauded, and NAACP Chairman White sent FDR a note thanking him "for all you did to insure a square deal for Negroes in the defense of our country." In the election, FDR managed to hold on to 67 percent of the black vote. FDR never delivered on his promise. While thousands of blacks served heroically in combat and support roles during the war, most were relegated to inferior positions and segregated units. Widespread racial integration in the military would have to wait for President Truman's executive order of 1948.

"You know I am a juggler, and I never let my right hand know what my left hand does," Roosevelt confessed in May 1942. "I may be entirely inconsistent, and furthermore I am perfectly willing to mislead and tell untruths if it will help win the war." Roosevelt's performance in the civil rights meeting illustrated one of the central operating principles of his protean executive style, a style that transformed the presidency, and the nation: a willingness to delay decisions, change his mind, keep his options open, avoid commitments, or even deceive people in the relentless pursuit of noble objectives. George Elsey, who as a young naval lieutenant helped run Roosevelt's secret wartime White House intelligence center, the Map Room, said, "Roosevelt had the habit of saying he was in agreement with whoever he was with and making them feel they had his full support, and he might well go off in another direction an hour later." "Roosevelt had a fairly creative relationship with the truth," noted Geoffrey Ward. "He could convince himself that what he was saying was the truth for the moment. He was a master at pleasing the visitors to his office."

Roosevelt's wife, Eleanor, who functioned mainly as an executive political deputy to her husband, saw this characteristic not as a strategy but as a personality flaw: "His real weakness," she commented, was "he couldn't bear to be disagreeable to someone he liked." "Franklin had a way, when he did not want to hear what somebody had to say, of telling stories and talking about something quite different." When FDR refused to inform Vice President Henry Wallace that he was being dropped from the ticket in 1944, Eleanor noted, "he always hopes to get things settled pleasantly and he won't realize that there are times when you have got to do an unpleasant thing directly, and, perhaps, unpleasantly." FDR crony Jim Farley spoke of the way "he forever put off things distasteful." Political boss and close FDR friend Ed Flynn wrote that FDR "did not keep his word on many appointments," and once hung up the phone on him after a perceived double-cross. Raymond Moley, a New Deal adviser, remarked, "Perhaps in the long run, fewer friends would have been lost by bluntness than by the misunderstandings that arose from engaging ambiguity."

Roosevelt's secret recorder began its trial run during an uneventful press conference on August 22, 1940, barely a month before the civil rights meeting. As soon as the press filed out of the Oval Office, in walked former newspaperman Lowell Mellett, who had just been named Roosevelt's assistant. The two had recently learned that Republican campaign operatives were about to publicize a group of bizarre and potentially embarrassing "Dear Guru" letters written by FDR's vice presidential running mate Henry Wallace to a White Russian cult leader, letters that could injure Roosevelt's reelection campaign. In retaliation, FDR was now considering unleashing a whispering campaign to promote a sex scandal against Wendell Willkie, who was thought to be having a longtime affair with a prominent New York book reviewer. The affair was fairly common knowledge in New York, and Willkie was still married to his wife while he spent extended periods with "the gal."

FDR waited until the door was closed, and then began speaking in a soft, theatrically conspiratorial voice, almost swallowing his words. He didn't want anybody else to hear, but he clearly had forgotten, or didn't care, that his brand-new experimental recorder was still humming along underneath his feet in the basement. "Ah, Lowell, on this, uh, thing, I . . . . Now, I agree with you that there is, so far as the old man [presumably FDR] goes, we can't use it publicly . . . You can't have any of our principal speakers refer to it, but people down the line can do it properly (raps desk). I mean the Congress speakers and state speakers, and so forth. They can use your material to determine the fact that Willkie left his old [several inaudible whispered words]. That's it. All right. So long as it's none of us people at the top. Now, all right, if people try to play dirty politics on me, I'm willing to try it on other people. Now, you'd be amazed at how this story about the gal is spreading around the country." Roosevelt compared the situation to that of former New York mayor Jimmy Walker, who, Roosevelt said, had an "extremely attractive little tart" for a mistress, and hired his estranged wife for $10,000 to appear publicly with him during a corruption trial. "Now, Mrs. Willkie may not have been hired," FDR speculated on the recording, "but in effect she's been hired to return to Wendell and smile and make this campaign with him."

In the end, the Republicans held their fire and did not publicize the "Guru letters," possibly because they were afraid of the type of counterstroke Roosevelt was considering on the recording, the first known electronic Oval Office recording in history. In turn, FDR never implemented the whispering campaign about Wendell Willkie's sex life. Roosevelt himself may also have feared triggering rumors about his own attachments to women other than his wife.

FDR's secret wiring of the Oval Office coincided with the dawn of the era of electronic surveillance by the U.S. government against its own citizens, a policy that began on FDR's order. A 1939 Supreme Court decision prohibited the use of wiretapping, but on May 21, 1940, three months before the Oval Office was wired, FBI Director J. Edgar Hoover received an authorization from Roosevelt directing him to use "listening devices" against people suspected of espionage and subversion. Although FDR intended the order to apply only to matters of extreme and imminent danger to national security (such as sabotage or espionage), Hoover used this document as his authorization to use wiretaps against a broad spectrum of targets for the next three decades. In 1975, a Senate investigation found evidence that Roosevelt authorized Hoover to tap the home telephones of several of his closest advisers, including Harry Hopkins. (FDR feared that Hopkins's wife was leaking anti-administration information to the Washington *Times-Herald*.)

Although the "FDR Tapes" cover only a microscopic portion of Roosevelt's time in office, they do illustrate a supreme reality of Roosevelt's presidency: he is completely in love with his job. Geoffrey Ward marveled, "He is trapped behind his desk and what is astonishing to me is what a good time he's having." "He was a most unusual man, one of the finest gentlemen I've ever known," said Dorothy Jones Brady, FDR's personal secretary and stenographer, who went to work for him as a twenty-one-year-old White House assistant in March 1933 and was with him until the day he died. "Every day you were there you knew that your number one job was to help people in trouble. He had a compassion that was like a magnificent obsession."

Just after taking office, Roosevelt moved quickly to distinguish his presidency from the image of Hoover's cold indifference. In 1932, Hoover launched an army attack against protesting veterans camped out on the Mall and burned down their camps. Frances Perkins reported, "When the veterans came to Washington in March 1933, in a similar, if smaller, march on the capital followed by an encampment, Roosevelt drove out and showed himself, waving his hat at them." He then sent Mrs. Roosevelt and aide Louis Howe out to meet with the veterans. "Above all," FDR directed, "be sure there is plenty of good coffee. No questions asked. Just let free coffee flow all the time. There is nothing like it to make people feel better and feel welcome." The veterans gradually drifted away peacefully.

James Roosevelt recalled one of his father's first White House executive orders after becoming president: "He circulated word to his staff, from the top secretaries to the telephone operators, that, if persons in distress telephoned to appeal for help of any sort, they were not to be shut off but that someone was to talk with them. If a farmer in Iowa was about to have his mortgage foreclosed, if a homeowner in one of the big cities was about to lose his home, and they felt desperate enough about it to phone the White House, Father wanted help given them if a way possibly could be found; he was keenly cognizant of the suffering he had seen on his campaign trips. Many such calls were taken—sometimes by me, when I was in the White House, and occasionally by Mother. Often ways were found to cut red tape with some federal agency. After Father's death, Mother received letters from strangers, who told her how, in the dark Depression days, they telephoned their president and received aid."

The rhythms of FDR's work pattern would vary little over the next twelve years. He awoke around 8:30 A.M., alone in an old-fashioned mahogany bed, threw a cape around the shoulders of his weather-beaten pajamas, and then, more or less simultaneously, ate a breakfast in bed of soft-boiled eggs, read through government reports, scanned the Washington, Baltimore, Chicago, and New York newspapers, got a quick health check from his doctor, Admiral Ross T. McIntyre, received Eleanor for some emergency request, and huddled with presidential aides like Harry Hopkins, "Pa" Watson, and Press Secretary Steve Early, plus Cabinet members and other officials, all while his valet bathed, shaved, and dressed him. Every morning FDR and his top officials received a package of clippings from some 700 newspapers, many of them hostile to the administration. Before long Roosevelt was stuffing the first of his forty daily Camel cigarettes into a soft-tipped ivory cigarette holder he used to protect his tender gums. Throughout the day, he used the holder as a theatrical prop, waving it around like a magician's wand, royal scepter, and orchestra baton to emphasize points and illustrate anecdotes.

Around 10:00 A.M. FDR was man-hauled into the wheeled chair, pushed into the elevator, and rolled down into the West Wing, now joined by a team of Secret Service men carrying baskets full of presidential work, and flanked by hyperactive Scottish terrier "Fala" trotting and yapping alongside. Once behind his desk, FDR would swing himself into a regular chair, and remain there as prisoner for much of the day, "a spider at the center of his web," as Geoffrey C. Ward put it, "where the world came to him."

THE OVAL OFFICE
SUMMER 1940

President Roosevelt with White House Staff
RE: *Routine Oval Office Business*
audio recordings on 35mm motion-picture film (RCA/Kiel machine)

Roosevelt's recordings capture his breezy, stream-of-consciousness Oval Office atmosphere of informality. In the first few weeks of his recording experiment, Roosevelt's machine recorded him tackling random slices of Oval Office business, shifting from one task to another with dizzying speed, interacting with his staff with effervescent charm.

AUGUST 22, 1940, MORNING

AIDE: The picture taken up at the park was fine. I saw it yesterday afternoon. It turned out fine.

FDR: Good. Fine. Fine. The sun came out, it was just right. I didn't need any paint on my face!

AIDE: That's the speech there, if you'd approve that. (*FDR reads and signs papers*)

FDR: Ask the Secretary of War and the Secretary of the Navy if they would approve a meeting here on Monday, and would they telephone to the Canadians and ask them if Tuesday would be all right instead of Monday to meet in Ottawa. I think that's a good idea, too.

Oh, look, get hold of Dan and tell Dan I want some maps on the [Presidential yacht] *Potomac* if they're not there already, charts, showing the entire layout of Newfoundland.

I want *large scale*. No small scale stuff. *Large scale stuff.*

Move them along. The east coast of Nova Scotia . . . .

Later, FDR reviewed lists of potential appointments to federal judgeships around the country, trying to steer clear of financial scandals allegedly connected to some of the candidates. In New Jersey, one candidate was supposed to be mixed up in illegal payoffs.

FDR: You been able to clear anything for Smathers?* (*signing papers*)

AIDE: Well, now, I want to tell you about Smathers.

He nominated a man by the name of Shalick. The story is that Shalick has paid him $10,000, and there is more scandal about Shalick, the probabilities are we're going to have to remove him as soon as it's time for his retirement. Violation of the Hatch Act.† It's in this report we want to show you.

Hague‡ says he's unfit, but Hague says he's also got to write you a letter that he's all right (*FDR laughs*) but it doesn't mean anything. Says he shouldn't be appointed . . . .

FDR: Right. I'll do this. It's very simple: send Boss Smathers a letter. "We cannot appoint Shalick. Give me another name."

Senator William Smathers of New Jersey, a rabidly pro-FDR New Deal supporter, in an ongoing feud with Jersey City Democratic boss Frank Hague.
†*The Hatch Act prohibits most political fundraising by federal officials.*
‡*Frank Hague.*

AIDE: Well, we've told him that . . . .

FDR: Appoint somebody else. I gave him three separate chances, every time. Number one man? No! Number two man? No! Number three man? No! Three strikes are out . . . .

In Oklahoma, the problem was an alleged sexual assault, and FDR faced the dilemma of whether to appoint an accused rapist to the federal bench. A former secretary of an Oklahoma judge accused him of raping her in his office. The judge maintained his innocence, but paid her a $3,000 settlement. Oklahoma Democratic senator Elmer Thomas was pushing hard for the appointment of the judge, one of his financial contributors. The whole mess could expose the Democrats to blackmail.

AIDE: In Oklahoma, they're still wanting a fellow appointed who's in trouble with his secretary for rape. Thomas is very urgent about it, said he'd take the responsibility and I said, well, now, look here, if they ask for the files on this man in the midst of a campaign and make it a national issue, you can't cover the nation. Well, he admitted that he might get into trouble . . . .

FDR: Oh. He's the fella that raped the girl in his office.

AIDE: And settled for three thousand dollars.

FDR: And settled for three thousand dollars, and he's led a clean life, so far as we know, ever since.

AIDE: Of course, the difficulty is everybody now wants to keep it very quiet, subject to blackmail now, the party is subject to blackmail.

Today, FDR passed over the accused judge, but changed his mind a few years later and appointed him to Federal District Court.

SEPTEMBER 6, 1940, 11:05 A.M.

GRACE TULLY:* Morning, Mr. President.

FDR: Morning, Grace!

TULLY: We're waiting for that update from the State Department as usual.

FDR: Yeah, they always send it at the last minute. (*signs papers*) I expected they would.

**Grace Tully was a longtime FDR personal secretary, and assumed number one status after the illness of Marguerite "Missy" LeHand in 1941.*

TULLY: Yeah, at the most inopportune time.

FDR: Now, is that all we've got? Got something for me to sign?

TULLY: Yessir, I'll bring it in.

FDR: Good, bring it in. (*reads document*) Now, what do we do about *this*? This is the damnedest thing I've ever read.

FDR now read aloud from a telegram sent by U.S. Minister Hugh G. Grant in Thailand to Secretary of State Cordell Hull. The telegram reported on an Asian trip by former FDR backer Roy Howard, head of the Scripps-Howard newspaper chain, now a Wendell Willkie supporter. Howard was spreading rumors that FDR was deteriorating mentally and physically. FDR seemed eager to retaliate, but was firmly kept in check by his press secretary, Steve Early, who convinced him this would be counterproductive.

FDR: "Accompanied by the leading American businessman in Siam, Howard called to see me at the legation with his friend and launched into a bitter attack on the president, accusing him of bad faith in inviting him, Howard, to go on a mission to South America, alleging that he, the president, was down and out physically and mentally, that he had made a mess of our foreign affairs during the crisis, and that he is desirous of leading the country into war . . . ."

Now, what do we do about a thing like that?

EARLY: Mr. President, I should think that the best thing to do with that would be to put it into the speech material file along with the other letters of record. I don't see that you can do anything else with it.

FDR: But it is interesting.

EARLY: Yes. Very much so, it ought to be made a part of that record . . .

APPOINTMENTS SECRETARY MARVIN MCINTYRE: When people see you when you go around, that refutes that physical stuff.

FDR: Yeah. I'm willing to admit my mentality's slipping, but that's all right! (*laughter in the room*)

MCINTYRE: The attorney general wants to speak to you after the Cabinet for a few minutes. Bob says its a very important thing . . . .

The Dutch Minister is sick, they say very seriously sick, and he says he has an urgent message for you, and he wanted to know if he could find some way, if he could phone you during the day.

FDR: Sure! Put him after lunch!

Roosevelt worked from two Oval Offices: the one in the West Wing, which he used for press conferences and formal, ceremonial meetings, and the Oval Room on the second floor of the White House mansion—also called the "Oval Study" or "the study." This was "the most important room of Roosevelt's presidency," according to White House historian William Seale. "There he worked, relaxed and there he conducted most of the important business of State." Frances Perkins watched the room quickly fill up "with everything that came his way—a Jefferson chair, another bookcase, another bench, another table, ship models and books and papers piled on the floor. Any room he used invariably got that lived-in and overcrowded look which indicated the complexity and variety of his interests and intentions."

FDR usually ate lunch at his desk with guests on card tables in front of sofas, some of which dated back to the days of Theodore Roosevelt. He regularly worked late into the evenings and weekends in the Oval Room, which was connected to his bedroom by a side door. From January 1942 to mid-1944 FDR went once or twice a day to the secret Map Room in the White House basement, a military and intelligence center inspired by Churchill's map room. Here Roosevelt could check the progress of troop movements and naval campaigns around the world on giant maps on the wall dotted with colored pins. He met every Monday with congressional leaders, held press conferences on Tuesday afternoons and Friday mornings, and Cabinet meetings every Friday afternoon. Roosevelt returned to the Oval Study at about 5:30 in the evening and then held court as mix-master at the nightly cocktail hour, where he would relax and gossip with his staff. Before turning in around midnight, he went through a bedtime folder of letters from ordinary citizens and chatted with his wife, who slept in a nearby room.

As a chief executive Roosevelt functioned not at the top of a pyramid, but at the center of a self-propelled whirlwind, as he smashed bureaucratic procedure, instigated open conflict between people and ideas, and sucked blizzards of data into his Oval Offices. He transacted much presidential business through short, informal memos on White House notepads, often simply dashed off in his own handwriting. Political scientist Frank Kessler described Roosevelt's accessibility: "One hundred or so persons could get to him directly by telephone without being diverted by a secretary. He employed no chief of staff and permitted few of his staffers to become subject matter specialists. Except for Harry Hopkins, to whom he turned almost exclusively for foreign policy assignments, staffers were assigned problems in a variety of areas."

Roosevelt soaked up new ideas and information ravenously from all directions, and his in-boxes were often piled high with reports sent to him directly from all corners of government. He preferred his memos and letters short ("Two short sentences will generally answer any known letter," he asserted), and if someone submitted an oversized document, he would ask, "Boil it down to a single page." If he liked a memo, he might read it back to the person who wrote it. Arthur M. Schlesinger, Jr., observed, "The first task of an executive, as he evidently saw it, was to guarantee himself an effective flow of information and ideas. An executive relying on a single information system became inevitably the prisoner of that system. Roosevelt's persistent effort therefore was to check and balance information acquired through official channels by information acquired through a myriad of private, informal and unorthodox channels and espionage networks."

The White House in FDR's early years was a remarkably modest operation: he had a primary staff of only around 100 and a $200,000 budget. To control costs, the offices were furnished with abandoned furniture from terminated federal agencies. When you walked into the West Wing lobby, if you looked closely you would see patches in the carpet. When you looked into Roosevelt's office, according to eyewitnesses, you could see him surrounded by assistants, signing a constant stream of papers and chatting on the phone. He would look up, see you, raise his huge hand into the air to wave while throwing his head back and shouting, "Come on in. We're doing a land-office business!" At the beginning of the war he bellowed to one visitor, "I can take anything these days!" An FDR friend observed: "This man functions smoothly because he has learned to function in chains." Washington attorney James Rowe, who became an FDR assistant at age twenty-eight, walked in to meet FDR for the first time in the Oval Office. Roosevelt smiled up at him and announced, "Jim, I want your advice," instantly creating a lifelong admirer.

Roosevelt was not afraid to admit when he didn't know something, an asset for any executive, especially crucial for a president. In one meeting he confessed, "I am still perfectly foggy about the whole thing. Can you differentiate between old mortgages and new mortgages?" After an aide phoned in a briefing from a meeting of economists, FDR hung up, then called back, "I don't understand it yet. Put it in a telegram." Roosevelt's tendency to hijack conversations led some officials to resort to a desperate strategy: they insisted on luncheon meetings, then waited for the exact moment when FDR stuffed his mouth with food to begin talking. When he wanted to end a conversation, FDR would say: "Well, I'm sorry, I have to run now!" FDR aide Samuel Rosenman mused, "I am sure it never struck him as a strange thing to say, even though he had not been able to walk since 1921."

FDR's Cabinet meetings were fairly useless, except as platforms for presidential pep talks. "You go into Cabinet meetings tired and discouraged," said one official, "and the president puts new life into you. You come out like a fighting cock." Afraid of leaks and scornful of committees, Roosevelt preferred to deal with department chiefs one-on-one. A Cabinet member asserted, "A Roosevelt Cabinet was a delightful social occasion, where nothing was ever settled." Labor Secretary Perkins, relishing her role as the first female Cabinet member, remembered things differently, at least early on. "Those early meetings were full of excitement, and always there was an easy give and take," she wrote. "He did not expect yes-men around him. He wanted a free expression of opinion, and it took place, under his leadership, in a stimulating atmosphere." FDR's Cabinet members were seasoned, heavyweight veterans of titanic turf wars. Management expert Peter Drucker considered the group a model: "Nine of its ten members were what we now would call technocrats—competent specialists in one area. That the exceptional team delivered an exceptional performance—not one financial scandal, for instance, despite unprecedented government spending—explains in large measure Roosevelt's own unprecedented hold on power and office."

FDR surrounded himself with many tough, strong, often cantankerous players like military Chief of Staff Admiral William Leahy, Cabinet Secretaries Stimson and Morgenthau, Press Secretary Early, and Interior Secretary Harold Ickes. Admiral Ernest King was reported to "raise holy hell" with FDR. During a group meeting at the White House, General George Marshall shot down a Roosevelt idea by announcing, "I am sorry, Mr. President, but I don't agree with you at all," startling FDR as well as Marshall's colleagues, who predicted career disaster for him. Instead, Roosevelt promoted Marshall over thirty-four more senior officers to be army chief of staff.

"There is nothing I love as much as a good fight," Roosevelt once declared, and the hallmark of his executive style was creative tension and controlled chaos. He thrived on managing through interpersonal competition and interdepartmental combat, and he delighted in pitting aggressive personalities against each other in open conflict. He apparently believed that the clash of people and ideas produced shocks to the bureaucracy necessary for creative solutions to cope with the emergencies of the Depression. "A little rivalry is stimulating," he explained. "It keeps everybody going to prove he is a better fellow than the next man. It keeps them honest too." "His favorite technique was to keep grants of authority incomplete, jurisdictions uncertain," wrote Arthur M. Schlesinger, Jr. "The result of this competitive theory of administration was often confusion and exasperation on the operating level; but no other method could reliably insure that in a large bureaucracy filled with ambitious men eager for power the decisions, and the power to make them, would remain with the president."

FDR's White House was a spectacle of gladiatorial warfare, a Roman coliseum of bloody showdowns. Roosevelt pitted Assistant Secretary of State Raymond Moley against Secretary of State Cordell Hull at the 1933 London Monetary and Economic Conference in a clash over tariff policy. Moley quit in disgust. Under Secretary of State Sumner Welles was in perpetual revolt against his boss Cordell Hull, with the apparent approval of Roosevelt. Commerce Secretary Jesse Jones and Agriculture Secretary Henry Wallace grappled in a debilitating wartime feud, as did many other agency and department chiefs.

The fighting got so intense at times that FDR was forced to intervene. At a Cabinet meeting in February 1935, Morgenthau blew up at Ickes over a secret investigation conducted by Interior into Treasury's handling of bids for the Post Office Annex building in New York City, also the turf of Postmaster General Jim Farley—a three-way shoot-out. During the meeting FDR wrote out a note and held it up to Morgenthau: "You must not talk in such a tone of voice to another Cabinet officer." He then pounded the table and told the three to get along. "I cannot have three Cabinet members disagreeing." Another three-way battle broke out in 1943, this time over tax policy. "Who is in charge?" one of the officials asked bitterly. Roosevelt smacked the table. "I am the boss. I am the one who gets the rap if we get licked in Congress . . . I am the boss, I am giving the orders."

In the heat of combat, FDR used his officials as surrogate combatants for himself, and he reserved the right to disassociate himself from the fray and withhold his support if the deputy was losing the battle. Frances Perkins recalled, "If you wanted to go out on a limb for some hobby or theory, he would never say no. He kept an open mind as to whether it was wise or unwise, but he reserved the right not to go out and rescue you if you got into trouble. He wanted you to understand that. Many, too timid to defend their own position, resented this." FDR told Cabinet members going on political missions during a campaign: "Say what you please. Use your own judgment. But if it turns out wrong, the blood be on your own head."

"He liked to have Harry Ickes and Harry Hopkins out there fighting in public, or Jesse Jones and Henry Wallace," said James Rowe, "because he could make a pretty good judgment on the reaction of the people or the newspapers or politicians." His tactics were often a mystery to his men. "You are a wonderful person but you are one of the most difficult men to work with that I have ever known," Ickes declared to his boss. "Because I get too hard at times?" Roosevelt asked. "No, you never get too hard but you won't talk frankly even with people who are loyal to you and of whose loyalty you are fully convinced. You keep your cards close up against your belly."

FDR once explained his philosophy to Morgenthau: "Never let your left hand know what your right is doing." Morgenthau asked: "Which hand am I, Mr. President?" FDR: "My right hand. But I keep my left hand under the table." In his diary, Morgenthau concluded: "This is the most frank expression of the real FDR that I ever listened to and that is the real way that he works—but thank God I understand him." Dean Acheson, as usual, was disgusted by Roosevelt's method: "One often reads of Franklin Roosevelt that he liked organizational confusion which permitted him to keep power in his own hands by playing off his colleagues one against the other. This, I think, is nonsense. Such is a policy of weakness, and Roosevelt was not a weak man. Furthermore, it did not keep power in his own hands, it merely hindered the creation of effective power by anyone."

To tackle the intractable problems of the Depression, FDR conjured up a blizzard of boards, agencies, and committees, many of them overlapping with existing departments. "The country needs, and unless I mistake, the country demands, bold persistent experimentation," he declared as the New Deal began. "We have new and complex problems," he said another time. "Why not establish a new agency to take over the new duty rather than saddle it on an old institution?" To provide some coordination to the proliferation of New Deal programs, FDR set up the National Emergency Council, a domestic super-cabinet that included Cabinet and agency chiefs that met regularly in the Cabinet Room. The meetings helped Roosevelt collect information, "knock heads together" and settle disputes on the spot.

FDR's New Deal executive style helped him collect multiple streams of opinions and information that had been "pre-tested" for debates in Congress, resulting in legislative triumphs like the Social Security Act of 1935. The Tennessee Valley Authority was a success, and the Public Works Administration and Works Progress Administration took 4 million people off relief rolls by 1936 and laid much of the physical plant for the country. By early 1936, stock prices and industrial production and payrolls doubled versus 1932. Overall though, much of the New Deal was a failure: the mammoth Agricultural Adjustment Act and National Recovery Administration projects were disappointments and were declared unconstitutional by the Supreme Court. By 1939, unemployment persisted at 9 million, and the unemployment rate stayed over 10 percent until the war.

"I wish you could be here for a week sitting invisibly at my side," Roosevelt once wrote to a friend. "It would not be a pleasant experience for you because you would get a shock every ten minutes." By early October 1940, inside Roosevelt's Oval Offices, the shocks were coming even faster. The presidential election was a month away, and Willkie was pulling even with Roosevelt in some polls, as the European war was threatening to turn global and pull in the United States.

THE OVAL OFFICE
OCTOBER 4, 1940, 11:00 A.M.

President Roosevelt with House Speaker Sam Rayburn and House Floor Leader John W. McCormack
RE: *State of the World and the Presidential Election*
audio recording on 35mm motion-picture film (RCA/Kiel machine)

Weeks before the presidential election, an embattled chief executive called his two top Democratic leaders in Congress to an Oval Office conference, really an FDR soliloquy. On the secret recording of the meeting, probably an accidental continuation of a press conference recording, the congressmen could barely get a word in edgewise. Arthur M. Schlesinger, Jr., wrote of the recording: "The listener almost feels the anxiety with which Sam Rayburn and John McCormack, the House Democratic leaders, wait for an opening so that they can slip in their own points. The president, imperturbable, deliberately oblivious, always in command, turning aside interruptions with his enigmatic 'Yeah'p,' talks everyone else down; while at the same time, one feels, he absorbs through mysterious antennae the points they are trying to make." Roosevelt offered a state-of-the-world review to the congressmen, speculating on Hitler's intentions and election politics, illustrating the interrelationship of domestic and foreign affairs on the eve of war.

FDR: And you see, look here now. The prime minister of Japan has just given out an interview which may or may not be true because they may deny it this afternoon, to the Scripps-Howard, uh, the INS* papers. In which, he says that Japan would regard it as an act of war if we were to give aid and comfort to any of the enemies of Japan. Now, what d'ya mean? What's the word "attack" mean? I don't

---

International News Service, predecessor of United Press International.

know. It's perfectly possible, not the least bit probable, I mean it's a, it's a, as [Vice President] Jack Garner would say, a one in ten shot, that Hitler and Mussolini, and Japan, united, might, ah, feel if they could stop American munitions from flowing to England—planes, guns, ammunition, anti-aircraft guns, and so forth, that they could lick England.

Now, they might send us an ultimatum (*raps his desk seventeen times through the next sentence*): "If you continue to send anything to England, we will regard that as an attack on us." I'll say: "I'm terribly sorry. We don't want any war with you. We have contracts, and under our neutrality laws any belligerent has a right to come and buy things in this country and take 'em away." They'll thereupon say: "Well, if after such and such a date you are continuing to ship munitions to England—and planes—we will regard you as a belligerent."

All right, what have we got to say on that? I'll say: "I'm terribly sorry. We don't consider ourselves a belligerent. We're not going to declare war on you. If you regard us as a belligerent, we're frightfully sorry for you, because we don't. Now, all we can say to you is that, of course, if you *act* on that assumption, that we're a belligerent, and make any form of attack on us, we're going to defend our own. Not war. We're going to *defend our own*. And nothing further." . . .

There will be in this country if that happens, a great deal of scared feeling, of panic. There will be a lot of people that'll say: "My God, we ought to keep some of these planes back here! We haven't got enough of these planes to defend ourselves! We ought not to send every other plane over to England. We haven't got enough anti-aircraft guns for Boston, and New York, and Washington, D.C.!"

Sure, it's perfectly true. And there'll be a demand that we *pull right in*, inside of ourselves, and keep everything we're making for our own defense. And that's just what they [the Axis powers] want [us] to do.

Now, this morning (*opens up newspaper*) you know there was a terrible attack on Lehman* because of what Lehman said—it's perfectly true, that the Axis powers—there's no question about it— would give anything in the world to have me licked on the fifth of November . . . .

Democratic New York Governor Herbert H. Lehman.

Roosevelt was correct in his suspicion—the Nazis mounted a major program of covert financial action to try to topple FDR in the 1940 election, working through German agents in the United States.

I would give anything in the world to get that fella [Republican Presidential candidate Wendell Willkie] licked.

Of course, the trouble with Willkie, as you know, his whole campaign—the reason he's losing strength, is that he will say anything to please the individual or the audience that he happens to be talking to. It makes no difference what he's promised first. [Unintelligible] come in and say, "Now, Mr. Willkie, please, will you, if elected, do thus and such?" "Of course I will!" Then somebody else comes in and he'll say, "Of course I won't!" [FDR himself was often criticized for the same behavior.]

THE OVAL OFFICE
OCTOBER 8, 1940, 4:20 P.M.

President Roosevelt with Staff
RE: *Threat of Japanese Attack on Hawaii*
audio recording on 35mm motion-picture film (RCA/Kiel machine)

Four days later, in an informal staff meeting right after a press conference on the afternoon of October 8, 1940, Roosevelt let out an explosive belly laugh and passed a newspaper clipping over to a visitor who was ushered in by his aides. FDR's attention was riveted on Asia, where Japanese troops were pouring into conquered territories in China and Indochina. It was over a year before Pearl Harbor, but Roosevelt was about to have a premonition of the tragedy that would finally plunge the United States into war.

FDR: Ah, look—here's one thing I wanted to ask my old friends, the Scripps-Howard papers about. Hah, hah, hah! [*Roosevelt laughed at his own joke—the chain was fiercely anti-FDR*]

Now, look, before you read that, I want to ask you this. Ah, Roy, the other day, received, Roy Howard, a telegram, apparently, which was published, I think U.P. [United Press] carried it—all of U.P. did—a telegram, as I remember it, from this chief of the Japanese press association.

VOICE: Mitsunaga.

FDR: What?

VOICE: Mitsunaga.

FDR: Uh-huh, right. Evidently an old friend of Roy's. In which Mitsuna-ga, or whatever his name was, said the damnedest thing that ever happened. I wouldn't refer to it because it would only stir up bad feeling in this country, and this country is ready to pull the trigger if the Japs do anything. I mean we won't stand any nonsense, public opinion won't, in this country, from the Japs, if they do some fool thing.

Now this Mitsunaga fella wires to Roy and says, ah, "there will be no war with the United States"—I'm quoting from memory—"on one condition, and one condition only (*bangs his desk*), and that is that the United States will recognize the new era in not the Far East but the East, meaning the whole of the East."

"Furthermore, that this recognition—there must be evidence of it, and the only evidence of this recognition the United States can give is to *demilitarize* all its naval and air and army bases in Wake, Mid-way, and Pearl Harbor!"

God, that's the first time that any damn Jap has told us to get out of Hawaii!

And that has me worried more than any other thing in the world, that a responsible—what?

VOICE: The question is how responsible Mitsunaga is. Now I know the head of the press association. He's an old-timer, he was in his day what we called a swashbuckler over there . . . .

FDR: Well, of course, we are worried, awfully worried about things today. There's this opening of the Burma Road on the seventeenth—that's a pretty definite challenge on the part of the British.

And the only thing that worries me is that the Germans and the Japs have gone along, and the Italians, for, oh, gosh. Five, six years without their foot slipping. Without their misjudging foreign opinion. They've played a damn smart game. Now the chance you could get from doing that all the time may be to do something foolish.

And the time may be coming when the Germans and Japs will do some fool thing. That would put us in. That's the only real danger of our gettin' in—is that their foot will slip.

The Oval Study, White House Mansion
December 7, 1941, 8:30 p.m.

President Roosevelt, Cabinet, and Congressional Leaders
RE: *Japanese Attack on Pearl Harbor*
stenographic transcription of meeting by White House stenographer

The disaster FDR feared finally fell upon Pearl Harbor in the morning light of December 7, 1941, after the breakdown of negotiations over the American oil embargo against Japan for its conquests in China and Indochina. U.S. code-breakers had picked up warnings of an attack, but the target was assumed to be the Malay Peninsula or the Philippines. Japanese planes swarmed over Pearl Harbor after 7:30 A.M., sank or damaged eight battleships and three cruisers, and killed over 2,000 men. Within hours the Japanese had also attacked the Philippines, Midway, Hong Kong, Malaya, Singapore, Bangkok, Shanghai, Thailand, and the distant U.S. outposts of Guam and Wake.

In the White House, Roosevelt had just finished lunch when Navy Secretary Frank Knox called with the news: "Mr. President, it looks as if the Japanese have attacked Pearl Harbor." FDR exclaimed, "No!" As Roosevelt raced to the Oval Office in his wheelchair to take command of the greatest military clash in history, a Secret Service man reported, "His chin stuck out about two feet in front of his knees and he was the maddest Dutchman . . . anybody . . . ever saw." Roosevelt soon moved to the second-floor Oval Study, and a direct phone line was patched in from Hawaii Governor Joseph Poindexter in Honolulu. At one point the governor yelled into the phone and Roosevelt cried: "My God, there's another wave of Jap planes over Hawaii right this minute!"

Roosevelt summoned his Cabinet to the Oval Study at 8:30 P.M., and as crowds thronged around the White House and a hazy moon hovered above in the winter night, rings of extra chairs were brought in to form horseshoes around Roosevelt's desk and a stenographer was called in to transcribe the meeting. Congressional leaders were asked to come at 9:00 P.M. As dozens of government leaders crowded around, Roosevelt gave them a comprehensive briefing, stopping to read from flash cables handed to him during the meeting.

FDR: The conversations were interrupted for six weeks to two months. They were then resumed, with the same objective in mind. Despite the Japanese move into Indo-China, they continued until about two weeks ago, when we received indications from various sources—Europe and Asia—that the German government was pressing Japan for action under the Tripartite Pact. In other words, an effort to divert the American mind, and the British mind, from the European field, and divert American supplies from the European theater to the defense of the East Asia theater. About two weeks ago we began to realize that the probability of Japan being in earnest was so slim that it was time to make a final and definite effort to pin them down on the one subject that they had never ever been pinned down on, and that was that they were to agree to cease their acts of aggression, and that they would try to bring the China war to a close.

The result was that the secretary of state sent a message on that point, to find out whether Japan would be willing to discuss or consider that point of nonaggression. That was the twenty-sixth of November. From that time on we were getting more and more definite information that Japan was headed for war, and that the reply to the secretary of state would be in the negative . . . .

And so the thing went along until we believed that under the pressure from Berlin the Japanese were about to do something . . . And so yesterday I sent a final message to the Emperor . . . The Japanese, we learned, were to bring the secretary of state today a reply to his note of November 26. Actually, in point of fact [?],* they telephoned to the State Department, after Hawaii had been attacked, for an appointment. They came to the State Department—they were given an appointment within three-quarters of an hour, and they actually arrived at the State Department one hour after the terrific bombing attack on the Island of Oahu.

Which of course was an act which is almost without parallel in relationships between nations, equaled only by the Japanese episode of 1904, when two squadrons—cruisers—lying in the Harbor of Korea [?] and without any warning—I think on a Sunday morning, by the way—Japanese cruisers sank all of them. . . .

And finally while we were on the alert—at eight o'clock—half-past seven—about a quarter past—half-past one, a great fleet of Japanese bombers bombed our ships in Pearl Harbor, and bombed

*Question marks and ". . ." are from the original transcript, representing uncertain and inaudible dialog, respectively.

all of our airfields. Shortly thereafter this was followed—about eleven o'clock, three hours later—by a third attack, which was not as violent, but most of the damage had already been done. The casualties, I am sorry to say, were extremely heavy. I cannot say anything definitely in regard to the number of ships that have been sunk. It looks as if out of eight battleships, three have been sunk, and possibly a fourth. Two destroyers were blown up while they were in dry-dock. Two of the battleships are badly damaged. Several other smaller vessels have been sunk or destroyed. The dry-dock itself has been damaged. Other portions of the fleet are at sea, moving towards what is believed to be two plane carriers, with adequate naval escort.

Eyewitness Frances Perkins reported "the president could hardly bring himself" to describe the slaughter, and had "physical difficulty" in getting the words out. She recalled FDR calling out to Navy Secretary Knox: "Find out, for God's sake, why the ships were tied up in rows." Knox sputtered, "That's the way they berth them!"

In addition to that, this afternoon, in Guam—Guam was being bombed by two squadrons of Japanese planes, and we know—and it is entirely possible that at this moment Guam—which was not defended except by a few marines, without much in the way of guns—in all probability has fallen to the Japanese.

Wake Island was also attacked, and we have no further word at the present time.

We believe that Manila was attacked, but that has not proved true, and it is possible that other ports of the Philippines—some ports in Mindanao—have been attacked. Those are merely reports.

. . . Three or four, probably, of the landing fields were very heavily bombed, and a very large number of aircraft were destroyed in the hangar, or on the fields.

I have no word on the navy casualties, which will undoubtedly be very heavy, and the best information is that there have been more than one hundred army casualties and three hundred men killed and injured.

I do not know what is happening at the present time, whether a night attack is on or not. It isn't quite dark yet in Hawaii. I suppose it's four o'clock in the afternoon, and it will probably be dark in a couple of hours . . . .

The fact remains that we have lost the great majority of the battle ships there. Of course, in the long run, probably most of them can be salvaged, or repaired, to take their place in the line of battle again. That, however, is a long process, and will last very many months, depending on the damage.

I think probably—Oh yes—one more thing—Out in Shanghai the one small gunboat we have there has been taken over by the Japanese, and a British gunboat has been blown up. We still have two hundred marines there . . . and we are not certain yet whether they have been gotten out or not. Probably not . . . .

The Dutch government had declared that a state of war exists between the Netherlands Indies and the Japanese.

The British cabinet is in session. I have heard nothing from them on that—just the fact. And at nine o'clock tomorrow morning, their time, a special session of the Parliament is being called. . . .

The entire leadership of the U.S. government was now crowding into the room, as Speaker Sam Rayburn, Republican Leader Joseph Martin, and various senators and congressmen joined FDR's Cabinet.

Under Secretary of State Sumner Welles, watching FDR manage the emergency, thought "he demonstrated that ultimate capacity to dominate and control a supreme emergency which is perhaps the rarest and most valuable characteristic of any statesman."

VOICE: Didn't we do anything to get—nothing about casualties on their side?

FDR: It's a little difficult. We think we got some of their submarines, but we don't know.

VOICE: Well, planes—aircraft?

FDR: We did get, we think, a number of their Japanese planes. We know some Japanese planes were shot down, but there again—I have seen so much of this in the other war. One fellow says he has got fifteen of their planes, and you pick up the telephone and somebody else says five. So I don't know what the report on that is, except that somewhere Japanese planes have been knocked down on the Island. I should say that by far the greater loss has been sustained by us, although we have accounted for some of the Japanese.

VOICE: There is a story coming over the radio that we got one of their airplane carriers.

FDR: I don't know. Don't believe it. It was reported about eight o'clock. I didn't believe it. A Japanese carrier has been discovered off the Panama Canal sunk by our forces. I wish it were true. But about the same time, the commanding officer in the Canal Zone said they were on the alert, but very quiet.

So that is literally everything I have got here. I think I have even covered the rumors as well.

Of course it is a terrible disappointment to be president in time of war, and the circumstances . . . came about most unexpectedly. Well, we were attacked. There is no question about that . . . .

Well, it is an awfully serious situation. There is a rumor that two of the planes—Japanese planes have a rising sun painted on them—but two of the planes were seen with swastikas on them. Now whether that is true or not, I don't know. It was a rumor, and therefore news until something a little more definite comes in. But that is rumor.

VOICE: I can't help wondering what we can do to do anything—

FDR: The only specific thing to do . . . our ships—we don't know what ships—are out trying to get the Japs at this moment . . . They can't send for fear of disclosing their position . . . .

VOICE: Well, they were supposed to be on the alert, and if they had been on the alert . . . I am amazed at the attack by Japan, but I am still more astounded at what happened to our navy. They were all asleep. Where were our patrols? They knew these negotiations were going on.

An eyewitness identified this voice as Senator Tom Connally of Texas, Chairman of the Senate Foreign Relations Committee, quoting him shouting as he slammed the desk with his fist: "How did it happen that our warships were caught like tame ducks at Pearl Harbor?" Purple-faced, he demanded, "How did they catch us with our pants down?" Roosevelt bowed his head and murmured "I don't know, Tom. I just don't know."

FDR: . . . Here is a dispatch from General MacArthur in the Philippines. All possible action is being taken here to speed defense. Pursuit planes are now reporting that by a counterattack about fifteen enemy planes north of the Far [?] in Central [?] . . . which mean that those Japs are over the Island of Oahu [?]. Report has been received that bombing attack . . . far end of the Island of Mindanao . . . In all probability . . . attack may come from the Japanese Mandated Islands, which lie to the west of the Philippines. The only damage caused, said the report, is a hangar of a civilian airport. A report has just been received of a bombing attack on Camp John Hayes at Baguio. . . .

Two hundred marines are in Northern China [?]. They have been asked by the Japanese army to disarm, to turn in all arms and ammunition, to assemble . . . The reply accepts the demands as of two o'clock today. That takes care of that. You have got the rest of it.

VOICE: That means two hundred of our marines are now prisoners of the Japanese?

FDR: Yes . . . .

VOICE: Well, Mr. President, this nation has got a job ahead of it, and what we have got to do is roll up our sleeves and win this war . . . .

FDR: We may have some very heavy losses. And the Japanese know perfectly well that the answer to her attack is proper strangulation of Japan—strangulation altogether . . . .

The fact is that a shooting war is going on today in the Pacific. We are in it . . . .

Captain Smith of the USS [?] received a telephone call at 4:15 this morning. Japanese naval officers stated over the telephone that a state of war exists between my country and yours. I am taking control over the USS [?]. That's the nearest official thing I have got, and that's a telephone message. I think we had better not say anything about it. Remember that out there it is nearly just about dawn. They are doing things, and saying things during the daytime out there, while we are all in bed.

VOICE: We are in bed too much.

VOICE: Well if that's—well, that's all we can say.

FDR: What?

VOICE: That is all we can say.

FDR: Yes.

After the meeting ended, FDR stayed at his desk late into the night conferring with smaller groups. Exhausted, he punched the table with his fist and, thinking of the scores of planes destroyed on the runways and in the hangars lined up cheek by jowl, he cried, "On the ground, by God, on the ground!"

Roosevelt's formula for managing the war was to set objectives and strategy, often in close cooperation with British Prime Minister Churchill, pick excellent commanders like Generals George Marshall and Dwight Eisenhower, and usually let them execute the war as they saw fit. During a conference at Pearl Harbor, Sam Rosenman looked through the window and saw Roosevelt in conference with military Chief of Staff William Leahy, Admiral Chester Nimitz, and General Douglas MacArthur. Rosenman described the scene as "the essence of Roosevelt's style as commander-in-chief—listening to his professionals, encouraging them to full discussion, asking questions. Perhaps he would adopt conciliation or compromise—but always the final decision was his. He seemed to be a part of the team rather than a civilian outsider—and the team accepted him as a member." Secretary of War Henry Stimson called FDR's record "unique in American war history for its scrupulous abstention from personal and political pressure."

Admiral William Leahy, who coordinated the mammoth military effort for Roosevelt from an office in the White House and met with him daily, reported that the major strategic decisions were Roosevelt's alone: "It was he (in conjunction with Churchill of course) who took the decision within a few weeks of Pearl Harbor that Germany, not Japan, must be beaten first, it was he who pressed for [Operation] Torch, the invasion of North Africa, as a preliminary to the assault on Europe, against the opposition of some of his own best advisers, like Stimson and Marshall; it was he who insisted that American ground troops must be put into combat against German ground troops as soon as possible; above all it was he who maintained persistent pressure on Churchill for the launching of [Operation] Overlord."

Frances Perkins wrote that during the war, FDR "administered by the technique of friendship, encouragement, and trust. This method of not giving direct and specific orders to his subordinates released the creative energy of many men. They looked to him for courage, for strength, for nobility of purpose, for the leadership that a democracy must have for its full effectiveness. His four-track mind proved invaluable. Without revealing war secrets from one group to another, he could keep many activities operating at top efficiency." Some patterns remained the same: Roosevelt still pitted bureaucrats against each other, and he often bypassed the chain of command to deal directly with military commanders. He could not resist periodically plunging into operational matters. At one point in the war, forty-seven federal agencies were reporting to Roosevelt personally, and in 1944 he lamented: "the details of this job are killing me." Henry Stimson contended, "One man simply could not do it all, and Franklin Roosevelt killed himself trying."

Some of Roosevelt's mistakes may have sprung from belief in his own invincibility; he may even have thought himself immortal. He stoically ignored his own physical collapse in 1944 and 1945, recklessly voyaged to Yalta as a very sick man in no condition to deal with Joseph Stalin, and negligently excluded his new vice president from all major decisions except those few made in Cabinet meetings. George Elsey observed that "he did not involve and inform the State Department as he should have on foreign policy matters that had long-range postwar implications. He even left some of his military leaders in doubt as he worked on major relationships with Stalin and Churchill along with Harry Hopkins."

Other Roosevelt failings affected entire populations. He delayed most action on civil rights, leaving it to his successor to desegregate the armed forces. He authorized the roundup and forced incarceration of 110,000 resident aliens and American citizens whose only crime was their Japanese ancestry. He allowed his State Department to engage in a systematic global slowdown of visa approvals that doomed thousands of Jews. Even in the context of the war, these actions are nearly unfathomable, given Roosevelt's lifelong progressive liberalism. In the warm light of the victory he did not live to see, Roosevelt might even have conceded these errors, or so one hopes.

Despite its failures and contradictions, FDR's creative, improvisational executive style liberated the energies of his government, his military, and the American people to believe in themselves again and conquer the impossible. Roosevelt's executive impact on the government and society was enormous. Though his techniques were often messy and unorthodox, he was chief architect of the executive and social services superstructures that blossomed from the ashes of 1932 and dominated national affairs for the rest of the century. His Reorganization Act of 1939 built the foundations of the modern Executive Office of the President. In 1933, the federal government employed 600,000 people; by January 1945 the number was 3.4 million civilians alone. Unemployment, at 8 million in 1940, plunged to 670,000 by 1944. The war not only ended the Depression, it transformed the American economy and created a vibrant American middle class. Years after FDR's death, Sam Rayburn declared, "He saved the nation, not once, but twice."

While he was working for FDR, budget director Harold Smith thought FDR was a very erratic administrator, but he later reversed himself. "Now I can see in perspective the 93 or 94 or 95 percent that went right—including the winning of the biggest war in history—because of unbelievably skillful organization and direction," Smith declared, adding "what we couldn't appreciate at the time was the fact that he was a real *artist* in government." Management expert Peter Drucker wrote, "Roosevelt knew that the main task of an American president is not administration. It is the making of policy, the making of the right decisions. And these are made best on the basis of 'adversary proceedings' to use the term of the lawyers for their method of getting at the true facts in a dispute, and of making sure that all relevant aspects of a case are presented to the court."

Like few other presidents except Washington, Lincoln, and his cousin Theodore, Roosevelt mastered the triple presidential roles of leader, politician, and executive. "Franklin Roosevelt threw me into completely new ventures which demanded original thinking," Henry Morgenthau, Jr., wrote in his diary. "Energy is contagious," noted John Gunther, "and Roosevelt's own glow of energy was energizing. He made almost everybody close to him feel bigger, heartier, more vigorous, by reason of his own luminous expansiveness."

For twelve years, what writer Hugh Gallagher called FDR's "splendid deception" of vigorous health worked perfectly: he was the most visible man in the world, but he went to his grave with only a handful of people knowing the extent of his paralysis. He never publicly mentioned his leg braces until his sad post-Yalta address to Congress a few weeks before his death. For a few moments during the war, though, FDR suddenly decided to break the spell, briefly pull the curtain down, and show off his infirmity. It occurred during a tour of Honolulu, in July 1944, when on the spur of the moment he ordered the Secret Service to wheel him into the halls of a veterans' hospital. The facility had wards of servicemen who had lost one, two, or more limbs in combat, and Roosevelt asked to be taken there. The patients had no warning Roosevelt was coming, and he ordered the guards to slowly roll him past the soldiers in their beds, so they could see his wheelchair and his legs, useless for the last twenty-three years.

Wearing a bright smile, Roosevelt slowly rolled through room after room, stopped at many of the beds and chatted with the stunned servicemen. As he was wheeled out of the hospital, Roosevelt was shaken and close to tears. But inside the hospital he left behind wards full of soldiers who now looked at their troubles differently. FDR lieutenant Sam Rosenman, following Roosevelt, saw soldier after soldier light up in surprise: "The expressions of the faces on the pillows as he slowly passed by and smiled showed how effective was this display of crippled helplessness."

FDR's Oval Office recordings abruptly stopped on November 8, 1940, the day of his last recorded press conference; there is no record why. Secure in his reelection victory a few days earlier, FDR may have no longer felt the need to record Oval Office activity, and the machine was quickly forgotten in the crush of White House business and the oncoming war. Author Kenneth S. Davis speculated that Roosevelt was "unprepared spiritually" to conduct extensive recordings. "His game-playing, fun-streaked penchant for secrecy and deviousness here collided with, and was halted by, his sense of justice and fair play, his gentleman's code of honor, and his remarkably acute sensitivity to political risks." The recordings were probably just an experiment conducted by a creative, improvisational executive, an experiment that ran its course.

J. Ripley Kiel's wired lamp stayed on Roosevelt's desk for the rest of his presidency, and through World War II, but no other recordings were ever found.

CHAPTER 2

Harry S. Truman
The Decisive Executive

*"I am here to make decisions, and whether
they prove right or wrong I am going to make them."*
HARRY TRUMAN, 1945

THE OVAL OFFICE
MAY 23, 1945, 4:00 P.M.

One by one, Harry Truman was lining up the members of Franklin Roosevelt's Cabinet and firing them.

"I propose to get the Cabinet officers I can depend on and have them run their affairs," Truman once explained, "and when I can't depend on them I'll keep on firing Cabinet members until I can get that kind." Truman later asserted that FDR's Cabinet was a "mudhole," and the people he inherited from FDR were "crackpots and the lunatic fringe." So now, just six weeks into his presidency, he was unleashing one of the bloodiest purges in presidential history.

Truman later confessed privately that he thought longtime Roosevelt crony and Treasury Secretary Henry Morgenthau, Jr., was a "blockhead" and a "nut"; Agriculture Secretary Claude Wickard was "a nice man, who never learned how his department was set up"; and Secretary of Labor Frances Perkins was "a grand lady—but no politician. FDR had removed every bureau and power she had." Even worse, she was a woman, and therefore had no business being in Harry Truman's Cabinet.

By the ninetieth day of Truman's term, all but four of FDR's Cabinet secretaries were thrown out the door and before long most of them were gone, too. "I want to keep my feet on the ground," said Truman, distancing himself as far as possible from his predecessor; "I don't want any experiments; the American people have been through a lot of experiments and they want a rest from experiments."

This afternoon, as members of the White House press corps were waved into the Oval Office to hear Truman read a statement on the latest round of firings at his eighth off-the-record press conference, they were unaware that FDR's Oval Office recorder was about to electronically capture their every word.

Days after his swearing in, Harry Truman was briefed on FDR's secret sound machine, still hooked up directly under the Oval Office. Truman was wary of such devices and may have thought the contraption was typical of FDR's sometimes duplicitous operating style. Once, when Truman suspected a Republican senator had used a recording device on him during a phone conversation, Truman barked, "I think it's outrageous for anyone to use them." Truman sometimes asked a stenographer to listen in on his phone conversations and take shorthand notes, but he always informed the other party. When an aide showed Truman some FBI transcripts made from Roosevelt wiretaps, Truman exclaimed, "I don't have time for that foolishness!"

Nevertheless, Truman was intrigued by FDR's recording device, in part because he was interested in electronic gadgets: he installed the first Oval Office TV set in 1947, and placed a bulky shortwave radio on the work desk behind him. Since Oval Office press conferences were recorded in shorthand by a stenographer in full view of the reporters, Truman probably thought it wasn't an ethical breach to authorize a secret test of the recording machine. Presidential press conferences were not yet broadcast, and, still under wartime rules, they were off the record unless the president gave reporters permission to quote him. On Truman's order, White House stenographer Jack Romagna walked down to the basement under the Oval Office, unlocked the storage room and switched the machine on.

Truman faced the reporters from behind a dark red mahogany desk that had been used by Presidents Theodore Roosevelt, Taft, Wilson, Harding, and Coolidge, wearing a double-breasted suit adorned with a World War I discharge button. He was a compact five-eight and 175 pounds, with warm hazel eyes and thick glasses that the chief White House usher said "magnified his eyes enormously, giving him a peering, owlish gaze." At sixty-one, he was the flesh and blood incarnation of the disappointments and promise of Middle America in the early twentieth century.

He grew up in small-town Missouri at the convergence of the American

West, South, and Midwest, swept the floors and bused tables at the malt shop on the town square, wooed and won the hand of a local girl from a well-to-do family, and spent ten years plowing the fields as a dirt farmer until going to war at the age of thirty-two.

As captain of an artillery battery charging into the slaughterhouse of the Meuse-Argonne, a single battle that killed 26,000 American troops, Truman quickly discovered two talents that would define his style as president: a skill for fast, instinctive decision making, and the ability to inspire fierce loyalty among his men. Nearly eighty years after the battle, Truman's chief mechanic, McKinley Wooden, reflected on his boss: "He was the best in the world. For the simple reason that he was a gentleman from the word go. If you soldiered, he got along with you. If you didn't, he gave you some trouble." Earlier that summer, in fact, Truman's men had panicked, broke, and ran under a nighttime barrage of German shells, and Truman chased, screamed, and swore at them until they stood their ground. "In combat, he was pretty cool," the 103-year-old Wooden recalled. "He gave you credit and he backed you up all the way." Truman later said that combat had taught him a crucial lesson: "There are a great many different factors that go into the making of a command decision, but in the end there has to be just one decision—or there is no command."

Truman's postwar career was a mixture of failure and comebacks: near-bankruptcy from the collapse of his haberdashery business, election as county commissioner, defeat for reelection, two years in a career wilderness as a membership salesman for the Kansas City Automobile Association, seven years as presiding judge of Jackson County, and ten years as a New Deal U.S. senator, when he gained national attention for investigating defense industry waste and fraud. "His personal and professional experience, like that of many men, had been an ambiguous blend of success and failure," wrote Truman historian Alonzo Hamby. "The security and confidence he had achieved were fragile."

After his surprise elevation to FDR's running mate, Truman spent his eighty-two days as vice president almost completely ignored by Roosevelt. Of his ascension to the presidency upon FDR's death on April 12, 1945, Truman noted, "I was handicapped by lack of knowledge of both foreign and domestic affairs—due principally to Mr. Roosevelt's inability to pass on responsibility. He was always careful to see that no credit went to anyone else for accomplishment." On his first full day as president, Truman entered the Oval Office at 9:00 A.M., sat down in FDR's chair, squirmed, rolled it back and forth, leaned back, let out a sigh, pulled up to the desk, and plunged into work. Admiral William Leahy brought in a pile of urgent papers. Leahy thought the pile looked taller than Truman in the chair. Another aide looked into the office and saw Truman swiveling in the chair, peering anxiously through his thick spectacles. That day Truman was heard muttering: "I'm not big enough. I'm not big enough for this job."

Harry Truman now sat in the cockpit of the world's first nuclear super-power and the wealthiest nation thus far in history, controlling almost 90 percent of the world's monetary gold. It was home to only 7 percent of the world's people, but commanded 42 percent of its income and half its manufacturing base. Truman had no grand vision, no master plan, only an in-box that was soon overflowing with the colossal challenges of postwar economic conversion, the demobilization of hundreds of thousands of American troops, and the emergency human needs of entire nations of refugees wandering the ruins of Europe. Above all, he would grapple with the inevitable clash between the two ideological empires of democracy and communism.

Harry Truman would have to master, somehow, this planet full of problems. But first he had to get rid of Franklin Roosevelt's Cabinet.

THE OVAL OFFICE
MAY 23, 1945, 4:00 P.M.

President Truman with Reporters
RE: *Cabinet Shake-up and the Climax of World War II*
audio recording on 35mm motion-picture film (RCA/Kiel machine)

On Truman's orders, FDR's secret recorder, which had laid unused but still hooked up to the Oval Office for the past four and a half years, was switched on for a test. Although Germany had surrendered two weeks earlier, the death of Adolf Hitler was not yet confirmed, and war with Japan was still raging—one of its bloodiest engagements was occurring on Okinawa. Truman greeted the reporters in his soft Missouri twang and then began firing off answers to their questions like a fast-draw artist—sometimes before they could even finish a question. The performance was a preview of Truman's crisp, sometimes impulsive executive style.

TRUMAN: How are y'all doing? Everybody here?

Well, I have some Cabinet changes I wanted to tell you about. Mr. Biddle's [Francis Biddle, the attorney general] resignation has been accepted, and Tom Clark of Texas will be appointed in his place as attorney general . . . .

I'm accepting the resignation of Miss Perkins as secretary of labor, and am appointing Judge Lewis B. Schwellenbach of Washington to be secretary of labor. Miss Perkins wrote me a very fine letter, and I wrote her a good one. You will receive copies of it.

Mr. Wickard's [secretary of agriculture] resignation is being accepted, and he is being appointed REA Administrator; and Congressman Clinton P. Anderson of New Mexico is being appointed secretary of agriculture . . . .

REPORTER: Are all these effective immediately—

TRUMAN: No—

REPORTER: —effective immediately, or June thirtieth?

TRUMAN: —the last of the fiscal year. These are all effective on June 30, except Mr. Wickard's. His takes effect as soon as he is confirmed as REA [Rural Electrification Authority] administrator. I have the resignation of Marvin Jones as war food administrator, and I'd like to read you the last two paragraphs of Mr. Jones's letter and comment on it . . . . (*Reads from letter*) Now Judge Jones is goin' back to the claims court on June thirtieth, and when he goes back and relinquishes the Office of War Food administrator, I expect to make the Secretary of Agriculture Food administrator. And I think that's about all, unless you have got some questions to ask me. (*laughter*)

REPORTER: I might say that's pretty good! . . .

REPORTER: Mr. President, did Mr. Morgenthau* offer his resignation this morning?

TRUMAN: No, he did not, and if he had, I wouldn't accept it.

REPORTERS: Mr. President, do you contemplate . . . Who was that? . . . We didn't hear that.

TRUMAN: Morgenthau.

REPORTER: What was the reply, Mr. President?

TRUMAN: He did not offer his resignation, and if he had, I wouldn't accept it.

REPORTER: Sir, do you contemplate any change in the State Department?

TRUMAN: I do not.

Henry Morgenthau, Jr., secretary of the Treasury.

REPORTER: Mr. President, were any of the resignations requested by you?

TRUMAN: They were not. I have the resignation of every member of the government who can resign since I have been president! (*laughter*) I can accept them or not as I choose.

REPORTER: Mr. President, would you clarify, please, the future status of Russia under lend-lease, now that the war in Europe is over?

TRUMAN: The—I don't care to discuss that. I think I covered it very thoroughly in the statement that was issued.

REPORTER: It left open one question, and that is whether or not Russia is getting any lend-lease now?

TRUMAN: Russia is getting the lend-lease that she has contracted to receive during the month of May.

REPORTER: How about, sir, when the protocol expires at the end of June?

TRUMAN: Well, let's wait and see what is necessary to be done at that time, then we will take care of it in a way which we think will be all right for the peace of the world.

REPORTER: When did cancellation of orders begin on lend-lease to Russia?

TRUMAN: The cancellation of lend-lease began as soon as the war ceased. It was not a cancellation, it was a readjustment because of the new conditions as they came about due to the collapse of Germany. The whole thing has to be gone into completely and thoroughly for all the nations, and I think it would be handled in a way that the country and the world will be helped by it . . . .

REPORTER: Mr. President, now that the war in Europe is over, has any arrangement been made for early release of the Italian armistice terms?

TRUMAN: I know nothing about it.

REPORTER: Mr. President, have you—can you inform us at all, on this status of German war prisoners, as to when they will cease being prisoners? Have you any plans—

TRUMAN: No, I can't.

REPORTER: —to make any statement on it?

TRUMAN: No, I can't. I can't do anything about that until we have an established government in Germany.

REPORTER: That might be for a generation.

TRUMAN: Well, your guess is as good as mine. (*laughter*)

Truman ended the conference with a joke about, of all people, Heinrich Himmler, architect of the Nazi death camps. The joke brought the house down.

REPORTER: Mr. President, a couple of weeks ago you told us you knew Hitler was dead, but you wouldn't give us very much detail about it. Can you give us any now?

TRUMAN: Yes, I think I can tell you why I thought Hitler was dead.

Himmler had told our minister in Sweden, through the—I think Prince Bernadotte of Sweden—that Hitler had had a stroke and that he wouldn't have but twenty-four hours to live. And I understood that whenever Himmler said anybody has just twenty-four hours to live, that's about how long he had!

(gales of laughter from the reporters)

That's what I based my statement on!

REPORTER: Does it still hold true? Is that the way you think he died— and when he died?

TRUMAN: I don't know a thing about his death any more than you do— only what I have seen in the papers.

REPORTER: Thank you, Mr. President.

TRUMAN: Not at all.

REPORTER: Twenty-four hours is all he had!

The conference ended, the reporters filed out of the room, and Truman relaxed. But underneath his office, the RCA recorder kept rolling as an informal staff meeting began. Although it is of extraordinarily bad quality, an often indecipherable recording, the sounds of Truman's early office atmosphere briefly drift through the late-spring afternoon noise of birds chirping loudly outside the Oval Office window and the cross-talk of White House radio communications bleeding onto the recording film. The sketch that emerges is of a gentle, humble, and vulnerable executive painfully aware of his limitations, and not afraid to share them with his staff.

The Oval Office was quiet. Truman murmured uncertainly, "I did the best I could do." One aide, referring either to the conference or to the Hitler joke, said "That was a fast one, all right!" Laughter.

Truman then said softly, "Well, if you feel all right, I do, but I don't know." A barrel-voiced man, possibly appointments secretary Matthew Connelly, said, "Oh, boss, that was good. Couldn't be better than that." He then asked to review some documents with the president: "We could take fifteen minutes now?" Truman replied, "Take all the time you want. Take all the time you want." A few moments of silence. The aide again volunteered support: "Boss, that was wonderful!"

"Was I all right?" Truman asked quietly.

Rose Conway, Truman's faithful and zipper-lipped personal secretary, now walked into the Oval Office, offering brightly, "I heard some very good compliments. Oh, you should have heard them . . . Oh, they were just—gosh!"

Truman now perked up and asked, "Were they?"

The barrel-voiced aide, referring to previous press conferences, said, "You looked quite good in those others, boss," but, he went on, this was "by far" the best. Conway added that his Himmler joke really went over well with the two *New York Times* reporters, and then presented the president with a long document to sign. As Truman flipped through the document, the aides assured him that "every word" of it had been checked. As he quickly scribbled his signature, evidently too pressed for time to fully review the paper, Truman laughed and said, "Well, I'll read this some day!"

When the staff meeting was over, Truman took Connelly, stenographer Jack Romagna, and a Secret Service man downstairs to the West Wing basement to inspect FDR's sound-on-film machine and listen to the playback of the press conference. As he stood in the cramped subterranean chamber underneath the Oval Office and listened to his own recorded voice on the RCA/Kiel machine, Truman immediately expressed doubts about the system. The whole exercise may have seemed devious and unseemly to him, and according to Romagna he declared, in effect, "I sure don't want anything to do with that." Only a few hours of other Truman Oval Office recordings exist, dating from 1945 and 1947. Less than three hours seem to include Truman's voice (although he's so soft-spoken it's hard to tell), and the segments are fragmentary and hopelessly unintelligible, the result of the machine's improper reinstallation into Truman's desk and at least two generations of duplication on inferior equipment. The recordings seem to be of random Oval Office activity, and probably were triggered accidentally or by Romagna occasionally test-running the machine.

In Truman's few surviving recordings, when Truman can be heard, what strikes the listener is how soft and gentle his voice sounds, the voice of a truly vulnerable man, a voice that almost disappears in the cavern of the Oval Office. Evidence of his soft-spoken, humble personality is found on one of the recordings, on an unknown date with an unidentified visitor: "I'm gonna need the support of everybody in order to get this job done. I didn't want it in the first place, but I've got it now, and I'm going to do the best I can. That's all I can do. And in order to get it done properly, we've got to have the support of every segment of the population." The recording provides a hint of the decisive but vulnerable executive style that was to guide Truman's performance for the next seven years, and trigger both great success and spectacular failures.

The trail of verbatim transcripts of Truman in action stops cold with the end of Truman's few test recordings. Like FDR, Truman actively discouraged verbatim note-taking in White House meetings to encourage candid discussions. Truman did, however, leave behind a personal record of his thoughts of the presidency in action in the form of an intermittent diary he wrote in longhand on plain paper and White House notepads. One of his early diary entries, on June 1, 1945, testifies to the grueling workload he endured for seven years: "Eyes troubling somewhat. Too much reading fine print. Nearly every memorandum has a catch in it and it has been necessary to read at least a thousand of 'em and at least as many reports. Most of it at night." He later estimated that he worked an average of seventeen hours a day, waded through a pile of paper six feet high every night, and signed 600 documents a day. Truman aide Clark Clifford remembered the president in the Oval Room upstairs working through piles of paperwork late at night while wearing an old-fashioned green eyeshade.

Truman also kept up an extensive correspondence with his wife, Bess, who often stayed at the Truman home in Independence, Missouri, to escape the stifling Washington summers and political climate. By all accounts Harry was madly, irrevocably in love with Bess. He asserted that she was "a full partner in all my transactions" and that he consulted her on all major decisions, including dropping the atom bomb, whether to intervene in Korea, and whether to launch the Marshall Plan. He also often reviewed speeches with "the boss," who made last-minute suggestions. Several of his early letters to her as president indicate his commonsense, homespun attitude toward the work of the presidency.

June 6, 1945: "Well I'm getting better organized now. My office force soon will be shaken out and so will my Cabinet when I've gotten State straightened out. War and Navy I shall let alone until the Japanese are out of the picture. It won't be long until I can sit back and study the whole picture and tell 'em what is to be done in each department. When things come to that stage there'll be no more to this job than there was to running Jackson County and not any worry. Foreign relations, national finances, reconversion, and a postwar military policy will be the big headaches—and they can all be solved if the Congress decides to help me do a bang-up job, and I believe they will do that. . . ."

June 12, 1945: "Just two months ago today I was a reasonably happy and contented vice president . . . things have changed so much it hardly seems real. I sit here in this old house and work on foreign affairs, read reports, and work on speeches—all the while listening to the ghosts walk up and down the hallway and even right here in the study. The floors pop and the drapes move back and forth—I can just imagine old Andy and Teddy having an argument over Franklin. Or James Buchanan and Franklin Pierce deciding which was the more useless to the country."

August 10, 1946: "I still have a number of bills staring me in the face. Byrnes called me from Paris this morning asking me not to veto a State Department reorganization bill, which I told Clark Clifford I was sure is a striped-pants boys' bill to sidetrack the secretary of state. Jimmy [James Byrnes, secretary of state] told me it wasn't but I'm still not sure. . . . It sure is hell to be president."

"I get up at five-thirty every morning," Truman told writer John Hersey in 1950. "Most people don't know when the best part of the day is: it's the early morning." Many mornings he would charge through the streets and parks of Washington on a vigorous power-walk for a mile or two at the military regulation pace of 120 steps per minute, swinging a rubber-tipped walking cane and accompanied by ten Secret Service guards, some wielding tommy guns. "I've been taking these walks for thirty years now. I got in the habit of getting up and moving around smart in the early mornings on the farm, and then when I got into politics, I couldn't stop," he explained as Hersey trotted alongside. "A man in my position has a public duty to keep himself in good condition. You can't be mentally fit unless you're physically fit. A walk like this keeps your circulation up to where you can think clearly. That old pump has to keep squirting the juice into your brain, you know."

When he got back to the White House, Truman worked out in the small White House gym and then ate a light breakfast with a shot of bourbon. He fit into suits he wore fifteen years earlier. As early as 7:00, he would enter the Oval Office, park his briefcase on the walnut desk, and dump out the papers he had worked on the night before. They would be routed back to their authors with notes like OK, HST, or THIS LOOKS GOOD TO ME, HST.

At 8:15 every morning early in his term, Truman received a special one- to two-page summary of State, War, and Navy intelligence, the first integrated report of its kind (dubbed "The President's Secret Daily Newspaper" by The New York Times). Between 8:00 and 9:00 A.M. Truman worked through correspondence and dictation with Rose Conway or popped into his staff's offices with decisions and papers. On his desk early on was a small oak plaque he inherited from FDR with three black buttons on it to summon secretaries, but instead he would hurry to the door and say, "Look, I want to dictate a few letters." The buzzers eventually disappeared.

If you went to visit Truman in the Oval Office, he would likely jump up to meet you at the door, ask "How are you?" as if he was really interested in knowing, and escort you to a chair. In contrast to FDR's office atmosphere of smooth, theatrical chaos, Truman was low key, meticulous, punctual, and soft-spoken. Unlike pack-rat FDR, Truman kept his desk neat, with papers squared off at right angles.

Truman's Oval Office walls were painted the same government regulation green as in FDR's time, but by the summer of 1945 all other traces of FDR were gone. Eventually, the famous thirteen-inch-long painted glass sign THE BUCK STOPS HERE appeared on the desk, a gift from Truman friend and U.S. marshal Fred M. Canfil, who saw a similar sign while visiting the Federal Reformatory at El Reno, Oklahoma, and asked the warden if one could be made for Truman. The saying originated in frontier days when poker players would pass around a buckhorn handled marker to indicate who would deal the cards. "We all understood what it meant," said aide Donald Dawson. Another sign on his desk displayed a motto of Mark Twain's, in Twain's own hand: ALWAYS DO RIGHT! THIS WILL GRATIFY SOME PEOPLE AND ASTONISH THE REST. Around Truman's desk blotter in neat rows were four clocks, a gold Shriner's membership plaque, a framed daily appointment list, a beat-up vacuum icewater pitcher inherited from FDR, a piece of granite from Mt. McKinley, a tiny totem pole, and a few magic charms and monkey figurines.

As Truman sat at the desk, on his right side hung a painting of Franklin Roosevelt, and straight ahead about thirty feet across the room, on the curved far wall, portraits were hung of the three liberators of the Western Hemisphere: George Washington, Simon Bolívar, and José de San Martín. Truman replaced Roosevelt's naval and river scenes with framed paintings of early airplanes. By the mantel was a large world globe given to him by Eisenhower that Ike used at his wartime headquarters. Truman would show off the globe by patting it and saying, "We won the war on this old globe; I hope we can win the peace on it, too." On a stand over on his left stood a small mounted statue of Truman's favorite president, Andrew Jackson.

Truman's secret weapon for building teamwork was "the morning meeting," a ritual that began in his first weeks as president and continued through the seven years of his presidency. Every morning at 9:00, Monday through Saturday, after his morning power-walk, Truman waved his top dozen White House staffers into the Oval Office, where they grabbed cane-backed chairs and formed a semicircle around his desk for a high-speed thirty- to sixty-minute staff meeting. During the sessions, he crisply handed out assignments from file slots on his desk labeled for each man. "The staff meetings were clearly joint efforts to share information, with the president conducting each one in a light and informal fashion," wrote speechwriter Ken Hechler. "News of topics discussed and assignments made quickly spread to all hands, and soon everybody felt a part of the unfolding drama." Hechler also recalled that "he encouraged people to be critical and constructive at the same time. The meetings created a team spirit that persisted throughout the day." Truman tried to keep his meetings as short as fifteen minutes, and he moved them along in a crisp manner while listening attentively and writing notes on a legal pad. "He was a voracious consumer of staff and government reports and documents," recalled George Elsey. "He didn't require much sleep, so he would read until midnight or later, and be up again and back at his desk by 5 or 5:30."

Truman started off with a very weak staff, a collection of burned-out FDR holdovers and his own low-wattage cronies. "Truman brought a bunch of incompetents down to the White House," said Robert Nixon, later a good friend of Truman's. "They didn't know first base from breakfast." Truman explained his predicament: "How can I bring big people into government when I don't even know who they are, and they don't know me?" The new president lamented, "I've had no broad contacts in life. The only people I knew to bring down to the White House were those that worked in my office on the Hill. All of whom were small-town people. That's all they were." Liberal journalist I. F. Stone described Truman's crew as "big-bellied good-natured guys who knew a lot of dirty jokes," and "Wimpys who could be had for a hamburger." Journalist Joseph Alsop wrote that the White House now resembled "the lounge of the Lion's Club of Independence, Missouri, where one is conscious chiefly of the odor of ten-cent cigars and the easy laughter evoked by the new smoking room story."

Among these cronies, military aide General Harry Vaughan stood apart. A loudmouthed wiseacre whose friendship with Truman stretched back to the army days, he was ostensibly Truman's military aide, but his main job appeared to be that of taxpayer-funded White House court jester, blasting seismic guffaws during Truman meetings, poker games, and cocktail sessions. Ken Hechler reported that "Vaughan was like a friendly puppy dog to all kinds of self-seekers. He'd invite lobbyists, outside interests, and those anxious to get something out of the White House. Then they would get Truman into trouble by bragging they had an inside track to the White House." Truman's chronic refusal to eject Vaughan and other episodes of perceived corruption and mini-scandals gave Republicans an easy and effective target in the 1952 campaign. When President Richard Nixon was mulling over who to fire from his White House in 1973, his own tape recorder captured him asserting, "The point is, whatever they say about Harry Truman, while it hurt him, a lot of people admired the old bastard for standing by people who were guilty as hell." Actually, few people did.

Eventually Truman built a first-class team, at least in the posts that counted most. Presidential scholar Stephen Hess noted, "Generally Truman picked superb people for the important jobs and ordinary or even unqualified people for the less important jobs." Truman appointed two of the giants of his age, Dean Acheson and George Marshall, to be secretary of state, and they both revered him. The imperious Acheson, schooled at Groton, Yale, and Harvard, made an improbable soul mate for the non-degreed Kansas machine politician Truman, but their close partnership yielded two of his first-term triumphs: the Marshall Plan and the Truman Doctrine. "The objective and its accomplishment is my philosophy, and I am willing and want to pass cred-it around," explained Truman. "The objective is the thing, not personal aggrandizement." Truman gave much of the credit (as well as the risk) for the rebuilding of Europe to Marshall, along with the program's name. "He didn't care who got the credit so long as the job got done," reported George Elsey.

"Harry S. Truman was a tidy man," observed Stephen Hess. "He was offended by Roosevelt's style as an administrator. He believed that govern-ment should be orderly. He did not believe in promoting rivalries between members of his administration. He believed intensely in the importance of loyalty as a unifying principle." You only had to glance at the president's "well-scrubbed, bandbox appearance, the starched handkerchief peeping out of the breast pocket of the sharply pressed double-breasted suit and showing the regulation four points," wrote Bert Cochran, "to realize that here was a person who valued orderliness and predictability." "In general, Truman pre-ferred administrative simplicity and sharply drawn lines of authority—all of which led up to him," observed historian Alonzo Hamby. "The very compact-ness of the staff made hierarchical levels of administration unnecessary and encouraged a collegial atmosphere. Rivalries existed, to be sure, but not vicious infighting. Truman expected his helpers to get along or get out."

Truman put together a smooth-running White House staff, a young, high-energy team of executives who were tightly bonded by their intense devotion to Truman. White House clerk William Hopkins explained, "Truman probably had the human touch to the greatest extent of any president I've worked for." "Each and every one of us had a close personal relationship with him," recalled Truman assistant David Stowe. "In my case, I felt that he was sort of like a second father to me; he was kind, he was decisive, he never bawled anybody out in public; if he had anything to say to them he always said it in private. A guy like that you just have to love." When Acheson had to leave the country when his wife was gravely ill, Truman called the hospital each day to check her status, and relayed the news to Acheson by transoceanic telephone. Acheson confessed, "Well, this is the kind of person that one can adore."

The love for Truman went deep down to the lowliest White House employees. A White House messenger explained: "The first thing you find out is that he calls you by name. You don't feel like some kind of a servant, but like a real human being. One day he was walking along with General George Marshall, and I tried to slip by quickly, but he stopped and introduced me to General Marshall in a way that seemed like I was somebody who was real important." A White House usher said, "When a butler or doorman or usher would enter the room, the Trumans would introduce him to whoever happened to be sitting in the room, even if it were a king or a prime minister." Ken Hechler explained, "He always made everybody feel they were a part of a great team. This extended not only to the staff members but also to the cooks and ushers and carpenters and electricians, all of whom just revered Truman because he knew about them as individuals and knew about their families."

Fifty years after going to work for Truman as special counsel, Clark Clifford still held a burning torch for his old boss. "I've worked for a number of presidents, and President Truman was the kindest and most thoughtful man of them all," Clifford remembered. "He had no bitterness in him. He was a very honest man, he played it straight, you could take his word, he would live up to it as if it were his bond. You always knew where you stood with him. If for any reason you had gotten off the track in some matter, he'd bring it up with you, not in a harsh manner, in a helpful and cooperative manner. The staff didn't break up into cliques and enmities like many administrations have, because he just wouldn't tolerate it. It was an exceedingly happy place to work, because the staff felt so much a part of what he was doing. He's the only President I know that when the time came to take a vacation, he took the vacation *with his staff!*"

"He always made people feel confidence in themselves," recalled Hechler. "He never engaged in put downs or criticisms of his staff. If we made a mistake, it was amazing the manner in which he handled it. It was amazing—he would just smile and say, 'Well, that's behind us.' It was a very human atmosphere. It was just like going to see your Uncle Dudley to go in and talk to him." George Elsey recalled Truman offering a "constant pattern of reassurance to his staff and Cabinet. When they were attacked, he'd say, 'Don't worry, they're just trying to get at me through you. You're doing a good job, keep it up!' He was always straightforward, open, and simple." Dean Acheson was struck by the equanimity Truman showed in his decision-making process. "He didn't make different decisions with different people. He called everyone together. You were all heard and you all got the answer together. He was a square dealer all the way through."

Truman's Oval Office executive style was relentlessly decisive. He tackled most every decision quickly and clearly, and worked through his in-box at machine-gun speed. In his memoirs, Truman wrote, "Within the first few months I discovered that being a president is like riding a tiger. A man has to keep on riding or be swallowed. The fantastically crowded nine months of 1945 taught me that a president either is constantly on top of events or, if he hesitates, events will soon be on top of him. I never felt that I could let up for a single moment." "You could go into his office with a question and come out with a decision more swiftly than any man I have ever known," according to Averell Harriman. "It almost seemed as though he was eager to decide in advance of thinking," Henry Wallace wrote in his diary. In sharp contrast to the circular decision-making style of patrician FDR, "Truman was a dirt farmer," said assistant Ken Hechler. "He plowed a straight furrow when it came to issuing directions and making decisions."

Once, during a poker game, Truman was handed a message about Yugoslav dictator Tito threatening to invade Trieste. Truman scanned the dispatch coolly and handed it back with the order: "Tell the son of a bitch he'll have to shoot his way in." Truman went back to his card game, the message went to Tito, and the threats ceased. When a railroad strike threatened to shut down the country in 1946, Truman called union leaders to the White House and declared, "If you think I'm going to sit here and let you tie up this whole country, you're crazy as hell." Then he anounced: "You've got just forty-eight hours—until Thursday at this time—to reach a settlement. If you don't I'm going to take over the railroads in the name of the government." The unions struck. Two days later Truman stood before Congress to ask authority to draft the striking workers. As he made the speech, a note was passed to him at the lectern. He announced: "Gentlemen, the strike has been settled." His sidekick Harry Vaughan commented: "He's one tough son of a bitch of a man." Truman aide David Bell recalled, "We hadn't expected very much, but as time went on we realized, here was a guy with a backbone of iron! Here was a guy who came from the middle of the United States and was not well educated, who was thoroughly up on the world, and was doing his damnedest."

White House clerk William Hopkins marveled that "nothing stays in the White House over forty-eight hours," and that Truman's flow of paper was "probably the best I have ever experienced." Truman's White House operating style focused tightly on efficiently gathering facts and making decisions. Truman assistant David Stowe commented, "Once he had the information he could make a decision and that was it; there was no delay, no fiddling around, no period of indecision while everybody wondered what was going to happen; he made the decision and [you] knew it was final."

"He was almost demonic in his habits of work and could labor to the point of being near the end of his nervous energy," wrote historian Robert Ferrell. Republican Senate leader Robert Taft said Truman was "a straightforward man and much franker than Roosevelt." Taft said, "He has the quality of decision which is a good thing in an executive," but he worried about Truman's lack of "education or background to analyze soundly the large problems which are before him." Truman worried, too: "I was always thinking about what was pending and hoping that the final decision would be correct. I thought about them on my walks. I thought about them in the morning and the afternoon and thought about them after I went to bed and then did a lot of reading to see if I could find some background of history which would affect what had to be done." Dean Acheson asserted of Truman, "Free of the greatest vice in a leader, his ego never came between him and his job."

Truman's ego and insecurities, however, did fuel a rapid-fire, hair-trigger executive approach that periodically threatened to cause him major problems during his presidency. A close friend of Truman's identified the paradox at the core of Truman the executive: "He is morally brave and intellectually honest. He is, curiously enough, both cocky and humble, if such a thing is possible." Dean Acheson commented, "President Truman's mind is not so quick as his tongue. He could not wait for the end of a question before answering it. Not seeing where he was being led, he fell into traps." At a news conference on November 30, 1950, he blundered into a firestorm when a reporter asked if there was active consideration of the use of the atomic bomb. Truman rashly tackled the question head-on: "There has always been consideration of its use. I don't want to see it used." Truman then gave the impression that General MacArthur had the power to order a nuclear attack in Korea on his own discretion. When the conference ended, reporters raced for telephones and filed panicked headlines that appeared throughout the world. Reaction in world capitals was confusion and near panic—British Prime Minister Clement Atlee jumped on a plane to Washington for an emergency conference to clarify the policy.

"Never kick a fresh turd around on a hot day," Truman is alleged to have said, and throughout his presidency he wrestled with a destructive temper that threatened his effectiveness as chief executive. Historian William Chafe explained that above all, "Truman wanted respect. His failure to get much of it throughout his political career produced an anger that fueled much of his campaigning and periodically blasted out at random targets." In his retirement, Truman would spin tales of titanic face-to-face showdowns with all manner of adversaries, but in reality he was almost always gentle and non-confrontational in person. Instead of head-on confrontation, Truman would scribble out furious, blistering letters to his enemies, lashing out at congressmen, newspaper publishers, and columnists, and usually file the letters away unsent. Truman's staff also served as safety valves for his fury. One day Truman ordered top assistant John Steelman to fire an official after an unauthorized statement to the press. Steelman stalled for a week, then said, "Mr. President, I've searched all over the world, I mean the world, and I can't find anybody to take his place." Truman, smiling, said, "Good. It's a good thing I have you to keep things in order when I fly off the handle."

Truman's first major decision, to detonate nuclear weapons over two Japanese cities to hasten the end of the Pacific war, was one of the most momentous choices in history, but for Truman it may have seemed virtually preordained. The project had attained tremendous momentum by the time Truman was sworn in. Historian Joan Hoff, former head of the Center for the Study of the Presidency, called it a "nondecision" and argued that "Truman did not have much choice about whether to employ the atomic bomb or to continue with plans to invade Japan. Both were served up to him by aides much more knowledgeable than he on these subjects. By the time the secret Manhattan Project, whose price tag was in excess of $2 billion, neared completion in the spring and summer of 1945, the atomic bomb had assumed status as a legitimate weapon among those few who knew about it—to be used when ready." George Elsey asserted that "Truman made no decision because there was no decision to be made. He could no more have stopped it than a train moving down a track."

As Truman matured in the job and gained confidence, he proved to be usually unafraid of dissent and conflicting opinions. He told top aide John Steelman, "The way you can be most helpful to me is to tell me exactly what you think and we'll understand each other." Assistant David Stowe noted that Truman "preferred to have the staff give the problem a thorough going over and to try to find answers—bring these recommendations into him for approval. However, if there were differences of opinion, he always wanted to know this; he didn't want us to feel we had to fight it out with somebody backing off, and then bring in a unanimous position." The recognition of Israel in 1948 was an example of Truman's style of encouraging discussion before a decision was made, according to aide Ken Hechler: "He brought in Clark Clifford to argue the case in favor, and Marshall the case against. He encouraged open debate. What he discouraged was backbiting among the president's staff." Staffer Donald Dawson agreed: "He was a man that sought advice, wanted to know all the facts, wanted to know both sides of any question, and if it took him a while to get it, he insisted on taking that time. For example, in the MacArthur removal, he called in all of the individuals concerned to Blair House, had a thorough discussion of the question back and forth across the table. Everybody had a chance to say what they wanted to say."

Truman's executive style contained an invisible flaw, however, and it would help trigger his biggest disaster. While he often welcomed dissent and debate, unlike FDR, Truman had no sure method for provoking it. His crisp emphasis on fact collection and teamwork served him well by effectively funneling information to his desk, but his executive style was so collegial that opposing points of view could be filtered out before they got there.

"When the president wants advice," a Truman associate noted, "he wants it in direct language: Do this or don't do that. He does not like treatises or arguments." Another Truman intimate agreed: "He likes things to run smoothly. He doesn't like his advisers to disagree." A Cabinet member asserted that "Mr. Truman does not have an inquiring mind. He does not ask many questions." Historian Richard Tanner Johnson noted that Roosevelt's competitive approach "tended to assume distortion and discounted the opinions of his advisers; he built a composite picture by collecting opposing views." "In contrast," argued Johnson, "Truman's system underplayed competition and tended to overlook conflict." Truman's system, Johnson concluded, "relied on what was coming up through the channels: it lacked a means to reach down and inspect for blockage." Truman's Korean War decisions exposed this flaw in tragic dimension.

On the night of June 24, 1950, American officials learned that the North Koreans had attacked South Korea. When Secretary of State Acheson called to confirm the invasion, Truman later recalled saying, "Dean, we've got to stop the sons of bitches no matter what." In the first few weeks of the crisis, Truman and his men met in a spirit of consensus enforced by Truman's resoluteness to stop the Communists. One participant called the atmosphere "the finest spirit of harmony I have ever known." After three months of bitter, inconclusive fighting, General MacArthur executed an audacious amphibious landing at Inchon, and led UN forces on a triumphant dash up the Korean peninsula toward the Chinese border. By September 27, MacArthur was consolidating his forces near the Yalu River border with China, and was authorized by Washington to unify the country as long as the Chinese or Russian Communists did not threaten to enter the fighting.

There were repeated warnings of coming disaster. Junior State Department officials such as Paul Nitze, "Chip" Bohlen, and George Kennan urged caution and advised against crossing the 38th parallel, but their dissent was kept away from Truman, and they were not invited to present their views to the president. On September 30, Chinese leader Chou En-lai issued one of several loud and clear public warnings: "The Chinese people absolutely will not tolerate foreign aggression, nor will they supinely tolerate seeing their neighbors being savagely invaded by the imperialists." On October 3, Chou called in the Indian ambassador and told him explicitly that if UN forces crossed the 38th parallel, China would send troops across the border to defend North Korea. In Washington, in an atmosphere of consensus with nobody playing the role of devil's advocate, Truman and his team discounted the warnings as bluffs and propaganda.

On October 12, Truman flew to Wake Island in the Pacific to confer with General MacArthur about Korea, but the trip seems to have been designed to beef up the president's image on the eve of a midterm election as much as for any meaningful policy review. When Truman bounded down the steps of his plane to meet the general, MacArthur declined to salute his commander. "You're goddamn right he didn't salute me!" Truman later exclaimed to eyewitness Vernon Walters, a military aide who was shocked at MacArthur's indiscretion but later realized it may have been because MacArthur hadn't met face-to-face with a superior in years.

After Truman spent an apparently uneventful forty minutes alone with MacArthur, the two sat down side by side in a small room for a group meeting with assorted aides and officials for less than hour and a half, in a pleasant, rambling, and perfunctory conversation, a meeting with no formal agenda and no in-depth preparation by Truman and his staff. "No new policies, no new strategy of war or international politics, were proposed or discussed," recalled MacArthur.

The stenographic transcript of this meeting is one of the exceedingly few near-verbatim records of Truman in action as president, and it was far from his finest hour. Eyewitness Vernon Walters, who described MacArthur as very deferential to Truman, said the purpose of the meeting was simply to get

MacArthur's opinion on what would happen in Korea. According to the transcript, MacArthur announced grandly: "I believe that formal resistance will end throughout North and South Korea by Thanksgiving. There is little resistance left in South Korea—only about 15,000 men—and those we do not destroy, the winter will." He declared: "In North Korea, unfortunately, they are pursuing forlorn hope. They have about 100,000 men who were trained as replacements. They are poorly trained, led, and equipped, but they are obstinate and it goes against my grain to have to destroy them. They are only fighting to save face. Orientals prefer to die rather than to lose face." Confident in his imminent victory and predicting "the greatest slaughter" if the Communists counterattacked, MacArthur stated, "It is my hope to be able to withdraw the Eighth Army to Japan by Christmas."

Truman said surprisingly little to MacArthur at the conference. He may have felt overconfident in America's global military superiority (to date, the nation had never lost a war) and insecure at the thought of debating with the supremely arrogant military superhero. Truman asked simply: "What are the chances for Chinese or Soviet interference?" MacArthur: "Very little. Had they interfered in the first or second months it would have been decisive. We are no longer fearful of their intervention. . . . We are the best." Incredibly, Truman and his men asked no follow-up questions on Korea and declined to probe MacArthur at all on his confident predictions. Truman happily declared that that it had been a most satisfactory conference, posed for photos, stuck a medal on the fairly bewildered general, and hightailed it back to Washington. Within two weeks, U.S. forces in northern Korea were starting to make scattered contact with Chinese troops.

Secretary of State Dean Acheson believed that Truman's National Security Council meetings in early November were examples of failed decision making. "Here, I believe, the government missed its last chance to halt the march to disaster in Korea. All the president's advisers in this matter, civilian and military, knew that something was badly wrong, though what it was, how to find out, and what to do about it they muffed," Acheson wrote. "I have an unhappy conviction that none of us, myself prominently included, served him as he was entitled to be served." At the core of the failure may have been what Yale University Professor Irving Janis called "groupthink," a syndrome he described as "the tendency for cohesive groups to foster a shared illusion of invulnerability, which inclines them to minimize risks."

Truman also failed to grasp an insight identified by management expert Peter Drucker: "Decisions of the kind the executive has to make are not made well by acclamation. They are made well only if based on the clash of conflicting views, the dialogue between different points of view, the choice between different judgments. The first rule in decision making is that one does not make a decision unless there is disagreement." Acheson noted: "We were frank with each other, but not quite frank enough."

On November 25, 1950, a force of 300,000 Chinese and 65,000 North Koreans charged across the Yalu and chased the stunned UN forces out of North Korea and nearly off the Korean peninsula into the ocean, subjecting MacArthur to one of the worst routs in American military history. The result was a long, bloody stalemate, followed by an inconclusive armistice that continued for over forty years.

Truman's presidency ended in a sad twilight. "After a year or so of the Korean War, it is sad to relate, Harry Truman came close to losing control of the government of the United States," wrote historian Robert Ferrell. His dismissal of General MacArthur in 1951 was wildly unpopular. Truman was blamed for losing China to the Communists, allowing the Soviets to gain the atomic bomb, causing the prolonged agony of the Korean War, and for scandals in various government agencies. Thanks in part to his often poor communications skills (his prepared speeches were as uncomfortable to watch as his early television appearances), Truman was chronically unable to project the public image of a strong chief executive. Historian Alonzo Hamby noted, "For far too much of his time in office, much of the public perceived him as erratic, petty, and a cut or two below his responsibilities. Yet he often felt suspicious of those around him, was capable of considerable vindictiveness, seethed with unfocused hostility, and, above all, dealt poorly with stress."

Truman's approval rating hit a low of 23 percent in late 1951, lower even than Nixon's bottom score of 24 percent in the depths of Watergate. In the 1952 election the American electorate, fed up with Truman and twenty years of Democratic hegemony, gave the presidency, the Senate, and the House of Representatives to the Republicans, delivering a whopping 55 percent vote to Eisenhower.

While most of Truman's progressive Fair Deal proposals were killed by Congress, Truman did manage to persuade legislators to preserve FDR's New Deal social programs, expand the Social Security rolls by 10 million, and fully fund the Marshall Plan. His rock 'em, sock 'em campaign attacks on the "do-nothing, good-for-nothing" Republican Eightieth Congress helped him win reelection in 1948. Southern Democrats buried his civil rights proposals, but Truman achieved one crucial victory with his Executive Order No. 8981, which began a steady desegregation of the armed forces that created a largely integrated military by the end of the Korean War.

To impose much-needed executive order on the sprawling bureaucracies bequeathed him by FDR, Truman backed the unification of the armed forces, the strengthening of the Joint Chiefs of Staff, and the creation of the Department of Defense, National Security Council, and the CIA. In the process, liberal historians charge, he overmilitarized the East-West conflict and spawned a runaway national security state. In his defense against later CIA abuses, Truman asserted: "The CIA was set up by me for the sole purpose of getting all the available information to the president. It was not intended to operate as an international agency engaged in strange activities." In an unsent letter to a critic in September 1952, Truman said of the loss of China: "Chiang Kai-shek's downfall was his own doing." He then rattled off what he considered his foreign policy successes: "The salvation of Greece and Turkey . . . the Berlin Airlift . . . the economic recovery of free Europe . . . NATO . . . the rehabilitation of the Philippine Republic . . . the Japanese Treaty and the Pacific Agreements." The 1949 Berlin Airlift was classic Truman decisiveness: he authorized 278,000 flights to supply the besieged city until the Russians backed down in frustration and lifted their blockade.

For seven years some of the toughest decisions of the century landed in Harry Truman's in-box, and he tackled each one head-on with a decisive executive style that was sometimes inelegant, impulsive, and overly collegial, but seasoned by a basic intellectual honesty and courage. General Joe Collins, a member of Truman's Joint Chiefs of Staff, stated: "I came to have tremendous admiration for this remarkable man. . . . He developed a rare talent for listening to his advisers in this field and quickly getting to the root of a problem. He was ever ready to hear both sides of a proposition and would balance them objectively and finally come up with a clear-cut, fearless decision." In his January 15, 1953, farewell address Truman said, "The president— whoever he is—has to decide. He can't pass the buck to anybody."

Truman's decisive executive style facilitated triumphs like the Marshall Plan, the Berlin Airlift, and the desegregation of the armed forces. When it failed, it helped trigger misjudgments in the Korean War, the failure of much of his legislative program, and the near meltdown of his presidency in 1951.

He left the Oval Office a hated man, but as time passed the American people began rediscovering Harry Truman, and before long they fell in love with him. Today Harry Truman is ranked high in the pantheon of presidential greatness by scholars and is a mythic figure to the American public, thanks in part to David G. McCullough's heroic 1992 biography *Truman*.

When Americans look at Harry Truman perhaps they see their own insecurities, their own humility, inconsistencies, and vulnerabilities, and their own humanity. Perhaps they also see Truman as the remarkable executive he was, a leader who was man enough to acknowledge his shortcomings and try to work through them as he battled the demons of inadequacy and stress, an ordinary American "country judge" capable of bending and shaping history at fundamental moments.

In a 1952 farewell tribute, George Marshall looked upon Truman and proclaimed: "The full stature of this man will only be proven by history, but I want to say here and now that there has never been a decision made under this man's administration, affecting policies beyond our shores, that has not been in the best interest of this country. It is not the courage of these decisions that will live, but the integrity of the man." Matthew Connelly concluded, "He had great administrative ability for one reason: he listened and he had judgment, and he wanted to know all the answers before he made a final decision. And I think that is my definition of a real executive."

Truman aide George Elsey felt that Truman left the Oval Office with his humility intact: "He came into office knowing that there was a hell of a lot he didn't know and he wasn't prepared for; and after nearly eight years of the presidency, I think he left the office still feeling unprepared." At the end of one long day, Truman grabbed a cocktail and groused, "They talk about the power of the president, how I can just push a button to get things done. Why, I spend most of my time kissing somebody's ass."

One day toward the end of 1948, though, Truman, feeling cocky, leaned back in his swivel chair, looked up toward the ceiling of the Oval Office, and offered a comment on his upset reelection victory that was also a fitting elegy for his presidency.

"I taught those sons of bitches a thing or two, didn't I?" said Truman slowly, punctuating every word.

During his presidency, Truman's handful of Oval Office test recordings were stored in the locked closet underneath the Oval Office, alongside FDR's recorder. Truman completely forgot about the recordings, never spoke about them publicly, and left them behind in the White House basement when his presidency ended in January 1953.

In the spring of 1954, a White House clerk came across a box full of the now-obsolete recordings during a renovation of the area beneath the Oval Office. The small partitioned recording room was dismantled, and on June 24, 1954, the Truman recordings left the White House on their way to the National Archives, where they would remain mostly forgotten by history.

No one knows what happened to the machine itself.

CHAPTER 3

Dwight D. Eisenhower
The Organized Executive

*"I have to sign so much god-damned paper
I haven't had a chance to read these days!"*

DWIGHT EISENHOWER,
OVAL OFFICE DICTAPHONE RECORDING,
JANUARY 7, 1955

THE OVAL OFFICE
JANUARY 7, 1955, 11:30 A.M.

The most powerful man in Congress was about to enter the Oval Office for a private meeting with the president. On the agenda: an issue that had tormented Dwight Eisenhower for the last two years, a problem he privately feared could "wreck the United States" and cause "chaos in international affairs." It was the beginning of Eisenhower's third year in the Oval Office.

As Senator Walter George, Democrat of Georgia, dean of the U.S. Senate, and chairman of the Foreign Relations Committee, entered the room, Eisenhower quietly flipped a concealed toggle switch, triggering an electrical current that ran through a wire out to a small light panel on his secretary Ann Whitman's desk adjacent to the Oval Office. On this signal, Whitman turned on a Dictaphone Dictacord A2TC machine hidden in a nearby storage closet. It was a two-foot-high, forty-five-pound machine designed for police, fire, emergency, and courtroom recordings featuring one thirty-minute recording deck on top of another, which fed sound signals onto nonerasable blue plastic Dictabelts.

"Well old friend! How nice of you to come in!" Eisenhower fired off the greeting like a friendly howitzer, and ordered the elderly senator to sit down as the Oval Office door closed.

For the next forty minutes, through a microphone concealed in the president's desk, Eisenhower's Dictaphone recorded their confidential discussion on the so-called Bricker Amendment, a resolution named for its author Senator John Bricker of Ohio. The resolution was a reaction by conservatives against both Roosevelt's concessions at the wartime Yalta conference and against U.S. entry into the United Nations, and would amend the Constitution to limit the president's power to make treaties. It was opposed by both Eisenhower and George, but supported by most of Eisenhower's fellow Republicans and many national organizations, including the American Bar Association, the VFW, and the United States Chamber of Commerce. Eisenhower believed that the amendment would subject all treaties of the past and future to endless challenges by states, a sure recipe for chaos.

The resolution had bedeviled Eisenhower since his first days as president, and through 1953 and 1954 he maneuvered strenuously behind the scenes to kill it. He spent untold hours writing substitute amendments himself, working over them word by word. He brought in constitutional lawyers, the secretary of state, the attorney general, and leaned on and cajoled Republican and Democratic lawmakers. Eisenhower "was a far more complex and devious man than most people realized, and in the best sense of those words," said a man who would know, Vice President Richard Nixon. "Not shackled to a one-track mind, he always applied two, three or four lines of reasoning to a single problem," Nixon wrote, and few problems bothered Eisenhower more than Bricker.

But the resolution would not die. A disgusted Eisenhower told his press secretary Jim Hagerty: "If it's true that when you die the things that bothered you most are engraved on your skull, I am sure I'll have there the mud and dirt of France during the invasion and the name of Senator Bricker." Now, the resolution was threatening to break out of committee and make a dash for the Senate floor. Ike wanted to kill it for good, and he needed Walter George to help him do it.

The recording of this meeting, from the first batch of Eisenhower Oval Office recordings ever found, was discovered forty-one years later, when, during research for this book, archivists at the Eisenhower Library were asked to search their holdings for Dictaphone material. Notations by Eisenhower's secretary, Ann Whitman, on memos for twenty-seven Oval Office meetings implying the existence of an Eisenhower recording system were first noted by government officials processing the President's Secretary's File (also known as the Ann Whitman Diary Series File) in the early 1970s. In 1979, Rice University history professor Frances Lowenheim widely publicized the memos and assumed "taping" system, but no tapes were ever found.

According to forty-five surviving pages of summaries and partial transcripts of the twenty-seven meetings, some of the key issues of Eisenhower's presidency were touched on in the recordings, including increasing aid to Vietnam, the excesses of Senator Joseph McCarthy, the Soviets getting the H-Bomb, and meetings with Secretary of State Dulles, senators and congressmen, labor leader George Meany, journalists, aides, businessmen, and heads of state Emperor Haile Selassie of Ethiopia and Queen Frederika of Greece. Also among the people Ike recorded was his own vice president, Richard Nixon. According to one memo, he switched on the recorder on June 29, 1954, to tape a meeting during which he gave Nixon a scolding for campaigning too aggressively against the Democrats. Eisenhower told Nixon that he was damaging the administration's efforts to achieve a bipartisan foreign policy.

Eisenhower's use of an Oval Office recorder was a closely held secret at the time, and even in 1979, in the wake of publicity generated by Professor Lowenheim, Ann Whitman dismissed the claim that Ike had a secret taping system. "Absolutely a lie," she insisted. She did say she remembered one attempt to use such a system but that the recording was bad and very difficult to transcribe. "I just gave up," she recalled. In an oral history dated 1991, the year before she died, Mrs. Whitman was slightly more forthcoming. "They put this monster in my office and, of course, it didn't work at all," she said. "He was supposed to push a button and the red light on my desk if he wanted me to listen in." She did concede that "we didn't want other people to know about it." In fact, according to the memos, Eisenhower conducted at least twenty-seven recordings from late 1953 and continued sporadically through 1955. Judging from the format and content of other memos, archivists have speculated that Eisenhower may have recorded as many as 100 meetings. Still, no trace of any tapes ever surfaced at the Eisenhower Library and the trail was assumed to end there.

In fact, Eisenhower left clues over the years pointing toward not only his practice of recording, but to the technology he used, which, as it turned out, was not a tape recorder as such. In a July 1954 Cabinet meeting, he laughed and announced, "You know, boys, it's a good thing when you're talking to someone you don't trust to get a record made of it. There are some guys I just don't trust in Washington, and I want to have myself protected so that they can't later report that I said something else." By now, secretarial monitoring of telephone calls was becoming increasingly common in government: Mrs. Whitman monitored Eisenhower's telephone conversations sporadically, while Secretary of State John Foster Dulles had his telephone conversations monitored and transcribed as a matter of routine.

The most direct clue to Eisenhower's Oval Office recording technology appeared in his bestselling World War II memoir published in 1948, *Crusade in Europe*. There he revealed that during the war, to keep track of decisions and details, he installed an "automatic recording system that proved most effective" as a management tool. "The method," wrote Eisenhower, "was a complete wiring of my war room with Dictaphones so placed as to pick up every word uttered in the room. Conversations were thus recorded on a machine just outside my office where a secretary instantly transcribed them into notes and memoranda for the benefit of my associates in the Operations Division. As a consequence, and often without further reference to me, the staff was able to translate every decision and agreement into appropriate action and to preserve such records as were necessary." Eisenhower was careful to add: "I made it a habit to inform visitors of the system that we used so that each would understand its purpose was merely to facilitate the execution of business." He was clearly impressed with the Dictaphone system's capabilities, reporting that it "saved me hours of work in the dictations of notes and directives and relieved my mind of the necessity of remembering every detail of fact and opinion that was presented to me."

In 1982, a retired former Dictaphone technician named John Raynor walked in unannounced to the Washington office of *Time* magazine's Hugh Sidey, the dean of modern presidential reporting, and told him that Eisenhower's fondness for Dictaphones stretched back to the early 1940s, when Eisenhower installed a Dictaphone to record his telephone calls at his office in the Pentagon. Raynor told Sidey that during Eisenhower's brief tenure as president of Columbia University in New York in 1950, Eisenhower called him in to place small microphones and a switch in the well of his mahogany desk to connect to a Dictaphone recorder at his secretary's desk. A cabinetmaker was called in to construct panels to conceal small microphones. Ike evidently tested the apparatus but couldn't get it to work properly. The following year, when Eisenhower was sent to Europe to command NATO forces, Raynor was packed off on a secret mission to fly Dictaphone recording gear to Ike's new headquarters, the Astoria Hotel in Paris, and wire up the general's office. He cleverly placed the microphones inside recessed grillwork at the front of the desk, so a guest facing Ike would be speaking almost directly into the invisible microphones. The story, appearing only in *Time*'s international edition, attracted relatively little attention.

In response to a research request for this book, Eisenhower Library archivists conducted an exhaustive search of their holdings, not for tapes or discs, but for Dictabelts, on the speculation that Eisenhower's use of them might have continued into the Oval Office. Finally, ten Dictabelts were located in storage shelves in the library's audiovisual department, one of which was labeled in Eisenhower's handwriting, "file in safe." In early 1997, an Eisenhower Library archivist hand-carried the Dictabelts to the Dictaphone Corporation technical center in Melbourne, Florida, to monitor an attempt to recover the contents of the Dictabelts, and to protect any national security or personal information that might be contained on them. The Dictabelts, which were severely creased from being folded into envelopes for over four decades, were also on a format the Dictaphone technician could not easily play back. Finally, they lashed together several period Dictaphone machines to do a jerry-rigged transfer, digitized the signal, adjusted the speed, and removed some of the surface noise.

It was then, forty-two years later, that the sounds of Eisenhower's Oval Office meeting on January 7, 1955, first returned to life.

When Senator Walter George sat down in the Oval Office that day, he faced a bald-headed, sparkling blue-eyed president who was sixty-four years old, had a ruddy, highly expressive face and spidery fingers, and was prone to chew restlessly on his eyeglasses or jump up from his desk and pace around the thick-piled green carpet as he grappled with the pressures of his job. "No man on earth knows what this job is all about," he told longtime colleague Field Marshal Bernard Law Montgomery. "It's pound, pound, pound. Not only is your intellectual capacity taxed to the utmost, but your physical stamina." Montgomery said of him: "He has the power of drawing the hearts of men towards him as a magnet attracts the bits of metal."

"Ike" Eisenhower was raised in the Kansas prairie town of Abilene, graduated first in his class of 275 officers at the army's 1926 Command and General Staff School, and went on to become one of the greatest military leaders of the twentieth century, commanding the victorious Allied invasions of North Africa and France. Despite his aw-shucks disclaimers, "I'm just a farm boy from Kansas" or "I'm just a simple soldier," Eisenhower was a Washington veteran, holding executive military posts in the capital during the Hoover years and into the New Deal era and then again at the start of World War II, gaining invaluable bureaucratic combat experience.

"From his West Point graduation in 1915, through World War II to NATO," historian Fred Greenstein noted, "his assignments either required organizational management or gave him vantage points from which to view and reflect on the problem of guiding large-scale collective endeavors."

Eisenhower once asserted, "I have been in politics, the most active sort of politics, most of my adult life. There is no more political organization in the world than the armed services of the United States." He had traveled through Asia, Central America, Europe, North Africa, the Soviet Union, China, and Japan and built personal relationships with many world leaders, including Stalin, Churchill, and Adenauer.

As an aide to the brilliant, flamboyant General Douglas MacArthur for seven years in the 1930s in Washington and the Philippines, Eisenhower suffered through the general's screaming fits, and learned much about how to be and how not to be a general. At the start of World War II he served as a Pentagon war planner under General George C. Marshall, whom he considered a perfect teacher: "I wouldn't trade one Marshall for fifty MacArthurs." Eisenhower absorbed Marshall's commonsense approach, emphasis on teamwork, and his philosophy that effective decisions required precise information, planning, and delegation.

During the next two years Ike honed his diplomatic and political skills by dealing successfully with some of the most impossible personalities of the twentieth century, among them Field Marshal Montgomery, General George Patton, and General Charles de Gaulle. His leadership skills culminated in the triumphant success of Operation Overlord, and his immense popularity and landslide election in 1952. Eisenhower saw his lack of partisan political attachments as a strategic advantage in the presidency. On a 1954 Oval Office recording, he argued: "I will make smarter political decisions than a lot of guys who are pros, because they have gotten used to the narrow quick advantage, rather than taking a look at the longer range."

When he took over the Oval Office, Eisenhower's overriding objectives were to restore domestic stability in the wake of the oscillations and low-level scandals of the Truman years, and to peacefully contain the global spread of communism without triggering combat with a newly nuclearized Soviet Union. He also had to organize and direct a government that was blossoming into gigantic proportions. The last time a Republican was in charge, the federal budget was under $4 billion; now it was over $85 billion.

Eisenhower's Oval Office was the sparsely furnished, no-nonsense headquarters of a "clean-desk man." The desk was appointed with only four pens, a blotter, two phones, and a silver tray set with a stone from each place the president had lived. Almost no paperwork was visible, but when a visitor asked him how he kept his desk so neat, he shyly pulled open the center drawer, which was overflowing with paperwork. In the president's line of sight on the wall opposite his desk was a painting of an Alpine hut on a brightly hazy and windy mountainside. On another wall, hung side by side, were portraits of General Robert E. Lee and President Abraham Lincoln. On the work table behind him was a fancy marble clock-barometer dating back to the Ulysses Grant administration.

A small black piece of wood on the desk captured the essence of Eisenhower's operating style. On it was inscribed a Latin saying attributed to sixteenth-century Jesuit general Claudio Aquaviva: SUAVITER IN MODO, FORTITER IN RE. On the back side was its English translation: GENTLY IN MANNER, STRONGLY IN DEED. Eisenhower explained: "I am not one of the desk-pounding type that likes to stick out his jaw and look like he is bossing the show. I would far rather get behind and, recognizing the frailties and requirements of human nature, I would rather try to persuade a man to go along—because once I have persuaded him, he will stick."

When Eisenhower's Dictabelt kicked on for the morning meeting with Senator George, the president greeted his guest and quickly got to the point.

THE OVAL OFFICE
JANUARY 7, 1955, 11:30 A.M.

President Eisenhower with Senator Walter George
Chairman, Senate Foreign Relations Committee
RE: *Congressional Action on the Bricker Amendment*
audio recording on Dictaphone A2TC machine

Forty-two years after Eisenhower secretly recorded this summit meeting with the most powerful man in Congress, the recording was discovered in the Eisenhower Library.

EISENHOWER: The point I wanted to talk to you about a little bit was this confounded Bricker Amendment which I see coming up to cause trouble again.

I've always of course been strong for the conviction that I believe that any treaty or any executive agreement that violates our Constitution ought to be null and void. I'm perfectly willing to say that. I have never yet, and I've lived with this now for almost two years, I've never yet found any language that goes beyond that which can satisfy the Bricker position without in my opinion, dangerously weakening the position of our country.

Even, in some of its aspects it brings us close to the French sort of thing, where there's no one in the executive in France in fact that has any real responsibility.

GEORGE: All right, all right.

EISENHOWER: I am certain, I think Senator Bricker is perfectly honest in his opinions, in his convictions. He's seen some abuse of power by the executive, which we've all seen.

GEORGE: Yes, that's true, that's quite true.

EISENHOWER: But some abuse of power, Senator, as I see it, can occur in any three-cornered government on world conditions of the moment. If there's a weak executive there's a strong and rather unified legislature, we can have circumstances arise that constitute abuse. We can have the judiciary—an invigorated judiciary that likes certain laws over others. So we have little ups and downs and little valleys and peaks. And by and large I think our Constitution has brought us along pretty well for 177 years. And I am perfectly safe with Section One of that resolution. But when they continue to take it further along, I find so far I have not been able to go along with it.

Now I wanted to have this little talk so that I could assure you personally that there is absolutely nothing personal about my view on this. I've listened. I've listened to every side. I've had the opposing people sitting in front of me here, I've had Senator Bricker, and the Attorney General.

As a matter of fact, I think Secretary Dulles at first didn't even want Section One, because he thought we'd have to find a new meaning for that. Why did they put that in? I said I'll vote for Section One, and I think that anyone that I know of now sees that probably we ought to do something definite to show that we're not trying to set a treaty or executive agreement above our Constitution. But the others, when they go beyond that, I get lost, Senator, I really get deeply concerned.

I know that you had convictions—we had a long talk this last year. And I know that coming from the judiciary you would have convictions. But you are not only the President pro tem, but you are I'm certain probably the most respected senator in the Senate.

GEORGE: Do you mind if I smoke?

EISENHOWER: Oh, no sir! You got matches? (*pulls open drawers*)

GEORGE: Yes, I've got matches.

EISENHOWER: I always keep matches around. Matter of fact, I only keep cigars around here for my friends. I never smoke, so I forget all about them.

GEORGE: I see those cigars by the stand. I'd offer you one of mine but they are not cigars.

EISENHOWER: Oh? They're just something that gives you the feeling of smoking?

GEORGE: "Cigar de-natured."

EISENHOWER: I'll be damned! It's a special cigar?

GEORGE: That's what it is. (*lights and puffs up his cigar*) Pardon me.

Now Eisenhower gently threatened to go over the heads of Congress and use his enormous popularity to appeal to the public for the resolution's defeat. Richard Nixon observed that "because of his military experience, he was always thinking in terms of alternatives, action and counteraction, attack and counterattack." But, Nixon also noted, "an Eisenhower characteristic was never to take direct action requiring his personal participation where indirect methods could accomplish the same result."

EISENHOWER: I would hope that because of your great judicial eye, that you would think this matter over and come back and see whether we couldn't avoid a situation where I feel it's necessary to go try to appeal to the country to keep legislators from approving it. I would hope and expect that we could have an honest meeting of the minds and trust the several branches of the government to work together through the years and not let one or two or three or four cases of violations here or there upset us and do something our Constitution couldn't very well recover from.

GEORGE: I can appreciate your attitude about it, Mr. President, and that you're concerned about it frankly. Now, last year we did have a talk, and I agreed with your position. I refused to go along with the rest of the resolution . . . .

EISENHOWER: We have a sort of philosophical paradox, or let's say a practical paradox. Our government was set up mainly to meet the situation of dealing with things abroad and things at home, so there is in our Constitution, you might say, built-in difficulties of interpretation. But nevertheless, we do know this: our Constitution was really devised because of the difficulty we got in when we couldn't get states to obey the treaties we were making with Britain. So here we are.

Eisenhower now took a passing shot at the man he felt was ultimately responsible for the Bricker mess, his former boss Franklin D. Roosevelt.

GEORGE: Oh, sir, I don't deny, I personally think that at least one president that I could name made very great errors in his way of dealing with this. But after all, he was a man of, almost an egomaniac in his belief in his own wisdom. Actually, when you come down to it, there is nothing in the Constitution that could have prevented Yalta and that could have prevented Potsdam and the others because they did not affect internal things . . . .

When Senator George mentioned the harm the amendment could do to Western European security, Eisenhower jumped in:

EISENHOWER: Oh, I'll tell you one thing, just while you remarked on that. It's a question, now you're talking about something which I gave some years of my life to. I'm sure that unless Western Europe unites very definitely in the economic and political fields, then Western civilization is darned near, well, I don't know, I'm not going to use such a strong word as "doomed"—but Western civilization in its struggle against communism is just fighting with handcuffs around it.
GEORGE: It's an unequal fight, there's no question about that . . . .

The president then argued that the Bricker Amendment could not prevent another Yalta, as many people have tried to tell him. Finally, the president quietly asked:

EISENHOWER: Senator, what do you think is the best procedure to follow with the Bricker Amendment now that he's introduced it to keep the pot from boiling all over?
GEORGE: I don't know that there's any procedure that can be followed except in the committee. I think Senator Kilgore* will be disposed not to bring it out, or let it come out, but a majority of them [on the

*Senator Harley Kilgore, D-WV, chairman of the Senate Judiciary Committee.

Judiciary Committee] will insist on bringing it up sometime because they do feel that Senator Bricker is entitled to his day in court.

Is there any way on Earth you can persuade Senator Bricker?

EISENHOWER: No, I don't think so.

GEORGE: I don't think there's any way, nobody unless the president can do it.

EISENHOWER: Well, I've tried, I've tried it, Senator. The only thing I would, if the Committee could keep it down to Section One.

GEORGE: Oh, I'll do that, I'll do that.

EISENHOWER: If they could keep it down to Section One, then we could all go along.

GEORGE: Oh, yes. We'll do the process that way. It clarifies the public mind on many issues.

EISENHOWER: You see, every time I get these long letters from the country it is, "I don't want a treaty to destroy our Constitution." Well, the assurance to the public would be right there in Section One: "No executive agreement, no treaty can violate the Constitution," period . . . .

The meeting broke up as Eisenhower extracted a promise from Senator George that he would talk to Bricker and other senators to try to postpone or limit the resolution. The Bricker Amendment soon petered out and died a quiet death, thanks in part to this kind of relentless, behind-the-scenes presidential maneuvering.

The president walked Senator George to the Oval Office door and returned to his desk. The room was silent for a time, then the president rustled papers and asked for his lunch to be brought in.

Instead of the relaxed, genial, grinning grandfather figure of the newsreels and television, a man capable of stupefyingly mangled syntax at press conferences, the Dictaphone had revealed an Eisenhower who was a lightning-quick conversationalist, sharp, barrel-voiced, diligent, a man who exerted a tight grip on the issues he cared most about, conserving his power, but not afraid to threaten to use it.

His chief military assistant General Andrew Goodpaster explained, "Eisenhower displayed two personas; the one which was public, the Chief of State role, then the 'indoor Eisenhower,' the role of Chief Executive." After a major global policy review in 1953, foreign affairs "Wise Man" George Kennan watched Eisenhower sum up all the arguments and marveled that he "showed his intellectual ascendancy over every man in the room."

Eisenhower's sunny but hesitant public image influenced the first wave of historical opinion against him in the 1960s, but as Eisenhower's presidential papers were published and his aides began speaking with historians, a gradual awareness dawned that Eisenhower was a much stronger closed-door chief executive than anybody had imagined.

The reappraisal of Eisenhower's leadership and executive style culminated in the publication of historian Fred Greenstein's 1982 book, *The Hidden-Hand Presidency*, which argued that Eisenhower used deliberate strategies "that enabled him to exercise power without seeming to flex his muscles," including a refusal to "engage in personalities," the selective practice of delegation, and building public support that transcended the nations' social and political divisions. Even liberal historian Arthur M. Schlesinger, Jr., joined in Eisenhower's rehabilitation, conceding, "Whatever his defects as a public leader, we may stipulate that behind the scene Eisenhower showed more energy, interest, purpose, cunning, and command than many of us understood in the 1950s; that he was the dominant figure in his administration whenever he wanted to be (and he wanted to be more often than it seemed at the time); and that the very talent for self-protection that led him to hide behind his reputation for muddle and to shove associates into the line of fire obscured his considerable capacity for decision and control."

After the meeting with Senator George, the Dictaphone kept rolling, catching the sounds of Eisenhower's Oval Office. Eisenhower grabbed a document on his desk and, exasperated, said, "Oh, now here's something else." An aide now quietly entered the Oval Office and explained that it was a finished letter to General Omar Bradley for his signature. Eisenhower, signing it without time to read it thoroughly, asked if the aide had checked the letter: "Well now, it's all right, is it?" The aide assured him it was OK.

As he signed the letter, Eisenhower muttered, "I have to sign so much god-damned paper I haven't had a chance to read these days!" The aide responded sheepishly: "I'm very careful with these things."

The two now quietly worked though a pile of paper.

Outside the Oval Office, Mary Jane McCaffree, press secretary to Mrs. Eisenhower and unofficial liaison between the president's West Wing and Mrs. Eisenhower's offices in the East Wing, was cooling her heels waiting for the signal to step in. She had to discuss a thorny issue with the president: invitation lists for two upcoming White House dinners, the vice president's and the Speaker's dinners scheduled for the week after next.

It was near lunch time but his food hadn't arrived yet, and Eisenhower, obviously spent from his meeting with Senator George, was getting cranky. His aide may have sensed this and dreaded the prospect of tackling a matter as detailed as the invitation lists. During the election campaign, on a visit to Philadelphia, when he was handed a twenty-five-page briefing on the city, Ike groused, "It only took a six-page directive to get me into Normandy." On another occasion he declared: "If a proposition can't be stated in one page, it isn't worth saying." Still, the aide decided to plunge ahead and announce Miss McCaffree: "There's one little thing. Mary Jane wants you to look at some lists of guests or something."

"Oh, for Christ's sake, I don't give a damn about this! Bring her in. Where is she?" Then, in an instant, Eisenhower's tone went from angry to friendly, as he may have realized she was within earshot just outside the door. He said sweetly, "Tell her to come in."

Eisenhower quickly flashed back to irritation as he carefully scrutinized the lists, name by name: "Well, why do you have to ask so many congressmen? I think it's silly . . . (*whistles*) Eighty-two on each of these? Good God! What is the maximum we can take? . . . Why do you have to have [Senator] George W. Malone? He's never voted on our side on any single thing! . . . Certainly some of them will be sick or dead or something . . . I think Mamie ought to give a *special* dinner . . . My God!"

"He had flashes of anger of great intensity," reported General Goodpaster. "There was a buzzer on my desk that he rarely used. It was never good news when that buzzer sounded. He got very angry whenever the armed services went into public print with rivalry or when they were trying to whip up a sense of danger in order to get additional weapons or when people came into the White House to propose a crash program. That was anathema to him. He said 'don't come in here and hold a pistol to my head. Where the hell were we when we should have been thinking about this?'" Goodpaster remembered being "taken apart a strip at a time by the president." If Goodpaster walked into the Oval Office with a well-prepared rationale "and I could convey it, fine. If it wasn't, I'd go out with a bigger agenda than I came in with, and in many cases we would then set up a meeting in his office because there was more to it than appeared in the proposal. But that's the mark of a superb executive."

"What the hell is this?" Eisenhower once barked at his son John Eisenhower, then on the White House staff. "Do you expect a president to sign a bunch of garbage like this?" On another occasion Eisenhower got irritated with aide Bobby Cutler for going on too long in a briefing session. The president snapped, "Dammit, Bobby, bring us issues and options so we can make some decisions here." After a screwup over a speech draft, he lamented, "If I had had a staff like this during the war we would have lost it." Even members of the animal kingdom weren't safe from Ike's temper. On his way to and from the office Ike would practice his golf shots in a putting green installed by the American Public Golf Association right outside the Oval Office. Truman had fed the resident squirrels and buried acorns and walnuts in the grass, creating generations of fat and happy varmints, which infuriated Eisenhower. "The next time you see one of those squirrels go near my putting green, take a gun and shoot it!" he ordered. The creatures were spared the firing squad, rounded up, and turned loose in a Washington park to an unknown fate.

Eisenhower customarily awoke in barracks tradition at the crack of dawn, around 6:00 A.M., and left the bedroom quietly to avoid disturbing Mamie. He then wolfed down a light breakfast on a tray while intently reviewing the Washington and New York newspapers and newsmagazines, and arrived at the Oval Office as early as 7:30. Late in the evening at the end of his first full day in the office, he wrote, "My first full day at the President's Desk. Plenty of worries and difficult problems. . . . The result is that today just seems like a continuation of all I've been doing since July '41—even before that." From 8:15 to 9:30, Eisenhower usually worked through documents or dictation with Ann Whitman. Ike would often challenge and argue over each item in a report, General Goodpaster reported, "a very intense give and take, all done in a very dignified and cordial way but very, very serious." Then came appointments through the day, often at fifteen-minute intervals.

Eisenhower preferred oral, in-person briefings, instead of on paper, which helps explain his habit of regularly holding large meetings. According to top assistant Sherman Adams, "He seldom exchanged written memoranda with me or with the Cabinet members or his staff. He preferred to get his information by talking with people who knew the issues involved in the matter he was considering. He listened intently, keeping the conversation brief and to the point with no wandering disgressions, interrupting now and then with a quick and penetrating question that brought the whole question into clearer focus."

Eisenhower usually worked straight through until 1:00 P.M., then had a business lunch and worked till 6:00 P.M. Unlike Truman, who left the Oval Office with a pile of paperwork, Eisenhower tried to leave a clean desk behind. After his heart attack in 1955, a small hideaway office with a bed was quietly set up just beside the Oval Office, where he periodically rested on doctor's orders. Following a cocktail, he joined Mamie for dinner on a tray while watching the nightly TV news, or ate in the West Sitting Hall with Mamie's mother, who lived with them in the White House. Through the evening he would look over some paperwork in his bedroom or the Oval Study and dabble with his paint brushes in a small studio before turning in to read Wild West stories in bed.

Eisenhower tried to refresh himself from the pressures of the job by taking frequent golf breaks, "stag" dinners, and fishing trips with his "gang" of tycoon friends, and most notoriously, long vacations. One epic vacation began in August 1955, drifted into late September, and showed no sign of ending until Eisenhower suffered a heart attack on September 24. That the government ran smoothly during his two-month convalescence testifies either to his luck or his organizational skill.

"Either you know how to manage or you don't," Eisenhower declared to Goodpaster, and his guiding executive principle was simply, organization itself; organization as a means, a method, and a goal. "Organization cannot make a genius out of an incompetent," he wrote in his memoirs. "On the other hand, disorganization can scarcely fail to result in inefficiency and can easily lead to disaster." Eisenhower defined the purpose of organization: to "simplify, clarify, expedite, and coordinate; it is a bulwark against chaos, confusion, delay and failure. Organization cannot of course make a successful leader out of a dunce, any more than it should make a decision for its chief. But it is effective in minimizing the chances of failure and in insuring that the right hand does, indeed, know what the left hand is doing."

Eisenhower was skeptical of FDR's executive style, disgusted with Truman's, and faulted both for bad organization. While observing one of FDR's feuds in 1933, Eisenhower wrote in his diary: "The mere fact that such a fight can begin and rage between two principal agents of the president, both responsible for important phases of his program for agricultural rehabilitation, is evidence of faulty organization."

"Truman didn't know any more about government than a dog knows about religion," Ike snorted, and he was horrified to learn that Truman had no chief of staff and that major government meetings happened on an unscheduled basis with no pre-staffed agenda. "For years I had been in frequent contact with the Executive Office of the White House and I had certain ideas about the system, or lack of system, under which it operated," he wrote. "With my training in problems involving organization it was inconceivable to me that the work of the White House could not be better systematized than had been the case during the years I observed it."

Eisenhower started organizing his presidency the minute he was elected, scheduling first-ever pre-inauguration Cabinet meetings at New York's Commodore Hotel. He saw one of his main jobs as an executive to be a leader at the conference table: in a 1948 memo as army chief of staff he wrote, "In organizing teams, personality is equally important with ability. . . . Leadership is as vital in conference as it is in battle." At his first Cabinet meetings, he ordered an agenda drawn up, minutes taken, and the discussions kept from wandering. He saw the meetings as a way of building teamwork and keeping himself and everyone else informed. He announced that he expected policy disagreements, but warned against personal disputes: "I hope that before we have gone very long each one of you will consider the rest of you here your very best friends in the world. . . . That is the perfect way." At the first post-inaugural meeting he told his Cabinet: "There is no use to try to conceal an error" and they should "advertise your blunders, then forget them."

An early memo to assistant Sherman Adams announced the style Ike would follow as president: "The marks of a good executive," Eisenhower wrote, "are courage in delegating work to subordinates, and his own skill in coordinating and directing their efforts." Adams's official title was assistant to the president—Ike avoided the term "chief of staff" because he thought politicians might think it sounded too military. Eisenhower charged Adams with overseeing White House schedules, patronage, personnel, speechwriting, Cabinet and congressional affairs, and, crucially, the flow of paper to his desk. "Eisenhower simply expected me to manage a staff that would boil down, simplify, and expedite the urgent business that had to be brought to his personal attention and to keep as much work of secondary importance as possible off his desk." Adams would also referee fights between Cabinet secretaries by pleading: "We must not bother the president with this. He is trying to keep the world from war."

Adams's role was central, but he was not all-powerful, as many critics charged at the time. Foreign relations was the exclusive joint empire of Eisenhower and super-heavyweight Secretary of State John Foster Dulles, press relations were managed by the ultra-professional Press Secretary Jim Hagerty, and the trusted General Goodpaster coordinated military and intelligence matters, working with the national security adviser. Goodpaster explained, "It was similar to what he did when he was in command in Europe, in the war, and then what he did when he was at SHAPE—block out wide areas, give policy direction, and then look to subordinates to handle the operations and the details, but having a chief of staff who knew how to be a chief of staff." Goodpaster argued that, contrary to widespread belief, "it was not on any strict military model," because "principal staff members were far from having the kind of definitive and hierarchical assignment of functions that you associate with the traditional and established military staffs."

Eisenhower scheduled four programmed "set piece" meetings each week, for two hours each: a breakfast with congressional leaders at 8:30 A.M. on Tuesdays, a press conference at 10:00 A.M. on Wednesdays, a National Security Council meeting at 9:00 A.M. on Thursdays, a Cabinet meeting at 10:00 A.M. on Fridays. Inspired by his observations of the British War Cabinet, Eisenhower set up the most organized and effective Cabinet of the century. A formidable weapon was Maxwell Rabb, an energetic, charming young Boston lawyer whom Eisenhower appointed as the first modern American Cabinet secretary. Rabb cleared an agenda with Eisenhower for every meeting, and afterward held a parallel meeting with Cabinet undersecretaries to ensure action and follow-up. Every three months a "Judgment Day" meeting was held, where secretaries reported their accomplishments and failures to the group.

General Goodpaster recalled, "He put a lot of authority on what he called his operating lieutenants. That's the heads of the departments and agencies, and then he growled a good deal if they brought their problems back to him, the problems that he thought they should solve over there." Once Eisenhower cut off an arcane discussion by Defense Secretary Charles Wilson by saying, "Charlie, you run Defense. We both can't do it, and I won't do it. I was elected to worry about a lot of other things than the day-to-day operations of a department." Eisenhower once told the Cabinet: "To make a mistake in judgment is excusable, but to make a mistake in preparation can't be excused."

After he left the presidency, Eisenhower explained that his Cabinet strategy was to share information and build teamwork: "Government cannot function properly if anybody who's in an important position is confined merely to his own particular function or field of direct interest. So when he would come back from any principal trip or had any great problem, I would insist that he give a briefing to all of the Cabinet so that they would know. So that if the secretary of the Interior were out making a speech about a dam, he wouldn't inadvertently say something that would affect our foreign relations." Cabinet member Harold Stassen observed: "There was never any doubt that he was in charge. He would call on people to comment. He made it clear that he wanted us to comment on each other's field of activity when we had something worth adding in the National Security Council and Cabinet. His fundamental strength was that he listened."

Since Eisenhower's Cabinet and National Security Council meetings routinely swelled to over thirty, forty, and fifty people, many outside observers (and some participants) faulted Eisenhower for being indecisive and managing by committee. But they missed the fact that, as his HEW Secretary Arthur S. Flemming said, "The Cabinet was used by Eisenhower as an advisory council and not as a policy-making body." Flemming added, "He is the only person who voted. He is the only person who made a decision." The Cabinet was a sounding board, not a decision-making body. Maurice Stans, Eisenhower's director of the budget, said he was "very strong in meetings, there was no doubt who was in charge. He was never indecisive. He always had the military attitude toward a problem—let's get it done and straightened out." Even Richard Nixon, who squirmed through eight years of Eisenhower meetings and griped that Ike saw his duty as "to be bored for his country as well as to lead it," conceded that "when it came to making a final decision, he was the coldest, most unemotional and analytical man in the world."

On the biggest issues of his presidency, those of war and peace, it was not in the formal Cabinet and NSC meetings where Eisenhower made decisions, but in the privacy of the Oval Office, in confidential, off-the-record conferences with small groups of his closest officials. On matters of national security involving State, Defense, and CIA, Eisenhower would spend a great deal of time burrowing into details with Dulles and others. "These were off-the-record meetings where he pulled together maybe three or four of the people directly involved," Goodpaster recalled. "The decision would be made," Goodpaster remembered, "then I would follow up." Ike delegated a great deal of work, but not the things that mattered most to him.

In foreign affairs, Eisenhower's executive style balanced public restraint with intense, hands-on maneuvering behind the scenes. In Korea, he brought the Communists to the truce table soon after becoming president by quietly implying that he would consider the use of nuclear weapons. But in a grotesque double-cross, hundreds of American prisoners of war were held back after the armistice was signed and all prisoners were supposed to be repatriated.

In late 1953, Eisenhower was personally briefed by the secretary of the army about hundreds of U.S. prisoners who "just disappeared from the camps." Eisenhower replied that he hadn't been fully aware of this during peace talks, saying, "Perhaps we should have insisted on their return as a precondition to the conference." In a December 1953 memo on file at the Eisenhower Library, President Eisenhower was said to be "intensely interested" in the fate of "the missing POWs," and that he wanted to be certain "everybody was doing all they could about it." Historians of the Korean War have speculated that Eisenhower feared going public with POW evidence to avoid triggering a war hysteria among Americans. "In a nuclear age, Eisenhower could not risk telling the Russians or the Chinese that we were willing to go to all-out war to get our prisoners back," congressional MIA investigator Al Santoli speculated in 1996.

A secret recording of a meeting on June 14, 1955, with Dulles and Indian UN Ambassador Krishna Menon captured Eisenhower trying to explore negotiations to return American POWs, using Menon as an intermediary with Communist China, with whom the United States had no diplomatic relations. "We know that there are—just in military uniform alone—people that have been seen or where we have reason to believe they have been captured—some 452," said Eisenhower, adding that "we know there are a great many more, unless something happened to them." The discussion went nowhere. Eisenhower wrote in a note to his file: "I have bluntly told him [Menon] . . . that the American people will not consider using the lives and freedom of their own citizens as a bargaining material." The fate of the P.O.W.'s was sealed, probably not by Eisenhower, but by Mao Tse-tung and Joseph Stalin, who likely used them not as hostages but as guinea pigs and sources of intelligence, to be tortured and disposed of.

Earlier that year, Eisenhower's hidden Dictaphone machine picked up an Oval Office discussion on another Asian hot spot, Vietnam, with visiting journalist Roy Howard of Scripps-Howard Publications, the same Roy Howard who so aggravated FDR on his Oval Office recordings a decade and a half earlier. Howard was paying Eisenhower a courtesy call before taking a trip to Asia, and much of their conversation dealt with tensions in the Formosa Strait between the Communist and Nationalist Chinese.

Eisenhower assured Howard that he was not planning to intervene in the crisis, and cited as an example his decision not to intervene at Dien Bien Phu, the French base in Indochina that was overrun by the Communists in May 1954. In the last weeks of the siege, Ike was urged by Dulles, the Joint Chiefs, Vice President Nixon, and others to authorize air strikes. Ike turned them down. On the recording, Ike said: "When we talk about Dien Bien Phu, maybe I need to tell you this, but I was one of the ones around here that was against the American air force going in! Hey, the boys, oh, the boys were putting the heat on me, you know. I was not willing to put the American prestige on one gol-durned thing in there that would put us forever on the side of a thing which you could see was every day deteriorating." Historian Stephen Ambrose noted that from then on, Ike's supporters could claim: "He got us out of Korea and kept us out of Vietnam."

"Bombs, by God. What does Anthony think he's doing? Why is he doing this to me?" Eisenhower's crisis-management skills faced a grueling multiple test in the last days of October 1956, when he was stunned to learn that, without any consultation with him, the British, led by his wartime colleague Prime Minister Anthony Eden, were joining the French and Israelis in launching a confused surprise attack on Egypt to reopen the Suez Canal. That summer, Lieutenant Colonel Gamal Abdel Nasser emerged as the leader of Egypt, and Ike offered to loan him $56 million to build the Aswan High Dam on the Nile. But the mercurial, nationalistic Nasser began flirting with Communist rulers in Moscow and Peking, prompting Eisenhower to cancel the loan and Nasser to seize the Suez Canal, cutting off Britain and France from their chief sources of oil. Now, the Soviets were simultaneously threatening to intervene militarily in support of Egypt and preparing to smash a mass democratic revolt in Hungary. On top of everything, Secretary of State Dulles was stricken with stomach cancer and hospitalized, and the U.S. presidential election was only days away. After quickly capturing the Gaza Strip and the Sinai Peninsula, the Israelis soon stopped firing. But on November 5, 1100 British and French paratroopers seized Egypt's Port Said at the mouth of the Suez, and the Soviets warned that the crisis could trigger World War III.

With Dulles out of commission, Eisenhower took personal charge of the Middle East crisis by supervising his State Department and United Nations delegations directly from the Oval Office, holding consultations with his military and intelligence brass, and conducting intensive diplomatic maneuvering with cables and transatlantic phone calls to pressure Eden and the French to disengage. At the peak of the fighting, on U.S. election day, Ike placed an overseas phone call to Eden and ordered Mrs. Whitman to come on the line and write down a verbatim transcript.

THE OVAL OFFICE
NOVEMBER 6, 1956, 12:55 P.M.

President Eisenhower and British Prime Minister Anthony Eden
RE: *Suez Crisis Cease-Fire*
"dead key" transcription of phone conversation

On the day of the U.S. presidential election, Eisenhower called Prime Minister Eden in London to discuss the climax of the Suez Crisis. Fighting still raged between British and French allies and the Egyptians. Fearing the Soviets would be pulled in and spark World War III, Ike wanted the fighting stopped.

Earlier that day, the hapless Eden was forced to declare a cease-fire (scheduled for the next day) just hours after his troops landed, in part because his government was running out of cash: the invasion had burned away $420 million of British reserves in a matter of days. Eden addressed Eisenhower like a junior officer speaking to a general.

EISENHOWER: This is a very clear connection.

EDEN: I can just hear you.

EISENHOWER: First of all, I can't tell you how pleased we are that you found it possible to accept the cease-fire, having landed.

EDEN: We have taken a certain risk, but I think it is justified.

EISENHOWER: Anthony, this is the way I feel about it. I have not ruminated over this particular situation at length. I am talking off the top of my head. You have got what you said you were going to get in that you have landed. It seems to me that from what—with regard to the cease-fire, and without going into any negotiations, I would go ahead with the cease-fire, not putting any conditions into the acceptance of the resolution and after cease-fire talking about the clearing of the canal and so on.

EDEN: We are going to cease firing tonight.

EISENHOWER: Could you not tell [UN Secretary-General Dag] Hammarskjöld that as far as the cease-fire arrangement is concerned, that that goes without condition.

EDEN: We cease firing tonight provided we are not attacked.

EISENHOWER: I see.

EDEN: What you may call the long cease-fire, the cessation of hostilities, that is more complicated.

EISENHOWER: Yes, it is more complicated. Talking about the technical troops of yours.

EDEN: They will cooperate with us in having a cease-fire tonight.

EISENHOWER: If I may make a suggestion, I would offer them to Hammarskjöld—but I would not insist that he take them.

EDEN: It is always a bit of working out with the allies and everybody else to get this thing—with some difficulty.

EISENHOWER: The point I want you to have in your mind is that the cease-fire tonight has nothing to do with technical troops. You cease anyway.

EDEN: Unless attacked.

EISENHOWER: The more permanent affair—we would like to know about the other thing.

EDEN: I have to go [to] my Parliament.

EISENHOWER: Oh, all right.

EDEN: In five minutes. Would you authorize me to say that you think this is helpful outside—

EISENHOWER: You can say that I called to say how delighted I was you found it possible to direct a cease-fire tonight so that negotiations could start.

EDEN: I am just getting it down—

EISENHOWER: How delighted I was that you found it possible to direct a cease-fire tonight which will allow negotiations to proceed from there on.

EDEN: Proceed—

EISENHOWER: Yes. Wait a minute. Well, I will tell you what I am trying to get at. I don't want to give Egypt an opportunity to begin to quibble so that this thing can be drawn out for a week. After the cease-fire it seems like the technical things of it would be settled very quickly, and when Hammarskjöld comes along with his people you people ought to be able to withdraw very quickly. He is getting Canadian troops—lots of troops—together.

EDEN: I hope you will be there. Are we all going to go out?

EISENHOWER: What I want to do is this. I would like to see none of the great nations in it [UN force]. I am afraid the Red boy* is going to demand the lion's share. I would rather make it no troops from the big five [powers]. I would say, "Mr. Hammarskjöld, we trust you. When we see you coming in with enough troops to take over, we go out."

EDEN: That is not too easy unless they have good force, you know.

EISENHOWER: I will tell you. If they have enough—and they attack, they attack the United Nations and its whole prestige and force—then everybody is in the thing. Then you are [not] alone.

EDEN: May I think that one over?

EISENHOWER: Now that we know connections are so good, you can call me anytime you please.

EDEN: If I survive here tonight I will call you tomorrow. How are things going with you?

*Red boy: the Soviet Union.

EISENHOWER: We have given our whole thought to Hungary and the Middle East. I don't give a damn how the election goes. I guess it will be all right.

EDEN: How is Foster?

EISENHOWER: Pretty good. He's making a pretty quick recovery.

EDEN: Wonderful.

EISENHOWER: All right. Thank you and go ahead with your meeting.

EDEN: Thanks so much.

Eisenhower won reelection that day by an overwhelming margin, but his party lost control of both houses of Congress. Hostilities in the Middle East stopped the next day, but the Soviets violently suppressed the Hungarian uprising. Eden was forced out of office in less than three months.

Eisenhower achieved his objectives: the fighting stopped, the British and French soon withdrew, American prestige in the area was enhanced, and the Soviets stayed out of the fighting. West Point historian Cole C. Kingseed argued that "the Eisenhower who emerged from the Suez crisis was a chief executive who was flexible and experimental in his decision making, not one tied to a rigid military model from which he seldom departed." Kingseed credited the outcome to "the force of his own personality, his bureaucratic skill, and his personal direction of an elaborate staff network that deferred all major decisions to the president before coordinating their execution. During the Suez crisis, Eisenhower proved himself to be a skilled and competent chief executive who dominated the decision-making process and placed the indelible imprint of his forceful leadership on United States foreign policy."

On the two biggest domestic challenges of the day, however, civil rights and McCarthyism, Eisenhower offered not forceful executive leadership but hesitation and avoidance. "Eisenhower evaded them both," wrote historian Arthur M. Schlesinger, Jr. "This may be in part because of his severely constricted theory of the presidency. But it was partly too because Eisenhower did not see them as compelling issues. He did not like to use law to enforce racial integration, and, while he disliked McCarthy's manners and methods, he basically agreed with his objectives." Both issues highlighted Eisenhower's distaste for risking political capital on public confrontation.

Ironically, Eisenhower's "hidden-hand" executive approach on civil rights did deliver some concrete achievements, but they were by definition underpublicized. Working through deputy Max Rabb, Eisenhower quietly but effectively integrated public facilities in Washington, D.C. (until then a staunchly segregated southern city), and removed remaining racial barriers in the navy, air force, army, and veterans' hospitals. "I really would like to get rid of discrimination," Eisenhower told Rabb. "But I want to avoid a repetition of FDR and Truman, where Southern Democrats filibustered it to death. I don't want publicity. I want results." Harlem Congressman Adam Clayton Powell was so impressed that he backed Eisenhower's reelection bid in 1956, but Eisenhower couldn't stop the Civil Rights Act of 1957 from being gutted by Southern Democrats. By neglecting his responsibility to educate the public on the issue (like most other presidents), wrote historian Stephen Ambrose, "he provided almost no leadership at all on the most fundamental social problem of his time," until he was forced to deploy paratroopers to enforce integration in Little Rock, Arkansas in 1957.

On the excesses of anti-Communist Senator Joseph McCarthy, Eisenhower chose a curious strategy of public avoidance and indirect backstage maneuvering. McCarthy eventually self-destructed, but surely Eisenhower could have found some way of using his immense popularity to finish him off sooner.

After his 1956 reelection, Eisenhower's last years in the Oval Office were increasingly tough. He suffered a stroke in 1957, the year Sputnik threatened to establish Soviet hegemony in space. In 1958, the Republicans were clobbered in midterm elections, and Sherman Adams was forced out in a scandal. In 1960, the U-2 fiasco scuttled Ike's dream of a farewell summit with the Soviets, the economy slumped, and John Kennedy defeated Richard Nixon in the presidential race. Eisenhower took the defeat as a repudiation of his presidency.

Eisenhower was arguably the last president to effectively organize his White House, and the last to get his arms completely around the federal government. He strengthened the Cabinet, National Security Council, and White House congressional, national security, and press offices to such an extent that R. Gordon Hoxie, chairman of the Center for the Study of the Presidency, argued: "Although Presidents Hoover, Roosevelt, and Truman had made some administrative reforms, Dwight D. Eisenhower was the principal architect of the institutional presidency."

Eisenhower was also the first president known to conduct secret and intentional Oval Office recordings of private meetings (excluding FDR and Truman's press conferences and probably unintended other recordings), although in a limited and sporadic fashion over less than twenty-one of his ninety-six months in office. His twenty-seven confirmed recordings are spread fairly evenly from his first known recording on October 21, 1953, until the last on June 14, 1955, the date of the MIA meeting. A few weeks later, Eisenhower was off to attend the July 1955 big power summit in Geneva. He returned to Washington for a few weeks and then went on vacation, suffering his heart attack in Colorado at the end of September. No firm evidence exists of any more recordings, except for a December 9, 1959, Oval Office meeting with Queen Frederika of Greece. In the filed minutes of that meeting, Ann Whitman referred to a "tape recording" of the meeting, although she may have used the term to refer generically to a Dictabelt (neither has been found).

Judging from his comments on the Dictaphone as a management tool and his 1954 advice to his Cabinet to make a record of important conversations, Eisenhower probably initially used his hidden Oval Office Dictaphone as an executive tool, a backup record-keeper to provide a measure of safety in the shark-infested Washington political waters. By the time he returned to a full schedule after his recuperation in the fall of 1955 and saw how smoothly his government functioned in his absence, he may have felt confident enough in the strength of his executive machinery to not have to worry about using his Dictaphone anymore.

In 1997, Eisenhower Cabinet member Harold Stassen noted, "He was President for eight years in which there were many critical international developments. The incredible thing was, in those eight years, no American soldier was killed or killed anyone else. It was more than luck. In more than one moment of tension he told [Defense Secretary] Wilson and the Joint Chiefs: 'You make it clear to all the commanders of all our forces that I don't want a single shot or bomb fired without my order.' He knew what it meant to start a war. He knew that the first time you shoot across a line it's awfully hard to control."

Eisenhower's supremely organized executive style helped him achieve the goals the American voters twice appointed him to achieve. The worldwide spread of communism was largely contained. The American economy boomed: the GNP rose 25 percent, and inflation averaged a minuscule 1.4 percent. Eisenhower managed to deliver three balanced budgets while sustaining the social programs of the New Deal. "Eisenhower gave the nation eight years of peace and prosperity," noted Stephen Ambrose. "No other president in the twentieth century could make that claim. No wonder that millions of Americans felt that the country was damned lucky to have him."

Eisenhower himself argued succinctly: "The United States never lost a soldier or a foot of ground in my administration. We kept the peace. People ask how it happened—by God, it didn't just happen, I'll tell you that."

It was Eisenhower's successors who would have to reap the whirlwinds of calamity that were gathering force just over the horizon of the 1960s.

CHAPTER 4

John F. Kennedy
The Rational Executive

*"You could have those bombs go off and
blow up fifteen cities in the United States."*

JOHN F. KENNEDY,
CABINET ROOM RECORDING
OCTOBER 22, 1962

THE CABINET ROOM
APRIL 18, 1961, 1:00 P.M.

"We are under attack by two Sea Fury aircraft and heavy artillery."

Commander José Pérez "Pepe" San Román was pinned down on a narrow Cuban beachead flanked by coral-scarred reefs and impenetrable swamps, calling into a field radio.

He and his force of 1,500 exiles from Brigade 2056 were trapped, surrounded, and being cut to pieces by curtains of tracer bullets and artillery fire from Fidel Castro's military. Now they were being betrayed by the United States government.

"Do not see any friendly air cover as you promised," San Román pleaded to his CIA contact stationed helplessly in a vessel offshore. "Need jet support immediately."

Inside the White House, John F. Kennedy stood in the Cabinet Room, a command post littered with bulletins of fresh disasters, and ordered American vessels to stay beyond sight of Cuba, away from the battle. To make his point, the forty-three-year-old president went to a map easel with navy ships represented by small magnetic figures, picked up one of the destroyers, and pushed it over the horizon. A U.S. Navy admiral standing nearby fumed in disbelief.

It was less than 100 days into his presidency and Kennedy's first test as chief executive was sliding into disaster. The invasion plan was inherited from Eisenhower, was supported by many of the top military and intelligence brass, and offered a swift, decisive solution to the thorn in the side of a hostile Communist dictatorship on America's doorstep. Later Kennedy would lament, "All the mysteries about the Bay of Pigs have been solved now but one—how could everybody involved have thought such a plan would succeed. I don't know the answer, and I don't know anybody else who does." Constant news leaks about the exiles' training camp gave Castro plenty of time to beef up his defenses. U.S. intelligence consistently underestimated the strength of Castro's air force jets versus the exile brigade's handful of World War II–era propeller planes. All the ships carrying reserve ammunition, supplies, and communications gear were blown up or chased away by Castro's air force.

Kennedy privately railed against "the experts" he claimed misled him into signing off on the plan: "How could I have been so stupid as to let them go ahead?" But the invasion, while probably doomed anyway, had its fate sealed when JFK repeatedly mismanaged and micromanaged it. He rejected the original CIA plan to seize the coastal Cuban town of Trinidad in an amphibious and airborne strike as "too spectacular" and "too much like a World War II invasion." He ordered planners to "reduce the noise level" and prepare a "quiet" landing, at night, with little visible U.S. support. Richard M. Bissell, Jr., the CIA officer running the invasion, noted that "the move from the heavily populated Trinidad to the remote Bay of Pigs made a mass uprising less likely and effectively negated the option of a retreat into the Escambray Mountains."

The world was witnessing not only a military, intelligence, and political failure but an epic management meltdown exacerbated by Kennedy's dangerously unstructured executive style. The White House planning meetings for the invasion were a tangle of confusion. According to the official postmortem analysis ordered by Kennedy, the Taylor Report, "Direction was given through ad hoc meetings of senior officials without consideration of operational plans in writing and with no arrangement for recording conclusions and decisions reached." For security reasons, paper copies of the constantly changing plan were never passed out, so on D-day the only place the full plan existed was inside Bissell's head. Junior staffers drifted in and out of unstructured, overlapping meetings. Kennedy aide Theodore Sorensen wrote that "no strong voice of opposition was raised in any of the key meetings, and no realistic alternatives were presented." Historian Arthur M. Schlesinger, Jr., a participant in the meetings, noted they "took place in a curious atmosphere of assumed consensus." He added: "One's impulse to blow the whistle on this nonsense was simply undone by the circumstances of the discussion."

At one meeting, instead of provoking debate or examining alternatives, JFK went around the room asking for simple yes or no votes. Most of the men blurted out "Yes," when in the words of Assistant Secretary of Defense Paul Nitze, "I should have had the guts to give a complicated answer." Under Secretary of State Chester Bowles wrote a strong memorandum to Secretary of State Dean Rusk opposing the CIA plan, but Rusk buried the memo instead of showing it to Kennedy. "My interpretation as to why Kennedy got into the Bay of Pigs is that he had never been an executive before," said Assistant Secretary of State Harlan Cleveland. "The last executive job he had had before becoming president was to be commander of a PT boat. He didn't know that the executive executes mostly by asking questions." Kennedy agreed: "I did not know enough to ask the right questions."

When someone suggested that Kennedy consider sending in U.S. troops to back up the exiles once they seized power, he erupted, "Under no circumstances! The minute I land one marine, we're in this thing up to our necks. I can't get the United States into a war and then lose it, no matter what it takes. I'm not going to risk an American Hungary. And that's what it could be, a fucking slaughter. *Is that understood, gentlemen?*" When the exiles hit the Cuban beaches on D-day, April 17, JFK refused to authorize air strikes to support them. Then he called Bissell to approve them, and in passing asked how many planes would be needed. "Sixteen," replied Bissell. "Well, I don't want it on that scale. I want it minimal." The number was cut down to six.

On the night of April 18, as his ammunition ran out, Commander San Román pleaded, "Please don't desert us . . . Do you people realize how desperate the situation is? . . . Tanks will hit me at dawn. I will not be evacuated. We will fight to the end here if we have to." His last radio message came the next day: "We have nothing left to fight with. How can you do this to us, our people, our country? Over and out." When the CIA broadcast a final refusal of aid, San Román replied, "And you sir, are a son of a bitch." Of the 1,500 exiles, a handful escaped, 1,189 were taken prisoner, and some 114 were killed.

Management expert Peter Drucker pinpointed the fatal contradictions Kennedy faced: "One specification was clearly Castro's overthrow. But at the same time, there was another specification: not to make it appear that U.S. forces were intervening in one of the American republics. That the second specification was rather absurd, and that no one in the whole world would have believed for one moment that the invasion was a spontaneous uprising of the Cubans, is beside the point." The mistake, Drucker concluded, was not bad advice from experts, but Kennedy's "failure to think through clearly the boundary conditions that the decision had to satisfy, and refusal to face up to the unpleasant reality that a decision that has to satisfy two different and at bottom incompatible specifications is not a decision but a prayer for a miracle."

"What happened in the end was that the original plan always called for American naval air support for the landing should it be necessary," said Treasury Secretary C. Douglas Dillon, formerly in charge of Cuba planning in Eisenhower's State Department and now on the Kennedy team. "The ships were there and the planes were ready to fly and when the time came the president said no." Dillon asserted that "the Bay of Pigs was the result of a lack of staffing. JFK thought he could organize the presidency better and abolish the National Security structure, and that led to the breakdown connecting and coordinating between the departments and the president . . . If Kennedy hadn't dismantled the National Security Council apparatus, it never would have happened." Robert Kennedy agreed: "The Bay of Pigs was the indication that we were not well organized." Kennedy had torn up Eisenhower's elaborate White House organization charts, which he felt made the presidency too bureaucratic and slow-moving.

The disaster exposed the risks of Kennedy's unstructured, improvisational style, a style that national security assistant McGeorge Bundy addressed in his own Bay of Pigs postmortem memo to Kennedy on May 16. "I hope you'll be in a good mood when you read this," Bundy began delicately. "We do have a problem of management; centrally it is a problem of your use of time. . . . We can't get you to sit still. . . . Truman and Eisenhower did their daily dozens in foreign affairs the first thing in the morning, and a couple of weeks ago you asked me to begin to meet you on this basis. I have succeeded in catching you on three mornings, for a total of about eight minutes, and I conclude that this is not really how you like to begin the day. . . . Right now it is so hard to get to you with anything not urgent and immediate that about half of the papers and reports you personally ask for are never shown to you because by the time you are available you clearly have lost interest in them."

JFK quickly, manfully shouldered blame for the disaster in public, declaring, "I am the responsible officer of the government." His fast admission of responsibility sharply boosted his approval ratings (a lesson few other presidents would learn: witness Johnson and Vietnam, Nixon and Watergate, Reagan and Iran-Contra). In private, however, Kennedy was furious—at the CIA, at himself, and at some of his own officials, who claimed to reporters that they had opposed the invasion. "We can't win them all," Kennedy mused, "and I have been close enough to disaster to realize that these things which seem world-shaking at one moment you can barely remember the next. We got a big kick in the ass—and we deserved it. But maybe we'll learn something from it." Sorensen recalled that "after the Bay of Pigs, he conducted national security operations in a different way. He was more skeptical of the recommendations which came to him from the experts. He challenged their assumptions, their premises, even their facts."

Until he entered the Oval Office, Kennedy had never managed an organization larger than a PT boat and a small Senate staff. Growing up in one of America's wealthiest families, Kennedy was seasoned in an atmosphere of Rooseveltian self-confidence by a patriarch who stimulated athletic and intellectual competition among his sprawling, viciously loyal band of children. After cheating doom in his heroic PT-109 rescue during World War II, the shadow of death was a constant companion for Kennedy, as siblings died and he battled his way through a series of debilitating illnesses. In Congress, Kennedy compiled an undistinguished record: he had written no major legislation, chaired no major congressional committees. But as a campaigner, as a debater, and as a personality, he was electrifying. When sworn in as president, he was now chief executive of a 2.35 million-employee organization.

Kennedy's cautious, pragmatic approach to governing stemmed from his tiny election margin; at only 112,803 more than Nixon, it was the smallest popular vote margin in history. "He did not feel that he had a strong, overwhelming mandate from the American people, and so he would rather be careful about picking the issues on which he wanted to make a fight," Secretary of State Rusk later recalled. Kennedy told his men, "If you're going to have a fight, have a fight about something. Don't have a fight about nothing." In an Oval Office discussion with reporters in December 1962 Kennedy observed, "There is no sense in raising hell, and then not being successful. There is no sense in putting the office of the presidency on the line on an issue, and then being defeated."

For much of his presidency, Kennedy would lurch from emergency to emergency as simmering domestic and international crises began detonating around him. The civil rights movement, excited by Kennedy's sympathetic rhetoric, entered a new phase of mass action. An emboldened Soviet Premier Nikita Khrushchev, after smelling blood at Kennedy's impotent performance at the Bay of Pigs and bullying him at a summit meeting in Vienna, geared up for showdowns in Berlin, Laos, Vietnam, and Cuba. In the wake of the Cuban Missile Crisis, the superpowers would sharply accelerate the nuclear arms race.

At 8:50 A.M. on his first full day as president, Kennedy sat alone in the empty Oval Office, flinching at the freshly painted green walls, pressing buzzers, and inspecting his desk drawers, which were empty except for a printed instruction sheet detailing what to do in case of nuclear attack. Soon he called in an aide, grinned at him, and asked, "What the hell do I do now?" When prospective budget director David Bell told him, "I've never run a large organization before," JFK responded, "Neither have I." Aide Ralph Dungan reported that Kennedy was "bored silly with normal day-to-day executive work. I attribute that to the fact that he always had a nanny, and he always had people around to pick up his knickers and dirty towels, and that's the way it worked." Kennedy eliminated the White House chief of staff slot, preferring to deal with his top staff and government officers directly, as the hub connecting to the spokes of a wheel. Kennedy explained: "I had different identities, and this was a useful way of expressing each without compromising the others. I know it's confusing at times, but it is very effective in governing. Franklin Roosevelt did the same thing, you know."

The Oval Office soon filled up with JFK mementoes; the famous SOS-bearing coconut from the PT-109 sinking, a huge antique scabbard on the wall, a collection of scrimshaw whale's teeth scattered on the shelves, his navy ID card in a glass ashtray. On his desk there appeared a plaque from Admiral Hyman Rickover given to commanders of Polaris nuclear submarines bearing a Breton fishermen's prayer, OH GOD, THY SEA IS SO GREAT AND MY BOAT IS SO SMALL. Also on the desk was an ashtray inscribed with Kennedy's fingerprints, a teasing gift from FBI Director J. Edgar Hoover. Kennedy was amused when he noticed the Oval Office floor chewed up by eight years of abuse from Eisenhower's golf cleats. *Time* magazine's Hugh Sidey recorded the early transformation of the room: "The pale-green walls were smothered in a coat of New England off-white. . . . A new stock of oak firewood was rushed in for the fireplace, which now crackled all the time. There were the marks of a navy vet: on the walls flanking the fireplace hung two naval pictures showing the 1812 battle between the *Constitution* and the British frigate *Guerriere,* and on the mantel was a model of the *Constitution.*"

Kennedy was a president who evidently suffered both from a galaxy of debilitating illnesses and an overwhelming compulsion to cheat on his wife. His medical problems were said to include venereal disease, Addison's disease, gastrointestinal problems, chronic colitis, recurring fevers, life-threatening spinal problems, and a persistent bladder and urinary infection, plus the side effects of multiple-drug "cocktails" of speed, vitamins, painkillers, and human placenta injected periodically by New York physician Max (Dr. Feelgood) Jacobsen, whose medical license was finally revoked in 1975. "In a lifetime of medical torment Kennedy was more promiscuous with physicians and drugs than he was with women," wrote Richard Reeves, who estimated that with afternoon naps and early bedtimes, JFK spent half his days as president in bed due to weak health.

In the early 1990s, the JFK Library unsealed Secret Service files of White House Police Gate Logs that gave credence to some of the mountains of posthumous charges of JFK's infidelity. Several White House visits in 1961 by Mafia girlfriend Judith Campbell were documented, confirming her accounts of a relationship with Kennedy that she said continued in other locations into 1962. Cryptic entries of "David Powers + 1" or "David Powers + 1 female" appear for the evening hours, supporting the speculation that presidential aide Powers, as Seymour Hersh charged in his 1997 bestseller *The Dark Side of Camelot,* procured for Kennedy a vast procession of women ranging from starlets to street hookers. JFK buddy LeMoyne Billings observed, "It never occurred to Jack that some of the women might be considered dangerous. They were never searched, never questioned in depth." While JFK's dalliances created huge risks to his political survival, his safety, and possibly to national security, no major impact on his executive performance has been proven.

Kennedy usually woke up at 7:30 or 8:00 A.M., then shaved in the bathtub to save time while reviewing documents on a board across the tub, causing staff members to sometimes receive waterlogged notes from the president. Around 8:45 he ate breakfast in his bedroom, at 9:00 or 9:30 he left the second floor of the mansion, sometimes with one or both of his children in tow, and rode an elevator to the first floor where he walked over to the Oval Office. Once in the office, JFK checked the newspapers and mail and read a three-thousand-word CIA briefing. Then he charged into a daylong stream of phone calls, ceremonies, and short meetings, usually fifteen minutes or less. He broke for lunch at 1:30, took a fifteen-minute dip in the White House pool heated to 90 degrees while a record player blared Broadway show tunes, did back exercises, took a nap until three or four, then went back to the Oval Office until around 7:00 P.M. He sometimes spent his afternoons working from the living quarters on the mansion's second floor, and at night he would often tackle paperwork while sprawled on a sofa in the comfortable West Sitting Room, laying papers out on the floor and making notes on yellow legal pads.

In his first days as president, Kennedy grabbed a walking cane and managed, in the Truman tradition, to slip away from the White House for a few walks around the snowy Washington streets and parks disguised in a plaid sports jacket, beat-up shoes, sunglasses, and a gray fedora. These were his last glimpses of what life used to be like as a relatively unknown backbench senator just a few years before.

Despite Kennedy's ice-cool outward detachment, he was a restless and driven executive, whom reporters and White House staffers nicknamed "the Tiger." Dean Rusk reported, "John Kennedy was an impatient fellow who didn't waste time. I learned to speak precisely to the point at hand, then shut up and go back to my office." JFK once snapped at a long-winded assistant: "Cut the commercials, get to the facts." One senator claimed that "when you see the president, you have to get in your car and drive like blazes back to the Capitol to beat his memo commenting on what you told him." C. Douglas Dillon, JFK's Treasury secretary, said Kennedy liked short personal meetings, not long memos or phone conversations. Dillon would frequently stride over from the nearby Treasury building, "go in for four or five minutes, get it done, and get out." One time Kennedy asked questions so quickly that an aide couldn't turn the pages of a report fast enough, so the aide simply pulled the document apart and spread it on the Oval Office floor.

"I'm interested in the little things, the details," Kennedy explained. "I want to know from A to B to C up until where it comes to me, where I have to make the decision." State Department veteran Charles "Chip" Bohlen marveled: "I never heard of a president who wanted to know so much." According to CIA official Richard Helms, he was the only president who asked to see raw intelligence cables. He even, on occasion, reviewed the expense accounts of White House staffers.

In an echo of FDR, the prince of bureaucratic disorder, Kennedy sometimes assigned the same task to different aides. "I can't afford to confine myself to one set of advisers," he once explained. "If I did that, *I* would be on *their* leading strings." JFK secretary Mrs. Lincoln saw this as Kennedy's way of stimulating competition: "Each person was unaware that the others were working on the same problem. In this way, he was sure to get an answer. The person who was the most efficient and most interested in doing the task promptly would be given more and more responsibility." According to White House aide Ralph Dungan, "He was not process oriented, he was goal oriented. If you were in the Oval Office transacting some item of business with him and something else flitted across his mind that was not in your general area of responsibility, he would say, 'Would you see that this is done.' Then you'd go out and call the person who's job it was and say the president wants this done. That happened all the time."

"His enormous energy permitted him to deal with a great many people on a bilateral basis, weaving their efforts into his tasks as he saw them," reported national security aide Walt Rostow. "His method was that of an extended family. He was part of a big family. It was the nucleus of his political organization." One of the few men in the Kennedy administration with extensive executive experience, Under Secretary of State Chester Bowles, the former governor of Connecticut and a founder of the advertising agency BBD&O said: "Management in Jack's mind, I think, consists largely of calling Bob [Kennedy] on the telephone and saying, 'Here are ten things I want to get done. Why don't you go ahead and get them done.'" Kennedy hated meetings, especially the huge, ritualized, set-piece conferences that can be endemic to the presidency. He rarely held formal National Security Council meetings and dispensed with most Cabinet meetings. British Prime Minister Harold Macmillan huffed at Kennedy's unstructured executive approach by claiming he spent "half his time thinking about adultery, the other half about secondhand ideas passed on by his advisers."

Despite Kennedy's contempt for bureaucratic procedure, his White House gradually settled into an operational rhythm. On Tuesdays Kennedy held a legislative strategy breakfast with congressional leaders. Every two weeks Kennedy held a press conference, and to prepare for each one, he conducted what was the main regular management exercise of his presidency: an intensive briefing session where he would wade through piles of briefing books and status reports. On the morning of the conference, he breakfasted for two hours with a team of advisers who drilled him in mock Q&A sessions. "It's like preparing for a final exam twice a month," Kennedy said. During the meetings, Kennedy would run down lists of items for action and follow-up, in what became a management meeting. The regular discipline of these sessions kept him on top of the myriad details of his presidency, and enabled him to keep up face-to-face personal contact with millions of TV viewers in press conference performances that were, by any measure, triumphant.

"He was an incendiary man who set most of the people around him on fire," said Dean Rusk, "and it was really fun to work with him." Rusk identified one of Kennedy's strongest executive weapons: a personality enriched by immense charm, intellectual integrity, and humor that forged his men into a Shakespearean band of brothers. Budget Director David Bell explained, "Kennedy was a magnificent natural leader. He was like a red-haired Irish sea-raider. Everyone had the natural feeling they'd follow him anywhere. He was quick and funny, and committed to all the right purposes. He was the guy you'd want to follow into the machine-gun fire." State Department official Pedro Sanjuan remembered, "When he came into the room, he was like the sun: he radiated confidence and victory."

Kennedy's special counsel and speechwriter Theodore Sorensen, first among equals in the band JFK brought into the White House from the Senate, recalled Kennedy's tactics for building an effective team: "He treated us more as colleagues or associates than employees. He made it clear that we were there to give advice as well as take orders." Domestic affairs assistant Myer Feldman asserted: "I can't imagine a better boss. He gave you enough discretion, but at the same time you knew you were going to have his support even if you did something a little bit wrong. He wouldn't criticize you in front of anybody else." Ralph Dungan recalled: "Everybody on the staff really liked and respected him. You'd really knock yourself out doing anything you could for him. He was terrific."

A story is told of Kennedy, working late in the Oval Office on a freezing cold night, looking out and seeing a Secret Service man shivering at his post in the garden just outside the windows. He opened the door and called out, "I don't want you out there in this terrible cold," and ordered him inside to "come in and get warm." The guard refused, saying such was his job. Kennedy soon came out with a heavy coat and announced, "I want you to put this on. You're not warm enough, I can tell." A few minutes later the president came out again, this time with a couple of cups of hot chocolate, and persuaded the guard to join him. The two sat down on the cold steps outside the Oval Office and drank the hot chocolate together. Years later the Secret Service man reportedly wept as he told the story.

In the summer of 1962, John Kennedy quietly installed the White House's first full-fledged secret recording network, a system of concealed switches, microphones, tape recorders, and Dictaphones that stretched through the Oval Office and Cabinet Room and into the White House mansion itself. Kennedy's motivation may have been to protect himself against second-guessing by his own officials. His secretary, Mrs. Evelyn Lincoln, recalled that "during the time of the Bay of Pigs, there were certain people who said before that they were for the operation and after said they were against it. He knew there was a crisis coming up with Cuba. So for history, he put in the tape recorder in order to take down the meetings."

On Kennedy's orders, the Secret Service turned the White House into a private recording studio. The agent in charge of the installation was Robert Bouck, whose duties as supervisor of the Protective Research Section included sweeping the Oval Office for bugging devices. Now, instead of sweeping for bugs, he was planting them. "Even at that time, recordings of conversations and phones were sort of frowned upon and it was generally not desired that it be advertised," Bouck recalled. Bouck's impression was that Kennedy wanted the taping system to gather material for his presidential memoirs. The Secret Service agreed to install the system, but insisted on not getting involved with controlling the actual taping process itself—that would be Kennedy's responsibility alone.

In July of that year, Bouck ordered Army Signal Corps personnel to buy the double-deck Tandberg reel-to-reel recording machine and tape monitor at a local Washington, D.C., electronics dealer, paying cash so there'd be no record of the transaction and no paper trail back to the White House. Then Bouck installed the recorders in a small 6-foot-by-8-foot locked storage room under the office of Mrs. Lincoln. Only Lincoln and Bouck had keys to the room. "I tried to place the microphones in locations where they could be easily hidden," said Bouck, "but yet, would be close enough to the center of discussion to record well. For instance, in the Cabinet Room, I placed them in light fixtures along the wall." He installed the ON/OFF switch under the Cabinet Room desk, within easy reach of Kennedy. The mikes could pick up sounds in a 15-foot radius and had their own battery power supply.

In the Oval Office, Bouck rigged the ON/OFF switch as a disguised feature right in the pen and pencil set on Kennedy's desk. When the president pressed down, the recorder kicked on. When he pressed it again at the end of the meeting, it stopped. Bouck fastened microphones into the kneewell of Kennedy's desk, set up another microphone station under the coffee table near the Oval Office fireplace, and installed a concealed switch in a nearby lamp. Finally, Bouck ran a microphone line down the colonnade and up into the second floor of the White House mansion into a sitting room where Kennedy sometimes held small meetings. He installed a microphone in a large coffee table in the middle of the room and a switch in a lamp table. (No recordings appear to have been made from this station.) Wires ran from all the concealed microphones down into the reel-to-reel tape recorder hidden in the storage closet in the basement of the White House West Wing. When the tape ran out, the back-up reel would start running and a light would flash on the timing monitor in Bouck's office, which he would check two or three times a day. Bouck would then go down to the closet, seal the used tape in a plain envelope, and walk it up to Kennedy's secretary, who locked the tapes in a special safe.

Without Bouck's knowledge, Kennedy expanded the recordings to include Oval Office phone calls. At about the same time as the installation of the taping system, a commercial model Dictaphone recorder was patched into the president's main phone line. The recorder was placed in a cabinet near the desk of Mrs. Lincoln and patched into the line connecting her phone to the president's. She switched the Dictaphone on upon receiving a light signal from Kennedy from a switch on his desk, much like Mrs. Whitman had for President Eisenhower. Early in his term, in fact, Kennedy had installed a Dictaphone in plain view on an Oval Office side table for dictation, and throughout the workday he would spin around and fire off short memos into the machine for Mrs. Lincoln to type out at the end of the day.

From July 1962 until his assassination, Kennedy recorded 260 hours of meetings and phone conversations, covering much of the most important activity of the second half of his abortive presidency. His tapes reveal a pragmatic, rational, cautious, hands-on executive facing crucial moments in history, including the eruption of civil rights onto the national agenda, the Cuban Missile Crisis, and the disintegration of America's early hopes in Vietnam. Only four people knew of the operation: agent Bouck, Kennedy, Evelyn Lincoln, and the White House Secret Service chief. Robert Kennedy and close JFK aides Kenneth O'Donnell and Dave Powers may also have known of the system, along with Jacqueline Kennedy. All of them kept the secret.

According to his press secretary Pierre Salinger, "John F. Kennedy had the facility to see the fact that life was not a black-and-white proposition, that there were a lot of gray areas in life." Kennedy's taping system was just one gray area in an ocean of moral flexibility that included charges that he, among other things, stole the 1960 election, lied about his health, systematically violated his marriage vows, consorted with a Mafia moll, and flirted with state-sponsored assassination attempts on Fidel Castro.

In addition to monitoring his White House officials and guests through his secret taping system, the Kennedys launched a campaign of electronic surveillance against political enemies, unfriendly reporters, and even some of their own staff members. Kennedy friend Ben Bradlee later exclaimed, "My God, they wiretapped practically everybody else in this town." To track down Pentagon news leaks, Attorney General Robert Kennedy approved wiretaps on two *New York Times* and *Newsweek* reporters in 1961 and 1962. "The FBI and the CIA had installed dozens of wiretaps and listening devices on orders and requests from the attorney general," reported Kennedy biographer Richard Reeves. "Transcripts of secret tapes of steel executives, congressmen, lobbyists, and reporters routinely ended up on the president's desk." The targets included Martin Luther King, Jr., anti-Kennedy author Victor Lasky, Kennedy's military assistant Godfrey McHugh, and national security official Robert Amory. Secretary of State Dean Rusk suspected FBI Director J. Edgar Hoover's bugging of Martin Luther King, and told Hoover in Kennedy's presence that if he discovered a microphone in his office or a tap on his phone, he would quit his job and announce the evidence in public.

The existence of a Kennedy White House taping system was revealed by the Kennedy Library in July 1973, in the wake of the firestorm over Nixon's system, but few details were revealed and the news generated little interest. "I know nothing about it," said Kennedy's national security assistant, McGeorge Bundy at the time, guessing that it was "a very private decision by President Kennedy." Historian and Kennedy aide Arthur M. Schlesinger, Jr., said at the time that such a secret taping system in Kennedy's White House was "absolutely inconceivable." "It was not the sort of thing Kennedy would have done," Schlesinger said. "I don't believe it happened," said former Kennedy Justice Department official Ramsey Clark, adding that, "It's a shameful thing to do. It's unacceptable that a president could ever condone, much less order, secret tapings."

Logs of Kennedy's tapes were not released until 1982, and when they showed that Kennedy had taped a wide variety of Washington figures, this time the media jumped on the story and people taped by Kennedy were stunned. Top Kennedy aide Theodore Sorensen, who was present for many of the taped meetings, said, "I'm dumbfounded." Former Senator William J. Fulbright, also taped, announced, "You feel as if you've been deceived to some extent." Senator Henry Jackson said, "It's a matter of right and wrong, and in our society, it is wrong to record someone without his consent." Former Representative Wilbur Mills: "It surprised me greatly—I didn't know he was that kind of fellow to take advantage of a person by taping his conversations without knowing it."

In 1962 and 1963, Kennedy recorded nineteen White House meetings and thirty-two phone conversations dealing with the increasingly turbulent issue of civil rights. In September 1962, the worst federal and state crisis since the Civil War was brewing in the state of Mississippi, which entered a state of virtual armed rebellion against the federal government over repeated attempts by air force veteran James H. Meredith to register as the first African-American student at the University of Mississippi, backed by a federal court order. On September 29, Kennedy called Mississippi Governor Ross Barnett to try to defuse the explosive situation developing at the university. Governor Barnett, an erratic segregationist hero, had appointed himself temporary registrar of "Ole Miss," and in three public showdowns backed by Mississippi state highway patrolmen and sheriffs, blocked Meredith from registering. Kennedy civil rights aide Burke Marshall recalled, "The governor was in rebellion one minute and the next minute not, depending on who he was talking to."

THE OVAL OFFICE
SEPTEMBER 29, 1962

President Kennedy and Mississippi Governor Ross Barnett
RE: *Integration of the University of Mississippi*
audio recording of telephone conversation on Dictaphone machine

On this call, an agitated, on-edge Kennedy tried to reason with fellow Democrat Barnett to prevent a violent showdown at the university. During the 1960 campaign, JFK criticized Eisenhower for vacillating in the 1957 Little Rock civil rights crisis: "There is more power in the presidency than to let things drift and then suddenly call out the troops," Kennedy charged. But now Kennedy had allowed events to drift toward an even more explosive outcome, and as he tried to avoid sending in troops, the ghosts of the Old South prepared to rise again.

Kennedy was firm and polite, but sounds so rational and detached that he could be discussing luncheon reservations at the Stork Club. The two talked past each other as Barnett (whom Bobby Kennedy called "an agreeable rogue") slipped and slid around the president with courtly congeniality. Toward the end of the call, the president and governor seemed to reach a tacit agreement to resolve the crisis.

BARNETT: . . . . I've taken an oath to abide by the laws of this state and our state constitution and the Constitution of the United States. And [Attorney] General, how can I violate my oath of office? How can I do that and live with the people of Mississippi? You know, they expecting me to keep my word. That's what I'm up against, and I don't understand why the court wouldn't understand that.

JFK: Governor, this is the president speaking.

BARNETT: Yes, sir, Mr. President.

JFK: I know it's your feeling about the law of Mississippi and the fact that you don't want to carry out that court order. What we really want to have from you, though, is some understanding about whether the state police will maintain law and order. We understand your feeling about the court order and your disagreement with it. But what we're concerned about is how much violence there's going to be and what kind of action we'll have to take to prevent it. And I'd like to get assurances from you that the state police down there will take positive action to maintain law and order.

BARNETT: Oh, we'll do that.

JFK: Then we'll know what we have to do.

BARNETT: They'll take positive action, Mr. President, to maintain law and order as best we can. We'll have 220 patrolmen and they'll absolutely be unarmed. Not a one of 'em'll be armed.

JFK: Well, no, but the problem is, well, what can they do to maintain law and order and prevent the gathering of a mob and action taken by the mob? What can they do? Can they stop that?

BARNETT: Well, they'll do their best to. They'll do everything in their power to stop it.

JFK: Now, what about the suggestions made by the attorney general in regard to not permitting people to congregate and start a mob?

BARNETT: Well, we'll do our best to keep 'em from congregating, but that's hard to do, you know.

JFK: Well, just tell them to move along.

BARNETT: When they start moving up on the sidewalk and different sides of the streets, what are you going to do about it?

JFK: Well, now, as I understand it, Governor, you would do everything you can to maintain law and order.

BARNETT: I'll do everything in my power to maintain order. And peace. We don't want any shooting down here.

JFK: I understand. Now, Governor, what about, can you maintain this order?

BARNETT: Well, I don't know. That's what I'm worried about, you see. I don't know whether I can or not.

JFK: Right.

BARNETT: I couldn't have the other afternoon.

JFK: You couldn't have?

BARNETT: There was such a mob there, it would have been impossible.

JFK: I see.

BARNETT: There were men in there with trucks and shotguns, and all such as that. Not, not a lot of 'em, but some we saw, and certain people were just, they were just enraged.

JFK: Well, now, will you talk—

Barnett: You just don't understand the situation down here.

JFK: Well, the only thing I got is my responsibility—

Barnett: I know you do.

JFK: —this is not my order, I just have to carry it out. So I want to get together and try to do it with you in a way which is the most satisfactory and causes the least chance of damage to people in Mississippi. That's my interest.

Barnett: That's right. Would you be willing to wait awhile and let the people cool off on the whole thing?

JFK: Till how long?

Barnett: Couldn't you make a statement to the effect, Mr. President, Mr. General, that under the circumstances existing in Mississippi, that there'll be bloodshed; you want to protect the life of James Meredith and all other people. And under the circumstances at this time, it just wouldn't be fair to him or others to try to register him at this time.

JFK: Well, then at what time would it be fair?

Barnett: Well, we, could wait a, I don't know. It might be in two or three weeks, it might cool off a little.

JFK: Well, would you undertake to register him in two weeks?

Barnett: Well, I, you know I can't undertake to register him myself.

JFK: I see.

Barnett: But you all might make some progress that way, you know.

JFK: (*laughs*) Yeah. Well, unless we had your support and assurance—

Barnett: I say I'm going to cooperate. I might not know when you're going to register him, you know . . . .

I might not know what your plans were, you see . . . .

JFK: Thanks, Governor.

Barnett: I thank you for this call.

JFK: Thank you, Governor.

When Attorney General Robert Kennedy and Barnett spoke the next morning, Sunday, September 30 at 10:45 A.M., the governor backed away from the recent tentative agreements and proposed a brand-new, highly theatrical plan: he would stand in front of a battle formation of 500 unarmed Mississippi highway patrolmen, sheriffs, and militia troops, stare down and physically block the U.S. Army from entering the university, all in front of the world press, giving Barnett an epic photo opportunity of heroic resistance to the federals. The army would draw weapons, the Mississippi forces would stand aside, and Meredith would be escorted in.

This was too much for the attorney general, who lost his patience and threatened that the president would reveal details of earlier secret phone negotiations with Barnett during his speech to the nation that night. "You broke your word to him," said Robert Kennedy. "You don't mean the president is going to say that tonight?" "Of course he is," said RFK. What he said next was the only known example of a presidential recording possibly being used against the person being recorded. "We've got it all down, Governor," said RFK, either an oblique threat to reveal recorded transcripts, or simply to release notes and details of the JFK/Barnett talks, either of which would have grievously embarrassed Barnett. The threat worked: Barnett abruptly proposed that Meredith be flown in and installed on the Oxford campus that night, and promised to help keep order.

Hoping that U.S. Federal Marshals and state highway patrolmen could handle the situation, JFK ordered some 20,000 U.S. Army troops to stand off at the Memphis Naval Air Station and other bases in the region. In late afternoon Sunday, truckloads of marshals borrowed from the Border Patrol and federal prison system arrived by truck caravan on the Oxford campus. The marshals formed a defensive semicircle around the front of pink brick Lyceum Administration Building at the center of campus, where Meredith was to register for classes the next day and Justice Department men were setting up a command post to direct the marshals. None of the federals realized that the building was a symbol of Mississippi pride, and its seizure was about the most provocative sacrilege anyone could imagine. The marshals were armed only with tear gas guns, gas grenades, and .38 caliber pistols, which they were ordered to keep holstered under their jackets.

When dusk approached, everything started falling apart. At 5:00 P.M. local time (7:00 P.M. Washington time), scattered groups of faculty and students appeared on the grove in front of the Lyceum to inspect the weird scene. At 6:00 P.M., boys in the Confederate uniforms of the "Ole Miss" college band, just returned from a football game in Jackson, paraded up and down the field, taunting the marshals. A group ran to the flagpole and hoisted the Confederate flag. A boy produced a bugle and blew cavalry charges. Groups surged onto the field in increasingly frenzied cheerleader calls: "Go to hell, JFK," "Two-four-one-three, we hate Kennedy!" "Go to Cuba, nigger lovers!" and the ominous "Just wait'll dark." Meredith was raced in through a side entrance and deposited in a dorm room several hundred yards away from the Lyceum, guarded by a team of marshals. He cracked his books and began studying. At 7:00 P.M., a boy ran up to the federal line in front of the Lyceum screaming, "Shoot me! Shoot me!" as pebbles and lit cigarettes began flying toward the marshals. A beautiful Ole Miss coed yelled at a gas-masked marshal, "You rubber-nosed motherfucker, where's your wife tonight—sleeping with a nigger?"

Shortly after 7:45, under a barrage of rocks, Chief U.S. Marshal Jim McShane, a tough ex–New York street cop and the veteran of seven shootouts with stick-up men (in three cases he shot the gun out of their hand), ordered gas guns "at ready." At 7:58 Oxford time a two-foot piece of lead pipe sailed down onto a marshal's steel helmet and smashed him to the ground. "Let 'em have it," cried McShane. "Gas!"

Moments later, inside the Oval Office, at 10:00 P.M. (8:00 Oxford time) John Kennedy went on the air in a national broadcast to appeal for calm in Mississippi, unaware that almost at that exact moment, his men were launching a fusillade of tear gas that marked the start of full-scale combat on the campus. Justice Department official Burke Marshall raced to the Oval Office to tell the president, but he'd already started the now-irrelevant speech. Wearing defective World War I gas masks, Mississippi state highway patrolmen caught between the rioters and marshals were sent reeling from the tear gas launched by the federals behind them. Some were knocked down by thick wads of padding expelled from the gas guns, others raced from the battlefield while ripping off the useless masks. One boy confronted a trio of fleeing patrolmen: "Shoot the Yankee, shoot! Give me your gun if you won't shoot."

THE OVAL OFFICE AND CABINET ROOM
SEPTEMBER 30–OCTOBER 1, 1962:
EST. 10:20 P.M.–3:00 A.M.

President Kennedy, Attorney General Robert Kennedy, and Aides
RE: *Riot in Oxford, Mississippi*
audio recording of meeting on Tandberg machine and Dictabelt phone
recordings

As 300 federal marshals faced off against an army of 2000 rioters across a battlefield illuminated by firebombs and tear-gas explosions, Kennedy's secret recording network documented its first crisis. While JFK and his men wisecracked in "top gun" style inside the White House, the Cabinet Room phone was patched into a pay phone inside the besieged Lyceum Building. The rioters attacked with shotguns, Molotov cocktails, and a hijacked bulldozer and fire engine, and repeatedly charged the marshals from behind Confederate flags, drawing them into hand-to-hand combat. Blood began flowing, and White House machismo was replaced by confusion and despair as the crisis slipped out of control.

RFK: (*on phone*) Have you got all the marshals there now? [Only the White House side of this continuously open phone line is audible.]

JFK: State police?

RFK: (*on phone*) How many've you got? And they're all there? Yeah. How are the state police? Yeah. Is the crowd getting bigger? Yeah. That's fine. Okay, well, I'll get back, I'll let you know.

JFK: What?

RFK: I think they have it in pretty good shape . . . . (*back on phone*) Oh, Ed?* Well, how's it look to you? Is it under control? Would you bring the Guard in? Are they mad at the marshals? Okay, well, I'm going to see if I can get these, yeah, troops started anyway. Yeah. We can see. Well, I think if they, you know, I think it's better that we can, can control the situation. I don't think it's worth screwing around.

JFK: It's going to be a long fall in Oxford, I think . . . . I think we oughta get the National Guard within, you know, shouting distance . . . .

RFK: Yeah . . . . We have control over the air. If you have gas, you got a pretty good operation going. They got five hundred marshals. You see, they're sitting there, and they're throwing iron—

JFK: Spikes?

RFK: —spikes, and they're throwing Coke bottles, and they're throwing rocks . . .

JFK: What's Barnett doing?

RFK: I suppose laughing at us. (*laughter in room*) . . . .

JFK: What are we waiting for, Cy Vance† to tell us how long it will take? . . . .

VOICE: This reminds me a little bit of the Bay of Pigs.

RFK: Yech! (*laughter in room*)

SORENSEN:‡ Especially when Bobby said we'd provide air cover! (*laughter*) . . . .

---

*Edwin Guthman, director of public information, Department of Justice.

†Cyrus Vance, secretary of the army.

‡Theodore Sorensen, speechwriter and counsel to President Kennedy.

RFK: (*on phone*) Is the gas coming in there?

VOICE: Now, what is next?

MARSHALL:* They gassed some of our own marshals.

JFK: Did they? . . .

RFK: (*on phone*) Well, would you favor that I had troops coming in there? Yeah? Well, they're on their way. Okay. No. Well, you can just say that. What about, is Nick† there? Well, I'd just like to find out what he's heard on the, getting that gas in there . . . .

VOICE: Evelyn's‡ got some beers in the refrigerator.

On JFK's order, army troops of the riot-trained 503rd Military Police Battalion were now moving toward Oxford to rescue the marshals and Meredith. At 9:02 Oxford time (11:02 D.C. time), the highway patrol again withdrew, leaving the marshals to the mercy of snipers, who, starting at 9:35, began knocking them down with shotgun blasts and birdshot.

MARSHALL: (*on phone*) Well, they're coming in. Why are they, have they walked out on you? They don't have any gas masks . . . . The gas should be there, there in a few minutes.

RFK: Is he, is that Nick?

MARSHALL: This is Ed.

JFK: How do we get the gas in and out of there? . . . . We have riots like this at Harvard just because some guy yells—! (*laughter*) . . . .

SORENSEN: We do have student riots like this and it is [unintelligible words], you ought to be prepared for the worst.

JFK: That's it. That's what we're preparing for. (*laughter*)

VOICE: Yeah, and evidently we got it.

JFK: Where is Nick? Is he up in the attic? (*laughter*) . . . .

VOICES: We should withdraw from there. Yeah, of course.

RFK: (*on phone*) Will ya? Do you want these troops in there? Yeah. I, okay. He got hit by what? Yeah. Is he gonna live? The state police have left? They're not thinking of putting them in?

MARSHALL: I just had a talk with the governor.

JFK: What did he say?

MARSHALL: He said they *can't* have pulled out . . . . I just spoke to the

---

**Burke Marshall, Justice Department civil rights official.*

†*Deputy Attorney General Nicholas Katzenbach, inside the besieged Lyceum Building.*

‡*Evelyn Lincoln, secretary to President Kennedy.*

governor and the governor just spoke to the highway patrol and that everything was under control.

RFK: (*on phone*) There's going to be a fight in the infirm—Have the marshals done pretty well?

MARSHALL: The bureau [FBI] says there are people coming in from out of town.

JFK: There are, huh?

MARSHALL: Yeah.

Just after 9:00 P.M. a tall figure in a white cowboy hat appeared on the edge of the battlefield, staring into the chaos. It was retired Major General Edwin A. Walker, who led Eisenhower's troops in the 1957 Little Rock integration crisis, but quit the army under fire after giving right-wing propaganda to his troops and was now a segregationist firebrand who proclaimed that the federal court order on Meredith was part of "the conspiracy of the crucifixion by anti-Christ conspirators of the Supreme Court."

Rioters clustered around the dazed, wild-eyed Walker like soldiers in Civil War movies: "We've got a leader now!" "General, will you lead us to the steps?" From atop a Confederate battle monument, Walker announced, "Don't let up now . . . you must be prepared for possible death. . . . Protest! Protest! Stand by your governor!" An eyewitness reported this was the turning point that pushed the riot out of control and triggered organized charges by hundreds of rioters in large groups. Oxford Episcopal minister Duncan Gray, who had been running around the battlefield confronting and disarming rioters, climbed up on the monument and pleaded with Walker to stop, but was pulled down and beaten by the mob. According to several eyewitnesses, Walker climbed down from the monument and led a charge himself.

RFK: General Walker's been out there, downtown, getting them, people stirred up. (*on phone*) Can we arrange to get him arrested?

JFK: By the FBI?

RFK: (*on phone*) Those [unintelligible], well, let's see if we can arrest him. I mean, tell the FBI need arrest warrant.

JFK: By the way, what's his crime?

SORENSEN: Incitement.

JFK: Inciting.

VOICES: Inciting insurrection. Obstruction of justice . . . .

JFK: General Walker, he is, imagine that son of a bitch having been commander of a division.

Voice: You're right.

JFK: Up until last year. And the army promoting him . . . . What are they saying, he's there now?

RFK: They're saying—

JFK: Where are they? Up around the third floor? Where are they? Are they in the administration building with Meredith?

RFK: No. Meredith is in another building.

JFK: Nobody knows where he is?

Sorensen: Not when you're guarding the administration building.

RFK: He'd got forty and fifty marshals. The gas is a quarter of a mile . . . .

JFK: I haven't had such an interesting time since the Bay of Pigs . . . .

Marshall: (*on phone, about midnight*) Hello? Yeah.

RFK: (*on phone*) Yeah. (*puts phone down*) They're storming where Meredith is.

JFK: Oh? The students are?

RFK: [unintelligible] They're storming where Meredith is.

Marshall: (*on phone*) I'll find out. [unintelligible] Yes. Yes. Yes.

JFK: Well, the other lines going?

RFK: (*on phone*) Hey, Nick?

JFK: Help necessary. You better try to stick and hold the line and then I suppose get [Meredith] in the car and start to see if they can, may not be able to move him out, I suppose.

Voice: Probably better if—

RFK: (*on phone*) We, you'd better move 'em all up and get, and see if we can't get them. Well, you go ahead and do it. All right. (*puts receiver down*)

Marshall: Bob, do we have any word on the MPs [military police]?

RFK: Yeah, they're on their way. You want to get Nick?

Voices: Hello? Hello.

O'Donnell:* You don't want to have a lynching.

O'Brien:† Yeah . . . .

O'Donnell: (*on phone, puts receiver down*) The marshals are now going to start firing . . . .

**Kenneth P. O'Donnell, JFK's appointments secretary.*

†*Lawrence O'Brien, JFK's chief aide for congressional affairs.*

PHONE CONVERSATION BETWEEN
PRESIDENT KENNEDY AND GOVERNOR ROSS BARNETT:
CALL 1 (NEAR MIDNIGHT, D.C. TIME)

Governor Barnett now offered to fly from the state capitol at Jackson up to the Oxford campus to try to address the crowds and defuse the tension in person, but he wanted Kennedy to remove Meredith first.

BARNETT: [recording starts mid-sentence]—the commissioner of the highway patrol to order every man he's got.

JFK: Yeah. Well, now, how long's that gonna take? We don't want somebody—

BARNETT: Well, I haven't been able to locate him.

JFK: You can't locate?

BARNETT: The, he went to, here's what happened. He went to the doctor's office with this man that was hurt. And he, I finally located him there after you told me to get at him to get more people, don't you see, if he needed 'em. And he thought then that fifty he had would be sufficient.

JFK: Yeah.

BARNETT: But I told him by all means to order out every one he had if he needed it.

JFK: Yeah.

BARNETT: And I'm certainly trying in every way—

JFK: Well, we can't consider moving Meredith as long as the, you know, there's a riot outside, 'cause he wouldn't be safe.

BARNETT: Sir?

JFK: We couldn't consider moving Meredith if you, if we haven't been able to restore order outside. That's the problem, Governor.

BARNETT: Well, I'll tell you what I'll do, Mr. President.

JFK: Yeah.

BARNETT: I'll go up there myself.

JFK: Well, now, how long will it take you to get there?

BARNETT: And I'll get, a microphone and tell 'em that uh, you have agreed to, for him to be removed.

JFK: No. No. No. Now, wait a minute. How long, wait a minute, Governor! Now, how long is it going to take you to get up there?

BARNETT: 'Bout an hour.

JFK: Now, I'll tell you what, if you want to go up there and then you call me from up there. Then we'll decide what we're gonna do before you make any speeches about it.

BARNETT: Well, all right. Well—

JFK: No sense in—

BARNETT: I mean, whatever you, if you'd authorize—

JFK: You see, we got an hour to go, and that's not, we may not have an hour. Won't it take you an hour to go up there?

BARNETT: This man has just died.

JFK: Did he die?

BARNETT: Yes.

JFK: Which one? State police?

BARNETT: A state policeman. [This was a false report.]

JFK: Yeah, well you see, we gotta get order up there, and that's what we thought we were going to have.

BARNETT: Mr. President, please. Why can't you give an order up there to remove Meredith?

JFK: How can I remove him, Governor, when there's a riot in the street, and he may step out of that building and something happen to him? I can't remove him under those conditions.

BARNETT: But, but—

JFK: Let's get order up there, then we can do something about Meredith.

BARNETT: —we can surround it with plenty of officials.

JFK: Well, we've gotta get somebody up there now to get order and stop the firing and the shooting. Then you and I will talk on the phone about Meredith.

BARNETT: All right.

JFK: But first we gotta get order.

BARNETT: I'll, I'll call and tell 'em to get every, every official they can.

JFK: That's right and then you and I will talk when they get order there, then you and I'll talk about what's the best thing to do with Meredith.

BARNETT: All right then.

JFK: Well, thank you.

BARNETT: All right.

PHONE CONVERSATION BETWEEN PRESIDENT KENNEDY AND GOVERNOR ROSS BARNETT: CALL 2 (AFTER MIDNIGHT, D.C. TIME)

JFK: . . . . I hear they got some high-powered rifles up there that have been shooting sporadically. Can we get that stopped? How many people have you got there? We hear you only got fifty . . . .

BARNETT: I'm doing everything in the world I can.

JFK: That's right. Well, we've got to get this situation under control. That's much more important than anything else.

BARNETT: Yes. Well, that's right. . . .

JFK: They called me a few minutes ago and said they had some high-powered rifles there. So we don't wanta start moving anybody around.

BARNETT: Mr. President, people are wiring me and saying, "Well, you've given up." I said, I had to say, "No, I'm not giving up, not giving up any fight."

JFK: Yeah, but we don't want to—

BARNETT: "I never give up. I have courage and faith, and we'll win this fight." You understand. That's just to Mississippi people.

JFK: I understand. But I don't think anybody, either in Mississippi or any place else wants a lot of people killed.

BARNETT: Oh, no. No. I—

JFK: And that's what, Governor, that's the most important thing. We want—

BARNETT: I'll issue any statement, any time about peace and violence.

JFK: Well, now here's what we could do. Let's get the maximum number of your state police to get that situation so we don't have sporadic firing. I will then be in touch with my people and then you and I'll be talking again in a few minutes about, see what we got there then.

BARNETT: All right.

JFK: Thank you, Governor.

THE CABINET ROOM

RFK: (*on phone*) Hello? Hello? Well, I think they have to protect Meredith now. Well, that's what I mean. They better fire, I suppose. They gotta protect Meredith. What? Yeah, they can't do anything. Is Meredith all right?

VOICE: Well I don't know if they can.

RFK: (*on phone*) They better protect Meredith now. But can you make sure he's protected, Dean?

JFK: He [Barnett] wants us to move him. And I said, "Well, we can't move him if the situation's like this." And he says, "Well, we'll take care of the situation if you move him."

RFK: I can't get him out. How am I gonna get him out?

JFK: That's what I said to him . . . .

It was "a terrible evening, because people were being shot," recalled Robert Kennedy. JFK, he added, "was torn between an attorney general who had botched things up and the fact that the attorney general was his brother." On the battlefield, Marshal Al Butler exclaimed, "That's not a riot out there anymore—it's an armed insurrection."

In the Cabinet Room, RFK now fielded a phone request from Katzenbach inside the Lyceum Building for the marshals to begin firing live ammunition, since rioters were starting to break into the building itself. Hearing this conversation, JFK told RFK (off the microphone) they were not to fire under any conditions, even if they were being overrun, except to save Meredith's life.

RFK: (*on phone*) Hey, Nick? I just got, Ramsey* asked me for, if they had permission to fire back? Do you have to do that? Well, can't they just retreat into that building? Is he safe over to your place? I think they can fire to save *him*. Now, can you hold out for an hour there? Can you hold out if you have gas? Is there much firing? Is there any way you could figure a way to scare 'em off? . . . . Damn army! They can't even tell if in fact the MPs have left yet . . . . Who've you got up at the other place [the dorm where Meredith was]. Yeah, but I mean, I think you want to get somebody that's up there that knows how important it is to keep Meredith alive. Yeah, but I mean it should be somebody that you know. And that should stay right by Meredith and, and shoot anybody that puts a hand on him . . . .

O'DONNELL: I have a hunch that Khrushchev† would get those troops in fast enough. That's what worries me about this whole thing . . . .

At the last minute, as tear gas ran out and rioters broke into the building, the cavalry arrived to support the marshals. Not the U.S. Army, still racing to the scene, but sixty local Mississippi national guardsmen of Troop E of the 108th Armored Cavalry Regiment commanded by Oxford insurance man Captain Murry Falkner (a nephew of famed writer William Faulkner), who fought their way through the combat onto campus carrying unloaded bayonet-tipped rifles and took up positions alongside the marshals.

---

*Ramsey Clark, Justice Department official.
†Soviet Premier Nikita Khrushchev.

O'BRIEN: They, they have sixty guardsmen there now. One of them was just wounded, so they know they're there.

JFK: One of the guards was wounded?

O'BRIEN: He said they just brought 'im in. So he says they estimate they've split it. He arrived in a group of sixty.

VOICES: You were right. What? That's good anyway. Yeah.

O'BRIEN: Sixty men. Sixty men under the command of a Captain Falkner . . . .

RFK: (*on phone*) They tell me the fellow from the London paper was killed. Well, they found him in back of some dormitories. Yeah.

French-English reporter Paul Guihard of Agence France Presse and the London Daily Sketch was last seen walking toward the Lyceum Building in the midst of the riot. His body was found after 9:00 P.M., shot dead at point-blank range, execution-style, with a bullet in his back. RFK now worried about how to handle the public relations fallout from the disaster-in-progress.

What about, what are we going to say about all this Ed? We're going to have a helluva problem about why we didn't handle the situation better. Yeah. Yeah, I know. Okay. Well, I think we're gonna have to figure out what we're gonna say. Right. You want to, oh, yeah. Well, you did terrific. I think it's just a question of the fact that I made a decision to send, Okay. Yeah. Want to hold on? . . . .

MARSHALL: (*on phone*) Ed? They can't get the trucks out to them. We're gonna try to land some [helicopters] on the campus. We're not. Yeah. We ought to do that. It's really a, yeah. I don't know if they've gone. Oh, he was there, all right, what he was doing, I don't, I don't know, Ed. Yeah, they did. Yeah, Okay. They've all been evacuated, I understand? Yeah. Real warring. No. God, that's dumb. That army, you know, they're just late. Well, they're in the air. Yeah. I don't think they do. They've got pistols . . . .

RFK: (*on phone*) Well, I just think that we're gonna take a lot of knocks, because people getting killed, the fact that I didn't get the people up there in time.

At midnight Oxford time the regular army still hadn't arrived. RFK later recalled "the evening would have been quite different if the troops had got-

ten there at the time that they were supposed to have gotten there. The army had botched it up." But it was the Kennedys who botched it up.

At 1:35 A.M. Oxford time (3:35 A.M. D.C. time), most of the regular army had still not made it to the campus, and a furious JFK sent a message to the army: "People are dying in Oxford. This is the worst thing I've seen in forty-five years. I want the military police battalion to enter the action. I want General Billingslea to see that this is done."

Kennedy cursed himself for not sending the troops in earlier. Finally, at 2:15 A.M. Oxford time (4:15 A.M. D.C. time), the regular army began arriving in strength and seized the university grounds. Within hours, some 20,000 U.S. troops invaded Mississippi. Fighting between the GIs and bands of rednecks continued until the early morning, when the troops swept the remnants of the riot off the campus and into the town square of Oxford. The fighting didn't stop until the army fired volleys of live ammunition over the rioters' heads. At 7:55 A.M., James Meredith, Marshal Jim McShane at his side, strode into the Lyceum to register and soon was attending his first class—American Colonial History. "The idea that we got through the evening without the marshals being killed and without Meredith being killed was a miracle," RFK later asserted. But two men lay dead and 200 were wounded, including scores of marshals and soldiers. The crisis was a watershed for the civil rights cause, as it forced Kennedy, who had been cautiously avoiding major action on the issue, to decisively commit himself to the struggle with a full-scale military invasion of Mississippi. Meredith graduated in 1963.

For Kennedy, the battle of Oxford was a near disaster, but it happened in the days just before TV networks could fully cover such an event live, and the few photos that survived of the mobs in Oxford were wiped off the nation's memory banks three weeks later by the Cuban Missile Crisis. Oxford was a case history in the cautious, pragmatic political and executive style that defined Kennedy's presidency. "Kennedy was decisive, though he never made a decision until he had to," wrote Richard Reeves, "and then invariably chose the most moderate of available options." "I don't think I ever react emotionally to a problem, but that doesn't mean I'm not emotional," Kennedy once explained. "It simply means I reason problems out and apply logic to them." On the recordings his tone of voice is always cool, confident, unemotional, and rational. While all of JFK's tapes are in a sense staged performances, since only he (and possibly RFK) knew the recorders were rolling, eyewitness testimony of Kennedy in action in untaped situations varies little from how he presents himself on the tapes.

The Cuban Missile Crisis in October 1962 was the singular achievement of John Kennedy's presidency—in the course of staring down both Soviet Premier Khrushchev and hard-liners among his own advisers, including furious members of his Joint Chiefs of Staff, Kennedy managed to carefully and rationally navigate the most dangerous crisis in Cold War history to a peaceful conclusion.

On the morning of October 16, 1962, Kennedy was in the White House living quarters in his bathrobe and slippers when he was greeted by his national security adviser, McGeorge Bundy. "Mr. President," said Bundy, "there is now hard photographic evidence which you will see, that the Russians have offensive missiles in Cuba." U.S. population centers were now coming under the crosshairs of Soviet nuclear warheads based just ninety miles offshore. Kennedy told Bundy to put together a meeting of his top advisers for later that morning. The missile crisis team, which varied in size around a core group of nine to fifteen aides, was dubbed the Executive Committee of the National Security Council, or ExComm.

The missile crisis showcased the strengths of Kennedy's maturing executive style, chiefly his talent for fostering intellectual interplay and creative tension among his advisers, and for creating an environment where people felt free to openly argue fact and opinion with one another without penalty. "The last thing I want around here is a mutual admiration society," Kennedy said one day, following a heated exchange between two aides in his presence. "When you people stop arguing, I'll start worrying." Pierre Salinger reported, "It was not an administration where the president's staff had to figure out what his position was before they went into a meeting and then make sure they followed that line." Former defense secretary and Kennedy adviser Robert Lovett observed, "President Kennedy had a quality which I have rarely seen in any holder of the chief executive office; that is, the willingness to have the person whose advice he sought answer with complete frankness and, if necessary, bluntness." Kennedy once explained, "I want all the input, but when they don't give it to me, I've got to dig into their minds."

At the time, JFK thought the chances of nuclear war were "fifty/fifty." They may, in fact, have been higher, since the Soviets had, unknown to the United States, secretly deployed at least ninety short-range tactical nuclear weapons in Cuba, in addition to the strategic launchers the United States knew about. These short-range weapons could have been fired at U.S. invasion troops as soon as they hit Cuban beaches, although how much discretionary authority the Russian commanders in Cuba had to launch them is unclear. Of the longer-range weapons, it was never clear how many had warheads and how many were ready to launch. During a tape-recorded meeting on October 23, JFK noted: "What we are doing is throwing down a card on the table in a game which we don't know the ending of," and as the crisis wore on both Kennedy and Khrushchev's ability to control the endgame threatened to slip away in the face of misunderstandings or by accident.

THE OVAL OFFICE AND CABINET ROOM
OCTOBER 16–27, 1962

President Kennedy and National Security Council Executive
  Committee
RE: *Soviet Nuclear Missiles in Cuba*
tape recording of meetings on Tandberg reel-to-reel machine

Kennedy's recordings of the Cuban Missile Crisis meetings, many of which were declassified only in the 1990s, reveal moments of great tension and occasional humor as he and his team grappled with the most crucial decision any president has ever faced—how to avoid triggering a nuclear war. The crisis also exposed the positive core of Kennedy's maturing executive style: self-control, a call for multiple opinions, the discipline to think several steps ahead, and the ability to put himself "in the other guy's shoes." Unlike the Bay of Pigs and Oxford crises (and later Vietnam), Kennedy's pragmatic, rational approach triumphed.

OCTOBER 16, 1962, 11:50 A.M.

At the first meeting, the ExComm gathered in the Cabinet Room for a briefing from Arthur Lundahl of the National Photographic Interpretation Center and CIA analyst Sidney Graybeal on aerial photographs of missile sites. The weapons in question were MRBMs, or medium-range ballistic missiles, and IRBMs, or intermediate-range ballistic missiles. Kennedy entered the room, sat down, and quietly flipped the hidden "record" switch under the Cabinet Room desk.

LUNDAHL: This is a result of photography taken Sunday, sir.
JFK: Yeah.
LUNDAHL: There's a medium-range ballistic missile launch site and two

new military encampments on the southern edge of the Sierra del Rosario in west central Cuba . . . .

JFK: How far advanced is this?

LUNDAHL: Sir, we've never seen this kind of installation before.

JFK: Not even in the Soviet Union?

LUNDAHL: No, sir . . . . But from May of 1960 on, we have never had any U-2 coverage of the Soviet Union, so we do not know what kind of a practice they would use in connection with this.

JFK: How do you know this is a medium-range ballistic missile?

LUNDAHL: The length, sir.

JFK: The what? The length?

LUNDAHL: The length of it. Yes . . . .

Mr. Graybeal, our missile man, has some pictures of the equivalent Soviet equipment that has been dragged through the streets of Moscow, that can give you some detail, sir.

GRAYBEAL: There are two missiles involved. One of them is our SS-3, which is 630 miles and on up to about 700. It's 68 feet long. These missiles measure out to be 67 foot long. The other missile, the 1,100 one, is 73 foot long . . .

JFK: Is this ready to be fired?

GRAYBEAL: No, sir.

JFK: How long, we can't tell, can we how long before fired . . . .

SECRETARY OF DEFENSE ROBERT MCNAMARA: . . . I think it is extremely important that our talk and our discussion be founded on this premise: that any air strike will be planned to take place prior to the time they become operational. Because, if they become operational before the air strike, I do not believe we can state we can knock them out before they can be launched; and if they're launched there is almost certain to be chaos, in part of the east coast or the area in a radius of six hundred to a thousand miles from Cuba . . . .

RUSK: I don't believe, myself, that the critical question is whether you get a particular missile before it goes off because if they shoot those missiles we are in general nuclear war . . . .

JFK: What is the, advant—, must be some major reason for the Russians to, set this up as, must be that they're not satisfied with their ICBMs. What'd be the reason that they would—

CHAIRMAN OF THE JOINT CHIEFS OF STAFF MAXWELL TAYLOR: What it'd give 'em is primarily, it makes it a launching base for short-range missiles against the United States to supplement their rather ineffective ICBM system, for example. There's one reason.

JFK: Of course, I don't see how we could prevent further ones from coming in by submarine. I mean if we let 'em blockade the thing, they come in by submarine . . . .

SECRETARY OF THE TREASURY C. DOUGLAS DILLON: I think that the chance of getting through this thing without a Russian reaction is greater under a quick strike than building the whole thing up to a climax . . . .

JFK: How effective can the take-out be, do they think?

TAYLOR: It'll never be 100 percent, Mr. President, we know. We hope to take out a vast majority in the first strike . . . I think we should be in a position to invade at any time, if we so desired . . . .

VICE PRESIDENT JOHNSON: I think the question with the [missile] base is whether we take it out or whether we talk about it, both, either alternative is a very distressing one, but of the two, I would take it out. Assuming that the commanders felt that way . . . .

RFK: I would say that you're dropping bombs all over Cuba if you do the second, air, and the airports, knocking out their planes, dropping it on all their missiles, you're covering most of Cuba. You're going to kill an awful lot of people, and we're going to take an awful lot of heat on it . . . .

JFK: I don't believe it takes us, at least, how long does it take to get in a position where we can invade Cuba? Almost a month? Two months?

McNAMARA: No, sir. No, sir. It's a bare seven days after the air strike, assuming the air strike starts the first of next week. Now, if the air strike were to start today, it wouldn't necessarily be seven days after today, but if, I think you can basically consider seven days after the air strike . . . .

JFK: I don't think we got much time on these missiles. They may be, it may be that we just have to, we can't wait two weeks while we're getting ready to, to roll. Maybe just have to just take them out, and continue our other preparations if we decide to do that . . . .

OCTOBER 16, 1962, 6:30 P.M. MEETING

JFK: . . . . He's [Khrushchev] initiated the danger really, hasn't he? He's the one that's playing God, not us . . . .

TAYLOR: I'd like to stress this last point, Mr. President. We are very vulnerable to conventional bombing attack, lower-level bombing attacks in the Florida area. Our whole air defense has been oriented in other directions. We've never had low-level defenses prepared for this country. So it would be entirely possible for MiGs to come through with conventional weapons and so some amount, some damage . . . .

DILLON: What if they carry a nuclear weapon?

JFK: Well, if they carry a nuclear weapon . . . you assume they wouldn't do that . . . .

RUSK: I would not think they would use a nuclear weapon unless they're prepared to generate a nuclear war. I don't think, I just don't see that possibility.

NATIONAL SECURITY ASSISTANT McGEORGE BUNDY: I would agree.

RUSK: That would mean that, we could be just utterly wrong, but we've never really believed that Khrushchev would take on a general nuclear war over Cuba . . . .

JFK: We certainly have been wrong about what he's trying to do in Cuba. There isn't any doubt about that. Not many of us thought he was going to put MRBMs in Cuba . . . .

I suppose they really, then they start getting ready to squeeze us in Berlin, doesn't that, you may say it doesn't make any difference if you get blown up by an ICBM flying from the Soviet Union or one from ninety miles away. Geography doesn't mean that much.

TAYLOR: We'd have to target them with our missiles and have the same kind of, of pistol-pointed-at-the-head situation as we have in the Soviet Union at the present time.

BUNDY: No question, if this thing goes on, an attack on Cuba becomes general war. And that's really the question, whether—

JFK: That's why it shows the Bay of Pigs was really right, if we'd done it right . . . .

OCTOBER 18, 1962, 11:10 A.M. MEETING

RFK: . . . . What is your preference, Tom?

THOMPSON:* My preference is let's blockade the [unintelligible] the declaration has already led the steps leading up to it. I think it's very

---

*Llewellyn ("Tommy") Thompson, ambassador-at-large and adviser on Soviet affairs.

highly doubtful that the Russians would resist a blockade against military weapons, particularly offensive ones, if at that point, if that's the way we pitched it to the world. [This turned out to be the plan Kennedy adopted.]

JFK: And what do we do with the weapons already there?

THOMPSON: Demand their dismantlement and say that we are going to maintain constant surveillance, and if they are not armed, we would then take them out, and then maybe do it. I think that we should be under no illusions that this would probably in the end lead to the same thing. But we would do it under an entirely different posture and background, and much less danger of getting up into the big war . . . .

As the ExComm debated possible responses, with a majority favoring an air strike against Cuba, one of the risks they faced was that any military move might provoke a Soviet counterstrike on Berlin. In that divided city, outnumbered U.S. troops faced surrounding Soviet bloc forces in a tense standoff. Under the NATO treaty, the United States was obligated to defend Berlin against a Soviet attack.

JFK: He'll grab Berlin, of course. Then either way it would be we lost Berlin, because of these missiles. . . .

RFK: What do we do when Khrushchev moves into Berlin?

BUNDY: If we could trade off Berlin and not have it our fault! *(laughter)*

McNAMARA: When we're talking about [Khrushchev] taking Berlin, what do we mean exactly? Does he take it with Soviet troops? I think there's a real possibility of that—we have U.S. troops over there where they do. If they fight, they fight, I think that's perfectly clear.

JFK: And they get overrun.

McNAMARA: Yes, they get overrun, exactly.

VOICES: Then what do we do? . . . Then we're in a general war . . . general war.

JFK: You mean nuclear exchange?

VOICE: Yessir . . . .

JFK: We've got to take some action. Because the alliance would disintegrate. Now, the question really is, is to what action would we take that lessens the chances of a nuclear exchange, which obviously is the final failure . . . .

OCTOBER 19, 9:45 A.M., CABINET ROOM, MEETING WITH SECRETARY OF DEFENSE AND JOINT CHIEFS OF STAFF

Kennedy had to manage tensions both with the Soviet Union and with his own military chiefs, most of whom opposed his blockade plan in favor of stronger military action. Leading their argument was Air Force Chief of Staff General Curtis LeMay, the blunt-talking, cigar-chomping air force commander who later wrote that the United States should threaten to bomb North Vietnam "back into the Stone Age." LeMay had little respect for Kennedy, and was appalled at his performance during the Bay of Pigs. A witness reported that JFK would have "fits" and be "frantic" when he met with LeMay because the general "wouldn't listen" and would make what Kennedy thought were outrageous proposals.

JFK: . . . . There's bound to be a reprisal from the Soviet Union, there always is—their just going in and taking Berlin by force at some point. Which leaves me only one alternative, which is to fire nuclear weapons, which is a hell of an alternative. We can have a nuclear exchange from all that's happening . . . .

TAYLOR: Well, I just have to say one thing, and then turn it over to General LeMay. We, we recognize all these things, Mr. President, but I think we'd all be unanimous in saying that really our strength in Berlin, our strength anyplace in the world, is really the credibility of our response under certain conditions. And if we don't respond here in Cuba, we think the credibility of our response in Berlin disappears.

JFK: That's right. Well, that's why we've got to respond. Now, the question is, what kind of response.

LEMAY: Well, I certainly agree with everything General Taylor has said. I'd emphasize a little stronger, perhaps, that we don't have any choice except direct military action.

If we do this blockade that's proposed, and political action, the first thing that's gonna happen is that the missiles are going to (*snaps his fingers*) disappear into the woods. Particularly your mobile ones. Now, we can't find them then, regardless of what they do, and then we're gonna take some damage if we try to do anything later on.

JFK: Can't there be some undercover now, in the sense of not having been delivered?

LeMay: There's a possibility of that, but the way they've lined these others up, now, I would say it's a small possibility. If they were going to hide any of them, you'd think they would have hid them all. I don't think they're hid. The only danger we have is that we haven't picked up some that were sittin' right around in plain sight. This is possible. If we do go out and do photography over 'em this'll be a tip-off, too.

Now, as to the Berlin situation, I don't share your view that if we knock off Cuba, they're gonna knock off Berlin. We've got the Berlin problem starin' us in the face anyway. If we don't do anything to Cuba, then they're gonna push on Berlin. And *push real hard!* Because they've got us *on the run!* If we take military action against Cuba then I think—

JFK: What do you think their reprisal would be?

LeMay: I don't think they're going to make any reprisal, if we tell them that the Berlin situation is the same as it's always been: if they make a move, we're gonna *fight.* I don't think it changes the Berlin situation at all, except (*voice dripping contempt*) you've gotta make one more statement on it.

So I see no other solution. This blockade and political action I see leading into war. I don't see any other solution. It'll lead right into war. This is almost as bad as the appeasement at Munich! (*dead silence in the room*)

Because if the blockade comes along, the MiGs are gonna fly, the IL-28s [Soviet aircraft] are gonna fly against us, and we're just gonna gradually drift into a war under conditions that are a great disadvantage to us, with missiles that can knock out our airfields in the southeastern portion, and if they use nuclear weapons, it's the population down there. We just drift into a war under conditions that we don't like.

I just don't see any other solution except direct military intervention—*right now!* . . .

Kennedy ignored LeMay's frontal assault and encouraged the other chiefs to speak up. Later in the meeting, one of the Joint Chiefs quipped to the president: "In other words, you're in a pretty bad fix at the present time!" JFK asked "What did you say?" The chief repeated, "You're in a pretty bad fix!" The room broke into laughter, then JFK fired back: "You're in with me!"

After Kennedy left the Cabinet Room, as they waited for their ride back to the Pentagon, the Joint Chiefs talked among themselves, behind the president's back. What they didn't know was that Kennedy's hidden microphones were picking up every word. Secretary McNamara lingered for a few moments, then left. The chiefs were alone. The door closed. Voices asked, "Is the coast clear out there?" "What do you gather he's gonna do?"

Soon the chiefs were voicing their disgust with Kennedy in bursts of blistering macho-speak:

JOINT CHIEF VOICE 1: You pulled the rug right out from under him!

JOINT CHIEF VOICE 2: Jesus Christ, what the hell did he mean?

JOINT CHIEF VOICE 1: I agree with you 100 percent. He finally got around to the word "escalation." That's the only goddamn thing that'll do the whole trick. It's been in Laos, it's been in every goddamn one. When he says "escalation," I say—somebody should keep him the goddamn thing piecemeal. That's our problem.

You go in there and frig around with the missiles, you're *screwed*. You go in there and frig around with the lift, you're *screwed*. (Voice 2: That's right!) You're *screwed, screwed, screwed*!

There's some goddamn thing, some way to see, to do the son of a bitch and do it *right*, and quit friggin' around. That was my position. Don't frig around and go take a missile out.

Goddamnit, if he wants you to do it, you can't fiddle around with taking out missiles. You can't fiddle around hitting the missile sites without taking out the SAM sites. You've got to go in and take out the goddamn things that are gonna stop you from doing your job! (*sounds of approval from other Chiefs*)

OCTOBER 22, 1962, 5:00 P.M.,
MEETING WITH CONGRESSIONAL LEADERS

As the U.S. military geared up to an intense DEFCON-3 global alert and prepared to shower the Soviet Union with the explosive power of 30 million tons of TNT, Kennedy met with nineteen congressmen at the Cabinet Room table before addressing the nation at 7:00 P.M. All through the day, air force planes had been flying around the country, picking up vacationing congressmen and racing them to Washington for the meeting. Kennedy told the congressmen that the Soviet Union had installed nuclear missiles in Cuba, and that he was going on national TV to announce a blockade of the island. To Kennedy's surprise the stunned legislators were interrupting him, attacking his plan, and demanding an immediate invasion.

Senator Russell:* . . . . Mr. President, I don't want to make a nuisance of myself, but I would like to complete my statement. My position is, these people have been warned . . . .

JFK: Senator, we can't invade Cuba—it takes us some while to assemble our force to invade Cuba. That's one of the problems we've got. We haven't wanted to surface the movement of troops beyond what has been surfaced in the last forty-eight hours. We have to bring some troops from the West Coast to assemble the force which would give us the 90,000-odd men who might participate in an invasion, it'll take some days . . . .

If we go into Cuba we have to all realize that we are taking the chance that these missiles which are ready to fire won't be fired. That's the gamble we should take. In any case we are preparing to take it. I think that is one hell of a gamble . . .

We may have the war by the next twenty-four hours. All I want to say is, we are going to move with maximum speed all of our forces to be in a position to invade Cuba within the seven-day period . . . .

A furious Senator Russell raised his voice at Kennedy, and the two briefly shouted at each other:

Russell: I think we're dying by attrition here. I'm through. Excuse me. I wouldn't be honest with myself if I didn't—*I hope you'll forgive me, but you asked for opinions!* (*during this sequence, JFK and Russell speak over each other*)

JFK: *No, I forgive you, but this is a very difficult decision we're faced with! I'll just tell you that. It's a very difficult choice we've got!*

Russell: Oh, my God, I know that. I'll tell you, the world's destiny will hinge on this decision!

JFK: That's right.

Russell: But it's comin' some day, Mr. President. Will it ever be under more auspicious circumstances? . . .

JFK: Now, when you talk about the invasion, first, excluding the risk

---

**Senator Richard Russell, D-GA, chairman of the Senate Armed Services Committee.*

that these missiles will be fired, we do have the 7 or 8,000 Russians there, we are going to have to shoot them up, and I think that it would be foolish to expect that the Russians would not regard that as a far more direct thrust than they're gonna regard on the ships. And I think that the end result will be immediately the seizure of Berlin.

Now, as I say, we may have to put up with all that. But I think that if you're talking about nuclear war, the escalation ought to be at least with some degree of control . . . .

Let me just say as I said at the beginning that the person whose course of action is not adopted is the best off. Because no matter what you do, some people say, well let's go in with an air strike. You could have those bombs go off and blow up fifteen cities in the United States. And they would have been wrong. . . .

RUSSELL: There's no use in waiting, Mr. President, the nettle is going to sting—

JFK: That's correct. I just think at least we start here, then see where we go. And I'll tell you that every opportunity is full of hazards. Now I'd better go make this speech. . . .

Shortly after the meeting, JFK muttered: "If they want this job, fuck 'em. They can have it—it's no great joy to me."

The next morning, October 23, Dean Rusk woke up to see sunlight beaming through his windows and thought, "Ah, I am still here. This is interesting." That day the stock market plunged, and in Florida there was a run on rifles and shotgun sales in sporting-goods stores. In Los Angeles, civil defense officials announced that stores would be closed for five days if a war occurred, sparking a stampede of housewives into supermarkets. In one store, hand-to-hand combat erupted over the last can of pork and beans. Kennedy asked a civil defense official, "Can we, maybe before we invade, evacuate these cities?" The air force dispersed hundreds of B-47 bombers to scattered civilian airfields to escape the first Soviet missile barrages, and 1,000 combat aircraft swarmed into Florida airbases to join over 100,000 troops poised to seize Cuba.

At this moment the power to launch U.S. nuclear weapons rested not only with the president, but with LeMay's deputy, Air Force General Thomas Power, head of the Strategic Air Command (SAC), a man who thought

Kennedy was a coward and who was considered a sadist even by LeMay. One of Power's subordinate commanders, Air Force General Horace Wade, said, "I used to worry about General Power. I used to worry that General Power was not stable. I used to worry about the fact that he had control over so many weapons and weapon systems and could, under certain conditions, launch the force." General Power had both the physical ability to launch American nuclear forces and, under war plans approved by Eisenhower and still in effect, had the legal authority to order a launch if the president couldn't be reached. Some 3,000 nuclear bombs were under the command of General Power, a man, who in the eyes of some who knew him, was "certifiably off the deep end," and "not the sort of person who could be counted on to follow strict orders of the political leadership during a nuclear crisis."

The risks of human or mechanical errors introduced the horrific possibility of an accidental nuclear launch. On the night of October 26, an American U-2 reconnaissance aircraft strayed deep into Soviet airspace over the Chukotskiy Peninsula when its navigation system failed. The pilot radioed his home base in a panic, "Hey, I think I'm lost. I may be over Siberia. For Christ's sake, tell me how to get home!" Soviet MiG interceptors were scrambled to chase and shoot down the plane. Responding to the U-2's SOS, several American F-102A interceptors, fully armed with Falcon air-to-air nuclear missiles ready to be fired at the pilot's discretion, were launched westward from Galena Air Force Base in western Alaska. While still over Siberia, the U-2 burned up its last fuel, "flamed out," and began to glide back toward Alaska, steadily losing altitude. Over the Bering Strait, one of the F-102As spotted the U-2 and escorted it down to a distant landing site on the Alaska coast.

At the height of the missile crisis, on October 27, technicians at a New Jersey radar post signaled the national command headquarters that a missile had been fired from Cuba and was about to land on Tampa, Florida. Other U.S. military commands were informed that a nuclear assault seemed to have begun. It was soon recognized as a false alarm, triggered by test software accidentally inserted into the radar screen.

Compounding the dangers of an accidental launch was the high level of combat alerts on both sides. On October 24, Defense Secretary Robert McNamara, at the direction of Kennedy, ordered the Strategic Air Command to a DEFCON 2 alert for the first and only time in its history, just one step down from DEFCON 1, or imminent war. DEFCON 3 had already been declared at the exact moment JFK's October 22 address to the nation began. The alerts boosted SAC's B-52 global nuclear patrol from twelve sorties per day to sixty-six and prepared U.S. missiles and bombers for an immediate large-scale nuclear strike; in the Pacific and European theaters QRA (quick reaction alert) aircraft were loaded with nuclear warheads and put on immediate take-off status.

Without the president's knowledge, and against procedure, SAC Commander General Power broadcast the DEFCON 2 message to his men on an open frequency so the Russians would pick it up, urging his pilots to be cautious and double-check all orders. In response, according to former Soviet military officers interviewed by Brookings Institution analyst Bruce Blair, the Soviet Strategic Rocket Forces received emergency orders to go on maximum combat alert, warheads were loaded onto ICBMs for a two-hour launch capability, and Soviet strategic bombers went on runway alert. On top of this, the commander in chief of the United Kingdom's Bomber Command, on his own initiative, ordered a full combat alert of all British nuclear weapons, including 140 V-bombers and 60 Thor missiles poised to strike 230 Soviet bloc targets in fifteen minutes or less.

By Saturday, October 27, according to Sorensen, "tempers were high and everyone was frustrated that the naval blockade was not working, and the hawks of the group were on the ascendancy again, in effect saying, 'We told you it would not work; we told you we had to bomb and invade, now let's do it.'" By now the Joint Chiefs were unanimously urging immediate military action, in part because of the difficulties of indefinitely maintaining a full alert. As if to illustrate their point, during the Saturday meetings, Kennedy received the alarming news that a U-2 spy plane had been shot down over Cuba.

When two conflicting letters from Khrushchev came in on Saturday, October 27, Kennedy ignored the belligerent one and responded to the more rational one, a tactic suggested by Soviet expert Lewellyn Thompson. Kennedy then deployed two highly secret back-up plans, not even telling the ExComm about them. First he sent his brother Bobby to propose to Soviet Ambassador Anatoly Dobrynin a mutual withdrawal of missiles from Cuba and Turkey. Then he approved a plan for UN Secretary-General U Thant to appeal for a mutual withdrawal. Either move would have enraged the hawks on Kennedy's civilian and military teams.

The back-up plans weren't needed. At 9:00 A.M. Washington time on Sunday, October 28, a message from Khrushchev was broadcast on American radio announcing that he had accepted the Kennedy terms on withdrawing the missiles. Dean Acheson, who quit the ExComm in protest over the blockade plan, thought Kennedy's meetings were "repetitive, leaderless and a waste of time." Acheson snipped: "It was just plain dumb luck." He may have been right, but a case can also be made that the crisis was a triumph for Kennedy's cautious, pragmatic executive style and his Oval Office atmosphere of encouraging productive creative tension and intellectual interplay to gather opinions and encourage open debate. Kennedy's tapes of the crisis illustrate his rational, low-ego approach, as he groped toward a solution, while trying to slow the escalation down and provide Khrushchev with a way out. ExComm member C. Douglas Dillon recalled, "He got input from everybody. We would argue in front of him. He wouldn't say anything, he would listen and learn, and then he'd take his decisions. He was very calm, very collected and impressive. He handled it beautifully. He made the right decisions."

As John Kennedy entered the final months of his life, the fault lines of two major issues, civil rights and Vietnam, opened up, and Kennedy's tape recorders caught him facing the new dangers of the mid-1960s with typical caution and ambiguity. On August 28, 1963, Kennedy invited the leaders of that day's historic civil rights March on Washington to the White House to salute the march's success and to review the status of legislation that later became the 1964 Civil Rights Act. Kennedy tape-recorded the meeting, which included Vice President Johnson and march organizers A. Philip Randolph and the Rev. Martin Luther King, Jr. Much of the meeting was occupied by Kennedy and Johnson glumly explaining how they couldn't muster the votes to get civil rights legislation through Congress in the current session, a depressing letdown from King's soaring "I Have a Dream" speech hours earlier.

In public statements just weeks before his death, Kennedy put forward contradictory views on Vietnam. There were now 16,732 Americans in Vietnam, and the war cost the United States half a billion dollars a year, but the Communists controlled 80 percent of the countryside. At time of his death, JFK was putting in motion a 1,000-man troop withdrawal, but there is no way of knowing what would have followed. At this point JFK had no Vietnam policy, but was trying to cobble together a stopgap solution, as he had done in Berlin and Laos, hoping to hold things together until after the 1964 election, when he would to be in a stronger position to decide to escalate, negotiate, or withdraw.

Events in Vietnam were quickly overwhelming Kennedy's cautious approach. In the wake of President Diem's repressive measures against Buddhists and other dissidents, army officers mounted a coup on November 1 and 2, and after a fourteen-hour firefight, captured and killed Diem and his brother, Ngo Dinh Diem. The coup was carried out with the tacit support of the United States, which was alarmed both by Diem's repressions and his flirtations with direct negotiations with the Communists. But when Kennedy was informed of Diem's death, General Taylor reported that the president "leaped to his feet and rushed from the room with a look of shock and dismay on his face which I had never seen before."

Just hours after the coup, a shaken Kennedy groped for direction as his Vietnam policy crumbled, but like two presidents after him, he found only despair. In a tape-recorded National Security Council meeting on November 2, Kennedy mused, "I didn't think there was that much hatred" for Diem. "We haven't got any report on what public reaction was to the assassination?" he asked. "The only reports we've had are jubilance in the streets," a voice responded. "Governor Harriman says if there was an election tomorrow and Lodge ran, he'd undoubtedly win." JFK waited a beat and dryly wisecracked, "I'm not so sure about that." The room exploded in belly laughter, as Lodge was a potential Republican presidential contender against JFK in the 1964 U.S. election. A voice called out over the laughter to clarify, "In Vietnam! In Vietnam!" Later in the meeting, when an official suggested they "get a story and stick to it" on the assassination, JFK replied, "Well, it ought to be a true story, if possible."

"Kennedy was the pragmatist par excellence," argued George Ball, adding that "although he sometimes alluded to conceptual ideas in his speeches, his main concern was action and day-to-day results." Dean Rusk explained, "He showed great flexibility of mind. It did not bother him, for example, that certain decisions might appear to be contradictory, and which called for different approaches. He was urbane, sophisticated, wary of dogma. He was skeptical of people who were always damned sure that they were right, because he understood the complexity and the complications of life."

JFK's detached pragmatism delivered mixed results in Congress, where he fell under the shadow of Lyndon Johnson, as do most presidents. Kennedy's success rate with Congress of 84.6 percent was the highest of any president, but many of his proposals, including the Civil Rights Act, simply didn't make it to a vote. A Democratic senator complained: "The president prides himself on being a pragmatist. I have never known him, in the Senate or in the White House, to display anything like ideological fervor. . . . So, although he sent us a program, he virtually abandoned it." Republican leader Everett Dirksen said that a JFK proposal had "all the impact of a snowflake on the bosom of the Potomac." Gerald Ford asserted: "He or his staff didn't conduct the best relations with Congress. They were sort of disorganized. He could charm the Congress, but he didn't work it." In the weeks before

Kennedy died, Congress had blocked almost his entire domestic program, and his popularity dropped from 83 percent after the Bay of Pigs fiasco, to 57 percent, due in part to growing southern resistance to civil rights. One victory was the Senate's passage of the Nuclear Test Ban Treaty, the first arms control agreement of the nuclear age.

Shortly after the assassination on November 22, 1963, journalist I. F. Stone wrote: "He died in time to be remembered as he would like to be remembered, as ever young, still victorious, struck down undefeated, with almost all the potentates and rulers of mankind, friend and foe, come to mourn at the bier. For somehow one has the feeling that in the tangled dramaturgy of events, this sudden assassination was for the author the only way out. The Kennedy administration was approaching an impasse, certainly at home, quite possibly abroad, from which there seemed no escape." The following year, the *New York Times*'s James Reston mused, "He always seemed to be striding through doors into the center of some startling triumph or disaster. He never reached his meridian: we saw him only as a rising sun."

Management expert Peter Drucker concluded that "for all the brilliance of its members, the administration achieved fundamentally only one success, in the Cuban Missile Crisis. Otherwise, it achieved practically nothing. The main reason was surely what its members called 'pragmatism'; that is, its refusal to develop rules and principles, and its insistence on treating everything 'on its merits.'" Historian James MacGregor Burns argued, "Kennedy accumulated tremendous personal popularity. The trouble is, popularity is not power. Power is the ability to move other people in government who may feel very differently from you. I don't think Kennedy ever found the secret of translating his personal popularity into fundamental legislative power or administrative power."

Kennedy's Oval Office tapes are the sound track for the heroic, carefully orchestrated visuals that flowed from his White House of a brilliant, funny, hard-working executive facing terrible crises with "grace under pressure," confidence, wisecracks, and existential cool. The problem is, as Hugh Sidey wrote in 1983, "He was the greatest actor of our time, dimming those mere celluloid performers like Ronald Reagan." It is impossible to tell if Kennedy would have lived on to be the potential Superman lionized by his faithful acolytes, or simply a "voguing" president, striking handsome poses in Italian-cut suits and a Palm Beach tan, but unable to master civil rights and Vietnam and the Cold War equipped only with an arsenal of romantic rhetoric and pragmatic caution. One wonders if Kennedy could have tackled the blossoming crises of the 1960s any better than his successors.

Whatever the judgments of historians and pundits, JFK towers above his competition with one crucial audience: the American people. He had the highest average Gallup approval ratings while in office of any president: his 70 percent beat his closest competitor, Eisenhower, by five points. In 1996, after thirty-three years of posthumous criticism, revisionism, sex and Mafia scandals, Kennedy won again, this time in a *New York Times*/CBS poll that asked which president Americans would pick to run the country today. Kennedy's winning 28 percent was more than double the number two choice (Ronald Reagan at 13 percent), and he buried FDR, Truman, and Lincoln, who shared a three-way tie at 8 percent.

Then, and now, Americans may look at Kennedy and see not only a leader and an image of themselves and their country as they might be, but a man who, with all his contradictions and weaknesses, was an intelligent, curious, rational executive in control of his ego and emotions. They may also see a chief executive who inspired hope in people the world over and who, when the door was closed, they could trust to make the right call.

When Secret Service agent Robert Bouck heard the news of Kennedy's murder shortly after 1:00 P.M. on November 22, 1963, he immediately went to the West Wing and began dismantling Kennedy's recording system. "I considered this a confidential thing between myself and the president and I had no idea of what the new president would think about a recording operation," explained Bouck. Working through the afternoon, he disconnected and pulled out the reel-to-reel recorders, removed the wires, and disconnected the microphones.

By the time the president's body returned to Washington that night, almost all traces of his taping system had vanished.

CHAPTER 5

Lyndon B. Johnson
The Controlling Executive

"I'm going to run over you."

LYNDON JOHNSON TO
SENATOR RICHARD RUSSELL ON CIVIL RIGHTS,
THE OVAL OFFICE, DECEMBER 1963

THE OVAL OFFICE
DECEMBER 20, 1963, 6:00 P.M.

Lyndon Johnson was breathing heavily into the phone, in deep, guttural snorts, the sounds a furious bull makes when circling a doomed matador.

On the other end of the line, bracing for Johnson's attack, was Democratic House Speaker John McCormack, who was trying to explain to Johnson why Congress wouldn't approve the foreign aid money he wanted, but was instead cutting funds by over 25 percent versus what it gave President Kennedy a year before.

A nearby Dictaphone patched into the president's Oval Office phone line was recording the conversation, part of a secret recording network Johnson began installing on his first day as president.

Johnson had been president for less than a month, but the recorder was capturing him assert his authority with unrestrained force. In his memoirs, Johnson recalled, "I knew I must break the legislative deadlock which had delayed most of President Kennedy's programs on Capitol Hill. Congressional foot-dragging and refusal to enact vitally needed legislation were developing into a national crisis. In all these areas time was the enemy. During my first thirty days in office I believe I averaged no more than four or five hours sleep a night."

Johnson started in on the congressman. "I don't believe that you can turn over to Mr. Kennedy $3.9 billion to run your foreign policy last year and turn me over $3 billion this year," he bellowed into the phone.

McCormack protested, "I'm just reporting to you what the situation is! I pleaded for $3.1 billion!" The Republican leader blocking the funds, Otto Passman, happened to walk into the room at this point, and LBJ blamed Passman for breaking an agreement with him. McCormack whispered to Johnson, "He just came in—you wanna talk to him?"

"Hell, no!" Johnson barked, loud enough for the whole room at the other end of the line to hear. "You know how I feel, I don't have any confidence in the man! I just don't trust him on anything. Far as I'm concerned, all my bets are off with him. I just think you oughta tell him that I think that they're endangering the future of their country, that everybody in the Joint Chiefs of Staff think that, the secretary of state thinks that and that's the only thing I know that's true!"

Sensing the coming onslaught, McCormack groaned, "Oh, God."

LBJ blasted away, now in full throttle: "I can't accept it any more than you could accept leaving the church and goin' out and becomin' an infidel! I just can't accept this because my country's at stake. And I'm not going to sign up with Passman, and I'm not going to sit idly by and let him wreck my country. And that's what he's doing! I think it's detestably wrong. I think it's shamefully wrong. I know foreign aid's unpopular. But I didn't want to go to the Pacific in '41, after Pearl Harbor. But I did. And I didn't want to let those Japs shoot at me with a Zero. But I did." Out of helplessness, McCormack then handed the phone to Democratic House Whip Carl Albert. Johnson greeted him with switchblade directness: "This is detestable. It's terrible. You're ruining the country." Albert pleaded, "What are you gonna do?"

Johnson's answer, delivered in the rich inflection of his native Texas hill country, came close to summarizing the executive style that helped him transfigure the nation by hammering through revolutionary civil rights legislation, and nearly tear it apart by pushing it into the abyss of Vietnam.

"We got an expression down in my country," Johnson said. "Fight him. Fight him till he's shitty as a bear!"

In this and in many legislative battles to come, Johnson's controlling style was victorious: he browbeat his men into extracting a written pledge from Passman to approve an extra $300 million in supplemental foreign aid.

"His executive style was just being in control," recalled his press secretary, George Christian. "He was his own press secretary. He was his own domestic affairs assistant. He was his own national security assistant. He was his own speechwriter. He always wanted to feel like he was totally in control."

Dean Acheson called Johnson "a real centaur—part man, part horse's ass." He was King Lear, Dr. Jekyll, Mr. Hyde, Captain Ahab, Moses, and Grendel, all stuffed into a scratching, belching, blustering, six-foot, two-inch 220-plus-pound explosive package. Russell Baker called him "a character out of a Russian novel, one of those human complications that filled the imagination of Dostoyevsky, a storm of warring human instincts: sinner and saint, buffoon and statesman, cynic and sentimentalist, a man torn between hungers for immortality and self-destruction." Veteran Johnson aide Horace Busby noted, "If you did not know Johnson, you would think he was nuts."

West German Chancellor Ludwig Erhard was supposed to have said to LBJ: "I understand you were born in a log cabin," to which the president responded, "No, Mr. Chancellor, you have me confused with Abe Lincoln. I was born in a manger." In fact, he was born in a small house beside a clutch of sycamore trees on the banks of the Pedernales River in Texas, the son and grandson of Texas state legislators. In an editorial in his college newspaper he declared one of his life strategies: "Personality is power; the man with a striking personality can accomplish greater deeds in life than a man of equal abilities but less personality." In 1932 he went to Washington as a congressional secretary, and became a protégé of fellow Texan, Senator Sam Rayburn, who persuaded FDR to appoint Johnson to be director of the National Youth Administration for Texas. Johnson used the New Deal post to propel himself into the House of Representatives at the age of twenty-nine, and outside of seven months in the navy, the U.S. Congress was his home ever after. Elected Democratic floor leader of the Senate in 1953, LBJ was infamous for eighteen-hour days and for relentlessly driving his staff to exhaustion and well beyond.

The bullets that ended John Kennedy's life ushered in a turbulent new era in American history, as Lyndon Johnson struggled with a doomed military crusade in Indochina and a social revolution at home. The Age of Johnson symbolically began in the spring of 1964 when in a speech at Ann Arbor, Michigan, he announced his Utopian vision of a "Great Society" of universal abundance. That fall, he was elected in his own right with the largest popular vote cast to date, and by the next year he had personally forced an impossible array of civil rights and social legislation through Congress. But simultaneously he was stumbling into the worst military disaster in American history, and his final days in office would see the fabric of American society being torn apart by riots, assassinations, and despair.

In the Oval Office, LBJ was a volatile, bullying, and often effective executive who pulverized his staff with sixteen-hour workdays and showered them with alternating streams of praise and verbal abuse. Johnson's aides tapped an inexhaustible reservoir of adjectives to describe him. Press Secretary George E. Reedy: "He was a man of too many paradoxes. Almost everything you find out about him you can find out a directly contrary quality immediately, and your problem is always which quality was real and which was assumed." Reedy, who worked for Johnson for fifteen years, called him "an insufferable bastard, a bully and a sadist." Bill Moyers, Reedy's successor, recalled, "He was thirteen of the most interesting and difficult men I ever met—at times proud, sensitive, impulsive, flamboyant, sentimental, bold, magnanimous, and graceful . . . at times, temperamental, paranoid, ill of spirit, strangely and darkly uneasy with himself. He owned and operated a ferocious ego, and he had an animal sense of weakness in other men."

A Kennedy aide who stayed on to help the new president reported: "LBJ was an emasculator, an egocentric son of a bitch. He kept us on to cover his ass until the election. Kennedy people stayed loyal to the institution. I think he was a rat, pure and simple. There was a real screw loose there. Vindictive. Kooky. He enjoyed administering pain to people. He loved it." Domestic policy aide Joseph Califano called his boss "brave and brutal, compassionate and cruel, incredibly intelligent and infuriatingly insensitive, with a shrewd and uncanny instinct for the jugular of his allies and adversaries." Another staffer said, "He is the only man who has ever made me feel that, like my father, he might at any moment take off his belt and strap me."

As president, Lyndon Johnson used the telephone like an assault weapon, firing off bursts of 75 to 100 calls per day. He reached for the phone when he woke up and fondled it as he went to bed. One morning, at 1:00 A.M., Johnson called Congressman Wayne Hays and asked, "Wayne, did I wake you?" The legislator replied, "No, Mr. President, I was just lying here waiting for you to call." The only way Vice President Hubert Humphrey could resist Johnson's hypnotic verbal attacks was by not answering the phone. "I've had ten calls from the man today," Humphrey groaned. "He has a new idea every thirty minutes and he calls me about it. I can't do anything he wants done because I don't have any time to get going between calls." George Reedy remembered, "He could practically crawl through that wire. And the full treatment really was an incredible thing. . . . It was a combination of badgering, cajolery, an enormous amount of statistical data, scraps of paper that might not seem so very relevant. And he was a great debater. God, he could debate."

At the end of his first full day as president, Johnson ordered an overhaul of the White House phone system, saying it was too slow—it took him ten full minutes to get Secretary of State Rusk on the line. He installed direct lines to his chief aides from phones on the Oval Office desk and coffee table, and his bedroom. At one point Johnson's Oval Office desk phone had forty-two different buttons, each for a different regular target.

In the swimming pool at his Texas ranch Johnson sailed specially ground-ed floating phones in the water to be seized whenever the urge struck him. He had three phones in his limousine, and one observer claimed Johnson could talk on all three while holding a conference in the car and barking instructions to the driver. One eyewitness reported: "He didn't just *pick* up the telephone; he *grabbed* the telephone. Secretaries say that he just grabbed the phone away from them while they were talking, cut off their conversation and dialed his number. And they would just be in tears. I think it was the thing that almost did him in, trying to look at three television stations at once and trying to talk over two or three telephones at the same time." LBJ once called CBS News when Walter Cronkite was in the midst of delivering the evening news and demanded to speak to Cronkite and be put on the air. "I don't give a damn where he is," Johnson fumed, "put him on the phone!" Unable to reach aide Califano in the men's room, LBJ yelled at a secretary: "I told you to put a phone in that toilet. I want that phone installed this morning. Do you hear me?" Phones were installed throughout Johnson's White House: under dinner tables, coffee tables, end tables, in bathrooms, and on windowsills.

"Johnson was the first Information Age president," said his deputy press secretary Tom Johnson, who later became president of CNN. In fact, LBJ was a stepfather of the Internet: funding for its initial working prototype first appeared as a Defense Department line item in Johnson's 1969 budget, but it didn't mature for another twenty-five years. That didn't stop Johnson from obsessively surfing the TV networks and wire services—he installed a three-screen color TV console with remote control in the Oval Office, along with two wire service tickers. Johnson often watched all three evening network TV newscasts, firing away with his remote control clicker to regulate the vol-ume. He inhaled mountains of information, sometimes opening the front panel and climbing into the ticker machines to get closer to the news as it was typed. After expanding his Dictaphone network, Johnson further revamped the Oval Office to suit his executive demands, often relying on high-tech features. He wheeled in the big mahogany desk he used in Con-gress, made in the Senate workshop at the turn of the century, and built in a panel with separate buzzers to summon stewards, secretaries, and a constant stream of Fresca. A canned music system was wired into the West Wing, and it sometimes surrounded the Oval Office with soft tunes, offering a soothing counterpoint to volcanic eruptions from the president.

"He was not the most sophisticated man in the sense of personal habits," close aide Jack Valenti admitted. "I mean, he'd scratch his ass or pick his nose, or go to the bathroom, and while he was taking a leak he'd just never stop talking." Congressman Richard Bolling thought "he was damn crude—

always scratching his crotch and picking his nose in mixed company." "His lapses from civilized conduct were deliberate and usually intended to subordinate someone else to his will," recalled Reedy. "He did disgusting things because he realized that other people had to pretend that they did not mind." Johnson even used the presidential toilet as a conference room. During a discussion on United Nations affairs, said Arthur Goldschmidt, "I stood at the bathroom door while he took a crap, then shaved and showered all the while continuing his conversation as though what he was doing was the most normal thing in the world." Johnson told Doris Kearns Goodwin of "one of the delicate Kennedyites who came into the bathroom with me and then found it utterly impossible to look at me while I sat there on the toilet. You'd think he had never seen those parts of the body before."

"You went with him into the bathroom," explained George Christian. "You stood there. He was always talking, always giving you instructions on what to do. While he shaved he talked to you, while he brushed his teeth he talked to you, while he was stuffing the toothpaste in his mouth. When he went to the bathroom he'd still be talking, when he got in the shower he'd still be talking. You were with him. It didn't make any difference to him what he was doing. He was conducting business. He thought he'd be wasting time if he did it any other way. These are private moments for most people. Nothing was private to him." During one bathroom conference, LBJ was spraying his teeth with a Waterpik filled with pink mouthwash. Christian recalled: "He was talking up a blue streak while he was doing his mouth. He turned his head toward us and squirted me from head to toe with that mouthwash. The president never said a word. He just went right back to his business. I had to spend the rest of the day smelling like Lavoris."

After suffering a massive heart attack in 1955, Johnson's doctors demanded that he stay in bed until 10:00 A.M., but Johnson evaded the order by waking up as early as 6:00 A.M., watching all three morning news shows on three separate TV screens, then working from his bed and toilet until the appointed hour, interacting with senior staffers. Johnson's mixture of work and bodily functions reached its crescendo in a story that was told of a man walking into LBJ's bedroom and witnessing a startling tableau: LBJ in action conducting business while lying on his side in bed, flanked by a nurse, Mrs. Johnson, a secretary, Bill Moyers, and others. While three TV sets blared at full blast, Johnson spasmodically manhandled the remote control clicker, yelled at Bill Moyers, and barked dictation at the secretary. Then the witness gradually realized why the nurse was there: in the midst of the chaos, she was administering an enema.

Although Johnson was usually on guard during his phone recordings (he initiated most of the 9,000-plus recordings one at a time by signaling to his secretary), Johnson's crudities sometimes shine through, and his rough, raw tone can be jarring for newer generations weaned on smooth, blow-dried politicians. He sometimes sounds like a cross between Foghorn Leghorn and John Wayne, an impossibly exaggerated caricature of himself. On a December 23, 1963, call to assistant for congressional affairs Larry O'Brien, Johnson, preparing for a White House Christmas party for congressmen who won't do what they're told, says: "Let's be over there and smile and shake hands and thank everybody and then just cut their dicks off and put it in your pocket when they do us this way." On February 9, 1964, he spoke to Jack Valenti about Texas votes: "I think I can take every Mexican in the state and every nigger in the state." On August 9, 1964, Johnson called clothing company president Joseph Haggar to shake him down for six pairs of pants: "If you don't want me running around the White House naked, you better get me some clothes. . . . Now, another thing, the crotch, down where your nuts hang, it's always a little too tight," LBJ instructed. "So when you make them up, give me an inch where I can let it out there, because they cut me. They're just like riding a wire fence." Among the host of other pungent quotes attributed to Johnson was one referring to a then-congressman and future president (this remark was untaped): "Ford's economics is the worst thing that's happened to this country since pantyhose ruined finger-fucking."

On November 22 and 23, 1963, Johnson began his recordings on an IBM office dictation magnetic belt, but the recordings were of poor quality and he switched to a Dictaphone on November 23. Johnson continued to use the Executive Office Building (EOB) office through November 25. When he moved into the Oval Office on November 26, he began using Kennedy's Dictaphone system, and gradually expanded it to cover two more secretaries' desks near the Oval Office, plus phones in the White House master bedroom, his office and bedroom at the LBJ Ranch in Stonewall Texas, and Camp David. In 1965, Johnson began recordings in the Situation Room, apparently in connection with a crisis in the Dominican Republic. He also sometimes used a portable system while traveling, including in the presidential helicopter. Late in his presidency, Johnson connected other recording devices to the Cabinet Room and the Little Study adjoining the Oval Office.

Johnson's Dictaphones were manually operated: "He buzzed us and we opened the door and he'd dangle his finger and move it around and around, and that would mean we should record the conversation," recalled Mrs. Juanita Roberts, one of Johnson's secretaries. "It was no great secret. It wasn't used to catch people. We didn't think we were doing something sinister. It was a working tool, a piece of equipment." Johnson was never quoted as to why he authorized recordings to be made, but transcripts of his conversations were used in regular White House operations. Jack A. Albright, chief of the White House communications office from 1965 to 1969, said the recordings were transcribed "on a daily basis," and the transcripts were circulated to Johnson's chief lieutenants.

Johnson also continued Kennedy's practice of wiretapping and secret taping for political purposes. Through the FBI, Johnson bugged opponents at the 1964 Democratic convention, and he approved the bureau's campaign of electronic surveillance against the Rev. Martin Luther King, Jr., and other civil rights activists. During the 1968 presidential campaign, Johnson authorized bugs against both candidates, Republican nominee Richard Nixon and Johnson's own vice president, Hubert Humphrey. FBI chief J. Edgar Hoover regularly spoon-fed juicy transcripts of King and others to the president, who despite sporadic pangs of conscience over such flagrant civil-liberties violations, devoured them.

Johnson recorded at least 700 hours of White House meetings and phone calls from November 1963 to late 1968, including approximately 9,420 phone calls totaling over 643 hours, most recorded on Dictaphones, and reel-to-reel recordings of meetings held in the Cabinet Room from late November 1967 through 1968. Johnson's tapes are a rich source of insight into his presidency, since Johnson's paper trail was surprisingly thin. "LBJ did not like to commit himself to writing," Robert A. Divine noted in a 1985 article on the LBJ Library. "Johnson preferred to deal with issues orally, face-to-face discussion or by telephone." When patched together, the LBJ recordings provide a remarkable, raw account of a presidency in action.

THE OVAL OFFICE
NOVEMBER 29, 1963, 8:55 P.M.

President Johnson and Senator Richard Russell
RE: *Formation of the Warren Commission*
audio recording of telephone conversation on Dictaphone machine

Johnson's controlling executive style was on symphonic display during this epic call to persuade a deeply reluctant Senator Russell to serve on the Warren Commission. Russell had been LBJ's boss, mentor, and father figure for years, but now LBJ barraged him with flattery, patriotism, kidding, and most of all, intimidation, to bend him to his will, illustrating his maxim that politics is "the art of making the impossible seem possible." To close the deal, Johnson invoked the specter of a nuclear holocaust.

The call showcases the mythic "Johnson Treatment." A victim recalled, "Lyndon got me by the lapels and put his face on top of mine and he talked and talked and talked. I figured I was either getting drowned or joining." Senator Barry Goldwater described the "half Johnson" as when he grabbed you by the arm, and the "full Johnson" as when he "hugged you by the waist and breathed into your mouth." "Telling Lyndon Johnson no," aide Bill Moyers said, "is like standing at the water's edge and shouting at the tide to go back." Senator Russell once commented: "That man will twist your arm off at the shoulder and beat your head in with it."

LBJ: Dick?

RUSSELL: Yes.

LBJ: I hate to bother you again but I wanted you to know that I made an announcement.

RUSSELL: Announcement of what?

LBJ: Of this special commission.

RUSSELL: Oh, you have already?

LBJ: Yes. May I read it to you . . . . (*reads statement*)

RUSSELL: Well, now Mr. President, I know I don't have to tell you of my devotion to you, but I just can't serve on that commission. I'm highly honored you'd think about me in connection with it, but I couldn't serve there with Chief Justice Warren. I don't like that man. I don't have any confidence in him at all. I realize he is a much greater man in the United States than anyone, and so you get John Stennis.*

LBJ: Dick, it's already been announced and you can serve with anybody for the good of America.

This is a question that has a good many more ramifications than on the surface, and we've got to take this out of the arena where they're testifying that Khrushchev and Castro did this and did that and kickin' us into a war that can kill 40 million Americans in an hour.

You would put on your uniform in a minute and the reason I've asked Warren is because he is the chief justice of this country and we've got to have the highest judicial people we can have.

The reason I ask you is because you have that same kind of temperament and you can do anything for your country and don't go giv-

---

*Senator John Stennis (D-MS).

ing me that kind of stuff about you can't serve with anybody. You can do anything!

RUSSELL: It is not only that. I just don't think the chief justice should have served on it.

LBJ: Well, the chief justice ought to do anything he can to save America and right now we've got a very touchy thing and wait until you look at this evidence. You wait until you look at this report. Now, I'm not going to lead you wrong and you're not going to be an Old Dog Tray*—

RUSSELL: I know that, but I have never—

LBJ: You've never turned your country down. This is not me. This is your country and the members of the special commission are the Chief Justice Warren, Senator Richard Russell, and I go right down the list now. I've got Allen Dulles, John McCloy, but you're my man on that commission and you're going to do it!

And don't tell me what you can do and what you cain't! Because I can't arrest you and I'm not going to put the FBI on you but you're god-damned going to serve, I'll tell you that! And A. W. Moursund† is here and he wants to tell you how much all of us love you. Wait a minute.

RUSSELL: Well, Mr. President, you ought to have told me you were going to name me.

LBJ: I told you. I told you the other day I was going to name the chief justice. I called you.

RUSSELL: You did not. You talked about getting somebody from Supreme Court. You didn't tell me you were going to name him . . . . Mr. President, please now.

LBJ: No. It is already done. It has been announced.

RUSSELL: You mean you've given that—

LBJ: Yes sir. I gave the announcement. It is already in the papers and you're on it and you're going to be my man on it and you forget that . . . .

I know you're going to have your reservations and your modesty, but now your president's asking you to do these things and there are some things I want you in besides civil rights and by God you're going to be in them because I can't run this country by myself.

RUSSELL: You know damned well my future is behind me and that is not entering into it at all.

---

* From 19th century composer Stephen Foster's song "Old Dog Tray," about a faithful canine.
† A. W. Moursund, Texas judge and friend of LBJ's, also in the Oval Office during this call.

LBJ: Well, your future is your country and you're going to do everything you can to serve America.

RUSSELL: I can't do it. I haven't got the time!

LBJ: All right, we'll just make the time.

RUSSELL: With all my Georgia items in there—

LBJ: Well, we're just going to make the time. There's not going to be any time to begin with. All you'll do is evaluate the Hoover report he's already made . . . .

RUSSELL: You're taking advantage of me but of course—

LBJ: No, no, no. I'm not taking advantage of you. I'm going to take a hell of a lot of advantage of you my friend, 'cause you made me and I know it and I don't ever forget. And I'm going to be taking advantage of you a good deal, but you're going to serve your country and do what's right . . . .

Why do you think I've done wrong now by appointing you on a commission?

RUSSELL: Well, I just don't like Warren.

LBJ: Well, of course you don't like Warren, but you'll like him before it is over with.

RUSSELL: I haven't got any confidence in him.

LBJ: Well, you can give him some confidence. God damn it, associate with him. Now you're not, you've got nothing to, I'm not afraid to put your intelligence against Warren's. Now, by God, I want a man on that commission and I've got one!

RUSSELL: I don't know about the intelligence, of course, and I feel like I'm being kidded, but if you think—

LBJ: Well, if you think, now Dick, do you think I'd kid you?

RUSSELL: If it is for the good of the country, you know damned well I'll do it. And I'll do it for you, for that matter. I still feel like it's sort of getting wrapped up—

LBJ: Dick, do you remember when you met me at the Carlton Hotel in 1952? When we had breakfast there one morning?

RUSSELL: Yes, I think I do.

LBJ: All right. Do you think I'm kidding you?

RUSSELL: No, I don't think you're kidding me, but I think, well, I'm not going to say anything more, Mr. President. I'm at your command.

LBJ: You damned sure going to be at my command. You're going to be at my command as long as I'm here.

RUSSELL: I do wish you'd be a little more deliberate and considerate next time about it, but this time, of course, if you've done this, I'm going to do it and go through with it and say I think it's a wonderful idea.

LBJ: Well, I'm not going to be any more deliberate than I've been about this 'cause I've been pretty deliberate but I'm going to have you on a good God damned many things that I have to decide and you're going to be America's representative and I don't want any special obligation. I just know you're going to call them as you see them and I've served under you and I don't give a damn if you have to serve with a Republican, if you have to serve with a communist, if you have to serve with a Negro, or if you have to serve with a thug, or if you have to serve with A. W. Moursund.

RUSSELL: I can serve with a communist, and I can serve with a Negro, I can serve with a Chinaman.

LBJ: Well you may have to serve with A.W. Moursund here.

RUSSELL: And if I can serve with A. W. Moursund, I would say, Mr. Chairman, I'm pleased to serve with you, Judge Moursund. But, well, we won't discuss it any further, Mr. President, I'll serve . . . .

LBJ: I just want to counsel with you and I just want your judgment and your wisdom, cause I haven't got any Daddy and you're going to be it. And you just forget it . . . .

RUSSELL: Well, you ought not to be so persuasive.

LBJ: Well, I think I ought to.

RUSSELL: I think you did wrong in getting Warren and I know damned well you did wrong in getting me, but I hope to do the best I can.

LBJ: I think that's what you'll do. That's the kind of Americans both of you are. Good night.

RUSSELL: Good night.

In person or on the phone, the Johnson Treatment was an overwhelming experience for its targets. One observer described it as "a boxer's bolo punch that comes from over his head." Hubert Humphrey described a meeting with Johnson as "an almost hypnotic experience. I came out of that session covered with blood, sweat, tears, spit—and sperm." Veteran LBJ aide Harry McPherson declared, "He has fifty reasons why he wants you to do something and you may have two reasons why you don't, and maybe you knock off ten of his fifty with your two, but he has still got forty left."

Johnson often used a gentler version of the Treatment on congressmen, and Johnson periodically offered his "love" to other men during phone conversations, sometimes signing off with "I love you." During a January 9, 1964, call to a flu-stricken Congressman Carl Albert, LBJ offered solicitously: "I just wanted to tell you that I loved you, and I hoped you were feeling good, and I missed you, and I missed you at the breakfast, and missed seeing you there yesterday. And I just want you to take care of yourself, and let me know anything in the world I can do." On an April 7, 1964, Dictabelt recording, he called Congressman Paul Rogers and begged sweetly for his support on a piece of legislation: "I just got to have your help on this farm bill, just got to, pardner . . . I just sure have got to have your help." Rogers, weakening steadily under Johnson's spell, asked, "Mr. President, may I do this? May I make a couple of calls and see what they think?" Like a determined, swooning suitor, Johnson offered soothingly: "Yes sir, yes sir, yes sir—Please stay with me—please stay with me."

LBJ's White House was a human meat grinder. Joseph Califano declared: "Johnson was a man-eater. He worked his staff incredibly hard." Johnson himself was "an incredibly hard worker," said Tom Johnson, a young White House press aide, "he worked two full days in one." Johnson split his marathon workday into two shifts: 7:00 A.M. to 2:00 P.M., then 4:00 P.M. to 9:00 P.M. In between, he napped in his pajamas in the Little Study next to the Oval Office, woke up, showered, and climbed into fresh clothes. "It's like starting a new day," he said. He expected senior aides to work straight through both shifts and into Saturdays, and rotated in teams of secretaries to handle the overload. "An eight-hour man ain't worth a damn to me," he said. According to Valenti, "His greatest strength was tenacity. When he was pursuing some cause or some issue, he never slept, he never let anybody else sleep." Around 11:00 or 11:30 P.M., he would get a rubdown from a naval aide and start plowing through a pile of 100-plus memos. He demanded a fresh stack of paperwork every night and every morning, a routine that sometimes triggered frantic searches by staff for material.

"Lyndon has a clock inside him with an alarm that tells him at least once an hour to chew somebody out," said a Johnson associate. A disgusted Bobby Kennedy, who served briefly as Johnson's first attorney general said, "He yells at his staff. He treats them just terribly. Very mean. He's a very mean, mean figure." Johnson played oppressive mind games with his staff. According to his in-house White House historian, Eric F. Goldman: "He would heap praise on a particular aide for a period, much to the discomfort of others, then, suddenly shift his attitude, giving the man no assignments, rejecting his suggestions in toto, scarcely speaking to him. Just as suddenly, the assistant would be lifted from hell and transformed into an angel again." "He was probably on the edge of paranoia," said David Bell, head of the Agency for International Development under Johnson. "He was almost over the edge a lot of the time. I always credited Mrs. Johnson enormously for keeping him within the bounds of reason and reality."

"I want loyalty," LBJ said of his staff. Of a man about to join his staff, he said, "I want him to kiss my ass in Macy's window at high noon and tell me it smells like roses. I want his pecker in my pocket." George Reedy compared Johnson's generally miserable office atmosphere to Kennedy's: "I attribute this to a hangover from the Irish clan system. You know, the Irish have this very strong in-group feeling. . . . And the Kennedy staff was a staff that always felt a certain degree of security. They might not be in favor with Jack Kennedy at any given moment or with the powers around Kennedy, but they knew that they would be taken care of one way or the other. This was one feeling that Johnson never gave to his staff people. They never had the inner feeling of security." There also, according to longtime LBJ aide Harry McPherson at the time, was "no sense of fun, no élan."

Johnson's lust for control sometimes led him into a quicksand of obsessive micromanagement. He reviewed equipment for the White House motor pool. He inspected staffers desks late at night. He tinkered with room thermometers and White House party invitation lists. He interrogated budget officials about crotch sizes in air force uniform trousers. "He had a tendency to get involved in almost everything," said Press Secretary George Christian. "He knew more about government than just about anybody around. He knew intricate details of the budget that presidents usually don't fool with." Eric Goldman reported that he devoted attention to "everything in the White House, minuscule as well as monumental in significance." Reedy contended that "it wasn't that he was overly concerned with details, it was just that when his mind focused on something, it focused in so thoroughly and completely that he would exhaust every branch of it. He ran everything into the ground."

Johnson had no chief of staff, preferring to interact directly with a top tier of some ten special assistants, relying often on high-energy young men like Joseph Califano, whom he installed as domestic policy czar to bypass old-line government institutions. David Bell, who worked for Truman, Kennedy, and Johnson, thought Truman's and Kennedy's executive styles were rooted in their experience as junior military officers, when they learned to delegate clearly and forge easy, trusting relationships with their men. In contrast, Bell observed, Johnson's formative experience in Congress created a style that "was a smothering, all-encompassing process of negotiation toward an effective solution conceived in legislative terms. Johnson would give you an instruction, and you'd go away to follow it up, and half an hour later he would be on the phone not just wanting to know how you were getting on, but with several additional ideas about how you ought to do it. He was constantly on your back. Dealing with him was a continuous floating crap game, a swirling process. It wasn't a sign of mistrust or doubt, it simply was his executive style. In many circumstances, the Johnson executive style was better calculated to get results—with Congress for example, he was a master." George Christian agreed: "His executive style was aimed at congressional programs. He was first and foremost a legislator."

Four months into Johnson's administration, the *New York Times*'s James Reston highlighted the difference between LBJ's and his predecessor's approach to Congress: "Kennedy was a back-row man in the Senate. He was never a leader there or in the House and even when he was president, he retained an inordinate respect for the committee chairmen and other elders of the Congress. When they growled, he paused and often retreated. President Johnson was not a back-row man in the Senate. He ran the place. . . . He is not so inclined to retreat. Kennedy put his arguments clearly and forcibly to the congressional leaders, but there was usually something detached and even donnish about his willingness to grant the merit in the other fellow's argument. President Johnson grants nothing in an argument, not even equal time." Veteran Washington hand and FDR aide James Rowe said, "If a senator didn't want to do something, saying, 'I'd love to, but it would just murder me in my state. I just can't do it,' Kennedy would say, 'Well, OK.' Now Lyndon Johnson would call that same fellow up and he knew what he was going to say. But before he could get his mouth open Johnson had him by the lapels, waving the American flag and saying, 'You've got to be a patriot,' and shove him out the door with a commitment."

A few weeks into his presidency, in a scene reported by Jack Valenti, LBJ called Senator Richard Russell into the Oval Office to demand his support for strong civil rights legislation in 1964. He positioned Russell on a small couch, towered over him, looked him in the eye, and announced: "Dick, you've got to get out of my way. I'm going to run over you. I don't intend to cavil or compromise. I don't want to hurt you. But don't stand in my way." Russell responded, "You may do that, but by God, it's going to cost you the South and cost you the election." "If that's the price I've got to pay," said Johnson, "I'll pay it gladly." Johnson pushed the 1964 Civil Rights Act through Congress, then ordered his men "to write me the goddamnest, toughest voting rights act that you can devise." When blacks everywhere got the right to vote, LBJ declared, "They'll have every politician, north and south, east and west, kissing their ass, begging for their support." An outmaneuvered Senator

Russell noted: "You know, we could have beaten John Kennedy on civil rights, but not Lyndon Johnson."

By 1965, LBJ was a Colossus climbing fast toward the summit of presidential greatness. In the November 1964 election he received the largest popular majority in history. Most of his Great Society programs were rammed through Congress in a nine-month burst of energy that Johnson boasted was "the greatest outpouring of creative legislation in the history of the nation," including landmarks like Voting Rights, Medicare, and Medicaid. "I think Johnson was a superb executive," argued Joseph Califano. "He wanted to know all aspects of a decision, all the possible implications, and he knew exactly how to marshal his forces to achieve his objective." LBJ's 93 percent success rate with Congress in 1965 was the highest ever measured for any president. In July 1965, he scored a commanding 70 percent approval rating from the American people.

Yet at the same moment, Johnson was stumbling through a series of decisions that triggered the biggest military and management debacle in American history. As he prowled the Rose Garden walking a pack of dogs in the summer of 1965, he abruptly blurted out, "I don't know what the fuck to do about Vietnam. I wish someone would tell me what to do."

Johnson inherited the Vietnam commitment from JFK in its late infancy—at the time of Kennedy's death, fewer than 100 of over 16,000 American advisers had been killed in combat. Determined to honor Kennedy's goals and stop communist expansion in Asia, LBJ slowly began to widen U.S. involvement in the war, but from the very beginning he had grave doubts about the adventure. Two days after Dallas, he told an aide, "It's going to be hell in a hand basket out there." He gazed at a corner of the ceiling and compared himself to a doomed catfish: "I feel like I just grabbed a big juicy worm with a right sharp hook in the middle of it."

THE OVAL OFFICE
MAY 27, 1964, 10:55 A.M.

President Johnson and Senator Richard Russell
RE: *The Vietnam War*
audio recording of telephone conversation on Dictaphone machine

Johnson called his old friend Senator Dick Russell to get his advice on the simmering Vietnam crisis, only to find that Russell was as lost as he was.

Russell: Pretty good. How are you, Mr. President?

LBJ: Oh, I'm, got lots of troubles.

Russell: Well, we all have those.

LBJ: I want you, I want to see what you, what do you think of this Vietnam thing? I'd like to hear you talk a little bit.

Russell: Well, frankly, Mr. President, if you were to tell me that I was off to settle it as I saw fit, I would respectfully decline and run on another ticket.

LBJ: (*chuckle*)

Russell: It's a damn worse mess that I ever saw. And I don't like to brag and I never have been right many times in my life, but I knew that we were to get into this sort of mess when we went in there. And I don't see how we're ever going to get out of it, without getting in a major war with the Chinese and all of them down there in those rice paddies and jungles. I just don't see it. It's—I—I—just don't know what to do.

LBJ: Well, that's the way I've been feeling for six months.

Russell: It appears that our situation is deteriorating and it looks like the more that we try to do for them the less that they want to do for themselves. It's just a sad situation. There's no sense of responsibility there on the part of the leaders that are bearing it . . . It's a helluva situation. It's a mess. And it's going to get worse, and I don't know how, what to do . . . .

LBJ: Well, I spend all my days with Rusk and McNamara and Bundy and Harriman and Vance and all those folks that are dealing with it and I would say that it pretty well adds up to them now that we've got to show some power and force, and that they do not believe—they're kind of like MacArthur in Korea; they do not believe that the Chinese Communists will come into this thing. And they don't know, and nobody can really be sure, but they, their feeling is that they won't, and in any event, that we haven't got much choice. That we are treaty bound, that we are there, that this will be a domino that will kick off a whole list of others, that we've just got to prepare for the worst. I don't think that the American people are for it . . . .

Russell: I just don't know. It's a tragic situation. It's just one of those places that you just can't win. Anything that you do is wrong . . . .

LBJ: You don't have any doubt that if we go in there, and get them up against a wall, the Chinese Communists are going to come in?

Russell: No doubt at all.

LBJ: That's my judgment, and my people don't think so . . . .

RUSSELL: I guess going in there with all the troops, I tell you it'll be the most expensive adventure that this country ever went into . . . .

LBJ: I just haven't got the nerve to do it. But I don't see any other way out of it.

RUSSELL: It's one of those things; heads I win, tails you lose.

LBJ: Well, think about it, and I'll call you again. I hate to bother you.

RUSSELL: It's a terrific quandary that we're in over there. We're in quicksand up to our neck, and I just don't know what the hell to do about it.

LBJ: I love you, and I'll be calling you.

RUSSELL: I'll see you, sir.

On a call to national security assistant McGeorge Bundy a half hour later, Johnson moaned, "This is a terrible thing that we're getting ready to do . . . . it's damn easy to get into a war, but it's going to be harder to ever extricate yourself if you get in."

THE OVAL OFFICE
JUNE 21, 1965

President Johnson and Defense Secretary Robert McNamara
RE: *Decision to Escalate U.S. Military Involvement in Vietnam*
audio recording of telephone conversation on Dictaphone machine

The August 1964 Gulf of Tonkin incident enabled Johnson to obtain a congressional "blank check" resolution authorizing increases in aid and manpower to Vietnam. In early 1965, he authorized a massive bombing campaign, Operation Rolling Thunder, to help the shaky South Vietnamese government defend against continuing Communist attacks. As soon as the bombing began, LBJ complained to the army chief of staff: "Bomb, bomb, bomb. That's all you know . . . you're not giving me any ideas and any solutions for this damn little pissant country." One day he groaned: "Vietnam is like being in a plane without a parachute, when all the engines go out. If you jump, you'll probably be killed, and if you stay in, you'll crash and probably burn."

In June 1965, as the bombing failed, LBJ reached a crossroads in history: whether or not to commit large numbers of U.S. combat troops to the war in Vietnam, as many of his advisers recommended.

On the eve of his decision, Johnson recorded a phone conversation with Defense Secretary Robert McNamara in which he clearly saw the tragedy to come. LBJ admitted that he was going into the Vietnam escalation with little hope of winning.

LBJ: It's gonna be difficult for us to very long prosecute effectively a war that far away from home, with the divisions that we have here, and particularly the potential divisions.

It's really had me concerned for a month, and I'm very depressed about it, 'cause I see no program from either Defense or State that gives me much hope of doing anything except just praying and gasping to hold on during monsoon and hope they'll quit, and I don't believe they're ever gonna quit, and I don't see how we have any way of either a plan for victory militarily or diplomatically.

And I think that's something you and Dean [Rusk] got to sit down and try to see if there's any people that we have in those departments that could give us any program or plan or hope. If not, we got to see if we, have you go out there or have somebody else go out there and take one good look at it and say to these here people, "Now you've changed your government about the last time. And this is it." Call the Buddhists and the Catholics and the generals and everybody together and say, "We're going to do our best," and be sure they're willing to let new troops come in and be sure they're not going to resent 'em. If not, why y'all can run over us and have a government of your own choosing. But we just can't take these changes all the time.

That's the Russell plan. Russell thinks we ought to take one of these changes to get outta there.

I don't think we can get out of there, with our treaty like it is and with all we've said, I think it would just lose us face in the world and I shudder to think of what all of them would say . . .

Just weeks after this call, Johnson approved the military's requests for a total of over 170,000 American troops to be deployed in Vietnam by the end of 1965. The notes of fateful group meetings in the Cabinet Room on July 21, 1965, that included almost the entire top civilian and military leadership of the U.S. government reveal Johnson asking all the right questions before deciding to escalate, constantly searching, as he did on many of his 1964 recordings, for advice and opinion.

"What has happened in the recent past that requires this decision on my part?" asked Johnson. "What are the alternatives? Also, I want more discussion on what we expect to flow from this decision. Discuss in detail. Have we wrung every soldier out of every country we can? Who else can help? Are we the sole defenders of freedom in the world? . . . What are the alternatives? We must make no snap judgments. We must consider carefully all our options." He asked the chairman of the Joint Chiefs of Staff: "What makes you think if we put in 100,000 men Ho Chi Minh won't put in another 100,000?" "This is important—can Westerners, in absence of intelligence, successfully fight Orientals in jungle rice paddies?" Johnson asked all the right questions, but his men had all the answers, or so they thought, intoxicated as they were by overconfidence and supreme ignorance of both the enemy and the magnitude of the coming slaughter.

During the meetings that day, Johnson repeatedly asked Under Secretary of State George Ball to make the case against escalation. But at this and many of the Vietnam meetings to come, doubts such as those expressed by Ball were torn to shreds by the arguments of Defense Secretary Robert McNamara and other war hawks. McNamara was the crown prince of the "best and brightest" advisers LBJ inherited from Kennedy, a supremely confident former president of Ford Motor Company, and Johnson was dazzled by him. George Reedy reported that for a time, Johnson "regarded Bob McNamara as the Messiah. He was holding conversations in which he was saying wistfully that he sure wished he could bring McNamara into the White House to run the country. McNamara . . . always had reams of figures at his fingertips and could rattle off statistics like a Hotchkiss machine gun." Of George Ball's role as a "designated dissenter," Reedy observed: "Strangely enough, an official devil's advocate is more likely to solidify the thinking of the president." Five minutes would be ritually reserved for Ball's criticism so the others could say "We heard both sides of the issue," but Reedy concluded, "They heard it with wax in their ears."

Despite a year of massive U.S. bombing and the insertion of more than 200,000 U.S. combat troops to the area, the Vietnam War ground into 1966 with no end in sight, and the divisions foreseen by LBJ on his June 21, 1965, recording opened up across the country. While the left wing called for a withdrawal, Republicans demanded even stronger military action. "If only I could get Ho in a room with me, I'm sure we could work things out," Johnson lamented, but Ho Chi Minh and his armies became the one thing Johnson could never control.

As the war ground on, Vietnam decisions were increasingly made not at the sprawling Cabinet and National Security Council meetings, but at a weekly lunch meeting between Johnson and a small group of his senior advisers known as the Tuesday Lunch Group, which met around Chippendale furniture in the quiet seclusion of the president's dining room on the second floor of the White House mansion. "That group never leaked a single note," Johnson boasted. "Those men were loyal to me. I could control them, but in those larger meetings, why, every Defense Department official and his brother would be leakers at one time or another." The few men who might express reservations on Vietnam gradually drifted away, and national security assistant Walt Rostow later realized, "The only men present were those whose advice the president wanted most to hear." The rarefied intimacy of the atmosphere may have excluded any free-wheeling strategic or policy debate on Vietnam, which the situation desperately needed.

"He was impatient about the inability or the unwillingness of senior advisers to agree among themselves," reported Secretary of State Dean Rusk. "He disliked the role of refereeing among senior colleagues." LBJ assistant Doris Kearns Goodwin wrote: "A typical discussion of the Tuesday lunch would begin with the alternative targets for bombing, continue with the increased lift capacity of the newest helicopters, move on to the quality of meat in the mess hall, and conclude with the production figures for waterproof boats, never once calling into serious question the shared assumptions about the nature of the war or its central importance to national security." "With but rare exceptions we always seemed to be calculating the short-term consequences of each alternative at every step of the process, but not the long-term consequences," recalled participant Bill Moyers. Johnson thought he created an atmosphere where dissent and conflicting opinions could flourish, but his personality seemed to smother chances of any real debate in meetings that were engineered instead to enforce consensus.

As the war ground on, Johnson searched in vain for military and diplomatic solutions. "I can't trust anybody," he lamented to an aide. "Everybody is trying to cut me down, destroy me." Vietnam soon drained effort and money from Johnson's cherished domestic programs. "He wanted to get out of Vietnam in the worst way," said Jack Valenti. "He wanted to spend the money to build the Great Society. Not to send supplies to some place 12,000 miles away, for God's sakes. He just couldn't disengage. Didn't know how to disengage without having the right wing of the Republicans saying, 'You cut and run, you coward, you're the first American president to lose a war.'" Tom Johnson, who attended many of the Vietnam meetings as LBJ's note-taker, recalled, "I never saw a leader who wanted to find a resolution to a problem so badly, yet the answer eluded him at every turn. There simply was no solution, diplomatic or military. He could never get Ho to respond directly."

LBJ and his advisers performed a *danse macabre* of over-optimistic reports and bogus casualty figures. To minimize civilian casualties and avoid triggering Chinese or Soviet involvement, U.S. pilots were shackled to a vast array of bombing restrictions for targets often picked or authorized by LBJ, who boasted his pilots could "not bomb an outhouse" without presidential approval. On many nights Johnson would jump out of bed at 3:00 A.M., put on his robe and padded slippers, grab a flashlight, and march down to the Situation Room in the White House basement to personally supervise bombing missions occurring on the other side of the world.

The U.S. military became prisoners of Johnson's executive style, which was perfect for passing bills but absurdly ineffective on the battlefield. He tried to run the war the way he ran Congress—punish, reward, bargain. Johnson's strategy, to inflict just enough calibrated pressure to deny the Communists victory but avoid Chinese and Soviet intervention, was well-intentioned, but totally backfired. "We had stopped the bombing, not once or twice, but eight different times from 1965 to the beginning of 1968," Johnson recalled. "Five other times we had ruled out attacks on military targets in or around Hanoi and Haiphong for extended periods. The net result of all these bombing pauses was zero. Indeed, it was less than zero for us, because the enemy used every pause to strengthen its position, hastily pushing men and supplies and equipment down the roads of North Vietnam for massive infiltration into the South."

On January 30, 1968, the Communists launched the Tet Offensive, a wave of surprise attacks across South Vietnam, including strikes on thirty-six of forty-four provincial capitals. A force of 1,000 Communists seized Hué, the religious and cultural capital. In the Saigon area, 4,000 troops attacked targets including the American embassy, where nineteen Vietcong commandos blasted into the compound with automatic weapons blazing and fought for six hours until they were finally killed by U.S. paratroopers lowered onto the roof by helicopter. Fierce fighting continued in Saigon for the next three weeks. Militarily, the offensive was a stalemate, but American public support for Johnson, and the war, nose-dived, and the pillars of American thinking on Vietnam were kicked away. After taking over from a disintegrating Robert McNamara, Johnson's new secretary of defense, Clark Clifford, launched an extensive review of American war policy and quickly realized the war could not be won. "After Tet, I assure you, there was no suggestion that we could see any light at the end of the tunnel," said Clifford.

THE CABINET ROOM
MARCH 4, 1968 5:33 P.M.

President Johnson and Senior Civilian and Military Advisers
RE: *United States Military Disengagement from Vietnam*
"President's Eyes Only" meeting minutes

At this historic meeting, Defense Secretary Clark Clifford stunned LBJ by announcing that the Vietnam War was being lost; the president should reject the military's latest request for 205,000 men and take steps to disengage. Clifford, one of the most formidable lawyers in Washington, "was the only person who had grasped the fact and who had the skill and the position to do something about it," said LBJ aide George Reedy. Clifford gently but methodically made his case in crisp, lean prose: "He spoke in soothing tones that sent everyone into a half-doze where they absorbed his words on a virtually subliminal basis," Reedy reported. Eventually, noted Reedy, LBJ and his officials would "turn against the war—and think it was their own idea." (Emphasis is from original meeting minutes.)

LBJ: As I told you last week, I wanted you to return today with your recommendations in response to General Westmoreland's[*] request. Among the things I asked you to study were the following questions.

  1. What particular forces are you recommending that we dispatch immediately? How do we get these forces?

  2. How soon could we formulate what we want from the South Vietnamese?

  3. What difficulties do you foresee with your recommendations, both with the Congress and financially?

    As I understand it, Clark Clifford, Secretary Rusk, and Rostow[†] and others have been meeting on these questions in conjunction with the Joint Chiefs of Staff.

ROSTOW: That is correct.

CLIFFORD: Paul Nitze[‡] and I started to work on this Friday night. As you could understand, with the time pressure we placed upon ourselves

---

[*]*General William Westmoreland, commander of U.S. forces in Vietnam.*
[†]*Walter W. Rostow, national security assistant.*
[‡]*Paul Nitze, deputy secretary of defense.*

there still may need to be refinements and adjustments to the program I will discuss.

We have tried to make this document clear and understandable.

The subject is a very profound one, and I consider it advisable to outline the difficulty we face and the central problem which your advisers see you facing.

As you know, from time to time, the military leaders in the field ask for additional forces. We have, in the past, met these requests until we are now at the point where we have agreed to supply up to 525,000 men to General Westmoreland.

He now has asked for 205,000 additional troops. There are three questions:

1. Should the president send 205,000?
2. Should the president not send any more?
3. Should the president approve a figure somewhere in between and send an alternative number?

Your senior advisers have conferred on this matter at very great length. There is a deep-seated concern by your advisers. *There is a concern that if we say, yes, and step up with the addition of 205,000 more men that we might continue down the road as we have been without accomplishing our purpose—which is for a viable South Vietnam which can live in peace.*

We are not convinced that our present policy will bring us to that objective . . .

For a while, we thought and had the feeling that we understood the strength of the Viet Cong and the North Vietnamese. You will remember the rather optimistic reports of General Westmoreland and Ambassador Bunker* last year.

Frankly, it came as a shock that the Vietcong–North Vietnamese had the strength of force and skill to mount the Tet Offensive—as they did. They struck thirty-four cities, made strong inroads in Saigon and in Hué. There have been very definite effects felt in the countryside.

At this stage, it is clear that this new request by General Westmoreland brings the president to a clearly defined watershed:

1. Do you continue to go down that same road of "more troops, more guns, more planes, more ships"?

Ellsworth Bunker, U.S. ambassador to the Republic of Vietnam.

2. Do you go on killing more Viet Cong and more North Vietnamese?

There are grave doubts that we have made the type of progress we had hoped to have made by this time. As we build up our forces, they build up theirs. We continue to fight at a higher level of intensity.

Even were we to meet this full request of 205,000 men, and the pattern continues as it has, it is likely that by March he [General Westmoreland] may want another 200,000 to 300,000 men, with no end in sight.

The country we are trying to save is being subjected to enormous damage. Perhaps the country we are trying to save is relying on the United States too much. When we look ahead, we may find that we may actually be denegating [*sic*] their ability to take over their own country rather than contributing to their ability to do it.

We recommend in this paper that you meet the requirement for only those forces that may be needed to deal with any exigencies of the next 3–4 months. March-April-May could be an important period.

We recommend an immediate decision to deploy to Vietnam an estimated total of 22,000 additional personnel. We would agree to get them to General Westmoreland right away. It would be valuable for the general to know they are coming so he can make his plans accordingly.

This is as far as we are willing to go. We would go ahead, however, and call up a sufficient number of men. If later the president decides Westmoreland needs additional reinforcements, you will have men to meet that contingency.

An eyewitness said Clifford's arguments had a "profound effect on President Johnson. He was dismayed, anguished, and torn by what Clifford was saying, because he realized the time had come to take a very different course." Johnson's next question illustrated his shock:

LBJ: Westmoreland is asking for 200,000 men, and you are recommending 20,000 or so?

CLIFFORD: The strategic reserves in the United States are deeply depleted. They must be built up. Senator Russell has said this. We do not know what might happen anywhere around the world, but to face any emergency we will need to strengthen the reserve . . . .

We also feel strongly that there should be a comprehensive study of the strategic guidance to be given General Westmoreland in the future.

We are not sure the present strategy is the right strategy—that of being spread out all over the country with a seek and destroy policy.

We are not convinced that this is the right way, that it is the right long-term course to take. We are not sure under the circumstances which exist that a conventional military victory, as commonly defined, can be had.

After this study is made—if there is no clear resolution in the actions of the next 3–4 months except long drawn-out procedure—we may want to change the strategic guidance given Westmoreland. Perhaps we should not be trying to protect all of the countryside, and instead concentrate on the cities and important areas in the country.

There will be considerably higher casualties if we follow the Westmoreland plan. It just follows that if we increase our troop commitment by 200,000 men, there will be significantly higher casualties . . . .

If we continue with our present policy of adding more troops and increasing our commitment, this policy may lead us into Laos and Cambodia.

The reserve forces in North Vietnam are a cause for concern as well. They have a very substantial population from which to draw. They have no trouble whatever organizing, equipping, and training their forces.

We seem to have a sinkhole. We put in more—they match it. We put in more—they match it. The South Vietnamese are not doing all they should do . . . .

I see more and more fighting with more and more casualties on the U. S. side and no end in sight to the action . . . .

We should consider changing our concept from one of protecting real estate to protecting people. We need to see if these people are really going to take care of themselves eventually. I am not sure we can ever find our way out if we continue to shovel men into Vietnam . . . .

We say, for example, that this is not the time to negotiate.

We have spent the last three days trying to reach a consensus. As we sat together and cross-fertilized, we have reached a general consensus on this.

Of course, if we had to vote on sending the straight 200,000 men or no men, we would come out all over the lot. We would be split all over the place.

But we wonder if we are really making progress toward our goal under the plan we have been following.

This is the overall approach we would recommend . . . .

SECRETARY RUSK: Mr. President, without a doubt, this will be one of the most important decisions you will have made since becoming president. This has implications for all of our society . . . .

On the negotiation front, I wish we had a formula to bring about a peaceful settlement soon. We do not . . . .

At the end of the meeting, Johnson finally rejected the military's troop request, marking the beginning of U.S. disengagement from Vietnam, a tortured, bloody process that would not be completed until 1974.

JOHNSON: Have you told Westmoreland you would only send this number and we could give no more by June 1?

GENERAL WHEELER: No, I will tell him after this meeting.

JOHNSON: Tell him to forget the 100,000. Tell him 22,000 is all we can give at the moment . . .

Johnson was so shaken by the implications of this meeting that he refused to speak with Clifford for several days.

Since late 1967, Johnson had been soliciting the opinions of a group of Establishment foreign policy mandarins led by former Secretary of State Dean Acheson known as the "Wise Men." Following the Tet Offensive, and after sitting through a series of pessimistic briefings from officials flown in from Vietnam, the Wise Men's consensus disintegrated. In a March 26, 1968, group meeting with Johnson, McGeorge Bundy summarized their views: "We can no longer do the job we set out to do in the time we have left and we must begin to take steps to disengage." Days after the meeting, Johnson formally rejected the military's request for 205,000 more troops, instituted a partial bombing pause, and withdrew from the 1968 presidential race.

In domestic affairs, Johnson left behind a mammoth legacy of mixed results. "What Lyndon Johnson was about during his presidency," declared Johnson's chief domestic affairs assistant Joseph Califano, "was social and economic revolution, nothing less." The Great Society had its success stories, including Head Start, the Job Corps, the Teachers Corps, Vista, the Vocational Education Act, the College Work-Study program, the Elementary and Secondary Education Act (which directed billions of dollars in aid to schools with poor children), the Fair Housing Act, the National Housing Act, Medicare, and Medicaid. But Johnson's "War on Poverty" fizzled out completely by the early 1970s. Johnson tried in vain to tighten the welfare rule that an unemployed husband must leave home in order for his family to obtain benefits, a failure that helped ignite new subcultures of poverty, dependency, and ruined families in the inner cities that Johnson had hoped to transfigure. His Model Cities program died almost before it was born, and other urban renewal projects inflicted more damage than they relieved. The crescendo of violence in Vietnam was mirrored by the eruption of full-scale race riots in over a hundred American cities, a police riot at the 1968 Democratic Convention in Chicago, and the assassinations of Bobby Kennedy and Martin Luther King.

"I made all the mistakes that one can make," Johnson reflected not long before he died. He realized, too late, that in his words, "the fella that has power is the one that uses it sparingly. Because you can throw it away very quickly with arrogance, hypocrisy, without consultation." The dissipation of Johnson's power was accelerated by the "credibility gap" brought on by his constant lying on Vietnam, and by his poor public communications skills. "Men are moved by love and fear," he claimed, "and the key to persuasion is to find the right measure of each to move them the way you want to." However, George Reedy said that eventually, "This mastery of debate technique actually hurt him in a very strange sort of way, because he'd throw himself into the most trivial arguments with all the same force that he would into the most important argument. He would argue just as hard to get a painter to reduce a bill for painting his house by forty dollars, as he would to get a civil rights bill through. And after a while, people would begin to get the impression that he wasn't sincere about anything."

"I can't stand the bastard," said Bobby Kennedy, "but he's the most formidable human being I ever met." Only a politician and executive as formidable, as passionate, and as controlling as Johnson could have rammed the Civil Rights Act of 1964 and the Voting Rights Act of 1965 through Congress so quickly and effectively, and in doing so, he may have spared the nation from even more turmoil than it did endure on civil rights in the 1960s. The legislation, which banned voting and job discrimination against minorities, were his towering achievements, and broke the national shackles of hypocrisy lingering since the Civil War, banishing a shame that Johnson, a southerner, felt deep in his bones. "He wanted to bring America to where it should be," said LBJ assistant Tom Johnson, "particularly on civil rights."

Of Johnson's many contradictions, the most tragic was that the most effective legislative executive America had seen in this century was also its worst military executive. The Vietnam War caused over 50,000 American fatalities, 200,000 wounded, 2,600 missing, over 3 million Vietnamese casualties, and half a trillion dollars wasted, while "guns and butter" economics ignited federal deficits, climbing interest rates, and inflation that would plague the country for years to come. Some 500,000 American boys and men followed Johnson into a nearly ten-year-long massacre he knew the United States could never win.

Lyndon Johnson's controlling executive style facilitated not the healthy debate and dissent that is the lifeblood of the presidency, but forced consensus, fear, and distortion. C. Douglas Dillon, one of Johnson's Wise Men, speculated that "everybody'd been so scared" of Johnson "that nobody would tell him the real news" from Vietnam until the shock of the Tet Offensive.

Johnson's anguish over the torments he knew would visit him in the Oval Office appeared on tape as early as August 25, 1964, in the first days of the Democratic National Convention in Atlantic City, when Johnson drafted a withdrawal statement and repeatedly threatened his aides that he was going to pull out of the running. "I don't think a white southerner is the man to unite this nation in this hour," he confessed. "I do not believe I can physically and mentally carry the responsibilities of the bomb, and the world, and the Nigras, and the South," he said, on the edge of tears. "I don't see any reason I ought to seek the right to endure the anguish of being here."

The recording machine then heard him confess the one thing he yearned for most, a treasure from the heart of his people that would stay forever out of reach until the day he was lowered to his grave.

"They think I want great power," he said.

"What I want is great solace and a little love, that's all I want."

"Love, a little love."

CHAPTER 6

Richard M. Nixon
The Strategic Executive

*"The whole hopes of the whole goddam world of peace, Ron,
you know where they rest. They rest right here in this damn chair."*

RICHARD NIXON,
APRIL 27, 1973, OVAL OFFICE RECORDING,
TO PRESS SECRETARY RONALD ZIEGLER

THE OVAL OFFICE, JUNE 30, 1971

"You're to break into the place, rifle the files, and bring them in," said Richard Nixon to his chief of staff H. R. Haldeman.

The president was ordering a felony and an impeachable offense, a full year before the Watergate burglary.

Nixon was also on the verge of stunning diplomatic breakthroughs to China and the Soviet Union. At the same time, he was laying the groundwork for the full withdrawal of U.S. troops from Vietnam, and gearing up for a campaign that would win him the greatest election landslide in American history.

But hidden away in the walls and furniture surrounding him was a secret known only to Nixon, Haldeman, and a handful of aides. It was a secret that would strangle and destroy Nixon's presidency by laying naked his fatal moral and executive flaws. For four months, a network of hidden microphones had picked up Nixon's most private and sensitive office conversations and fed them into voice-activated tape recorders. Not even Rose Mary Woods, Nixon's longtime secretary, was allowed to know of the taping. "I say things in this office that I don't want even Rose to hear," Nixon told Haldeman.

The microphones were everywhere.

Five were built right into Nixon's desk, two were hidden on either side of the Oval Office fireplace, two were placed in the Cabinet Room under the table near the president's chair, and four more were installed in his hideaway office in the Executive Office Building. The mikes were wired into electronic devices that combined their signals into the input of Sony 800B reel-to-reel recorders hidden in locked storage closets nearby, which transmitted the sound signals onto 1,800-foot-long reels of tape. The president's telephones in the Oval Office, the EOB office, and the Lincoln Sitting Room on the second floor of the White House mansion were also wired for sound, and the following year his desk and telephones at Aspen Lodge at Camp David were, too.

To compensate for Nixon's clumsiness, the systems in the Oval Office, the EOB, and the Camp David study were sound activated, and telephone recordings started whenever a call was placed. The only recording station controlled manually was the Cabinet Room, which could be activated by Nixon by flipping a hidden switch, or, since he usually forgot, by Haldeman's aide Alexander Butterfield, who had a switch in his office. The system was installed and maintained by agents of the Technical Security Division of the Secret Service.

Nixon's taping had its origins during the presidential transition in late 1968, when FBI Director J. Edgar Hoover told Nixon that LBJ had bugged Nixon's campaign plane, and then warned him, "When you get into the White House, don't make any calls through the switchboard. Johnson has it rigged, and little men you don't know will be listening." H.R. Haldeman, who was in the meeting, recalled that Hoover then told Nixon that "Johnson had installed electronic facilities that enabled his people to secretly monitor phone calls made through the switchboard. Not only that, but he had taping facilities that recorded his Oval Office conversations—and allowed aides nearby to monitor such conversations, live." When Hoover left, Nixon told Haldeman: "We'll get that goddam bugging crap out of the White House in a hurry."

In later years, Nixon told different stories about how he found out about Johnson's bugging. In one version, he asserted that in a post-election visit to the White House in 1968, LBJ got down on the floor in his bedroom, pointed to recording devices allegedly installed by JFK, and said, "Dick, they are voice activated." In another version, Nixon claimed to reach under the presidential bed to find a slipper one day early in his term and discovered a dangling microphone. "I discovered a mass of wires and cables underneath Johnson's bed," Nixon wrote in his memoirs. "I was told that some were for his telephones, some were remote control wires for the TV sets, and some were for tape-recording equipment connected to the phones. I asked that they all be removed."

Gradually, Nixon began having second thoughts. Not quite two years into his first term, in 1971, Nixon decided to build the most comprehensive White House taping system ever. One impetus, ironically, was Johnson, who told Nixon that he shouldn't have removed the taping capability in the first place, since his own recordings were proving very helpful in writing his memoirs. Nixon, with a keen eye both to history and to literary market potential, took the point, and concluded, after a few Oval Office experiments with note-takers, that any transcribing had to be surreptitious, or candid conversation would be inhibited.

Finally, there was the matter of Henry Kissinger, Nixon's brilliant, mercurial national security adviser. According to Haldeman, the tapings were "a final attempt by a frustrated Nixon to pin down the opinion of Henry Kissinger and other advisers who often seemed to come up with their own versions of both their own and the president's positions on controversial military and foreign policy questions." According to Haldeman, Nixon believed that "Henry's view on a particular subject was sometimes subject to change without notice," especially when talking to reporters. Kissinger in turn often recorded his calls with Nixon and others, either electronically or through use of a "dead key"—an unheard note-taker on the line. Of Nixon's taping, Kissinger would later quip, "It was a high price to pay for insurance."

On this day, June 30, 1971, as the tape machine quietly rolled forward in its secret compartment, it was apparent that Nixon had mostly forgotten about it, the tapings now blended invisibly, untranscribed, into his office routine. "As impossible as it must seem now," Nixon wrote in his memoirs, "I had believed that the existence of the White House taping system would never be revealed." The tape registered Nixon's fear that the Brookings Institution, a liberal think tank, might possess documents harmful to his Vietnam policies. Two weeks before, when the *New York Times* began running leaked excerpts of the classified Defense Department documents known as the "Pentagon Papers" that were critical of the Kennedy and Johnson war policies, Nixon authorized formation of an anti-leaking and covert operations squad, later known as "the Plumbers," to plug any further leaks. On the day this tape was made, the Supreme Court had turned down the White House's request to stop further public disclosure of the Pentagon Papers.

Nixon spoke in a series of broken, fragmentary outbursts evoking a 1930s gangster film. "They have a lot of material," Nixon said to Haldeman. "I want, the way I want that handled, Bob, is through another way. I want Brookings, I want them just to break in! Break in and take it out! You understand?"

Haldeman responded, "Yeah, but you gotta have somebody to do it."

Nixon: "Well, don't discuss it here." Now almost shouting, Nixon exclaimed, "You're to *break into the place, rifle the files,* and *bring them to me!*" Haldeman sputtered, "Talking about breaking in, is it a Defense Department-approved, security—?" Nixon: "Just go in and *take it!* Go in around eight or nine o'clock. And I mean *clean it out!*"

Although Henry Kissinger and then–Defense Secretary Melvin Laird were listed on the National Archives log as attending this meeting along with Attorney General John Mitchell, neither recalled this outburst in 1996 when the tape was released, and they may have already left the room when it occurred. "I have no such recollection," said Kissinger. "Nixon often said exalted things that people didn't think would be done." Laird agreed: "I don't think Haldeman would have carried it out." As it turned out, no break-in was reported, but the night security guard at Brookings remembered that at eight o'clock that night, the time Nixon ordered a break-in, two unidentified men appeared in the building's lobby, asking to go to the office of Morton Halperin, one of the likely places that damaging papers would be held. The men said they were expected, so the guard needn't call upstairs. The guard refused to let them proceed, and the men turned on their heels and disappeared.

The Brookings break-in tape, and many other of Nixon's tapes, vividly illustrate not only an Oval Office veering into a twilight zone of moral jeopardy, but a lacerating executive flaw that would accelerate Nixon's self-immolation: at different times he gave contradicting orders to different people, sometimes expecting that his orders would not be carried out. The resulting tangle of confusion and illegality would interconnect with his tapes and hurl Nixon out of the Oval Office. "Nixon was the weirdest man ever to live in the White House," Haldeman later wrote. "Many problems in our administration arose not solely from the outside, but from inside the Oval Office—and even deeper, from inside the character of Richard Nixon. I soon realized that this president had to be protected from himself." Haldeman, reported Nixon speechwriter William Safire, "*had the responsibility not to carry out orders* he felt were ill-conceived or badly put."

Just days after his inauguration, Nixon asked his wife to arrange for two Dictaphones to be installed in his bedroom, one for current memoranda and one for memos for the file. Nixon also placed Dictaphones in the Oval Office, in the EOB office, aboard Air Force One, and at the Western White House. Before long, Nixon was governing, in part, by Dictaphone. In September 1969 Haldeman wrote in his diary: "P is all of a sudden enamored with use of the Dictaphone and is spewing out memos by the carload, plus about double the volume of news summary marginal comments."

Nixon sensed the dangers of his ambiguous executive style and even tried to institute a system to correct for it. On one of his Dictaphone memos, dated June 16, 1969, he revealed his own awareness of the maze of conflicting and fantasized orders: "I have an uneasy feeling that many of the items that I send out for action are disregarded when any staff member just reaches a conclusion that it is unreasonable or unattainable. I respect this kind of judgment. On the other hand, I want to know when that kind of decision is made. In the future, I want you to keep a checklist of everything I order and I want you to indicate what action has been taken (and I want no long memoranda indicating why it can't be taken) and particularly I want to know when the action that I have ordered has *not* been taken."

"With Nixon," said Henry Kissinger, "you never knew how many games were being played simultaneously." Indeed, the brighter lights on Nixon's staff understood Nixon's executive ambiguity and compensated for it. Nixon had an "extremely complex personality," said his deputy national security assistant Brent Scowcroft. "You have to understand that to understand things like his ordering a break-in at the Brookings Institution. He was blowing off steam. He didn't mean it, his people knew that, and Brookings was never broken into. Anyone who was around Nixon a lot knew that he had a penchant for hyperbole. People who don't know that react in horror to imagine that a president of the United States could order a break-in of an institution. This is a man who is very convoluted in his emotions. You have to understand the distortions that produces." William Safire asserted that "orders are not always orders, even when they are couched in command nomenclature and issued with the crackle of authority. Sometimes they are ways of unwinding or of stimulating suggestions, and occasionally they are merely thoughts spoken aloud."

Alexander Haig, Kissinger's assistant and Haldeman's successor as Nixon's chief of staff, said of Nixon: "He agonized over every decision a great deal more than other presidents I have known—'on the one hand, on the other hand.' Most of the tapes are sheer, utter hogwash. People read them as though they were an expression of the intentions and directions of a man. They weren't. A lot of people are like that, they like to let off steam, and say a lot of crazy things just to get a counter to see how the listener is going to react to it. They were macho fantasies to build his confidence. My God, if I had done everything Richard Nixon told me to do, I'd probably be in Leavenworth today!" Haig reported that he would placate Nixon's outbursts by saying "Right, boss, let's think about it. We'll talk about it in the morning." Overnight, Haig said, "These crazy things usually disappeared." According to Nixon speechwriter Ray Price: "He has always needed people around him who would help the lighter side prevail, who, when he issued an outrageous order, would quietly let it sit for a while until he calmed down, and then either ignore it or ask him whether he really wanted it done."

Haldeman recalled Nixon barking out "petty, vindictive orders" such as when a senator made a speech critical of the Vietnam War: "Put a twenty-four-hour surveillance on that bastard." Nixon buzzed him on the intercom within ten minutes: "What have you done about it?" Haldeman delayed the order until Nixon asked with a half-smile, "I guess you never took action on that, did you? Well, I guess it was the best thing." "Nixon's indirect method of operation simply could not be gauged by an outsider," wrote Kissinger. "There was no way of telling what Nixon had put forward to test an interlocutor and what he meant to be taken seriously; and no outsider could distinguish a command that was to be followed from an emotional outburst that one was at liberty to ignore—perhaps was even expected to ignore." Nixon once sent Secretary of State Rogers a note to "fire everybody in Laos" for disobeying orders. Rogers sat on it, and a few weeks later told Nixon he hadn't implemented the order. Nixon, who couldn't remember giving the order in the first place, smiled and said, "Oh, hell, Bill, you know me better than that."

In 1969, during a presentation of federal agency budgets, Nixon barked: "Cut 'em by half. They're utterly useless—cut 'em by 30 percent! . . . They're not worth a damn—cut 'em by 25 percent!" Later he said to one of the presenters, then–Deputy Budget Director James Schlesinger, "Look. I don't know how much these agencies should be cut. When I say these things, I'm just trying to strengthen your hand in dealing with the agencies. If you report back that the president says cut 'em in half, they're going to be more amenable to cuts." Schlesinger recalled, "It was not intended that he be taken literally. But when you told the agencies that the president thought they should be cut, you got their attention, I'll tell you!"

The unspoken understanding that Nixon's orders were not always to be taken seriously soon collided with a contradictory reality: Nixon's White House "corporate culture" was one of macho obedience and can-do efficiency, where, said his daughter Julie Nixon Eisenhower, "Loyalty was demanded of all, not judgment." Nixon national security aide Robert McFarlane noted: "With Nixon, toughness was an article of faith. You got no points for losing gracefully. The name of the game was winning, and people who compromised were seen as wimps."

Nixon's anger was rooted in his hardscrabble California youth, growing up in a poor family headed by a stern father, watching two brothers die of tuberculosis while battling his own crippling and unfathomable insecurities. "What starts the process really are laughs and slights and snubs when you are a kid," Nixon recalled. "But if you are reasonably intelligent and if your anger is deep enough and strong enough, you learn that you can change those attitudes by excellence, personal gut performance, while those who have everything are sitting on their fat butts."

Nixon's burning, angry ambition powered a fast-track trajectory up the right wing, anti-Communist arc of the postwar Republican party: congressman at thirty-three, United States senator at thirty-seven, and Eisenhower's vice president at thirty-nine. Nixon attorney Leonard Garment said, "Over the years, Nixon observed politics very closely; it's not a tea party or a love match, but a form of combat. Part of what fueled him to be effective was anger, ambition, and the appetite for revenge—the knowledge that unless you made yourself fearful to your enemies, they would savage you."

Tape-recorded examples of Nixon venting his dark side are legion. One day late in his first term, in a staff meeting, Nixon railed against Democratic senators: "One day we will get them—we'll get them on the ground where we want them. And we'll stick our heels in, step on them hard and twist . . . Henry knows what I mean. Get them on the floor and step on them, crush them, show no mercy." On a tape released in 1993, Nixon agreed with Haldeman's suggestion that it could be a good idea to recruit "eight thugs" from the Teamsters Union to physically attack antiwar protesters: "They've got guys who will go in and knock their heads off," said Nixon. "Sure," says Mr. Haldeman, "murderers . . . they're going to beat the shit out of some of these people." On a September 15, 1972, tape, Nixon growled: "This is a war. . . . I want the most comprehensive notes on all those who tried to do us in. . . . They didn't have to do it. . . . They are asking for it and they are going to get it. We have not used the power in this first four years as you know. . . . We have not used the [FBI] and we have not used Justice, but things are going to change now."

On tapes made public in 1996, Nixon ordered the flagrant abuse of the Internal Revenue Service, following the logic that earlier presidents had used the agency for political purposes. On May 13, 1971, he announced to Haldeman and domestic affairs adviser John Ehrlichman his criteria for a new I.R.S. commissioner: "I want to be sure he is a ruthless son of a bitch, that he will do what he's told, that every income tax return I want to see I see, that he will go after our enemies and not go after our friends." On a May 28, 1971, recording Nixon could be heard launching a portion of the extensive political intelligence and spying program that culminated in the Watergate break-in. "That's why I want more use of wiretapping," the president whispered. "Are we dealing adequately with their candidates, tailing them and so forth? It should not be on and off," Nixon said to Haldeman. "Keep after 'em."

Nixon's secret taping occurred against the backdrop of extensive illegal wiretapping orchestrated by the FBI at the behest of the Nixon White House. The taps began to protect national security secrets, but spiraled out of control. "The taps of National Security Council aides and journalists were designed to ensure the administration's control over the flow of news and the formation of policies," wrote historian Stanley Kutler. "But wiretapping was also a basic tool of the plan to maintain surveillance over potentially subversive domestic elements, particularly antiwar and civil rights activists. The efforts were extensive and violated both the letter and the spirit of the law." In his memoirs, Nixon argued that the tappings were fewer in number than those ordered by the Kennedys. The Nixon tapings and tappings also coincided with an epidemic of other White House electronic monitoring and surveillance. Top White House aides routinely taped and manually recorded conversations with each other and the outside world.

Nixon's anger extended to the military's prosecution of the lingering nightmare of the Vietnam War. Like Johnson, Nixon swore, "I won't be the first president to lose a war," and in May 1972, as he and Kissinger pursued peace negotiations and phased U.S. combat troop withdrawals, Nixon, whose military experience was limited to a World War II tour as a poker-playing junior supply officer in the backwaters of the Pacific, lashed out at the tactics of his generals in a recording of a memo to Kissinger and Haig.

MAY 19, 1972

President Nixon to Henry Kissinger and Alexander Haig
RE: *Military Insubordination in Vietnam*
audio recording of memorandum on Dictaphone machine

In this scorching Dictabelt memo, Nixon charged that his orders were not being carried out, and accused the air force of near-mutiny. To blunt a fierce new Communist offensive, and to strengthen his position for the upcoming Moscow Summit, Nixon had ordered a ferocious bombing blitz of his own, targeting the areas of Hanoi and Haiphong for the first time since 1968, with an armada of 150 warships and over 1,000 planes.

NIXON: I am thoroughly disgusted with the consistent failure to carry out orders that I have given over the past three and a half years, and particularly in the past critical eight weeks, with regard to Vietnam. It is easy, of course, to blame the bureaucracy for failing to carry out orders. But we always have the problem of the bureaucracy. It is our responsibility to ride the departments hard to see that when I give an order it is carried out faithfully, or that I am told as quickly as it is known that the order is not being carried out, and why that is the case.

I refer specifically to the fact that I have ordered, on occasion after occasion, an increase in the quantity and quality of weapons made available to the South Vietnamese. All that we have gotten from the Pentagon is the run around and a sometimes deliberate sabotage of the orders that I have given. I want it clearly understood, that from now on the moment that I find another instance where there is such insubordination the man who will be held responsible, and whose resignation will be requested, will not be the Ollie down the line in the woodwork but the man at the top, whoever he is.

The performance in the psychological warfare field is nothing short of disgraceful. The mountain has labored for seven weeks and when it finally produced, it produced not much more than a mouse. Or to put it more honestly, it produced a rat. We finally have a program now under way but it totally lacks imagination and I have no confidence whatever that the bureaucracy will carry it out. I do not simply blame Helms* and the CIA. After all, they do not support my policies because they basically are for the most part Ivy League and Georgetown-society oriented. On the other hand, the Pentagon deserves an even greater share of the blame. After all, they are supposed to take orders from the commander-in-chief. The trouble is that we left too many of the McNamara people around in high places and they are constantly sabotaging everything we are trying to do.

Finally, I have told Henry today that I wanted more B-52s sent to Vietnam. I want this order carried out, regardless of how many heads have to roll in carrying it out. Even though the bomb load is smaller until they can be remodeled, the psychological effect of having 100 more B-52s on the line in Vietnam would be enormous. I either expect this order to be carried out or I want the resignation of the man who failed to carry out the order when it was given.

The crowning insult to all this injury is to have the military whine around to Agnew that they were not getting enough support from the

*Richard Helms, director of Central Intelligence.

commander-in-chief in giving them targets they could hit in North Vietnam.

I want you to convey directly to the air force that I am thoroughly disgusted with their performance in North Vietnam. Their refusal to fly unless the ceiling is 4,000 feet or more is without doubt one of the most pusillanimous attitudes we have ever had in the whole fine history of the U.S. military. I do not blame the fine air force pilots who do a fantastic job in so many other areas. I do blame the commanders who, because they have been playing "how not to lose" so long, now can't bring themselves to start playing "how to win." Under the circumstances, I have decided to take the command of all strikes in North Vietnam in the Hanoi-Haiphong area out from under *any air force jurisdiction whatever*. The orders will be given directly from a naval commander whom I will select. If there is one more instance of whining about target restrictions we will simply blow the whistle on this whole sorry performance of our air force in failing for day after day after day in North Vietnam this past week to hit enormously important targets when they had an opportunity to do so and were ordered to do so and then wouldn't carry out the order.

The examples I have given above are only a small number of those that I could point to if I had the time. What I am saying is that I want some discipline put into our dealings with the State Department, with the Pentagon and with the CIA, and I want that discipline enforced rigidly from now on out. I want you to convey my utter disgust to Moorer,* which he in turn can pass on to the Chiefs and also convey it to Abrams† and Bunker‡ in the field. It is time for these people either to shape up or get out.

JANUARY 5, 1973
TIME UNKNOWN, BETWEEN 7:38 AND 7:58

President Nixon and Charles Colson
RE: *Secret Monitoring of Henry Kissinger's Phone Calls*
audio recording of telephone conversation on Dictaphone machine

---

Admiral Thomas Moorer, chairman, Joint Chiefs of Staff.
†*General Creighton Abrams, commander of U.S. forces in Vietnam.*
‡*Ellsworth Bunker, U.S. ambassador to the Republic of Vietnam.*

Nixon's management system broke down when staffers such as domestic affairs adviser Charles Colson managed to slip around Chief of Staff Haldeman and feed the boss's dark side. Haldeman wrote of Colson: "In between his official projects, he was inside the Oval Office listening enthusiastically to Nixon's outraged pleas for action against various persons or organizations and promising, 'Yes, sir, I'll do that for you tomorrow morning.'"

An illustration of Nixon's executive style going haywire is found on this recorded phone conversation, when Colson reported on the results of a secret tracking system he placed, on Nixon's orders and without Haldeman's knowledge, on Kissinger's phone calls to monitor his contacts with the press. Rather than finding a way to evade or soften the order as more experienced staffers would have done, Colson had carried it out enthusiastically, and the results inflamed Nixon's anger:

COLSON: Mr. President, after we started keeping a log on Henry's calls, this should be in total confidence, because Henry should never know this.

NIXON: What did you find out?

COLSON: After we started keeping the log we found [columnists] Rollie [Roland] Evans and Joe Kraft and [*Time* magazine's] Jerry Schecter and those kind of people.

NIXON: Was Joe Kraft on the list?

COLSON: Oh, yes. January second.

NIXON: Joe Kraft, January second? And you saw his column today!

COLSON: Yeah, and how. So you know where that comes from. But we have not yet found the *New York Times*, the problem being that we didn't keep a log until I ordered it on January 1.

NIXON: Well, just keep the log from now on.

COLSON: Now, they're going to keep the log on people . . . . The hypocrisy of it is that he was sighing to me on Sunday that "we must not talk to anybody." Then he picks up the phone and calls Joe Kraft. So if—

NIXON: Sunday being—

COLSON: It was the thirty-first.

NIXON: So he called up Joe Kraft on Tuesday.

COLSON: Yep.

NIXON: And Joe Kraft writes an article yesterday that knocks the bejesus out of us. In which Henry indicated that. Now I think Henry oughta be taken on, on, calling, just say, "Henry, did you, have you talked to Kraft?"

COLSON: Yeah, I can hit Henry on that.

NIXON: No, no, I want you to ask him, I said, Joe, "Henry, gee this is a terrible article. Have you talked?" And if he lies on that, I wanna know. Will you do it?

COLSON: Yessir, I can do that.

NIXON: It's very important that I know that.

COLSON: I won't be able to get him tonight. I'll probably have to get him in the morning.

NIXON: Oh, God, no. I don't mean tonight. But some time tomorrow, you know, before say—I don't want him too irritated before he goes to Paris [peace talks]. Just say "What the hell, did anybody in your shop talk to Kraft?"

He called him, or did Kraft call Henry?

COLSON: No, he called Kraft, it's an outgoing call. He called Kraft.

NIXON: I'll be *God damned!*

COLSON: The incoming calls we couldn't even monitor.

NIXON: *He called Kraft! I'll be a son of a bitch!*

COLSON: It was outgoing. The incoming calls you can't always check.

NIXON: That is *unbelievable!* Have you told Haldeman?

COLSON: No.

NIXON: Tell him tomorrow.

COLSON: I haven't even told Haldeman—

NIXON: OK.

COLSON: —we're checking it.

NIXON: All right. Call him tomorrow. Well, it's good that you're checking it.

Against such avalanches of venom, a man like Chief of Staff Haldeman, whose previous executive experience was that of running a regional office of the J. Walter Thompson advertising firm, eventually relented; in time, he seemed to feed it. "The White House staff's attitude to the president resembled that of an advertising agency—whence indeed most came—to an exclusive, temperamental client," wrote Kissinger. "They were expediters, not balance wheels. And once the machine started skidding, they accelerated its descent over the precipice rather than braking it in time."

On most mornings Nixon took the two-and-a-half minute walk from the White House residence to arrive at the Oval Office by 8:00 A.M. While his faithful manservant Manolo poured Nixon a cup of coffee, Muzak drifted softly through the halls of the West Wing to enforce the atmosphere of quiet, orderly isolation, and Nixon intently scoured the thirty- to sixty-page bound news summary prepared overnight by his staff. The briefing book summarized news and editorials from fifty-two newspapers, plus capsule versions of the network TV news broadcasts. "I don't get bogged down in any part of the news," Nixon explained. "My much maligned and praised news summary covers all aspects of it: the newspapers, TV news, radio, the newsmagazines, and the monthly magazines. I can scan the report in as little as ten minutes and know more than if I had read the *New York Times* all the way through. I tell the staff to leave out the puff pieces and the personal criticism. I am an issue man."

The News Summary was a primary management tool for Nixon, who would jot action notes in the margins. According to historian Stephen Ambrose, "He governed through notes. Nixon found it difficult to give orders face-to-face, to fire someone, to express his wishes and give his commands in a meeting. Even at age fifty-seven, in short, he remained a shy Quaker boy, one who hated personal confrontation and avoided it if at all possible. So he gave his orders via his News Summaries. 'H—do this,' he would write, or 'E—do that.' Some of Kissinger's most important marching orders came in the margins of the News Summaries."

Nixon's first meetings of the day were with Kissinger and Haldeman, who would scribble notes on a yellow legal pad, charge out of the office, and use the pad as his bible of instructions for the day. Haldeman was a humorless paragon of order and efficiency, the ultimate no-nonsense account executive, and as Nixon's chief operating officer, he tightly controlled White House paperwork, staffing and scheduling, and—crucially—everyone's access except Kissinger (and eventually, Colson). "Every president needs a son of a bitch and I'm Nixon's," said Haldeman. According to Julie Nixon Eisenhower, "My father wanted Bob Haldeman to be the sole conduit to him." In 1971, Nixon told his Cabinet: "From now on, Haldeman is the lord high executioner. Don't you come whining to me when he tells you to do something. He will do it because I asked him to and you're to carry it out."

Nixon's mornings were consumed with formal meetings from 9:30 until noon, when a half-hour was set aside for "fanny patting" photo ops with members of Congress. He did not relish this part of the job, as he was stumped for chitchat and pathologically shy. Sometimes he would end these meetings by thrusting a small presidential gift to a visitor and mumbling a weak joke like, "Give this to your wife or your secretary, whatever you prefer." He often lunched alone at his Oval Office desk or in a small adjoining ante-room. The menu never varied: a slice of canned Dole pineapple, a scoop of Knudsen's cottage cheese, and a couple of Rye Crisp crackers, washed down with a glass of skim milk. "Some like to bat ideas around with aides over lunch," Nixon later explained, "but I generally preferred to get analysis from others in writing, not because I disliked fellowship but because I tried not to mix fellowship with work. Besides, most smart people express themselves better in writing than orally." One intimate said Nixon functioned "as the senior partner of a law firm who reviews the work of his underlings. He is issue-oriented, not management-oriented."

After lunch, Nixon often charged across the street and up the steps of the Executive Office Building into his hideaway office. Here he installed the Oval Office desk Eisenhower used, but Nixon could usually be found hun-kered down in a yellow silk armchair with his feet spread out on an ottoman, scribbling on yellow legal pads, flanked by a Dictaphone and telephone, strategizing, reorganizing the world balance of power, and batting around impeachable offenses with his staff. "I usually work here from three to six in the afternoon," he explained to a visitor. "When important decisions are to be made, I have to withdraw sometimes." His staff tried to free him up to spend Wednesday afternoons in the hideaway office for strategic thinking and chewing over "the big plays," particularly on foreign policy, which Nixon saw as his main responsibility. "All you need is a competent Cabinet to run the country at home," he said. "You need a president for foreign policy." He often worked into the evenings in the Lincoln Sitting Room in the southeast cor-ner of the White House mansion while listening to heroic orchestral music on the hi-fi: Tchaikovsky, Rachmaninoff, the scores from *Victory at Sea* and *Dr. Zhivago*. The rug became spotted with small burns from his pipe when Nixon nodded off in the chair.

In this cocoon of semi-isolation, Nixon was virtually shielded from per-sonal debate and criticism. "He was very shy, a loner in many respects," observed his second vice president, Gerald Ford, "and he seemed to prefer dealing with paperwork than dealing with people." "Nixon could be very decisive," wrote Henry Kissinger. "Almost invariably during his presidency his decisions were courageous and strong and often taken in loneliness against all expert advice. But wherever possible, Nixon made these decisions

The first wired Oval Office: FDR began electronic recordings in the Oval Office to protect himself in press conferences, like this one in 1939. The recording control box was placed in the top left drawer of the desk. *Associated Press*

FDR's secret recorder under construction: Inventor J. Ripley Kiel builds FDR's sound-activated recording machine in his laboratory, 1939. The high-tech device was an ancestor of the tape recorder. *Courtesy Sharon R. Kiel and Barbara Kaley*

FDR's recorder ready for installation under the Oval Office: The three-and-a-half foot machine was installed in a secret chamber. The recordings were not found for nearly forty years. *Courtesy Sharon R. Kiel and Barbara Kaley*

The decisive executive: Harry Truman tested FDR's recorder in the mid-1940s. Every morning after Truman's power-walk, the White House staff circled around his desk for a high-speed action meeting. Secretary of State Dean Acheson (shown at right with Truman and U.S. High Commissioner for Germany John J. McCloy) said of Truman, "This is the kind of person that one can adore." *Harry S. Truman Library*

Eisenhower's Oval Office Dictaphone, 1955: A state-of-the-art, double-decked "Dictacord" enabled Ike to record a one-hour meeting on non-eraseable plastic Dictabelts, which were lost to history until they were discovered in the Eisenhower Library forty-one years later during the research for this book. *Courtesy Dictaphone Corporation*

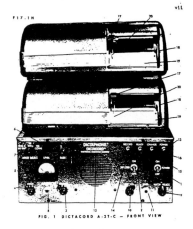

The organized executive: Dwight Eisenhower secretly bugged the Oval Office with a Dictaphone. The microphone is hidden in Ike's desk. He was "a far more complex and devious man than most people realized, and in the best sense of those words," said his vice president, Richard Nixon. With Secretary of State John Foster Dulles briefing the nation on the Suez Crisis, 1956. *Dwight D. Eisenhower Library*

JFK installs the first White House taping network: In 1962 Kennedy wired his Oval Office and Cabinet Room with hidden tape recorders. The on/off switch is hidden in the pen and pencil set near JFK's right hand. The desk is wired with hidden mikes. "He spent half his time thinking about adultery," said British Prime Minister Harold Macmillan, "and the other half about secondhand ideas passed on by his advisors." *John F. Kennedy Library*

Kennedy's triumph: JFK and his men manage the aftermath of the Cuban Missile Crisis, October 29, 1962. The room is bugged, but nobody knows except JFK and Attorney General Robert Kennedy (*far left*). JFK has flipped a switch under the table and is recording the meeting through microphones hidden in the wall behind him. "He was an incendiary man who set most of the people around him on fire," said his secretary of state, Dean Rusk (*to the left of Kennedy*), "and it was really fun to work with him." *John F. Kennedy Library*

JFK's recording studio: A tiny mike is stashed underneath Kennedy's coffee table, and is connected to tape recorders in the basement by wires running through a hidden hole in the floor. An on/off switch is built into one of the lamps by the fireplace. *John F. Kennedy Library*

Lyndon Johnson assumes the position: He was "a real centaur—part man, part horse's ass," said Dean Acheson. LBJ used the telephone like an assault weapon, firing off bursts of 75 to 100 calls per day. He recorded 9,200 hours of phone calls on a network of Dictaphones and tape recorders. *Lyndon B. Johnson Library*

The first electronic surfing president: LBJ lusted ravenously for electronic information, and planted TVs and news tickers right in the Oval Office. Here he is watching three networks at once. *Lyndon B. Johnson Library*

King in his court: LBJ's doctors ordered him to stay in bed until 10 A.M., so he used his bedroom and toilet as conference rooms. *Lyndon B. Johnson Library*

Nixon's taping system: Five microphones (M-1 through M-5) were placed in the president's desk. Two others (M-6 and M-7) were located in the wall lamps on each side of the fireplace. The taping system also included other rooms in the White House, the old Executive Office Building, and Camp David. *National Archives*

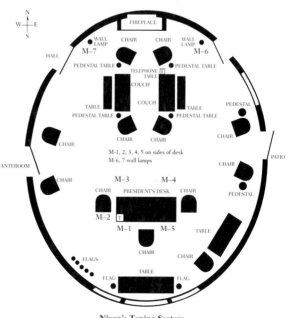

Nixon's Taping System

Source: National Archives

The collegial executive: Gerald Ford inherits the ruins of the presidency. "He saved the country," argued Kissinger. Here he tackles paperwork in August 1976 while a bust of Truman peers over his shoulder. Ford thought Nixon's microphones had been taken out of the office. He was in for a shock. *Gerald R. Ford Library*

The molecular manager: Jimmy Carter banned White House taping, but kept a tape-recorded diary. He tracked White House newspaper subscriptions and charged his staff $1.75 for breakfast. "At times," wrote Zbigniew Brzezinski (*left*), "I thought he was like a sculptor who did not know when to throw away his chisel." *Jimmy Carter Library*

The visionary executive: Ronald Reagan abdicated control of many details but worked hard on what he considered most important: U.S./Soviet affairs and public and congressional persuasion. "I had an agenda I wanted to get done," he explained. "I came with a script." With National Security Adviser John Poindexter and Chief of Staff Donald Regan in 1986. *Ronald Reagan Library*

The Reagan tapes: Reagan quietly resumed tape recordings of presidential phone calls routed through the basement Situation Room. With Defense Secretary Caspar Weinberger and General Robert T. Herres in 1987, discussing Persian Gulf tensions. He also began videotaping Oval Office meetings, tapes first discovered during research for this book. *Ronald Reagan Library*

The diplomatic executive: The Gulf War was a crisis custom-engineered for Bush: "I've been training all my life for this." Here Joint Chiefs Chairman Colin Powell tells Gen. Norman Schwarzkopf to shut down the war on Bush's order after only 100 hours of combat, February 27, 1991, as Chief of Staff John Sununu, Deputy National Security Adviser Robert Gates, and Defense Secretary Richard Cheney look on. According to a Bush aide, "Anyone who taped would have been shot." *George Bush Library*

The Clinton tapes: The 1997 release of Clinton's White House TV tapes revealed a president exerting a firm grip on his reelection campaign while skating on the edge of the law. Here Clinton greets fund-raiser Johnny Chung in the Oval Office. *White House TV*

The chaotic executive: "Hell, you work for Bill Clinton," said James Carville, "you go up and down more times than a whore's nightgown." On the eve of his final impeachment vote in the Senate in February 1999, the specter of secret Clinton phone tapes briefly appeared. Inside the Oval Office, Clinton was a reckless, energetic and often effective executive. *White House Photo*

in solitude on the basis of memoranda or with a few very intimate aides. He abhorred confronting colleagues with whom he disagreed and he could not bring himself to face a disapproving friend."

"Nixon had a bewildering combination of great grace and amazing awkwardness in dealing with people face-to-face," wrote Haldeman. "He hated to see people who needed either to be persuaded personally or forced to take action." Nixon aide Donald Rumsfeld contended that "only a person like that could have made what I consider to be an enormous mistake in imposing wage and price controls on the United States. There was no experience in our country at all with peacetime wage and price controls. They didn't work. They were ill-advised in the first instance. He did it with an exceedingly limited number of people advising him." The flip side of Nixon's executive style, said Rumsfeld, "was the secret breakthrough to China. It didn't leak, and in that instance, his approach worked brilliantly."

Among the Nixon Presidential Papers at the National Archives in College Park, Maryland, is a box of files called "President's Personal File, Materials Removed From President's Desk 1969–1974." The files include many of the legal-pad "think pieces" he scribbled out during his long periods of solitude, and reveal the ruminations of a brooding strategist capable of plotting breakthroughs to China and the Soviet Union, but also hint at the surreal distortions of an executive spending too much time with himself.

September 7, 1969: "Each day a chance to do something memorable for some one . . . need to be good to do good . . . Need for joy, serenity, confidence, inspirational . . . Set example, inspire, instill pride." January 8, 1970: "Make people have a memorable experience each day . . . Spiritual; add element of lift to each appearance." November 15, 1970: "I have learned about myself and about the presidency. From this experience I conclude: The primary contribution a president can make is on Spiritual Lift—not material solution. The staff—particularly K & H—with my active cooperation have taken too much of my time in purely material decisions which could be left to others." During one rambling evening monologue with Haldeman, Nixon bellyached he was spending too much time signing documents and reading briefing papers, and he yearned for even more time to concentrate, read, and think deep thoughts on major decisions.

By 1970, Nixon's isolation was so tight that desperate congressmen would comically blurt out proposals to him during fifteen-second handshaking sessions on a reception line. That year Nixon had only three direct lines on his phone (Haldeman, Ehrlichman, and Kissinger), and only four Cabinet officers had direct phone access: Defense Secretary Laird, Secretary of State

Rogers, Labor Secretary George Shultz, and Attorney General John Mitchell. By now Rogers and Laird were rarely seeing the president, and Nixon was largely running the government through just four men: Kissinger, Haldeman, Ehrlichman, and Colson. Liberal Republican Congressman Paul McCloskey, Jr., said at the time, "For the president to isolate himself from all criticism, from differing opinion is a dangerous thing. Hell, every time I see the president the band has been playing "Hail to the Chief" and everyone has been bowing and scraping. That's not the real world. I see no one who has the guts to stand up to the president and say 'You're wrong.'"

Nixon's eight-year tour as vice president gave him a superb up-close observation post on the presidency of master-organizer Eisenhower. Before taking office, Nixon vowed to run a decentralized presidency. He intended to conduct few Cabinet meetings, since he found those in the Eisenhower administration "ineffably boring." "For one thing, I would disperse power, spread it among able people. Men operate best only if they are given the chance to operate at full capacity," he stated. "I would operate differently from President Johnson. Instead of taking all power to myself, I'd select Cabinet members who could do their jobs, and each of them would have the stature and the power to function effectively." Not long into his first term, however, Nixon became suspicious that his Cabinet officers were "going native" and becoming more loyal to their bureaucracies than to him. So he reversed himself and pulled all power into the White House, with eventually disastrous results.

"Time is a person's most important possession," wrote Nixon in his retirement. "How he makes use of it will determine whether he will fail or succeed in whatever he is undertaking." But as president, Nixon was one of the most prodigious time-wasters in history, squandering precious hours, days, and months on counterproductive, Byzantine interadministration scheming, ham-handed spin control, and misguided micromanagement. Nixon regularly intervened in the most trivial of details, including White House police uniforms, menus, wine lists, and music at state events. After no Cabinet members called to congratulate him after a speech on Kent State, he petulantly canceled their White House tennis court privileges. After Nixon complained that he didn't have enough thinking time, Haldeman dictated in his diary: "Main problem is how he'd use the time if it were made available. Right now he generally wastes it on trivia."

Another colossal time-waster was Nixon's obsession with the media and his unceasing struggle to influence press coverage with positive "PR." Commerce Secretary Maurice Stans claimed Nixon "was mentally overcharged with the feeling that some of the media were his enemies." Budget director

James Schlesinger said that Nixon "tended to brood excessively about criticism and to take it personally, as a personal affront. This fed a depth of suspicion that people were out to get him. As he brooded about that, it tended to interfere with the time he would devote to real decisions."

The biggest time-waster of all, of course, was Watergate, which hijacked Nixon's presidency from early 1973 to his resignation in August the following year. Haldeman's diary entries show the paralysis striking abruptly in mid-April. April 16: "Another all-Watergate day, as they generally tend to be now." April 17: "Today was another major Watergate day." April 26: "Another day all shot on the Watergate." "Even a labor-intensive president has only about three hundred sixty working hours a month," Nixon wrote. "When you consider the challenges and crises he faces at home and abroad, wasting even an hour of that time is an intolerable sacrifice of the world's scarcest resource." He proved his point with Watergate, which was both an ethical failure and a colossal management meltdown.

In June 1972, Nixon campaign operatives were captured trying to bug the Democratic national headquarters at the Watergate complex, and for the next two years, Nixon and his men tried to contain the blossoming political disaster. At the end of a meeting on the night of April 15, 1973, Nixon stood up from his desk, moved to a corner, lowered his voice, and confessed to White House counsel John Dean that it was probably stupid for them to have discussed clemency for Watergate burglar E. Howard Hunt at an earlier meeting. At that moment, Dean later told investigators from the Senate Watergate Committee, he somehow sensed that the president might be trying to avoid a tape recorder hidden in or near his desk. That summer, the investigators showed White House aide Alexander Butterfield memos they received from Nixon that looked like verbatim transcripts. Remembering Dean's suspicions, they asked Butterfield if Nixon recorded any of his meetings.

Butterfield's answer, which he repeated in public testimony on July 16—that Nixon maintained an elaborate recording system that picked up thousands of hours of White House meetings and phone calls—electrified Washington and triggered a constitutional crisis that tore down Nixon's presidency in little more than a year. Shock turned to anger as portions of the tapes were made public and revealed a White House obsessed with punishing political enemies, fighting the press, and covering up presidential involvement in Watergate. The tapes captured the president discussing the payment of hush money to Watergate burglars working for Nixon's reelection committee, exploring the obstruction of justice, and ordering a cover-up of White House involvement in the scandal.

On July 19, 1973, Nixon was in Bethesda Naval Hospital recovering from surgery at the same time the existence of his taping system was made public. He jotted a note on a bedside pad: "Should have destroyed the tapes after April 30, 1973." Since the tapes were not yet subpoenaed, he probably could have destroyed them legally as his own personal property, but his attorney Leonard Garment argued that a bonfire would look like an admission of guilt, and Nixon agreed. Besides, Nixon actually clung to the hope that there were enough contradictory statements in the tapes to save him, statements like "Tell the truth," "This is the first I ever heard of this," "I know nothing about Watergate," and the infamous "It would be wrong."

In 1991, Nixon mused bitterly, "For every remark that I probably shouldn't have made, there are hundreds that are good and positive and show what we were up against and what we were trying to do. But does the press show these? No. Do they even put the questionable remarks in context? No. Or do they even show that a few sentences later I take it all back? No." Close readings and listenings to his full tapes, however, reveal that he was doing a variety of things, all fairly simultaneously: game-playing, testing the reactions of his men, spouting macho fantasies, conspiring to commit crimes, taking it back, and contradicting himself. This mire of conflicting and fantasized orders was gasoline on the fire of Watergate.

THE OVAL OFFICE
MARCH 21, 1973, 10:12 A.M.

President Nixon, John W. Dean III, and H. R. Haldeman
RE: *Watergate Cover-up*
audio recording of meeting on Sony reel-to-reel machine

This is the tape that prompted the Watergate grand jury to consider indicting Nixon for conspiracy.

Nixon's presidential counsel and attorney John Dean briefed the president on a criminal conspiracy to obstruct justice being run "right out of the White House." Instead of buzzing his secretary to call the police, Nixon meandered and game-played through a murky exploration of hush money, perjury, and blackmail. As usual in this type of meeting, Nixon issued contradictory statements, and while he never clearly orders the payment of hush money to the Watergate burglars, he confirms the drift of the Watergate cover-up. The meeting can be construed either as appropriate to a Mafia social club, or, as Nixon says at the end, a review of "various options" before deciding on "the right plan."

When Nixon was forced to release transcripts of this and other tapes on April 30, 1974, public support for him collapsed. The tape is a case study in both moral weakness and Nixon's fatally convoluted executive style.

DEAN: The reason that I thought we oughta talk this morning is because in our conversations, I have the impression that you don't know everything I know and it makes it very difficult for you to make judgments that only you can make on some of these things and I thought that—

NIXON: In other words, I've gotta know why you feel that we shouldn't unravel something?

DEAN: Let me give you my over-all first.

NIXON: In other words, your judgment as to where it stands, and where we would go.

DEAN: I think that there's no doubt about the seriousness of the problem which we've got. We have a cancer within, close to the presidency, that's growing. It's growing daily. It's compounded, growing geometrically now, because it compounds itself. That'll be clear if I, explain, you know, some of he details of why it is. Basically, it is because (1) we're being blackmailed; (2) people are going to start perjuring themselves very quickly that have not had to perjure themselves to protect other people and the like. And there's no assurance—

NIXON: That it won't bust?

DEAN: That that won't bust . . . .

Dean then outlined intelligence-gathering operations conducted by Nixon 1972 campaign operatives. He described a meeting with Attorney General John Mitchell and Nixon White House and campaign aide G. Gordon Liddy during which "Liddy laid out a million-dollar plan that was the most incredible thing I ever laid my eyes on: all in codes, and involved black-bag operations, kidnapping, providing prostitutes to weaken the opposition, bugging, mugging teams." The plan was not approved, but Nixon observed, "Then you have a problem—I was saying as to the criminal liability in the White House." Dean then speculated that the June 17, 1972, Watergate break-in was approved when "Mitchell probably puffed on his pipe and said, 'Go ahead,' and never really reflected on what it was all about."

DEAN: Now what has happened post–June 17? Well, I was under pretty clear instructions not to investigate this, but this is something that could have been disastrous on the election if all hell had broken loose. I worked on a theory of containment—

NIXON: Sure.

DEAN: To try to hold it right where it was.

NIXON: Right . . . .

DEAN: All right, then they [the Watergate defendants] started making demands. "We gotta have attorneys' fees. We don't have any money ourselves, and you're asking us to take this through the election." All right, so arrangements were made through Mitchell, initiating it, in discussions that I was present, that these guys had to be taken care of. Their attorneys fees had to be done. Kalmbach* was brought in. Kalmbach raised some cash.

NIXON: They put that under the cover of a Cuban Committee, I suppose?

DEAN: Well, they had a Cuban Committee and they had, some of it was given to Hunt's† lawyer, who in turn passed it out. You know, when Hunt's wife was flying to Chicago with $10,000 she was actually, I understand after the fact now, was going to pass that money to one of the Cubans—to meet him in Chicago and pass it to somebody there.

NIXON: [unintelligible] but I would certainly keep that cover for whatever it is worth.

DEAN: That's the most troublesome post-thing because Bob [Haldeman] is involved in that; John is involved in that; I am involved in that; Mitchell is involved in that. And that is an obstruction of justice . . . .

Here's what's happening right now. What sort of brings matters, one, this is going to be a continual blackmail operation by Hunt and Liddy and the Cubans. No doubt about it . . . .

All of these things are bad, in that they're problems, they're promises, they are commitments. They are the very sort of thing that the Senate is going to be looking most for. I don't think they can find them, frankly.

NIXON: Pretty hard.

---

*Herbert W. Kalmbach, personal attorney to Nixon.

†E. Howard Hunt, Jr., former CIA agent and White House consultant and Watergate conspirator.

DEAN: Pretty hard. Damn hard. It's all cash.

NIXON: Well, pretty hard I mean as far as the witnesses are concerned.

DEAN: All right, now, the blackmail is continuing. Hunt called one of the lawyers from the reelection committee on last Friday to meet with him over the weekend. The guy came in to see me to give a message directly to me. From Hunt to me for the first time.

NIXON: Is Hunt on bail?

DEAN: Hunt is on bail. Correct. Hunt now is demanding another $72,000 for his own personal expenses; another $50,000 to pay his attorneys fees; $120,000. He wanted it as of the close of business yesterday. 'Cause he says, "I'm going to be sentenced on Friday, and I've got to get my financial affairs in order." . . .

Hunt has now made a direct threat against Ehrlichman.[*] As a result of this, this is his blackmail. He says, "I will bring John Ehrlichman down to his knees and put him in jail. I have done enough seamy things for he and Krogh,[†] they will never survive it."

NIXON: Was he talking about Ellsberg?[‡]

DEAN: Ellsberg, and apparently some other things. I don't know the full extent of it.

NIXON: I don't know about anything else . . . .

DEAN: People around here are not pros at this sort of thing. This is the sort of thing Mafia people can do: washing money, getting clean money, and things like that. We just don't know about those things, because we are not criminals and not used to dealing in that business.

NIXON: That's right.

DEAN: It's a tough thing to know how to do.

NIXON: Maybe we can't even do that.

DEAN: That's right. That's a real problem as to whether we could even do it. Plus there is a real problem in raising money. Mitchell has been working on raising some money, feeling that he's one of the ones with the most to lose. But there is no denying the fact that the White House, and Ehrlichman, Haldeman, and Dean are involved in some of the early money decisions.

---

[*]*John Ehrlichman, former chief domestic affairs assistant to President Nixon.*
[†]*Egil "Bud" Krogh, former chief assistant to Ehrlichman.*
[‡]*Daniel J. Ellsberg, former Pentagon consultant, provided Pentagon Papers to the New York Times; his psychiatrist was the target of White House–approved burglary.*

NIXON: How much money do you need?

DEAN: I would say that these people are gonna cost a million dollars over the next two years.

NIXON: We could get that. On the money, if you need the money you could get that. You could get a million dollars. And you could get it in cash. I know where it could be gotten. I mean, it is not easy but it could be done. But the question is who the hell would handle it?

DEAN: That's right.

NIXON: Any ideas on that?

DEAN: Well, I think that is something that Mitchell ought to be charged with.

NIXON: I would think so too.

DEAN: And get some pros to help him . . . .

NIXON: What do you need? You don't need a million right away, but you need a million? Is that right?

DEAN: That's right.

NIXON: You need it in cash. Okay. Do you want to put that through, I am just thinking out loud here for a moment. Would you put that through the Cuban Committee?

DEAN: No.

NIXON: It is going to be cash—how if that ever comes out, are you going to handle it? . . .

DEAN: Let me continue a little bit right here now. When I say this is a growing cancer, I say it for reasons like this. Bud Krogh, in his testimony before the grand jury, was forced to perjure himself. He is haunted by it . . . .

NIXON: What did he perjure himself on, John?

DEAN: Did he know the Cubans. He did.

NIXON: He said he didn't?

DEAN: That's right. They didn't press him hard.

NIXON: Perjury is an awful hard rap to prove . . . .

Just looking at the immediate problem, don't you have to handle Hunt's financial situation damn soon?

DEAN: I think that is, I talked with Mitchell about that last night and—

NIXON: It seems to me we gotta keep the cap on the bottle that much. In order to have any options.

DEAN: That's right.

NIXON: Either that or it blows right now?

DEAN: That's the question . . . .

    If this thing ever blows, and we are in a cover-up situation? I think it would be extremely damaging to you and the—

NIXON: Sure. The whole concept of administration justice. We cannot have— . . .

DEAN: I can just tell from our conversations that these are things that you have no knowledge of.

NIXON: The absurdity of the whole damned thing, buggings and so on. Let me say I am keenly aware of the fact Colson, et al., were doing their best to get information and so forth and so on. But they all knew very well they were supposed to comply with the law. No question about that! . . .

    What are your feelings yourself, John? You know pretty well what they'll all say. What are your feelings toward the options?

DEAN: I am not confident that we can ride through this. I think there are soft spots.

NIXON: You used to feel comfortable.

DEAN: Well, I feel, I felt, I felt comfortable for this reason. I have noticed . . . that everybody is now starting to watch after their behind. Everyone's pulling in. They're getting their own counsel. More counsel are getting involved. How do I protect my ass.

NIXON: Well, they're scared. . . .

    Talking about your obstruction of justice role though, I don't see it. I can't see it.

DEAN: Well, I have been a conduit for information on taking care of people out there who are guilty of crimes.

NIXON: Oh, you mean like the blackmailer.

DEAN: The blackmailer. Right.

NIXON: Well, I wonder if that part of it can't be, I wonder if that doesn't, let me put it frankly: I wonder if that doesn't have to be continued? Let me put it this way: let us suppose that you get the million bucks, and you get the proper way to handle it, and you could hold that side?

DEAN: Uh, huh.

NIXON: It would seem to me that would be worthwhile.

DEAN: Well, that's one problem.

NIXON: I know you have a problem here. You have the problem with Hunt and his clemency . . . .

DEAN: I am not sure that you will ever be able to deliver on the clemency. It may just be too hot.

NIXON: You can't do it politically until after the '74 elections, that's for sure. Your point is that even then you couldn't do it.

DEAN: That's right. It may further involve you in a way should not be involved in this.

NIXON: No. It is wrong that's for sure . . . .

Now, let me tell you. We could get the money. There is no problem in that. We can't provide the clemency. Money could be provided. Mitchell could provide the way to deliver it. That could be done. See what I mean? . . .Well, if you had it [money], how would you get it to somebody? . . .

HALDEMAN: (*Haldeman has now entered the meeting*) That was the thing that we thought Mitchell ought to be able to know, how to find somebody who could do all that sort of thing, because none of us know how to.

DEAN: That's right. You got to wash the money. You can get $100,000 out of a bank, and it all comes in serialized bills.

NIXON: I understand . . . .

All right. Fine. And my point is that I think it is good, frankly, to consider these various options. And then, once you decide on the plan, John, and you had the right plan, let me say I have no doubts about the right plan before the election. You handled it just right. You contained it. And now after the election we have to have another plan, because we can't for four years have this thing, we're going to be eaten away. We can't do it . . . .

Hours after this conversation, $75,000 was delivered to Hunt's lawyer, according to grand jury testimony. The next day Mitchell told Ehrlichman that Hunt was not a problem any more. On June 4, 1973, after Dean had been talking to Watergate prosecutors for eight weeks, Nixon's tape recorder caught him worrying about this tape: "I mean, God, maybe we were talking about a cover-up—Watergate, I really didn't, I didn't know what the hell—I honestly didn't know . . . It's not comfortable for me because I was sitting there like a dumb turkey." "That's a tough conversation. Unless Haldeman explains it—which he will." Haldeman did try to explain the tape in a way that would clear Nixon of the cover-up—and Haldeman was indicted for perjury.

Nixon's credibility was further torpedoed with the discovery of the "eighteen-and-a-half-minute gap" on a tape of an Oval Office meeting between Nixon and Haldeman on June 20, 1972. A panel of experts reported to Federal Judge John Sirica on January 15, 1974, that it had concluded unanimously that at least five, and perhaps as many as nine, "separate and contiguous" erasures were made by hand-operated controls. When a Watergate prosecutor asked if the erasures could have been accidental, an expert testified that "it would have to be an accident that was repeated at least five times."

THE OVAL OFFICE
JUNE 23, 1972, 10:04 A.M.

President Nixon and H. R. Haldeman
RE: *Watergate Investigation: "Smoking Gun" Tape*
audio recording of meeting on Sony reel-to-reel machine

Nixon's hopes were dashed with the belated release, on August 5, 1974, of the infamous "smoking gun" tape, which was recorded six days after the Watergate break-in and captured Nixon approving a plan by his staff to stop the FBI's investigation of the burglary. Since some of the Watergate burglars were involved in the CIA's Bay of Pigs operation years earlier, the cover-up plan was to call in the FBI and tell them to back off their investigation at the president's request, by making Watergate seem connected to CIA and national security secrets. This tape was the fatal blow that tore down Nixon's presidency. President Eisenhower once told Nixon that he had "learned a long time ago" that if you made a mistake, "don't try to be cute or cover up. If you do, you will get so entangled you won't know what you're doing."

HALDEMAN: Now, on the investigation, you know the Democratic break-in thing, we're back in the problem area because the FBI is not under control, because Gray* doesn't exactly know how to control 'em and they have, their investigation is now leading into some productive areas, because they've been able to trace the money, not through the money itself, but through the bank sources, the banker himself. And, and it goes in some directions we don't want it to go . . . .

L. Patrick Gray, former acting director of the FBI.

Mitchell came up with yesterday, and John Dean analyzed very carefully last night and concludes, concurs now with Mitchell's recommendation that the only way to solve this, and we're set up beautifully to do it, ah, in that and that, the only network that paid any attention to it last night was NBC, they did a massive story on the Cuban thing.

NIXON: That's right.

HALDEMAN: That the way to handle this now is for us to have Walters* call Pat Gray and just say, "Stay to hell out of this—this is ah, business here we don't want you go to any further on it." That's not an unusual development, and ah, that would take care of it.

NIXON: What about Pat Gray—you mean he doesn't want to?

HALDEMAN: Pat does want to. He doesn't know how to and he doesn't have, he doesn't have any basis for doing it. Given this, he will then have the basis. He'll call Mark Felt† in and the two of them, and Mark Felt wants to cooperate because he's ambitious—

NIXON: Yeah.

HALDEMAN: He'll call him in and say, "We've got the signal from across the river to put the hold on this." And that'll fit rather well because the FBI agents who are working the case, at this point, feel that's what it is, this is CIA.

NIXON: But they're tracing the money to 'em.

HALDEMAN: Well they've traced it to a name, but they haven't gotten to the guy yet.

NIXON: Would it be somebody here?

HALDEMAN: Ken Dahlberg.‡

NIXON: Who the hell is Ken Dahlberg?

HALDEMAN: He gave $25,000 in Minnesota and, ah, the check went directly in with, to this guy Barker.

NIXON: It isn't from the Committee, though, from Stans?§

HALDEMAN: Yeah. It is. It's directly traceable and there's some more through some Texas people that went to the Mexican bank which

---

*Lieutenant General Vernon Walters, CIA deputy director.

†W. Mark Felt, FBI deputy associate director in 1972.

‡Kenneth H. Dahlberg, former treasurer, Finance Committee to Reelect the President.

§Maurice Stans, former secretary of commerce, former chairman, Finance Committee to Reelect the President.

they can also trace to the Mexican bank—they'll get their names today. . . . They'll stop if we take this other step.

NIXON: All right.

HALDEMAN: And they seem to feel the thing to do is get 'em to stop.

NIXON: Right, fine. . . . Good. Good deal. Play it tough. That's the way they play it and that's the way we are going to play it. . . .

Other matters were discussed, then the conversation circled back to the cover-up plan. This was the passage that finished Nixon's presidency.

When you get in these people, say, look. The problem is that this will open the whole, the whole Bay of Pigs thing, and the president just feels that, ah, I mean without going into the details of it—don't, don't lie to them to the extent to say that there's no involvement— but you'd say this is sort of a comedy of errors [brief unintelligible sound, possibly "bizarre to handle"], without getting into it. The presidents' belief is it's gonna open up the whole Bay of Pigs thing up again. And because these people are playin' for keeps. And that they should call the FBI in and say that we the country don't go any further into this case, period!

Nixon resigned the presidency on August 9, 1974 , and fled to California, leaving the tapes behind on White House property. He later mused, "I brought myself down. I have impeached myself."

For Nixon-haters, his tapes are the gift that never stops giving. Recordings released in 1996 and 1997 sound like a carnival of crimes-in-progress as Nixon and Haldeman toss off criminal schemes like Bonnie and Clyde, planning shakedowns, break-ins, and payoffs. On July 1, 1971, Nixon again fantasized Don Corleone–style about burglarizing the Brookings Institution and gathering dirt to discredit Democratic presidents: "Who is going to break into the Brookings Institution? . . . Who is going to be in charge of looking over the Pentagon Papers, the papers on the Cuban Missile Crisis, on the Bay of Pigs, on World War II and Korea? Who the hell is doing that and pulling out everything that might embarrass members of the Establishment? See? Who's going to do that? . . . I need a man, a commander, an officer in charge here in the White House that I can call when I wake up, as I did last night, at two in the morning, and I can say, 'Now, look here, I want to do this, this, this and this. Get going.' See my point?"

Buried in Haldeman's diary in an entry dated January 15, 1971, is a passage that highlights a personal and executive flaw that may have prevented Nixon from rescuing his presidency before it was too late. Said Nixon: "You don't capture people by surrendering to them," Haldeman recorded. "They capture you. It's extremely important that the leader never be in the position to allow the impression that he was wrong." Nixon's successor, Gerald Ford, observed, "Most of us have hidden flaws . . . in Nixon's case, that flaw was pride."

Like all Oval Office tapes, Nixon's recordings by definition offer an incomplete and thereby distorted picture of his presidency. In his case his recordings not only captured everything, but his worst tapes were released first, and are still being released today, a quarter century later. Almost two-thirds of Nixon's tapes, 2,338 hours, remain to be processed by the National Archives. Perhaps some of them will restore some honor or balance to Nixon's never-ending recorded legacy of confusion and disgrace. Compare Nixon's system to the Kennedy taping system, which was carefully and manually controlled by JFK, who rarely forgot the machines were running. Kennedy's tapes contain no scandal, no major embarrassments, and almost no presidential cursing (he periodically swore, but almost never on the tapes). Both Eisenhower and Kennedy administration officials explored the overthrow of foreign governments by the CIA, acts at least as egregious as the boneheaded Watergate burglary, but no corresponding tape recordings have been found.

"Nixon was so much more than Watergate," wrote historian Joan Hoff, "and Watergate so much more than Nixon that his diehard critics can only simplistically conflate them." What Nixon's tapes miss completely is the fact that Nixon was capable of being a surprisingly complex, sophisticated strategic executive on both domestic and foreign policy. "He was a bold, innovative, high-risk president," wrote historian Stephen Ambrose, "who had succeeded in bringing a majority of his countrymen with him on adventures into wholly new areas—most obviously, the opening to China, détente with the Soviets, and the beginning of arms limitations." No tapes have been released of Nixon and Kissinger planning the China and Soviet breakthroughs or engineering the beginnings of the Middle East peace process, events equally as historic as the Watergate abuse of power.

In foreign policy, Nixon's weird personality and executive style interacted with Kissinger's strengths and weaknesses to achieve often stunning results. "Kissinger and Nixon both had degrees of paranoia," said longtime Kissinger assistant and Bush secretary of state Lawrence Eagleburger. "It led them to worry about each other, but it also led them to make common cause on perceived mutual enemies. They developed a conspiratorial approach to foreign policy management." While making war against real and perceived enemies, including many inside their own government, Nixon and Kissinger initiated a bloody, protracted, but eventually complete withdrawal from Vietnam, phasing down U.S. troop levels from Johnson's 500,000 to less than 25,000 when a peace agreement was finally signed. They suddenly reorganized the world balance of power by opening up to China, and improved the U.S./Soviet superpower relationship. They negotiated major arms control agreements, including the beginnings of the SALT [Strategic Arms Limitation Talks] process. They orchestrated two Middle East disengagement agreements between Israel, Egypt, and Syria, and mediated a war between Greece and Turkey.

Distracted as he was by foreign affairs, Nixon's domestic achievements were few and far between, and his approach to economic policy was muddled. Even so, his domestic initiatives were surprisingly progressive, and sometimes bore the marks of a keen strategist. He quietly and effectively implemented Supreme Court–ordered school desegregation in the South. "By 1974 only 8 percent of black children in the South were attending all-black schools, down from 68 percent in the fall of 1968," Nixon noted proudly in his memoirs. Although Kennedy and Johnson articulated the concept of affirmative action, Nixon was the first to widely implement it in government contracts. Nixon's generally strong environmental record included support for the Clean Air Act, and he even pursued Native American rights and reforms. Nixon briefly supported a radical approach to relieving poverty by establishing a minimum income through cash payments to poor families, but the plan was shot down by Congress along with almost all his other domestic proposals. Part of the problem was that, as Gerald Ford observed, Nixon's staff "viewed Congress in much the same way that the chairman of the board of a huge corporation regards his regional sales managers."

"How can one evaluate such an idiosyncratic president," asked historian James MacGregor Burns, "so brilliant and so morally lacking?" Former Republican senator Barry Goldwater happily accepted the challenge, declaring flatly: "He was the most dishonest individual I ever met in my life. President Nixon lied to his wife, his family, his friends, longtime colleagues in the U.S. Congress, lifetime members of his own political party, the American people, and the world."

The paradox of Nixon's strategic executive style was that the brooding, solitary, and often experimental ruminations that immolate him on his Oval Office tapes are the same impulses that fueled the Machiavellian blood-sport power politics that facilitated his reelection landslide, propelled him into the Kremlin to clink glasses and sign arms control agreements with Brezhnev, and brought him, in one astonishing moment, into the Forbidden City and face-to-face with Mao Tse-tung. Elliot Richardson, who was fired by Nixon for refusing to fire Watergate special prosecutor Archibald Cox, called Nixon "a man of remarkable intelligence, and great power of the intellect," who "had it within his grasp to be our greatest post–World War II president," but whose many good qualities could "give way very quickly to manipulation and ruthlessness."

Our greatest postwar international strategist-president was simultaneously a grieviously dysfunctional executive. His tortured personality created a fractured, twisted executive apparatus that exacerbated his weaknesses and liberated his darkest angels and those of much of his top staff. In time, he had no devil's advocates, only his own devils, and they devoured him.

Nixon never realized that among the most crucial responsibilities of a chief executive and a president are to set a moral tone and to give clear instructions to his staff, and he failed spectacularly in both departments.

For a few seconds in 1973, though, the fog lifted and Nixon briefly saw the truth he seemed to have forgotten during his entire five-and-a-half-year occupation of the Oval Office.

As John Dean laid out the turgid, confused litany of the Watergate cover-up during the infamous March 21 tape, Nixon mused into the hidden microphone: "First, because I am an executive, I am supposed to check these things."

CHAPTER 7

Gerald R. Ford
The Collegial Executive

"Rhetoric is cheap. Decision making is pretty hard."
GERALD FORD, 1976

ASPEN LODGE, CAMP DAVID
SEPTEMBER 1, 1975

Gerald Ford was about to do something no other president is ever known to have done.

He was going to electronically record a conversation—*and tell the other side he was doing so.*

It was almost halfway through Ford's abbreviated presidency, and Secretary of State Henry Kissinger was calling from Jerusalem. After months of on-and-off shuttle negotiations, Kissinger had just clinched an agreement between Israel and Egypt on an Israeli withdrawal from the Sinai Peninsula, the hottest foreign issue facing the White House that summer. The breakthrough was crucial to stabilizing the region in the aftermath of the October 1973 War, and it helped lay the groundwork for the Camp David Accords of 1978.

The process had been grueling for Ford and Kissinger. Six months earlier, they thought they'd persuaded Israeli Prime Minister Yitzhak Rabin and Egyptian President Anwar Sadat to agree to a deal. Then in March, the framework that both sides agreed to in principle broke down when the Israelis refused to withdraw behind the crests of two strategic mountain passes. The collapse occurred when, incredibly, no one could come up with accurate maps that clearly indicated where the passes were located. Ford angrily threatened to "reassess" America's relationship with Israel, a move which backfired, provoking fierce attacks both from American Jewish groups and their congressional supporters and caused the Israelis to dig their heels in even further. Fearing another Mideast war, Ford and Kissinger stuck with the negotiations.

Then, on June 1, during a meeting with Ford in Salzburg, Sadat suggested that the impasse be broken by a Sinai buffer zone policed by U.S. civilian monitors. Ford agreed. The following week, when Rabin visited with Ford and Kissinger at the White House, Ford cleverly suggested the buffer zone concept to Rabin without mentioning it was Sadat's idea. Rabin bought it, and the final deal was hammered out by Kissinger in August.

The two calls President Ford made from Camp David on this day, September 1, to Kissinger and Rabin, and an aborted call to Sadat (the two could barely hear each other because of a bad connection) are the only recordings ever found of Gerald Ford in action as a working president, and there's a good chance they are the only ones that ever will be. Ford's press secretary Ron Nessen recalled, "Coming on the heels of Watergate, Ford gave very firm instructions to have any and all taping equipment removed. I don't know of anything that was recorded." Presidential counselor Robert Hartmann wrote: "Ford issued strict orders against phone-tapping. So far as I know there was none. I even left my dictating machine at home." Soon after taking office, in fact, Ford stood before Congress and pledged, "There will be no illegal tappings, eavesdroppings, buggings, or break-ins by my administration." Because of the historical significance of the calls to Kissinger and Rabin, Ford authorized the White House Communications Agency to record them.

The recording captures a moment in the birth of the Mideast peace process, an excruciating journey that would continue through Camp David, the Israeli invasion of Lebanon, the Oslo Accords, the assassination of Rabin, and the beginnings of Palestinian self-rule. The recording also offers a hint of the executive style of a career politician and legislator, who, despite a public image of blockheaded, stumbling gracelessness, often proved to be an effective chief executive behind the scenes, applying a natural executive portfolio of common sense, decency, and sound judgment. Brent Scowcroft, his national security adviser, asserted: "President Ford was not a great intellect but that is not a prime requisite for being president. A great president needs to possess two qualities: the first quality is courage, the courage to make a decision and then stick with it. Gerald Ford did that perhaps better than anyone else. When he made a decision he did not worry about it. The decision had been made and he could move on to the next problem or issue."

Ford greeted his secretary of state in his characteristically flat, earnest, halting, and lightly midwestern-accented voice.

ASPEN LODGE, CAMP DAVID
SEPTEMBER 1, 1975

President Ford and Henry Kissinger
RE: *Egyptian-Israeli Disengagement: Sinai II Accords*
audio recording of telephone conversation on reel-to-reel tape machine

This phone recording, discovered in the Ford Presidential Library twenty-two years after it was made, captured Ford congratulating his secretary of state on successfully concluding a protracted round of shuttle diplomacy between the Egyptians and Israelis.

KISSINGER: Hello, Mr. President.

FORD: Henry, how are you?

KISSINGER: I am fine. How nice to hear from you.

FORD: The same to you. I have just been warned by Ron [Press Secretary Ron Nessen] that I have to tell you—and later when I talk to the Prime Minister and to the president—that WHCA [White House Communications Agency] is recording this conversation. You don't have any objections, I trust?

KISSINGER: No, I don't have any objection.

FORD: I think they wanted it for historical purposes.

KISSINGER: Right.

FORD: Let me say very, very deeply how very grateful I am for the tremendous effort that you have made in this last round of negotiations, but I know how long and how hard and how devotedly you have spent many, many hours, not only with me but with Prime Minister Rabin and President Sadat.

I think this is a great achievement, one of the most historic, certainly of this decade and perhaps in this century. And I know that the American people will be most grateful for the successful efforts that you made. I just want to express it very strongly and very deeply for myself.

KISSINGER: I appreciate this very much, Mr. President, and of course, we have spent more time on the Middle East—you and I—than on almost any other problem . . . .

FORD: It is in the best interests of not only the two countries ourselves but, in my judgment, Henry, one of the great achievements for the world at this time.

KISSINGER: I think it gives peace a chance in this area, and the consequences, as the U.S. pointed out repeatedly, of stalemate were simply unacceptable.

FORD: I am sure there will be some critics, but I think in all honesty they have to understand what the alternatives would have been.

KISSINGER: Exactly, Mr. President. That is the problem, that the continuation of the stalemate would have had both military and economic consequences for the world that we had to do something about.

FORD: You are leaving very shortly, as I understand, for the actual initialing.

KISSINGER: I am going to see Prime Minister Rabin now, and then we are going to initial the documents.

FORD: Right.

KISSINGER: Then shortly after that, I will go to Egypt to meet with President Sadat and participate in the initialing of the documents there.

FORD: You will actually carry the documents with you to Alexandria, then?

KISSINGER: Exactly, the documents and maps.

FORD: I am going to call the prime minister after talking with you, and I will express to him my appreciation, but if you will do it in person for me, I would also be very grateful.

KISSINGER: I will do that, Mr. President, and I look forward very much to seeing you on Thursday.

FORD: You are getting in Wednesday night, as I understand?

KISSINGER: That is right. I am getting in Wednesday night about nine or ten o'clock.

FORD: Well, I will be at the airport to meet you.

KISSINGER: Thank you very much.

FORD: And it is arranged for us to have a [congressional] bipartisan leadership meeting on Thursday morning at 8 A.M.

KISSINGER: Good.

FORD: And I am sure that their reaction will be the same as mine, that this is a great achievement for not only the parties involved but for the world as a whole, and I just can't express deeply enough my appreciation for your own magnificent efforts in this area.

KISSINGER: Mr. President, we have worked together on this, and your strong support and your leadership and your talks with Sadat and Rabin made this possible.

FORD: You go over there and participate with the prime minister, give him my best, and at the same time give Nancy* my very best.
KISSINGER: Thank you, and the best to Betty.†
FORD: Thank you very much, and we will see you Wednesday night.
KISSINGER: See you Wednesday night.
FORD: Okay. Thanks, Henry.

Mrs. Nancy Kissinger.
†*Mrs. Betty Ford.*

Twenty-one years later, after listening to the tape, Henry Kissinger made a surprising assertion about Gerald Ford: "To work with, he was the best president. I've seen a lot of them." Kissinger explained: "Ford's style of operation was very professional." Compared to Nixon's Byzantine game-playing, Kissinger found that Ford "knew exactly what the issues were, he would listen to all of his people. If there were disagreements, he'd get everybody together, he would ask good questions. He'd make a decision and not fret about it. He never lost his temper. He never was egotistical. It was a great joy to work with him." Kissinger added, "Look, I think Nixon was an outstanding president. But a very complicated man. Now with Ford, what you see is what you get. You knew no games were being played. You knew that if there was something on his mind he'd tell you. You knew you could tell him what was on your mind. There'd be no second-guessing of a decision."

Brent Scowcroft, who was picked by Ford to replace Kissinger as national security adviser in early 1975, described Ford as the "antithesis" of Richard Nixon. "He had a very straightforward personality, simple in the best sense of the word. There is no guile, no convolution, no complexity in Gerald Ford. He was comfortable in who he was. He is the only man to become president who didn't seek to become president. He was not a man who was trying to feed his ego or searching to fulfill himself. He already was fulfilled. He was very able to make decisions. And once he made the decision, he never looked back. Richard Nixon did. He would keep analyzing—was it the right decision, should he have done the other."

After Nixon's bizarre farewell speech and helicoptered ascension to oblivion on August 8, 1974, Ford walked into the White House to take the oath of office at noon (he had technically been president for twenty-five minutes already, ever since Nixon's resignation letter was delivered to Secretary of

State Kissinger). He proclaimed that "truth is the glue that holds government together" and that "our long national nightmare is over." When he sat down at his desk in the Oval Office for the first time, though, he faced two potential new nightmares: how to repair the damage of a shattering constitutional crisis, and how to correct an economy in serious trouble. He met first with congressional leaders to offer cooperation, then with White House staff, then with economic advisers, declaring that his top priority was to conquer inflation. That first night, since the Nixons' things hadn't all been moved out yet, the Fords went back to sleep at their Virginia home.

The next day, Americans were treated to the sight of a slippered president in baby blue pajamas looking for the *Washington Post* on his front porch before the world media. Ford was an archetypal midwesterner: sunny, hale, and hearty; an Eagle Scout, football star, World War II Navy vet, Yale Law School graduate (graduating in the upper third of his class), and a conservative U.S. representative for thirteen terms, rising to become House Republican leader. Representative Paul N. McCloskey, Jr. (R-CA), said: "There is a basic trust which Jerry Ford inspires in those who work with him." Former senator Charles Goodell observed: "It's very difficult to think of negatives about Jerry Ford, unless you say he's too nice a guy." It was this last quality that was decisive in his selection as successor to Nixon's disgraced vice president, Spiro Agnew—he was one of the few men in Washington whom practically nobody disliked.

As his car approached the city of Washington that morning, what few Americans realized was that they were about to get a president who was perhaps the most qualified operations and budget executive in the federal government. Lyndon Johnson alleged that Ford was "so dumb he can't fart and chew gum at the same time," but Ford had spent a quarter century in Congress, twelve of them on the House Appropriations Committee, the "boiler room" of the U.S. government, where every year, thousands of government programs were presented, scrutinized, budgeted, and revised. As president, Ford would give a tour de force briefing on the federal budget for press and government officials, rattling off figures with authority and precision, like a corporate CEO. One bureaucrat marveled, "God, but he is good at this." "Ford possessed a vast amount of practical knowledge and an intellect that could quickly absorb details of complex issues," wrote his press secretary Ron Nessen. "At a thousand congressional meetings, Ford's specialty was picking his way through the budgets of the Pentagon, State Department, and CIA. He considered this expertise to be the best training for the presidency."

Ford stepped into a critically damaged presidential office. Watergate had shaken the core of American constitutional government. Power was suddenly swinging away from the Oval Office to Capitol Hill: Congress was passing a series of legislation that crippled the president's traditional executive power in foreign affairs, including the War Powers Resolution, which sharply limited his ability to deploy troops overseas. Ford had to preside over the humiliating final evacuation of American forces from Indochina. At the same time, the removal of wage and price controls combined with the Arab oil embargo to spike inflation to 11 percent by the time Ford took office.

Before he went home to Virginia that first night, Ford and aide Bob Hartmann walked into the Cabinet Room, fumbled around for the light switch, and surveyed the layout. Hartmann asked Ford which president's portrait should be hoisted up in the place of honor. "Truman," Ford replied quickly, identifying his hero and fellow midwesterner. He soon installed a bust of Truman just behind him in the Oval Office to gaze over his shoulder through the day, along with busts of Lincoln. Ford banished the loud, defiant gold and blue colors of Nixon's Oval Office in favor of restrained beige and rust patterns. He placed his Pacific battle medals and ribbons in a small display on a ledge. On his right he installed Bronco Buster, a Frederic Remington bronze of a cowboy struggling to stay on a tossing horse. Rembrandt Peale's heroic painting of George Washington soon appeared on the wall.

Ford usually woke up at 5:30 A.M. ("eating and sleeping are a waste of time," he said), pumped away on his exercise bike until 6:00 A.M., and started work by 8:00 A.M. He had the same lunch most days: a ball of cottage cheese soaked in A1 steak sauce, sliced tomato or onion, and a small scoop of butter pecan ice cream. The Oval Office was his main work space, but he used the small side office to his left for peace, quiet, and the occasional meeting. He usually had lunch in the side office, watching edited tapes of the previous night's newscasts.

In meetings, Ford would thoughtfully puff on his pipe while others spoke, then lean forward to comment and summarize. James Reston, writing in the *New York Times*, noted that Ford reached out to critics and opposing points of view: "Unlike Nixon, he didn't pretend he was always right, but dealt with the facts, and again unlike Nixon, kept in touch with his opponents." Ford, continued Reston, "does not shut himself off in the White House, but brings everybody in—the Republicans and Democratic leaders, old buddies from his days on Capitol Hill, friends and critics from the newspapers, radio, and television." One aide said Ford "preferred to have contact with people who were recommending the decisions and to talk it over at the table and to have a lively debate."

Ford's first days in the White House were nearly ruined by two close calls that could have easily exploded in his face. Both involved Oval Office taping.

On the second day of Ford's administration, Ford aide Benton Becker looked out the window of his temporary office in the Executive Office Building and saw a convoy of air force trucks lined up to the basement entrance of the White House West Wing. Men were loading file cabinets and sealed boxes onto the trucks. Becker went down to ask what they were doing, and learned that they were taking former President Nixon's records to be airlifted to Nixon's office in San Clemente. Becker suspected that crucial Watergate evidence was in the boxes, including Nixon's Oval Office tapes. "Who authorized this shipment?" he asked the officer in charge. "I answer to General Haig," the officer replied. Becker, who was volunteering legal services to Ford and as such had no official White House authority, tried to locate Haig or any other responsible official, but couldn't find anyone. So he convinced the Secret Service that no records should leave the White House without the authorization of Ford. The soldiers were ordered to unload their trucks and drive away. Nixon never regained possession of his tapes.

Eight days later, Becker was having lunch in the White House Mess when he made another startling discovery. A high-ranking Secret Service official offered him a tour of the White House West Wing basement. Becker readily agreed. In a casual, passing comment, the official said, "You know, the microphones are still in the Oval Office." Becker nearly choked. Almost simultaneously, Ford aide Robert Hartmann was told by an informant that "the president ought to know that his Oval Office is still bugged, and you should know that any of these telephones may be bugged, if certain parties just ask the Secret Service to do it." A stunned Hartmann called Becker, who was taken by his Secret Service contact to a room in the basement. When the door was unlocked and opened, according to Becker, there was taping equipment, still in place over a year after Nixon's taping was officially stopped. He then learned that two microphones remained in the presidential desk and two more were still hidden in the walls behind the brass fixtures on the other side of the Oval Office. The wires were cut, but the bugs were still in position. If publicized, they could cause Ford, who had issued strict orders against bugging, a firestorm of embarrassment.

Becker and Hartmann walked in on Ford in the middle of a meeting to tell him the news. "I was very upset," recalled Ford. "Even though I had issued a directive, nothing had been done to remove the equipment. All they did was turn off the equipment. Now that was a step in the right direction, but somebody from behind the scenes could have gone back in and turned the equipment back on. As far as I know that never happened, but the fact that the potential existed bothered me." Hartmann recalled, "The president's jaw tightened. I knew the sign. He slammed what he was reading on the desk, hard enough to rattle the sturdiest microphones." Ford exclaimed, "Dammit! They told me definitely there weren't any—that they'd all been removed long ago. Back when Butterfield first told the Ervin committee that there were tapes." That night the Secret Service dug out the microphones, and the Oval Office was repainted and replastered by the next morning.

Ford soon realized he had to project the image of a strong chief executive: "I wanted to be personally involved in the day-to-day operations. I felt there had not been enough such involvement in the case of my predecessor. . . . I wanted to convey the impression that I was involved and on top of what was taking place." Soon he was tackling the piles in his in-box with Trumanesque speed. At the time, staff secretary Jerry Jones reported that it took only two or three hours for a piece of paper to enter and leave Ford's office: "President Ford is much faster at making decisions than President Nixon, and I have served both. Also, President Ford sees a lot of people in making a decision, while President Nixon saw few or none."

Kissinger described Ford as much more hands-on than Nixon. "Nixon just focused on the general principles," he explained. "Ford went through all the details. He had daily meetings. But he'd never make a decision just on my say-so. If there was disagreement among his advisers, we all got together, he heard us out, he made his decision. Nixon only really wanted to talk about objectives. Ford wanted to know each stage of the negotiation."

The first weeks of the administration were chaotic: there was no shake-down transition period to smooth out bugs, information got to Ford haphazardly, and his carryover vice presidential staffers clashed with Nixon holdovers. Press Secretary Nessen recalled that the staff "was a strange mixture of leftover Nixon people, people from his congressional and vice presidential offices, new people he hadn't worked with before, and [Vice President Nelson] Rockefeller people." Ford's schedule was fouled up repeatedly. On one occasion, a delegation of forty Rotarians from Grand Rapids, Michigan, showed up in the West Wing to greet their old buddy Congressman Jerry while President Ford was huddled in the Cabinet Room with his National Security Council on nuclear weapons strategy. The Rotarians were sadly ushered away.

Ford started off trying to operate through a "spokes of the wheel" White House staff structure similar to his congressional office, with a variety of aides reporting to him directly, but it proved unworkable. Ford recalled,

"Everyone wanted a portion of my time, my accessibility was making me fair game for ridiculous questions, and the 'spokes of the wheel' structure wasn't working well. Without a strong decision maker who could help me set my priorities, I'd be hounded to death by gnats and fleas." "For a time, after Haig departed, the White House was close to anarchy," Nessen recalled. "Literally, no one was in charge of the staff. Advisers wandered in and out of the Oval Office, often taking up the president's time with minor matters." "Eventually, we got away from that type of confusion," said Ford lieutenant Richard Cheney. "As time went on, the president himself became a much more efficient manager of his time and the resources available to him."

At the core of Ford's problems, and successes, as president was a personality and an operating style of extreme collegiality, conditioned by his years of congressional service. "He arrived as the instant president, but with a long background as a successful legislator," argued Donald Rumsfeld, Ford's chief of staff and later defense secretary. Suddenly, "he was in a position that was not legislative but executive. For a person who had been in Washington for thirty years, who knew the town, knew the issues, knew the people—it was understandably impossible for him to believe that most everything he did to become a successful legislative leader was of relatively little value if he wanted to be successful as an executive." Ford aide Robert Hartmann noted that "the person who is drawn to a career as a legislator is usually not the type of person who rises to the top of a corporate or military structure. The essence of the legislator is compromise."

Ford's personality was seemingly devoid of bitterness or rancor. "I have never seen anyone more immune to criticism than Gerald R. Ford," wrote speechwriter John J. Casserly. "He simply accepts it like water rolling off his back in a swimming pool; it is part of the action." This magnanimousness helped Ford navigate through the disaster he triggered just one month into his presidency with his pardon of Richard Nixon. Almost overnight, his approval rating plunged from 71 to 49 percent. "I thought there would be greater forgiveness," Ford lamented. "It was one of the greatest disappointments of my presidency that everyone focused on the individual instead of on the problems the nation faced." Ford made the decision, which in large part cost him a second term, in solitude, without soliciting the opinion of advisers. According to aide James Connor, the experience taught Ford that he needed a system to organize the flow of information and advice into the Oval Office. "It wasn't hard to convince him after the pardon that he damn well better get something like that fast or his presidency was going to be even shorter that it turned out to be."

"Ford had a great executive talent which is a rare one; the ability to find and recruit good people," said Press Secretary Nessen, pointing to strong staff and Cabinet choices like Don Rumsfeld, Dick Cheney, Ed Levi, Carla Hills, George Bush, Dr. Alan Greenspan, James Baker, and Bill Simon. Reflecting on the 1991 Gulf War, Time's Hugh Sidey wrote: "Of the eight men in George Bush's war council, four were brought in directly or shoved along in their journey by Ford. Two others arrived at the fringes of power during Ford's brief tenure, and their talents were allowed full play in the meritocracy." Ford also appointed a fairly strong Cabinet (although it included too many Nixon carryovers) and restored the Cabinet secretariat, which had fallen into disuse since the days of Eisenhower.

"I've been criticized, and I think this is somewhat legitimate, that I don't like to hurt people's feelings," said Ford, explaining his reluctance to fire Nixon people. "And that's my nature, and I guess you're not going to change it. I haven't in sixty-one years." The results were debilitating personnel clashes and executive confusion at the beginning of his presidency, the last things Ford needed. "With Nixon, you had to try to save him from his worst instincts," said a Nixon veteran. "With Ford, you have to try to save him from his best instincts." "How can you get mad at a president who's too nice for his own good?" asked Press Secretary Ron Nessen. Ford ordered his staff: "Don't push people around. Treat them the way you want to be treated. Be courteous." To new speechwriter John Casserly, Ford said: "You write simply. I like simple words and a simple style. Your stuff is damn good. You keep writing the way you do, and I promise that I will become a better speaker," and broke into a smile. "This is a humble man," Casserly recalled thinking.

Ford aide James Cannon reported: "He worked quietly and patiently at the daily presidential tasks with a kind of genial intensity, and from a personal background of solid, if old-fashioned, American values. He knew who he was, and he was very comfortable with who he was. There was not a trace of insecurity about him." While speaking with Brent Scowcroft one day, he suddenly asked, "What does UNESCO do?" After hearing the explanation, Ford said, "Well, thanks, Brent. I was wondering about it the other day, and I thought I would ask you."

Ford's greatest weakness, according to Ford himself: "I am probably too easygoing on people that work for me . . . I tend to overlook." Nessen described one of Ford's rare outbursts of discipline, this one occurring at a staff meeting two months into the administration. Fed up by news leaks, Ford exclaimed: "I'm damn sick and tired of a ship that has such leaky seams. We are being drowned by premature and obvious leaks." In another meeting, during a flurry of anti-Kissinger stories, Ford punched his desk and said, "Goddamn it, I don't want any more of this." But Ford rarely got tough with his staff and rarer still did he fire anyone.

Ford faced no major foreign crises as president, and only three relatively minor ones: the humiliating final U.S. evacuation from Saigon, a smaller evacuation of Americans from the outbreak of civil war in Beirut, and on May 12, 1975, the seizure of Americans on board the U.S. merchant ship *Mayaguez* by Cambodian Khmer Rouge Communists. "We've got a little crisis," Ford announced to his Oval Office guests that Monday morning. Coming as it did after the breakdown of the Sinai talks and in the middle of the New York City fiscal emergency, the *Mayaguez* crisis hit Ford's White House at a time when it needed a victory, and Ford and his men seized the opportunity to assert Ford's untested crisis management skills and toughness.

In declassified records of White House meetings and phone calls during the crisis, participants seem to be as concerned with bellicose posturing and inflicting punitive damage on Cambodia as much as with the actual rescue. Kissinger advised: "Let's look ferocious." In one phone conversation, Ford told Brent Scowcroft: "I think we should just give it to them." Scowcroft: "To show them we mean business." Still fresh in their minds was not only the recently concluded Vietnam nightmare, but the seizure of the U.S. intelligence ship *Pueblo* by North Korea in 1968 and yearlong imprisonment and torture of its crew. Historian John Robert Greene wrote, "Evidence also suggests that the Ford White House believed that their actions were being watched closely by North Korea hoping for another sign of U.S. weakness in Southeast Asia to use as a pretense for launching a second invasion of South Korea." The net result, as one official put it, was "there wasn't a dove in the place."

THE CABINET ROOM
MAY 12–14, 1975

President Ford and National Security Council
RE: *Khmer Rouge Seizure of USS* Mayaguez
National Security Council Meeting Minutes

National Security Council meeting minutes of the *Mayaguez* crisis reveal a Gerald Ford confident in command, snapping off orders to dispatch the carrier USS *Coral Sea*, pull together an amphibious task force, conduct photo surveillance, and issue demands for the release of ship and crew. This was the Ford the public never saw: not a flat-footed blockhead slipping head-first down airplane stairs or creaming innocent bystanders with wayward golf shots, but a strong closed-door CEO, probing his men for facts, expressing anger at information foul-ups, repeatedly clarifying and summarizing the situation.

MAY 12, 12:05 P.M. MEETING

FORD: Please go ahead, Bill, and bring us up to date.

CIA DIRECTOR WILLIAM COLBY: The U.S. container ship *Mayaguez* was seized by the Khmer Communists about 3:15 P.M. local time about seven or eight miles from the Cambodian island of Poulo Wei in the Gulf of Thailand. The ship was able to transmit at least two messages picked up in Jakarta and Manila after the boarding but communications from the ship were quickly broken off.

The ship was en route to a Thai port from Hong Kong.

At last report the ship was being taken to the port of Kompong Som, about sixty miles away, under escort by a Khmer Communist gunboat . . . . We have no hard information on why the Khmer Communists seized the ship as it was en route from Hong Kong to Sattahip, Thailand.

The ship was some sixty miles southwest of Kompong Som, but within eight miles of the island of Poulo Wei, claimed by the Khmer Communists . . . .

A Panamanian charter vessel was seized by the Khmer Communists last week in roughly the same area, but was subsequently released.

FORD: When?

COLBY: We are not sure . . . . There is evidence that some forces landed on at least one of these islands.

FORD: What is the best estimate of where the ship is now?

COLBY: It was proceeding under its own steam at what we estimate to be about ten miles an hour. Considering when it was picked up, it would be in or near the port now.

DEFENSE SECRETARY JAMES SCHLESINGER: When I left the Pentagon, the ship was already only about ten miles out.

FORD: What are our options?

SCHLESINGER: We can have a passive stance or we can be active. We can do such things as seizing Cambodian assets. We can assemble forces.

We could seize a small island as a hostage. We might also consider a blockade. All these options would have to be scrutinized by the Congress because, while you have inherent rights to protect American citizens, you would soon run into the [requirement to notify Congress] . . . .

KISSINGER: As I see it, Mr. President, we have two problems:
—The first problem is how to get the ship back.
—The second problem is how the U.S. appears at this time.
Actions that we would take to deal with one of these problems may not help to deal with the other. For example, I think that if they can get us into a negotiation, even if we get the ship back, it is not to our advantage. I think we should make a strong statement and give a note to the Cambodians, via the Chinese, so that we can get some credit if the boat is released. I also suggest some show of force.
What do we have in the neighborhood of the incident?

SCHLESINGER: We have the *Coral Sea*, which is now on its way to Australia for ceremonies.

FORD: How long would it take to get there?

SCHLESINGER: About two to three days.

FORD: Do we have anything at Subic [U.S. naval base at Subic Bay, Philippines]?

AIR FORCE GENERAL DAVID JONES: We have the carrier *Hancock* and other vessels, but it would take about a day and a half at least to get them down there.

KISSINGER: We may not be able to accomplish much by seizing their assets, since they are already blocked. Perhaps we can seize a Cambodian ship on the high seas. But I think that what we need for the next forty-eight hours is a strong statement, a strong note and a show of force.

SCHLESINGER: That would mean turning around the *Coral Sea* . . . .

FORD: I think we should turn the *Coral Sea* around. We should get everything organized in Subic Bay. We should make a strong statement at once before the news hits from other sources. We should also get a full photo run of the island and of the harbor where the ship is.

VICE PRESIDENT NELSON ROCKEFELLER: May I say something?

FORD: Please.

ROCKEFELLER: I think this will be seen as a test case. I think it will be judged in South Korea. I remember the *Pueblo* case. I think we need something strong soon. Getting out a message and getting people ready will not do it.

I think a violent response is in order. The world should know that we will act and that we will act quickly. We should have an immediate response in terms of action. I do not know if we have any targets that we can strike, but we should certainly consider this. If they get any hostages, this can go on forever . . . .

Now you can take action before you begin to get protests. I believe the authorities there only understand force. There is an old Chinese saying about a dagger hitting steel and withdrawing when it hits steel, and that is the impression that we should convey.

FORD: I think that that is what we will do. We will turn around the *Coral Sea.* We will get the mining ready. We will take action.

KISSINGER: If it is not released by Wednesday, we will mine.

ROCKEFELLER: Public opinion will be against it in order to save lives. Is there anything we can do now?

SCHLESINGER: We can sink the Cambodian navy.

CLEMENTS*: We could hit the patrol ship.

ROCKEFELLER: Or we could seize the island.

RUMSFELD: When did we get word of this?

INGERSOLL†: At 5:15 at the National Military Command Center.

KISSINGER: I agree with the vice president that we should show a strong position. We should also know what we are doing so that it does not look as though we want to pop somebody. We could mine their harbors. This will not get the ship. Or we could take the ship, or we could scuttle it . . . .

FORD: We have now looked at the options. We will issue a statement and we will send a message. We will turn around the *Coral Sea.* We will get a task force assembled at Subic and maybe get it under way. Perhaps we will scramble a force to take the island.

I would like to get something straight now. Brent told me at 7:45 that the ship had been seized, but there should be a quicker way to let us know this.

SCOWCROFT: I agree. That is when I heard of it.

RUMSFELD: I also.

KISSINGER: I was not told until my regular staff meeting this morning,

*William P. Clements, Jr., deputy secretary of defense.
†Robert S. Ingersoll, assistant secretary of state.

and then it was mentioned as an aside.

SCHLESINGER: This is a bureaucratic issue. The NMCC [National Military Command Center] did not become alarmed because it was not a U.S. Navy vessel.

FORD: This would be all right in ordinary times but not now . . . .

SCHLESINGER: What kind of clarification would you want us to use regarding the authority and your relation with the Congress?

FORD: There are two problems:
  —First, the provisions of summer, 1973
  —Second, the War Powers.

Ford was referring to the War Powers Act, passed the year before at the height of the Watergate crisis, which required the president to notify Congress at least forty-eight hours prior to troop deployments.

Regarding the military options, I would like to know how they would be hamstrung and what we want to do. I can assure you that, irrespective of the Congress, we will move . . . .

Let us review it again. Within an hour or so, there will be a public statement. Let us make an announcement ahead of time, and a tough one so that we get the initiative. Let us not tell Congress that we will do anything militarily since we have not decided. I think that it is important to make a strong statement publicly before the news gets out otherwise . . . .

All right. Let us get a message to the Chinese government as soon as possible . . . .

KISSINGER: To bomb, even from Clark [air base], we would be in trouble. This is a symptom of Vietnam. We can bomb from Guam with B-52s or from the carriers. But we should know what we are doing. I am more in favor of seizing something, be it the island, the ship, or Kompong Som.

FORD: This has been a useful discussion. Thank you. I will look forward to seeing the options.

MAY 13, 1975, 10:22 A.M. TO 11:17 A.M. MEETING

FORD: Bill, will you please bring us up to date.

COLBY: The *Mayaguez* is at anchor just off Koh Tang Island, about thirty miles southwest of Kompong Som.

Until late yesterday evening, the ship was being held near where it was seized in the vicinity of Poulo Wei Island, about forty miles further to the southwest.

Shortly after midnight, however, an American reconnaissance aircraft observed the ship at Koh Tang Island. At least two U.S. reconnaissance aircraft have reported receiving small arms fire from a gunboat, and from the *Mayaguez* itself . . . . The latest U.S. reconnaissance flights observed the crew being transferred from the ship via a tugboat to Koh Tang and then being led off toward the interior of the island . . . .

FORD: I do think we have to be certain of our facts. Overnight, Brent gave me a series of different reports that we were getting about the ship's location and about what was happening. We have to be more factual or at least more precise in pointing out our degree of knowledge. What do we know now? How certain are we of the facts with which we are dealing? . . .

JONES: I talked to the commander in Thailand who was in contact with our reconnaissance aircraft. Through this commander, I have the following report from the aircraft. He said that the ship had one anchor up, and one down . . . . Our experts tell us that it is very improbable that the Cambodians can run this ship, so that if there is any indication that the ship is moving, it must be the Americans who are running it.

RUMSFELD: How do we know these things? How do we know that it was the *Mayaguez* that your reconnaissance aircraft saw? . . . .

JONES: It is a positive identification. As I said, the anchors are up and down . . . . Some boats have come alongside. Through fighter runs, we kept them off. Some, however, did get to the boat. We saw some people getting off and going to the island. Then we saw them on the island. They had their heads between their legs. They appeared to be Caucasians . . . .

We can, if necessary, disable the ship. We can hit it a beam, just off the stern. We will not hit people that way. We can do that with pretty high confidence that we can stop the ship from sailing under its own power . . . .

FORD: I am very concerned about the delay in reports. We must have the information immediately. There must be the quickest possible communication to me . . . .

I have a question about that from my World War II experience. That destroyer would have been operating at flank speed for about thirty-six hours. In those days it would not have much fuel left when it arrived at its destination. We would not want it to be dead in the water.

SCHLESINGER: It will not be in that condition. In any case, the carrier will arrive the following morning and it will be able to refuel . . . .

ROCKEFELLER: May I say something?

FORD: Yes.

ROCKEFELLER: I do not think the freighter is the issue. The issue is how we respond. Many are watching us, in Korea and elsewhere. The big question is whether or not we look silly . . . .

RUMSFELD: This is a different set of times from what we were given earlier.

SCOWCROFT: Right.

FORD: I have to go to meet with some congressional people. Can somebody please put all this down so that we have it in writing? (*Schlesinger showed the schedule to the president.*) The *Coral Sea* gets in at eight. What about the *Holt*?

JONES: We are trying to speed it up . . . .

SCHLESINGER: Landing on the ship is to send them a signal. If we start to hit the boats, they know we are up to something. They could kill the Americans, but I doubt it. We have the element of surprise.

FORD: Let's get the facts on the times lined up.

ROCKEFELLER: We do not want a land war in Cambodia.

That evening, a navy jet fighter circling Koh Tang Island prepared to sink a boat that refused to respond to warning shots. Suddenly the pilot spotted a concentration of huddled figures on the deck. The pilot radioed to his superiors, "I believe I see Caucasian faces." The call was bounced up the chain of command into the White House Situation Room, from where the message was relayed into Ford's NSC meeting. "They actually had the pilot on the line," remembered Scowcroft. "I went into the Cabinet Room and described to the president what the situation was." Ford recalled, "If we told the pilot to strafe the boat or sink the boat, we might be losing everything." He ordered, "Let the boat go. Do not fire." The boat turned out to be holding the Mayaguez *crew.*

THE CABINET ROOM, MAY 14, 1975, 6:30 P.M.
PRESIDENT FORD AND BIPARTISAN
CONGRESSIONAL LEADERSHIP

On May 14, Ford approved a plan try to rescue the crewmen of the *Mayaguez*. One unit of marines, from the destroyer *Holt*, would attack the island of Koh Tang, the other would storm the *Mayaguez* by being lowered from helicopters. Over opposition from Defense Secretary Schlesinger and the Joint Chiefs, Ford approved the bombing of targets on the Cambodian mainland to prevent the resupply of Communist forces and, evidently, to inflict punitive damage.

As the operation was unleashed, Ford called the congressional leadership into the Cabinet Room for a briefing. Flanked by aerial photos and maps of the combat zone and State and Defense Department experts, Ford led them through a thirty-five-minute briefing. Some of the legislators were furious both by Ford's plan to bomb the Asian mainland just a year after the end of the Vietnam War, and by his not consulting them prior to launching hostilities, as the War Powers Act required. Ford had ordered the air strikes on Cambodia two hours before this meeting.

FORD: Let me thank you for coming at such short notice. I thought it important to fill you in on the chronology and tell you my decision. I do this to comply with the War Powers Act and in order to keep you abreast of developments. [He went over the chronology of events.]

At noon on Wednesday, we sent a message to the UN that Cambodia was responsible if they didn't release the ship and crew.

At 3:00 P.M., we had another NSC. Here I directed the following. It is most important that you not reveal this.

(1) Marines to land on the *Holt* and board the ship.

(2) Marines to land on the island.

(3) Aircraft from the *Coral Sea* to attack selected military targets at Kompong Som, where their navy is, and at Ream, where there is an airfield.

These operations should begin everywhere simultaneously.

KISSINGER: We published the note to the [UN] Secretary-General as the quickest way to get it delivered in Phnom Penh. We haven't heard anything from Cambodia since the beginning. We delivered

216 • INSIDE THE OVAL OFFICE

it to the Chinese and the Cambodians, so we know it was received.

SCHLESINGER: On the boarding party is the crew, EOD [explosive ordnance disposal], and interpreter. The island landing is simultaneous. It should be under way by nine.

ALBERT:[*] Could Americans be on the boats that will be destroyed?

FORD: There is no way of knowing.

VOICE: Which way were they heading?

FORD: To the mainland. They ignored our warning.

MANSFIELD:[†] Why are we going into the mainland of Asia again when we practically have the boat in our custody?

FORD: There are aircraft and boats in the area. The operation is designed to prevent these forces from interfering with our operations.

MANSFIELD: Is there any information that there are any Americans on the mainland?

FORD: Only that pilot report.

MANSFIELD: Where are the thirty-nine?

FORD: We are not sure where they are.

BYRD:[‡] Couldn't we have intercepted the boat some other way?

FORD: There were no surface ships there until today . . . .

VOICE: Suppose we don't find the Americans? We can't let them take Americans off our ships and keep them.

VOICE: You're talking about an invasion of the mainland.

CEDERBURG:[§] I'm saying it is not acceptable.

EASTLAND:[‖] That's an invasion. Hell, I'm for it.

VOICE: Are we just going into Koh Tang shooting?

FORD: We are going in to insure that none of these assets can be used.

McCLELLAN:[#] Do we have to fire before we know we have to?

FORD: If I were not to, I would be negligent.

McCLELLAN: Can't we wait?

EASTLAND: No, we can't.

ALBERT: The charges on the Floor are that you have violated the law.

FORD: I have the right to protect American citizens . . . .

---

[*]*House Speaker Carl Albert, D-Oklahoma.*
[†]*Senate Minority Leader Mike Mansfield, D-Montana.*
[‡]*Assistant Democratic Senate Leader Robert Byrd, D-West Virginia.*
[§]*Representative Elford Cederberg, R-Michigan.*
[‖]*Senator James Eastland, D-Mississippi.*
[#]*Senator John McClellan, chairman of the Appropriations Committee, D-Arkansas.*

BYRD: Did we give Cambodia a deadline?

KISSINGER: No. We thought it not productive to give them that kind of warning so they could take counteraction.

MANSFIELD: I have to express my concern that we are once again invading by air the Asian mainland. We have plenty of force and I think it will not have a salubrious outcome.

VOICE: I am the author of the Church-Case Amendment. I disagree with Mike. The act wasn't designed to condone piracy but for other purposes. I think the actions were proper.

BYRD: Why were the [congressional] leaders not consulted before the decision to strike the mainland? I'm for getting the ship back, but I think you should have given them a chance to urge caution.

FORD: That's a good question and I'll answer. It is my constitutional responsibility to command the forces and to protect Americans. It was my judgment, based on the advice of the JCS, that this was the prudent course of action. Had we put the marines' lives in jeopardy by doing too little, we would have been negligent. It is better to do too much than too little.

BYRD: My only question is why didn't you at least give them [congressional leaders] a chance to express their reservation?

FORD: We have a separation of powers. The president is the commander-in-chief so long as he is within the law. I exercised my power under the law and I complied with the law. I would never forgive myself if the marines had been attacked by 2,400 Cambodians.

Ford ended the briefing by asking the congressmen to pray for "the very best."

The *Mayaguez* rescue operation ran into trouble quickly. U.S. Marines hitting the beaches of Koh Tang Island ran into fierce fighting from an unexpectedly large Cambodian force. Fifteen marines were killed in the first hour, and eight helicopters were shot down, including one carrying all the unit's radios. "We were lucky all of the marines did not get killed," said one general. Minutes after the bombing runs on the Cambodian mainland began, forty-eight marines from the USS *Holt* stormed onto the *Mayaguez*, only to find no one aboard. Lacking any reliable way of communicating with the Cambodian authorities, the White House then announced publicly that that the U.S. would stop the military operation when the Cambodians announced the release of the crew. An hour later a navy pilot saw the crew of the *Mayaguez* shaking white flags on a fishing boat, and minutes later they were safe on board the USS *Wilson*.

Casualties were high: fifteen U.S. Marines dead, three missing, fifty wounded, another eighteen air police and five crewmen killed in a helicopter accident in Thailand while supporting the operation. In fact more men were killed in the rescue than were on the *Mayaguez*. "The bombing of the Cambodian mainland comes dangerously close to being irresponsible," argued historian John Robert Greene. "Never completely sure of the whereabouts of the crew but faced with evidence that they might have been moved to the mainland [the "Caucasians on the bow" report], Ford nevertheless ordered the bombing, an action taken despite the possibility that the crew might be lost in the process. . . . It can be argued that Ford threw caution to the wind when he agreed to a plan to retrieve the crew of the *Mayaguez*—a plan that was a punitive operation born of a political need."

"All of a sudden, the gloomy national mood began to fade," he recalled. "*Mayaguez* wasn't the only reason, of course; the economy was improving at a rapid rate, but the net effect was that I felt I had regained the initiative, and I determined to do what I could with it."

Despite the *Mayaguez* boost, Ford's chronically collegial, "nice guy" style placed great stresses on his ability to govern effectively. Factional inter-administration warfare and power struggles, a problem in any administration, were especially rampant in Ford's. "During my fifteen months at the White House, I came gradually and reluctantly to the conclusion that Gerald Ford and his staff were unprepared and unable to assume the full power of the presidency," reported Ford speechwriter John Casserly. According to Casserly, "The Ford White House 'team' lacked unity and internal discipline. Unlike the staffs of elected presidents, Mr. Ford's staff had not been forged in the heat of a lengthy political campaign, where team strengths are solidified and weaker members winnowed out."

"I am appalled by the amount of time Ford's men devoted to fighting with, plotting against and leaking bad stories about each other," observed Ford's press secretary Ron Nessen. "I can't believe other administrations squandered as much effort on it as we did." At least five concentric staff factions competed for power and attention: the "Old Boy Network" from Ford's congressional career, the "Grand Rapids Crowd" of longtime friends, a group of younger aides, a Rockefeller faction of policy specialists, and holdover Nixon people. Longtime Ford aide Robert Hartmann blamed the failures of the Ford administration on the Nixon leftovers. To Hartmann, "There was never, for all thirty months he was president, a truly Ford Cabinet or Ford Staff. There was an incompatible, uncontrolled, contentious collection of Praetorians, many bitterly resentful of the few old Ford loyalists who hung on to the end. [They] stubbornly shielded Jerry Ford from his better self."

In one meeting, Ford's top advisers complained to him about "internal anarchy" in his White House. One aide, Bryce Harlow, declared, "Now, Mr. President, if you have to fire 'em all, you have got to put a stop to it." The plea fell on deaf ears, as Ford saw the problem as leaks, not staff anarchy. "The nice guy approach doesn't always work," noted Ron Nessen.

Finally, after fifteen months in office, Ford announced a major personnel shake-up. He fired his outspoken, independent Secretary of Defense James Schlesinger and replaced him with Chief of Staff Donald Rumsfeld. He relieved Kissinger of his post as national security adviser, freeing him up to concentrate on being secretary of state (he'd held both jobs until now). Kissinger's deputy Brent Scowcroft got the NSC job. Ford fired CIA Director William Colby (who Ford felt had gone too far in opening up closets full of agency "skeletons" to public view) and installed George Bush in his place. Sniping and skirmishing continued into the election year of 1976, however, threatening Ford's reelection effort with wasted energy and confused campaign messages. "President Ford's candidacy is threatened by internal strife among the workhorses that make a campaign go," reported Tom Jarriel of ABC News. "Most feel, as one put it, that 'the president has not taken charge of this place.'"

Ford came very close to squeaking through to another term: he came back from thirty-three points behind Jimmy Carter in polls taken in the summer of 1976 to within one percentage point of victory on the eve of the election. "Nothing in life is more important than the ability to communicate effectively," Ford later wrote, but in the campaign, Ford was crippled by his flat, plodding speaking style, and he was unable to project the image of strong leader. In a TV debate with Carter, Ford made the inexplicable mistake of insisting that there was no Soviet domination of Poland. He meant that the Polish people's spirit was free, but Ford's stubbornness in clinging to his original phrasing made him look foolish, and may have cost him the election.

By most measurements, Ford is considered the least historically significant of the modern presidents—his exceedingly short term in office is remembered for the suicidal Nixon pardon and little else. When asked how he would summarize his presidency, Ford said modestly that he wanted to be remembered as a "nice person, who worked at the job, and who left the White House in better shape than when he found it." But Henry Kissinger offered a stronger, and perhaps more accurate epitaph: "He saved the country. He took over in a very difficult period and he steered us through great problems in so understated a manner and with such decency. He's never been given adequate credit for it, because people forget how easily it could have been otherwise."

Ford did rack up some real achievements: he managed to make slow, steady progress on improving the economic mess Nixon left him, including 12 percent inflation, mainly by killing most of the spending bills sent him by the overwhelmingly Democratic Congress. The *Wall Street Journal* editorialized, "He wielded the veto more often than any other modern president, holding a profligate Congress in check and falling only a veto or two short of curing the energy mess. By the time he left office inflation was down to 5 percent and real economic growth was 6 percent." Although the Nixon/Ford/Kissinger policy of détente withered in the mid-1970s under relentless assault from congressional enemies, Ford made progress in superpower relations, personally negotiating the 1974 Vladivostok Agreement, which broke a two-and-a-half-year impasse and set the stage for new SALT agreements. Ford and Kissinger brokered an interim peace accord between Israel and Egypt, and initiated an historic turn in U.S. policy toward southern Africa, committing the American government to supporting majority rule for black Africans.

What the world could not see was that inside the Oval Office, Jerry Ford possessed that rarest of executive talents, a skill rarer still among presidents: the ability to improve and grow. His decency and humility prevented him from cracking his staff's heads together, but in other ways, he got better at the job.

"President Ford came into office with wonderful training and success that didn't suit him for an executive function," said his chief of staff and defense secretary, Donald Rumsfeld. "He started out functioning basically like a legislator. Every day he was president he got better at being an executive. Within a year he became an exceedingly good executive. He began to delegate effectively, to become more strategic, instead of being consumed with what was in his in-box. He was an excellent president in the second half of his term and he would have been an even better president had he been reelected." Rumsfeld's successor Richard Cheney reported, "By the end of his presidency he was a very tough customer to deal with. If papers were not prepared properly and were not in on time, he canceled the meeting."

"His first and foremost problem was he really hadn't thought of being president," said Ford's first staff chief Alexander Haig. "He was about to retire. He really wasn't sure he could be president. This terrible burden was thrust upon him. By the time he realized he was doing the job well, it was too late for him."

Ford proved that a president can be too collegial, too patient, even too decent an executive inside the Oval Office. At times, a president has to be ruthless, cold-blooded, and brutal.

To Jerry Ford's credit as a human being, these talents were beyond him.

CHAPTER 8

Jimmy Carter
The Technocrat Executive

*"I'm an engineer at heart, and I like to understand details
of things that are directly my responsibility."*

JIMMY CARTER, 1976

CAMP DAVID
SEPTEMBER 15, 1978

Anwar Sadat was furious. The Egyptian president had packed his bags, ordered a helicopter, and was storming out of Camp David, taking the future of Mideast peace with him.

After ten days of excruciating, truculent negotiations with Israeli Prime Minister Menachem Begin mediated by President Jimmy Carter, Sadat decided that an Israeli-Egyptian peace treaty was now impossible, that Begin wasn't sincere, and that the risks he took in coming here weren't worth it any more. So he and the entire Egyptian negotiating team were now assembling on the porch of their cabin to say farewell and await the chopper.

A white-faced Secretary of State Cyrus Vance burst in on Carter with the news. Carter was mortified. Before him flashed a dark vision of what might be, a Soviet-Arab alliance that would threaten Israel and the United States for years to come. Carter looked out to the mountains outside his window, said a prayer, and then, without knowing why, switched to formal clothes for the walk over to Sadat's cabin. Carter could understand Sadat's feelings: at one point during the proceedings, Begin so aggravated him that he privately called the Israeli leader a "psycho."

The negotiations were so difficult and complex that Carter's national security adviser, Zbigniew Brzezinski, proposed to the president that the

Americans secretly monitor and tape-record the quarters of the Israeli and Egyptian delegations to gather intelligence on their negotiating strategy. Carter shot down the proposal, and did not allow any recordings to be made of any White House or presidential activity, secretly or otherwise, at any point during his presidency. (The Egyptians and Israelis feared such surveillance anyway, and conducted their strategy sessions while wandering deep in the woods of Camp David.) Given Carter's moral code and the post-Watergate mania over taping, his no-taping policy was understandable.

Carter did, however, follow a daily ritual of tape-recording throughout his presidency. At the end of most of his workdays, he dictated his personal thoughts into a handheld audiocassette recorder, and had these notes transcribed by his secretary, Susan Clough. In one entry, Carter reflected on his own frustrations with Menachem Begin during pre–Camp David meetings earlier that year: "I told him that peace in the Middle East was in his hands, that he had a unique opportunity to either bring it into being or kill it. . . . My guess is that he will not take the necessary steps to bring peace to Israel—an opportunity that may never come again."

When Carter arrived at Sadat's cabin, he pulled Sadat inside and coldly warned him of the consequences of his action, in the clearest and toughest of terms: "It will mean first of all an end to the relationship between the United States and Egypt. There is no way we can ever explain this to their people. It would mean an end to this peacekeeping effort, into which I have put so much investment. It would probably mean the end of my presidency because this whole effort will be discredited. And last but not least, it will mean the end of something that is very precious to me: my friendship with you. Why are you doing it?" Shaken but still furious, Sadat explained that the Israelis were provoking the breakdown as a trick, in order to lock Sadat into the concessions he already made and use them as the starting point in future negotiations. Carter said to stick with him another day or two, pledging that he would not let this happen. Sadat then stared at Carter and said, "If you give me this statement, I will stick with you to the end." Sadat stayed.

For the next two days Carter hurled himself into negotiating sessions, elbowing aside his own specialists and huddling up with Israeli and Egyptian technical experts to review and rework maps and legal documents. On the night of Saturday, September 16, Brzezinski wrote in his notes: "He is driving himself mercilessly, spending most of his time either debating with the Egyptians or the Israelis or drafting and revising texts that are being submitted to him. He has single-handedly written the proposed document for the Sinai formula." Senior Carter aide Jack Watson observed: "You cannot find two personalities more different than Begin and Sadat. Sadat was almost a mystic. Begin was like a Talmudic scholar. And Carter was in the middle. He was able to delve down into the thousand-year history and show Begin and Sadat that he understood the historical bases of their positions." To succeed, Watson said, "required enormous in-depth knowledge of the subject, enormous patience, incredible mediation skills, high credibility with Begin and Sadat, and the ability to sustain effort." It also required a style like Carter's, which old Washington hand "Tommy the Cork" Cochran called "the smile and the dagger—very smooth, very tough."

On Sunday, September 17, 1978, an exhausted Carter hammered out the final details of the agreement with Carter and Begin, and the three helicoptered to the White House for the signing ceremony. According to Zbigniew Brzezinski, "The outcome was a triumph of Carter's determined mastery of enormous detail and of his perseverance in sometimes angry and always complex negotiations. He showed himself to be a skillful debater, master psychologist, and a very effective mediator. Without him, there would have been no agreement." Carter "played the role of draftsman, strategist, therapist, friend, adversary, and mediator," declared National Security Council official William Quandt. As the conference ended, however, Carter and Sadat thought Begin agreed to an indefinite freeze on Israeli settlements in the West Bank and Gaza pending agreement on self-government. Begin later insisted he agreed only to a three-month freeze. Without any verbatim notes or recordings, the dispute was unresolved and would cause problems for the next twenty years.

The Camp David Accords were the zenith of Carter's presidency and the triumph of his skills as the best technician and planner of any modern president. Carter was the first engineer president since Hoover, and he was the ultimate technocrat executive. It was Carter's style as a technocrat that would help trigger the greatest achievements and worst mistakes of his narrowly won presidency.

On his first day as president, with the sounds of his inaugural parade ringing in his ears, Jimmy Carter stood inside the White House mansion after a quick check of his new living quarters, wanting to go straight to his new office. He had no idea where it was. "I never saw the Oval Office till after I was elected president," he explained. He then simply announced to his Secret Service detail that he was going to the Oval Office, and followed them down the hall. Once alone, Carter looked around the office to ponder the immensity of what he faced. He was not a politician by nature, but a manager and an engineer—and now he stood at the controls of the most complex organization ever built—the U.S. government. And he was in rapture. "The newness of each detail," Carter wrote of his first afternoon in the Oval Office, "made those hours one of the most exciting afternoons of all."

Carter would preside over a transitional presidency, symbolizing the death of the New Deal and Imperial Presidency eras and the dawn of a new age of limited government, fiscal and social conservatism. His term would be consumed largely with trying to manage an energy crisis that sparked runaway inflation: when Carter was sworn in, the country was suffering the worst natural-gas shortage in history, and his presidency ended with oil shocks triggered by upheaval in Iran. Carter also faced the intractable challenge of forging a centrist governing coalition with a sharply rebellious Congress as the parties were polarizing to the extremes—Democrats to the McGovernite Left, Republicans to the Reaganite Right.

In a reflection of his roots as a populist, small-town Democrat, Carter put a replica of Truman's THE BUCK STOPS HERE sign on his desk. A painting of Truman was hung in the Cabinet Room. Carter moved quickly to tear down the trappings of the imperial presidency that climaxed with Nixon: he carried his own suit bag on trips, placed daughter Amy in public school, banned the playing of "Hail to the Chief," turned down White House thermostats, sold the presidential yacht *Sequoia,* cut limousines of the White House staff, and slashed all White House salaries (except his own) by 10 percent.

It was common for Carter to be at his desk at 5:30 A.M., and he could often be found, in his blue jeans, working late into the evening, voraciously consuming forests of paperwork. "He worked a driven, disciplined, twelve- to sixteen-hour day," said his vice president, Walter Mondale, "did his work way into the night, and was always ready for every meeting." Carter used the Oval Office mainly for ceremonies, and preferred to work out of the small study next door, especially early in his term. For the Oval Office, he brought in from retirement the old desk made from the timbers of the ship *Resolute,* which Queen Victoria had given to President Rutherford B. Hayes, last used by JFK. In the study, classical music played all day long on a Panasonic phonograph, the selections chosen by Carter's secretary, who typed up the playlist on yellow three-by-five cards for Carter's reference: Bach, Verdi, Puccini, Mozart. On his desk was a Bible, as well as a memento reading (like the one on JFK's desk) OH, GOD, THY SEA IS SO GREAT AND MY BOAT IS SO SMALL.

The sign was a gift from Carter's hero, Admiral Hyman Rickover, the "father of the nuclear navy" and like Carter, a cold, methodical technocrat. A young Georgia-bred navy man who graduated in 1946 (ranking 59 in a class of 820) from the United States Naval Academy, Carter was rejected for a

Rhodes Scholarship. He asked to be transferred to Rickover's command, considered among the toughest in the navy. Although he later implied that he was a nuclear scientist, he spent only a year in the nuclear submarine program and took one non-credit semester of nuclear physics 101 at Union College in Schenectady, New York. He left the navy to help with the family business, becoming a farmer and small-business manager. "I like to run things," Carter announced. His family farm and peanut warehouse eventually grossed $2.5 million.

Carter served in the Georgia Senate from 1963 to 1967, and in 1966 he was defeated in his bid to become governor of Georgia. In despair, he became a born-again Christian, a transformation that redefined his world-view and affected virtually everything he did from then on. He ran again for governor in 1970, and won, compiling a record as an efficient managerial governor. He enforced "zero-based budgeting" on the Georgia bureaucracy, cut the number of agencies from 300 to 22, and left office with a $50 million budget surplus without raising taxes. In the process he demonstrated contempt for the sleazy aspects of political patronage and privilege, and refused to toady to the state legislature. In a preview of his presidency, his relations with the Georgia legislature were often fractious.

Hamilton Jordan, then Carter's executive secretary, said Carter "is not easy to get close to. He doesn't have enough time in his life to let people get close. He doesn't understand the personal element in politics, though nobody is better at campaigning." Historian Erwin Hargrove wrote, "At the core of Jimmy Carter's political personality was the imperative for mastery. His life was to be a testing ground on which he would prove himself, and he was to do it alone. This was the source of his strength and his weakness as a political man. His great achievements—winning the presidential campaign and his foreign policy successes—were personal achievements."

People who worked with Carter marveled at his raw intellect: "When it came to understanding the issues of the day, Jimmy Carter was the smartest public official I've ever known," noted House Speaker Thomas "Tip" O'Neill. "The range and extent of his knowledge were astounding; he could speak with authority about energy, the nuclear issue, space travel, the Middle East, Latin America, human rights, American history, and just about any other topic that came up." Carter's secretary of state, Cyrus Vance, observed, "I think of all the presidents I've worked with—and I've worked with many—in terms of sheer intellect, he had more brain power than any of them." Adviser Hedley Donovan noted, "He could master masses of material, the more technical and statistical the better, and it would stay mastered." Carter's sister,

Ruth, described him as "a very logical, methodical, punctual, well-programmed man with a mind like a steel trap. I would not say that he's particularly creative or innovative." During the campaign, Carter worked through an issues book covering Abortion to Zero-based budgeting, discussing the issues not in priority order, but in alphabetical order.

Whenever Jimmy Carter's management style is discussed, the ghost of his White House tennis courts rises up to haunt and chase him through the halls of history. No story better illustrates the charge that Carter was a relentless micromanager besotted with detail than the charge that he personally controlled the schedule for the White House tennis courts. It is an irresistible image: a president keeping a chart on his desk, approving court reservations, reviewing requests for mixed doubles and tournaments, fiddling with pencil marks while Angola and Afghanistan burn. The truth is slightly more complicated.

In 1978, former chief Carter speechwriter James Fallows publicly accused Carter of personally approving tennis court requests sent to him by memo. Carter denied it, but conceded that he did direct his secretary to "receive requests from members of the White House staff" to avoid having two parties trying to play at once. Professor Stanly Godbold of Mississippi State University, who studied Carter's presidential records extensively, concluded that "Carter did schedule the tennis courts, usually through his secretary Susan Clough. Former presidents usually restricted the courts to First Family use, mostly to avoid hassles. Carter felt it was a shame not to share the courts with his staff and Cabinet. Carter tried to work out a plan where they could use the tennis court and swimming pool also, out of generosity." Carter's press secretary Jody Powell called it "a classic case of no good deed goes unpunished. He wanted to make the courts available to other people when he wasn't using them, so he said, schedule it through his secretary Susan Clough. It was a fairly decent thing to do."

While Carter may not have literally scheduled the White House tennis courts himself, an inspection of the President's Secretary's File at the Carter Presidential Library, his daily "out-box" does reveal a stark reality: Jimmy Carter wasn't just a micromanager—he was a *molecular* manager, inspecting tiny pieces of White House operations and poking his nose into minute details down to the subatomic particle level.

As soon as he assumed command of the White House, Carter submerged and saturated himself in detail, probing and burrowing for statistics, appendixes, and back-up charts, more numbers, more data. He did not come up for air for four years. "You can overwhelm yourself with minutia," said Jerry Ford, now watching Carter from the sidelines. "Anyone who works hard—and Carter has a reputation for that—is inclined to dive into everything. You can't do that." Carter knew the risks of his style and resolved to himself to improve: in a tape-recorded diary entry at the beginning of his term, he said he hoped he would delegate more than he did as governor, since "it's just not within the bounds of human capability to go into as much detail as I did in Georgia." But as his files and his staff reveal, he couldn't help himself, and he soon was running the White House like his peanut warehouse.

On his first day in office Carter received a memo from cousin Hugh Carter, Jr. (known by some as "Cousin Cheap"), whom he had installed to watch White House expenses and administration. The memo offered a detailed breakdown of the White House motor pool fleet. Carter demanded in a note on the margin, "Why so many?" On February 5, Carter fired off a note to Hugh: "There are about thirty people working at Blair House. Have person in charge confirm need for this many." On February 7, he asked another staffer: "Explain the barber shop staffing/pay to me." During the next few weeks, Carter personally signed off on individual White House staff travel requests, including pre-advance work for Town Meeting sites, sometimes challenging them with margin notes, and approving them with the caveat: "Let it be commercial, tourist." Until his seventh month in office, Carter personally reviewed a detailed monthly breakdown of staff travel. In Carter's defense, both Eisenhower and Kennedy expressed interest in individual expense reports at one time or another.

Carter's frugal obsession with details was in part a legitimate attempt to control what he saw as an out-of-control White House budget. He was also congenitally cheap, and he seemed to relish flaunting his parsimony. At early breakfast meetings with Congress, Carter authorized only dry rolls and coffee. The legislators protested and demanded eggs. (For once, Carter was weak: they got their eggs.) At a summit meeting at Carter's pond house in Plains, Georgia, twenty of the top economists and bankers in America suffered for hours without food, snacks, or even water. The president of the Bank of America reportedly locked himself in a bathroom while trying to slurp water from a faucet. At his weekly presidential breakfasts with senior staff in the Cabinet Room (always preceded by Carter saying grace), Carter charged each of the participants $1.75.

In a move that seems silly by any measurement, Carter in his first days in the Oval Office ordered up no less than three separate reports on newspaper and magazine subscriptions in the White House for his personal review. On the first report, Carter asked for an addendum to cover subscriptions in the

White House mansion, canceled everybody's Sunday papers, and decreed that people in adjacent offices must share their newspapers. "Be strict," he commanded in the margin. On the follow-up report on mansion subscriptions, Carter fastidiously crossed out newspapers allocated for himself, ushers, and guests and painstakingly marked up the report with check marks and notes before ordering yet another analysis. One Carter aide defended him as trying to set an example on cost control, but Carter was making decisions down to the hundreds and tens of dollars, judgments that surely could have been delegated. "At times, I thought he was like a sculptor who did not know when to throw away his chisel," noted Brzezinski.

"Carter had a tremendous appetite for detail," asserted Joseph Califano, Carter's secretary of health, education and welfare. "I'd send him a seventy-five-page document on welfare reform, and he'd send it back to me with two or three decisions checked off on each page." Frank Carlucci, then the number two man in the CIA, said, "He was an intelligence briefer's delight, because he loved to absorb information. How well he integrated that information is another question. He was taken by total personal surprise when the Soviets invaded Afghanistan. The CIA was not surprised—we warned him it was coming. But he just couldn't believe the Russians would do it." Robert Kimmitt, then a national security aide, reported that after reviewing the foreign assistance budget, Carter returned the presentation sheets not only with questions, but with notations and grammatical and spelling corrections as far back as the appendix pages. "On the one hand it made you feel good that he was reading what you prepared as closely as he did," said Kimmitt, but "he may have lost sight of the forest for such intimate interaction with the trees." A Pentagon official, also pondering forests and trees, said of Carter: "My God, he was a leaf man!"

In his first two years, Carter functioned as his own budget director, ordering over twenty-eight different presidential reorganization studies and calling in experts two and three levels down in the budget hierarchy to scrutinize financial minutia. Early in his term, officials from the Office of Management and Budget (OMB) were stunned to find out that they were going to brief the president on the defense budget instead of his senior staff. In one meeting that started at 3:00 P.M. and ran for the next eight hours, the president consumed all the data the budget bureaucrats could throw at him.

"Carter governed by memo," reported historian Stanly Godbold. "He liked to operate one-on-one, he didn't give his people much chance to bounce ideas off one another, outside of ritualized Cabinet meetings." In his memoirs, Carter explained his reliance on memos as a time-saver, noting that he could read a memo in a matter of moments and achieve the same result as a five- or ten-minute meeting. "At times, Carter could also be extremely pedantic," wrote Zbigniew Brzezinski. "Memos addressed to him would come back with penciled corrections of spelling mistakes or grammatical improvements." He was America's first politically correct president: on his copy of a proposed form letter to Cabinet members ("Dear Mr. Secretary") he intoned: "Do not use the sexist address."

"The president liked to have decision memoranda," said Carter's agriculture secretary, Bob Bergland. "He didn't really like to mix it up in a meeting. He didn't like to debate or listen to arguments; he was very uncomfortable in that area." Bergland's department once sent Carter an agricultural initiative document with a twelve-page executive summary, 100 pages of detailed documentation, and 600 pages of charts. "President Carter called me up on a Saturday afternoon and asked me about chart 3 on page 412. I was embarrassed because I hadn't read it. To be honest with you, I had no intention of reading it." Bergland reported that his colleagues in the Defense Department were "flabbergasted" at Carter's ravenous lust for data. "Harold Brown, the secretary of defense, was telling me one time that there was some national defense issue with documentation that went into hundreds of pages and the president read it all and wanted more." Bergland concluded, "He didn't care about people's opinions. He wanted to know what the facts were and he wanted to see the hard data." "He was an engineer," said Bergland, "and he delighted in seeing pieces and parts. He wanted to see everything move, but he wanted to inspect all the pieces." "President Carter wanted to know every detail about everything," recalled Carter's secretary of education, Shirley Hufstedler. "He knew all the details about all the programs of all the departments, whether it was the Department of Defense, the Department of State, or the Department of Education. He had studied them all, and, believe me, that is a chore."

In meetings, Carter would often show off his mastery of detail. In one conference, when energy industry officials proposed a cost hike that appeared small in percentage terms, Carter rejected the plan by declaring that one tenth of a percent equated to $10 billion. Another time, Carter rattled off budget figures for military programs that the Joint Chiefs of Staff did not know. One staffer convinced Carter to stop such exhibitions on the grounds that he was badgering the experts and ran the risk of blocking the flow of information. Pedro Sanjuan, who joined the White House staff to work on the Panama Canal treaties, said Carter was "a very strange man, who gave you the impression of being humble and deferred to people in the room, but wanted everybody to know he had done his homework and had read things." A Carter assistant said he "had the pride an uneducated man takes in his intelligence. History and experience were not important to him. He had the vain belief that he could move into an area and master it."

Former Vice President Walter Mondale said that Carter "seemed to have that engineer's method of describing things. If you asked about the car, he'd want to tell you how to build an engine. He figured that if he told you the details, the central and sometimes very technical arguments, then honest minds would be driven by the power of the calculation. Of course it doesn't work that way." In his own defense, Carter later explained: "I spent hour after hour studying the structure of the federal government in preparation of the budgets and really did a lot of detailed work on the budgets because I felt that this was one of the managerial weapons or tools that I had to exert my influence in a definitive way. And my budget came through Congress relatively intact."

Carter's displays of technical mastery sometimes backfired in meetings, like one with the chiefs of the auto companies on pollution-control devices. Energy Secretary James Schlesinger recalled: "Carter was very concerned about the subject and had studied it very carefully because he cared very deeply about the environment. His presidential style tended to be to hector and to preach more than other presidents have done in private meetings. He told the auto executives immediately what was distressing him. He said he was very disturbed that we hadn't made more progress in limiting pollution from automobiles and expressed his annoyance at what he considered the failure of these companies. 'Why don't you use the new Japanese converter?' asked Carter. The heads of the auto companies looked blank. They had brought along a technical expert from the University of Michigan. Pretty soon there was a conversation between the president and the professor about the merits of this Japanese converter. The executives knew very little of the technical aspects. But Carter, by God, understood the technical issues! I just marveled at this—first, that a president of the United States would take the time to master this kind of detail, and second, that he would waste so much time to do it. The meeting was a failure, because while Carter demonstrated he knew more than the auto executives about their business, he did not induce them to be supportive of White House policy. It just annoyed them."

At the root of Carter's troubles was the paradox that he was the country's chief political executive, but he hated politics. "Carter's anti-political attitudes used to drive me nuts, because you couldn't get him to grapple with a political problem," said Mondale. "Carter thought politics was sinful," Mondale observed. After being denied a long list of federal appointments, an amazed House Democratic majority leader Jim Wright of Texas drawled, "The president thought there was something tawdry—tawdry—about the idea of political appointments." Wright often met with Carter, and had the feeling that Carter didn't listen to him. "He may suffer from the delusion that elected officials are all a bit corrupt," Wright speculated. By Carter's one-year anniversary as president, public support for him was collapsing, and Carter's response, according to his assistant Peter Bourne, was "to work ever harder, putting in even longer hours reading memos and studying option papers—as much as 300 per night. Increasingly, however, the public interpreted his style as conveying an attitude of moral superiority."

"He was a proud man, very certain of his moral and intellectual superiority," contended Betty Glad, professor of government at the University of South Carolina. Pope John Paul II once recalled a conference with Carter by smiling and saying: "You know, after a couple of hours with President Carter I had the feeling that two religious leaders were conversing." Carter's attorney general, Griffin Bell, recalled, "I was in the room when he fired [UN Ambassador] Andy Young, and it was terrible to have him talk to Andy the way he did . . . President Carter was big on using the word 'disgrace,' and he accused Andy Young of bringing disgrace on him when he met with the PLO." Press Secretary Jody Powell saw Carter's virtuous streak as an asset: "One of his strengths, before, during and after his presidency is that sense of moral purpose. You always felt like he was trying to figure out what the right thing to do was, in the finest sense of the word." "Behavior Carter enthusiasts attribute to high integrity was often the product of stubbornness instead," noted Leo Ribuffo, historian at George Washington University. "Carter rejected the imperial presidency, yet in this respect, he was an imperious president."

A crippling by-product of Carter's executive style was his repeated failure to effectively organize his White House. One disillusioned aide sniped that the Carter White House was "like a movie set for a Marx Brothers picture, only instead of four brothers, there were about a dozen." Carter brought a tough, loyal cadre of Georgians into the White House with him, but apart from chief domestic policy adviser Stuart Eizenstat, none of them had any significant Washington experience. And it showed. Aide Bourne wrote, "By filling jobs with people who had no federal government experience, or who were weak, ineffectual, or there solely through loyalty to Jordan, Carter was denied the range of talent and expertise he desperately needed in dealing with Washington."

Compounding his staff's inexperience was Carter's decision to forego a chief of staff and rely on a "spokes of the wheel" structure for his White House staff, with a dozen or so top aides reporting directly to him. Carter explained, "That's the way I structured my warehouse, that's the way I structured my governor's office, and that's the way I structured the White House." Jimmy Carter was, in effect, his own Haldeman. "Policy, politics, and strategy was to come together only in the Oval Office," wrote Bourne. "He did not want someone, like [Jack] Watson, with a broad range of talents, integrating and synthesizing under him. Much less did he want an old Washington hand, with political standing in his own right, in that role." Bourne cited an ex–Georgia congressman, who said, "Carter did not like to have people around him whom he felt intimidated by, who he felt were smarter than he."

Carter's "spokes of the wheel" management structure was doomed from the start. "It was a mistake for all of us not to have had a strong official chief of staff at the outset," said Jody Powell. "Carter didn't want to put one person in a position to control the flow of information and access to him." Mondale explained: "Try as hard as he could, there just wasn't time enough to handle the presidency with the mass of people expecting direct access."

Eventually, Carter brought in heavyweight Washington pros like Robert Strauss and Lloyd Cutler to beef up his staff. But inexplicably, he appointed Hamilton Jordan, longtime "first among equals" of the staff and mastermind of Carter's come-from-nowhere election triumph, as official White House chief of staff. This was a colossal mismatch, since Jordan, while a gifted political strategist, by his own admission had almost none of the administrative skills required for his new job. Jordan spent much of the Carter years ducking charges of arrogance and insensitivity to inside-the-Beltway codes of behavior. Carter tried to compensate for his staff's Washington inexperience by giving veteran Capitol insider Vice President Walter Mondale and his seasoned staff an unprecedented degree of influence and proximity, an experiment that, despite inevitable strains, helped Carter.

Carter's dealings with his Cabinet as a body, like most presidents, were troubled. Carter picked a team of Washington pros, exhorted them to play as a team, gave them authority to pick their own deputies, and began meeting with them as a group once a week, preceded by a prayer breakfast in the White House mess. Cabinet meetings "were almost useless," according to Zbigniew Brzezinski, "the discussions were desultory, there was no coherent theme to them." During the meetings Brzezinski would knock off his pile of weekly newsmagazines by reading them under the table. After a while, Carter held fewer and fewer Cabinet meetings. Starting in June 1977, Carter conducted weekly 7:30 A.M. presidential breakfasts in the Cabinet Room to review foreign policy, and it became a key decision-making forum. The major players included Vance, Mondale, Brzezinski, Defense Secretary Harold Brown, and Hamilton Jordan.

An example of failed teamwork was the ongoing feud between Carter's reserved, cautious Secretary of State Cyrus Vance and his outspoken, activist National Security Adviser Brzezinski. "Zbig would sit at his side," recalled Hamilton Jordan, "stimulating new ideas, creating long-range plans, and sifting through the mountains of foreign policy papers that regularly came to the White House for the president. Vance would be the diplomat, meeting with ambassadors and foreign dignitaries: the manager, trying to control the sprawling State Department bureaucracy; and the implementer, responsible for making policies work. The president-elect was not worried about conflicts, and relished their different ideas and lively debate. The roles were clear to him. Zbig would be the thinker, Cy would be the doer, and Jimmy Carter would be the decider." "I deliberately chose advisers with disparate points of view," explained Carter. "I wanted the very conservative, stable, and cautionary reaction of the State Department on the one hand and the more dynamic, innovative advice from the National Security staff on the other hand. Sometimes the two points of view conflicted. But in foreign policy and defense, the final decisions were always mine. I wanted a broad assortment of opinions before I made a judgment."

The Vance-Brzezinski tensions however, more often produced debilitating friction rather than creative sparks. According to Mondale, the two "were fighting all the time." Brzezinski complained that Vance "preferred to litigate issues endlessly, to shy away from the unavoidable ingredient of force in dealing with contemporary international realities, and to have an excessive faith that all issues can be resolved by compromise." Vance, in turn, concluded, "It was an unsatisfactory relationship between myself and the national security adviser on a number of things—not all of them—but particularly on U.S.-Soviet matters. I think it hurt the president." Carter's naïveté soon extended to superpower relations. In March 1977, two months into his term, he packed Vance off to Moscow carrying a surprise public proposal for deep cuts in nuclear weapons, without the usual quiet prior preparation between diplomats. The Russians instantly shot down both the proposal and a backup plan and sent Vance home empty-handed. It took two years to draft a new SALT agreement.

In a move that was until then without precedent in American history, Carter invited his wife, Rosalynn, by most accounts an influential and effective activist First Lady, to attend Cabinet meetings. During the sessions she sat by the door taking notes, and soon she was even attending national security briefings for the White House staff. "I thought it was important for me to know generally what was going on," Mrs. Carter later explained. "I had campaigned all over the country telling people what my husband was going to do; also, when I went out I had press conferences, and the reporters would ask me what he was doing. I needed to know." Some members of the Cabinet resented the intrusion, though. Secretary of Agriculture Bob Bergland said, "People thought that they were sort of being snooped on." The move illustrated a surprising insensitivity to the dynamics of teamwork and to the egos of his own Cabinet members.

Carter's shortcomings were to bear bitter fruit in his relations with Congress, which were, at least on the surface, a comic opera of ineptitude and screw-ups. Carter faced a huge challenge in the Ninety-fifth and Ninety-sixth Congresses—although his fellow Democrats controlled two-thirds of the seats, the post-Watergate climate left them unusually rebellious and assertive. To make matters worse for Carter, who had dealt in Georgia with a more pliable, one-party legislature that met only a few weeks a year, the structure of power in Congress suddenly fragmented from 22 committee chairmen to 172 subcommittees, making congressional relations an exponentially more complex process. Into this turmoil Carter resolutely blundered, armed with a flood of legislative proposals and a disaster-prone congressional relations staff. In an act of supreme naïveté, Carter decided to tackle a host of contentious and long-delayed national priorities all at the same time, including the Panama Canal treaties; energy conservation; industrial deregulation; and tax, welfare, civil service, and Social Security reform. Carter himself conceded, "There is no doubt I gave Congress too heavy an agenda—twelve or fifteen important issues the first year I was in. I would have been better off in the public's estimation as well as with Congress if I had narrowed those down to one or two."

To manage this torrent of action, Carter appointed a congressional relations staff that was, in the words of Agriculture Secretary Bergland, "an unmitigated disaster." Bergland explained: "They were amateurs in a lot of ways but they were honest about it. His government was really loaded with honest amateurs. It got off to a terrible start. . . . The president brought in people to run the Congressional Relations Office who didn't know the Speaker of the House, Tip O'Neill." Carter chose trusted Georgian Frank Moore to head up his lobbying effort, and a close Carter associate remembered: "I knew the Carter administration was finished the day I heard Moore was to be in charge of congressional relations." Moore went on to become a respected and successful lobbyist, but his first days in Congress were murder. Carter aide Jack Watson recalled, "We made a lot of mistakes. Frank got better and better at it and ultimately put together an effective team on Carter's behalf in the House and Senate. We built an impressive domestic record, but Lord knows how much incoming fire we took from the Hill on our inexperience, our ineptitude, our lack of knowledge."

In one of their first meetings, Carter told House Speaker "Tip" O'Neill how he handled the Georgia legislature by bypassing them and appealing directly to the people. O'Neill replied, "Hey, wait a minute. You have 289 guys up there [the House Democrats] who know their districts pretty well. They ran against the administration, and they wouldn't hesitate to run against you." Carter said, "Oh, really?" O'Neill's appeals for extra tickets at inaugural festivities were denied by Jordan, causing a furious O'Neill to begin calling Jordan "Hannibal Jerkin." Before long, congressmen were complaining of phone calls ignored, patronage requests rejected, and form letters from Cabinet members. In 1978, a House leader griped that the White House people "think we're just a pack of crooked whores."

Just weeks into his presidency, Carter blind-sided and enraged Congress by chopping out fifteen water projects from his 1978 budget plan without prior consultation. One legislator said, "I was so mad and embarrassed I couldn't see straight." The Senate voted to reverse the move by a vote of 65-24. When O'Neill pushed hard for the B-1 bomber in the House, he thought he was supporting Carter. Two days into the debate, Carter announced he was against the bomber, and told O'Neill just ten minutes before the announcement. In the summer of 1978, the White House fired a close friend of O'Neill's. O'Neill read the news in the paper then furiously banished Carter's congressional aide from his office. Democratic Majority Whip John Brademas was infuriated at not being consulted on Carter's policy on Turkey, and accused the White House of having "all the finesse of an alcoholic hippopotamus."

The ultimate responsibility for all these missteps, of course, was Carter's. "Carter was not a buddy," said Walter Mondale. "He did not approach it that way. No backslapping, and he did not want to deal with the Congress from a bargaining-type psychology where they would give something and he'd give something, they'd get a deal and go out and get it done." Jack Watson observed, "Carter has an almost irresistible inclination to approach problems as an engineer would—identify its components, set out the options for its solution, take into account the economic and political considerations, choose the best option and then do it. His approach wasn't nearly as collegial as Congress would have liked it to be. He was respectful and accessible to members of Congress, but he was in many cases uncompromising. It was regarded by many as arrogant."

A former Democratic senator said, "This was an important aspect of the Carter enigma: how somebody so bright could fail to understand the full importance, like it or not, of Congress. He could be tireless on the phone with congressmen and brilliant in informal briefing sessions with them, but he never made them feel he was entirely comfortable with them. He wasn't." "He felt morally superior to Congress," asserted presidential adviser Hedley Donovan. A Carter associate explained: "He viewed political problems as cube roots. . . . if you find the right answer and use your powers of logical deduction that was it. You didn't waste a lot of time persuading people about it."

"Presidential power," maintained presidential historian Richard Neustadt, "is the power to persuade," and few presidents seemed less capable of persuasion than Jimmy Carter. UN Ambassador Donald McHenry said, "In close person-to-person contact, he was an impressive figure. Indeed, he was one of the most impressive figures that I have known. That is, Jimmy Carter in this room would be a great communicator. Double the size of this room and he would be a disaster." Walter Mondale lamented Carter's shortcomings as a public educator: "He tended to speak to the public in the language of an engineer, and he recoiled against using emotion, poetry, and the rest. I believe that because of that, his appeal to the general public was not a strong one, and in many ways he was unable to convince the public that he was not somebody weak, uncertain, timid—which he wasn't at all."

At the end of two years in office, Carter seemed to be losing control of his White House. Cabinet members were unsure of priorities and took positions independent of Carter's, like Califano's aggressive anti-smoking campaign. Carter's first energy plan, which required new taxes, was put together without involving Treasury Secretary Michael Blumenthal. Carter's Domestic Policy Council took liberal positions while his Office of Management and Budget veered toward a conservative line. White House staffers backstabbed Cabinet members in the press.

In June of 1979, with gas lines sprouting around the country, Carter fled to Camp David in a state of spiritual exhaustion and tried to prepare a speech to the nation that would push his energy plan through Congress. Twenty-four hours before the speech, Carter told his staff to call the networks and cancel it, without explanation. Rumors spread through world capitals that something was wrong with Carter, triggering a sharp plunge in the dollar. Then Carter, in one of the strangest self-criticism exercises in memory, invited a parade of notables from outside the government to be flown up to Camp David in a foolish spectacle to tell him what he was doing wrong. For ten days the helicopters shuttled to his mountain retreat, packed with clergy, union officials, governors, business tycoons, professors. For ten days Carter earnestly absorbed the criticism, diligently taking hundreds of pages of notes on yellow legal pads.

When he came down from the mountaintop, Carter staggered into yet another self-imposed disaster when on July 17 he demanded the resignations of his entire Cabinet and top White House staff. One horrified White House official exclaimed, "We've burned down the house to roast the pig." Massachusetts Democratic Party chairman Chester Atkins quipped: "The mouse that roared is still a rodent." Democratic Congressman Charles Wilson of Texas exclaimed: "Good grief! They're cutting down the biggest trees and keeping the monkeys!" Republican Whip Ted Stevens of Alaska announced on the floor of the Senate: "Some of us are seriously worried that he might be approaching some sort of mental problem."

At the same time, newly appointed Chief of Staff Hamilton Jordan passed around a competence and loyalty questionnaire and ordered that one be filled out for every executive branch employee making over $25,000. The form asked for information like what time the person showed up at work, "How bright is this person?" and "List three things about this person that have disappointed you," as well as ratings of "uncomfortable" [sic] and "savy" [sic]. Transportation Secretary Brock Adams tossed his questionnaires in the trash. By the end of that week, resignations were accepted from five Cabinet officers, and Carter, instead of looking tough, looked pathetic. That year, Carter registered the lowest Gallup job approval rating of any president in history, only 19 percent, beating the previous record holders Nixon (24 percent) and Truman (23 percent).

The end of Carter's presidency was agonizing: the oil crisis ignited stratospheric inflation and interest rates, and the American hostage misery consumed Carter's attention and energy. When Ronald Reagan asked the American electorate, "Are you better off today than four years ago?", the people answered with a resounding, "Hell, no." The hostage crisis vividly captured the bleak image of Carter's impotence as chief executive, as he decided to cancel his campaign activity and turn the Oval Office into a round-the-clock command bunker for running the hostage negotiations. Instead of an in-charge, compassionate executive, Carter looked like a hostage himself. "The more the president becomes a captive to the immediate pressures on him, the more he may become drawn away from the more significant but more remote and long-run problems of his time," wrote historian James MacGregor Burns, identifying a root cause of Carter's difficulty. "The more practical, pragmatic, and operational he becomes, the more he is victim of events rather than shaper of events."

Ambassador McHenry argued that Carter approached the hostage crisis "in the same manner that he approached other problems, and involved himself in the slightest of details. He followed up on every avenue, whether or not it had much likelihood of success." Secretary Bergland remembered seeing a "devastated" Carter give a 7:00 A.M. briefing to the Cabinet after the aborted Desert One rescue operation in April 1979: "He was drained emotionally and he was drained physically. He was a beaten man. It was really from that day hence that he withdrew to the Rose Garden. He wouldn't come out to campaign."

As soon as Carter's presidency ended, experts began issuing the bleakest of judgments: "He just never got his act together," said R. Gordon Hoxie, chairman of the Center for the Study of the Presidency. "The Carter administration was not a disaster," argued Carter adviser Hedley Donovan, "but it came close to the guaranteed minimum presidency." "History will treat him more kindly than the American people did, but there was nothing epochal about his presidency, nothing really remarkable," said Democratic Party powerhouse Clark Clifford in 1981. "Jimmy Carter was a man who came from nowhere, flashed across the political firmament, had some solid accomplishments in his four years but ultimately failed to establish a political base. Then the people, at their first opportunity, returned him to Georgia. There was nothing exceptional about it, no new theory of government was presented. It was just one of those rare moments that historians will rack their brains to understand and explain."

When measured as an all-around executive, Carter seemed to fail handsdown. He never came close to grasping Peter Drucker's dictum that "effective executives concentrate on the few major areas where superior performance will produce outstanding results. They force themselves to set priorities and stay with their priority decisions. They know they have no choice but to do first things first—and second things not at all. The alternative is to get nothing done." Historian Phillip G. Henderson argued that Carter's "spokes of the wheel" structure conflicted with his big agenda, revealing a "profound internal contradiction of his administration. On the one hand, he wanted to decentralize the actual exertion of executive authority. However, his failure to foster teamwork among his Cabinet secretaries meant that issues percolated right back into the Oval Office."

The story might have ended there, with Jimmy Carter run out of town on a rail. But a few years after he left the White House, like Lazarus, Jimmy Carter began to rise. He started becoming a better president. Around the mid-1980s, as macro-manager Ronald Reagan's limitations became painfully visible and Carter's post-presidential achievements began piling up, presidential experts and the media began reappraising him. Carter's strengths as a negotiator and long-range planner, previously obscured, began coming into view.

In addition to the Camp David Accords, Carter's foreign affairs achievements include the Panama Canal treaties, SALT II (unratified by the U.S. Congress, but adhered to by the U.S. and the Soviet Union), recognition of China, the transition to majority black rule in Zimbabwe, the Tokyo trade agreement, a healthy trade surplus, and the elevation of human rights to the international agenda. In a 1988 editorial titled "Jimmy, We Hardly Knew Ye," the *Wall Street Journal* traced the beginnings of Reagan's economic and military programs to Carter's policies, especially "the appointment of Paul Volcker as chairman of the Federal Reserve and the start of the military buildup following the Soviet invasion of Afghanistan." In response to the 1979 Soviet attack on Afghanistan, Carter proposed annual increases of 5 percent in military spending, launching the beginning of the defense buildup of the 1980s.

"Every single strategic offensive weapon that Ronald Reagan deployed in the 1980s was able to be deployed because Jimmy Carter kept the programs alive," asserted career CIA official Robert Gates. "The only exception was the B-1, because Carter had already given approval for the Stealth bomber and didn't see any reason to have both." "He was deeply conservative fiscally. He *hated* to spend money." Gates listed Carter's forgotten achievements: "Jimmy Carter in many respects laid the foundation for much of what Ronald Reagan would do. He was the first president to approve restrictions on the transfer of technologies to the Soviet Union. The first President to put sanctions and limits on U.S./ Soviet trade. . . . It was Jimmy Carter, not Ronald Reagan, who first launched covert action against the Soviets in Central America." According to Gates, Carter approved covert CIA aid to the mujahedin guerrillas in Afghanistan six months before the Soviets invaded.

Jimmy Carter was, retroactively, one of the heroes of the Gulf War, thanks to his skills as a military planner and technocrat. Decisions made by Carter and Secretary of Defense Harold Brown in the late 1970s to push high-tech weapons and tactics helped set the stage for America's victory against Iraq twelve years later. The Tomahawk cruise missile, in development under Nixon and Ford but accelerated by Carter and Brown, achieved a 98 percent success rate in the Persian Gulf conflict. "The basic idea that the U.S. would rush to defend moderate Mideast states from attack was outlined in the Carter Doctrine, espoused in 1980," reported the *Wall Street Journal* in January 1991, "and the plans for getting the troops there in a hurry were put in place by Secretary Brown the year before, when he launched the Rapid Deployment Force, a multiservice organization that Mr. Weinberger [Reagan defense secretary Caspar Weinberger] later transformed into the Central Command." Carter also championed development of the Stealth bomber, which was used to deadly effect in the war. Although Reagan's buildups in funding, spare parts, training, aircraft carriers, and Patriot missiles were also decisive, Harold Brown argued, "When I hear commentators saying that the credit for these weapons go to the Reagan administration, I say 'Credit for what? The B-1 bomber and Star Wars?' They're not involved in this war."

Even Carter's much-lamented problems with Congress recede with the passage of time as the gap between perception and reality narrows. "When you look at the bottom line on Congress," said Jack Watson, "you find to many people's utter astonishment, that his success rate was very impressive." When measured by *Congressional Quarterly,* Carter's respectable overall success rate with Congress of 76.6 percent beats Eisenhower, Nixon, Ford, and Bush, and is the same ballpark as master manipulator LBJ's 82 percent.

Carter left Reagan a nightmarish economic situation to grapple with, with inflation at 13.5 percent, and the bank prime lending rate hitting an unbelievable 21.5 percent. Yet Carter left behind domestic achievements as well: strong economic growth (despite record interest and inflation rates), a decrease in the budget deficit as a percent of GNP, relatively low unemployment (the total number of Americans working increased by 8 million, although the unemployment rate was 7 percent at the end of his term), civil service reform, and the rescue of the Social Security system from bankruptcy.

Carter also engineered the Alaska Lands Bill (stalled for twenty years, it doubled the size of America's national parks in one stroke), and backed the $1.6 billion Super Fund legislation to finance toxic-waste disposal, plus coal strip-mining legislation and child abuse and child welfare bills. He also racked up strong records in minority recruitment, judicial appointments, and the environment. "We deregulated oil and gas, airlines, railroads, trucks, the financial institutions, and communications, including radio and television," argued Carter in 1988, and "in general, even including the airlines, U.S. industry and consumers have gained substantial benefits from deregulation." Carter's energy policies cut consumption, boosted production, and helped create an oil surplus by the mid-1980s, much too late for Carter to enjoy the political benefit.

Walter Mondale concluded that "under Carter we always front-loaded pain and back-loaded pleasure. We did what we had to do. We paid a heavy price for it and the country benefited, and so did Ronald Reagan."

Jimmy Carter the technocrat demonstrated that no matter how skilled a president is technically, he must set achievable goals, and he must inspire and lead his government and people to achieve them. As Carter's Panama Canal negotiator Sol Linowitz said, Carter "could have been great if he had managed the presidency better."

Carter spent his last two days in the Oval Office in feverish, sleepless, round-the-clock negotiations to get the hostages safely out of Iran. After nearly four years of a total ban on any Oval Office recordings of the working presidency, Carter suddenly waived the restriction and allowed network TV cameras to film him at work in his last hours in the office. On the tapes, Carter can be seen calmly, methodically working the phones, piecing together a complex global patchwork of details to finalize the release.

At 8:06 A.M. on his last day as president, Carter heard from Deputy Secretary of State Warren Christopher that the hostages' plane was cleared for takeoff at the airport in Teheran. But in a final act of torment, the Iranians were holding the jet and delaying the takeoff until after the inauguration of incoming President Ronald Reagan. The news crushed Carter. "He was as near despair as I have ever seen him," a top Carter assistant reported. "It was incredible agony."

Carter was so overwhelmed and upset that he had to be physically helped by his staff as he walked away from the Oval Office for the last time.

CHAPTER 9

Ronald Reagan
The Visionary Executive

*"Good Lord. Oh, Lord. Damnit, it is an evil empire!
It's time to say it again!"*

RONALD REAGAN, OVAL OFFICE,
WHITE HOUSE TV VIDEOTAPE, APRIL 1, 1985

THE CABINET ROOM
OCTOBER 25, 1983, 10:00 A.M.

It was Ronald Reagan's first taste of combat and the first U.S. military action since the end of the Vietnam War. Inside the White House, on the president's secure phone line and in his private meetings, audiotapes and videotapes were rolling as he loosed the most powerful military machine in history upon the island micro-nation of Grenada.

Reagan was having a terrible week. In Lebanon on October 23, a smiling man in a truck sped past the gates of the U.S. Marine barracks at the Beirut Airport, crashed into the first-floor lobby, and blew up the building, killing 241 marines. Reagan later called it "the saddest day of my presidency, perhaps the saddest day of my life." On the same day, in cities across Europe, 2 million people marched to protest Reagan's plan to deploy intermediate-range nuclear missiles against the Soviets.

At 5:15 A.M. on Saturday, October 23, Secretary of State George Shultz and National Security Adviser Robert McFarlane woke up Reagan at his golfing vacation cottage in Augusta, Georgia, to tell him that the Organization of Eastern Caribbean States had issued an appeal for the United States to intervene in Grenada, which was nearing a state of anarchy after marxist Prime Minister Maurice Bishop was executed by radicals in his own government.

On Grenada were an unknown number of Cubans building an airport, and 1,000 U.S. citizens, most of them students at the St. George's Medical School.

Reagan was seventy-two years old and he was leading troops into battle for the first time. After a middle-class, midwestern upbringing, Reagan went to California to seek his fortunes as a contract movie player and sat out World War II making training films in Hollywood. Years later, as president, he confided to his UN Ambassador and conservative soul mate, Jeane Kirkpatrick: "You know, Jeane, a lot of people criticize me because I'm an actor. But there are a good many times when I ask myself how anybody but an actor could hold this job for long." His movie career was lackluster. He came close to cracking the A-list in 1941 with an Oscar-caliber performance in *Kings Row* and enjoyed an accompanying sharp boost in popularity and salary. But the war intervened and afterward he was relegated mostly to forgettable B-movie, second-banana roles where Reagan, in the words of one Hollywood producer, "always had the manner of an earnest gas-station attendant." Hollywood taught him the fundamentals of connecting with an audience, but as he entered middle age, the roles dried up and he switched to TV hosting and advertisements. His first career, and his life, hit rock bottom in 1954 when his agent booked him for a two-week stint as an emcee for a floor show at a Las Vegas hotel, doing slapstick sketches and a monologue of poetry. He took the booking because he needed the work.

Reagan rebounded with two new careers, as professional speaker and chief executive, and the experiences positioned him superbly for the Oval Office. First, as corporate spokesman for the General Electric company from 1954 to 1962, Reagan traveled the "mashed potato" circuit, giving patriotic speeches with the blessing of GE's right-wing CEO, diligently honing and perfecting his speaking style until he became one of the most effective stump speakers in the country.

Next, during eight years as governor of California, a state whose GNP would rank it as the seventh largest country in the world, he transformed himself into a seasoned, engaged, and pragmatic chief executive. Apart from a stint as president of the Screen Actors Guild, at fifty-two, it was his first executive job. Despite his deeply conservative principles, he signed a liberal abortion law, charmed and bargained with a Democratic legislature, launched a major reform of the California welfare system, and turned a $200 billion budget deficit into a $500 million surplus, in part by raising taxes. In the governor's office in Sacramento, he developed a clean-desk, board-of-directors system of governance, relying heavily on a strong staff and cabinet. "Let's roundtable it with the fellas," he would say if a proposal got to him prematurely. He also developed a fondness for tightly focused "mini-memos" laying out problems and solution options. "If you can't reduce it to one page," he told an assistant, "you may not understand the problem."

According to then–Defense Secretary Caspar Weinberger, Reagan worried about the risks of the Grenada military action, both to U.S. troops and to civilians, and questioned the military closely on troop levels, potential casualties, risks, and alternatives. "But once he concluded the operation was necessary he was absolutely first-rate. He gave full heed to the military's recommendations. He was decisive. He was very firm. He was very much an ideal commander in chief." Howard Baker, later Reagan's chief of staff, explained, "When he made a decision, it was very prompt and crisp." Reagan wrote, "I asked McFarlane how long the Pentagon thought it would need to prepare a rescue mission on Grenada. He said the Joint Chiefs of Staff believed it could be done in forty-eight hours." Reagan said, "Do it."

On the night of October 24, an assault force of over 5,000 U.S. combat troops was steaming toward the 133-square-mile island, and Reagan, back in the White House with his senior civilian and military brass in the second-floor yellow Oval Room (the same room where Roosevelt held his post–Pearl Harbor briefing), was briefing the bipartisan congressional leadership on the invasion. But two problems arose. Most of the congressional leaders, including those from his own party, were arguing against the strike.

Then, in the middle of Reagan's briefing, British Prime Minister Margaret Thatcher came on the telephone. And she was hopping mad. Grenada was a part of the British Commonwealth, but no one had bothered to tell her the island was about to be invaded by her staunchest ally. Reagan excused himself and went next door into a small study adjoining his bedroom and picked up the phone. A few dozen yards away, personnel in the Situation Room in the basement floor of the West Wing patched the call through to Reagan's phone. Few people knew at the time that the Situation Room was home to a recording capability that had been quietly resumed in Reagan's first days in the White House.

"Early on in the administration Reagan was presented with the option of continuing or not continuing the phone tapings in the Oval Office for national security purposes," said his first-term Deputy Chief of Staff Michael Deaver. "And obviously tapings were a very controversial subject ever since the Nixon days. But Reagan could see the value of it, not so much for history, but for accuracy. If you were dealing with interpreters and government leaders and talking about issues of vital concern, maybe involving lives, he saw the value of it, and readily agreed to continue the tapings."

Reagan's taping system was intended mainly as a management back-up, to create a record from which accurate memorandums of conversation, or "memcons," could be made, especially when translation was involved. The taping, however, was a closely held secret, and the White House denied it was happening at the time it was going on. In February 1982, in the wake of reports on Roosevelt's and Kennedy's recordings, White House Director of Communications David Gergen announced: "The only conversations that I can detect or find that are being recorded are conversations with the press. . . . We are not recording his private conversations," Gergen declared flatly. In fact, the taping was kept a total secret to all but the most senior Reagan officials.

The Situation Room patched the Thatcher call through to Reagan in the White House mansion, and National Security Adviser McFarlane picked up on an extension and listened in. A furious Thatcher expressed her anger that she had not been consulted by the Americans in advance of the invasion of the island. Reagan took the blame. "She was really quite bitter, almost shrill about our doing this," said McFarlane. Thatcher said, "I don't think you should do this." Reagan graciously said, "I'm sorry that there's been some miscommunication, I hope you can understand that this is a matter of great importance not only to the security of the area but also to the American students at the medical school." Thatcher pressed on: "Ron, I simply cannot understand this. This is going to create enormous problems. I must ask you to reconsider." A disturbed but resolute Reagan come out of the room and reported: "She doesn't agree with us, she thinks this is not the right thing to do, and I told her it was too late, I had made the decision." A few hours later, at 5:36 A.M., 400 marines from the helicopter carrier *Guam* landed at Pearls Airport on the western shore of Grenada, and thirty-six minutes later, U.S. Army Rangers parachuted onto the uncompleted runway at Point Salines on the southeastern tip of the island.

In addition to the Situation Room recordings, another taping operation was in place in Reagan's White House, and it was used continuously from 1982 until Reagan's last moments in the Oval Office. It was conducted by a then little-known Defense Department audiovisual crew known as White House Television, part of the White House Communications Agency. The crew, authorized by Congress to a provide a historical record of the presidency in action, was a successor to various photographers from the U.S. Army, U.S. Navy, and Interior Department who had been shooting still and film coverage of presidents as far back as FDR. In 1982, the unit began shooting color video and sound of Reagan's public and ceremonial duties, including speeches, campaign trips, and ceremonial White House activities.

The White House TV crew also began shooting footage of Reagan in action in closed presidential meetings, after the press had been dismissed and the meetings had started. Reagan, supremely comfortable with cameras and always pressed for time, would often start the meeting while the crew was still in the corner of the room shooting, and the crew stayed in the room as long as the first five or ten minutes, sometimes longer. From 1982 to 1989, roughly 800 hours of video were shot of Reagan in working meetings, including encounters with congressmen, heads of state, private citizens, and his own staff, and Cabinet and National Security Council officials. The footage was sealed for years and mostly forgotten until Reagan library archivists made the tapes available for research for this book. The taping was not a secret to the people in the room, but these were working meetings, closed to the press and public.

THE CABINET ROOM
OCTOBER 25, 1983, 10:00 A.M.

President Reagan and Cabinet
RE: *Launching the Invasion of Grenada*
videotape recording of meeting by White House TV

In the first hours of combat, a White House TV crew captured an in-charge Reagan briefing his Cabinet on the Grenada invasion. The tape shows Reagan with his cheeks flushed, excited, alert, and very much in command. "He was a man of extraordinary self-confidence," said UN Ambassador Jeane Kirkpatrick. "The confidence was more in his mission than himself. He was not an arrogant man—he was modest, direct, straightforward." Despite the recent slaughter of 241 marines in Lebanon and the unfolding danger in the Caribbean, Reagan, as always, started the meeting off with a joke. Then, flanked by Secretary of Defense Caspar Weinberger and Secretary of State George Shultz, Reagan addressed his Cabinet officers in his signature husky baritone, peeking occasionally at a note card, but conducting the briefing mostly unscripted.

REAGAN: We have been having meetings at all odd hours and planning going on.

I wanna tell you, if you ever have a chance to go on a golfing weekend with George Shultz (*laughter in room*) do it! Because it's so great when at 2:30 in the morning they tap you on the shoulder and say, "Get up and come out in the other room, we've got to have another meeting." The next day I think it was a little later than that.

No, seriously. You all know the situation that's been going on in Grenada and the concern that we've had for a long time about that country's Cuban connection.

On October 12, or 13, to keep things straight, Bishop, the prime minister, was put on house arrest. Then a crowd estimated at 10,000, which is one tenth of the whole country's population, arrived at that house in support of him, and that crowd was fired upon by the people who had arrested Bishop. They are really leftist thugs. And they took him and his Cabinet prisoners. They later executed him and several of his cabinet members. They fired into the crowd, they killed people including children. The only semblance of law on the island is a twenty-four-hour curfew with orders to shoot on sight.

Now we have about 1,000 Americans there, several hundred of them are in the St. George medical schools. They have been confined to the school by the authorities for safety because of this curfew.

Grenada and five other countries in the Eastern Caribbean are members of a thing called the Organization of Eastern Caribbean States. And they met several days ago, or maybe they had been meeting longer than that, with the exception of Grenada because it has no government to speak of. These nations then appealed—all of them are former colonies of Great Britain—they then appealed to Jamaica and Barbados to join them with whatever military forces they could put together, to restore order and to protect their own people on the island of Grenada.

Now before this ever happened, before we ever knew that anyone else was interested in this, we had a force, the rotation force of marines, on its way in a flotilla of ships to Beirut. We have diverted that, turned that task force, that flotilla to go into the [Caribbean] area and simply stand by someplace within immediate range, in case we had to make an immediate evacuation of our Americans.

On October 23, we got a request from the OECD [Reagan meant OECS, for Organization of Eastern Caribbean States], it was an urgent plea, to join them, because these countries have lived so peacefully, one of them, two of them don't even have any military at all, and the others just have a few. They have joined together and as I said, asked these other two and asked the OECD [sic] plus Jamaica and Barbados, made this urgent plea to the United States to join them in a joint effort to restore order to Grenada . . . .

You're going to find this hard to believe, but with all of these early morning meetings and everything else, we have managed to keep one thing in the administration from leaking.

And at 5:15 this morning, the joint force landed at two spots on Grenada: paratroopers in the south, the marines, and this other multiple force in the north, secured both airports, they're eight miles apart, the one at the south tip of the island and then the operational one, the one that the Cubans have been building is up further north.

Both airports are under our control. We have secured the school for the safety of the people.

There is, now, firing and combat going on.

There have been casualties, they have been evacuated to the USS *Guam*. I'm going to see if we've got any update on reports here in a minute and have others talk to you.

But it was our feeling in making this decision, and believe me it wasn't easy, and certainly in the face of what had happened in Lebanon, to order a thing of this kind.

But first of all was our consideration for our own people. And second was, once this urgent plea had come to us, none of us believed that there was any way that the United States could say no to that without in the eyes of the world revealing that when the chips were down, we backed away.

I don't know what credibility we would have in the Middle East or anyplace else if we had done that.

We believe we've taken the right action. We hope we'll be shortly out of there . . . .

After two days of unexpectedly heavy fighting, U.S. forces rescued the American medical students, captured Bishop's killers, and restored order to the island. The human cost totaled nineteen Americans and forty-five Grenadians killed, including twenty-five civilian fatalities in the accidental bombing of a mental hospital. Although critics pointed to the vast imbalance of forces (Reagan's first secretary of state, Alexander Haig, later snorted that "the Provincetown police force could have conquered Grenada"), the action sent a strong signal to the Soviet Union that Reagan would not tolerate Communist interference in the Western Hemisphere. The invasion, in George Shultz's words, "caused people to see that the U.S. would use its military power for strategic purpose."

The conquest of Grenada also illustrated a little-known reality of Reagan's executive style: in those areas of the presidency that he cared about most and chose to focus on, he was capable of being a hands-on, decisive, engaged, and effective chief executive.

"I had an agenda I wanted to get done," explained Reagan. "I came with a script." Like few other presidents, Ronald Reagan entered the Oval Office with a clear vision of where he wanted to lead the country, on a mission he had been pursuing for twenty years. "He had goals which were already articulated in his speeches in 1961 that he was still pushing as president," observed Jeane Kirkpatrick. "Ronald Reagan had a strategic vision and a sense of historical optimism that was unparalleled by any other president I worked for," said CIA official Robert Gates. "His sense of strategy and timing and negotiation were superb." Domestic policy adviser Martin Anderson noted, "He established two top priorities. The first was to rebuild America's military strength. The second was to rebuild America's economic strength. All other issues, important as they might be, were rigorously relegated to the sidelines."

Reagan's entire presidency was geared to exploit his strengths as a visionary communicator and steer him away from energy-consuming operational details that Reagan thought belonged in the hands of capable deputies. First-term Deputy Chief of Staff Michael Deaver claimed, "All he worried about from the time he got up in the morning to the time he went to bed at night was how he was going to communicate the things he believed." "Harry Truman said the main job of the presidency is persuasion," said Reagan. "I couldn't agree more." A longtime Reagan friend noted, "He created images on the movie screen and then he had a job of creating a vision for G.E.—of having people see things as he sees them. He's had years and years of experience of creating visions."

The Oval Office was Ronald Reagan's greatest stage, a theater in the round where he projected a hypnotic spell of incandescent optimism that rippled out around the world. It was also one of Reagan's most powerful management tools. "Visitors to the Oval Office are coming to see the most powerful man in the world," said Reagan national security aide Geoffrey

Kemp. "They are all scared silly." In hundreds of hours of White House TV videotapes, Reagan can be seen gripping stupefied, rubber-legged visitors at the door, ranging from beauty queens to senators and foreign leaders, greeting them joyfully, steadying and pulling them into the historic office, soothing their terror with a joke, and melting their resistance with a husky, mellow personal charm that rivaled Roosevelt's and Kennedy's on their best days. His entire being glowed confidence and warmth. The combination of Reagan's charisma, seared-in suntan, and the high windows and brilliant interior lighting of the room created a powerful illusion: inside Reagan's Oval Office *the sun always shined.*

In his first moments in the Oval Office as president, Reagan parked a sign on his desk for all to see: THERE'S NO LIMIT TO WHAT A MAN CAN DO OR WHERE HE CAN GO IF HE DOESN'T MIND WHO GETS THE CREDIT. It was joined by another sign which proclaimed the strategy of relentless optimism that would govern the office for the next eight years: IT CAN BE DONE. If you looked closely at an oval-shaped crystal memento at the front of his desk, you'd see etched in small letters a slogan that invoked the flexibility and pragmatism of John Kennedy, with a line from Kennedy's inaugural: LET US NEVER NEGOTIATE OUT OF FEAR, BUT LET US NEVER FEAR TO NEGOTIATE. The sign was an early clue to the startling developments that were to come in superpower relations.

For the next eight years, Reagan carried in his suit coat pocket a white laminated card that contained the authentication codes for launching a nuclear attack. If necessary, Reagan would insert the card into the suitcase-sized nuclear "football" device discreetly carried around by a military aide hovering a few feet away twenty-four hours a day, and missiles would fly around the world, bringing much of it to an end. Seven presidents before him had similar authority (except theoretically for a few hours in the late 1970s when Jimmy Carter accidentally left the card in his jacket pocket and it was sent to the dry cleaners). Reagan was not only outraged by the concept of nuclear "mutual assured destruction," but he had a radical vision of disarmament. Conservatives dismissed him as naïve; liberals were certain he was insincere. Other presidents might have harbored similar hopes, but Reagan actually thought he could make the vision a reality.

To sharpen the theatrical impact of the Oval Office, on Reagan's order the walls were given a fresh coat of off-white paint, the cornice and woodwork were coated in a bright, pure white, and new sofas and Chippendale chairs were installed, all upholstered in white (Nancy Reagan claimed to have found beer cans and sandwiches in the drawers left behind from the previous inhabitants). Western art was brought in, including bronzes by sculptors Frederic Remington and Charles Russell.

Reagan sat in the same chair he did at the governor's office in Sacramento, and worked from the same *Resolute* desk used by Kennedy and Carter. To accommodate Reagan's burly 6-foot 1-inch, 185-pound frame, the desk was raised a few inches. "Out of respect for this office and the events which transpired in it, I almost never removed my suit coat," recalled Reagan. "Somehow, casual attire seemed out of place here." In the Cabinet Room, sculptures of Benjamin Franklin and George Washington were brought in. Harry Truman's portrait was replaced by Dwight Eisenhower and Calvin Coolidge. "Eisenhower is up there because I beat him for $10 the first time we played golf," quipped Reagan.

Right in front of his place at the Cabinet Room table, Reagan parked a long revolving wooden sign that read YES, NO, and MAYBE. Within arm's reach was an immense Waterford crystal jar of Jelly Belly brand jellybeans. During meetings, he would grab a fistful, lay them down on the table in neat rows, and discreetly pop them one at a time. Offering the jar to others, he'd ask brightly: "Would you like a quick energy boost?" The jar would then begin a long journey around the table, as sheepish government officials took turns plunging their arms into the candy jar.

"It's true hard work never killed anybody, but I figure, why take a chance?" quipped Reagan, whose schedule was ruthlessly geared to preserving his energy. It was an understandable goal for the oldest man ever elected president, who at the midpoint of his presidency was seventy-five years old, fully ten years older than the standard retirement age. No one has ever proven a correlation between long work hours and presidential effectiveness: witness the meltdown of the hardest-working modern presidents, Lyndon Johnson and Jimmy Carter. "He does not devote large chunks of time to peripheral issues," said Harvard presidential scholar Roger Porter, who spent five years on Reagan's White House staff. "That is one of the keys to his success."

Reagan saw Jimmy Carter as a blueprint for precisely how not to do things in the Oval Office. "The problem with Carter," Reagan told an aide before election, "is that he tries to do everything at once and he tries to do too much of it himself. If we win we are going to set priorities and do things one at a time." Several months into his first term he told *U.S. News & World Report:* "There is no way you could do this job and involve yourself in the details. You'd stop each day at about the first item on the agenda and spend the rest of the day on that."

Reagan woke up around 7:00 or 7:30 A.M., scanned the morning TV shows and the papers, including the *Washington Post, New York Times,* and *USA Today,* paying closest attention to his "hometown" *Los Angeles Times* and local conservative favorite, *Washington Times.* He got to work by 9:00 and knocked off by 5:00 or 5:30, joking about "burning the midday oil." "He was a very disciplined person," said Howard Baker, Reagan's 1987–88 chief of staff. "He was the most punctual man I ever met. He was in the office at 9:00 A.M. You could set your watch to it. He'd have lunch in the small study next to the Oval Office, usually alone, thin soup, some crackers. At exactly 6:00 P.M. he'd go up to the living quarters, put on his jumpsuit and work out on his Nautilus machines for an hour." Reagan often took both Wednesday and Friday afternoons off, taking the helicopter to Camp David for the weekend. On Sundays he'd bring back a supply of acorns and walnuts from Camp David and sometimes in the middle of meetings he would get up and toss them out to the squirrels in the Rose Garden.

Through the day, Reagan fastidiously checked off each item on his agenda with a pencil. At the start of a meeting, he would slip small cue cards out of his suit pocket. The little scripts were not just the tools of a former actor, but those of a well-prepared chief executive who wanted to be sure he set the agenda for each meeting. Reagan's was a heavily scripted presidency, right down to the president's chitchat with visitors. On the very few occasions Reagan lost his temper, the cause was usually an overloaded schedule. "He hated to keep people waiting," explained Geoffrey Kemp. "He figured that if someone was coming all the way to see the president of the United States, it was the height of rudeness for the president to be late." If he was over-booked, Reagan would throw his glasses down on the desk and mutter some cross words to no one in particular. That was usually the end of it. He rarely drank or smoked and usually had dinner in his pajamas with Mrs. Reagan on TV trays while waching their favorite programs.

One of the most effective and feared weapons in Reagan's executive arsenal was his wife, Nancy, who periodically stepped in as an invisible adviser, enforcer, and hatchetwoman, usually on major policy or personnel issues. "She has always had more influence than people generally realize," said top Reagan aide Michael Deaver. Mrs. Reagan saw the need to compensate for what she called her husband's "soft touch" in personnel matters, and she was believed to play a key role in the ousters of National Security Adviser Richard Allen, Secretary of State Alexander Haig, Cabinet secretaries James Watt and Raymond Donovan, and Chief of Staff Don Regan. Her policy instincts were shrewd: she pushed her husband toward his stunning, historic rap-prochement with the Soviet Union. She also intervened in 1984 campaign and debate strategy, an election that saw Reagan reelected in the greatest Republican landslide in U.S. electoral history.

Domestic affairs aide Martin Anderson described Reagan as a "closet workaholic." Chief of Staff Donald Regan reported, "Every afternoon he went home complete with material—homework: briefing books, intelligence briefings, reports from State, DOD, materials submitted by Cabinet officers, legislative analysis on whether or not he should sign a particular bill. When he brought that stuff back at 8:50 or 8:55 in the morning, he not only had parts underlined, but pages annotated. You knew that he had done his homework." Reagan was actively involved in the preparation of major speeches— they were written by others, of course, but Reagan honed them to a fine edge by polishing and editing, by adding folksy parables, and by constant rehearsal. The bigger the speech, the more he worked on it: he made significant edits, for example, on his November 14, 1985, speech to the nation on departing for the Geneva summit. Additionally, reported Deaver, "I don't think, at least when I was in the White House, there was ever an American killed in the line of duty that Ronald Reagan either didn't physically see the widow, the husband, mother, father, whatever, or call them on the phone. . . . He would sit at that desk for hours and hours and hours making those phone calls."

Reagan's defenders argued that, far from being, as Clark Clifford anointed him, an "amiable dunce," Reagan was capable of being a strong executive. "He was a hard worker and a quick study," said William Clark, Reagan's Sacramento chief of staff and number two in Reagan's parade of six national security advisers. "He was highly deliberative, and far better informed than most of those around him who had not worked with him for a long period of time recognized. He had fantastic recall. He would amaze us at times." Clark's predecessor Richard Allen declared: "Reagan never, never minded being underestimated. He never felt insulted. That gave him an armor plating." Jeane Kirkpatrick asserted, "In my experience he was always prepared. He knew the issues and he had thought about them. He called on people and he asked questions. This is the way he liked to inform himself—opinions embodied in people. Ronald Reagan was interested in the whole pattern of international power."

A random inspection of dozens of Reagan's diary files at the Reagan Library reveals not a somnambulant shirker, but a seventy-something man who took a round of live ammunition in the chest in his second month on the job and went on to endure a tough daily schedule of frequent high-pressure private meetings and public events, plus a regular schedule of presidential functions at night, plus weekly radio addresses on Saturdays and sometimes more functions on the weekends, topped off with regular bursts of national and international travel. In retrospect, given the killing pace any modern president has to endure and Reagan's advanced age, it seems the height of responsibility that he paced himself as he did. "Show me an executive who works long, overtime hours," he told journalist Charlie Rose in 1980, "and I'll show you a bad executive."

Reagan was capable of making decisions with decisiveness and force, especially early in his presidency. In his first year he surprised everyone, including his own officials, by firing the nation's air traffic controllers after they declared a strike. To wrap up a 1983 National Security Council debate over whether to launch an anti-Castro shortwave radio operation, Reagan gave the go-ahead, then declared the matter closed by announcing: "Listen, I want you folks to know I don't want any delays or reevaluations because I'm a stubborn bastard!" During an impasse in nuclear arms talks early in his presidency, Reagan instructed his negotiator Paul Nitze: "You just tell the Soviets that you're working for one tough son of a bitch." "He didn't hesitate to make the tough decisions," said Jeane Kirkpatrick. "I think it's because he was not a work in formation when he came into the White House, he was making judgments against a well-defined policy view. He was also much brighter than people imagined, and an exceptional listener."

A dramatic example of Reagan decisiveness came during the climax of the Battle of Beirut in August 1982. Earlier that summer, after years of torment from cross-border terror attacks, Israeli Defense Force (IDF) tanks smashed through United Nations barricades in the fragrant hills of South Lebanon and raced northward toward PLO headquarters in the slums of West Beirut in a final attempt to eradicate Yasser Arafat and his fighters. Starting on July 21, Israeli planes bombed West Beirut for seven consecutive days, causing heavy civilian casualties. On August 4, Israeli armored units lunged into West Beirut under cover of heavy artillery fire. Reagan sent a stern warning to Israeli Prime Minister Menachem Begin to comply with a truce, but Begin declared the attacks would continue until the PLO was evacuated from Beirut.

As Israeli artillery pounded PLO positions, furious U.S. negotiator Philip Habib stood by a window at the U.S. ambassador's residence overlooking the city and screamed into a satellite phone patched through to both Secretary of State Shultz in Washington and Deputy Chief of Mission Bill Brown in Jerusalem. Habib yelled that the shelling must stop. Brown was also patched through to Begin on another line, who calmly denied that there was any shelling. "Oh, yeah?" said Habib, who thrust his phone out the window and broadcast the sounds of eight artillery barrages launched within thirty seconds from Israeli artillery batteries just below him.

In the early morning hours of August 12, the IDF began a daylong incineration of West Beirut from air, land, and sea, in a final spasm of vengeance against lightly armed PLO guerrillas dug into their hijacked capital. Shells and bombs showered the city like rain. In less than nine hours 44,000 artillery shells slammed into the souks and apartment buildings of the once-thriving city. Habib called Washington on the satellite phone and begged Shultz to intervene, exclaiming: "The city is being destroyed, and America is being blamed for it. It is all going up in smoke! Tell Begin to stop it or else! Israel is destroying the negotiation in its final moments!" Unable to cross Beirut under heavy artillery fire to confer with the PLO, Habib, now wondering what was left to negotiate if Beirut was destroyed, instead paid a visit to Mother Teresa's East Beirut mission. Mother Teresa consoled Habib, saying she would pray to the Virgin Mary for him. When Habib left the meeting, he said, he looked up to the evening sky and "watched the Israeli air force drop sticks of bombs on Beirut from 10,000 feet."

In the Oval Office, Reagan had enough. For weeks he had been following gruesome TV footage of civilian casualties from the battle, and it sickened him. "It was an outrage in Reagan's mind," said Robert McFarlane. "He felt very passionately about the deaths of those women and children on television." Michael Deaver marched in from his office next door and announced to Reagan that he intended to resign, saying, "I can't be a part of this anymore, the bombings, the killing of children. It's wrong. And you're the one person on the face of the earth right now who can stop it. All you have to do is tell Begin you want it stopped." At about 10:00 A.M. Washington time, Reagan picked up the phone to his secretary and said, "Get me Menachem Begin." Begin, in the midst of a fractious cabinet meeting, refused to take the call. An hour later Begin's return call finally came through. The Israeli Cabinet had just voted for a cease-fire, but Begin had not yet confirmed that IDF firing had stopped.

Almost shouting, Reagan gripped the receiver with white knuckles and exclaimed, "Menachem, I cannot understand this! I want you to stop it! We will help you find a longer-term solution, but right now, I want you to stop this. It is senseless. It is to no useful purpose. I want you to stop it! Menachem, I must tell you that if you don't, we're going to have to undertake a very fundamental review." McFarlane recalled, "Over the next few minutes, he excoriated the Israeli prime minister for the air attacks, and warned him, in terms as severe as I had ever heard him use, that unless the attacks ceased immediately, the United States would have to reassess its relationship with Israel." Reagan proclaimed, "Our entire relationship is at stake!" He was as angry and emotional as anyone had ever seen him. "Menachem, this is a holocaust!" said Reagan to Begin, himself a Holocaust survivor. Begin, for once barely able to get a word in edgewise, responded in a voice dripping with sarcasm, "Yes, Mr. President, I'm aware of what a holocaust is." Reagan signed off by ordering Begin, "It has gone too far. You must stop it." Minutes later, Reagan sent a furious confirming cable to Begin.

Twenty minutes passed. Then Begin called back to confirm he had given the order to stop firing and there were no jets over Beirut. "Mr. President, we've stopped the shelling," Begin said. "I have just talked with the minister of defense and the chief of staff. Now there is no firing at all." Reagan bade the prime minister farewell: "Menechem, shalom." Reagan hung up the receiver, looked at his men, and said, "I didn't know I had that kind of power." Soon Habib hammered out a truce, and U.S. Marines entered Beirut as part of a multinational force to protect and escort the PLO out of the city.

In Reagan's first years in the Oval Office, he paid very close attention to congressional relations, and it paid off spectacularly early on, yielding congressional success scores rivaling LBJ's. Despite Reagan's hard-core conservative principles, he pragmatically negotiated and compromised with Congress on taxes, defense, social programs, and the budget. Day after day, he summoned busloads of legislators to the Oval Office, assiduously charmed them, and followed up with phone calls. Michael Deaver recalled, "He was indefatigable when it came to working at some of those bills and those congressional issues. And, if you looked at the eight years, you would probably see a big part of his time was personal salesmanship." "He's a very likable person," said the Democratic chairman of the House Banking Committee. "His style of communicating is superb. He's simple and direct." One congressman remembered a meeting with Jimmy Carter: "We had barely got seated and Carter started lecturing us about the problems he had with one of the sections of the bill. He knew the details better than most of us, but somehow that caused more resentment than if he had left the specifics to us." When the same congressman met with Reagan, "He patted me on the back and told me how much he needed and appreciated my vote. He said that I should call if I needed anything."

Filed away at the Reagan Library are boxes full of "talking points" memos for calls to congressmen that Reagan methodically worked through, often marking them up with his handwritten notations. On a call sheet to Congresswoman Jean Ashbrook on a tax bill: "I don't know—she's asking herself what [her late husband] John would have done. She's very sincere and will truly soul search." Senator Jack Danforth on MX missile funding: "He's with us." Congressman Bob Davis on tax reform: "Swallows hard and says yes." Congressman Bill Archer on the budget: "This call was almost forty minutes of sheer frustration. He believes a $110 billion deficit is the end of the world." Congresswoman Margaret Heckler: "She's supportive to the extent she can be. She has a very tough race in her district . . . asked me to understand if here & there she had to protect herself. I said I did." Congressman Bill Goodling on MX funding: "I think he's OK. (Don't Congressmen ever say yes or no?)"

Nineteen eighty-one was a triumphant year for Reagan in Congress, and he overwhelmed congressional Democrats on all fronts. In pushing the centerpiece of his program, a major tax overhaul, Reagan repeatedly instructed his team: "Do what is necessary to get the program adopted. Don't back off. Find out what needs doing and do it. Period." The bill passed, as did Reagan initiatives from defense spending increases and foreign aid to selling AWACS planes to Saudi Arabia.

In a number of meetings through Reagan's first term, White House Television cameras rolled in the Oval Office and Cabinet Room as Reagan started arm-twisting meetings with legislators. In the Oval Office, riveted and spellbound congressmen sank deep down in the low sofas as an elevated Reagan held court by the fireplace like a benevolent sun king, putting forth his arguments with his powerful, husky baritone charm. These meetings were among Reagan's greatest command performances as president, but since they were closed to the press and to most of his own White House staff, they played only to the tiniest of audiences.

THE CABINET ROOM
SEPTEMBER 28, 1983, 10:45 A.M.

President Reagan and House Republicans
RE: *U.S. Marine Deployment in Lebanon*
videotape recording of meeting by White House TV

This videotape of a closed-door meeting captured super-salesman Reagan strong-arming congressmen to vote in favor of an agreement authorizing U.S. Marines to remain in Lebanon for another eighteen months as part of the Multinational Force. For this brief moment, things were looking bright in Lebanon. Three days earlier, the warring factions agreed to a cease-fire and negotiations in Geneva, and the Beirut International Airport had just reopened. Reagan made his case confidently, forcefully, pointing at the legislators and warning them that if they voted against the agreement, Americans would die.

REAGAN: In 1974, when Lebanon fell apart, that has complicated things, because the PLO, born out of the refugees there in Lebanon, began their terrorist actions across the northern border into Israel. Which finally led, as we know, to this Israel invasion to, actually not an attack on the Lebanese, but an attack to drive the PLO out . . . .

We've come a long way since then, and I don't believe that there's any Arab state, other than possibly the one that's causing the trouble today, Syria, that has not agreed that they can negotiate and sit down and that peace can come to the Middle East. But first we had to quiet this thing in Lebanon . . . .

The idea was that the Multinational Force would, then as the others withdrew, Israel and Syria and the PLO, the PLO was ushered out as part of the fighting, they have been infiltrated back in and are a presence again there. But the idea that we would help provide stability, and then as the Lebanese army moved out, to reassert the Lebanon's government's control over its own territory . . . .

Remember this about the Middle East. There is no way—first of all, every government of the United States since 1948 and the creation of Israel has gone on record pledging its support for the continued existence of Israel as a nation. I don't believe there's any way that we can walk away from our moral obligation to Israel itself.

But, also, Japan, Western Europe, and to a lesser extent ourselves, it would be a traumatic experience for us, as we found out in the oil boycott, if the Middle East was denied to the Western world. It would be sheer disaster for Europe and Japan because that's where virtually all of their energy comes from for all of their industry. So with the Soviet Union stirring the pot as it has been for years and with its eye on the Middle East, not because it needs the oil—the Soviet Union is the biggest oil producing country in the world.

There's no way that we can stand back. That's why, as I say, it hasn't just been altruism—it's been in our own interest to try and bring peace and stabilize that area. Now, the stabilization begins with

Lebanon. And I can tell you the words from the ambassador of Lebanon are that the cease-fire and this attempt now to get together and resolve the Lebanese situation by those warring factions is due to this agreement on this resolution, this compromise agreement. This is what has convinced them that it's time to maybe settle things.

I think that to amend this, I think to reduce down the time, could only torpedo the negotiations that are going on. Syria would be encouraged to believe that particularly in an election year coming up that there'd be no reason for them not to continue to harass—and I think it would cost us more American lives.

We'd have to cut and run.

Reagan's hardball pitch worked—Congress passed the agreement the next day. But a month later, terrorists blew up the marine barracks at Beirut Airport, killing 241 Americans. Three months later the Lebanese government and military disintegrated, and U.S. troops were withdrawn.

THE OVAL OFFICE
APRIL 17–20, 1985

President Reagan and Congressional Leaders
RE: *Aid to the Nicaraguan Contras*
videotape recordings of meetings by White House TV

Seeds of near-destruction: White House videocameras caught a moment in the birth of the Iran-Contra scandal as Reagan entered two of his toughest weeks in the Oval Office. In the same week, a controversy erupted over Reagan's plan to visit Bitburg, Germany, for a ceremony at the graves of 2,000 German soldiers including forty-nine members of Hitler's elite guard, the Waffen SS. Reagan stubbornly refused to change the trip, incurring a hail of protests from Jewish and veterans' groups. Reagan had recently arm-twisted Congress into funding twenty-one new MX missiles, but Democrats were rallying for a showdown over Central America.

Now, Reagan was corralling parades of congressmen into the Oval Office to lean on them to fund a paltry $14 million in "humanitarian aid" for the *contra* anti-Communist guerrillas in Nicaragua, a cause very dear to Reagan's heart. Reagan proposed that if the marxist Sandinistas agreed to peace talks mediated by the Catholic Church, the

U.S. would limit *contra* aid to non-military items. But Reagan threatened that if the talks stalled, he would resume military shipments to the rebels. Reagan did not know it, but his spell over Congress was about to vanish.

APRIL 17, 1985: MEETING WITH DEMOCRATIC HOUSE MEMBERS, 3:30 P.M.

REAGAN: Good to see you. Well, come on in! Well, thank you! All right.

Well, thank you, first of all, for coming down. I appreciate it very much. I appreciate also the fact that most of you, or almost all of you, have been most supportive on this same subject, or had you guessed that I wanted to talk about the *contras*? (*laughter*)

I just wanted to, I know that some of you have had some misgivings about some of the things that have happened.

Our plan was one that we thought trying to break this deadlock with the Sandinastas. The support has been wonderful from the Contadora countries and from their neighbors down there . . . The *contras* offered to negotiate as onetime members of the revolution, to get back to the goals of the revolution. And the Sandinistas said no.

So we've came up with this plan. The other day someone came back and brought a verbal message from the pope. He thinks we're doing right . . . .

The tape just caught Reagan in two errors as he oversold his plan. He exaggerated when he implied that the Contadora leaders of Mexico, Colombia, Panama, and Venezuela supported his plan: they had only mildly endorsed his call for a cease-fire and negotiations, and had rejected his threat of military aid to the contras. *The pope did not support the Reagan plan, either. When word of this claim reached Pope John Paul II, the Vatican quickly and emphatically denied that he had given Reagan any such message, especially a plan with military aspects.*

APRIL 18, 1985: MEETING WITH REPUBLICAN SENATORS, 11:00 A.M.

REAGAN: Come in, sit down! (*Reagan showed the senators the pro-*contra *message*)

Well, now, I assume you're all coming in to strongly support whatever I've advocated! If not, why, I'll make a certain pitch to you.

I do think that opening line is the truth. I think what is at issue today is whether we're voting for or against a plan, we're really voting are we going to have another Cuba, a Marxist-Leninist totalitarian country as we have now in Nicaragua, on the mainland of the Americas, or are we going to hold out for people who want democracy.

I think that the issue is as clear-cut as that.

I know that they have got one of the biggest disinformation programs going in the country we've ever seen. And we brought up this plan, this idea, to refute the thought that we're somehow sneaking around here hoping for a military overthrow of the government.

All we're asking is a restoration of the revolution that overthrew Somoza. And on the *contra* side are people and leaders who participated in that revolution, men who were imprisoned by the Sandinistas who got in and just did what Castro did in Cuba many years ago, and that was had a revolution and then double-crossed his fellow revolutionaries in order to institute what he had always intended, this kind of a totalitarian government. And we think that this plan, which was borne of the fact that the *contras* themselves several weeks ago offered to lay down their arms if the Sandinistas would negotiate with them and let them come in and try for a peaceful reconciliation and the restoration of the aims of the revolution, which were given to the Organization of American States during the revolution, appealing for them to persuade Somoza to step down, which he did. And on that basis, the Sandinista government refused their offer, and we picked it up.

And we've gotten the [support of] leadership of the Contadoras, we've gotten the leadership, the presidents of the neighboring countries, all of them . . . .

APRIL 18, 1985: MEETING WITH
DEMOCRATIC SENATORS, 2:00 P.M.

SENATOR PATRICK LEAHY: You're our senior guy here, Fritz, you sit with the president. (*to Senator Hollings*)

REAGAN: What I have here, really, is something of yours. They gave me a copy of it, too. You're getting one.

LEAHY: In what way, Mr. President?

REAGAN: See all these people?

Reagan held up a framed statement from an international pro-contra group: "An Urgent Message from Europeans to Congress: Support the Nicaraguan Resistance," signed by eighty-nine European political and intellectual leaders. The statement was part of a communications blitz orchestrated by White House Communications Director Pat Buchanan to build support for the contras.

It includes people like Winston Churchill III and J. Malcolm Fraser, the former prime minister of Australia, all these, from all over Europe and everything, they have come here to present to the Congress of the United States an "Urgent Message" signed by all of them asking you to support the Nicaraguan Resistance.

The opening line says, "Democracy itself is at stake in Nicaragua. After four years of dictatorship, the FSLN, the totalitarian ruling party, has not succeeded in breaking the resistance of the Nicaraguan people."

They came here and visited the White House this morning and gave me this one. You'll be getting one up there for all of you.

LEAHY: Framed?

REAGAN: I don't know whether they'll frame yours or not (*laughter*) but mine was framed. I just thought you'd like to see this, because they've talked me into it. I believe now, that we ought to go that way.

VOICE: They had to twist your arm about it! (*laughter*)

LEAHY: Max Friedersdorf* had you on the doubtful list just before?

REAGAN: Leaning! (*laughter*)

VOICES: Leaning—leaning!

REAGAN: Well, listen, let me seriously though, talk here for just a minute and then let me hear from all of you.

First of all, I regret that in some circles, present company excepted, I regret very much the—this is kind of being placed over into a Democrat/Republican context.

I think this is one of those situations where traditionally, we've always closed ranks at the water's edge.

And it does have to do with our national security.

Max Friedersdorf, Reagan's chief congressional lobbyist.

The reason for posing this plan came, was inspired by, the fact that several weeks ago, the *contras* offered to lay down their weapons and enter into discussions, negotiations regarding a peaceful reconciliation to simply restore the goals of the original revolution.

And today, contrary to what all this disinformation program says, the bulk of those *contras* and their leaders are also veterans of that revolution who fought against Somoza . . . .

Days after these meetings, the Senate voted to approve the funding, but the House killed the plan, and with it Reagan's hopes for contra *aid from Congress. The defeat reflected Reagan's declining effectiveness with Congress: his batting average declined from a very strong 82 percent in 1981 to 43 percent in 1987, the second lowest ever recorded. After this defeat, Reagan, desperate to rescue the* contras, *ordered his national security officials to find a way to keep the* contras *alive "body and soul," which triggered covert actions that snowballed into the Iran-Contra scandal.*

There were three Reagan White Houses. The first, which ran from 1981 to 1985, was run by a "troika" of aides: Chief of Staff James Baker (handling operations), counselor Ed Meese (policy), and Deputy Chief of Staff Michael Deaver (image, public appearances, and First Family affairs). The group was often effective in exploiting Reagan's strengths and protecting him from his weaknesses. James Baker said the team was successful because "we were able to present the president with all viewpoints. Also, we had a system that was very effective in preventing end-runs. We had a rule that any Cabinet officer or high-level official could see the president alone any time they wanted to. But the president had to debrief one of the three of us so we would know what was going on."

The second Reagan White House lasted from 1985 to early 1987 and was supervised by ex–Treasury Secretary Donald Regan, formerly a highly successful CEO of Merrill Lynch. This period saw an historic thaw in U.S.-Soviet relations, but also saw Reagan's National Security Council run off the rails and trigger the Iran-Contra scandal. The third Reagan White House ran from 1987 to 1989, was managed by Howard Baker and then his deputy Kenneth Duberstein, and national security assistants Frank Carlucci and Colin Powell, and focused both on repairing the damage incurred by Iran-Contra and consolidating progress on U.S.-Soviet affairs.

Don Regan took command in an abrupt job switch he organized with a burned-out James Baker, who took Regan's slot as secretary of the Treasury, and Michael Deaver, who was departing to become a lobbyist. Deaver announced to Reagan, "I've found [you] someone your own age to play with." Reagan accepted the switch as a fait accompli, in part because he loved the company of multimillionaire Wall Street powerhouse Regan. "He's a lot like Reagan's friends in California," said an old Reagan friend, "a self-made guy from a poor section of Boston, tough, direct, and successful." The take-charge Regan ruffled many feathers with his brash style, and was accused of cutting off access to Reagan. A staff veteran of Reagan's first term said at the time, "It's clear that Regan's calling the shots. He's the de facto national security adviser, the de facto legislative strategist . . . the de facto president."

The delicate staff equilibrium that protected Reagan was shattered, although nobody realized it at the time, especially Reagan. Michael Deaver reflected that Reagan had "grown to rely on a small group of people that had come with him from Sacramento, Ed Meese and I, Lyn Nofziger and others, had been around him for twenty years. And we all left. And I think it didn't dawn on him that while the system was going to stay pretty much the same, these were people who didn't understand him or the way he operated." All the men who had formed a protective shield around Reagan in the first term by now were gone or relegated to the sidelines. "Reagan's management style is unique," wrote Reagan adviser Martin Anderson, "making it possible for him to achieve legendary changes in economic policy and nuclear weapons strategy, magically and seemingly without effort. But it is a style with danger-ous flaws that were masked until the Iran-Contra affair exposed them and nearly destroyed his presidency. It is a high-risk style. . . . When it works, it is spectacular. When it fails, it is also spectacular."

Suddenly, with the death of the troika, Reagan's executive flaws were exposed to a dangerous degree. Chief among them was his implacable adher-ence to a narrow agenda, fueled by a detached passivity that, according to some of his aides, veered toward indolence. "He was a highly intelligent man who, when confronted with big workloads and easy workloads, would always pick the easy workloads," said Richard Allen, Reagan's first national security adviser. White House aide Jonathan Miller stated, "Reagan is like a great racehorse that performs well when you have a jockey that knows how to use a whip. If you don't use the whip, he'll just loaf." "His decisions were more visceral than cerebral," said Reagan's first secretary of state, Alexander Haig. "He had a set of convictions; it was very hard to shake him from them. He was stubborn. He was also lazy. He didn't like to work too hard." "He was flat-out not a detail man," said Howard Baker. "He didn't want to be over-loaded with information. He wanted it presented to him in understandable form. I always had the impression that once he had absorbed it and made a decision it was sort of like a computer dump—it just went away." Reagan's energy level flagged as the years went on: he was already the oldest president in history, and White House TV recordings from 1982 to 1989 clearly show a gradual, natural slowdown in his physical and mental alertness as the years progressed.

Reagan's White House resembled FDR's coliseum of warring gladiators, but unlike FDR, Reagan would not jump in and manipulate the spectacle. Reagan hired tough, strong officials, watched them frequently cut each other to pieces, and rarely intervened. "When the staff were all organized and in sync with each other, Reagan's strengths could be magnified and the whole country benefited," argued Reagan national security aide Geoffrey Kemp. "When the staff was fighting with each other, it was a disaster. Because he simply was unable or unwilling to intervene and crack heads. Whoever got to him last usually got the last word." "Everybody leaked on everybody in that administration," noted Robert Gates.

The chaos of Reagan's official family feuds did have benefits: through the friction and clashes of debate, Reagan was sure of hearing all the arguments, and by not penalizing officials for speaking their minds, he assured himself a steady stream of opinion and information. Reagan claimed that fostering dissent was a deliberate strategy. "I use a system in which I want to hear what everybody wants to say honestly," Reagan explained to *Fortune* magazine in 1986. "I want the decisions made on what is right or wrong, what is good or bad for the people of this country. I encourage all the input I can get." "More than anybody it's ever been my experience to know," recalled James Baker, "President Reagan made people feel good. We'd come out of the most divisive Cabinet confrontations and once the president had made a decision, he would rule in such a way that the loser never felt like he was beaten, never humiliated, never embarrassed. He made it very clear to everybody that they would never prejudice themselves with him by arguing forcefully for the point of view that they thought was right." "Reagan not only was aware of the contentions and the conflicts between his senior advisers," asserted Robert Gates, "he encouraged them and he allowed them to continue, because he found value in them."

But interadministration feuding and leaking was epidemic under Reagan, as pragmatic aides battled conservative policy hawks for Reagan's soul, plunging knives into each others' backs and bellies in White House meetings, on the front pages of the *Washington Post,* and in back alley showdowns. "It's terrible," said one foreign policy official. "You have no president and you have feudal barons, and it's very bad." CIA Director William Casey called James Baker "a liar." Secretary of State George Shultz clashed with Casey and UN Ambassador Jeane Kirkpatrick. Like champion sumo fighters, Shultz and Secretary of Defense Weinberger were locked in intense, shrill debates over arms control, superpower relations, and Middle East strategy, debating endlessly in front of Reagan. In one arms control meeting in the Situation Room, Shultz, so enraged by hostile leaks, sat with his arms folded and refused to talk to anybody.

In the face of these struggles, Reagan often withdrew. At a meeting of the Economic Policy Council in 1984, the secretaries of State and Agriculture raised their voices and waved their arms at each other, prompting others to join in a raging debate. Reagan sat at his place at the table, focusing quietly on picking licorice jelly beans from his big crystal jar. "He doesn't function well if there are tensions," said Mrs. Reagan. "He likes everybody to like one another and get along." Reagan's third national security adviser, Robert McFarlane, said, "He really disliked personal confrontation. It wasn't a matter of his not seeing value in the competition between Cabinet officers. But he was always quite upset about the shrillness between Cap [Weinberger] and George [Shultz]." Reagan biographer Lou Cannon traced Reagan's withdrawals to his coping with his father's alcoholic eruptions as a child: "In this respect he was a classic adult child of an alcoholic who had learned early in life to retreat from discord and unpleasantness."

Jeane Kirkpatrick recalled "sharp, sometimes bitter debate" between Reagan's national security team, including Shultz, Weinberger, Casey, Joint Chiefs Chairman General John W. Vessey, and herself. "Reagan liked that fine," she contended; "he actually encouraged the big debates between Shultz and Weinberger. He wanted to hear the strongest case to be made for both sides." But the missing ingredient was follow-up. "The president would make decisions three, four, five times, and they would never be implemented," Kirkpatrick recalled. "What was missing was the president saying, 'Now do it, or do it this way. Cut it out. Don't do that.'" "I sat through many meetings down in the Situation Room in the basement where Reagan was brought in because we needed a picture of him there presiding," said National Security Council Mideast expert Geoffrey Kemp, "but it made no difference on the endless fighting between Weinberger and Shultz for instance. He would hardly say anything, and then he'd have to leave to go to another meeting." Reagan once admitted to watching *The Sound of Music* on TV instead of reading his briefing books for the 1983 Williamsburg economic summit.

To budget director David Stockman, Reagan "seemed so serene and passive," and "gave no orders, no commands; asked for no information; expressed no urgency." Stockman recalled that whenever there was an argument, Reagan would smile and say: "Okay, you fellas work it out." Martin Anderson remembered: "Essentially, he just responded to whatever was brought to his attention and said yes or no, or I'll think about it." One aide marveled: "He does not know in any specific way what most of us do or how we do it." Donald Regan maintained that "Reagan seldom criticized, seldom complained, never scolded. Not even the Iran-Contra debacle could provoke him into harsh words, much less subordinates who had let him down. Never—absolutely never in my experience—did President Reagan really lose his temper or utter a rude or unkind word. Never did he issue a direct order, although I, at least, sometimes devoutly wished he would."

When Frank Carlucci walked out of his first meeting with Reagan as his new national security adviser, a meeting in which Reagan had not given any clear guidance, Carlucci turned to his deputy Colin Powell and quipped, "Gee, Colin, I didn't think we signed on to run the country." "You didn't always get crisp guidance from Ronald Reagan," said Carlucci. "We would go back to our office and say, "Now where do you *think* the president would have come out?" He placed great faith in his subordinates. That was what exposed him to the abuses of Iran-Contra."

Reagan's detached, gentle "niceness" caused some of his officials to yearn for a boss who would blow his stack at least once in a while. "There's never been any discipline or rewards from higher up, no matter what you do," one aide lamented in 1987. "I've never heard 'Good job,' or been chewed out." "Nobody ever feared the old man," Ed Rollins observed, identifying one of Reagan's executive Achilles' heels. "He had their affection but not their respect." Reagan hated to fire people, as do most presidents. Donald Regan explained, "He could not bring himself to look somebody in the eye and say OK, you son of a bitch, if that's the way you want it, you've got it—You're fired." The result was that administration officials had to waste a great deal of time scheming and maneuvering, often with the help of Nancy Reagan, to finally push people overboard when Reagan couldn't act.

The Iran-Contra affair exposed the risks of Reagan's executive style, including his frequent detachment and over-delegation of authority. It was a tangled fiasco that severely damaged Reagan's presidency and triggered a congressional reprimand of Reagan's dangerously lax management style. The affair saw the breakdown of Reagan's national security apparatus, as NSC officials sold 2,004 TOW antitank missiles and spare parts to Iran in exchange for three American hostages in Lebanon, with some $3.8 million in profits going to secretly fund the Nicaraguan *contras*. The freed hostages were quickly replaced by three more kidnapped Americans. Reagan directly approved the arms sales to Iran as part of a deliberate strategy to improve relations with Iran and to facilitate the release of the hostages, but it is not clear if Reagan approved the diversion of profits to the *contras*.

In a White House organizational chart of the period, National Security Adviser John Poindexter, who supervised the Iran-Contra operation, is shown reporting to *both* Regan and Reagan—a bureaucratic confusion that led Poindexter, in effect, sometimes to report to neither of them. The responsibility for this muddle was Ronald Reagan's, since he signed off on it. Reagan admitted that "no one kept proper records of meetings or decisions," so he could not recall if he signed off on the first Israeli arms delivery to Iran before or after it occurred. "Reagan had a total incapacity to manage even the mildest detail," argued veteran White House official James Schlesinger. "He was an executive who could not execute. We probably have not had as good a chief of state since George Washington, but he was a dreadful, dreadful chief of government. He really didn't know what was going on most of the time. Therefore he was subject to manipulation by whomever he trusted."

Reagan's trusting, passive executive style left him wide open for both manipulation and miscommunication. A longtime Reagan aide said, "I'm a firm believer that he was at fault for not trying to find out what was going on, but to him it was just one act in a many-ringed circus, and it was either not communicated to him or it was communicated in a way that he just didn't connect." Veteran NSC insider Brent Scowcroft said that the reorganized second-term White House exacerbated Reagan's biggest executive flaw: "He does not have an inquiring style about him." Scowcroft speculated that Reagan could have approved the diversion of arms profits to the *contras* without realizing it.

The report of Reagan's own Tower Commission which investigated the scandal charged "at no time did he insist on accountability and performance review." The report noted, "The president's management style is to put the principal responsibility for policy review and implementation on the shoulders of his advisers. Nevertheless, with such a complex, high-risk operation and so much at stake, the president should have ensured that the NSC system did not fail him. He did not force his policy to undergo the most critical review of which the NSC participants and the process were capable." The majority report of the congressional committee investigating Iran-Contra was even tougher, accusing Reagan of virtual negligence for allowing an "out of control" NSC staff to hijack covert operations from the CIA, and for not ensuring that the law was obeyed. In a White House where few officials feared being fired or disciplined, the hijacking should have surprised no one. Late in 1987, Republican Senator William Cohen of Maine, a member of the investigating committee, said it would be a "waste of time" to talk to Reagan because "with Ronald Reagan, no one is there. The sad fact is we don't have a president."

At the same time that Reagan's presidency was nearly melting down over the relatively peripheral issue (to Reagan) of Iran-Contra, Reagan was achieving stunning breakthroughs on what he, along with every other post-war president, considered to be the number one job of his presidency: it was a job he often managed in a very hands-on style through both terms. "The president loved seeing the raw intelligence on the Soviet economy," said former National Security Adviser John Poindexter. "The anecdotal intelligence especially—factories that were shutting down for a lack of spare parts, hard currency shortages, food lines—interested him greatly and helped determine his belief that the Soviet economy was in monumental trouble." Both CIA Director William Casey and the NSC staff had weekly packages of raw intelligence hand-delivered to Reagan's in-box.

Reagan's close management of U.S.-Soviet affairs is vividly demonstrated by a remarkable series of handwritten letters on file at the Reagan Library, letters to Soviet leaders Brezhnev, Andropov, Chernenko, and Gorbachev at the climax of the Cold War. Banishing his experts, Reagan sat down and painstakingly wrote out the long, heartfelt letters to the Soviet leaders, assuring them of his sincerity and strong desire for peace and arms reduction. This highly personal diplomacy followed Reagan's theory that "sometimes the easiest way to get some things done is for the top people to do them alone and in private."

With the emergence of Mikhail Gorbachev in 1985, a new superpower relationship developed and eventually flourished over five historic summit meetings, powered by a surprising personal chemistry between Reagan and the new Soviet leader. Behind Reagan's bellicose anti-Communist rhetoric was a flexible, pragmatic negotiator who was convinced he could negotiate the end of the arms race. Incredibly, that's exactly what he did, though it would take his successor's term and the collapse of the Soviet Union in 1991 to complete the process. Snapshots of Reagan's evolving attitudes toward the Soviet Union appear in White House TV footage shot from the midpoint of his presidency through his last year.

The Oval Office and Cabinet Room

President Reagan and Administration Officials and Congressmen
1985–1987
RE: *U.S./Soviet Relations*
videotape recordings of meetings by White House TV

April 1, 1985: The Oval Office, Meeting with James Buckley, President of Radio Free Europe, and National Security Advisers, 9:45 a.m.

RE: *Smuggled Message From Soviet Women Imprisoned in Gulag*

Radio Free Europe president James Buckley strode into the Oval Office this morning to hand Reagan a message from 100 Russian women buried in the Soviet gulag prison system for human rights activity. The women, who had been on hunger strike, smuggled out a message for Reagan printed on tiny pieces of rolled-up rice paper, in letters so small "you almost needed a magnifying glass to read them," according to Buckley. Reagan was a big supporter of Radio Free Europe and Radio Liberty, which broadcast uncensored news and information in dozens of languages into the Soviet bloc. As the president sat Buckley down by the fireplace, Vice President Bush looked on from a nearby couch. Reagan appeared stunned and upset by the message.

Buckley: Mr. President, this is a rather remarkable item. Are you familiar with the word *samizdat* [Russian term for underground press]?
Reagan: Yes. (*riveted*)
Buckley: That's what it looks like. That is a message to you from 100 women who are locked in the pokey for having done such things as Helsinki Watch and so on.
　　This is what they say: "We women political prisoners congratulate you on your reelection to the post of president of the U.S.A. We look with hope to your country which is on the road of freedom and respect for human rights. We wish you success."
　　This is a schedule of the hunger strikes that they scheduled September through December of last year in commemoration of Helsinki Days and things of that sort. (*hands documents to Reagan*)

REAGAN: Oh, golly. (*Reagan closely examines the documents through the rest of the meeting*)

BUCKLEY: This in here is further documentation of who they are and where their camp is. That was smuggled out, Lord knows how.

REAGAN: There's no way to thank them, 'cause they'd probably get in trouble?

BUCKLEY: Actually, these people want to be publicized. Why have a hunger strike if the world doesn't know.

REAGAN: For heaven's sakes.

BUCKLEY: One way or another, they will be alerted to the fact you read it, either by explicit name—if it can be smuggled out, I assume it can be smuggled back in.

REAGAN: They don't mean for us to do something about acknowledging this publicly?

BUCKLEY: No. One way or another we'll let them know that you personally received it.

BUSH: How did it get to you, Jim?

BUCKLEY: George, those are some of the questions . . . (*brief tape cut as video crew moves*) unofficial documents, because people know that once it reaches us, it can reach the world, because we broadcast back into the country.

REAGAN: That's the actual size? Golly, how could anyone write that small?

Good Lord. Oh, Lord. Damnit, it is an evil empire!

It's time to say it again!

BUCKLEY: May I quote you?

REAGAN: Yes, yes you may! It is! We've just been talking in here about the Nicholson thing. That's the difference. [Reagan was referring to U.S. Army officer Major Arthur D. Nicholson, Jr., part of a liaison team operating in East Germany under the rules of a 1947 access agreement, who, the previous week, was shot by a Soviet sentry and allowed to bleed to death when the Soviets prevented first aid from reaching him.]

You can't really say that down to the people's level. I'm sure the people of Russia are outgoing, probably very very nice, warm people. But the system—*is barbarism!*

The emotional impact of the message lingered—in private, Reagan talked about the message from the imprisoned Russian women for days.

December 11, 1987: The Cabinet Room, President Reagan and Congressional Leadership, 8:30 a.m.

RE: *U.S./Soviet Summit in Washington*

The turning point in the end of the Cold War occurred at the Reykjavík summit in October 1986, when long hours of negotiations produced progress on human rights and missiles in Europe but stalled finally on Gorbachev's insistence on blocking Reagan's cherished Strategic Defense Initiative. "I've said again and again that SDI wasn't a bargaining chip," a furious Reagan told the Soviet leader. "There is no way we are going to give up research to find a defense weapon against nuclear missiles." Reagan slammed his briefing book shut while Gorbachev was in mid-sentence, stood up and ended the conference. "The meeting is over," he said. As Reagan put on his overcoat, a dazed Gorbachev asked, "Can't we do something about this?" "It's too late," said the president as he walked out of the summit.

The walkout was a turning point: Gorbachev soon dropped his SDI demand and a new summit in Washington in December 1987 accelerated the thaw in U.S.-Soviet relations. "I think Gorbachev was ready to talk the next time we met—in Washington—because we had walked out on him at Reykjavík and gone ahead with the SDI program," said Reagan. At the Washington summit the two leaders signed the INF agreement eliminating nuclear missiles in Europe, and planned both a new summit in Moscow and the beginnings of the strategic arms reduction process. On this tape Reagan briefed a Cabinet Room full of congressional leaders on the summit. As Reagan walked in the room, they greeted him with cheers and a standing ovation, prompting a vintage Reagan wisecrack.

Reagan: What, did they run one of my old movies last night?

In addition to signing of the treaty, we covered fully our four-part agenda, to include human rights, regional conflicts and bilateral issues.

I'll just give you—keep on eating—I'd just like to give you a brief summary of our talks, and then I'll ask Howard [Baker, chief of staff] and Colin Powell to elaborate further. George Shultz, by the way, is on his way to Europe right now to brief our Allied leaders.

We started right off on Day one on human rights, and there is movement and resolution with individual cases in which prisoners who will be released or exit visas granted and I'm encouraged by his assurance of more substantial movement in the future which I hope to see become a reality.

We have been, if you don't know, we have been instead of just talking generally on it, we have from every source names that come in to us of people that are separated, husband and wife and that sort of thing, or anything else, and we put lists together and we furnish them as requests from us that they take action on those cases. There has been quite a response to that.

On the regional conflicts, I spoke very candidly to him on the issue of Afghanistan. While he assured me of the desire to withdraw their troops, we couldn't get around to setting a date as to when that would begin or end. There was some discussions he means to have about what follows their withdrawal, the coming together of neutral government in Afghanistan. We talked about that, and he made it plain in his mind that there will be a date set for leaving and the completion of their departure . . . .

On arms control, we of course signed not just an arms control treaty, but an arms reduction treaty, as you know, that won't just put a ceiling on the growth of nuclear weapons, but actually abolishes that particular class of weapons.

A major achievement was a good set of instructions to our negotiators in Geneva to conclude a START agreement. We're working on that. We'll have it preferably in time to be signed at the Moscow summit. There's no question, we've agreed, all of us, that there will be such a meeting and it's up to us to set the date on it. We're simply waiting until we know more about things like the economic summit.

On defense and space, we came to an agreement that protects our ability to develop and deploy SDI.

So I'm really satisfied with the results of the summit. I think we achieved our objectives . . . .

June 14, 1988: The Cabinet Room, President Reagan and Congressional Leadership, 9:30 a.m.

RE: *U.S./Soviet Summit in Moscow*

At the Moscow summit, NSC aide Paul Stevens's job included transcribing the notes of private conversations between Reagan and

Gorbachev. "I was absolutely awestruck because there is no one who could have spoken with greater forcefulness than Ronald Reagan. This was representation at a presidential level of our country in as fine a fashion as you could ever find it. That's not the Reagan that a lot of people dismissed him as. But it certainly is the Reagan that he was behind the scenes very often to me." When he returned from the summit, Reagan briefed congressional leaders.

REAGAN: We won't be disturbed by the media, so we'll get right to it.

I know that some of you've probably seen some hints in the media about a summit in Moscow just recently. I wanted to add a personal observation or two here.

The channels of communication I think between our two governments are wide open and I hope we can keep it that way and allow my replacement to build on the achievement so far.

I think it's clear that Gorbachev really wants to restore the Soviet economy. It's a terrific job and it will take him a long time if he succeeds at all, because he's got opposition there, very obviously so.

He also appears to be interested in political reform, although it's a little harder to pick out exactly what he has in mind with that.

In any event, though, we've seen progress, yet at the same time I think that we have to consider them an adversary, because of their foreign policy and controlled society at home, until there is more substantial evidence that we can look at them differently.

We know the power of the word and we know the importance of being able to speak directly to the Soviet people without their government in between. Because I was pleased on my trip to convey the support of the American people directly to the dissidents and refuseniks struggling for their human rights and also to the clergy with regard to freedom of religion and all.

There were no objections—I don't think they stood off and cheered or clapped, I mean the [Soviet] government, but I did it with their full knowledge that I was doing this.

Now I'm out of town again, I'm heading out on Sunday, I'll be leaving for the economic summit with our allies. It's the eighth and final one for me. I'm thinking back to that first one, and then realize how far we've come. (*Reagan shook his head in a gesture of amazement*)

Before he resigned as Reagan's third national security adviser, Robert McFarlane shook his head and said, "He knows so little and accomplishes so much." Years later, McFarlane's bewilderment grew. In 1991, he mused, "Jimmy Carter just by default left him this legacy of a readiness on the part of the American people to spend money on national security. Number two, he happened to serve at a time when the Soviet Union collapsed. He contributed to that, but he is the beneficiary of something that was not of his own creation, at least not entirely. All in all, and I'm just talking about foreign policy, there isn't anything you can really say that Ronald Reagan—by dint of intellect and skill in diplomacy or imagination—did." "You couldn't figure him out like a fact," wrote George Shultz, "because to Reagan the main fact was a vision."

Reagan's struggle to achieve his vision of a soaring American economy was only partly fulfilled. When he took office, the economy was in its worst shape in forty years. Under Reagan the longest expansion in U.S. peacetime history occurred, without serious inflation, creating over 16 million new jobs. The inflation rate, 12.5 percent in Carter's last year, was down to 4.4 percent percent in 1988, and the unemployment rate was reduced from 7.1 percent to 5.5 percent, while the prime interest rate fell nearly six points to 9.3 percent percent. In the process, Reagan's military spending spree ignited huge deficits, and tripled the national debt to $2.7 trillion. "Every budget that I submitted to the Congress is lower than what the Congress was proposing," Reagan argued in 1991, "and every one of my budgets was put on the shelf, and they called it dead on arrival."

In his last Oval Office interview as president, Reagan was asked to describe his presidency in one line. "We won the Cold War," he said quickly. Richard Allen argued, "The democratization of the world occurred under Ronald Reagan. Not only eventually in Russia and the Soviet bloc, but Taiwan, the Philippines, Korea, all of Latin America democratized." Robert Gates argued, "It was Ronald Reagan who made the critical strategic decisions to return to negotiating with the Soviets, first in arms control, and then in negotiating solutions to a number of Third World conflicts, beginning with Afghanistan." In 1991, Margaret Thatcher announced simply, "He won the Cold War without firing a shot." In a 1996 *New York Times*/CBS poll, Reagan was ranked the number two president among Americans when asked who they'd want to run the country today. He placed second only to John Kennedy, and beat the next three (FDR, Truman, and Lincoln) by a wide margin. Scholars already revising their estimates of Reagan upward: in a 1997 *Chicago Sun Times* poll of historians, he ranked in the top third, at number ten.

Reagan was not a totally detached and disengaged executive. In what he considered the most important functions of the presidency—superpower and congressional relations and communicating with the public—he was hands-on and effective in pursuing his radical vision. It was the narrowness of his executive agenda and attention that nearly killed his presidency.

Ronald Reagan's executive style was too trusting in human nature, and he clung to a flawed understanding of the chief executive's role. Halfway into his presidency, as the Iran-Contra scandal was about to break, he told *Fortune* magazine, "I believe that you surround yourself with the best people you can find, delegate authority, and don't interfere as long as the overall policy that you've decided upon is being carried out." By adopting this system he abdicated his responsibility to inspect his subordinates' work, to prod, to follow up, to ask tough questions, to clarify, to challenge assumptions, and most of all, to insist on accountability from his people.

Reagan demonstrated that even the greatest visionary must have his dreams tethered to an effective system for managing them. As an operational executive he was dangerously incomplete, but as a visionary executive in a turbulent time, America will see few stronger than Ronald Reagan.

In his last moments in the Oval Office, Reagan wrote a note to incoming president George Bush on a notepad inscribed DON'T LET THE TURKEYS GET YOU DOWN and stashed it in the desk drawer. Spotting National Security Adviser Colin Powell, Reagan reached into his coat pocket and pulled out the white laminated card he had carried with him for the past eight years containing the nuclear launch codes. "Oh, who do I give these to?" Powell told him a military aide would take it from him after the new president was sworn in, but thanks in large part to Reagan's work, the card was now almost irrelevant. These last moments in the office were captured by the quiet, ubiquitous White House TV crew.

Reagan sadly looked around one last time at the now darkened and bare office.

He reached down to touch the desk, threw his shoulders back, and marched out the door.

CHAPTER 10

George Bush

The Diplomatic Executive

*"You know, every day, many important papers come across that desk
in that marvelous Oval Office, and very few items remain there for long.
Got to keep that paper moving or you get inundated. Your snorkel
will fill up and there will be no justice."*

GEORGE BUSH, 1991

THE OVAL OFFICE STUDY
JANUARY 17, 1991, 7:00 P.M.

George Bush sat in the small private study next to the Oval Office with his
top White House aides, firing a remote control at the TV, his suit jacket
draped over a chair. On the other side of the world, the event he said he had
"been training all his life for" was beginning.

Across the Middle East, 527,000 American soldiers and 200,000 coalition
troops were preparing to pulverize Iraqi armed forces and expel Saddam
Hussein from Kuwait. In the moonless desert sky southeast of Baghdad, the
first in a wave of a hundred $1 million-a-piece, terrain-hugging Tomahawk
cruise missiles was speeding toward Baghdad at low altitude, five minutes
from impact, an onboard computer adjusting its flight path by checking its
radar with digitally scanned topographic maps and gently rotating its wings to
guide it within a few feet of its target.

As the clock in the president's study struck seven o'clock, a U.S. pilot in
a $100 million F-117A Stealth bomber above Baghdad squeezed a button on
his joystick and launched a 2,000-pound, laser-guided penetrator bomb
straight down through the center of the concrete roof of Iraq's International
Telephone and Telegraph Building. Seconds later it was followed by two

high-explosive bombs fired by Stealths following closely behind. The bombs flew through the hole in the roof and detonated from inside the building, blowing its top off and decapitating much of Iraq's communications network.

Throughout the Gulf region, Allied attack jets and helicopters, electronic warfare planes, refueling tankers, and decoy drones were surging into the skies in a vast ballet of high technology, a symphony of strategic planning, tactical complexity, and precision timing. With Vice President Dan Quayle, National Security Adviser Brent Scowcroft, and Chief of Staff John Sununu by his side, George Bush clicked through the channels in his shirt-sleeves, jumping from CNN to ABC, where reporter Gary Shephard in Baghdad broadcast from his hotel window that he saw the bombs destroying the communications building.

Moments later, when the TV networks reported the skies over Baghdad were ablaze with antiaircraft fire and flying bombs, Bush remarked, "This is just the way it was scheduled." He turned to his press secretary, Marlin Fitzwater, and directed him to announce to the world that the liberation of Kuwait had begun. "Go ahead and do it, Marlin." Moments later the world heard CNN reporters Bernard Shaw, John Holliman, and Peter Arnett broadcasting from the ninth floor of Baghdad's Al Rashid Hotel, crawling on their hands and knees, peering out the window, and exclaiming, "Something is happening outside . . . we're getting starbursts . . . in the black sky . . . they're coming over our hotel. You can hear the bombs now . . . we just heard—whoa! Holy cow! That was a large airburst that we saw! . . . This feels like we're in the center of hell."

Outside Bush's office, a White House TV video crew was shooting the scene through the window, but they were not allowed into the room. As vice president, Bush spent seven years fidgeting and squirming in the background as White House TV crews shot footage of President Reagan in the White House (the filming began in 1982). Now, as president, although he was warm and friendly with the crews, he was letting them into less substantive White House activity. Additionally, according to both Bush's Chief of Staff John Sununu and his National Security Adviser Brent Scowcroft, no other recordings of any kind ever took place in the work sessions of George Bush's White House: no video or audio recordings of meetings, no head-of-state telephone recordings, nothing.

The no-taping policy was typical of Bush's highly cautious and secretive management style, and one Bush aide said, "Anyone who taped would have been shot, there would have been a fight for the gun, and I would have pulled the trigger." Like Carter, however, Bush did keep a tape-recorded personal diary. According to presidential historian and Bush biographer Herbert Parmet, Bush began the practice when he was U.S. envoy to China in 1975, and when he began running for president in 1986, he periodically carried a minicassette machine in his breast pocket to make diary recordings. So far the tape transcripts have been made available only to Parmet (he was not allowed to make copies, and could only make notes from them in Bush's post-presidential office).

"You work your ass off, get credit for stuff you're barely involved in and none at all for things you've put together behind the scenes," Bush mused back in 1980 while losing the presidential nomination to Ronald Reagan. "Domestic problems drag you down and nag all the time. You're up in the polls and down and then up again. But sooner or later something major happens, something abroad that only we can do something about. Then you show if you can cut it." That something was now happening to Bush in the strategic crucible of the Persian Gulf. Over and over again during his presidency, Bush declared, "The single most important job of the president is the national security of the United States," and ever since the August 1990 invasion of Kuwait, when an angry Bush declared "this will not stand," he saw the Gulf crisis as the defining event of his presidency and of the post–Cold War era. "I've resolved all the moral issues in my mind," Bush told his staff. "It's black and white, good versus evil."

"Bush's decision to commit U.S. troops in the Gulf War was a pure Bush decision," said John Sununu, "in the sense that he made it clear to a military that constantly appeared reluctant to accept the responsibility of going to war, that that was what we were going to do." According to Sununu, Bush "literally had to look senior military advisers in the eye and say that's what we're going to do." "You have to remember that people like George Bush who play on the world stage don't think like the rest of us," said a Bush confidante at the time. "One part of him, frankly, welcomes the challenge. This is exactly the kind of high-stakes, history-making decision he hoped he would have the opportunity to make, and he has a quiet confidence that there is nobody better qualified to make it."

Bush was right: on paper, no one in the world had a bluer-chip pedigree for the Oval Office than his. As the youngest combat pilot in the World War II navy, he flew fifty-eight missions and lost four planes to enemy fire or malfunctions. After graduating from Yale in 1948, the Philips Andover–educated Bush, son of a wealthy Wall Street broker–cum–U.S. Senator from Connecticut, seasoned in moderate Republican WASP patricianism and noblesse oblige (Bush spent part of the Depression being driven to Greenwich Country

Day School by chauffeur), packed up a 1947 Studebaker and drove all the way to Texas to stake his claim as an entrepreneur oilman. He started out as an equipment salesman, and within five years he was co-owner and president of Zapata Off-Shore Co. Bush enjoyed the experience, but as *Fortune* magazine reported, "Bush's company did not exactly boom. New competitors with more money surged past it. When he sold Off-Shore to run for Congress in 1966, Bush's share of the company brought about $1 million."

His political career, as two-term Texas congressman, UN ambassador, Republican Party chief, envoy to China, CIA director, and globe-trotting vice president, honed his skills as a faithful, non-ideological organization man with a diplomatic, collegial executive style that stressed personal relationships, loyalty, and secrecy, and allowed disagreements as long as they were settled privately. "One would think that Bush's broad-based experience in business, government, and international affairs would help in presidential decision-making," wrote Ann Reilly Dowd in *Fortune* magazine in 1988. "His greatest managerial strength is a fine talent for inspiring affection and trust. A warm, personable man who seems genuinely to care about fellow humans, Bush has been a much-loved boss, building team spirit and morale in difficult situations. Still, he is not a manager who intentionally shakes things up."

As UN ambassador and as China envoy, Bush did not make major decisions, not with a boss like Henry Kissinger. Stephen Hess, senior fellow at the Brookings Institution and author of *Organizing the Presidency,* observed that Bush's executive résumé, while wide, was not extremely deep. "The vice president's office is not much of a managerial proposition," said Hess. "The UN ambassador gives speeches. The CIA is something worth managing, but he was only there for a year." In 1975, Bush took over a CIA that had been shaken to its core by revelations of illegal domestic spying and foreign assassination plots, and by most accounts did a capable job. Thomas Ashley, a former Ohio congressman and friend of Bush's since college, said, "Bush wasn't intellectually penetrating at the CIA, but what he did for morale in a year was astonishing."

As Ronald Reagan's vice president for eight years, Bush had an office just down the hall from the Oval Office, access to presidential briefings and meetings, and a weekly private meal with Reagan. He had a ringside seat for the action, but he was neither a main administration player nor a Reagan intimate: the Bushes were hardly ever invited to the upstairs White House residence to socialize, thanks in part to reportedly frosty relations between Nancy Reagan and Barbara Bush. From this vantage point, however, Bush was able to gain invaluable operational knowledge of the presidency, and he built a global network of friendships with current and future world leaders. When he entered the Oval Office, Bush had more than 2,000 people in his Rolodex.

In interviews before taking office, Bush described his planned management style as a reaction to his predecessors. He said he planned to be fully briefed, but not to get bogged down in micro-decisions: "Jimmy Carter got credit for knowing everybody who played on the White House tennis court," Bush asserted, "and President Reagan has been a master delegator. I think I would be somewhere in between." "I think you have to delegate because nobody can be expected to know everything about everything," he told another interviewer. "Government is too complex, the problems too enormous. But I think I'd be good in setting a philosophical direction, setting certain objectives, delegating authority and then staying in touch, and I've always done that, in something as complicated as the CIA, or for the short period of time I was in business." In the Gulf War, Bush proved true to his plan.

On the second day of the Gulf air war, Bush sat down for a briefing in "the tank," a super-secure conference room used by the Joint Chiefs at the Pentagon. Bush grilled his brass, poring over maps, satellite photos, and gun-camera video footage that amplified starlight by a factor of 25,000. He probed for updates, damage assessments, contingency plans. Joint Chiefs Chairman Colin Powell had crisp answers for each Bush salvo, and after a half hour, Bush jumped up and adjourned by cracking, "Hey, I'm going to have to do some more micromanaging of this thing." The generals belly laughed in relief: this was one commander in chief who was not going to hover over their shoulders like a raven and second-guess their decisions, like Lyndon Johnson.

Colin Powell later reflected, "I think we were blessed with a group of political leaders, a president, and a secretary of defense who . . . allowed the military to participate in the decision-making process from the very beginning, and allowed me as chairman to be a part of the inner sanctum, so there was, as close as possible, integration between political issues and political thinking and military issues and military decisions." Recalling his Vietnam agonies, retired Admiral Thomas Moorer noted: "This is so different from Vietnam, it's out of this world." Gulf battle commander Lieutenant General Gary Luck declared George Bush "was a hero to all of us. He did not tie us down." Bush carefully avoided any direct communication with coalition field commander General H. Norman Schwarzkopf, dealing instead with Powell and Defense Secretary Dick Cheney. When Iraq fired SCUD missiles against Israel, Bush pointedly shunned rushing to the West Wing and stayed in the White House residence to dine with his EPA administrator, an image that was carefully spoon-fed to the press.

Behind the public relations spin was an intensely hands-on chief executive, "a sponge for detail" according to one staffer, who periodically barged into the White House Situation Room to grab raw intelligence cables, stayed glued to his television for war news, and spent up to 80 percent of his day huddled up with his "Gang of Eight" War Council—Powell, Chief of Staff Sununu, Defense Secretary Dick Cheney, Secretary of State James Baker, National Security Adviser Brent Scowcroft, Deputy National Security Adviser Robert Gates, and Vice President Dan Quayle, periodically joined by CIA Director William Webster and Press Secretary Marlin Fitzwater. In classic Bush tradition, it was a tight, cohesive, and leak-free group. "We were all friends," James Baker recalled. "We had all worked together before in one capacity or another. It worked very smoothly. And that was a function of President Bush's executive management style."

While Bush did not intervene in the military tactics of the war, diplomacy, however, was a radically different matter. The Gulf War demonstrated why people at the State Department called Bush "The Mad Dialer" and Bush aides called him "the Rolodex President." Since his first days in the Oval Office, Bush had been methodically, compulsively telephoning his fellow heads of state around the world, to wheel and deal, discuss policy, or just say "Hi." Bush had 190 such phone conferences, in addition to meeting with other world leaders 135 times, all in his first year alone. In August 1989, when Lebanese terrorists threatened to execute hostage Joseph Cicippio, Bush telephoned Kings Hussein of Jordan, Fahd of Saudi Arabia, and Hassan of Morocco; Prime Ministers Margaret Thatcher of Britain and Turgut Ozal of Turkey; Chancellor Helmut Kohl of West Germany; Presidents Hosni Mubarak of Egypt and Chadli Bendjedid of Algeria; plus the pope, to ask for their intercession with Iran and Iranian-supported terrorists. There were some embarrassing slip-ups: one day a man impersonating Iranian President Ali Akbar Hashemi Rafsanjani bluffed his way through the White House switchboard into speaking with Bush by phone, and during the Tiananmen Square crisis in Beijing, Bush could not get any of his "good friends" in the Chinese leadership to come to the phone.

"He would turn to the phone at any opportunity to talk to his counterparts," recalled Brent Scowcroft. "It played an enormous role in building U.S. leadership and building confidence on the part of his counterparts around the world in his decisions. They knew what his thinking was and they had confidence, even if they didn't necessarily agree with the decision he was making." As an example, Scowcroft cited the Panama invasion of 1989.

"By the time we sent forces into Panama to take Noriega, he had talked on the phone, unassociated with this crisis, to almost all of the heads of state in Latin America," Scowcroft said. "As a consequence, there was relatively little outcry at the fact that we had intervened in Panama. They were disposed to give him the benefit of the doubt. He used that in every crisis—with Chancellor Kohl and the unification of Germany, with both Gorbachev and Yeltsin in the last days of the Soviet Union, with the coalition in the Gulf War." Assistant Secretary of State John Bolton recalled, "The career people at the State Department used to call him the 'Mad Dialer' because of his frequent calls to foreign leaders. In fact, it's pretty clear that Vernon Walters, the U.S. ambassador to Germany at the time, resigned because he was tired of hearing from the German Foreign Ministry that the president had been on the phone to Chancellor Helmut Kohl again and that they had agreed on some other aspect of U.S.-German bilateral relations."

As soon as Iraq invaded Kuwait, Bush raced into his "speed-dial mode," burning up the phone lines to Moscow, Bonn, Paris, Tokyo, London, Cairo, and Jerusalem in bursts of concentrated energy that rivaled his infamous rounds of "golf polo" (eighteen holes in less than two hours). Two days after the invasion in August 1990, Bush rattled off the dizzying array of leaders he was phoning. Among them: President Ozal of Turkey, Japanese Prime Minister Kaifu, Prime Minister Mulroney, President Mitterand, Chancellor Kohl, and Prime Minister Thatcher.

A Bush aide said Bush "knew twenty-four hours after the invasion that the first step would be making this an international effort." "By Thursday," the aide said, "the orders started flooding out of the Oval Office. The president had all of these diplomatic pieces in his head. The UN piece. The NATO piece. The Middle East piece. He was meticulous, methodical and personal." A crucial Bush call to Prime Minister Toshiki Kaifu persuaded Japan, which imported 12 percent of its oil from Kuwait and Iraq, to join the allied embargo, a very tough decision for Japan. During a call with French leader Mitterand, the two made word-by-word revisions to the UN sanctions resolution. "No memos were required," said an aide. "It was all in his head. He operated exactly opposite of how Reagan worked. He knew the military thrust should follow the diplomatic. He knew that to be effective, the lineup against Saddam had to be perceived as more than just the rich West against a poor Arab."

By the end of November 1990, when the UN Security Council passed Resolution 678 authorizing the use of force to expel Iraq from Kuwait, Bush and Baker had cobbled together an extraordinary global coalition by phone from the Oval Office, with troops from almost all Arab countries including Egypt, Syria, and Saudi Arabia; thirteen NATO nations including England and France; former Warsaw Pact countries like Czechoslovakia, Poland, and Bulgaria; and even developing nations like Bangladesh, Senegal, Somalia, and Zaire. Japan offered financial assistance, and the Soviets kicked in with moral support. Assistant Secretary of State Bolton remembered Bush as "an incredibly hands-on president in foreign policy" and recalled times when, sitting in Secretary of State Baker's office, Bush would be on the phone instructing Baker on UN Security Council procedure. "Baker would hold the phone away from his ear so I could hear the president's conversation and write down what I was supposed to do. When I say a hands-on approach, I mean a hands-on approach."

During the Gulf buildup, air war, and ground war, Bush stayed glued to the phone in international hand-holding sessions, consulting with Gorbachev, trading news with Mubarak and Major, sympathizing with Fahd, holding the coalition together, telling them "where he's coming from," and asking "where they're coming from," as he put it. When SCUD missiles began slamming onto Israel, his phone stroking of Israeli leader Yitzak Shamir helped keep the Israelis from counterattacking and triggering a wider war. After five and a half weeks of bombardment and 100 hours of ground combat, coalition forces chased Iraq out of Kuwait, the United States suffered only 124 dead, and "a quick, decisive and just victory" was achieved, according to Bush.

There was controversy over the war's finale: at one point Schwarzkopf claimed that he had preferred continuing the fighting for at least several hours to encircle and destroy fleeing Iraqi Republican Guards (he and Bush's brass then denied it), and critics charged that coalition forces should have conquered Baghdad and somehow captured Hussein. In the final hours of the war, Bush, under pressure from Saudi Arabia and Egypt to conclude the conflict, and sensitive to images of a continuing mass slaughter of Iraqi troops, did press the military for estimates of how quickly the war could be ended.

Bush contended that the military supported the timing of the war's end, that UN objectives had been achieved, and that a longer war would have fractured the coalition. He explained: "I was very careful in being sure that the military supported the cessation of the fighting. It was stated to me clearly by General Powell, who indeed talked on the phone to General Schwarzkopf from my office, that the time had come to stop the fighting. The goal was to kick Iraq out of Kuwait, and the goal, in the opinion of our top fighters, had been achieved." Powell reflected, "We had done the right thing, he believed, and we had prevailed. The only way to have avoided this outcome was to have undertaken a largely U.S. conquest and occupation of a remote nation of 20 million people. I don't think that is what the American people signed up for."

The Gulf War was also the zenith of George Bush's career, a dizzying glimpse of a summit he would never see again.

The first time George Bush entered the Oval Office as president, he walked around and inspected it as if he'd never been there before. He sat down at the presidential desk, pulled open the drawer, and found the note Reagan placed there a few hours before. It read, "Dear George, You'll have moments when you want to use this particular stationery. Well, go for it. George, I treasure the memories we share and wish you all the very best. You'll be in my prayers. God bless you and Barbara. I'll miss our Thursday lunches. Ron." Bush read the note to himself, smiled, and said, "What a sweet man." He moved the *Resolute* desk to his second office on the second floor of the White House, and wheeled his vice presidential desk into the Oval Office, and soon its drawers were crammed with baseball gloves and tennis balls.

Bush usually jumped out of bed at 5:30 in the morning, after six and a half hours of sleep, to the sounds of country and western music on the radio. He began scanning newspapers and morning TV news shows in bed with Barbara, then made it over to the Oval Office study by 6:30 or 7:00 to watch CNN and review the *Washington Post, New York Times, Wall Street Journal, USA Today* (for box scores), New York's *Daily News* and *Post,* and his home-town *Houston Chronicle,* while downing a breakfast of coffee, grapefruit, and cereal. He'd spend the next hour alone, calling aides, reading, or banging out typewritten messages to his Cabinet and staff on blue "From the President" note cards. According to Scowcroft, "He reads and scans a lot of news stories as a check on the bureaucracy and to see how his policies are being under-stood and interpreted." During the day he popped his head in on Press Sec-retary Fitzwater's office: "How are the overnights, Marlin?"

Between 8:00 and 8:15 A.M. began the morning meeting, a ritual that Sununu called "the catalyzing meeting, on a daily basis, of George Bush's management of the presidency." The key players were Sununu, Quayle, Scowcroft, and Gates. First came an overnight intelligence briefing, then a national security briefing, a domestic affairs briefing, and a group "round robin" discussion, which was over by 10:00 A.M. Bush was highly assertive and engaged in these sessions. In the intelligence briefings the old spymaster would often jump in to fire off questions or challenge the data as it was reported to him. "Bush managed the presidency through a very onion-layered structure," recalled Sununu. "There was a layer closest to the president: myself, General Scowcroft, and the vice president. We'd meet every morning and within that group, anything went. People would argue back and forth. It was a group of people who had a lot of respect for each other, who wouldn't leak. The next layer was the Cabinet."

If a guest walked in on Bush in the Oval Office, Bush could often be found doing several things at once, like writing personal notes while holding an informal staff conference. He'd greet a visitor with a big grin, and perhaps give him a playful squeeze. According to Powell, "Bush had a knack for putting people at ease when they entered the Oval Office . . . 'Hi, Dick, hi, Colin. Did you hear the one about the psychiatrist—'." Vice President Dan Quayle observed, "He always wanted people to be comfortable. During a meeting he'd pour cream in people's coffee or offer them Velamints." Bush would surprise visitors with his prep-school manners by pouring beverages himself: "This is coffee, this is tea. Would you like cream and sugar?" During meetings, Bush would drape out his cowboy-booted legs while fiddling with a silver-and-black monogrammed Swiss Army knife. If a staffer argued a point too long, he'd cut in with a stock wisecrack: "If you're so damned smart, how come you aren't president of the United States?" "He's very direct with his questions," reported Sununu. "If he doesn't understand it, he asks the question why, or how, or where."

Like JFK, Bush sometimes plunged deep down in the bureaucracy for information. John Sununu observed, "He is just as likely to pick up the telephone and call a staff member three layers down to get an answer as he is to call the chief of staff and have the chief of staff go chase it. Or he'll pick up the phone and call somebody in a department." James Baker recalled, "Bush came up through the system, so he knew how to reach down directly and tap those resources." One top aide said that Bush performed as "his own chief of staff" and "his own best intelligence agent." Such tactics were not always productive: in the midst of an attempted coup against Panamanian dictator Manuel Noriega that preceded the successful U.S. invasion, Bush turned the Oval Office into a war room filled with raw CIA data and battle maps, while answering calls from the field. Bush was soon swamped with conflicting information and the coup failed. During the U.S. invasion of Panama, Bush called up the CIA's operations center at midnight to ask an amazed desk officer if Noriega had been caught yet.

Bush's Oval Office was a hurricane of hyperactive motion—phone calls, brain-picking sessions, unscheduled meetings. According to presidential personnel director Chase Untermeyer, Bush not only left his in-box empty every night, he cleaned it out several times a day. Through the day, Bush often rearranged the schedule and added impromptu discussions. Deputy Chief of Staff Andy Card, a former Reagan aide, noticed, "Reagan was comfortable with structured events. Bush invites spontaneity. He manages by walking around." "His instinct is to return as many phone calls as possible, to drop in on his buddies in Congress, initiate a lot of calls, even in the middle of meetings, to anybody he thinks can shed light on a subject he's interested in," observed Craig Fuller, Bush's vice presidential chief of staff. "He's also prone to overcommit himself when any of his thousand best friends ask him to do things." "And yes, he likes to check who's playing on the White House tennis court and horseshoe pit, who's flying on Air Force One, and who's sitting next to whom at White House dinners," reported *Fortune*'s Ann Reilly Dowd. "During the development of his 1991 budget, he made about seventy relatively micro decisions, most of which would have been settled by staff in the Reagan years."

In the Cabinet Room, Bush replaced a portrait of the quasi-conscious Calvin Coolidge with one of Bush's fellow hyperkinetic Republican Yankee-turned-Westerner Theodore Roosevelt, and installed two sculptures of TR in the Oval Office. Bush returned memos with extensive margin notes and edits, and was notorious for marking up most everything that came through his in-box. Bush usually left the Oval Office around 6:45, but on many nights from 8:00 P.M. to 10:00 P.M. he locked himself up in his study on the second floor of the White House, signing memos, reading briefing papers, and, as he did since he was a young Texas oilman, writing twenty to forty personal notes per night to friends and supporters the world over. Bush regularly flooded the in-boxes of top aides like Scowcroft, who worked until 10:00 P.M. to clear his desk, only to be greeted the next morning by a fresh mountain of memos and cables from the president. On the way back from London after a 1989 NATO summit, Bush dashed off forty thank-you notes to his staff.

Bush was obsessed with maintaining secrecy and preventing leaks. The *Washington Post*'s David Hoffman contended this was because Bush was "a throwback to the patrician 'wise men' of the U.S. foreign policy establishment, the men who guided the United States from the period after World War II through the Vietnam War." "They were diplomats and businessmen who believed they had been endowed with the education and experience to perform in the public's best interests but often without the public's knowledge," Hoffman wrote at the end of Bush's first year. Bush regularly swore his aides to secrecy, and kept secrets himself even from his top tier of advisers, compartmentalizing information so that only he knew the full picture. When National Security Adviser Brent Scowcroft flew to China on a secret post-Tiananmen visit with Chinese leaders, Bush didn't even tell Chief of Staff Sununu about it. Sununu's aides accidentally found out, infuriating Bush. After a rare leak, about a summit with Gorbachev at Malta, an angry Bush announced to his officials: "If we cannot maintain proper secrecy with this group, we will cut the circle down."

Former Vice President Dan Quayle reported that Bush was "intellectually very curious, and wanted to know all sides of a problem." "I've been to Cabinet meetings when [they have] been a show-and-tell," Bush remarked, taking a not-so-subtle shot at Reagan's style. "We don't do ours that way." To expose Bush to conflicting ideas, his aides organized policy debates, or "scheduled train wrecks," during which officials would go at it while Bush took notes on a legal pad and interjected with questions, in a process called "multiple advocacy" by Bush aide and Harvard presidential scholar Roger Porter. "I've known pretty well how I want to reach decisions," said Bush, "get good, strong, experienced people, encourage them to express their views openly, encourage them not to hold back." "He doesn't want filters," said one official.

In sharp contrast to Reagan, Bush ran a non-ideological White House, where obedience, loyalty, and collegiality were valued most. "There are no ideologues around George Bush," said one aide. "He can't abide people who know they have all the answers." Another adviser reported, "George Bush is very loyal to people, more than to ideas." Bush's staff, like his vice president Dan Quayle, was, by and large, just like Bush: prudent, loyal, buttoned-down operations men, not ideological crusaders. And in Quayle, Bush may have seen a younger version of himself: a capable, gracious, enthusiastic second banana. Bush took pains to include Quayle in top-level decision making and meetings, and a series of reports on Quayle by the *Washington Post*'s Bob Woodward and David S. Broder argued that Quayle was more effective than commonly believed at the time. Despite his rocky public performances, Quayle's legislative experience served Bush well as a boost to his political antennae inside the White House and at their weekly breakfasts.

In 1997, a former Bush adviser dismissed Bush's pre-presidential team as "bland, upper-class, middlebrow, tennis-playing second-raters." At the time, one aide described Bush's White House as "very small, very clubby. There's lots of camaraderie, humor, and male bonding. That's how the boys defuse tension and avoid burnout." Duke University presidential scholar James David Barber observed, "Bush wants twins around him, and that can be dangerous." A famous exception to Bush's legion of WASP gentility was John

Sununu, the former governor of New Hampshire who helped engineer Bush's pivotal 1988 victory in that state. Sununu soon developed a suffer-no-fools, take-no-prisoners reputation as Bush's "pit bull–bad cop" chief of staff who made the trains run on time and deflected criticism away from Bush. Former Vice President Quayle traced the beginnings of Bush's biggest troubles as president to Sununu's forced departure at the end of 1991.

Quayle recalled that Bush "didn't mind varying viewpoints, but he didn't want a lot of tension." Quayle wrote that "Bush wanted to avoid friction. He didn't mind debate within his administration, but he was very bothered by any reports of people not getting along." Quayle observed, "Bush was very compartmentalized, with lots of people, from national security staff to political people feeding directly into him. This sometimes made it difficult for John Sununu because in a way Bush was his own chief of staff. He'd pick up the phone and get the information, insights, or gossip he wanted from any source. His in-box was always full. He loved reading the briefing papers, listening to people, absorbing information, and making decisions." "George Bush always was willing to listen to people," recalled Sununu. "But once he listened and gave everybody a chance to have their say, he was very willing to come down with a clear decision. It made my life rather easy, because I was always operating with clear-cut directives. George Bush was very at ease with himself. Some presidents hammer themselves with doubts. He didn't."

Bush tolerated and even stimulated debate with his official family, as long as it didn't get too personal, messy, or public. "I thank my lucky stars that we can fight like cats and dogs in Cabinet meetings, but once I make a decision, move on as a team," Bush declared. He wanted his officials to close ranks behind him, often remarking, "Loyalty is not a character flaw." At Bush's first pre-inaugural Cabinet meeting at Blair House, he pulled out a list and read what he called "The Marching Orders," including: "Think big . . . Challenge the system . . . Adhere to the highest ethical standards . . . Be on the record as much as possible . . . Be frank . . . Fight hard for your position . . . When I make a call, we move as a team." *New York Times* columnist William Safire complained that "the absence of creative tension has generated little excitement or innovation: no stewing, all stewarding. We miss the Rooseveltian turbulence that often leads to original thinking."

The undisputed heavyweight of Bush's White House squad was the secretary of state, fellow Texan and longtime friend James Baker, a formidable bureaucratic player and media manipulator, widely regarded to have been an effective White House chief of staff during Reagan's first term. Bush and Baker were on the phone constantly, in a relationship some described as brotherly in both closeness and competitiveness. "Baker dots every *i* and crosses every *t*," noted one observer, "and the president likes people there who dot the *i*'s and cross the *t*'s." "This office intimidates people," Bush explained as he waved his hand around the Oval Office. "They walk in here and say, 'I'll go tell this son-of-a-gun,' and they walk in and they don't tell the son-of-a-gun. I've been through it on the other side, walking through that door. And it's different." According to Bush, close friends like Baker knew they "can come and say what they think and nobody's going to bark their head off. And they will not be intimidated by the seal on the ceiling.'" Baker asserted that "President Bush, like President Reagan, really wanted to hear your honest opinion. You never got in trouble by telling him something he didn't want to hear."

One rare exception to Bush's collegial White House atmosphere occurred when former football hero and then–Secretary of Housing and Urban Development Jack Kemp followed Bush and Baker into the Oval Office to lobby them in favor of recognizing Lithuania. An aggravated Baker, so the story goes, snapped, "Fuck you, Kemp!" Kemp then dove across the Oval Office for Baker's throat, then chased him down for a tackle until National Security Adviser Scowcroft heroically threw his body between the two Cabinet officers to prevent a fistfight.

Ronald Reagan, now watching Bush from the sidelines, reportedly sniped at his former deputy: "He doesn't seem to stand for anything." Reagan later denied making the statement, but it was clear to all that Bush had no compelling agenda, no clear-cut philosophy, and no framework to capture and communicate his ideas. When he declared for presidency in October 1987, Bush announced, "I am a practical man. I like what's real. I like what works . . . I do not yearn to lead a crusade." During the 1988 campaign, he acknowledged, "I am no mystic, and my leadership will not be the most charismatic, but I'm not sure we need a lot of razzle-dazzle." Bush suffered in the shadow of the mythic communicator Reagan, and one Bush aide said: "He refuses to be managed. He refuses to do theatrical things. He refuses the bigger-than-life mode. If he gets a hint of it, he resists it." In his inaugural, Bush defiantly intoned in stanzas of empty windiness: "Some see leadership as high drama and the sound of trumpets calling, and sometimes it is that. But I see history as a book with many pages, and each day we fill a page with acts of hopefulness and meaning. The new breeze blows, a page turns, the story unfolds."

Even if Bush did have a clear domestic agenda, he would have had a terrible time communicating it, as he was crippled by a flat speaking style punctuated by bursts of tortured syntax, goofy giddiness, and frantic hand and body motions. "Fluency in English is something that I'm often not accused of," he admitted in a 1989 toast to Pakistani Prime Minister Benazir Bhutto. "I'm not good at expressing the concerns of a nation," Bush admitted to interviewer David Frost. "I'm just not very good at it." Barbara Bush noted, "The camera shrinks him and makes him seem small." Bush once announced, "Hey, listen, right now things are going pretty good, but tomorrow it will be another kind of ball game. So just keep doing your best. Back to my mother —do your best. Do your best." In 1989, when asked in a White House press conference how he would justify an invasion of Panama to Gorbachev, Bush embarked on a classic Bushian voyage of mangled speech: "Look, if an American marine is killed—if they kill an American marine, that's real bad. And if they threaten and brutalize the wife of an American citizen, sexually threatening the lieutenant's wife while kicking him in the groin over and over again, then, Mr. Gorbachev, please understand, this president is going to do something about it."

Dan Quayle recalled, "What his administration never had in four years was a credible communications strategy. His staff would get bogged down in detail and forget about the big picture. Bush was a problem solver. Everyone would bring their problems, large and small, for him to resolve. Very seldom would there be a long strategy session focused on what direction the president wanted the country to take." A Republican close to Bush observed, "This is a White House consumed with day-to-day tactics, much like the president is. At the morning staff meetings, all you heard is what's up, what's going on, what do we have to react to today. It's not how do we want to approach the next week, the next several weeks."

In the months after the Gulf War victory, many Americans abruptly shifted their concern to domestic affairs, but it was painfully obvious that it was not where Bush's heart was. For one thing, he had to deal with the strongest opposition Congress any president had to face in memory. Bush confessed, "I enjoy trying to put the coalition together and keep it together. I can't say that I just rejoice every time I go up to talk to my good friend [Dan] Rostenkowski about what he's going to do about taxes." Bush's strategy with Congress was to bludgeon most of the legislation that was sent to him—he vetoed more bills than any modern president, and he had the worst overall batting average with Congress of any president since *Congressional Quarterly* began measuring with Eisenhower. A former Reagan official who also advised Bush groused: "On a scale of one to ten, the president's rhetoric is an eight, his bills are fours, and his lobbying is zero." Bush domestic policy became, in the words of a Republican activist, "All stop and no go." Bush's patrician gentility hobbled him from locking horns with Congress. Bush "finds it hard to get emotionally involved in passionate dislike of one side or another," said Bush friend Thomas Ashley. "He's not a confrontational guy; he'd rather get along."

In March 1991, with the Gulf War victory still fresh, Bush scored a near 90 percent approval rating, the highest measured for any president in history. But the pinnacle was built on sand, and when it shifted, Bush came crashing down, a victim in part of a destructive overconfidence and euphoria that gripped his White House. "After Desert Storm, everyone in the White House was now making plans to be working six more years," said Bush's Secretary of Veterans' Affairs Edward Derwinski. "They also thought that they themselves had planned Desert Storm. There were many runaway egos. When the polls showed the president at 85 percent in public support, the complacency and smugness were shocking, and they never shook it off. They never understood that it was possible to be beaten." Dan Quayle reported that "midway through what we still thought would be only George Bush's first term, his administration had begun to appear merely competent, without any driving creed. We were, in some minds, turning into the caretakers of the Reagan revolution, appearing unable to keep up with the changes in the country's circumstances." By May 1992, Bush's approval score had swan-dived to 40 percent.

In sharp contrast to Bush's foreign affairs achievements, his domestic agenda stumbled almost out of the gate. In his first 100 days, as his budget plan faltered, bad preparation helped torpedo his nomination of the allegedly hard-drinking and womanizing Senator John Tower as secretary of defense, the first time in thirty years that the entire Senate rejected a president's Cabinet nominee. Bush's domestic strategy was one of caution, avoidance, and icy detachment, focused on passing a bare minimum agenda of "kinder, gentler" legislation such as the Americans with Disabilities Act and the Clean Air Act. "I don't want to do anything dumb," he repeatedly announced. "I expect in this job I'll make plenty of mistakes, but I don't want to make the wrong mistakes." Quayle reported, "In many areas—including education, health care, and the environment—we were reluctant to advocate much, since Congress probably wouldn't pass the legislation anyway; if it did, it would load it up with so much additional spending, going so far beyond what we had intended, that we would have been better off doing nothing."

In the closing days of 1991, Bush's reelection campaign, and his presidency, began a long meltdown of staff chaos and organizational confusion. Ironically, the same executive assets that won the Gulf War—strategic planning, clear objectives, contingency planning—deserted Bush's reelection campaign. Bush repeatedly told his aides that there was no way he could be beaten by a "failed governor of a small state" like Bill Clinton. In December 1991, Transportation Secretary Sam Skinner took over as chief of staff, replacing the departed John Sununu. "There was a lot of staff chaos, we sometimes got too bogged down in details, and we never had a communications strategy," said Dan Quayle. "We should have had a Domestic Desert Storm, with two or three priorities."

"No one could make a decision," wrote Press Secretary Marlin Fitzwater of both the Bush campaign and White House staffs, "the president should have fired us all." Fitzwater recalled that "during the first months of 1992, when the president should have been getting ready to mount a tough reelection drive, he was more or less serving as his own chief of staff, doing everything from scheduling to making foreign policy decisions." On September 4, 1992, Bush persuaded James Baker to leave his secretary of state post and take charge of both the campaign and the White House, but it was far too late.

As his reelection campaign neared, Bush was haunted by two immense perception problems. The first was the ghost of his 1990 budget deal with Congress, when he repudiated the "Read my lips: no new taxes" pledge he proclaimed at the 1988 Republican convention in favor of spending cuts and tax increases. The deal was the largest deficit reduction package before or since, but was widely percieved as a flip-flop and a broken promise. Second, in March 1992, Bush and his men interpreted an uptick in the economy as meaning that no new economic action was needed. Bush's Secretary of Agriculture Clayton Yeutter recalled, "When Bush and others in the administration began speaking of a recovery, no one believed them. It did not feel like a recovery for the large number of people who were unemployed or frightened about losing their jobs. As a consequence, we slid along this recessionary bottom with people saying, 'The president is disengaged—he does not know what is happening around the country. We are in the midst of a recession and the president doesn't know it.'"

Bush and his team gambled that a hands-off approach to the economy would work, and they were within days of being right: the economy grew by a full 5.7 percent in the fourth quarter of 1992, but the news came just after the election, too late for Bush. "Reductions in the deficit and interest rates came too late to help Mr. Bush at the polls," contended Bush's Treasury Secretary Nicholas Brady, "yet these reductions, paid for in blood by the Bush administration, were perhaps the essential component of the economic expansion we enjoy today." Looking back in 1997, Bush lamented: "I lost in '92 because people still thought the economy was in the tank and that I was out of touch and that I didn't understand that. And the economy wasn't in the tank and I wasn't out of touch, but I lost. But I lost." Bush not only lost, he was flattened, receiving only 37 percent of the popular vote, the worst percentage showing by an incumbent since William Howard Taft in 1912.

Bush left behind a foreign policy legacy that extended beyond Desert Storm and its ambiguous conclusion. His activist approach, while often tactical and ad hoc, helped stop and reverse the nuclear arms race, strengthened the NATO alliance, achieved progress in Latin American debt financing, pushed forward the GATT and NAFTA accords later implemented by the Clinton administration, and facilitated German reunification and the democratization of Eastern Europe. "This is a legacy which by itself would qualify President Bush as one of our nation's great diplomatists," said Lawrence Eagleburger, Bush's final secretary of state.

"I would submit to you that the national security apparatus worked better under President Bush than any other president since World War II," argued James Baker in 1997, five years after Bush left power. "The world changed dramatically those four years. The Cold War ended, we had the end of the East/West confrontation, the reunification of Germany, we fought a major war in the Gulf, another war in Panama. We began a Middle East peace process that is continuing today. He did all of this without all of the backbiting and backstabbing and trashing and infighting and leaking that has characterized most presidents' national security apparatus."

Robert Gates, Bush's deputy national security adviser (1989–1991) and CIA director (1991–1993), asserted, "It was always Bush who was pushing for new initiatives and new approaches, particularly with respect to the Soviet Union." Gates argued, "Most people say this is a guy who lacked vision, a guy who had no strategy, who may have dealt fairly well tactically with some of these issues. But it was Bush who set the tone on German reunification. It was Bush alone who made the strategic decision that the United States would support prompt German reunification, to the horror of both the French and the British, including Margaret Thatcher, even most of the people in the U.S. government, all of whom thought he was moving much too fast. I believe it was George's statecraft, his day-to-day management of foreign policy and his relationship with other leaders that made a very unstable, revolutionary period seem a lot less dangerous than it really was."

"Was he a man of vision?" asked Scowcroft. "You bet he had vision, but he did not articulate it." "My mother told me, George, no one likes a braggadocio," Bush explained at the 1997 Hofstra University conference on his presidency. Typically, Bush refused to visit the site of the torn-down Berlin Wall, to avoid gloating and risk offending the Soviets.

In his inaugural address, Bush declared, "There are times when the future seems thick as a fog; you sit and wait, hoping the mists will lift and reveal the right path." But on domestic affairs, Bush sat and waited for most of his presidency, and instead of lifting, the mists enveloped him and carried him back to Texas.

Bush's defeat was not only a saga of bad political calls, but also a cautionary tale of overconfidence and what can happen when an executive plays mainly to his strengths and avoids his blind spots and his least favorite parts of the job—in Bush's case, domestic affairs and public persuasion. Some executives can get away with it. In the Oval Office it can be fatal.

"I think I will be remembered for being president at a time of historic change in the world," Bush said in 1997, "and if I were editorializing, I hope people would say, 'Well, they handled this pretty well. Got it right.'"

If you searched the United States for an executive to engineer America's part in the transformation of the post–Cold War world, you'd have a hard time finding one more skilled than George Herbert Walker Bush.

But the American people could never see the strongest side of diplomat-executive Bush, the closed-door, hands-on-the-throttle, effective management of America's role in a world turning upside down.

CHAPTER 11

Bill Clinton
The Chaotic Executive

"Dear God, help me."

BILL CLINTON, OVAL OFFICE VIDEO RECORDING,
DECEMBER 15, 1994

THE OVAL OFFICE
DECEMBER 15, 1994, 7:50 P.M.

"Wait a minute! Wait, wait, wait!"

Bill Clinton's eyeglasses were perched on the tip of his nose, and his huge head and arms were flying around in multiple directions as he called out to his staff from behind the same *Resolute* desk used by Presidents Hayes, Kennedy, and Reagan. Inside the Oval Office, a White House TV videotape was quietly capturing the private pandemonium of Bill Clinton ten minutes before a speech to the nation, as his presidency hit rock bottom.

It was over three years before anyone had heard of Linda Tripp or Monica Lewinsky.

The Oval Office was festooned with festive Christmas trimmings and bright poinsettia, but the White House atmosphere was funereal. In the midterm election five weeks earlier, Newt Gingrich's Republicans clobbered Clinton with the "Contract with America" and seized control of both houses of Congress for the first time in forty years.

The Oval Office was packed with electrical cables, dropcloths, and scurrying aides as the president scribbled frantically on the draft of his speech to the nation proposing a "middle-class bill of rights." A few feet away, a technician fiddled with a TelePrompTer, struggling to insert the president's latest changes. At 8:00 P.M., the TV networks were scheduled to cut into their signal and broadcast live from the Oval Office. But now, with ten minutes to go, Bill Clinton was improvising.

"It could be a pivotal speech," Dan Rather intoned solemnly from his anchor desk in New York. "This is a decisive hour for the president . . . he is attempting to reconnect with voters." On NBC, Tom Brokaw was proclaiming the moment "the formal beginning of Clinton II," adding it was Clinton's attempt "to reclaim a place in the hearts of American voters."

Two weeks earlier, on the evening of December 1, Clinton had gathered his closest advisers together to survey the shambles of his nearly dead-in-the-water presidency, which was blasted by Republican commercials that "morphed" Democratic candidates into Bill Clinton's face, to deadly effect. "On a scale of one to ten with ten being nuclear war, it was about a 9.6 if you were a Democrat," said assistant George Stephanopoulos of Clinton's midterm drubbing.

During the meeting, one adviser told Clinton, "You're going to have to take clearer stands." Clinton detonated in a purple-faced rage: "Goddamn it," he shouted, "don't tell me about taking clearer positions. You want to talk about why we lost the election? You want to talk about why? Because the DNC didn't do its part. We didn't have a message." He griped, "I get treated like a mule. Whenever I'm at my desk I end up with these lists of people to call. I'm supposed to call every junior congressman about every vote. I'm the legislator in chief. It's wasted time, because the American people don't know I'm doing this stuff. And I shouldn't have to do it. I don't have time to think." White House Chief of Staff Leon Panetta interjected that Clinton was always yakking on the telephone, which provoked yet another tantrum. Clinton was notorious for his Vesuvian temper, which would erupt (and often soon recede) at senior aides like Stephanopoulos, National Security Adviser Anthony Lake, counselor Bruce Lindsay, and various young lieutenants close to the Oval Office. Aides reported screaming fits by Clinton, and one official warned, "You don't want to be in the room when Clinton gets angry."

Six minutes to go until the speech. At the *Resolute* desk, Clinton was lopping off entire paragraphs, rewriting sentences, and adding new lines. A portrait of Andrew Jackson gazed sternly at the spectacle, as did the Rembrandt Peale portrait of George Washington perched over the marble-manteled fireplace; a bronze bust of Benjamin Franklin by Jean-Antoine Houdon; busts of Clinton's presidential heroes Jefferson, Lincoln, both Roosevelts, Truman, and Kennedy; and a pair of American eagles, one in the Prussian blue Oval Office carpet and one on the domed ceiling above. On the table behind Clinton's desk was an identical copy of Ronald Reagan's IT CAN BE DONE sign, a little bronze frog, a Winston Churchill figurine, and a toy model of the

Clinton-Gore campaign bus, along with framed family pictures of Hillary and Chelsea Clinton and his mother, Virginia Kelley. The rugs and furniture were appointed in bold, sharp colors of Prussian blue, golds, and reds that celebrated the youthful energy of its chief executive, but there had been no major architectural changes made to the office since FDR moved into it in 1934. The four cane-backed chairs were in use since Herbert Hoover's time.

"That's not what we had on that other copy," said Clinton, scribbling on his speech draft as aides and technicians scurried around the office in a caffeinated, overcharged atmosphere of barely controlled panic. Clinton, a pale and puffy near-220 pounds despite almost daily morning jogs of three to five miles, called out to chief speechwriter Don Baer, "We're going to take the first paragraph out, Don." Baer replied apprehensively, "You are? The whole first paragraph?" "Yeah. I think that's OK, don't you?" said Clinton. Resigned, Baer groaned, "Yeah, sure." The president was on edge, talking very fast: "And we also took another paragraph out. That'll save us time. All right, I want you to, who's going to do the TelePrompTer? Can you hear me? All right. Let's go. Ready? Close the doors please. Close the door, please, everybody be quiet—I gotta talk!" Clinton began a quick read-through of the speech.

"Turn it!" Clinton snapped at the TelePrompTer operator, waving his hand. "Stop, stop," Clinton said abruptly, making a time-out signal with his hands. He rewrote another line as an aide ran over to straighten out his jacket. "We should say we can *pay* for the middle-class bill of rights. OK? Right there. We got time to do that?" The technician cautioned: "You have about four and a half minutes left." An aide crept toward the desk and knelt down to gently coach the president: "A little flat." Clinton replied: "Flat, isn't it—too fast?" Aide: "No. It's flat. This is a great line. Work the camera a little more. Bite into it a little more." Clinton whipped out a pen, shuffled papers, and continued reworking the speech.

Clinton's high-wire performance tonight was typical: for his first State of the Union address in February 1993, the speech draft was hammered together by speechwriters working an all-nighter, with Clinton ordering revisions throughout the afternoon. As he drove onto Capitol Hill that night, Clinton was still making changes by hand inside the limousine. The computer disk containing the speech was barely loaded into the TelePrompTer in time, and just minutes into the address Clinton began improvising on the spot as he stood before Congress. An amazed presidential aide commented, "He's riffing. He's making this up." In heart-stopping congressional showdowns in 1993, he came within a few seconds of losing his budget and deficit-reduction plans. His 1995 State of the Union speech preparation was equally chaotic: last-second overhauls resulted in a speech that both Clinton and his wife were dissatisfied with, and a planned thirty- to forty-minute address ballooned into a ninety-minute mess.

Three minutes to go. An aide ordered all cell phones and beepers out of the Oval Office. Someone called out to Clinton: "Energy." Clinton unbuttoned his jacket, blew his nose and asked the group: "Does it look OK? Ready? How much time?" Voice: "Two minutes to the president." An aide offered soothingly: "Just look real natural. Talk to the people. You don't really have to act or do anything. Be yourself." The countdown: "45 for the president . . . 35 for the president . . ." The room suddenly hushed, Clinton closed his eyes, took a deep breath, sighed heavily, and muttered softly, "Dear God, help me."

The networks cut to the Oval Office, Clinton pursed his lips in a theatrical grimace of sincerity and delivered his speech. At 8:10, a technician declared, "Mr. President, we're clear." Clinton's eyes darted around the room, plaintive for approval. He asked, "OK? Did it look good? Did you like it? Did you like it?" His staffers, crowded by the fireplace, clapped and cheered: "Great job! Terrific! You didn't miss a beat!" A relieved, happy Clinton entered the victory huddle and announced, "Well, I had more energy!"

He'd made better speeches before, and the theme of this one, a middle-class bill of rights, was soon forgotten. But in the coming weeks and months, Clinton, the perennial "Comeback Kid," painstakingly rebuilt his presidency. Two weeks after the speech, Clinton retreated to Camp David to consult with three of the nation's top self-help gurus, including *Seven Habits of Highly Effective People* author Stephen Covey, self-styled celebrity minister Marianne Williamson, and granite-jawed gargantuan performance coach and infomercial czar Tony Robbins ("Thirty days to mastering your emotions! Your physical body! Your relationships! Your finances!").

Clinton tried to improve his executive style by delegating more work, scheduling more "think time," giving meetings a sharper focus, and better organizing the White House. He earnestly read piles of books on the presidency and studied videotapes of Ronald Reagan in action. He chucked his unflattering micro-short running pants. He walked taller and looked more presidential. He began slenderizing himself with a low-fat diet, eventually slimming down to 200 pounds. He moved the nucleus of White House decision making from the often packed, frenzied conference room atmosphere of the windowless Roosevelt Room in the West Wing to the stately, historic yellow Oval Room in the White House mansion.

To reposition and repackage himself for reelection, Clinton hired Dick Morris, the political uber-strategist who had navigated his journey back from political extinction in Arkansas. Clinton supervised a $45 million advertising blitz produced by White House ad men and funded by the Democratic Party, personally reviewing and signing off on advertising copy portraying him as an executive president hard at work in the Oval Office while dithering Republicans gridlocked Congress. "Buy it," Clinton ordered. "The president controlled all of this," said George Stephanopoulos. "He knew what had happened to him, and he knew Dick had the skills to clean it up. Like Franklin Roosevelt, consciously or not, Clinton strove to create an atmosphere of creative tension. For good reason. We were stuck in the trees, thinking tactically and not strategically. Dick provided energy and a strategic vision that we needed."

In late 1995, Clinton challenged Newt Gingrich to two "High Noon," belly-to-belly, *quien es mas macho* showdowns over the federal budget. He stared the Speaker down in the Oval Office as a government shutdown deadline approached and announced: "If you want this budget signed, you'll have to put someone else in this chair. I will not now, not ever, sign this budget. I think it's bad for America." The government shut down twice. Clinton not only remained standing, he used the showdowns to help get reelected.

Slowly, Clinton forced up his Gallup job approval rating from a dismal 40 percent just after the speech in December 1994 into the low 50s in 1995, then into the high 50s in 1996, until it broke into the 60s in 1997 and stayed there straight through his impeachment ordeal in 1998 and 1999. He swerved to the political center and right, seized the initiative from Republicans on everything from the economy, crime, and welfare reform to soccer-mom values, V-chips, and school uniforms, and crushed Bob Dole in the November 1996 election, the first time a Democrat was reelected to a second term in sixty years. It was the triumph of a master politician and a political executive the likes of which the Oval Office had never seen before.

"Hell, you work for Bill Clinton, you go up and down more times than a whore's nightgown," observed adviser James Carville. "Energy in the executive," Alexander Hamilton wrote in the *Federalist Papers,* "is a leading character in the definition of good government," and few American presidents have had more intellectual and physical energy than Bill Clinton, the youngest president since John Kennedy. It was an energy channeled through a messy, chaotic, and yet often effective executive style by a seeming indestructible president.

When they elected William Jefferson Clinton president in 1992, American voters fired their most accomplished diplomat and hired their greatest domestic policy wonk. They also elected an executive with a rich portfolio of skills invaluable to running the Oval Office. Clinton possessed strong talents for learning, listening, absorbing and synthesizing information, empathizing and communicating, as well as nearly inexhaustible levels of energy and stamina. He also believed that he could constantly revitalize his presidency through the force of effort and hard work. "If you have energy and sort of an inner determination that keeps you at the task," Clinton explained, "I think you can re-create political capital continuously throughout the presidency. I have always believed that." He was right. Through his two terms, he defied the laws of political physics, bouncing into tremendous highs and lows like he was bungee-jumping off a roller coaster and kept snapping back.

Clinton's first glimpse of the Oval Office came on July 24, 1963, when as a sixteen-year-old delegate from Hope, Arkansas, chosen to attend an American Legion "Boy's Nation" leadership conference, he stood in the sweltering heat of the Rose Garden just outside the office and waited for President Kennedy. Clinton's traveling salesman father William Blythe died in a car accident before his son was born, and Clinton may have seen in the super-heroic popular images of Kennedy a glimmer of the father he never knew. Inside the Oval Office that day, Kennedy was in the midst of a bitter struggle with the Joint Chiefs of Staff over their opposition to the Nuclear Test Ban Treaty (in a Dictabelt-recorded phone call, he enlisted former President Harry S. Truman's help in the struggle), but when he stepped out on the porch to address Clinton and his colleagues, he graciously welcomed them and said, "We want you to feel very much at home," an invitation Clinton was to take most literally.

When Kennedy descended into the Rose Garden to greet the delegates, Clinton elbowed his way to the front of the line, thrust out his hand, and greeted the president with a handshake, their eyes meeting, Kennedy nodding to Clinton with a bemused smile. The moment was captured for the ages by White House photographers, and footage of the encounter, evoking an Arthurian anointing of a young chevalier, was played to a thunderous ovation at the 1992 Democratic Convention. Clinton left the White House that day in a state of bliss; an eyewitness reported Clinton announcing on the bus back to the University of Maryland dormitory, "Someday I'm gonna have that job. Someday I'm gonna be president."

Clinton spent most of the next three decades in relentless pursuit of that goal, coming back to Washington a year later to attend Georgetown University, going on to Oxford as a Rhodes Scholar and then to Yale Law School, getting elected as the nation's youngest governor at age thirty-two in 1978. During an unsuccessful lunge for Congress in 1974, Clinton, then a law professor, exhibited a hands-on-the-throat, neck-deep-in-details executive style that would carry through to the White House. "The principal strategist and tactician in that campaign was Bill Clinton," said former Arkansas legislator David Matthews, then a Clinton volunteer. "I haven't seen a candidate who's better at running his own show."

After two years as governor, Arkansas voters, angry over Clinton's lack of focus and perceived arrogance, most notably in jacking up car and truck license fees, tossed him out of office. Chastened, he mounted the first of many comebacks and was elected again in 1982, and appointed take-charge Betsey Wright as chief of staff. She ran his second term with sharp efficiency, and berated him into focusing on a short, manageable agenda. As a progressive, consensus-building centrist Democrat facing a structurally weak legislature (it was only 10 percent Republican and met for sixty days every other year), Clinton achieved mixed results, making strides in areas like education, health care, and jobs while raising residents' pride in Arkansas, which remained one of the poorest states in the nation. He was elected chairman of the National Governors' Association in 1986, and in 1991 was voted the nation's most effective governor by his peers.

In Clinton's first term as governor he made bold, decisive moves often ahead of the curve of public opinion, a habit that nearly killed his career, so in his second incarnation he switched gears and became a virtuoso of the high political arts of consensus-building, compromise, gregariousness, and empathy. In doing so he gained a Rooseveltian reputation for placating visitors into thinking he agreed with them when he didn't. Clinton's "instinct to try to make you feel good . . . sometimes leaves people hanging," said former Clinton education adviser Don Ernst. "Sometimes, decisions don't get made." "It's almost impossible not to be charmed by him, and it's almost impossible not to be disappointed by him," a longtime Clinton lieutenant said. After a perceived double-cross by Clinton in 1990, Arkansas labor leader J. William Becker issued the classic phrase, "The guy will pat you on the back while pissing down your leg."

In 1992, Clinton campaigned for the presidency as the nation's best-informed, most energetic domestic policy expert, a crusading "agent of change" from America's heartland, determined to break through the "brain-dead politics" of the two parties. He withstood the multiple detonations of Gennifer Flowers, draft-dodging, and "didn't inhale" to achieve a 43 percent plurality over George Bush and Ross Perot. His campaign organization became the model for his White House: crash, panic, and burn "War Room" command posts fueled by pizza, Coke, Doritos, and frantic twenty- and thirty-somethings laboring for a chief executive with a kung-fu management grip. On "everything from policy to strategy to schedule," said Clinton campaign issues director Bruce Reed, "he makes the final call."

"I felt like the dog that chased the pickup truck," Clinton told friends in the days before his inauguration. "I got it; now what am I going to do?" He decided, in his first months as president, to try to do everything, just as he did in his first term as governor. He exuberantly charged out of the gate and ran straight into a series of fiascoes, many of them triggered by sloppy management and poor preparation. "His management style," said one close associate at the time, "just doesn't work at this level of government." Part of Clinton's problem was that he broke a twelve-year Republican hammerlock on the executive branch, and Democratic White House pros who still had pulses were exceedingly hard to find. Of his top staff, only National Security Adviser Tony Lake had ever worked in the White House before.

Two days after his swearing-in, Clinton was forced to withdraw his nomination of Zoë Baird for attorney general after finding out she had hired an illegal alien as a maid. Soon, his second choice, Kimba Wood, had to back out because the White House hadn't fully investigated her nanny-hiring practices either. A few months later, Clinton's nominee for assistant attorney general for civil rights, Lani Guinier, had to be withdrawn after controversy erupted over her writings on race-based voting preferences, a debate the White House might have managed if Clinton's staff had done the proper homework. One week into his term, without doing any political spadework with Congress or the military brass, Clinton proclaimed that gay Americans would no longer be discharged from the armed forces. A blizzard of opposition forced him to back down to an ambiguous "don't ask, don't tell" policy by that summer, angering all parties concerned. In May 1993, the fumble-fingered firing of White House travel office personnel turned into a public relations disaster and tragically combined with a host of other political and personal problems to help trigger the suicide of White House counsel Vince Foster in July 1993.

Clinton's early fiascoes were the direct product of an executive style that intentionally thrived on chaos, multiple advisers, and multiple sources of information to feed his lust for data, opinions, and ideas. In 1992, he became enamored with the book *Lincoln on Leadership,* and he told *Time* magazine why he saw Lincoln's presidential style as a model for his own. "The key to being an effective political leader is getting around. Lincoln was always out and about picking up information. He wasn't a prisoner in the White House," Clinton said. "You've got to go find the facts for yourself, and many of the good ones come from outside your inner circle. If I make it, the hardest thing will be to keep reaching out. A strict, formal structure just won't cut it. There's too much you miss if you don't forage around yourself." This sounded much like the romantic management disorder of his hero John Kennedy, but the bitter experiences of Ford and Carter should have taught Clinton that the presidency had now grown far too enormous to be run through a "spokes of the wheel" structure without a strong chief of staff.

Sure enough, as soon as he sat down in the president's chair, Clinton broke down all the potential barriers to information in his White House, and in the process he kicked away the supporting beams of structure and management that might have protected him against some of his early mistakes. Thomas "Mack" McLarty, Clinton's nominal first chief of staff, told his boss one day: "What I'll never understand is how a man with such genius for organizing his thoughts and articulating them could be so disorganized in managing himself." A White House adviser commented in November 1993: "There is no system there. There is no real management. Everyone in the place rushes to one fire to put it out while five more smolder somewhere else." "They are good at takeoffs, passable at stopping crash-landings," said a Democratic strategist, "but everything in-between gets lost." "The fundamental problem was that there was no organization chart," said Clinton's second chief of staff, Leon Panetta. "No chain of command. People were not sure who they reported to. There were people with titles like 'counselor to the president' who had no definitive responsibilities. They wandered the halls and in and out of meetings giving advice but never had to deliver. There was an aura of chaos."

"The president is into everything, wants to decide everything, wants the details of everything," said one official during Clinton's first year. "He wants to hear various aspects of the issues," said domestic policy aide Carol Rasco, "the ups, downs, pros, cons. He wants to hear everything from everybody." "The fundamental problem is that he gets to see too many people before deciding, he ends up doing the staff work himself and there are too many decisions for him to make," an administration official lamented in mid-1994. "A lot of decisions are put on his desk without all the facts," the staffer continued. "He's a very hands-on president." McLarty noted, "President Clinton is inclusive by nature, he likes to get a lot of opinions, a lot of information." A cabinet member said, "He's like a kid—he wants to do everything at once." "He doesn't want to do everything," asserted campaign aide Bruce Reed in 1992, offering a subtle distinction, "he just wants to know everything." For his first budget, Clinton spent days huddled with budget director Leon Panetta, side by side, reviewing items line by line. After one marathon budget meeting, Clinton exclaimed to his exhausted staff: "That was fun!"

"He's the great synthesizer," said a White House staffer, and it was a title Clinton was proud to claim. "If I have brought anything to the presidency," Clinton said, it was "a feel for how all these issues fit together and why. You know, fighting for the V-chip or regulating cigarette advertisements or trying to help communities adopt stiffer standards on truancy and curfews and all that, that's part of a security environment that's a piece of what we're trying to do with antiterrorism and nonproliferation." The connection between Joe Camel and nuclear weapons is hard to trace, but if anyone could do it, Clinton could. "He has a subtle mind," one aide contended. "It wrestles with complex issues. He understands complexity. That complexity is often at odds with concreteness."

"Clinton is not sequential," said one White House observer. When you put a list in front of some people—setting forth what is most important and what is least important—they go down the list. Clinton goes around the problem. He circles it and circles it." An ex–Clinton staffer described Clinton's decision style in similar, nonlinear terms: "If you go to him and say, 'We must do A or B,' he'll say, 'Can't we do A and B? Or something else?'" An assistant said, "You do not stick a twenty-page memo on his desk and at the bottom it says 'yes' or 'no.'" One adviser said: "Clinton never stops thinking." Another stated, "His decision-making style is not to make a decision the way others do—toting up the costs and benefits. He makes a decision when he absolutely has to. Sometimes when he must make a decision that he's not ready to make, the decision doesn't get made."

One friend of Clinton's who knew him for twenty-five years, said: "They've got to get somebody to manage the president, hands on, full time. This is a guy who has to be told to do his homework and eat his spinach and get to places on time." A Cabinet officer said: "He doesn't want hierarchy. He doesn't want a strong chief of staff. He doesn't want a single economic adviser. He wants all kinds of advisers swirling around him constantly." Labor Secretary Robert Reich wrote: "B doesn't give a fig for formal lines of authority. He'll seek advice from anyone he wants to hear it from, for as long as he thinks he's getting what he needs." Longtime White House adviser David Gergen observed: "Everybody goes down the court and anybody can shoot."

Clinton "is the meetingest fellow I know," marveled Treasury Secretary Lloyd Bentsen. In Clinton's first two years he set up a semi-permanent camp in the windowless Roosevelt Room across the hall from the Oval Office, with groups so large, as one official claimed, they could have been "held in Yankee Stadium," in grueling super-marathons of endurance. By 8:00 or 9:00 P.M., staffers would groan as Clinton said, "let's continue," and the sessions droned on for hours more. Brief updates stretched into two-hour Clinton colloquies that often provoked "analysis paralysis," where issues were studied to death without decisions being made. Teams of staffers hashed out issues in front of

Clinton while he scarfed down hamburgers, French fries, and pizza and slurped on diet cola.

"Clinton didn't want debates settled before reaching his desk," reported staff secretary John Podesta. One aide called Clinton "the staffer-in-chief." "He really loves the intellectual give-and-take," said another. "But the time pressures and political pressures are such that he can't afford that anymore." Clinton was a proud practitioner of "management by wandering around," energetically roaming the halls of the West Wing, popping in on lieutenants to wrestle over policy arcana or shoot the political breeze. His inclusive, accessible, and informal style extended to the Oval Office, where many staffers (and, most infamously, young interns) felt comfortable appearing without an appointment. In March 1993, the *New York Times* called Clinton's White House "a mix of pure policy with controlled pandemonium."

In March 1993, Clinton admitted that "I may have overextended myself" and vowed to "focus anew" on the "big things." In May 1993, as Clinton's popularity plunged, Ross Perot sniped from the sidelines that Clinton was such a bad executive that "you wouldn't consider giving him a job anywhere above middle management" in the corporate world. At the beginning of Clinton's first summer in the White House, as fiascoes continued erupting around him, a dazed Clinton observed, "One of the things that you risk when you try to get a lot of things going in a hurry—and we tried to get a lot of things going in a hurry because four years passes in a hurry—is that you wind up having people work very, very hard but maybe getting a little out of focus." His congressional allies agreed: when a Democratic legislator asked Clinton to "stop the policy-a-day nonsense," the room full of congressmen applauded.

For the first year and a half of Clinton's term, the chief of staff title was held by Clinton's childhood buddy Thomas "Mack" McLarty, a Fortune 500 CEO whose style was so diplomatic and deferential that his nickname was "Mack the Nice." McLarty enforced little discipline on the White House staff, in line with Clinton's wishes. A campaign consultant said of McLarty and Deputy Chief of Staff Mark Gearan: "If Mack or Mark were really angry at you, you wouldn't wet your pants. So how scared do you think [Congressman] Danny Rostenkowski is going to be?" "What the president needs is an enforcer," a Cabinet member agreed, "someone who can keep him in line, keep him from wandering off onto topics that haven't been thought through. I love him—he's my friend—but my goodness, he can't stop talking." By late 1993, McLarty was resorting to pulling Clinton out of discussions by the arm and passing him notes like, "Get to the point, Haiti, and wrap this up."

The management chaos in Clinton's early White House caused chronic personnel turmoil and sloppiness: many jobs remained unfilled, staff turnover was high, and inexperienced party operatives like Craig Livingston were put in sensitive jobs like head of personnel security, which triggered the FBI files mini-disaster. In the early summer of 1993, Clinton shuffled his staff to try to improve internal coordination and external communications. He brought in Washington Beltway veteran David Gergen to help shape the White House message and "help me interpret Washington" (or, as Clinton privately fumed, "the fucking Washington crowd"). To bolster Chief of Staff McLarty's dangerously loose grip on White House operations, Clinton appointed Roy Neel, then Vice President Al Gore's chief of staff, to the post of deputy chief of staff for administration.

Despite the reshuffle, Clinton allowed anarchy to reign supreme. Nobody was exactly sure who was supposed to do what. Coordination between domestic, national security, and congressional policy groups was almost nonexistent. Gergen left within a year. The White House operations job became a game of musical electric chairs. Neel was gone in six months, replaced by Phil Lader. Lader was gone in nine months, replaced by Erskine Bowles. Before long Bowles was gone, too (he would return later as chief of staff). "He'd like more order, but he doesn't want it at the expense of shutting out people he wants to see, friends or advisers," according to one aide. "He feeds on hearing from different people. He sifts. He wants a debate. He makes us talk it through. He doesn't want a staff situation where he gets a yes or no, boxes to check off."

In November 1993, when asked on NBC's *Meet the Press* about polls that showed over 70 percent of Americans thought the country was going in the wrong direction, Clinton acknowledged that his lack of focus was a liability: "I think in a way it may be my fault. I go from one thing to another. So we have one moment on national service, the signature idea of my campaign, and it happens, but it happens in the middle of all these other things, so nobody knows it happened. I think that's a big problem." That month Clinton worked assiduously to pass NAFTA, a struggle many thought he would lose. "Give me that 'no' list," said Clinton to his staff, "I know who I can get off that list." One aide recalled, "He knew which buttons to push on which members. He had the feel in his fingertips. He looked at the undecideds leaning against. We made a pool of ten. He got five. It was personal relations. Only experience gets you that." He did, however, allow NAFTA opponents to build up a powerful head of steam that nearly derailed the vote. "We've had too many near-death experiences in here," one administration official said of the constant crisis atmosphere. "We gotta figure out a system so people's hearts aren't stopping in sheer terror all the time."

Clinton began his presidency with a power structure the likes of which the White House had never seen, a ruling troika of policy super-wonks operating from three independent power centers: the Oval Office, Vice President Gore's office, and the empire known as "Hillaryland," which was split between Mrs. Clinton's cramped second-floor office and her staff's offices in the Executive Office Building across the street.

From January 1993 to mid-1994, Bill Clinton's chief operating officer, enforcer, consigliere, and virtual chief of staff was Hillary Rodham Clinton, easily the most powerful First Lady of the modern era. Mrs. Clinton asserted herself far beyond any First Lady before her. She was out-front, in-charge, and in-your-face, reaching for power and influence on the national stage light years beyond what Eleanor Roosevelt or Rosalynn Carter ever attempted. The previous power–First Ladies were content to travel extensively, advise their husbands behind the scenes, and mostly stay away from policy, at least publicly. Hillary Clinton decided, with her husband's blessing, to try to transform the concept of First Lady and enlighten the world with the "Politics of Meaning."

In the first two years of Clinton's term, Mrs. Clinton's influence was everywhere. She helped supervise office assignments for the West Wing, planted herself on a second-floor office a few dozen yards from the first-floor Oval Office (the first time ever a First Lady set up shop in the West Wing). She signed off on senior White House personnel appointments, helped choose federal judges, and reportedly blocked the hiring of white male candidates in favor of female and minority candidates. She took charge of the administration's response to the Whitewater and travel office fiascoes, scoring dismal results.

Like the president, Mrs. Clinton was a master policy analyst. Unlike him, she was a "closer" who knew when to cut a meeting short and when to shoot people in the kneecaps, including her husband. One top White House staffer called it "the most complicated relationship I have ever seen between two people." Early in the administration, she would tongue-lash the president in front of other people, attacks he withstood without responding. "I want to see a plan," she demanded at one economic policy meeting.

One Clinton official said that Mrs. Clinton could plunge a knife into you with an expression that said, "I've already thought about that." Another official reported that she sometimes demonstrated a "kind of Nazi-ish feeling" of "get on the program or get off the train." "The president sits in the middle of the table, the vice president right across from him, and Hillary wherever she wants," reported one aide. "And the refrain we have all gotten used to is, 'What do you think, Hillary?'" Another staffer explained: "A speech that gets a rewrite, get Hillary. A speech that needs to be given, get Hillary. The president has a problem he wants to chew over, get Hillary. The point is you never go wrong getting Hillary."

The young residents of "Hillaryland" were fiercely loyal to Mrs. Clinton: her staff closed ranks around her in constant crises and refused to leak to the press, like the rest of the White House did. She endeared herself to them with solicitude about their personal lives, pranks like wearing a necklace of flashing Christmas tree lights, and goofy phrases like, "Okey-dokey, artichokey," and "Miss Patty, you're as cute as a bug in a rug today." Until 1998, Mrs. Clinton was often unable to inspire affection in many segments of the public, and a Republican pollster claimed in early 1995 that his polls indicated she was "an asset to women eighteen to thirty-four and a liability to everybody else. She is still a role model to young women, particularly working women. But she reminds most men of their first wife—or mother-in-law."

In a series of gigantic tactical blunders, Mrs. Clinton decided, with her husband's enthusiastic approval, to totally overhaul the national health care system, a $1 trillion Rubik's Cube of intractable problems. She assembled a 500-person task force and traveled around the country conferring with Native American spiritual healers and consultants, set up a "War Room" command post in the Executive Office Building, and held closed meetings with as many as 100 of her staff at a time, some of which started as late as midnight and stretched on for days.

Mrs. Clinton excluded both key administration officials and influential senators from the health care plan's development, infuriating Republicans. The resulting 1,000-page, 240,000-word bill, which even its authors had trouble explaining, was cleanly torpedoed by Republicans, who ridiculed the plan as "socialized medicine" and displayed a comical Rube Goldberg organization chart to prove their point. Clinton couldn't generate enough votes to even budge the plan out of committee, and it was declared dead by all parties in mid-1994. One aide concluded: "The person who's in charge shouldn't sleep with the president, because if you sleep with the president, nobody is going to tell you the truth." Clinton explained, "I knew that she could manage a long, complex, highly contentious process [involving] something people care a lot about." In a major understatement, he conceded, "The reaction was more negative than I thought. I will admit, I underestimated this." On developing the plan in secret, Clinton admitted, "In retrospect, I think that was a mistake."

In late 1994, a defeated Mrs. Clinton retreated from the public policy arena and banished herself from most White House operations meetings. Despite her private yearnings to affect what she called "systemic change," the health care mess marked the death of her public policy role. She continued to exert influence behind the scenes, helping to recruit Dick Morris to rescue and reelect her husband in 1996 and helping craft the winning "center-values" campaign positioning strategy. In late 1997, Mrs. Clinton reemerged in the public spotlight with a new, less controversial cause, child care, and a softer, humbler, and more inclusive style, and in 1998 her popularity ratings skyrocketed in the wake of the Lewinsky mess.

From the start of Clinton's presidency and through both his terms, an effective collaboration blossomed between Clinton and Vice President Al Gore, whose polish, brainpower, inside-the-Beltway experience, and steady, confident forcefulness behind the scenes were ideal executive complements to Clinton's inexperience and volatility.

Clinton regularly ended meetings by offering the floor to Gore to deliver the wrap-up, and often put Gore on the Oval Office speakerphone to tag-team congressmen. "His voice is heard on every policy decision the president makes," according to a top White House staffer, "and there are large areas of policy which the president effectively has ceded to him," including the environment, Reinventing Government, and technology policy. A senior Clinton aide claimed, "He does more to make this place work than anyone knows." The vice president played a central role in foreign affairs, too, forming close ties with Egyptian President Hosni Mubarak and South African President Nelson Mandela, and acting as point man in supporting Russian reforms by nurturing a strong partnership with Russian Prime Minister Victor Chernomyrdin. Gore tackled substantive assignments, challenged the president in closed-door meetings, and earned the president's respect and confidence, all rare achievements for a vice president. Gore seemed bulletproof until his mealy-mouthed "no controlling legal authority" response to campaign finance inquiries in March 1997 exposed his vulnerabilities.

In June 1994, with anarchy continuing to grip his White House, Clinton announced a major shakeup of his staff, appointing budget chief and congressional veteran Leon Panetta as chief of staff and pushing McLarty downstairs to become counselor to the president. A Clinton adviser sniped: "What the president needs is someone who knows how to manage Congress, knows how to manage the media, and knows how to manage Clinton. Mack couldn't do any of the three. "Clinton recognizes his own mistakes," Panetta said. "His fear is that he has been seeing a repetition of his first term as governor, when he was involved in an awful lot of issues. Management became very chaotic. He ended up micromanaging." Panetta announced to reporters: "The one thing he wants is tough management."

Panetta's first move was to ask for a White House organizational chart. No one had one. "As far as I know, anybody who walked down the hall walked in" to the Oval Office, he recalled. Panetta quickly seized control of the president's schedule and appointments, and tried, not always successfully, to clear all access to the Oval Office, even by close advisers like George Stephanopoulos and National Security Adviser Anthony Lake, as well as prepare agendas for meetings and conduct "dress rehearsals" before seeing the president. In taking the chief of staff job, Panetta extracted promises from the Clintons and Gore that he had their confidence and the authority to make decisions, including hiring and firing. In his first days on the job, however, Panetta wandered into a typical fog of Clintonian confusion when ambiguous comments he made with McLarty on a joint *Meet the Press* appearance led many to believe he was going to fire Press Secretary Dee Dee Myers. Myers protested to Clinton in an emotional Oval Office meeting (Clinton wept), she kept her job, and Panetta's authority was undercut even before he got started.

In a replay of the Baird, Wood, and Guinier fiascoes of 1993, staff sloppiness in background checking of Henry W. Foster, Jr., to be Surgeon General provoked total confusion over his history of performing abortions, dooming his chances for Senate approval. "Look at the past week and weep," groaned an adviser about a continuing lack of focus at the White House. "Even without the Foster fiasco, I'd like to know what the country is supposed to think the president really cares about based on the past week? They're always complaining the president can't get the message out. Well, what is the message? Abortion? Immigration? Crime?" A Democratic congressional supporter complained, "One of President Clinton's main problems is people don't know what the core is, what he stands for, because if you talk about everything, then you talk about nothing." Democratic Senator Joseph R. Biden, Jr., of Delaware asserted that "no deep thought was given before the nomination was sent up." Democratic Senator Barbara A. Mikulski agreed: "That's just the way this White House is." House Speaker Newt Gingrich, still triumphant from the 1994 midterm election rout of Clinton, chimed in gleefully, "Ask yourself, two years into an administration, how could they be this grotesquely wrong and how could they stumble into a fight of this proportion."

As the first inaugurated post–Cold War president, Clinton made no effort to hide his preference for tackling domestic issues over foreign affairs. His first year was dominated by the humiliating images of American soldiers being dragged through the streets of Mogadishu and the U.S. Navy retreating before a mob of Haitian rent-a-thugs at Port-au-Prince. "Clinton is very bright and capable, as good at foreign policy as the next guy," said foreign policy mandarin Paul Nitze, "But he gives the impression of not caring about it." In his first term, Clinton, busy with NAFTA and budget battles, canceled his international security briefings so often that CIA Director James Woolsey, an occasional participant, simply boycotted them altogether.

Clinton claimed to have learned from his early foreign policy stumbles, explaining, in late 1994, "First of all, it's a more disciplined, tightly focused process now than it was in the first year. The weekly meetings with the national-security team, which we have now even when some of the principals are gone, enable us to take a long view. We've also allocated slightly more time every day for the national-security briefing, and it's amazing what a difference—it's another fifteen minutes to thirty minutes over and above the base-line time we normally give it. Now, it's forty-five minutes." Clinton was miraculously lucky not to have any major foreign policy crises into his sixth year in office, and as time progressed, Clinton did improve: he and his team patched together fragile peace accords for Bosnia, Israel and the Palestinians, and Ireland. In 1998, Clinton shored up ties with China during a state visit in which he also managed to speak out for human rights.

Clinton's passion for policy debate and hands-on-the-throat management of congressional relations paid off spectacularly in his first two years, when he won on big issues like his budget package, crime bill, Brady Bill, NAFTA, and GATT, and passed a host of Democratic initiatives backed up during the Bush years. Although his crime bill was battered and his health care initiative collapsed before coming to a vote, Clinton's 86.4 percent success rates with Congress in both 1993 and 1994 were beaten only three times before (Eisenhower's 89 percent in 1953 and LBJ's 88 percent in 1964 and 93 percent in 1965). On NAFTA, Clinton squared off against organized labor and anti-NAFTA forces in his own party, worked the phone, and wheeled and dealed like LBJ. Senator James Exon, a member of the budget committee, marveled: "Certainly I would have to rate Bill Clinton as the best salesman that I guess I've ever seen."

Clinton's congressional liaison Howard Paster reported, "He has had them jogging, had them on Air Force One, had them over for breakfasts, dinners, movies." "He asks a lot of questions," one aide said of Clinton. "He probes to find out where they are. He listens. He talks about policy the way other people talk about baseball. He doesn't close the deal, but moves the deal quite a long way along, creating a climate in which a deal can be closed." In one meeting with legislators, Clinton ticked down a long list of statistics and said, "You know I love this stuff." "The president was far more successful than the public perception," said Senate Majority Leader George Mitchell. "He's extremely knowledgeable on the issues, more so than any other president. He knows the subject better than members of Congress. You speak to him directly on the issues, not through aides. He works hard at it. He spends a lot of time with members and with me. I call him up and say, 'Call Senators A, B, C.' He does it."

During budget negotiations in the winter of 1995, House Speaker Newt Gingrich said Clinton was the "most powerful setter of mood" he'd ever met. Whenever he entered Clinton's Oval Office, Gingrich was overwhelmed by Clinton's seductive, overpowering charm. After meeting with Clinton, Gingrich claimed, "I need two hours to detoxify." The *Washington Post's* David Maraniss wrote that "Gingrich found himself caught in a trance, believing that Clinton wanted an agreement and that they were on the verge of reaching one. In the end, he realized too late that he had been utterly outmaneuvered and outsmarted by Clinton: The public would believe that it was Clinton, and not the Congressional Republicans who really wanted to end the deficit." Gingrich sputtered: "There is this residual belief on the part of the American public that no one can be as baldly and totally dishonest as he is capable of being. I mean, it's stunning."

When Gingrich's Republicans stormed into Congress in 1995, Clinton's success rate plunged to 36.2 percent that year, the lowest of any president in *Congressional Quarterly's* forty-seven-year measuring history. In classic Clinton roller-coaster style, his congressional box score rebounded to 55 percent in 1996, the biggest comeback in history, holding close to 54 percent in 1997 and dropping to 51 percent in 1998. Clinton scored victories in budget showdowns late in 1995, his support of a major welfare reform bill in the summer of 1996, and a budget compromise in 1997, but his chronically disorganized style contributed to his November 1997 defeat on "fast track" trade legislation, during which he lurched into potential lame-duck status. Citing constituent concerns, 80 percent of congressional Democrats bolted from Clinton. "The White House didn't have a clue as to what was motivating members," said Democratic Representative Nancy Pelosi of California. "They were pushing all the wrong buttons." Clinton delayed lobbying Congress for months, infuriated legislators by ignoring their concerns, and waited too long to introduce a bill, leaving the field wide open for organized labor to seize the initiative. "It reminds me of how I got my term papers done in college," one presidential adviser moaned about Clinton's procrastination.

The release of the White House TV "Coffee Tapes" in October 1997, triggered by research for this book and a resulting investigation by *Washington*

Post reporter George Lardner, Jr., exposed humiliating images of a president groveling for cash and the sloppiness and confusion of a White House whose left hand often didn't know what its right hand was doing. The tapes, made by the same White House TV unit that started taping Ronald Reagan in 1982, were belatedly discovered by an overworked White House staff that claimed it had forgotten the tapes existed. A furious Republican Senator Fred Thompson, leader of the Senate campaign finance inquiry that had periodically asked for such records, fumed, "They thwarted our subpoenas, misinformed and misled us." Ironically, Clinton was said to have had a special fondness for the White House Television crews because it was their predecessors in a naval film unit who captured now-epic footage of Clinton shaking hands with President Kennedy in July 1963.

The Coffee Tapes give an inside view of Clinton as a highly exuberant, energetic political executive exerting a micromanagement grip on his reelection campaign, gleefully exploiting arcane campaign finance loopholes and fraternizing with big cash contributors to avoid the $1,000 limit on individual donors by diverting money to issue-based "soft money" campaign funds. The tapes were a numbing, Kafkaesque series of presidential suck-up sessions for money, as Clinton relentlessly charmed donors while skating along a thin line of legality, offering banalities like "Hi, nice tie" on an endless loop to any man who looked like he had cash in the bank.

One sequence, shot on June 18, 1996, showed Clinton shaking hands with John Huang, who was later charged with helping foreign nationals make illegal campaign contributions, offering him a friendly, "Hi, John." At a May 1, 1996, Oval Office coffee, Clinton charmed a group of five donors, and four of them soon contributed $100,000 each. At another 1996 coffee event, Clinton stressed the effectiveness of the soft money campaign, telling a group of contributors: "The fact that we've been able to finance this long-running constant television campaign where we were always able to frame the issues—most of it's been actually quite positive, not a big negative hit on the Republicans, but just trying to show the differences in what we were trying to achieve—has been central to the position that I now enjoy in the polls." Federal election law prohibits fund-raising in White House work areas, but Clinton officials defended the coffees by pointing out that no overt solicitations were made. "They're not incriminating," said a White House aide of the Coffee Tapes, "they're just . . . pornographic."

From 1996 into 1998, Clinton's job approval ratings held strong in the mid-60s, as Americans seemed willing to forgive his weaknesses as long as he stayed on top of his job. In May 1996, *New York Times* White House correspondent Todd S. Purdum wrote of the "paradox" of Clinton: "One of the biggest, most talented, articulate, intelligent, open, colorful characters ever to inhabit the Oval Office can also be an undisciplined, fumbling, obtuse, defensive, self-justifying rogue. His strengths and weaknesses not only spring from the same source but could also not exist without one another. In a real sense, his strengths are his weaknesses, his enthusiasms are his undoing and most of the traits that make him appealing can make him appalling in the flash of an eye."

By early 1998, it appeared that Clinton had improved and grown in office. Although he repeated his mistakes, he seemed capable of learning from them, and tried to compensate for his weaknesses. Moving into his second term, for example, he brought millionaire entrepreneur Erskine Bowles back to the White House as chief of staff. Following Panetta's lead, Bowles imposed stronger discipline and accountability on Clinton's notoriously anarchic staff. As Clinton's sixth year in office began, his officials spoke wistfully of "legacy items" they hoped would define his chapter in the history books: the elimination of the deficit, the strongest peacetime economic expansion in history, a restructured welfare system, the rescue of Social Security.

Then, suddenly, on January 21, 1998, a bomb named Monica Lewinsky landed on Bill Clinton's head. A bizarre new chapter in American history began as the first real-time presidential sex scandal erupted, complete with secret phone tapes, XXX-rated performances in the Oval Office study, and intense media scrutiny of presidential DNA deposits. Presidents used to have the luxury of decades (or in Thomas Jefferson's case, centuries) of breathing room before their sexual misbehavior was publicly confirmed. Now it was happening with Internet speed, as grand jury leaks landed on the World Wide Web within seconds.

The messy, ultra-high-risk, edge-of-disaster style that defined Clinton's executive performance pervaded his private life as well, and the detonation of the Lewinsky scandal threatened the presidency with global ridicule. For the first time in history, Congress impeached an elected president. The "Monica effect" paralyzed Washington through 1998, derailing Clinton's plans for a tobacco settlement, the expansion of Medicare, a patient's bill of rights, and campaign finance reform. All were consumed, at least temporarily, by the Monica firestorm.

The Lewinsky affair illustrated that the Oval Office may be the world's most public office, but it includes surprisingly broad zones of physical privacy. Only one peephole looks into it, on the door leading from the president's secretary's office. It was often used by Clinton staffers to see when meetings were about to break up, but it doesn't give a complete view of the office. Secret Service agents are usually posted outside another Oval Office door that opens up to the West Wing office corridor, but that door doesn't contain a peephole. Consequently, retired Secret Service agent Lewis Fox, who was posted outside the door on a weekend afternoon in 1995, was unable in early 1998 to verify whether Clinton and Lewinsky were completely alone during forty minutes they spent together.

The president's movements are tracked through an elaborate system of electronic monitors, allowing his guards and aides to identify his location on the White House grounds, but the system is not believed to extend inside the Oval Office suite of offices. There is a peephole on the west door to the hallway leading from the Oval Office to the bathroom, pantry, presidential dining room, and connecting secluded outdoor patio, but this is traditionally a private area that few visitors enter without the president's invitation. In February 1998, *U.S. News & World Report* reported of a "little-known tunnel leading from under the Oval Office to the basement of the family quarters," another potential area of presidential privacy.

The most private spot in the area is the presidential study immediately west of the Oval Office. The small office was built by Eisenhower for post-heart attack napping and was used by many presidents who followed, including Clinton, who retreated there to nap, read, listen to CDs and, on some ten occasions from 1995 to 1997, have sex with Monica Lewinsky. All of the Clinton/Lewinsky contacts described by the Starr Report as "sexual encounters that involved some form of genital contact" occurred in the study, the hallway outside the study, or the bathroom across the hall. "Ms. Lewinsky stated," according to the Starr Report, "that the hallway outside the Oval Office study was more suitable for their encounters than the Oval Office because the hallway had no windows."

The acts of extramarital sex with an intern and lying under oath to subvert a sexual harassment lawsuit would have gotten Clinton fired from the U.S. military and a great many corporations. But to the astonishment of Republican strategists, they were offenses that many Americans seemed capable of forgiving Clinton for, as he doggedly pursued the strategy that got him reelected: projecting the image of a diligent executive focusing on his job while his enemies dithered. The American people rewarded him with job approval ratings that roared along at robust levels through 1998 and into 1999.

After ten months of excruciating, embarrassing ordeal, the paralyzing spell of Monicagate lifted in part with a remarkable succession of Clintonian triumphs in the fall of 1998. Over the course of a few weeks, he brokered a major budget deal with Congress that included $1.2 billion to hire 100,000 new teachers, arm-twisted the Israelis and PLO into signing the Wye River Accords, and saw his party cruise to a historic midterm reelection victory, the first time since 1934 that the party controlling the White House scored net gains in Congress.

The midterm election also saw the full symbolic resurrection of Mrs. Clinton as a potent political force, as she barnstormed the country for Democratic candidates to exultant crowds and ignited speculation over what could be a golden political future, independent of her husband's. If that wasn't enough, within weeks Newt Gingrich resigned as House Speaker and Attorney General Janet Reno ruled against appointing a special prosecutor to investigate Vice President Gore's 1996 fund-raising activities.

On February 12, 1999, the strange, steamy melodrama of Clinton's impeachment finally culminated in his acquittal in the Senate. But at the eleventh hour, a dark apparition appeared in the shadows, and for a brief moment it threatened to hijack the story into an unfathomable new direction. It was the specter of secret White House taping.

Two weeks earlier, at least two Republican senators received sketchy information from unnamed government sources about the possible existence of a taping capability that could have captured Clinton's phone conversations. Within days the rumors were being discussed on Fox News. White House Press Secretary Joe Lockhart denied that any secret White House taping occurred, while acknowledging that "we certainly have the ability to tape some phone calls," such as a press phone interview to provide reporters with a transcript. He added that phone calls with foreign leaders weren't routinely taped.

On February 9, less than three days before the final impeachment vote, Senate Majority Leader Trent Lott sent Independent Counsel Kenneth Starr a letter saying that the Senate had learned of the possibility that such secret tapes may exist, and referred the matter to Starr's office for follow-up. The next day, Press Secretary Lockhart repeated the denials: "From everything that I've been able to gather from talking to people within the Administration, there is no recording system, there are no tapes, there are no transcripts." He went on to deny knowledge of "any system that's either built in or not built in."

However, Senator Jon Kyl (R-Arizona), a member of the Select Committee on Intelligence, told the February 10, 1999 *Arizona Republic*: "There are different agencies and it was one of those agencies" that conducted the taping, adding, "incidentally, it may have been more than one of those agencies."

"Here you have a case going forward, and at issue are a lot of different inter-
pretations of phone conversations," Kyl continued, alluding to disputed conversations involving Clinton, Lewinsky, and presidential confidant Vernon
Jordan. "Now you have people who have reason to know that the tapes exist
and they say, 'Wait a minute, shouldn't someone know about this?'"

Several theories were floated in the press as to who may have conducted
such taping. One theory envisioned a hypothetical U.S. counterintelligence
operation monitoring phone transmissions to investigate spying activities of a
foreign government in Washington. One senator, cited by *Newsday*, mentioned
that military personnel might be taping Clinton to determine whether he was
being secretly blackmailed. In other words, Clinton could have been taped
without his knowing it, perhaps even by members of his own government.

If such a system existed, so then would the possibility not only of presidential phone sex tapes, but of tapes of disputed Clinton calls with Lewinsky
and Jordan. A tape of a December 17, 1997 Clinton-Lewinsky call, for example, might prove—as House prosecutors charged and Lewinsky denied—that
Clinton had asked Lewinsky to conceal their relationship after telling her that
her name was on a witness list in the Paula Jones sexual harassment case.

An official with hands-on knowledge of Clinton's White House phone
systems told *The White House Bulletin* that the capability to tape presidential phone conversations most certainly did exist.

The source explained that there are three phone systems the president
can use: a secure military "command and control system" run by the Defense
Department's White House Communications Agency (WHCA), and two relatively less secure systems: a cell phone frequency and local phone company
lines Clinton reportedly installed in the Oval Office and White House mansion as soon as he became president in 1993, lines that bypass the White
House switchboard and can't be taped, at least from inside the White House.
The WHCA circuit is believed to have the capability of being digitally
recorded. "In the case of a head of state phone call," the source contended,
"that would probably go over the command and control circuits. And in order
to insure that there wasn't a missed translation, that type of call is usually
recorded so everyone involved in the call, if they needed to, could go back
and revisit it."

The *White House Bulletin*'s source speculated that it was possible that
Clinton used the WHCA line for Lewinsky and Jordan calls because he was
frequently urged to "use that system, simply because we have safeguards on
it that would protect him from being overheard by people he didn't want to
be overheard by." On the other hand, the source said that Clinton didn't nec-

essarily trust the WHCA system: "My sense was that with President Clinton, the less he has to deal with WHCA, the more comfortable he felt. He would grab an aide's cell phone rather than use the phone in his limousine." Also, since WHCA staff are supposed to record calls only if they're asked to, and are not in the habit of eavesdropping on presidential conversations, such tapes may not exist.

In the end, Republicans, facing inevitable defeat in the Senate vote and unwilling to risk further infuriating an impeachment-weary public, simply referred the matter to special prosecutor Ken Starr. The possibility of secret Clinton tapes receded back into the historical vapor, at least for the moment.

William Jefferson Clinton's improvisational, seat-of-the-pants style of governance would make political science and management professors sick, but it helped him constantly reinvent, reposition, and reinvigorate himself while managing the messy, chaotic business of policy and politics. Clinton proved to be an often effective president, presiding over major trade, crime, and budget bills, a successful reelection, a balanced budget, strong job growth, and a booming economy and stock market, all accomplished in the midst of chronic sloppiness, scandals, and, in the twilight of his administration, the dagger blow of impeachment.

"I'm a lot like Baby Huey," Clinton announced prophetically to Newt Gingrich during a get-acquainted meeting on the White House Truman balcony in 1993. "I'm fat. I'm ugly. But if you push me down, I keep coming back. I just keep coming back." The following year, Clinton mused in the Oval Office, "I'm not perfect, but I work hard and I get things done."

Bill Clinton demonstrated that in the eyes of many Americans, inside the Oval Office, competence is more precious a commodity than character.

The Wired Presidents

*"I always wondered about that taping equipment
but I'm damn glad we have it, aren't you?"*

RICHARD NIXON TO H. R. HALDEMAN
OVAL OFFICE RECORDING, APRIL 25, 1973

THE WHITE HOUSE MAP ROOM
AUGUST 17, 1998, 12:40 P.M.

Bill Clinton shifted nervously in his chair in the historic Map Room in the basement of the White House mansion as White House TV cameras prepared to record his deposition in the Monica Lewinsky investigation. Standing a few feet away was Special Prosecutor Ken Starr. Fifty-six years earlier, Franklin Roosevelt and Winston Churchill sat in this same room, gazed at giant battle maps, and plotted the rescue of world civilization. Today, the world's most powerful chief executive was being asked to confess his most intimate sexual behavior to a grand jury, on a tape that would soon be broadcast to the entire planet.

A technician pressed the RECORD button, the president rose to put his hand in the air to swear to tell the truth, and sat down. Over the next five hours, Clinton rambled and stumbled through an excruciating marathon of confession, evasion, and denial: "That depends on what the definition of the word 'is' is" . . . "something funny is going on here" . . . "I may have been confused in my memory" . . . "you're dealing with in some ways one of the most mysterious areas of human life" . . . "it depends on how you define 'alone.' "

Clinton's ordeal marked the completion of the symbolic arc of White House taping, the return of an arrow fired by Franklin Roosevelt in 1940 that had already sliced through Richard Nixon. Nearly six decades since the first secret White House recording in history captured FDR toying with a sex scandal that could destroy his enemy, President Clinton was in danger of being destroyed himself, not by his own tapes like Nixon, but by a sex scandal ignited by the taped phone confessions of an intern to her confidante, recordings initiated by Clinton's enemies and turned against the White House. Secret tapings began as a covert exertion of presidential power, but they became potential agents of presidential destruction. If presidents ever needed a reminder to be careful whom they sleep with and talk to, especially when menaced by an extremely zealous federal prosecutor, Clinton's predicament provided it in spectacular detail.

The Oval Office is the world's most dangerous office: a single phrase can send armies across borders, send financial markets into shock, or change history. It is little wonder that many presidents experimented with the option of White House taping to provide a small margin of security to protect themselves against their enemies, even those lurking in their own administrations. The tapes and transcripts many of these presidents left behind, incomplete and imperfect as they are, offer glimpses of how their public political and leadership skills were enhanced or sabotaged by their closed-door executive skills—how well they managed the executive power the Constitution gave them in the day-to-day pressure cooker of the Oval Office.

Every president since FDR has had to confront one of the central executive dilemmas of the office: how to get an accurate record of what is said in the White House, but at the same time not restrict the flow of candid and confidential advice by telling people they are being recorded. The way each man dealt with this dilemma reflects the executive styles that governed their presidencies. FDR began his recording experiment soon after he realized the United States was on the verge of becoming a global superpower; he secretly bugged the Washington press corps to assure he wouldn't be misquoted, and inadvertently captured other Oval Office business as well. Roosevelt tested the practice over three months, but sensitive to the political risks, he discarded it. Harry Truman got a look at FDR's machine, tried it out, and shut it down. Period. To have done otherwise would have required a deviousness and complexity that were completely beyond the straight-shooting country judge.

Dwight Eisenhower stashed a hidden Dictaphone in the Oval Office as a backup executive tool, an insurance policy to protect himself in the turbulent arena of brute-force power politics. John Kennedy was the producer and director of the White House's first full-fledged secret recording network, and he knew exactly when and who to tape. He concentrated mainly on the most heroic and dramatic moments of his presidency, and in keeping with his cautious executive style, he always remembered when the tape was running. Lyndon Johnson recorded the rough music of his most beloved instrument of manipulation: his own voice on the telephone.

Richard Nixon, the consummate strategist and dysfunctional tactician, installed equipment to record all the sounds of his offices and then forgot about it. He soon discovered that White House taping is a devil's bargain, and his tapes preserved for all time the desolate agony of his accidental self-crucifixion. Nixon and his heirs fought a quarter-century legal campaign to block and delay the release of the tapes he commissioned, but they, like all White House tapes, should belong not to Nixon, but to the people who paid for the Dictaphones, Dictabelts, reel-to-reel recorders, reel-to-reel tape, microphones, mixers, monitors, cables, and technicians, the same people who paid Nixon's salary—the American taxpayers.

For post-Watergate Presidents Ford, Carter, and Bush, the decision to forbid all secret White House taping was automatic, and given Ford's decency, Carter's morals, and Bush's caution, it was an easy choice. Ronald Reagan's White House television cameras were installed to create a historical record in his favored medium of projecting visions, while his telephone recordings were designed to give him a margin of safety during potentially high-risk conversations with other world leaders. Like most other White House taping systems, his Situation Room audio recorder was installed not for entrapment but for self-protection.

While Bill Clinton has not been accused of secret White House recordings, he proved to be the most reckless president ever on tape, next to Richard Nixon. Clinton demonstrated how to exploit campaign finance law loopholes in full view of White House TV video cameras. Even though he was afraid his phone was being bugged by a foreign government, he engaged in repeated bouts of phone sex with an emotional young White House intern and left tape-recorded phone messages on her answering machine. Finally, Monica Lewinsky was trapped in a tape-recorded FBI sting. Clinton thrived on chaos, but he was nearly overwhelmed by it.

Clinton discovered not only that presidents no longer have any hope of privacy, but that a lone citizen like Linda Tripp, armed only with a vendetta and a Radio Shack phone recorder, can trigger a campaign of surveillance and manipulation that could threaten a president with ejection from the Oval Office. One of the cosmic ironies of Clinton's Lewinsky ordeal was that the entire episode was triggered by a secret taping operation that was illegal under the law of Tripp's home state of Maryland, punishable by up to five years in jail and a $10,000 fine. Maryland, along with some eleven other states, requires the consent of all parties to a phone call being taped. Maryland even makes an additional distinction against making an illegal tape for commercial gain, as Tripp, a lucrative book deal in mind, was very likely doing.

Presidential White House taping itself has always been legal. Until 1968, federal law on the issue was ambiguous, and there was no clear-cut prohibition against recording face-to-face or phone conversations to which one was a party. With passage of the 1968 Omnibus Crime Control and Safe Streets Act, federal law required only one-party consent to recordings. Today, federal law, Washington, D.C., law, and the law in thirty-eight states allow taping with only one-party consent. In almost all cases, however, it is illegal to intercept or record the conversations that one is not a party to, as a Florida couple found out when they intercepted and recorded a conference call captured on a police radio scanner in December 1996. On the call, House Speaker Newt Gingrich and other Republican leaders were overheard strategizing responses to ethics charges against Gingrich, a seeming violation of a Gingrich pledge not to organize a political response. Since the federal wiretap law was amended in 1986 and 1994 to extend the ban on third-party recordings to include cellular and cordless phone conversations, the couple pled guilty to violating the statute and were fined $500.

Secret taping is in a sense a betrayal of trust, a violation of the American ethic of freedom of speech in the sense that it restricts the freedom to choose whom one speaks freely to. Lyndon Johnson, in the midst of a secret Oval Office phone-taping spree on a scale never seen before or since, once mused to an assistant, "The worst thing in our society would be to not be able to pick up a phone for fear of it being tapped." His comment echoes the ambivalence many of the taping presidents must have felt, which compelled them to keep the practice secret. The ultimate extreme extensions of presidential taping were the wiretapping campaigns conducted *outside* the White House by JFK, LBJ, and Nixon, tappings that began as national security measures but began mutating into abuses of presidential power.

The dilemmas of presidential taping and tapping reflect the tension between the open society sanctified in the Bill of Rights and the runaway national security state of postwar America, where government agencies such as the FBI, the CIA, and the super-secret National Security Agency (NSA) have routinely intercepted and tracked private conversations in the fight against communism, crime, terrorism, and other foreign and domestic threats.

Presidential recordings are, of course, only a symbolic tip of the iceberg of surveillance and electronic espionage that is increasingly a tool of doing business for individuals, companies, and governments. The FBI recently asked phone companies to plan for an expansion of the bureau's wiretapping ability to be able to conduct up to 60,000 simultaneous phone taps and traces in the fight against crime. Court-authorized government wiretaps (75 percent for drug investigations) reached a record 2 million individual private conversations in 1997. The little-known Foreign Intelligence Surveillance Act (FISA) allows not only for secret wiretaps but for searches of a home when the owner is away, if the FBI can convince a secret FISA court in Washington that there is probable-cause evidence that the target is a national security threat or a foreign agent. In the twenty years since the program began, the bureau made 10,000 such requests and all but one were approved (a single tap request can result in many conversations being tapped on that line). FISA wiretaps now exceed those conducted by regular law enforcement.

"We're on the precipice of developing a Big Brother Society," said Donald Haines, a privacy expert for the American Civil Liberties Union. "That's not a metaphor but a reality." Concealed cameras and microphones are proliferating throughout American society. Video surveillance cameras are quietly popping up not just in their traditional locations at banks and stores but in mass transit systems, schools, stadiums, even city streets. Over sixty American cities use video surveillance in public places for security purposes. In New York City alone, there is video monitoring of parks, subway platforms, public pools, and a trial program on buses. It is legal in forty-six states for employers to hide cameras in bathrooms and locker rooms.

Even before the Tripp/Lewinsky mess, security industry experts were reporting a surge in demand for listening devices from private industry and individuals. Recordings are being initiated by executives, attorneys, police officers arresting suspects, company whistleblowers, workers trying to prove sexual harassment, and couples suspicious of each other or of their nannies. Advances in surveillance and security device technologies are occurring at dizzying speed. At a New York "spy shop," for $30 you can buy a palm-sized microcassette recorder that can easily be sneaked into a meeting, or a credit card–sized recorder for $800 that will pick up voices ten feet away when it's buried in your purse or suit pocket. In 1997, federal law enforcement authorities raided and shut down the Spy Factory, the largest national chain of retail stores selling high-tech personal security devices, for selling thousands of illegal third-party bugging and wiretapping devices, including tiny transmitters hidden in ballpoint pens and calculators.

The reason secret taping is so popular is that it works. Armed with wiretaps and bugs, the FBI came close to breaking the back of organized crime in the 1980s and 1990s. In 1995, the bureau busted one of the largest price-fixing conspiracies in history. Their case was built on secret recordings of a 1993 meeting in Tokyo's Palace Hotel between representatives of Archer Daniels Midland and three Asian companies. In corporate America, secret monitoring and taping is a routine cost of doing business: sales of security cameras alone are approaching $6 billion per year. Testifying before Congress against workplace privacy proposals, a representative of the National Association of Manufacturers said "random and periodic silent monitoring" was "a very important management tool." Companies now routinely tape-record customer service calls, after cryptically warning the caller that "this call may be monitored or taped for quality purposes."

Employees are using secret tapes against their companies to document corporate wrongdoing. A Texaco staffer taped white executives making racist remarks in company meetings, and the release of the tapes triggered a national scandal and frantic company reforms. Some companies are so worried by this trend that they're prohibiting secret taping by employees even in states where it is legal, and counterattacking employees in states that require all-party consent. In California, for example, a Bank of America technician trying to document sexual harassment by a female employee released more than 160 taped conversations with co-workers. The bank sued him for invasion of privacy and breaking California's all-party consent law, won a trial-court victory, and in 1994 a state appeals court upheld a $132,000 fine against the employee.

In late 1997, reporter Timothy W. Maier of *Insight on the News* magazine (affiliated with *The Washington Times,* a conservative daily) broke an extraordinary story accusing U.S. intelligence agencies of staging a massive bugging operation during the 1993 APEC summit of fifteen Asia-Pacific leaders in Seattle hosted by President Clinton, with data passed from the White House to big Democratic corporate donors. The story, which was denied by the White House, was based on tips from concerned "high-level sources" in the intelligence and law enforcement communities, who described a top secret operation run by the FBI in conjunction with the NSA and several other agencies.

"There were bugs placed in over 300 locations," said one informant, who alleged that "just about every room was bugged." At least 10,000 conversations were reportedly recorded. Vehicles, phones, hotel rooms, and conference centers were reportedly bugged with wireless mikes placed in flowerpots, lamps, and rental cars. Even a charter boat carrying the heads of state was allegedly monitored by agents with electronic-listening equipment. The agents were told it was a national security operation to protect the leaders' safety, but the article alleged that economic espionage data collected by the bugs was channeled through bureaucratic layers and wound up in the hands of Democratic National Committee operatives, who used the information "to create business and financial opportunities and as part of fund-raising operations."

If true, the bugging of the APEC conference was just an opening shot in the new age of global economic espionage that may be a key part of the U.S. intelligence community's post–Cold War annual $28 billion charter, which even includes spying against allies like Japan and France. The year after the APEC summit, during automobile negotiations in Tokyo, U.S. trade representative Mickey Kantor was accompanied by a team of CIA and NSA analysts, who sifted through intelligence gathered in part by American electronic eavesdropping equipment. The intelligence included intercepted private conversations between Japanese business and government officials. "It was a remarkable performance," said a top U.S. official, "because the U.S. intelligence agencies finally realized this was the World Series—the arms control talks of the new age." A 1995 operation in Europe didn't go as smoothly: the French caught and expelled the CIA Paris station chief and four undercover American officers, one of whom was caught trying to bribe his way into bugging the French phone system.

The president of the United States today sits at the pinnacle of a gigantic, highly secret global network of electronic surveillance that, unknown to most Americans, is believed to periodically intercept worldwide phone conversations, faxes, and electronic-mail messages. The network, known as ECHELON, is an outgrowth of Cold War electronic espionage and is based on a secret 1948 agreement between the United States, Britain, Canada, Australia, and New Zealand to share electronic intelligence. Collecting vast amounts of data with a network of spy satellites, ground-based interception bases, and supercomputers, ECHELON reportedly uses keyword scanning to search, for example, for words or codes connected to terrorism or drugs, and alerts human operators for further analysis. According to a 1998 report by the European Parliament, all phone calls, faxes, and e-mails throughout Europe are subject to "routine and indiscriminate" monitoring by ECHELON.

Such measures may be necessary in a world populated by Osama bin Laden, Saddam Hussein, and international networks of drug dealers, terrorists, pedophiles, and gangsters, but the potential for abuse of such a system is staggering. Already the ECHELON system is rumored to be collecting data on civilian entities, including businesses, governments, and organizations such as Greenpeace and Amnesty International. According to British European Parliament official Glyn Ford, "Information collected [by ECHELON] has apparently been used by U.S. companies to win commercial contracts, against all the rules of competitiveness and to the detriment of European and Japanese firms."

We are not yet facing techno-tyranny, but the day is fast approaching when governments, in response to political, military, or economic crises, could quickly reprogram such monitoring systems and bring entire populations under strict political surveillance. The question Americans now face is how much freedom and privacy we are willing to trade in exchange for lessening our exposure to real and catastrophic dangers, and how intrusive, ubiquitous remedies such as electronic surveillance can exist in a society that values freedom above all. Referring to NSA surveillance techniques a quarter century ago, Senator Frank Church warned "that capability at any time could be turned around on the American people and no American would have any privacy left, such [is] the capability to monitor everything: telephone conversations, telegrams, it doesn't matter. There would be no place to hide."

"I know the capacity that there is to make tyranny total in America," Church declared, "and we must see to it that this agency and all agencies that possess this technology operate within the law and under proper supervision, so that we never cross over that abyss. That is the abyss from which there is no return."

The new dangers of twenty-first-century technology and disorder illustrate that the presidency is an executive job like no other on earth. As vice president, Al Gore was struck by the "unrelenting intensity of decision making. A typical CEO of a Fortune 500 company will have two to three gut-wrenching decisions a week to make."

"The president and vice president will have six to eight decisions every day," Gore said, "but there is no time in between for a sigh of relief." Ironically, some presidents, such as John Kennedy and Gerald Ford, had next to no real executive experience before entering the Oval Office.

The presidency requires an impossibly wide array of responsibilities: head of state, military commander, chief political officer, director of foreign affairs, legislative strategist, national father figure, global leader, and international toastmaster. No single human being could hope to synthesize and master all these pieces all of the time. A supreme paradox of the presidency is that the most dangerous executive office in history has been home to some of the world's most inept executives: witness Lyndon Johnson's epic mismanagement of Vietnam and the tragi-comedy of Richard Nixon's Watergate.

Today, the White House operates under the dangerous absurdity that almost no one who works there keeps good records, since everybody is afraid of being subpoenaed. The fate of many Clinton officials has shown that the closer you work to the Oval Office, the higher the risk that the memo you write may soon appear in court or on CNN's and MSNBC's Web sites, your career will explode, and your bank account will be hijacked to pay for lawyers' fees. The risks of incomplete White House records can be enormous. During negotiations at Camp David, Jimmy Carter had neither electronic nor manual verbatim note-takers rolling when he thought Menachem Begin agreed to an indefinite freeze on Israeli settlements in the West Bank. Begin insisted he agreed only to a temporary freeze. What followed was twenty years of bitter disputes between Israelis and Palestinians over the issue. In the wake of Iran-*Contra,* a befuddled Ronald Reagan complained that no one kept proper records of key meetings and decisions, and therefore he couldn't figure out the truth of the scandal.

To help protect against such dangers, the business offices of the White House should be fully wired with a high-quality backup audio recording network, the tapes to be consulted only by the president to clarify, when necessary, the sometimes critical question of who said what to whom in the White House. The system would be revealed publicly in a routine White House announcement, and the tapes automatically sealed for twenty years, to be opened earlier only by a court or congressional order. Officials would hesitate to say things they wouldn't want to see repeated in a court of law, but maybe that's a good thing. The system could eventually blend into the woodwork and the natural rhythms of productive debate and opinion might, hopefully, flourish. It's not a perfect solution, but the risks of an Oval Office operating in a fog of executive confusion are unacceptably higher. For the rest of the White House, a zone of complete privacy should be created within which First Families can live the personal lives they deserve to keep private.

The tapes resulting from an openly, fully wired White House, as a simple extension of good record keeping, will add to our historical understanding of the men and women we hired to work there. After twenty years have passed, we will then be able to draw our own conclusions, not only on what kind of job was done, but what sort of human beings sat behind the Oval Office desk.

The business of politics is the clash of people and ideas, and when presidents succeed, it is often because they provoke and orchestrate the conflict effectively. In his retirement, Harry Truman argued that the most important requirement of a president is that "he must be a fundamentally honest man—intellectually and every other way. An intellectually honest man," he argued, "will usually succeed in any line of business he takes up."

If the parade of men who followed Herbert Hoover in and out of the Oval Office have taught us one fundamental lesson, it is the truth of Truman's insight. Leadership skills, intelligence, political instincts, and charisma are all crucial to winning and holding on to the Oval Office. But the glue that holds them together and governs executive success in the job is intellectual honesty: a president's conscious or unconscious ability to face up to his own flaws and mistakes and to try and adjust for them by installing people and systems to correct his weaknesses, and by stimulating and managing debate, dissent, and the free flow of information and opinion, especially when it conflicts with his own.

In the final analysis, it is the power of intellectual honesty that is the heartbeat of the Oval Office—and the lifeblood of the radical experiment called American democracy.

Acknowledgments

My fiancée Naomi reignited this project and has been an inexhaustible source of support and enthusiasm ever since. I am forever thankful I met her one sunny summer afternoon in Central Park. My parents, Bill and Marilou, my sister, Kate, and her husband, Joe Hooper, have also been sources of constant support and advice.

I'm most grateful to Mel Berger at the William Morris Agency, who made this book possible.

At Kodansha America, I thank my superb editor Deborah Baker, Minato Asakawa, Nancy Cooperman-Su, Brian Desmond, Elizabeth Bennett, Maria Carola, Jim Nichols, and Cicely Ignatowski for their terrific support.

In 1982, I read an extraordinary cover article in *American Heritage* magazine, "The FDR Tapes," written by Professor Robert J. C. Butow and edited by historian Geoffrey C. Ward. It told the story of Professor Butow's accidental discovery in 1978 of a box full of primitive, experimental audio recordings of President Roosevelt in action in the Oval Office during the late summer and fall of 1940, at the FDR Library in Hyde Park. I resolved to visit Hyde Park some day to listen to the recordings, and then promptly forgot about them.

Eleven years later, I retraced Butow and Ward's pilgrimage up to a soundproof audio room at Hyde Park to listen to the FDR recordings and was astonished by what I heard. Here was Roosevelt as I'd never heard him—live, unscripted, and unguarded in the privacy of the Oval Office, bantering with his staff and visitors at a crucial point in his presidency, a creative, exuberant chief executive at the peak of power. Butow and Ward were most generous in helping me retrace their footsteps up to Hyde Park and to the ancient Roosevelt Oval Office recordings. I am very appreciative of the time they spent with me and the research and insights they shared.

I especially thank the people who were interviewed for this book. They are listed on page 338. Any errors of fact or interpretation are, of course, my responsibility.

Dorothy Jones Brady, personal secretary to Franklin Roosevelt from 1933 to 1945, waived her lifelong "passion for anonymity" and spent many hours helping me from her Virginia headquarters overlooking the Potomac River in Virginia, flanked by an oil portrait of John Paul Jones given to her by FDR. She has been a source of laughter, insights, and fact-checking in helping me imagine FDR's Oval Office atmosphere. In 1996, she returned to the White House for the first time in over fifty years to attend a reception for the FDR Memorial ceremonies, and she was, I hear, the star of the party in the East Room. She called me that night to give me a report, and I wish her old boss could have heard it. He would have roared.

In 1995 Ambassador William vanden Heuvel, president of the Franklin D. Roosevelt Foundation, commissioned the high-tech audio restoration of the FDR Oval Office recordings, using the advanced CEDAR (Computer Enhanced Digital Audio Restoration) computer software. This enabled entire paragraphs of hitherto inaudible Roosevelt Oval Office dialogue to become clear, and breathed fresh life into the fascinating but often murky antique recordings.

Audio engineer Don Grossinger supervised audio work on many of the tapes for this book, and provided the skill and equipment to enable exact DAT (Digital Audio Tape) copies of Oval Office recordings to be made at the Roosevelt, Truman, and Reagan Presidential Libraries. He has been a valued supporter and adviser on this book, as has been his partner Kate Lynch.

The Research Center at Time Inc. in New York is near-paradise for anyone writing a book of this kind. They must have the best subject and biography files, periodical holdings, online resources, and staff in the business, all in one easy-to-use command center. Anyone writing a non-fiction book should take a tour there as their first order of business. I especially thank Lany McDonald, Lynn Dombek, Patricia Clark, Bob Paton, Brenda Cherry, Karen McCree, Charlie Lampach, Jennifer Barry, Evelyn Cunningham, Pamela Wilson, Carol Weil, Andi Ramos, Theresa Ott, Elias Rodriguez, Steven Rotter, Annette Rusin, Pam Brooks, Sharon O'Brien-Powers, Angela Thornton, Diane Francis, Lu-Anne Castello, Bill Hooper, Soraya Behesti, Terryl Williams, Blake Goodman, Ed Power, Sam Brintle, Mary Pradt, Claude Boral, and James Macove.

Carol L. Fleisher of fleisherfilm was my writing and producing partner on, and director of, the A&E Investigative Reports Special *The Secret White House Tapes,* which was based in part on this book. She is a great pleasure to work with. I also thank Michael Cascio and Gayle Gilman of the A&E network, and series host Bill Kurtis of Kurtis Productions.

Pedro Sanjuan, veteran of the Kennedy, Johnson, Nixon, Ford, Carter, and Reagan administrations and a former UN official, is director of the Institute of East-West Dynamics in New York and a spiritual godfather of this book, offering advice, insights, and introductions. Ambassador Maxwell Rabb in New York has offered enthusiasm and friendship during this project, and with his keen memory and eye for detail, described Eisenhower's Cabinet meetings, which he helped run.

At the Herbert Hoover Presidential Library in West Branch, Iowa, Dwight Miller, Jim Detlefsen, and Pat Wildenberg helped me piece together the 1929 White House fire.

At the FDR Library in Hyde Park, New York, former director Verne Newton offered insights and enthusiasm from the start. I appreciate his help and that of the superb staff at the FDR Library, including Ray Teichman, Mark Renovitch, and Bob Parks. Elizabeth Safly at the Truman Library in Independence, Missouri, may be not only the most helpful archivist I've met, but also the most fun to be with. I think I know why—she worked there when Harry Truman ran the shop. Her fellow archivists Dennis Bilger and Pauline Testerman were a big help, as was retired archivist Philip Lagerquist, who did detective work on the fragmentary Truman recordings back in 1982.

At the Eisenhower Library in Abeline, Kansas, archivist James Leyerzapf searched his vast collection, and one day in October 1996 found the first Eisenhower Oval Office Dictabelts, forty-two years after Ike flipped the switch to start his secret Dictaphone machine. His patience and thoroughness in piecing together the available history of the materials are very much appreciated. I thank Eisenhower Library Director Dan Holt for his strong support in locating and rescuing the Dictabelts, and also for letting me examine Eisenhower's then-unpublished pre-presidential papers. Archivist David Haight hand-carried the Eisenhower Dictabelts to the Dictaphone technical laboratory in Florida and oversaw their transfer to modern audio tape. His fellow archivists Cathy Struss and Mack Teasley were also a big help in the rescue and recovery of these extraordinary recordings. Thanks also to retired archivist Dr. John Wickman.

At the JFK Library at Columbia Point in Boston, archivists Jim Cedrone, Stephanie Fawcett, Alan Goodrich, and historian Sheldon Stern were of assistance. I first visited the LBJ Library on a business trip to Austin, Texas, in 1984 and was overwhelmed by the scale of the library and its subject. Twelve years later, the archivists there were a pleasure to deal with. Director Harry Middleton was very helpful in explaining the history of the Johnson recordings. Archivists Linda Hanson, Tina Houston, Regina Greenwell, Mary Knill, and Philip Scott deserve special thanks.

John Powers at the Nixon Presidential Materials Project in College Park, Maryland, is the National Archives leading authority on presidential recordings, and was a great source of facts and ideas in my research. I also thank Nixon Project Director Karl Weissenbach and archivist Steve Greene.

At the Gerald R. Ford Library in Ann Arbor, Michigan, audiovisual archivist Kenneth Hafeli called me up one day with the surprising news that after searching his holdings, he had found several Ford telephone recordings that the Library didn't even know they had in their collection. Archivist William McNitt and his staff guided me to the minutes of the *Mayaguez* meetings.

Bob Bohannon and David Stanhope at the Carter Library in Atlanta steered me toward the fascinating Carter "out-box" file and other treasures in their holdings. Carter Center historian Steven Hochman answered questions on Carter's tape-recorded diary.

At the Reagan Library, audiovisual archivist Steve Branch wheeled up the first Reagan White House TV videotapes from his vault during my first visit in early 1996, and kept me hooked for several weeks with fresh discoveries from his remarkable collection of White House TV tapes of closed presidential meetings, which I was amazed to learn nobody had delved into before. I also thank archivists Diane Barrie, Greg Cumming, Donna Dillon, and Rod Soubers for their advice and their help, along with Larry Bumgardner and Lynda Schuler of the Reagan Foundation.

Thanks to Doug Thurman and John Keller at the National Archives Office of Presidential Libraries in Washington, D.C., and Bush Presidential Library Director David Alsobrook and Bush Library archivist Mary Finch. For arranging White House press passes, I thank the White House Press Office.

Historian and researcher Lynn Watson Powers went through the Jimmy Carter "out-box" file in Atlanta for me, and with her trained eye, identified some fascinating material.

I thank the family of the late J. Ripley Kiel, inventor of FDR's sound-on-film machine, including Mrs. J. Ripley Kiel, Barbara Kiel Kaley, and Sharon R. Kiel, for sharing his letters, photographs, and files with me.

I also thank Chizuko Moriyama; Shigeo Moriyama; Miki Moriyama; Adam Bellow; Lynn Bodges and Don Joyner of the Dictaphone Corporation; Gordon Hoxie of the Center for the Study of the Presidency; Augusto Failde; Lee Certilman; Herman Eberhardt; Brian Maloney; Mark Cerulli; David Starr; HBO's Colin Callender, Kerith Putnam, Sharon Werner, and Susan Ennis; Peter Hannaford; Robert Ferrell; Elena Song; Walter Isaacson; Professor Maurice Crane and John Shaw of the G. Robert Vincent Voice Library at Michigan State University; State Department historian David Humphrey;

Herbert Parmet; Steve Riggio of Barnes & Noble; Joanie Jenkins; Jerry Fabris of the Thomas Edison Home; Timothy Maier; Alan Koenigsberg of *Antique Phonograph* magazine; C. J. Wilson; Ann Moore of the Benjamin Harrison Home in Indianapolis; Elbert Hilliard and Ann Webster of the Mississippi State Department of Archives and History; Edmund Morris; Mason Funk; Mark Hoover; Mimi and Ralph Rosnow; Connie, Hari, and Kerry Mithalal; Betsy Harkavy; Frank Gannon; Jesse Raiford; George Lardner; Santi Visalli; Mark Hoover; and Wayne Furman and Elie Weitsman of the New York Public Library.

Source Notes

ABBREVIATIONS USED IN NOTES

OH	Oral History
NYT	*New York Times*
WP	*Washington Post*
WSJ	*Wall Street Journal*
USNWR	*U.S. News & World Report*
PSQ	*Presidential Studies Quarterly*
Powers Paper	National Archives paper on presidential recordings by archivist John Powers, "The History of Presidential Audio Recordings and the Archival Issues Surrounding Their Use," 1996
A&E Fleisher interview	Carol L. Fleisher interview for A&E special *The Secret White House Tapes*
FDRL	Franklin D. Roosevelt Library, Hyde Park, NY
HSTL	Harry S. Truman Library, Independence, MO
DDEL	Dwight D. Eisenhower Library, Abilene, KS
JFKL	John F. Kennedy Library, Boston, MA
LBJL	Lyndon B. Johnson Library, Austin, TX
NPMP	Richard M. Nixon Presidential Materials Project, College Park, MD
GRFL	Gerald R. Ford Library, Ann Arbor, MI
JCL	Jimmy Carter Library, Atlanta, GA
RRL	Ronald Reagan Library, Simi Valley, CA
PPF	President's Personal File
PSF	President's Secretary's File

Oral histories are from the presidential libraries corresponding with the chapter, except where indicated. Tape and meeting transcripts are all prepared from source tapes, transcripts, or documents from the respective presidential libraries unless otherwise noted. In some cases, tapes were played for former White House aides to help identify dialogue and speakers on the tapes. Since dates are provided in the text, recordings transcribed and quoted in the text are not sourced separately. Researchers wanting to order tapes or transcripts when available should contact archivists at the corresponding presidential library. All ellipses in transcripts represent edits for space by author (except for Pearl Harbor meeting, noted separately). All tapes and transcripts of White House business should be considered unofficial, imperfect, and speculative, no matter who does the transcribing.

INTERVIEWS

By author (1996–1999): Bradley Nash, George Elsey, Milton Lipson, Geoffrey C. Ward, Robert J. C. Butow, Verne Newton, Dorothy Jones Brady, Sharon Kiel, Barbara Kaley, McKinley Wooden, John Steelman, Clark Clifford, Donald Dawson, David Stowe, Ken Hechler, David Bell, Vernon Walters, Vernice Anderson, Max Rabb, Mary Jane McCaffrey Monroe, Andrew Goodpaster, Elmer Staats, Stephen Benedict, Maurice Stans, Harold Stassen, Dan Holt, Hugh Sidey, Theodore Sorensen, Ralph Dungan, Myer Feldman, Pedro Sanjuan, Robert Bouck, Edwin Martin, Sheldon Stern, Harry Middleton, Bruce Blair, Raymond Garthoff, C. Douglas Dillon, Nicholas Katzenbach, James Meredith, William Simmons, Murry Falkner, Michael McShane, Al Butler, Bishop Duncan Gray, George Christian, Joseph Califano, John Powers, Tom Johnson, Henry Kissinger, Raymond Price, Alexander Butterfield, Alexander Haig, James Schlesinger, Donald Rumsfeld, Robert Hartmann, Benton Becker, Ron Nessen, Zbigniew Brzezinski, Jack Watson, Professor Stanly Godbold, Jody Powell, Richard Allen, Donald Regan, Frank Carlucci, Howard Baker, Jeane Kirkpatrick, Edwin Meese, William Clark, Caspar Weinberger, Robert McFarlane, Paul Stevens, Pamela Naughton, Rhett Dawson, James Buckley, Geoffrey Kemp, Brent Scowcroft, John Sununu, Robert Gates, James Baker, and Dan Quayle. Several other individuals preferred to remain anonymous.

By Carol L. Fleisher for A&E special (fall 1996): Geoffrey C. Ward, Dorothy Jones Brady, Bruce Blair, Raymond Garthoff, Theodore Sorensen, Burke Marshall, Jack Valenti, Robert Dallek, Gerald Ford, Michael Deaver, Stanley Kutler, and Stephen Ambrose.

PREFACE
AMERICA'S CHIEF EXECUTIVES CAUGHT ON TAPE

ix   Background of Kiel recorder installation in Oval Office: letter, J. Ripley Kiel to R.J.C. Butow, February 2, 1982, courtesy Professor Butow, Barbara Kiel Kaley, and Sharon R. Kiel.

ix   FDR's schedule, late summer 1940: Stenographers Appointment Book, August 1940, FDRL.

ix   Invincible summer: Albert Camus wrote, "In the depths of winter, I finally learned that within me there lay an invincible summer." The phrase has been used by several writers in connection with FDR, including Kenneth S. Davis in his 1974 book *Invincible Summer: An Intimate Portrait of the Roosevelts, Based on the Recollections of Marion Dickerman* (New York: Atheneum, 1974).

x   "largest going concern": Truman farewell address, January 15, 1953, Universal newsreel.

xi   "I remember the headlines": Richard Nixon, 1983 interview by Frank Gannon, videotape at Richard M. Nixon Library and Museum, Yorba Linda, CA.

American presidents had a periodic love affair with recording equipment ever since April 18, 1878, when Rutherford B. Hayes invited Thomas Edison to a White House sleepover to demonstrate his brand-new tinfoil phonograph machine. Hayes was thrilled with the device, and the two stayed up until 3 A.M. making some of the world's very first sound recordings, which have never been found. The first sound recording was made by Thomas Edison on December 6, 1877 ("Mary Had a Little Lamb"), just over four months before his White House visit.

There is the faintest echo of an even earlier White House recording but it is almost certainly an acoustical mirage. It is the story, believe it or not, of a "Lincoln Tape." The tale, which sometimes circulates among collectors of antique recordings, concerns French inventor Edward Leon Scott de Martinville, who in the 1860s invented the "Phoneautograph," a tributary ancestor of the phonograph. A person spoke into the machine's horn, and the sound passed through a stretched diaphragm connected to a bristle, which traced a graphic pattern onto lampblack-coated paper rolled around a rotating cylinder, creating a "sound picture" on paper. The story goes that Scott visited Washington in 1865, stopped by the White House and persuaded Lincoln to speak into his machine. If he did, and the graphic survived with enough detail, it might be possible to digitally synthesize some remote approximation of Lincoln's voice, or a "Lincoln Tape." No such record has ever been found. The story of a "Lincoln Tape" could be dismissed as fantasy, except for the fact that Edward Leon Scott de Martinville did visit Washington at least once, in 1866 (the year after Lincoln's death), and sold a Phoneautograph to the Smithsonian, which has the receipt on file today. Only fragmentary records of Lincoln's visitors were kept, but he did set aside time each day for callers who showed up at the White House unannounced. If Scott had shown up at 1600 Pennsylvania Avenue one day the year before with his machine, there's a good chance he would have been moved to the front of the line and ushered up to Lincoln's second-floor White House office—Lincoln was fascinated by mechanical gadgets.

(Sources: *Antique Phonograph Monthly* 86 [1992], p. 7; Allen Koenigsberg, editor *Antique Phonograph Monthly,* interview by author; Louis H. Hertz, *Antique Collecting for Men* [New York: Galahad, 1978], p. 270; Oliver Read and Walter L. Welch, *From Tinfoil to Stereo: Evolution of the Phonograph* [Indianapolis: H.W. Sams, 1959], pp. 3, 4, 6; Jerry Fabris, Edison Historic Site administrator, interview by author, January 30, 1996.)

Copies survive of audio recordings of speeches purported to have been made in the 1890s by Presidents Grover Cleveland and William McKinley on early cylinder recorders, but they are probably reenactments by turn-of-the-century actor-brothers Len and Harry Spencer. A short greeting to the 1898 Pan American Exhibition attributed to retired President Benjamin Harrison survives, and it may be the oldest surviving recorded presidential voice. Theodore Roosevelt, William Howard Taft, Woodrow Wilson, and their successors all made sound recordings of speeches, mainly of campaign addresses that were copied and sent around the country in the days before radio. Calvin Coolidge was the first to use a recording device in presidential business; in 1924 he installed a Dictaphone dictating machine on the presidential yacht to enable him to work away from the White House.

(Sources: 1996 author interviews with Allen Koenigsberg; Library of Congress audio expert Sam Brylawski; Professor Maurice Crane and John Shaw of the G. Robert Vincent Voice Library at Michigan State University; Ann Moore of the Benjamin Harrison Home in Indianapolis, IN; Lynn Bodges of Dictaphone Corp.)

xi   "it is exceedingly difficult": Robert Dallek, A&E Fleisher interview, October 15, 1996.

xi   "There is noble talk": Richard Nixon, *RN: The Memoirs of Richard Nixon* (New York: Grosset & Dunlap, 1978), p. 996.

xi   "I've served seven presidents": CNN, *Inside Politics,* November 18, 1996.

xi   "Every journey into the past": *Forbes,* November 4, 1996, p. 400.

xi   "You didn't say that, I did" and "If you want to use the tapes": Leon Friedman and William F. Levantrosser, *Watergate and Afterward: The Legacy of Richard M. Nixon* (Westport, CT: Greenwood Press, 1992), p. 275.

xii "wrong for presidents to tape visitors": Kathleen Sterritt and Carla Hall, "Personalities," *WP,* February 6, 1982, p. C3.

xii "could learn more about the way the government really works": Doris Kearns Goodwin, *Lyndon Johnson and the American Dream* (New York: Harper & Row, 1976), p. 412.

xii "that politics is not a science": Geoffrey C. Ward, A&E Fleisher interview, October 8, 1996.

PROLOGUE

The Oval Office on Fire

1   Details of Herbert Hoover's Oval Office and White House Christmas Eve fire of 1929: news coverage of fire in Vertical File at Herbert Hoover Presidential Library, West Branch, IA, including December 25–29, 1929, *NYT, WP, New York Post, New York Herald Tribune, and New York World;* White House physician Joel T. Boone OH; William Seale, *The President's House: A History, Volume II* (Washington, DC: National Geographic Society: White House Historical Society, 1986), pp. 893–95.

1   History of presidential offices since Washington: Seale, *The President's House: A History, Volume II,* pp. 7, 8, 32.

1   "almost too peaceful and luminous": Theodore H. White, *The Making of the President, 1960* (New York: Atheneum, 1961), p. 371.

1   Substantial recovery under way and latest figures indicated a normal year: David Burner, *Herbert Hoover: A Public Life* (New York: Knopf, 1979), p. 248.

3   National income dove from $81 billion to $39 billion, 13 million people unemployed, food riots across country, relief stations running out of money: Frances Perkins, *The Roosevelt I Knew* (New York: Viking Press, 1946), pp. 182, 183.

3   273,000 families evicted: Stephen Hess, *Organizing the Presidency* (Washington, DC: Brookings Institution, 1976), p. 27.

4   1 million roamed the country in boxcars: Richard Norton Smith, *An Uncommon Man: The Triumph of Herbert Hoover* (New York: Simon & Schuster, 1984), p. 29.

4   Banks closed or suspended in twenty-three states: ibid., p. 160.

4   "The presidency is not merely": to Ann O'Hare McCormick, "Interview with Franklin D. Roosevelt," *NYT Magazine*, September 11, 1932, p. 1.

4   "a gibbering idiot": Smith, *An Uncommon Man*, p. 52.

4   "a chameleon on plaid": ibid.

4   "Hoover and Roosevelt prepared" and "The president doesn't want": Frank Freidel, *Franklin D. Roosevelt: Launching the New Deal* (Boston: Little, Brown, 1973), p. 26.

4   November 17, 1932, Hoover-FDR phone call: Freidel, *Launching the New Deal*, pp. 26–27.

5   "Let's concentrate on one thing": Smith, *Uncommon Man*, p. 155.

5   "Nobody leaves before the president": Smith, *Uncommon Man*, pp. 153, 154.

5   The country was in "a hell of a fix": Smith, *Uncommon Man*, p. 161

5   FDR postinaugural walk: Norman Sweetser home movie footage, FDRL. Newsreel footage of the ceremony cut off at the end of Roosevelt's speech, but Sweetser, an NBC radio technician located near the foot of the Capitol steps, was shooting a black-and-white home-movie camera up at the podium from ground level at the front of the V.I.P. spectator area. He continued shooting as Roosevelt walked down the ramp toward his car.

5   Roosevelt's first moments in the Oval Office: Rexford Tugwell, *The Democratic Roosevelt: A Biography of Franklin D. Roosevelt* (Garden City, NY: Doubleday, 1957), pp. 270–71.

CHAPTER 1

FRANKLIN D. ROOSEVELT: THE CREATIVE EXECUTIVE

6   "The country needs": Arthur M. Schlesinger Jr., "The Real Roosevelt Legacy," *Newsweek*, October 14, 1996, p. 43.

6   Given the significance of the September 27, 1940, meeting, FDR may have recorded it intentionally. His schedule for this day lists two fifteen-minute appointments between the press conference and the civil rights meeting, and neither of the two appointments shows up on the recordings, leading one to suspect the recorder was stopped and then started. However, notations by the White House press stenographer indicate that the civil rights meeting

occurred directly after the press conference. If so, FDR's schedule was rearranged at the last minute (it often was) and the recorder simply rolled on.

The FDR recordings were first uncovered in 1978 by University of Washington history professor Robert J. C. Butow, while he was conducting research at the FDR Library. After Butow good-naturedly complained to the staff about having to wade through boxes of documents, he joked, "When are you going to let me listen to the FDR tapes?" To Butow's surprise, the archivists then told him about some obscure audio recordings in their collection that nobody knew much about. Before long, Butow was listening to disc copies of recordings of Oval Office business captured by FDR's sound machine over a period of eleven weeks in 1940.

Professor Butow managed to track down both Henry Kannee and his successor as White House stenographer, Jack Romagna, the two men who had hands-on experience with the machine. According to them, FDR evidently wanted to keep an audio record of press conferences during what could be his last few months in power, to defend against misquotation (and possibly to help him write his memoirs). Butow published a cover story about the recordings, "The FDR Tapes," in *American Heritage* magazine in its February/March 1982 issue. *American Heritage* commissioned a partial audio restoration of the often poor-quality recordings using noise suppression techniques of the period, a process supervised by Professor Mark Weiss, an audio expert who had consulted for the government on the Watergate tapes.

These more detailed transcriptions were made possible by a 1995 CEDAR (Computer Enhanced Digital Audio Restoration) high-tech digital noise reduction process commissioned by the Roosevelt Foundation. Restoration work in 1996 and 1997 by fleisherfilm for the A&E special *The Secret White House Tapes* used the CEDAR and NoNoise processes, which removed much of the sudden impulse noises, background "crackle," and hissing and buzzing that plagued the recordings, which were several generations removed from the original 35mm film. The results were significant; entire paragraphs of dialogue, previously overwhelmed by noise, were recovered and made audible. Walter White's extensive comments, for example, earlier too faint under noise damage to be audible, are now understandable.

A glimpse of FDR's recording system appeared in John Gunther's 1950 book *Roosevelt in Retrospect* (New York: Harper, 1950), which contained a cryptic passage on page 145: "Evidence exists that after the war began all conversation at his desk was secretly recorded, of course with his knowledge and consent." Gunther may have been speculating from newspaper accounts in the days after Roosevelt's death of reporters noticing some kind of radio apparatus in Roosevelt's desk drawer. What they saw, in all likelihood, was the control box for the Kiel/RCA machine.

When possible, start times for FDR recordings are estimated by timing the recordings back to the start time of the recorded press conferences as published in the FDR Press Conference file at the FDR Library.

6   Walter White 1/64th black, death of Walter White's father: "Black's White," *Time*, January 24, 1938, p. 9.

7   "His mind does not follow easily": Warren F. Kimball, *The Juggler: Franklin Roosevelt as Wartime Statesman* (Princeton, NJ: Princeton University Press, 1991), p. 14, citing Henry Stimson Diary, December 18, 1940, Yale University Library.

7   FDR's physical condition: Joel Achenbach, "Why Things Are," *WP*, November 4, 1994, p. F5; Geoffrey C. Ward, interview by author, October 1, 1996; Geoffrey C. Ward, *A First-Class Temperament: The Emergence of Franklin Roosevelt* (New York: Harper & Row, 1989), pp. 780–85. FDR quotes on his condition are from *WP*, November 4, 1994, p. F5.

7   Description of FDR's desk: inspection of desk at FDRL; White House Desk diagram, FDRL; "The President's Desk Is Covered With Gimcracks," *Life*, August 10, 1942, pp. 8–9.

7   Clutter so thick papers waited six months: White House clerk William Hopkins quoted in Robert H. Ferrell, *Harry S. Truman: A Life* (Columbia: University of Missouri Press, 1994), p. 181.

7   "He has a big head": Gunther, *Roosevelt in Retrospect*, p. 22.

8   1934 Oval Office renovation: Seale, *The President's House: A History, Volume II*, p. 947.

8   "furnished somewhat more elaborately": ibid.

8   FDR covered Oval Office walls with naval and Hudson River prints: Freidel, *Launching the New Deal*, p. 272.

8   "FDR was supremely confident": Geoffrey C. Ward, interview by author, October 1, 1996.

8   "had a maturing effect": James MacGregor Burns, *Roosevelt: The Lion and the Fox* (New York: Harcourt, Brace, 1956), p. 67.

9   FDR speculated in a dizzying series of schemes: Smith, *An Uncommon Man,* p. 51; Burns, *The Lion and the Fox,* pp. 83–84.

9   "As war administrator, as businessman": Burns, *The Lion and the Fox,* pp. 83–84.

9   "a spiritual transformation" that "purged the slightly arrogant attitude": Frances Perkins, *The Roosevelt I Knew* (New York: Viking Press, 1946), p. 29.

9   "What is needed is a wide previous experience in government": letter from FDR to C. Hustis, September 20, 1928, PPF, FDRL.

9   FDR "could keep all the balls in the air": William E. Leuchtenburg, "Why the Candidates Still Use FDR as Their Measure," *AH*, February 1988, p. 42.

9   Hitler planning invasion of Britain after raiding London with 1,500 aircraft per day; German troops in Czechoslovakia, Poland, Denmark, Norway, Holland, Belgium, and France; FDR evaded Congress and granted fifty warships to Britain: Burns, *The Lion and the Fox,* pp. 440–42.

9   Japan consolidating in China and Manchuria: ibid., pp. 146, 176, 443.

9   30,000 Japanese troops in Indochina, 15,000 Japanese occupied Hanoi: *New York Herald Tribune,* October 8, 1940, p. 4.

9   Army ranked eighteenth in the world: Doris Kearns Goodwin, *No Ordinary Time: Franklin and Eleanor Roosevelt: The Home Front in World War II* (New York: Simon & Schuster, 1994), p. 23.

10   Willkie dodging eggs, rotten vegetables and lightbulbs: Kenneth S. Davis,

FDR: Into the Storm: 1937–1940, A History (New York: Random House, 1993), p. 613.

10   Willkie pulling even with FDR in New York as Democratic and labor bosses and the *New York Times* deserted Roosevelt: Burns, *The Lion and the Fox,* p. 445.

10   History and details of FDR recording machine: R.J.C. Butow, "The FDR Tapes," *AH,* February/March 1982, pp. 10–15; R.J.C. Butow, "How FDR Got His Tape Recorder," *AH,* October/November 1982, pp. 109–12; Verne Newton, FDRL director, and Mark Renovitch and Raymond Teichman, archivists, interviews by author; R.J.C. Butow and Geoffrey C. Ward, interviews by author; papers of J. Ripley Kiel (courtesy Barbara Kiel Kaley and Sharon R. Kiel); FDRL Presidential recordings Vertical File; inspection of recordings and FDR desk at FDRL.

10   "the very first recording device": letter, J. Ripley Kiel to R.J.C. Butow, February 2, 1982, courtesy Professor Butow, Barbara Kiel Kaley, and Sharon R. Kiel.

11   "With all their technical imperfections": *AH,* February/March 1982, p. 9.

11   Political and military background for FDR meeting with civil rights leaders, aftermath of meeting: *AH,* February/March 1982, p. 23–24; Kearns Goodwin, *No Ordinary Time,* pp. 161–72. Roosevelt appears to have taken no notes during the meeting (on other recordings the sensitive microphone machine clearly picks up the sharp sounds of FDR writing on the desk). The evidently disgusted Knox and silent Patterson quickly slipped out of the Oval Office without a word on follow-up, and Roosevelt plunged into another meeting, this one with a delegation from England (the recorder soon cut off).

13   "It was remarkable enough": Geoffrey C. Ward, A&E Fleisher interview, October 6, 1996.

13   "The trouble with the president": David McCullough, *Truman* (New York: Simon & Schuster, 1992), p. 328, citing Harold Ickes diary, December 16, 1944, Library of Congress.

17   "He could charm an individual or a nation": Dean Acheson, *Present at the Creation: My Years in the State Department* (New York: Norton, 1969), notes p. 1.

18   White House October 9, 1940, press release; NAACP October 11 press release; Randolph and White letters to White House: PPF, FDRL.

18   FDR held on to 67 percent of the black vote: Nancy J. Weiss, *Farewell to the Party of Lincoln* (Princeton, NJ: Princeton University Press, 1983), p. 288.

19   "You know I am a juggler": Henry M. Morgenthau, Jr., Presidential Diary, May 15, 1942, Morgenthau Papers, FDRL.

19   "Roosevelt had the habit of saying he was in agreement": George Elsey, interview by author, June 11, 1996.

19   "Roosevelt had a fairly creative relationship with the truth": Geoffrey C. Ward, A&E Fleisher interview.

19   "His real weakness": Kearns Goodwin, *No Ordinary Time,* p. 23.

19   "he always hopes to get things settled pleasantly": Jonathan Daniels, *White*

House Witness, 1942–1945 (Garden City, NY: Doubleday, 1975), p. 257.

19 "he forever put off things distasteful": Gunther, *Roosevelt in Retrospect*, p. 42.

19 FDR "did not keep his word on many appointments": ibid., pp. 52, 53.

19 "Perhaps in the long run": Kearns Goodwin, *No Ordinary Time*, p. 78.

19 Background and aftermath of August 22, 1940, recording: *AH,* February/March 1982, pp. 20–22; Steven V. Roberts, "Tapes Offer a Rare Glimpse of the Private F.D.R.," *NYT*, March 2, 1988, p. 1.

20 FDR wiretapping: Richard G. Powers, *Secrecy and Power, The Life of J. Edgar Hoover* (New York: Free Press, 1987), p. 237; "Hoover's Political Spying for Presidents," *Time*, December 15, 1975, p. 10.

21 "He is trapped behind his desk": Geoffrey C. Ward, A&E Fleisher interview.

21 "He was a most unusual man": Dorothy Jones Brady, interview by author, May 15, 1996.

21 "When the veterans came to Washington": Perkins, *The Roosevelt I Knew*, p. 112.

21 "He circulated word to his staff": James Roosevelt and Sidney Shalett, *Affectionately, FDR: A Son's Story of a Lonely Man* (New York: Harcourt, Brace, 1959), pp. 254, 255.

22 FDR routine: Dorothy Jones Brady and Verne Newton, interview by author; Burns, *The Lion and the Fox*, p. 381; James MacGregor Burns, *Roosevelt: The Soldier of Freedom* (New York: Harcourt, Brace, 1970), pp. 22, 23; John Morton Blum, *From the Morgenthau Diaries, 1928–1938* (Boston: Houghton Mifflin, 1959), p. 69; Nathan Miller, *FDR, An Intimate History* (Garden City, NY: Doubleday, 1983), pp. 345, 348; Grace Tully, *FDR, My Boss* (New York: Charles Scribner's Sons, 1949), p. 77.

22 Every morning FDR received a package of clippings: *AH,* February 1988, p. 48.

22 FDR cigarette routine: Burns, *Soldier of Freedom,* p. 433; Miller, *FDR: An Intimate History,* p. 274.

22 "a spider at the center of his web": Geoffrey C. Ward, interview by author, October 1, 1996.

24 FDR appointed federal judge: "Senate Confirms Judgeship," *Washington Herald,* June 9, 1943.

26 Roosevelt worked from two Oval Offices: author interviews with Dorothy Jones Brady and Verne Newton.

26 "the most important room": Seale, *The President's House: A History, Volume II,* p. 985.

26 "with everything that came his way": Kearns Goodwin, *No Ordinary Time,* p. 35.

26 He ate lunch at his desk with guests on card tables: Seale, *The President's House,* p. 985.

26 FDR worked late in the Oval Room: Dorothy Jones Brady, interview by author, May 15, 1996.

26   FDR went to the secret Map Room: Seale, *The President's House,* p. 989.

26   FDR explained his use of notepads or "chits" during a conference with the Senate Military Affairs Committee on January 31, 1939, a transcript of which is in the PPF, FDRL.

26   "One hundred or so persons could get to him directly": Frank Kessler, *The Dilemmas of Presidential Leadership: Of Caretakers and Kings* (Englewood Cliffs, NJ: Prentice-Hall, 1982), p. 60.

27   "Two short sentences will generally answer": Burns, *The Lion and the Fox,* p. 381.

27   "Boil it down to a single page": Gunther, *Roosevelt in Retrospect,* p. 125.

27   He might read a memo back to the person who wrote it: ibid.

27   "The first task of an executive": Arthur M. Schlesinger, Jr., *The Age of Roosevelt, Volume 2: The Coming of the New Deal* (Boston: Houghton Mifflin, 1958), p. 522.

27   Small staff and budget, abandoned furniture, patches in carpet: Juan Cameron, "The Management Problem in Ford's White House," *Fortune,* July 1975, p. 80.

27   "Come on in": Miller, *FDR: An Intimate History,* p. 276.

27   "I can take anything these days!": Gunther, *Roosevelt in Retrospect,* p. 314.

27   "This man functions smoothly": Miller, *FDR: An Intimate History,* p. 288.

27   "Jim, I want your advice": Hugh Sidey, "The Power of Charm," *Time,* April 11, 1983, p. 21.

27   "I am still perfectly foggy": Minutes of the Executive Council and National Emergency Council, Meeting 9, FDRL.

27   "I don't understand it yet": Gunther, *Roosevelt in Retrospect,* p. 115.

27   Luncheon meetings: Miller, *FDR: An Intimate History,* p. 277; Gunther, *Roosevelt in Retrospect,* p. 55; Burns, *The Lion and the Fox,* pp. 328, 329.

27   "Well, I'm sorry, I have to run now!"; "I am sure it never struck him": Samuel I. Rosenman, *Working with Roosevelt* (New York: Da Capo Press, 1972), p. 37.

28   "You go into Cabinet meetings tired": *AH,* February 1988, p. 42.

28   "A Roosevelt Cabinet": Gunther, *Roosevelt in Retrospect,* p. 131.

28   "Those early meetings": Perkins, *The Roosevelt I Knew,* p. 153.

28   "Nine of its ten members": Peter F. Drucker, "Six Rules for Presidents," *WSJ,* September 22, 1993, p. 20.

28   King would "raise holy hell": Gunther, *Roosevelt in Retrospect,* p. 45.

28   "I am sorry, Mr. President": Kearns Goodwin, *No Ordinary Time,* p. 22.

28   "There is nothing I love as much as a good fight": Gerald Ford, *A Time to Heal: The Autobiography of Gerald R. Ford* (New York: Harper & Row, 1979), p. 408.

28   "A little rivalry is stimulating": Burns, *The Soldier of Freedom,* pp. 342–43.

28   "His favorite technique was": *AH,* February 1988, p. 42.

29   Roosevelt pitted Moley against Hull at London Conference: Congressional Quarterly, *Powers of the Presidency* (Washington, DC: Congressional Quarterly, 1989), p. 9.

29   Welles in revolt against Hull: Burns, *The Soldier of Freedom,* p. 465.

29   Jones/Wallace feud: ibid., p. 341.

29   February 1935 Cabinet meeting: Blum, *From the Morgenthau Diaries*, pp. 88–91.

29   "I am the boss": Burns, *The Soldier of Freedom*, pp. 364.

29   "If you wanted to go out"; "Say what you please": Perkins, *The Roosevelt I Knew*, p. 137.

29   "He liked to have Harry Ickes": Burns, *The Soldier of Freedom*, p. 364.

29   "You are a wonderful person": Burns, *The Lion and the Fox*, p. 374.

30   "Never let your left hand know": Blum, *From the Morgenthau Diaries, 1928–1938*, p. 254.

30   "One often reads of Franklin Roosevelt": Dean Acheson, *Present at the Creation: My Years in the State Department*, (New York: Norton, 1969), p. 47.

30   "The country needs, and, unless I mistake, the country demands": Arthur M. Schlesinger, Jr., "The Real Roosevelt Legacy," *Newsweek*, October 14, 1996, p. 43.

30   "We have new and complex problems": *AH*, February 1988, p. 42.

30   New Deal successes: Gunther, *Roosevelt in Retrospect*, p. 284.

30   New Deal failures, unemployment persisting: Gunther, *Roosevelt in Retrospect*, p. 284; and Raymond S. Franklin, in Herbert D. Rosenbaum and Elizabeth Bartelme, eds., *Franklin D. Roosevelt: The Man, the Myth, the Era, 1882–1945* (Westport, CT: Greenwood Press, 1987) p. 119.

30   "I wish you could be here for a week sitting invisibly at my side": Burns, *The Soldier of Freedom*, p. 66.

31   "The listener almost feels the anxiety": *AH*, February/March 1982, p. 9.

33   the Nazis mounted a major program of covert action: David Stout, "How Nazis Tried to Steer U.S. Politics," *NYT*, July 23, 1997, p.17.

33   Fragmentary, barely audible comments on the October 4, 1940, recording suggest that the visitor might have been then–pro-FDR columnist Walter Winchell. Press Secretary Early introduced the guest by saying to FDR: "I told Walter he could have a few minutes," and FDR joshed, "That's OK, Walter almost works for the government, too!"

35   Pearl Harbor background: Burns, *The Lion and the Fox*, pp. 460, 461; Burns, *The Soldier of Freedom*, pp. 158–67; R.J.C. Butow, "How Roosevelt Attacked Japan at Pearl Harbor: Myth Masquerading as History," *Prologue* (National Archives), Fall 1996, pp. 209–13.

35   "Mr. President, it looks as if the Japanese have attacked": Burns, *The Lion and the Fox*, p. 461.

35   Roosevelt racing to the Oval Office in his wheelchair to take command of the war, "His chin stuck out": R.J.C. Butow, "Pearl Harbor Jitters," *Prologue* (National Archives), Winter 1991, p. 390.

35   Pearl Harbor meeting background, quotes: Richard M. Ketchum, "Yesterday, December 7, 1941," *AH*, November 1989, pp. 54–67, Kearns Goodwin, *No Ordinary Time*, p. 292.

35   The transcript of the meeting on December 7, 1941, between President Roosevelt, the Cabinet, and congressional leaders was printed in *Hearings before the Joint Committee on the Investigation of the Pearl Harbor Attack, 79th*

Congress (Washington, DC: U.S. Government Printing Office, 1946) Part 19, pp. 3503–507.

37 Perkins recollections of meeting: Kearns Goodwin, *No Ordinary Time,* p. 292.

38 "he demonstrated that ultimate capacity": *AH,* November 1989, p. 60.

39 "How did it happen?": *AH,* November 1989, p. 68.

40 "On the ground!": ibid.

41 "the essence of Roosevelt's style": Samuel I. Rosenman and Dorothy Rosenman, *Presidential Style: Some Giants and a Pygmy in the White House* (New York: Harper & Row, 1976), p. 391.

41 "unique in American war history": Burns, *Soldier of Freedom,* pp. 492, 493.

41 "It was he (in conjunction with Churchill of course)": Gunther, *Roosevelt in Retropect,* pp. 326, 327.

41 "administered by the technique": Perkins, *The Roosevelt I Knew,* p. 381.

41 Forty-seven federal agencies reporting to Roosevelt; "the details of this job are killing me": Richard Tanner Johnson, *Managing the White House* (New York: Harper & Row, 1974), p. 35.

41 "One man simply could not do it all": Gunther, *Roosevelt in Retropect,* p. 329.

42 "he did not involve and inform the State Department": George Elsey, interview by author, June 11, 1996.

42 FDR's executive impact: Burns, *Soldier of Freedom,* pp. vii, 343; Kearns Goodwin, *No Ordinary Time,* pp. 624–27.

42 "He saved the nation": Rosenman, *Presidential Style,* p. 427.

42 "Now I can see in perspective": A.J. Wann, *The President as Chief Administrator: A Study of Franklin D. Roosevelt* (Washington, DC: Public Affairs Press, 1968), p. 251.

43 "Roosevelt knew that the main task": Peter F. Drucker, *The Effective Executive* (New York: Harper & Row, 1967), p. 149.

43 "Franklin Roosevelt threw me into": Blum, *From the Morgenthau Diaries 1928–1938,* p. xiii.

43 "Energy is contagious": Gunther, *Roosevelt in Retrospect,* p. 314.

43 Visit to Honolulu veterans' hospital, "The expressions of the faces": Rosenman, *Presidential Style,* p. 392.

44 "His game-playing, fun-streaked": Davis, *FDR: Into the Storm,* p. 616.

CHAPTER 2
HARRY S. TRUMAN: THE DECISIVE EXECUTIVE

45 "I am here to make decisions": Alonzo Hamby, *Man of the People: A Life of Harry S. Truman* (New York: Oxford University Press, 1995), p. 313.

45 "I propose to get the Cabinet officers": Patrick Anderson, *The President's Men* (Garden City, NY: Doubleday, 1968), p. 91.

45 FDR's Cabinet was a "mudhole"; "crackpots and the lunatic fringe": Bert Cochran, *Harry Truman and the Crisis Presidency* (New York: Funk & Wagnall's, 1973), p. 120.

45   Truman jibes at FDR Cabinet members: Hamby, *Man of the People* p. 306.

46   "I want to keep my feet on the ground"; "I don't want any experiments": Cochran, *Harry Truman and the Crisis Presidency,* p. 120.

46   Truman recording press conference: Ron Ostroff, "A Look at Truman's Tapes Sheds Light on Presidential Recordings," *Kansas City Times,* September 13, 1982, pp. 1, 9, 17.

46   Truman was briefed on FDR's sound recording machine: letter from Jack Romagna to Benedict K. Zobrist, March 7, 1982, Presidential Recordings Vertical File, HSTL.

Philip Lagerquist, a former Truman Library archivist, guessed that Truman's recordings date only from 1945 and 1947, with most of them occurring in 1945. Recordings were "done at random times and for no discernible reasons," Lagerquist concluded, a notion supported by the fact that the sounds that can be made out seem to be of routine Oval Office business. The recordings may also have been initiated as tests, perhaps by Romagna, who later said he periodically ran the machine to keep it in working order in case some emergency use was required (Romagna letter to Zobrist).

Photos of Truman's Oval Office in April and May of 1945 show the Kiel lamp still on the Oval Office desk (chronological photo file, April–August 1945, HSTL). One of Truman's Oval Office recordings consists entirely of workmen's tests as they install the recording microphone in Truman's Oval Office desk, and very audibly screw the mike into the telephone. The workmen, possibly Army Signal Corps technicians, perform voice countdowns from different spots in the Oval Office to test sound levels, and call down to a colleague at the controls of the machine in the chamber under the Oval Office. One of the workmen refers to V-E Day as being the day before, which places the reinstallation at May 8, 1945 (Truman Oval Office recording, 74-2/200X, HSTL).

46   "I think it's outrageous for anyone to use them": Robert J. Donovan, *Tumultuous Years: The Presidency of Harry S. Truman, 1949–1953* (New York: Norton, 1982), p. 358.

46   Truman asked a stenographer to listen in on phone conversations: Romagna letter to Zobrist, March 7, 1982.

46   "I don't have time for that foolishness!": "Hoover's Political Spying for Presidents," *Time,* December 15, 1975, p. 10.

46   Truman was intrigued: Romagna letter to Zobrist, March 7, 1982. Early in his presidency, James Forrestal, who was then secretary of the navy and later secretary of defense, suggested to Truman that Cabinet meetings be recorded in shorthand. Truman discussed the idea with aide Matthew Connelly, who talked him out of it, saying, "They're not going to speak for that record, where if they could speak off the cuff, they will say more and you will have closer cooperation between them." (Matthew Connelly OH, p. 131.) Truman agreed, and the result is that virtually no verbatim records of Truman in action survive.

46   Installed the first Oval Office TV set, and placed a bulky shortwave radio on the work desk: Oval Office exhibit, HSTL.

46   Truman faced the reporters from mahogany desk, wearing a double-breasted suit adorned with World War I discharge button: "The First Ten Days," *Time*, April 30, 1945, p. 18.

46   physical description of Truman: Hoxie, *Command Decision and the Presidency: A Study in National Security Policy and Organization* (New York: Reader's Digest Press, 1977), p. 79.

47   "He was the best in the world"; "In combat, he was pretty cool": McKinley Wooden, Chief Mechanic, Battery D, American Expeditionary Force, U.S. Army, 1917–1919 (ret.), interview by author, May 15, 1996.

47   "There are a great many different factors": Hoxie, *Command Decision and the Presidency*, p. 79.

47   "His personal and professional experience": Hamby, *Man of the People*, p. 484.

47   "I was handicapped by lack of knowledge": HST Diary, May 6, 1948, Post-Presidential File, HSTL.

47   Truman's first working moments in the Oval Office: Robert H. Ferrell, *Harry S. Truman: A Life* (Columbia: University of Missouri Press, 1994), p. 184; David G. McCullough, *Truman* (New York: Simon & Schuster, 1992), p. 328.

48   "I'm not big enough": Robert J. Donovan, *Conflict and Crisis: The Presidency of Harry S. Truman, 1945–1948* (New York: Norton, 1977), p. 15.

48   U.S. statistics: William Manchester, *The Glory and the Dream: A Narrative History of America* (Boston: Little, Brown, 1974), p. 1251.

51   This press conference was also published in Truman's Presidential Papers.

52   Truman Oval Office conversation with staff: Truman Oval Office recording, 74-7/700X, HSTL. This May 23 recording also catches Truman signing a document so fast he didn't fully read the text, a management weakness that tripped him up several times as president. In fact, twelve days earlier, he was handed an order restricting the wartime lend-lease program. Truman signed the order without reading and absorbing it fully, triggering a fiasco when aggressive U.S. officials implemented the order strictly, turned ships bound for American allies around at sea and enraged the Russians and British, compelling Truman to reverse the order (Hamby, *Man of the People*, p. 319). In the fall of 1946, Commerce Secretary and liberal leader Henry Wallace submitted a controversial foreign policy speech to Truman. The speech asserted that a "get tough" policy with Russia would not work, a view opposite to that of Secretary of State Byrnes. Truman did not grasp the implications and briskly approved it. Wallace gave the speech, which triggered a tidal wave of negative press coverage, and eventually Wallace's resignation. Truman wrote to his mother: "Never was there such a mess and it is partly my making. But when I make a mistake it is a good one" (Donovan, *Conflict and Crisis,* pp. 223–28).

52   Truman went downstairs to inspect machine, "I sure don't want anything to do with that": Romagna letter to Zobrist, March 7, 1982.

52   Truman recordings details: Powers Paper p. 10, retired HSTL archivist Philip Lagerquist, interview by author, June 2, 1996.

52 "I'm gonna need the support of everybody": Truman Oval Office recording, 74-6/600X, HSTL.

53 "Eyes troubling somewhat": HST diary entry, June 1, 1945, PSF, HSTL.

53 Truman worked seventeen hours a day, waded through six feet of paper every night, signed 600 documents a day: Diary entry, February 20, 1952, PSF, HSTL.

53 In the Oval Room upstairs: McCullough, *Truman*, p. 557.

53 "a full partner in all my transactions": Karen O'Connor, Bernadette Nye, Laura van Assendelft, "Wives in the White House: The Political Influence of First Ladies," *PSQ,* Summer 1996, p. 837.

53 Reviewed speeches with "the boss": Ken Hechler OH, p. 166; George Elsey OH, p. 189.

53 "Well I'm getting better organized now": letter to Bess Truman, June 6, 1945, Robert H. Ferrell, *Dear Bess: the Letters From Harry to Bess Truman, 1910–1959* (New York: Norton, 1983), pp. 514–15.

53 "Just two months ago today": ibid.

54 "I still have a number of bills staring me in the face": ibid, p. 530.

54 "I get up at five-thirty every morning"; "I've been taking these walks for thirty years"; "A man in my position has a public duty": John Hersey, "Mr. President: Quite a Head of Steam," *The New Yorker,* April 7, 1950, pp. 42, 43, 51.

54 Truman physical and office routine: ibid.; and Hamby, *Man of the People,* p. 293; "Truman Gets Busy," *Life,* December 13, 1948, p. 38; Francis H. Heller, ed., *The Truman White House: The Administration of the Presidency, 1945–1953* (Lawrence: Regents Press of Kansas, 1980), pp. 78, 116, 117; *Time,* April 30, 1945, p. 18.

54 daily report: Arthur Krock, "The President's Secret Daily Newspaper," *NYT,* July 16, 1946.

54 Truman Oval Office detail: historian Herman Eberhardt, interview by author, December 10, 1996 (researched and designed HSTL Oval Office replica, 1996); John Hersey, "Mr. President: Ten O'Clock Meeting," *The New Yorker,* April 14, 1951, p. 38; Guide to the White House Gallery and Oval Office Reproduction, HSTL, December 1995, p. 4; Kenneth Hechler, *Working with Truman: A Personal Memoir of the White House Years* (New York: Putnam, 1982), p. 17; McCullough, *Truman,* pp. 402, 403; "The President's Desk," *Parade* magazine, May 22, 1949, p. 8.

55 Truman's BUCK STOPS HERE sign is a bit of an Oval Office mystery. Close Truman aide Donald Dawson recalls seeing it on Truman's desk every day (interview by author, June 10, 1996). Other Truman aides interviewed in the late 1990s also remembered seeing it at times on the desk, but their memories were foggy. Of the thousands of government photos at the Truman Library showing the desk from 1945 to 1953, not one has been found that showed the sign. Perhaps Truman removed the sign when pictures were taken, or kept the sign on a side table or in a drawer as a conversation piece. The sign resides today at the Truman Library.

55 "We all understood what it meant": Donald Dawson, letter to author, August 13, 1997.

55 Truman morning meeting detail: John Steelman, George Elsey, David Stowe, Donald Dawson, and Ken Hechler, interviews by author, June 1996. Steelman added, "Teamwork was great with him."

56 "The staff meetings were clearly joint efforts": Hechler, *Working with Truman*, p. 19.

56 "he encouraged people to be critical": Ken Hechler, interview by author, June 14, 1996.

56 "He was a voracious consumer": George M. Elsey OH, p. 31.

56 "Truman brought a bunch of incompetents"; "How can I bring big people into government": Ferrell, *Truman, A Life*, p. 219.

56 "big-bellied good-natured guys": Cochran, *Harry Truman and the Crisis Presidency*, pp. 124, 125.

56 "the lounge of the Lion's Club of Independence": McCullough, *Truman*, p. 365.

56 "Vaughan was like a friendly puppy dog": Kenneth Thompson, ed., *The Truman Presidency: Intimate Perspectives* (University of Virginia: The Miller Center, 1984), p. 58.

57 "The point is, whatever they say about Harry Truman": Richard Nixon, Oval Office tape recording, April 14, 1973.

57 "Generally Truman picked superb people": Stephen Hess, *Organizing the Presidency* (Washington, DC: Brookings Institution, 1976), p. 45.

57 "The objective and its accomplishment is my philosophy": HST Diary, May 6, 1948, Post-Presidential File, HSTL.

57 "He didn't care who got the credit": George Elsey, interview by author, June 11, 1996.

57 "Harry S. Truman was a tidy man": Hess, *Organizing the Presidency*, p. 44.

57 "well-scrubbed, bandbox appearance": Cochran, *Truman and the Crisis Presidency*, p. 126.

57 "In general, Truman preferred administrative simplicity": Hamby, *Man of the People*, pp. 305, 306.

57 "Truman probably had the human touch": William Hopkins OH, JFKL, p. 10.

57 David Stowe on Truman: Stowe OH p. 32, and David Stowe, interview by author, June 12, 1996.

58 Truman called the hospital each day, "Well, this is the kind of person that one can adore": McCullough, *Truman*, p. 755.

58 "the first thing you find out is that he calls you by name": Hechler, *Working with Truman*, p. 20.

58 "When a butler or doorman or usher": Donovan, *Conflict and Crisis*, p. 148.

58 "He always made everybody feel they were a part of a great team": Ken Hechler, interview by author, June 14, 1996.

58 "I've worked for a number of presidents": Clark Clifford, interview by author, February 12, 1997.

58   "He always made people feel confidence in themselves": Ken Hechler, interview by author, June 14, 1996.

58   "constant pattern of reassurance to his staff and Cabinet": George Elsey, interview by author, June 11, 1996.

59   "He didn't make different decisions": McCullough, *Truman*, p. 755.

59   "Within the first few months I discovered": Harry S. Truman, *Memoirs, Volume II: Years of Trial and Hope* (Garden City, NY: Doubleday, 1956), p. 13.

59   "You could go into his office with a question": Donovan, *Tumultous Years*, p. 24.

59   "It almost seemed as though he was eager to decide": ibid.

59   "Truman was a dirt farmer": Ken Hechler, interview by author, June 14, 1996.

59   "Tell the son of a bitch he'll have to shoot his way in": Hechler, *Working with Truman*, p. 53.

59   "If you think I'm going to sit here": Ferrell, *Truman: A Life*, p. 231.

59   "Gentlemen, the strike has been settled": ibid., p. 231.

59   "He's one tough son of a bitch of a man": McCullough, *Truman*, p. 501.

59   "We hadn't expected very much": David Bell, interview by author, June 12, 1996.

60   "nothing stays in the White House over forty-eight hours": William Hopkins OH, p. 87.

60   "Once he had the information": David Stowe OH, p. 30.

60   "He was almost demonic in his habits of work": Ferrell, *Truman: A Life*, p. xi.

60   "a straightforward man and much franker than Roosevelt": Donovan, *Conflict and Crisis*, p. 62.

60   "I was always thinking about what was pending": Ferrell, *Truman: A Life*, p. 182.

60   "Free of the greatest vice": McCullough, *Truman*, p. 755.

60   "He is morally brave and intellectually honest": "Mr. Truman After Five Years: Sizing Up His Faults and Merits," *USNWR*, April 14, 1950, p. 17.

60   "President Truman's mind is not so quick as his tongue": Cochran, *Harry Truman and the Crisis Presidency*, p. 135.

60   "There has always been consideration of its use": Donovan, *Tumultous Years*, pp. 308–10.

61   "Never kick a fresh turd around on a hot day": Merle Miller, *Lyndon, an Oral Biography* (New York: Putnam, 1980), p. 541.

61   "Truman wanted respect": Hamby, *Man of the People*, p. 637.

61   Truman ordered Steelman to fire official; "Mr. President, I've searched all over the world": John Steelman, interview by author, June 10, 1996.

61   Joan Hoff on Truman's "nondecision"; "Truman did not have much choice": "Panel on Three Biographies of Harry S. Truman," *PSQ*, Summer 1996, pp. 860, 861.

61   "Truman made no decision": McCullough, *Truman*, p. 442. In a 1963 letter to a journalist, Truman explained, "It was done to save 125,000 youngsters on the American side and 125,000 on the Japanese side from getting killed and

that is what it did. It probably also saved a half million youngsters on both sides from being maimed for life." "I have no regrets and, under the same circumstances, I would do it again" (unmailed letter to Irv Kupcinet, August 5, 1963, PSF, Post-Presidential Files, HSTL). Joan Hoff asserted that Truman had estimates of U.S. fatalities in an invasion of Japan ranging only from 20,000 to 46,000, not the figures of up to a million casualties Truman cited (*PSQ*, Summer 1996, p. 860, 861).

61   "The way you can be most helpful to me": John Steelman, interview by author, June 10, 1996.

61   "preferred to have the staff give the problem a thorough going over": David Stowe OH, p. 29.

62   "He brought in Clark Clifford": Ken Hechler, interview by author, June 14, 1996.

62   "He was a man that sought advice": Donald Dawson, interview by author, June 10, 1996.

62   "When the president wants advice"; "He likes things to run smoothly"; "Mr. Truman does not have an inquiring mind"; "seldom reaches out for ideas": *USNWR*, April 14, 1950, pp.13, 14. A businessman added: "The late President Roosevelt had no real grasp of economics, business or fiscal policy. But he was a thinker. When something was explained to him, he put his mind to it and followed. He'd interrupt and say, 'Wait a minute now; let me get straight on that.' Mr. Truman hears you, or appears to, then says, 'OK, that's fine.' But you know he hasn't really grasped what you were saying" (ibid., p. 15).

62   Roosevelt's competitive approach "tended to assume distortion"; Truman's system "relied on what was coming up through the channels": Richard Tanner Johnson, *Managing the White House* (New York: Harper & Row, 1974), p. 60.

62   "Dean, we've got to stop the sons of bitches": Hamby, *Man of the People,* p. 534.

62   "the finest spirit of harmony I have ever known": Irving L. Janis, *Victims of Groupthink: A Psychological Study of Foreign Policy Decisions and Fiascoes* (Boston: Houghton Mifflin, 1972), p. 51.

63   Korea and Wake Island background: Philip C. Jessup, "The Record of Wake Island—A Correction," *The Journal of American History,* March 1981, pp. 866–70; John Edward Wiltz, "Truman and MacArthur: The Wake Island Meeting," *Military Affairs,* December 1978, pp. 169–76; Donovan, *Tumultuous Years,* pp. 278, 279; Ferrell, *Truman: A Life,* pp. 324–32; McCullough, *Truman,* pp. 798–808, Janis, *Groupthink,* pp. 48–71; Vernon Walters, interview by author, March 18, 1997.

63   "You're goddamn right he didn't salute me!": Vernon Walters, interview by author, March 18, 1997.

63   The Wake Island transcript appears in *Foreign Relations of the USA,* 1950, U.S. State Department, pp. 948–60. Truman was later accused of planting Anderson in the room to secretly "bug" the meeting, but both Walters and Anderson, interviewed in 1997, convincingly dismissed the charge, as have most historians who studied the episode.

63 Walters said the purpose of the meeting to get MacArthur's opinion: Vernon Walters, interview by author, March 18, 1997.

64 U.S. forces making contact with Chinese troops: Dean Acheson, *Present at the Creation: My Years in the State Department* (New York: Norton, 1969), p. 469; Ferrell, *Truman: A Life*, p. 327.

64 "Here, I believe, the government missed its last chance": Acheson, *Present at the Creation*, p. 466.

64 "the tendency for cohesive groups": Janis, *Groupthink*, p. 60.

64 "Decisions of the kind the executive has to make": Peter F. Drucker, *Management: Tasks, Responsibilities, Practices* (New York: Harper & Row, 1974), p. 472.

65 "We were frank with each other, but not quite frank enough": Acheson, *Present at the Creation*, p. 468.

65 "After a year or so": Ferrell, *Truman: A Life*, p. 358.

65 "For far too much of his time in office": Hamby, *Man of the People*, pp. 483, 484.

66 "The CIA was set up by me": letter to William B. Arthur, June 10, 1964, Post-Presidential Secretary's Office Files, HSTL.

66 "Chiang Kai-shek's downfall was his own doing": unsent letter to Arthur Krock, September 11, 1952, Ferrell, *Off the Record*, p. 271.

66 "I came to have tremendous admiration": Janis, *Groupthink*, p. 53.

66 "The president—whoever he is—has to decide": Truman farewell address, January 15, 1953, Universal newsreel.

67 "The full stature of this man": David McCullough, *Truman*, p. 614.

67 "He had great administrative ability": Matthew J. Connelly OH, p. 453.

67 "He came into office": George M. Elsey OH, p. 48.

67 "I taught those sons of bitches a thing or two": Hamby, *Man of the People*, p. 469.

67 Removal of Truman recordings from White House: White House memo from chief clerk William Hopkins to General Carroll, June 18, 1954, Presidential Recordings Vertical File, FDRL. In interviews, Professor Robert Butow and retired Truman Library archivist Philip Lagerquist speculated that the Kiel recording machine was removed from the White House by the RCA Corporation some time around the late 1940s, but no records have been located confirming its actual fate.

CHAPTER 3

Dwight D. Eisenhower: The Organized Executive

68 Eisenhower feared Bricker amendment could "wreck the United States": Eisenhower memcon of April 28, 1954 meeting with Joseph T. Meek and Senator Dirksen, Ann Whitman Diary Series File (AWDSF), DDEL.

68 Eisenhower feared Bricker amendment could cause "chaos in international affairs": Dwight Eisenhower, *Mandate For Change: The White House Years 1953–1956* (Garden City, NY: Doubleday, 1963), p. 281.

68   The description of Eisenhower's recording system and reconstruction of his recording procedure is derived from the recordings themselves (located in 1996 and restored by the Dictaphone Corporation in 1997); a 1991 Ann Whitman OH at the DDEL; 1996 author interviews with Dictaphone technical director Don Joyner, who supervised the transfer; DDEL archivists James Leyerzapf, Mack Teasley, and David Haight; and *Time*'s Hugh Sidey, who wrote of the recordings in the September 6, 1982 international edition of *Time*. From listening to the recordings, Joyner concluded that the microphone was concealed on or in the desk. This is likely, since the microphone picks up loudly and sharply the sounds of Eisenhower scribbling on papers. Mrs. Whitman described a "button" on Ike's desk as the trigger of the signal to turn it on, but she said her memory of the system was "perfectly foggy." Contemporaneous Dictaphone technical literature for the A2TC, supported by Dictaphone's Joyner, indicated that a toggle switch was the standard device (although technicians could have rigged up a button for Ike instead). Additional details were obtained from "President Ike Liked a Mike," *Time*, November 5, 1979, p. 33; and Ron Ostroff, "Secret Tapes Provide a Glimpse at Life in Two Administrations," *Kansas City Times*, September 13, 1982, p. 1; and Francis L. Lowenheim, "Eisenhower had own secret tapes," *Houston Chronicle*, October 21, 1979, p. 1.

An archivist at the Eisenhower Library has speculated that the actual number of recorded meetings might exceed one hundred, based on the format and content of other memos in the Ann Whitman Diary Series File. An inspection of the file supports this, as at least one hundred additional memos contain verbatim dialogue in a format identical to the original twenty-seven memos, though there is no explicit reference to a recording.

The Eisenhower Dictabelts recovered in 1996 were found inside White House envelopes with notations indicating five 1955 Oval Office meetings, three of which correspond with dates and people listed on the original list of twenty-seven meetings believed to have been recorded by Eisenhower: Congresswoman Frances Bolton, January 19, 1955; industrialist Paul Hoffman, March 5, 1955; and journalist Roy Howard, February 24, 1955. Two of the meetings were not on the original list: the meeting with Senator George, and a January 4, 1955, recording of the president with Commerce Secretary Sinclair Weeks. One of the envelopes had the notation "file in safe" in Eisenhower's own hand. The discovery of the Dictabelts was reported by George Lardner, Jr., "Eisenhower Secretly Recorded Oval Office Sessions," *WP*, March 15, 1997, p. 6.

69   Bricker Amendment background: Eisenhower, *Mandate for Change*, pp. 277–85.

69   "complex and devious"; "Not shackled to a one-track-mind": Richard Nixon, *Six Crises* (Garden City, NY: Doubleday, 1962), p. 172.

69   "If it's true that when you die": Stephen E. Ambrose, *Eisenhower: The President* (New York: Simon & Schuster, 1984), pp. 154, 155.

69   Notations of recordings: AWDSF, DDEL. For example:

"October 21, 1953: Large portions of the tape were completely garbled. The noise of the machine itself is so great that the words, while loud enough, cannot be understood. acw"

"November 7, 1953: 9:00 appointment with secretary of commerce. First time any adequate use of 'gadget' for recording conversations made. It is now fine and a complete verbatim report of the conversation could be made—but the work! Anyhow here are the highlights of this conversation (apparently the president did not turn his switch until conversation was underway)."

"April 28, 1954: Interview with Senator Dirksen and Joseph T. Meek, Republican candidate for Senate from Illinois. The interview had been underway approximately 5–10 minutes before monitoring took place. Tape on conversation is filed."

"December 9, 1959: Attached is as much substance as could be gained from tape recording of conversation with the president and Queen Frederika on December 9."

70 "Absolutely a lie": "Ike's Secretary Denies Extensive Use of Tapes," *Washington Star*, October 24, 1979.

70 Whitman on recorder: Ann C. Whitman OH, DDEL, pp. 4, 5.

70 "You know, boys, it's a good thing": Ambrose, *Eisenhower*, p. 203.

70 Whitman monitored Eisenhower's telephone conversations; Dulles had phone conversations monitored and transcribed routinely; Dulles File contains 13,000 telephone memos: letter from DDEL archivist David J. Haight to LBJL archivist John Powers, May 11, 1995, courtesy John Powers. By early 1954 the practice of "dead key" phone transcriptions was so widespread that the White House circulated a warning throughout the executive branch that the practice not be abused and that the other party should be informed ("Monitoring of Telephone Calls" memo July 16, 1954, AWDSF, DDEL).

71 He installed an "automatic recording system"; "a complete wiring of my war room with dictaphones"; "I made it a habit to inform visitors of the system"; "saved me hours of work": Dwight Eisenhower, *Crusade in Europe* (Garden City, NY: Doubleday, 1948), p. 38.

The Dictaphone was invented around the turn of the century, and by the 1920s it had become the leading brand of office recording equipment for government and industry. Thousands of Dictaphones were used during World War II by the U.S. government and military, for dictation, radio intercept work, and interrogation of prisoners. General Patton used a Dictaphone throughout the European campaign. In the late 1940s, wax Dictaphone cylinders were replaced by much sturdier plastic Dictabelts, the kind Ike used in the Oval Office.

71 Hugh Sidey's account of Dictaphone technician John Raynor; Eisenhower's wiring of Columbia and NATO offices: Hugh Sidey, "Ike's Beautiful, Bugged Desk," *Time* international edition, September 6, 1982. No Eisenhower recordings from this or any other pre-presidential period have been found.

72 Physical description of Eisenhower: "Eisenhower: Man in Motion," *Time*, January 18, 1954, p. 21.

72   "No man on earth knows": December 17, 1954, memo, "President with Field Marshal Montgomery, November 24, 1954," AWDSF, DDEL.

72   "He has the power of drawing the hearts of men": Ambrose, *Eisenhower*, p. 17.

72   Graduated first in his class: Fred I. Greenstein, *The Hidden-Hand Presidency: Eisenhower as Leader* (New York: Basic Books, 1982), p. 11.

72   "I'm just a farm boy from Kansas"; "I'm just a simple soldier": Ambrose, *Eisenhower*, pp. 18, 19.

72   "From his West Point graduation": Greenstein, *The Hidden-Hand Presidency*, p. 101.

73   "I have been in politics": Michael R. Beschloss, *Eisenhower: A Centennial Life* (New York: HarperCollins, 1990), p. 30.

73   Eisenhower's travels and relationships: Ambrose, *Eisenhower*, pp. 18, 19.

73   Suffered through MacArthur's screaming fits; "I wouldn't trade one Marshall for fifty MacArthurs": Chester J. Pach, Jr., and Elmo Richardson, *The Presidency of Dwight D. Eisenhower* (Lawrence: University Press of Kansas, 1991), pp. 5, 6, 7.

73   "I will make smarter political decisions": memorandum of recorded conversation with journalist Merriman Smith, November 23, 1954, AWDSF, DDEL.

73   Federal budget figures: William Manchester, *The Glory and the Dream* (Boston: Little, Brown, 1974), p. 649.

73   Description of Eisenhower's Oval Office: Robert J. Donovan, *Eisenhower: The Inside Story* (New York: Harper, 1956), p. 206; Virgil Pinkley with James F. Scheer, *Eisenhower Declassified* (Old Tappan, NJ: Revell, 1979), p. 275; Charles J.V. Murphy, "Eisenhower's White House," *Fortune*, July 1953, p. 75.

74   "GENTLY IN MANNER" plaque on Eisenhower's desk: Eisenhower, *Mandate for Change*, p. 148.

74   "I am not one of the desk-pounding type": Ambrose, *Eisenhower*, p. 623.

76   "because of his military experience": Nixon, *Six Crises*, p. 169.

76   "an Eisenhower characteristic was": ibid., p. 172.

78   "Eisenhower displayed two personas": Andrew Goodpaster, interview by author, July 3, 1996.

79   "showed his intellectual ascendancy": Andrew Goodpaster OH, p. 118.

79   Strategies "that enabled him to exercise power": Greenstein, *The Hidden-Hand Presidency*, pp. 57, 58.

79   "Whatever his defects as a public leader": Arthur M. Schlesinger, Jr., *The Cycles of American History* (Boston: Houghton Mifflin, 1986), p. 390.

79   Eisenhower Oval Office activity after the meeting with Senator George on January 7, 1955, is a continuation of the Dictabelt recording, the machine simply kept running. Mary Jane McCaffree Monroe, who entered the Oval Office during this recording, provided background for the meeting in an interview with the author, March 8, 1997. Like most Eisenhower officials, she hadn't the faintest idea that Ike stashed a microphone in the Oval Office.

80   "It only took a six-page directive": "How Ike Runs His Jobs," *USNWR*, August 20, 1954, p. 39.

80   "If a proposition can't be stated in one page": *Fortune*, July 1953, p. 77.

80 "He had flashes of anger of great intensity": Andrew Goodpaster, interview by author, July 3, 1996.

80 "taken apart a strip at a time": Oral History with the Eisenhower White House, DDEL, pp. 57, 58.

80 "I'd go out with a bigger agenda": ibid.

80 "What the hell is this?": Pach and Richardson, *The Presidency of Dwight D. Eisenhower*, p. 44.

81 "Dammit, Bobby, bring us issues and options": Oral History with the Eisenhower White House, DDEL, p. 16.

81 "If I had had a staff like this during the war": Ann Whitman memo to file, May 10, 1955, AWDSF, DDEL.

81 "The next time you see one of those squirrels": Ambrose, *Eisenhower*, p. 75.

81 Eisenhower routine: Ambrose, *Eisenhower*, pp. 26–28, 72; William Hopkins OH, JFKL, p. 11; *Fortune*, July 1953, p. 176; Andrew Goodpaster OH, p. 78; Greenstein, *The Hidden-Hand Presidency*, p. 35; James Hagerty OH, p. 225.

81 "My first full day at the President's Desk": Eisenhower, *Mandate for Change*, p. 112.

81 "a very intense give and take": Kenneth Thompson, ed., *The Eisenhower Presidency: Eleven Intimate Perspectives of Dwight D. Eisenhower* (University of Virginia: The Miller Center, 1984), p. 73.

81 "He seldom exchanged written memoranda": Sherman Adams, *Firsthand Report: The Story of the Eisenhower Administration* (New York: Harper, 1961), p. 70.

82 "Either you know how to manage or you don't": Andrew Goodpaster OH, p. 42.

82 "Organization cannot make a genius": Eisenhower, *Mandate for Change,* p. 114.

82 "simplify, clarify": Dwight D. Eisenhower, *Waging Peace, 1956–1961: The White House Years* (Garden City, NY: Doubleday, 1965), p. 630.

82 "The mere fact that such a fight can begin": Chief of Staff Diary, December 9, 1933, Pre-Presidential Papers, DDEL.

82 "Truman didn't know any more about government": Ferrell, *Truman: A Life*, p. 391.

82 "For years I had been in frequent contact": Eisenhower, *Mandate for Change*, p. 87.

82 "With my training in problems involving organization": ibid.

83 Commodore Hotel meetings: Greenstein, *The Hidden-Hand Presidency*, p. 105.

83 "In organizing teams, personality is equally important with ability": ibid., p. 119.

83 "I hope that before we have gone very long": Ambrose, *Eisenhower*, p. 37.

83 "There is no use to try to conceal an error"; "advertise your blunders": ibid, p. 45.

83 "The marks of a good executive": "Memorandum for Governor Adams," September 29, 1953, AWDSF, DDEL.

83   "Eisenhower simply expected me to manage a staff": *NYT,* June 25, 1961.

83   "We must not bother the president with this": Robert J. Donovan, *Eisenhower: The Inside Story* (New York: Harper, 1956), p. 71.

83   "It was similar to what he did when he was in command in Europe," and "it was not on any strict military model": Andrew Goodpaster OH, Columbia University, p. 31.

84   Eisenhower Cabinet strategy and method: Maxwell Rabb, interview by author, April 11, 1997.

84   "He put a lot of authority": Andrew Goodpaster OH, p. 42.

84   "Charlie, you run Defense": Cole C. Kingseed, *Eisenhower and the Suez Crisis of 1956* (Baton Rouge: Louisana State University Press, 1995), p. 14.

84   "To make a mistake in judgment is excusable": "Eisenhower's Management and Decision-Making Style," *PSQ,* Fall 1983, p. 306.

84   "Government cannot function properly": Dwight D. Eisenhower OH, The John Foster Dulles Oral History Project, Princeton University, July 28, 1964, p. 13.

84   "There was never any doubt that he was in charge": Harold Stassen, interview by author, August 26, 1997.

84   Eisenhower's meetings routinely swelled to over thirty, forty and fifty people: see agendas and invitee lists for Cabinet Meetings and National Security Council meetings, 1955–1960, AWDSF, DDEL.

85   "The Cabinet was used by Eisenhower as an advisory council": Thompson, *The Eisenhower Presidency,* pp. 236–37.

85   "very strong in meetings": Maurice Stans, interview by author, January 15, 1996.

85   "to be bored for his country as well as to lead it": Tom Wicker, *One of Us: Richard Nixon and the American Dream* (New York: Random House, 1995), p. 396.

85   "when it came to making a final decision": Nixon, *Six Crises,* pp. 169, 170.

85   "These were off-the-record meetings": Andrew Goodpaster OH, Columbia University, p. 35.

85   Communists held back hundreds of American prisoners of war: Memorandum from Dr. Craig to Elmer Staats, "Interview with Rastvorov (former MVD) concerning U.S. Prisoners of War in the USSR," January 31, 1955, declassified April 9, 1996, Project Russia Papers, DDEL; Philip Shenon, "U.S. Knew in 1953 North Koreans Held American P.O.W.'s," *NYT,* September 17, 1996, pp. 1, 5; Al Santoli, congressional MIA investigator, interview by author, November 5, 1997.

85   Eisenhower briefed about hundreds of U.S. prisoners who "just disappeared": *NYT,* September 17, 1996, p. 1.

85   "perhaps we should have insisted on their return": Bruce W. Nelan, "Lost Prisoners of War: Sold Down the River?" *Time,* September 30, 1996, p. 45.

85   Eisenhower was said to be "intensely interested" in the fate of "the missing P.O.W.'s": *NYT,* September 17, 1996, p. 5.

85   "In a nuclear age, Eisenhower could not risk": ibid.

86   This excerpt is from a memo quoting a recording of the meeting between

Eisenhower, Dulles, Krishna Menon, and G. Lallubhai Metha, June 14, 1955, AWDSF, DDEL.

86   "I have bluntly told him": Eisenhower memo to file, July 14, 1955, AWDSF, DDEL.

86   Eisenhower urged to authorize air strikes: Ambrose, *Eisenhower*, p. 185; Dwight D. Eisenhower OH, The John Foster Dulles Oral History Project, Princeton University, pp. 25, 27.

86   "When we talk about Dien Bien Phu": Oval Office audio recording, February 24, 1955, 2:15 P.M., President Eisenhower with Roy Howard, RE: Vietnam, DDEL.

86   "He got us out of Korea and kept us out of Vietnam": Ambrose, *Eisenhower*, p. 185.

86   "Bombs, by God": Kingseed, *Eisenhower and the Suez Crisis*, p. 81.

87   Suez background: Eisenhower, *Waging Peace*, pp. 58–93; Kingseed, *Eisenhower and the Suez Crisis*, pp. 26–80.

87   This Eisenhower-Eden transcript was published in *Foreign Relations of the United States, 1955–1957*, Vol. XVI, U.S. State Dept., pp. 1025–1027.

       In an interview for this book, General Andrew Goodpaster, who was in the Oval Office for this and other Eisenhower-Eden phone conversations during the Suez crisis, concluded that the transcript was prepared by Ann Whitman listening in on the president's phone line.

90   "the Eisenhower who emerged from the Suez crisis"; "the force of his own personality, his bureaucratic skill": Kingseed, *Eisenhower and the Suez Crisis*, p. 154.

90   "Eisenhower evaded them both": Schlesinger, *The Cycles of American History*, p. 390.

91   Eisenhower and Rabb tackle segregation: Maxwell Rabb, interview by author, April 11, 1997; Eisenhower, *Mandate for Change*, p. 235; Ambrose, *Eisenhower*, pp. 126, 308, 309.

91   "I really would like to get rid of discrimination": Maxwell Rabb, interview by author, April 11, 1997.

91   "he provided almost no leadership at all": Ambrose, *Eisenhower*, p. 192.

91   "Although Presidents Hoover, Roosevelt, and Truman": *PSQ*, Fall 1983, p. 589.

92   "He was president for eight years": Harold Stassen, interview by author, August 26, 1997.

92   Inflation averaged 1.4 percent a year from 1953 to 1960: Steve Neal, "Why We Were Right to Like Ike," *AH*, December 1985, p. 53.

92   "Eisenhower gave the nation eight years": Ambrose, *Eisenhower*, p. 627.

92   "The United States never lost a soldier": William A. DeGregorio, *The Complete Book of U.S. Presidents* (New York: Barricade Books, 1993), p. 542. Eisenhower was omitting U.S. combat deaths and MIA's from the final months of the Korean War, which occurred at the start of his first term. Also, one U.S. soldier was killed during the otherwise uneventful 1958 intervention in Lebanon (Pach and Richardson, *The Presidency of Dwight D. Eisenhower*, p. 193).

CHAPTER 4

JOHN F. KENNEDY: THE RATIONAL EXECUTIVE

93 "We are under attack"; "Do not see any friendly air cover"; Need jet support immediately": "Cuba: The Massacre," *Time,* April 28, 1961, p. 21.

93 Kennedy stood in the Cabinet Room: Peter Wyden, *Bay of Pigs: The Untold Story* (New York: Simon & Schuster, 1979), p. 267.

94 Bay of Pigs background: Taylor Report (Paramilitary Study Group), Memorandum No. 1, "Narrative of the Anti Castro Cuban Operation Zapata," National Security Files, Cuba, JFKL, pp. 7–19; Irving L. Janis, *Victims of Groupthink: A Psychological Study of Foreign Policy Decisions and Fiascoes* (Boston: Houghton Mifflin, 1972), pp. 14–47; Wyden, *Bay of Pigs,* pp. 266, 267, 303; Haynes Johnson with Manuel Artime and others, *The Bay of Pigs: The Leaders' Story of Brigade 2506* (New York: Norton, 1964), pp. 150–162; Linda Robinson, "The Price of Military Folly," *USNWR,* April 22, 1996, pp. 53–56; Richard Benedetto, "An Invasion of Bad Ideas," *USA Today,* June 23, 1997, pp. 4, 5.

94 "All the mysteries about the Bay of Pigs have been solved": Hugh Sidey, *John F. Kennedy, President* (New York: Atheneum, 1964), p. 126.

94 "How could I have been so stupid": Michael R. Beschloss, *The Crisis Years: Kennedy and Khrushchev, 1960–1963* (New York: Edward Burlingame Books, 1991), p. 132.

94 JFK's micromanagement of assault; "too spectacular"; "too much like a World War II invasion"; "reduce the noise level": Wyden, *Bay of Pigs,* pp. 100, 121.

94 "the move from the heavily populated Trinidad": Richard M. Bissell, Jr., *Reflections of a Cold Warrior: From Yalta to the Bay of Pigs* (New Haven: Yale University Press, 1996), p. 172.

94 The only place the plan existed was in Bissell's head: Wyden, *Bay of Pigs,* p. 317.

94 "no strong voice of opposition was raised": Theodore C. Sorensen, *Kennedy* (New York: Harper & Row, 1965), p. 304.

94 "took place in a curious atmosphere": Arthur M. Schlesinger, Jr., *A Thousand Days: John F. Kennedy in the White House* (Boston: Houghton Mifflin, 1965), p. 250.

95 "One's impulse to blow the whistle on this nonsense": ibid., p. 255.

95 "I should have had the guts to give a complicated answer": Wyden, *Bay of Pigs,* pp. 14, 149.

95 "My interpretation as to why Kennedy got into the Bay of Pigs": Gerald S. and Deborah H. Strober, *Let Us Begin Anew: An Oral History of the Kennedy Presidency* (New York: HarperCollins, 1993), p. 156.

95 "I did not know enough": Hugh Sidey, "A Little Experience is . . . Useful," *Time,* April 18, 1977, p. 13.

95 "Under no circumstances": Beschloss, *The Crisis Years,* p. 114.

95 "Well, I don't want it on that scale": Wyden, *Bay of Pigs,* p. 170.

95 Pepe San Román's final messages: Johnson, *The Bay of Pigs,* pp. 150–62;

USNWR, April 22, 1996, p. 56; *USA Today,* June 23, 1997, p. 5; Taylor Report, section 65.

95   "One specification was clearly Castro's overthrow": Peter F. Drucker, *The Effective Executive* (New York: Harper & Row, 1967) pp. 133, 134. The CIA Inspector General's secret post-mortem of the Bay of Pigs operation, released only in 1998, blamed CIA incompetence for the disaster, not JFK's cancellation of the air strike.

96   "What happened in the end": C. Douglas Dillon, interview by author, March 17, 1997.

96   "The Bay of Pigs was the indication": RFK OH, p. 602.

96   Kennedy tore up Eisenhower's organization chart: C. Douglas Dillon, interview by author, March 17, 1997.

96   "I hope you'll be in a good mood when you read this": Richard Reeves, "The Lines of Control Have Been Cut," *AH,* September 1993, p. 65.

96   "We can't win them all": Schlesinger, *A Thousand Days,* p. 290.

97   "after the Bay of Pigs": Theodore Sorensen OH, p. 23.

97   A 2.35 million-employee organization: William Manchester, *Portrait of a President: John F. Kennedy in Profile* (Boston: Little, Brown, 1962), p. 43.

97   "He did not feel that he had": Dean Rusk OH.

97   "If you're going to have a fight": Dean Rusk, as told to Richard Rusk, *As I Saw It* (New York: Norton, 1990), p. 293.

97   "There is no sense in raising hell": "Conversation with President Kennedy," joint network TV broadcast interview, December 12, 1962.

98   "What the hell do I do now?": Hugh Sidey, "Majesty in a Democracy," *Time,* December 1, 1980, p. 18.

98   "I've never run a large organization before": Richard Reeves, *President Kennedy: Profile of Power* (New York: Simon & Schuster, 1993), p. 666, citing Bell OH, pp. 1–3.

98   "bored silly with normal day-to-day executive work": Ralph Dungan, interview by author, April 14, 1997.

98   "I had different identities": William Manchester, *One Brief Shining Moment: Remembering Kennedy* (Boston: Little, Brown 1983), p. 64.

98   JFK Oval Office detail: Kenneth P. O'Donnell and David F. Powers with Joe McCarthy, *Johnny, We Hardly Knew Ye* (New York: Pocket Books, 1973), pp. 250–51; Sorensen, *Kennedy,* p. 375; Oval Office exhibit, JFKL.

98   JFK found the floor chewed up by Eisenhower's golf cleats: Lawrence E. Knutson (AP), "The Oval Office," *The Free Lance-Star* (Fredricksburg, VA), June 6, 1994, p. D3.

98   "The pale-green walls": Hugh Sidey, *John F. Kennedy, President* (New York: Atheneum, 1964), p. 62.

98   JFK medical problems: James N. Giglio, "Past Frustrations and New Opportunities: Researching the Kennedy Presidency at the Kennedy Library," *PSQ,* Spring 1992, pp. 371–73; Reeves, *Profile of Power,* pp. 36, 42, 43.

98   "In a lifetime of medical torment": Reeves, *Profile of Power,* p. 36.

99   White House Police Gate logs: *PSQ,* Spring 1992, p. 374.

99   Hersh on Powers: Seymour M. Hersh, *The Dark Side of Camelot* (Boston: Little, Brown, 1997), pp. 227, 230.

99   "It never occurred": *PSQ,* Spring 1992, p. 374.

99   JFK daily routine: Sorensen, *Kennedy,* pp. 366–76; Schlesinger, *A Thousand Days,* pp. 664–91; Manchester, *Portrait of a President,* pp. 40, 41; Sidey, *John F. Kennedy, President,* pp. 62, 212; James N. Giglio, *The Presidency of John F. Kennedy* (Lawrence: University Press of Kansas, 1991), p. 256; Stober and Stober, *Let Us Begin Anew,* pp. 150–54; William Hopkins OH, p. 1; author interviews with C. Douglas Dillon (March 17, 1997), Theodore Sorensen (August 6, 1996), Myer Feldman (April 20, 1997).

      In the early 1990s, historian James J. Best studied JFK's daily appointment books, or "diaries," at the JFK Library and concluded "according to the diaries, he was in the office by 9:30 most mornings" and met with advisers "until 7:00 or 7:30 each night." Best noted that "when Kennedy worked, he worked very hard, interacting frequently with advisers; when he vacationed he rarely interacted with people outside his immediate family and close friends." These records were kept by appointments secretary Kenny O'Donnell and updated by White House secretaries. Unless O'Donnell and the secretaries were systematically forging the records (which can't be totally ruled out in O'Donnell's case since he was the most viciously loyal soldier in Kennedy's "Irish Mafia"), the case that JFK's private life interfered with his executive performance remains to be proven. James J. Best, "Who Talked With President Kennedy? An Interaction Analysis," *PSQ,* Spring 1992, pp. 351–54.

99   Kennedy worked from mansion: Manchester, *Portrait of a President,* pp. 40, 41.

99   Kennedy slipped away for a few walks: "New Folks at Home," *Time,* February 10, 1961, p. 15.

100   JFK nicknamed "the Tiger": Sidey, *John F. Kennedy, President,* p. 218.

100   "John Kennedy was an impatient fellow": Rusk, *As I Saw It,* p. 293.

100   "Cut the commercials, get to the facts": former Kennedy aide who requested anonymity, interview by author.

100   "when you see the president": Manchester, *Portrait of a President,* pp. 12, 13.

100   JFK liked short personal meetings, Dillon would "go in for four or five minutes": C. Douglas Dillon, interview by author, March 17, 1997.

100   Kennedy asked questions so quickly the aide couldn't keep up: "The Closest Look Yet at J.F.K.," *Life,* April 28, 1961, p. 36.

100   "I'm interested in the little things": Ralph G. Martin, *A Hero for Our Time: An Intimate Story of the Kennedy Years* (New York: Macmillan, 1983), p. 425.

100   "I never heard of a president": Beschloss, *The Crisis Years,* p. 71.

100   The only president who asked to see raw intelligence cables: Reeves, *Profile of Power,* p. 670.

100   He reviewed expense accounts of White House staffers: Manchester, *Portrait of a President,* p. 52.

100   "I can't afford to confine myself": Schlesinger, *A Thousand Days,* p. 123.

100 "Each person was unaware that the others": Evelyn Lincoln, *My Twelve Years With John F. Kennedy* (New York: D. McKay Co., 1965), p. 5.

100 "He was not process oriented": Ralph Dungan, interview by author, April 14, 1997.

100 "His enormous energy": Walt W. Rostow, *The Diffusion of Power: An Essay in Recent History* (New York: Macmillan, 1972), p. 128.

101 "Management in Jack's mind": *AH*, September 1993, p. 62.

101 Rarely held formal NSC meetings, dispensed with Cabinet meetings: Theodore Sorensen, interview by author, August 6, 1996.

101 "half his time thinking about adultery": Beschloss, *The Crisis Years*, p. 227.

101 Every Tuesday morning Kennedy held a breakfast with congressional leaders: Theodore Sorensen, interview by author, August 6, 1996.

101 The main management meeting of his presidency: ibid.

101 "It's like preparing for a final exam": Sorensen, *Kennedy*, p. 325.

101 "He was an incendiary man": Strober and Strober, *Let Us Begin Anew*, p. 156.

101 "Kennedy was a magnificent natural leader": David Bell, interview by author, June 12, 1996.

101 "When he came into the room, he was like the sun": Pedro Sanjuan, interview by author, September 14, 1997.

102 "He treated us more as colleagues": Sorensen, *Kennedy*, p. 374.

102 "I can't imagine a better boss": interview with Myer Feldman, April 20, 1997.

102 "Everybody on the staff really liked and respected him": Ralph Dungan, interview by author, April 14, 1997.

102 Story of Kennedy, Secret Service man, and hot chocolate: Giglio, *The Presidency of John F. Kennedy*, p. 257; Martin, *Hero for our Time*, p. 245.

102 Details of Kennedy taping system installation and operation, locations of microphones, subjects taped, Robert Bouck quotes: Robert Bouck, interviews by author and A&E Fleisher interview, October 1996; Stephanie Fawcett, JFKL archivist, interview by author, April 21, 1997; *Presidential Recordings, 1962–1963, Finding Aid*, JFKL, 1994; "On the Record—Literally," *Time*, February 15, 1982, p. 16. Evelyn Lincoln quote is from the JFKL Finding Aid.

There are 127 audio tapes in all, with a running time of about 248 hours, covering 300 separate meetings and conversations. The earliest tape is July 30, 1962, and the latest is November 8, 1963. Kennedy also recorded 275 of his phone conversations onto 73 Dictabelts, totaling 12 hours of conversation. JFK recorded calls and meetings on Berlin, China, Laos, the Middle East, the Nuclear Test Ban, the Chinese-Indian border clash, NATO, Latin American and African affairs, foreign aid, the space program, agricultural subsidies, labor disputes, and the tax cut of 1962, and conversations with Senator Barry Goldwater and other congressmen, Soviet ambassador Anatoly Dobrynin, retired General Douglas MacArthur, and former Presidents Truman and Eisenhower, among others.

While Kennedy's Dictabelt material is usually of good audio quality and many of the taped meetings are understandable, it was far from a perfect system. John Powers, a National Archives official who has studied the tapes, wrote: "Voices too close to the microphones are distorted; voices too far away from the microphones are inaudible. Some participants mumbled, while others yelled. The microphones picked up many background noises such as helicopter rotor noise, air conditioning, clattering of cups, scribbling of pens, and rustling of papers, to name a few, that obscured the recordings of the conversations. The microphones in the kneewell of the president's desk in the Oval Office also recorded loud and clear the president's knees and legs knocking against the desk."

104 "John F. Kennedy had the facility to see the fact": Pierre Salinger OH, p. 92.

104 Kennedy wiretapping: Reeves, *Profile of Power*, p. 709; *Time*, "Hoover's Political Spying for Presidents," December 15, 1975, p. 10.

104 "My God, they wiretapped": Reeves, *Profile of Power*, p. 304.

104 "The FBI and the CIA had installed": ibid.

104 targets of Kennedy wiretaps: ibid., pp. 304, 709.

104 Rusk suspected bugging, warned Hoover: Beschloss, *The Crisis Years*, p. 71.

105 1973 reactions of McGeorge Bundy, Arthur M. Schlesinger, Jr., and Ramsey Clark to news of JFK taping: John Kifner, "Kennedy Aides Unaware That Talks Were Taped," *NYT*, July 19, 1973, p. 1.

105 1982 reactions of Theodore Sorensen, William Fulbright, Henry Jackson and Wilbur Mills: Harrison Rainie, "Camelot Records with Original Cast," *Daily News* (New York), February 5, 1982, p. 2.

105 Details of Oxford crisis: Katzenbach OH p. 104-23; "The Edge of Violence," *Time*, October 5, 1962, pp. 15-17; "Though the Heavens Fall," *Time*, October 12, 1962, pp. 19-22; Robert Massie, "What Next in Mississippi?" *Saturday Evening Post*, November 10, 1962, pp. 18-23; Walter Lord, *The Past That Would Not Die* (New York: Harper & Row, 1965), pp. 1-4, 139-232; Arthur M. Schlesinger, Jr., *Robert Kennedy and His Times* (Boston: Houghton Mifflin, 1987), pp. 340-51; Taylor Branch, *Parting the Waters: America in the King Years, 1954-63* (New York: Simon & Schuster, 1988), p. 662-69; Reeves, *Profile of Power*, pp. 355-64; Schlesinger, *A Thousand Days*, pp. 940-48; Sorensen, *Kennedy*, pp. 483-88; Theodore Sorensen and Burke Marshall, A&E Fleisher interviews; James Meredith, Rev. Duncan Gray, Edwin Guthman, former Citizens Council leader William Simmons, former Army Lt. Donnie Bowman, former Mississippi National Guard Capt. Murry Falkner, former U.S. Marshal Al Butler, Nicholas Katzenbach, former *New York Times* senior reporter Claude Sitton, and Jim McShane's son Michael McShane, interviews by author, 1998. Also: transcripts of Cabinet Room and Oval Office, 1998, recordings, September 28-October 1, 1962, JFKL.

Since the exact sequence and timing of the Oxford recordings were often not specified on the original tapes, they are estimated from contemporary and historical accounts of the crisis as well as from comments on the recordings themselves. The Cabinet Room recordings of this crisis are often very hard to understand, and sometimes parallel conversations or phone calls occur simultaneously with the main drift of conversation. These excerpts are based on the tapes and on a transcript prepared by the JFK Library, and follow the main conversation. This is a perfect example of why all transcripts of White House recordings should be considered tentative and speculative, including the identification of individual speakers.

105 "The governor was in rebellion one minute": Burke Marshall, A&E Fleisher interview.

106 "There is more power in the presidency": "Though the Heavens Fall," *Time*, October 12, 1962, p. 20.

106 "an agreeable rogue": Edwin O. Guthman and Jeffrey Shulman, eds., *Robert Kennedy In His Own Words: The Unpublished Recollections of the Kennedy Years* (New York: Bantam, 1988), p. 159.

109 "You broke your word to him": Lord, *The Past That Would Not Die*, p. 194.

110 "You rubber-nosed motherfucker": interview with former U.S. Marshal Al Butler.

118 "a terrible evening"; "was torn between": Guthman and Shulman, eds., *Robert Kennedy in His Own Words*, p. 161.

118 JFK ordering marshals not to fire: ibid., p. 162.

119 "the evening would have been quite different": ibid., p. 167.

120 "People are dying in Oxford": Lord, *The Past That Would Not Die*, p. 3.

120 "The idea that we got through the evening": ibid., p. 165.

120 "Kennedy was decisive": Reeves, *Profile of Power*, p. 19.

120 "I don't think I ever react emotionally": Martin, *A Hero for Our Time*, p. 43.

121 "The last thing I want around here": Pierre Salinger, *With Kennedy* (Garden City, NY: Doubleday, 1966), p. 64.

121 "it was not an administration": Strober and Strober, *Let Us Begin Anew*, p. 158.

121 "President Kennedy had a quality which I have rarely seen": Lewis J. Paper, *The Promise and the Performance: The Leadership of John F. Kennedy* (New York: Crown, 1975).

121 "I want all the input"; JFK discussing Truman's decision-making style: Martin, *A Hero for Our Time*, p. 425.

121 JFK thought chances of nuclear war were "fifty/fifty": Theodore Sorensen, A&E Fleisher interview.

121 Background and details of Cuban Missile Crisis: Reeves, *Profile of Power*, pp. 370–423; Sorensen, *Kennedy*, pp. 667–718; Schlesinger, *A Thousand Days*, pp. 801–30; Dino A. Brugioni, *Eyeball to Eyeball: The Inside Story of the Cuban Missile Crisis* (New York: Random House, 1991), pp. 358–61; Janis, *Groupthink*, pp. 132–58; *The Air Force Response to the Cuban Missile Crisis* (undated), USAF Historical Division Liason Office; Tom Morgenthau, "At the Brink of Disaster," *Newsweek*, October 26, 1992, p. 39; *Time*, October–November 1962; Robert McNamara comments on ABC *Nightline*, October 24, 1996; C. Douglas Dillon, Theodore Sorensen, Edwin Martin, Bruce Blair, Raymond Garthoff, interviews by author.

121 Soviet tactical nuclear weapons in Cuba: Robert McNamara comments on ABC *Nightline*, October 24, 1996. According to former CIA analyst Dino Brugioni, the SS-4 missiles in Cuba, which had the range to hit Washington, had warheads at their launch sites and could have been fired within a few hours of an order from Moscow (*Newsweek*, October 26, 1992, p. 39).

127 "back into the Stone Age"; LeMay contempt for JFK and vice versa: Thomas Coffey, *Iron Eagle: The Turbulent Life of General Curtis LeMay* (New York: Crown, 1986), pp. 356, 357.

129 In their 1997 book *The Kennedy Tapes: Inside the White House During the Cuban Missile Crisis* (Cambridge, MA: Belknap Press of Harvard University Press), Ernest R. May and Philip D. Zelikow identified Voice 1 as General Shoup and Voice 2 as General LeMay.

131 "If they want this job": Beschloss, *The Crisis Years,* p. 481.

131 "Ah, I am still here": Rusk, *As I Saw It,* p. 235.

131 Stock market plunge, Florida panic, Los Angeles stampede: "The Backdown," *Time,* November 2, 1962, pp. 27, 29.

132 "I used to worry": Scott D. Sagan, *The Limits of Safety: Organizations, Accidents, and Nuclear Weapons* (Princeton, NJ: Princeton University Press, 1993), p. 150, citing Air Force Oral History interview with Wade.

132 Bruce Blair quotes: A&E Fleisher and author interviews, fall 1996.

132 Eisenhower conditional predelegation of nuclear launch authority: Bruce G. Blair, *The Logic of Accidental Nuclear War* (Washington, DC: Brookings Institution, 1993), pp. 48, 49.

132 "certifiably off the deep end"; "not the sort of person who could be counted on": A&E Fleisher interview with Bruce Blair.

132 U-2 strays over Siberia: Sagan, *The Limits of Safety,* pp. 136, 137.

132 "Hey, I think I'm lost": Rusk, *As I Saw It,* p. 242.

132 New Jersey radar post false alarm: Sagan, *The Limits of Safety,* p. 6.

132 DEFCON, Soviet, and U.K. alerts: Blair, *The Logic of Accidental Nuclear War,* p. 24; Raymond L. Garthoff, *Reflections on the Cuban Missile Crisis* (Washington, DC: Brookings Institution, 1987 and revised 1989 version), p. 37; Sagan, *The Limits of Safety,* pp. 62, 63, 65, 72, 73; U.S. Air Force, *The Air Force Response to the Cuban Crisis* (undated report, presumably soon after crisis, consulted at National Security Archive, Washington, DC), pp. 18, 19; A&E Fleisher interviews and author interviews with Bruce Blair and Raymond Garthoff.

DEFCON details: Sagan, *Limits of Safety,* pp. 64, 65, citing 1962 U.S. Air Force documents. Details of this alert are often misreported, including the claim that SAC went on DEFCON 2 alert on its own. McNamara initiated the alert on October 24 on Kennedy's authorization. DEFCON 2 is often referred to as "one step down from nuclear war," when there were in fact three alert levels beyond DEFCON 2: DEFCON 1 ("Cocked Pistol: war is imminent and may occur momentarily"), and two final, maximum alerts, Defense Emergency ("Hot Box: a major attack upon U.S. forces overseas, on allied forces in any theater, or a covert attack of any type upon the United States and confirmed by a unified or specified commander or higher authority"), and Air Defense Emergency Warning Red ("Big Noise: attack by hostile aircraft/missiles upon the continental United States, Alaska, Canada, or Greenland is imminent or taking place").

In Montana, Minuteman missiles "were rushed into operational status," according to Blair, "and in doing so, we cut corners on safety and safeguards so it was much easier than it should have been for a crew at the very bottom of the chain of command to launch those missiles" (A&E Fleisher interview with

Bruce Blair). Generals Power and LeMay reportedly tried to rush the thermonuclear 9 megaton B-53 gravity bomb into service at the Bunker Hill Air Force Base, even though it contained a safety defect that increased the risk of accidental detonation (Sagan, *The Limits of Safety,* pp. 72, 73). A civilian Pentagon official ruled it not safe and blocked the request. On October 26, at 4:00 A.M., without the ExComm's knowledge, an Atlas ICBM was fired on a previously scheduled test launch from Vandenberg Air Force Base, running the risk of looking like the first wave of an enemy attack on Soviet radar screens (ibid., pp. 78, 79).

133 "tempers were high and everyone was frustrated": Theodore Sorensen, A&E Fleisher interview.

133 JFK October 27 back-up plans: Rusk, *As I Saw It,* pp. 240, 241.

133 "repetitive, leaderless and a waste of time": Beschloss, *The Crisis Years,* p. 455.

134 "It was just plain dumb luck": Rusk, *As I Saw It,* p. 242.

134 "He got input from everybody": C. Douglas Dillon, interview by author, March 17, 1997.

134 August 28, 1963 meeting: Cabinet Room tape recording, JFKL.

134 JFK ambiguous statements on Vietnam: John Galloway, ed., *The Kennedys & Vietnam* (New York: Facts on File, 1971), p. 41.
    Senator Mike Mansfield and JFK aide Kenneth O'Donnell said that Kennedy told them in a 1963 meeting that he agreed on the need for a total military withdrawal from Vietnam, but said "I can't do it until 1965—after I'm reelected" (ibid., p. 51).

134 Vietnam and coup background: *NBC News White Paper: Vietnam Hindsight* (1971); Roger Hilsman, *To Move a Nation: The Politics of Foreign Policy in the Administration of John F. Kennedy* (New York: Dell, 1967), pp. 517–20; John M. Newman, *JFK and Vietnam: Deception, Intrigue and the Struggle for Power* (New York: Warner Books, 1992), pp. 378–416.

135 "leaped to his feet": Maxwell D. Taylor, *Swords and Ploughshares* (New York: Norton, 1972), p. 301.

135 "Kennedy was the pragmatist par excellence": George W. Ball, *The Past Has Another Pattern: Memoirs* (New York: Norton, 1982), p. 167.

135 "He showed great flexibility of mind": Dean Rusk OH, p. 389.

135 "The president prides himself": "Kennedy and Congress: Score for the Next Six Months," *USNWR,* July 17, 1961, p. 41.

135 "all the impact of a snowflake": James D. Barber, *The Presidential Character: Predicting Performance in the White House* (Englewood Cliffs, NJ: Prentice-Hall, 1972), p. 319.

135 "He or his staff didn't conduct the best relations with Congress": Stober and Stober, *Let Us Begin Anew,* p. 145.

136 Congress blocked JFK's domestic program, popularity dropped from 83 to 57 percent: Thomas A. Bailey, "Johnson & Kennedy: The 2,000 Days," *NYT Magazine,* November 6, 1966, p. 31.

136 "He died in time to be remembered": Galloway, ed., *The Kennedys & Vietnam,* p. 49.

136 "He always seemed to be striding through doors": James Reston, "What

Was Killed Was Not Only the President but the Promise," *NYT Magazine,* November 15, 1964, p. 24.

136 "for all the brilliance of its members": Drucker, *The Effective Executive,* p. 125.

136 "Kennedy accumulated tremendous personal popularity": ABC News, *JFK: A Special Presentation* (1983).

136 "he was the greatest actor of our time": Hugh Sidey, "He Asked Me to Listen to the Debate," *Time,* November 14, 1983, p. 69.

137 New York Times/CBS poll: Marjorie Connelly, "Americans Are Still Voting for J.F.K.," *NYT,* August 18, 1996, section 4, p. 4.

137 "I considered this a confidential thing": Robert Bouck, interview by author. After JFK's murder, Bobby Kennedy seized the tapes and maintained control over them through Mrs. Lincoln. He commissioned some transcripts to be made (which turned out to be often inaccurate) and may have consulted them in preparing his bestselling memoir of the Cuban Missile Crisis, *Thirteen Days: A Memoir of the Cuban Missile Crisis* (New York: W.W. Norton, 1969). The tapes were deeded to the government in 1976, and transcripts and tapes were periodically declassified and released by the Kennedy Library from 1983 to 1998. In 1993 the *Boston Globe* reported that withdrawals of an unknown number of tapes were made over the years by George E. Dalton, a representative of the Kennedy family, presumably material of a personal nature. Philip Bennet, "Mystery Surrounds Role of JFK Tapes Transcriber," *The Boston Globe,* March 31, 1993, p. 1.

CHAPTER 5

LYNDON B. JOHNSON: THE CONTROLLING EXECUTIVE

138 "I'm going to run over you": Michael Oreskes, "Civil Rights Act Leaves Deep Mark on the American Political Landscape," *NYT,* July 2, 1989, p. 16.

138 LBJ phone conversation with McCormack and Albert appears on December 20, 1963 Dictabelt, LBJL.

138 "I knew I must break the legislative deadlock": Lyndon B. Johnson, *The Vantage Point: Perspectives of the Presidency, 1963–1969* (New York: Holt, Rinehart & Winston, 1971), p. 21.

139 "His executive style was just being in control": George Christian, interview by author, June 24, 1997.

140 "a real centaur": Kenneth Turan, "The Hexagon" (review of Walter Isaacson and Evan Thomas, *The Wise Men*), *Time,* October 27, 1986, p. 98.

140 "a character out of a Russian novel": Robert Dallek, "My Search for Lyndon Johnson," *AH,* September 1991, p. 88.

140 "If you did not know Johnson": Hugh Sidey, "Was Lyndon Johnson Unstable?" *Time,* September 5, 1988, p. 22.

140 "I understand you were born in a log cabin": William E. Leuchtenburg, "A Visit With LBJ," May/June 1990, *AH,* May 1990, p. 64.

140 "Personality is power": James David Barber, *Presidential Character: Predicting Performance in the White House* (Englewood Cliffs, NJ: Prentice-Hall, 1972), p. 137.

141   "He was a man of too many paradoxes": Todd S. Purdum, "Facets of Clinton," *NYT Magazine,* May 16, 1996, p. 36.

141   "an insufferable bastard": George E. Reedy, *Lyndon B. Johnson: A Memoir* (New York: Andrews and McMeel, 1982), p. 130.

141   "He was thirteen of the most interesting": Bernard J. Firestone and Robert C. Vogt, *Lyndon Baines Johnson and the Uses of Power* (Westport, CT: Greenwood Press, 1988), p. 350.

141   "LBJ was an emasculator": interview with former aide to JFK and LBJ who requested anonymity.

141   "brave and brutal, compassionate and cruel": Joseph Califano, *The Triumph and Tragedy of Lyndon Johnson: The White House Years* (New York: Simon & Schuster, 1991), p. 10.

141   "He is the only man who has ever made me feel": *AH,* September 1991, p. 86.

141   Reached for phone when he woke up and fondled it as he went to bed: Eric F. Goldman, *The Tragedy of Lyndon Johnson* (New York: Knopf, 1969), p. 21.

141   "Wayne, did I wake you?": anecdote told by Liz Carpenter (former press secretary to Mrs. Johnson), *The Johnson White House,* C-Span broadcast, April 1997.

141   "I've had ten calls from the man today": Jack Bell, *The Johnson Treatment: How Lyndon B. Johnson Took Over the Presidency and Made It His Own* (New York: Harper & Row, 1965), p. 40.

141   "He could practically crawl through that wire": George E. Reedy OH, p. 47.

141   Ordered an overhaul of the White House phone system: LBJ Daily Diary, November 23, 1963, LBJ- Kennedy Assassination and Transition file, *America Since Hoover Collection,* National Archives, consulted at FDR Library.

141   He installed direct lines to his chief aides: Califano, *Triumph and Tragedy,* p. 25.

142   Floating phones: Bell, *The Johnson Treatment,* p. 32.

142   Phones in his limousine; LBJ phone technique in limo: Goldman, *The Tragedy of Lyndon Johnson,* pp. 21, 22.

142   "he didn't just pick up the telephone": Merle Miller, *Lyndon: An Oral Biography* (New York: Putnam, 1980), p. 535.

142   "I don't give a damn where he is": CBS network broadcast, *Cronkite Remembers,* May 23, 1996.

142   "I told you to put a phone in that toilet": Califano, *Triumph and Tragedy,* p. 26.

142   Phones installed throughout Johnson's White House: Hugh Sidey, "Gadgetized White House Pleases the POTUS," *Life,* August 26, 1966, p. 38B.

142   "Johnson was the first Information Age president": Tom Johnson, interview by author, November 19, 1997.

142   "He was not the most sophisticated man": Miller, *Lyndon,* p. 539.

142   "he was damn crude—always scratching his crotch": Miller, *Lyndon,* p. 541.

143   "He did disgusting things": Reedy, *Lyndon B. Johnson: A Memoir,* p. 157.

143 "I stood at the bathroom door while he took a crap": Miller, *Lyndon,* p. 540.

143 "one of the delicate Kennedyites": Doris Kearns Goodwin, *Lyndon Johnson and the American Dream,* p. 241.

143 "You went with him into the bathroom": George Christian, interview by author, June 24, 1997.

143 Johnson's morning work schedule: ibid.

143 Presidential enema story: Miller, *Lyndon,* pp. 539, 540.

144 "Ford's economics is the worst thing": ibid., p. 541.

144 Details of Johnson recording system: Harry Middleton, LBJL director; Mary Knill, Linda Hanson, Regina Greenwell, LBJL archivists; John Powers, Nixon Project archivist, interviews by author, 1997 and 1998; Powers Paper; LBJL recordings finding aids.

Johnson's use of electronic recordings in the White House gradually tapered off through his years in the Oval Office. In his first weeks as president, he recorded heavily, recording over 800 phone calls in just 39 days. In 1964, he kept up the hectic pace, recording over 4,600 conversations. Starting in 1965, his recordings dropped off abruptly: that year he taped only 1,780 conversations. In 1966, the number was down to 1,240, and by 1967 it was down to 350, increasing a bit the following year to about 560.

It is not clear why the recordings dropped off, but it is known that LBJ's secretaries disliked the major diversion of energy required by having to make transcripts. According to National Archives presidential recordings expert John Powers, "Members of the White House staff suggested that Johnson, in constant fear of leaks during his second term, was afraid that the existence of the Dictaphone system would become known. Therefore, he used the system infrequently and carefully." In January 1968, Johnson had the White House Communications Agency (WHCA) install a reel-to-reel recording system in the Cabinet Room and the small lounge office next to the Oval Office otherwise known as the "Little Study," or "Little Lounge," originally built for Eisenhower's post-heart attack naps and now used by LBJ for intimate, close-quarters meetings. In the Little Lounge, two microphones were installed, and a switch was built onto a control panel that also summoned aides and refreshments. In the Cabinet Room, tiny lapel pin-sized microphones were drilled into the bottom of the long desk, which were fed into a mixer in the middle of the bottom of the table. The ON/OFF switch was on a control panel within LBJ's reach, like the one in the Little Study. Wires from the mixer were drilled through the Cabinet Room floor down into to the West Wing basement, into recorders located in a locked storage cabinet controlled by WHCA. Johnson ordered the White House Dictaphone systems and the recording system in the Little Lounge removed at the end of his term, and when he left the White House in January 1969 he took his tapes with him.

LBJ assistant Mildred Stegall reported that LBJ considered the recordings very sensitive material. "On average of once every six months from 1964 until his death he would ask me for my assurance that this material was in a secure vault. He repeatedly stressed that no one was to have access to it." Johnson also used the transcripts in preparing his presidential memoirs.

The existence of LBJ recordings was first publicly confirmed in mid-1973, in the wake of national interest in Nixon's taping system. On January 29 of that year Stegall turned over the collection of recordings and some accompanying transcripts to the director of the LBJ Library, Harry Middleton, with the stipulation that President Johnson, who had died seven days earlier, wanted the material to be closed for research until fifty years after his death.

In 1992, in response to the President John F. Kennedy Assassination Records Collection Act of 1992, the Johnson Library prepared a special opening of recordings and transcripts of telephone conversations, consisting of the recordings and transcripts of all recorded phone calls from November 22, 1963, through December 31, 1963, as well as conversations from selected later periods in the Johnson administration. This series was opened in installments from September 30, 1993, through April 15, 1994.

Now that LBJ's fifty-year seal was broken, LBJ Library Director Middleton decided to continue to open the material. At this time, he decided he had the authority to break the seal and start processing the collection for public release, believing it was "historically very important," and he informed Mrs. Johnson of his plan. In 1993, the National Security Council approved Secretary of Defense Robert McNamara's request for access to LBJ recordings on Vietnam in preparation for his book, *In Retrospect*. Five excerpts from these recordings were used in McNamara's book and were released in mid-1995. In 1996, in response to a research request for this book, three of Johnson's Cabinet Room recordings from 1968 were opened up (since corresponding transcripts had already been published in the State Department's *Foreign Relations of the U.S.* series), covering Vietnam peace talks and the Russian invasion of Czechoslovakia, including meetings with Secretary of Defense Clark Clifford, Secretary of State Dean Rusk, Republican leader Everett Dirksen, and Soviet ambassador to the U.S. Anatoly Dobrynin.

In 1997, the Johnson Library made two major new releases of Johnson recordings, now in chronological installments from early 1964 to August 1964. These conversations covered a wide variety of topics, including congressional action on Great Society legislation; foreign policy developments, particularly in Vietnam and Laos; the beginnings of the 1964 presidential campaign and the murder of three civil rights workers in Mississippi. An additional release, mainly of September/October 1964 tapes, occurred in September 1998.

Sometimes, Johnson made veiled references to taping on the tapes themselves. During a 1964 conversation with FBI Director J. Edgar Hoover, Johnson playfully needles, "Edgar, I don't hear you well. What's the matter, you got this phone tapped?" Hoover muttered unconvincingly, "I should say not, Mr. President." During a March 9, 1964, phone call to his friend and New York attorney Edwin Weisl Sr., Johnson complained, "It sounds like you're way down in the walls somewhere." Weisl: "Can you hear me now?" Johnson: "Yeah, we must have four or five lines tapped here." According to LBJ aide Tom Johnson, "Taping was suspected, but not known, by 95 percent of the staff."

144 "He buzzed us and we opened the door": *The Kansas City Times*, September 13, 1982, p. 1.

145 "LBJ did not like to commit himself to writing": David C. Humphrey, "Searching for LBJ at the Johnson Library," The SHAFR Newsletter, June 1989.

146 "Lyndon got me by the lapels": Barber, The Presidential Character, p. 79.

146 "half Johnson": Richard Tanner Johnson, Managing the White House (New York: Harper & Row, 1974), p. 172.

146 "Telling Lyndon Johnson no": Hugh Sidey, "Two Years in Office: Measure of the Man," Life, December 3, 1965, p. 56.

146 "That man will twist your arm off": Orville Freeman quoting Richard Russell, Kenneth Thompson, ed., The Johnson Presidency: Twenty Intimate Perspectives of Lyndon Johnson (University of Virginia: The Miller Center, 1986), p. 143.

149 "a boxer's bolo punch": Harry McPherson OH, p. 17.

149 "an almost hypnotic experience": Califano, Triumph and Tragedy, p. 55.

149 "He has fifty reasons": Harry McPherson OH, p. 27.

150 "Johnson was a man-eater": Joseph Califano, interview by author, July 10, 1997.

150 "an incredibly hard worker": Tom Johnson, interview by author, November 19, 1997.

150 Johnson's work habits"; "It's like starting a new day": Goldman, The Tragedy of Lyndon Johnson, pp. 21, 22.

150 "An eight-hour-a-day man": Vaughn Davis Bornet, The Presidency of Lyndon B. Johnson (Lawrence: University Press of Kansas, 1983), p. 38.

150 "his greatest strength was tenacity": Jack Valenti, A&E Fleisher interview, October 15, 1996.

150 "Lyndon has a clock inside him": Paul F. Boller, Jr., Presidential Anecdotes (New York: Oxford University Press, 1981), p. 309.

150 "He yells at his staff": Guthman and Shulman, Robert Kennedy In His Own Words, p. 412.

150 "He would heap praise": Frank Kessler, The Dilemmas of Presidential Leadership: Of Caretakers and Kings (Englewood Cliffs, NJ: Prentice-Hall, 1982), p. 63.

151 "He was probably on the edge": David Bell, interview by author, June 12, 1996.

151 "I want loyalty": David Halberstam, The Best and the Brightest (New York: Random House, 1972), p. 434.

151 "I attribute this to a hangover": George Reedy OH, p. 43.

151 "no sense of fun, no élan": Harry McPherson OH, p. 30.

151 He inspected White House motor pool, staffers desks, thermometers, party lists: Goldman, The Tragedy of Lyndon Johnson, pp. 22, 23.

151 Interrogated officials on crotch sizes in Air Force uniforms: Hugh Sidey, "Beyond the Facts and Figures" Time, February 2, 1976, p. 11.

151 "He had a tendency to get involved": George Christian, interview by author, June 24, 1997.

151 LBJ devoted attention to "everything in the White House": Goldman, The Tragedy of Lyndon Johnson, p. 22.

151 "it wasn't that he was overly concerned with details": George Reedy OH, p. 6.

151 "was a smothering, all-encompassing process": David Bell, interview by author, June 12, 1996.

152 "His executive style was aimed at": George Christian, interview by author, June 24, 1997.

152 "Kennedy was a back-row man": James Reston, "The Girl Who Settles Down With the Old Beau," *NYT*, March 20, 1964, p. 43.

152 "If a senator didn't want to do something": Thompson, *The Johnson Presidency*, p. 275.

152 "Dick, you've got to get out of my way": Michael Oreskes, "Civil Rights Act Leaves Deep Mark on the American Political Landscape," *NYT*, July 2, 1989, p. 16.

152 "write me the goddamnest, toughest voting rights act": Miller, *Lyndon*, p. 371.

153 "You know, we could have beaten John Kennedy on civil rights": Orville Freeman quoting Richard Russell, Thompson, *The Johnson Presidency*, p. 143.

153 "the greatest outpouring of creative legislation": David E. Rosenbaum, "20 Years Later, the Great Society Flourishes," *NYT*, April 17, 1985, p. 23.

153 "I think Johnson was a superb executive": Joseph Califano, interview by author, July 10, 1997.

153 93 percent success rate with Congress in 1965 was the highest ever measured for any president: *Congressional Quarterly*, December 19, 1992, p. 3896.

153 70 percent approval rating: "At the Perigee," *Time*, July 9, 1965, p. 19.

153 "I don't know what the fuck to do": Lloyd C. Gardner, *Pay Any Price: Lyndon Johnson and the Wars for Vietnam* (Chicago: Ivan R. Dee, 1965), p. 221.

153 Fewer than 100 American advisers had been killed in combat: Lester Sobel, ed., *South Vietnam: U.S.-Communist Confrontation in Southeast Asia, 1961–1965* (1966), p. 78.

153 "It's going to be hell in a hand basket": Gardner, *Pay Any Price,* p. 95.

153 "I feel like I just grabbed a big juicy worm": ibid.

155 "Bomb, bomb, bomb": Halberstam, *The Best and the Brightest*, p. 684.

155 "Vietnam is like being in a plane without a parachute": Gardner, *Pay Any Price*, p. 221.

157 Quotes from July 21, 1965, meeting: U.S. State Department, *Foreign Relations of the United States, 1964–1968* (Washington, DC: U.S. Government Printing Office, 1996), p. 189–95.

157 LBJ "regarded Bob McNamara as the Messiah": George Reedy OH, p. 33.

157 "Strangely enough, an official devil's advocate": Lewis J. Paper, *The Promise and the Performance: The Leadership of John F. Kennedy* (New York: Crown, 1975), p. 116.

157 "If only I could get Ho in a room with me": Richard Goodwin, "The War Within," *NYT*, August 21, 1988, p. 48.

158 "That group never leaked a single note": Kearns Goodwin, *Lyndon Johnson and the American Dream*, p. 320.

158 "The only men present": Frank Kessler, *The Dilemmas of Presidential Leadership: Of Caretakers and Kings* (Englewood Cliffs, NJ: Prentice-Hall, 1982), p. 106.

158　"He was impatient about the inability": Dean Rusk OH, p. 8.

158　"A typical discussion of the Tuesday lunch": Kearns Goodwin, *Lyndon Johnson and the American Dream,* p. 321.

158　"With but rare exceptions": Janis, *Groupthink,* p. 103.

158　"I can't trust anybody": D. Jablow Hershman, Julian Lieb, "Does the White House Need a Shrink?" *WP,* February 2, 1989, p. C3.

158　"He wanted to get out of Vietnam in the worst way": A&E Fleisher interview with Jack Valenti.

158　"I never saw a leader": Tom Johnson, interview by author, November 19, 1997.

159　"not bomb an outhouse": Colin Campbell and Bert Rockman, *The Bush Presidency: First Appraisals* (Chatham, NJ: Chatam House Publishers, 1991), p. 116.

159　LBJ nighttime visits to Situation Room: Richard Goodwin, *Remembering America* (Boston: Little, Brown, 1988), p. 415.

159　"We had stopped the bombing, not once or twice": Johnson, *The Vantage Point,* p. 241.

159　Tet Offensive detail: Townsend Hoopes, *The Limits of Intervention: An Inside Account of How the Johnson Policy of Escalation in Vietnam Was Reversed* (New York: David McKay, 1969), pp. 139–41, 214–18; Irving Bernstein, *Guns or Butter: The Presidency of Lyndon Johnson* (New York: Oxford University Press, 1996), pp. 474, 475.

159　"After Tet, I assure you": Clark Clifford OH, p. 3.

160　Clifford "was the only person who had grasped the fact"; "He spoke in soothing tones": George E. Reedy, *Twilight of the Presidency* (New York: World Publishing, 1970), p. 149.

160　President Johnson and senior advisers meeting on Vietnam: "Notes of the president's meeting with senior foreign policy advisers, the Cabinet Room, 5:33 P.M., March 4, 1968," LBJL, declassified October 12, 1994. According to the LBJ Library, this meeting was not recorded.

By now, Johnson had supplemented his extensive electronic recording operation by including a manual note-taker in his meetings: press assistant Tom Johnson, who took extensive notes of almost 200 Johnson White House meetings from October 1967 to January 1969, including meetings with Alabama Governor George Wallace and Soviet Premier Alexi Kosygin. Johnson also took notes for most of the key Vietnam meetings. (Unlike Johnson's hidden recorders, Tom Johnson was kept in full view of the participants.) According to Tom Johnson, his notes "were intended as summaries, not word-for-word transcripts, not for historians. They were for LBJ's eyes only and were never circulated to anybody but LBJ."

The president wanted a record of important meetings turned around quickly, so Tom Johnson, who said he was "not a skilled note-taker," used a note-taking system called "speedwriting," which condensed words and phrases to catch the most significant passages. When the meetings were over, the young Johnson would race to his office for his secretary to type up the notes fast enough to make the deadline for the president's night reading the same evening. The notes were then filed away in a classified safe. Tom Johnson, interview by author, November 19, 1997. Notes of the March 4, 1968 meeting are courtesy of Tom Johnson.

164 "We can no longer do the job": Tom Johnson's notes of March 26, 1968 meeting, LBJL.

164 On April 3, 1968, Robert F. Kennedy and Theodore Sorensen met with Johnson in the Cabinet Room to discuss Kennedy's plans to campaign for the presidency. The story was later told by Richard Nixon (in a 1983 videotaped interview with Frank Gannon, for example) and others that LBJ tried to tape the meeting, in part to preserve his delight in telling arch-enemy Bobby that he wasn't going to endorse him. When Johnson asked to hear the tape, an ashen-faced Jack Albright of the White House Communications Agency told Johnson that the tape was completely unintelligible—instead of conversation, there was a steady buzzing noise for the duration of the conference. Kennedy apparently had brought a briefcase into the Cabinet Room and placed it at his feet. Albright told Johnson that RFK probably scrambled the recording of the meeting "with an electronic buzzer" or jamming device.

164 "What Lyndon Johnson was about": Califano, *Triumph and Tragedy*, p. 12.

165 Results of Great Society: *NYT,* April 17, 1985, p. A23. Conservative analyst Charles Murray observed that social spending took the biggest jump not in Johnson's years, but during the expansion of Great Society programs during the Nixon administration, when welfare and disability eligibility rules were relaxed and funding for the Food Stamp, Medicaid, and Social Security programs was dramatically increased.

165 "I made all the mistakes that one can make"; "The fella that has power": CBS Television broadcast, "Five Presidents on the Presidency," 1973.

165 "Men are moved by love and fear": Califano, *Triumph and Tragedy*, p. 104.

165 "This mastery of debate technique actually hurt him": Reedy OH, p. 47.

165 "I can't stand the bastard": Goodwin, *Remembering America,* p. 415.

166 "He wanted to bring America": Tom Johnson, interview by author, November 19, 1997.

166 "everybody'd been so scared": C. Douglas Dillon, interview by author, March 17, 1997.

CHAPTER 6

RICHARD M. NIXON: THE STRATEGIC EXECUTIVE

167 "The whole hopes of the whole goddamn world": Oval Office tape recording, April 27, 1973.

167 The Brookings break-in tape, along with over 95 percent of Nixon's secret recordings, was blocked from public release by a twenty-year, multimillion dollar legal campaign by Nixon. The tape was released only in late 1996, thanks to the efforts of University of Wisconsin history professor Stanley Kutler, who waged a long legal struggle of his own to get the tapes opened to the public.

Nixon recorded a grand total of just over 3,700 hours on his taping systems. (The often quoted total of 4,000 hours is a "ballpark" number.) This figure excludes recordings of dictation, memoranda, and diary entries made on other Dictaphones. Nixon's Dictaphone diary recordings are held by the private Nixon Library and are closed for research. The paper component of much of Nixon's Dictaphone work dictation and memoranda has been opened over the years by the National Archives, but the recordings themselves, while on file, are closed and cannot be listened to.

Of the 3,700 hours of Nixon tapes, the original "Watergate Special Prosecution Force" segment is 60 hours. In 1993, 3 hours of "Abuse of Governmental Power" recordings were opened. In 1996, another 201 hours of "Abuse of Power" recordings were opened. In 1997, 154 hours of Cabinet Room tapes were opened. The National Archives has returned 830 hours of recordings to the Nixon estate, by law, as personal material. The tapes can only be listened to at the National Archives in College Park, MD. The National Archives is now processing the remaining tapes. Under the terms of an agreement between the Nixon estate and the government that ended the suit by Kutler, most of these tapes will be made public in the near future.

Basic source materials consulted for the Nixon Watergate and "abuse of power" tapes quoted in this chapter are the source tapes themselves, listened to at the National Archives in College Park, MD, plus Nixon's April/May and August 1974 releases of transcripts to Congress and the public; *Time* magazine and Senate investigating committee transcripts of the original tape releases; *WP, NYT,* and CNN coverage in 1996 and 1997 on the newest tape releases; and Stanley Kutler's 1997 book, *Abuse of Power: The New Nixon Tapes* (New York: Free Press, 1997). A good source for background on the history of the tapes is Seymour M. Hersh's article in *The New Yorker,* December 14, 1992, p. 7. A rare essay defending Nixon's tapes appeared in *American Spectator,* March 1998, authored by Nixon Library Executive Director John Taylor.

Perhaps the best summary of the contents of the murky, sometimes impenetrable recordings was offered by Nixon's attorney Leonard Garment when he explained that the tapes are "all in code." "Essentially," said Garment, "what Nixon was trying to do was to bring Haldeman and Ehrlichman to the execution chamber without having to give them sedatives or tie their hands. He knew just what he was doing; he had that capacity for that brain of his to work on two, or three, or four levels." Unless Nixon could "get them to go quietly, peacefully and loyally," he concluded, "they would kill him" (Gerald S. and Deborah H. Strober, *Nixon: An Oral History of His Presidency* [New York: HarperCollins, 1996], p. 400).

167   "I say things in this office that I don't want even Rose to hear": H. R. Haldeman and Joseph DiMona, *The Ends of Power* (New York: Times Books, 1978), p. 196.

168   Details of installation of Nixon taping system, operation, locations of microphones: Powers paper, Nixon Project finding aids, Alexander Butterfield, interview by author, November 7, 1996.

168   "When you get into the White House": Haldeman, *The Ends of Power,* p. 80.

168   "Johnson had installed electronic facilities": ibid., p. 80.

168   "We'll get that goddam bugging crap out of the White House": ibid., p. 81.

168   "Dick, they are voice activated": Monica Crowley, *Nixon Off the Record* (New York: Random House, 1996), p. 17.

168   Nixon claimed to discover a mike under bed: Richard Nixon, interview by Frank Gannon, 1983.

168   "I discovered a mass of wires": Richard M. Nixon, *RN: The Memoirs of Richard Nixon* (New York: Grosset & Dunlap, 1978), p. 368.

168   Nixon ordering LBJ's bugs out of the White House: Jonathan Aitken, *Nixon: A Life* (London: Weidenfeld and Nicolson, 1993), p. 495; Walter Isaacson, *Kissinger: A Biography* (New York: Simon & Schuster, 1992), p. 160.

169   LBJ told Nixon he shouldn't have removed taping capability: Aitken, *Nixon: A Life*, p. 496.

169   Experiments with note-takers: ibid., p. 497.

169   "a final attempt"; "Henry's view": Haldeman, *The Ends of Power*, p. 194.

169   "It was a high price to pay for insurance": Isaacson, *Kissinger: A Biography* pp. 494, 495.

169   "As impossible as it must seem now": Nixon, *RN*, p. 900.

170   "I have no such recollection"; "I don't think Haldeman": "Tapes Show Nixon Ordering Theft of Files," *NYT*, November 22, 1996, p. 16, quoting *San Fransisco Examiner* article, November 21, 1996.

170   nighttime visit by unidentified men to Brookings Institution: Daniel Schorr, *NPR Weekend Sunday*, January 12, 1997.

170   "Nixon was the weirdest man": "Quotation of the Day," February 17, 1978, Section 2, p. 1.

170   *"had the responsibility not to carry out orders"*: William Safire, *Before the Fall: An Inside View of the Pre-Watergate White House* (Garden City, NY: Doubleday, 1975), p. 285.

170   Asked his wife to arrange for two Dictaphones: Memo from Richard Nixon to Mrs. Nixon, January 25, 1969, PPF, Memoranda from the President, 1969–1974, NPMP.

170   "P is all of a sudden enamored with use of the Dictaphone": H. R. Haldeman, *The Haldeman Diaries: Inside the Nixon White House* (New York: G. P. Putnam's Sons, 1994), p. 8.

171   Dictabelt Memo from Richard Nixon to H. R. Haldeman, June 16, 1969: PPF, Memoranda from the President, 1969–1974, NPMP.

171   "With Nixon you never knew": Henry Kissinger, interview by author, May 7, 1997.

171   "extremely complex personality": Brent Scowcroft, interview by author, November 12, 1996.

171   "orders are not always orders": Safire, *Before the Fall*, p. 286.

171   "He agonized over every decision": Alexander Haig, interview by author, November 25, 1996.

171   "He has always needed people around him": Raymond Price, *With Nixon* (New York: Viking, 1977), p. 29.

172   "Put a twenty-four-hour surveillance on that bastard": Haldeman, *Ends of Power*, pp. 88, 89.

172   "Nixon's indirect method of operation": Henry A. Kissinger, *Years of Upheaval* (Boston: Little, Brown, 1982), p. 111.

172   "fire everybody in Laos"; "Oh hell, Bill, you know me better": Safire, *Before the Fall*, p. 286.

172   "Cut 'em by half"; "It was not intended that he be taken literally": James Schlesinger, interview by author, September 22, 1996.

172   "loyalty was demanded of all": Stanley I. Kutler, *The Wars of Watergate: The Last Crisis of Richard Nixon* (New York: Knopf, 1990), p. 86.

172   "With Nixon, toughness was an article of faith": Robert McFarlane, interview by author, June 30, 1997.

172   "What starts the process": Tom Wicker, *One of Us: Richard Nixon and the American Dream* (New York: Random House, 1995), p. 9.

173   "Over the years, Nixon observed politics very closely": Strober and Strober, *Nixon: An Oral History of His Presidency*, p. 56.

174   "The taps of National Security aides": Kutler, *The Wars of Watergate*, p.121.

174   "I won't be the first president to lose a war": Stephen E. Ambrose, *Nixon*, vol. 2, *The Triumph of a Politician, 1962–1972* (New York: Simon & Schuster, 1989), p. 388.

177   "In between his official projects": Haldeman, *Ends of Power*, p. 59.

178   "The White House staff's attitude": Kissinger, *Years of Upheaval*, p. 97.

179   Nixon routine: Strober and Strober, *Nixon: An Oral History of His Presidency*, pp. 74, 75; Juan Cameron, "Richard Nixon's Very Personal White House," *Fortune*, July 1970, pp. 57–59.

179   "I don't get bogged down in any part of the news": Jerrold Schechter, "The Private World of Richard Nixon," *Time*, January 3, 1972, pp. 18, 19.

179   Nixon News Summary: "Inside the White House: How Nixon Runs Things Now," *USNWR*, April 23, 1973, p. 39.

179   "He governed through notes": Ambrose, *Nixon*, vol. 2, *The Triumph of a Politician*, p. 410.

179   "Every president needs a son-of-a-bitch": ibid.

179   "My father wanted Bob Haldeman": Kutler, *The Wars of Watergate*, p. 84.

179   "From now on, Haldeman is the lord high executioner": Haldeman, *The Haldeman Diaries*, p. 7.

180   "Give this to your wife or your secretary": Haldeman, *Ends of Power*, pp. 70, 71.

180   "Some like to bat ideas around with aides over lunch": Richard M. Nixon, *In the Arena: A Memoir of Victory, Defeat and Renewal* (New York: Simon & Schuster, 1990) p. 156.

180   "as the senior partner of a law firm": Jack Anderson, "Isolation of Nixon Is Being Increased," *WP*, June 24, 1970, p. D15.

180   EOB routine: *Time*, January 3, 1972, pp. 18, 19; Price, *With Nixon*, p. 70.

180   "All you need is a competent Cabinet": Forrest McDonald, *The American Presidency: An Intellectual History* (Lawrence: University Press of Kansas, 1994), p. 338.

180   Rug became spotted with burns: Sarah Booth Conroy, "Habitation Speculation: Will There Be Presidential Talk?" *WP*, November 8, 1992, F1.

180   "He was very shy": Gerald R. Ford, *A Time to Heal: The Autobiography of Gerald R. Ford* (New York: Harper & Row, 1979), p. 35.

180   "Nixon could be very decisive": Henry A. Kissinger, *White House Years* (Boston: Little, Brown, 1979), p. 45.

181   "Nixon had a bewildering combination": Haldeman, *The Ends of Power*, p. 70.

181   "only a person like that": Donald Rumsfeld, interview by author, April 23, 1997.

181   Congressmen would blurt out proposals: "How Nixon's White House Works," *Time*, June 8, 1970, p. 16.

181   Nixon had only three direct lines on his phone: ibid, p. 18.

181   Only four Cabinet officers had direct phone access: ibid.

182   Rogers and Laird were rarely seeing the president, and Nixon was largely running the government through just four men: Ambrose, *Nixon: The Triumph of a Politician*, p. 410.

182   "For the president to isolate himself": *Time*, June 8, 1970, p. 19.

182   "ineffably boring": Wicker, *One of Us*, p. 396.

182   "For one thing, I would disperse power": Earl Mazo and Stephen Hess, *Nixon: A Political Portrait* (New York: Harper & Row, 1968), pp. 314–15.

182   "I would operate differently from President Johnson": Stephen Hess, *Organizing the Presidency* (Washington, DC: Brookings Institution, 1976), pp. 105–6.

182   "Time is a person's most important possession": Nixon, *In the Arena*, p. 121.

182   "Main problem is how he'd use the time": Haldeman, *The Haldeman Diaries*, p. 131.

182   "was mentally overcharged": Maurice Stans, interview by author, April 23, 1997.

183   "tended to brood excessively": James Schlesinger, interview by author, September 22, 1996.

183   "Another all-Watergate day": Haldeman, *Haldeman Diaries*, p. 641.

183   "Today was another": ibid., p. 642.

183   "Another day all shot": ibid., p. 661.

183   "Even a labor-intensive president": Nixon, *In the Arena*, p. 126.

183   April 15, 1973 encounter between Nixon and Dean, Dean's suspicion of taping system: Sam J. Ervin, Jr., *The Whole Truth: The Watergate Conspiracy* (New York: Random House, 1980), pp. 186, 187.

184   "for every remark that I probably shouldn't have made": Monica Crowley, *Nixon in Winter* (New York: Random House, 1998), p. 288.

184   March 21 tape triggered Watergate grand jury to recommend Nixon's indictment: *Time*, May 20, 1974, p. 31. Special prosecutor Leon Jaworski talked them out of it, arguing that he wasn't sure if a sitting president could be indicted.

190    $75,000 delivered to Hunt's lawyer: "Further Tales from the Transcripts," *Time*, May 20, 1974, p. 32. Tapes released in 1996 indicate Nixon knew of

payments to Hunt as early as August 1, 1972. See Stanley Kutler, *Abuse of Power*, p. xvi.

191 "it would have to be an accident": Kutler, *The Wars of Watergate*, p. 431.

191 Congressional reactions: Kutler, *The Wars of Watergate*, p. 525; Stephen E. Ambrose, *Nixon*, vol. 3, *Ruin and Recovery, 1973–1990* (New York: Simon & Schuster, 1991), p. 335; Ervin, *The Whole Truth*, p. 279.

191 "don't try to be cute or cover up": Ambrose, *Nixon*, vol. 2, *The Triumph of a Politician*, pp. 576, 577.

191 Even the seemingly irrefutable "smoking gun" tape was partially contradicted by yet another Nixon tape, this one a Dictabelt recorded in the study at his Western White House on July 6, 1972, just two weeks later. That day Nixon spoke by phone to acting FBI director Pat Gray, who complained about White House attempts to frustrate the FBI inquiry into Watergate. Later, Nixon asserted, "I told Gray emphatically to go forward with his full investigation," after deciding no national security matter was at stake. After the conversation with Gray, Nixon then dictated a July 6 diary entry in which he reported ordering complete White House cooperation with the FBI inquiry: "Certainly the best thing to do is to have the investigation pursued to its normal conclusion." Nixon concluded, "As I emphasized to Ehrlichman and Haldeman, we must do nothing to indicate to Pat Gray or to the CIA that the White House is trying to suppress an investigation. On the other hand we must cooperate with the investigation all the way along the line." No tape of the Gray call has surfaced: as Nixon's bad luck would have it, the San Clemente phones were not tapped.

When Nixon released the contents of the "smoking gun" tape, he tried to include details of the Gray call in his statement, but Nixon's lawyers threatened to walk off the job if he did. The diary tape has played continuously as part of an exhibit at the private Nixon Library at Yorba Linda, CA, to prove Nixon's innocence in the cover-up. What it really demonstrates is Nixon's familiar executive habit of issuing contradictory instructions. See Kutler, *The Wars of Watergate*, p. 537; and Nixon, *RN*, pp. 650, 651.

193 "I brought myself down": Richard Nixon interview by David Frost, 1977.

194 "You don't capture people": Haldeman, *The Haldeman Diaries*, p. 233.

194 "Most of us have hidden flaws": Gerald R. Ford, *A Time to Heal*, p. 35.

194 "Nixon was so much more than Watergate": Joan Hoff-Wilson, *Nixon Reconsidered* (New York: Basic Books, 1994), p. 346.

194 "He was a bold, innovative": Ambrose, *Nixon: The Triumph of a Politician*, p. 653.

195 "Kissinger and Nixon both had degrees of paranoia": Theodore Draper, "Little Heinz and Big Henry," review of Walter Isaacson's book *Kissinger*, *NYT Book Review*, September 6, 1992, p. 19.

195 "By 1974 only 8 percent of black children in the South": Nixon, *RN*, p. 443.

195 "viewed Congress in much the same way": Elizabeth Frost, ed., *The Bully Pulpit: Quotations from America's Presidents* (New York: Facts on File, 1988), p. 41

195 "How can one evaluate such an idiosyncratic president": Arthur M.

Schlesinger, Jr., "The Ultimate Approval Rating," *NYT Magazine*, December 15, 1996, p. 48.

195   "He was the most dishonest individual I ever met": Barry M. Goldwater with Jack Casserly, *Goldwater* (New York: Doubleday, 1988), p. 255.

196   "a man of remarkable intelligence": Tom Wicker, "Nixon Revisited," *NYT*, November 23, 1987, p. A23.

196   "first, because I am an executive": Richard M. Nixon, *Submission of Recorded Conversations to the Judiciary of the House of Representatives by Richard Nixon*, April 30, 1974, p. 203.

CHAPTER 7
GERALD R. FORD: THE COLLEGIAL EXECUTIVE

197   "Rhetoric is cheap": "I Don't Expect to Lose," interview, *Time*, January 26, 1976, p. 12.

197   Background of Sinai accords: John Robert Greene, *The Presidency of Gerald R. Ford* (Lawrence: University Press of Kansas, 1995), pp. 154, 155.

198   "Coming on the heels of Watergate": *Los Angeles Times*, October 29, 1979, p. 14.

198   "Ford issued strict orders": Robert T. Hartmann, *Palace Politics: An Insider's Account of the Ford Years* (New York: McGraw-Hill, 1980), p. 199.

198   "President Ford was not a great intellect": Kenneth W. Thompson, ed., *The Ford Presidency: Twenty-two Intimate Perspectives of Gerald R. Ford* (University of Virginia: The Miller Center, 1988), p. 310.

199   Transcripts of these recordings were published in Ford's Presidential Papers, 1975, pp. 1279–81.

201   Kissinger quotes on Ford: Henry A. Kissinger, interview by author, May 7, 1997.

201   "antithesis"; "He had a very straightforward personality": Brent Scowcroft, interview by author, November 12, 1996.

202   Morning of August 9, 1974: "Enter Ford," *Time*, August 19, 1974, p 13A.

202   "There is a basic trust": Israel Shenker, "Ford a Traditionalist Who Believes in Home, Family, Hard Work and Patriotism," *NYT*, August 9, 1974, p. 8.

202   "It's very difficult to think of negatives": ibid.

202   "so dumb he can't fart and chew gum": Richard Reeves, *A Ford, Not a Lincoln* (New York: Harcourt Brace Jovanovich, 1975), p. 25.

202   "God, but he is good at this": Hugh Sidey, "Beyond the Facts and Figures," *Time*, February 2, 1976, p. 11.

202   "Ford possessed a vast amount": Ron Nessen, *It Sure Looks Different from the Inside* (Chicago: Playboy Press, 1978), p. 164.

203   Ford's first days in the Oval Office: *Time*, August 19, 1974, pp. 13, 14.

203   Ford and Hartmann in the Cabinet Room: Robert Hartmann, interview by author, September 5, 1996.

203   Ford's Oval Office decorations: Hugh Sidey, "Subtle Changes in the Oval Office," *Time*, January 13, 1975, p. 16.

203 Ford routine, "eating and sleeping are a waste of time": John R. Hersey, *Aspects of the Presidency* (New Haven: Ticknor & Fields, 1980), pp. 178, 202; additional detail from Ron Nessen, interview by author, April 25, 1997.

203 "Unlike Nixon, he didn't pretend": James Reston, "Nobody's Mad at Jerry," *NYT*, March 9, 1975, p. 17.

203 "preferred to have contact with people": Bernard J. Firestone and Alexej Ugrinsky, eds., *Gerald R. Ford and the Politics of Post-Watergate America* (Westport, CT: Greenwood Press, 1993), p. 233.

204 Air force moving Nixon materials out of White House: Benton Becker, interview by author, June 1, 1996; James Cannon, *Time and Chance: Gerald Ford's Appointment with History* (New York: HarperCollins, 1994), p. 365.

204 Story of Nixon microphones in Ford Oval Office: Gerald Ford, A&E Fleisher interview; Benton Becker, A&E Fleisher interview and interview by author, June 1, 1996; Robert Hartmann, interview by author, September 5, 1996; Hartmann, *Palace Politics*, pp. 198, 199.

205 "I wanted to be personally involved": Firestone and Ugrinsky, *Gerald R. Ford and the Politics of Post-Watergate America*, p. 200.

205 "President Ford is much faster": John J. Casserly, *The Ford White House: The Diary of a Speechwriter* (Boulder: Colorado Associated University Press, 1977), p. 48.

205 "Nixon just focused on the general principles": Henry A. Kissinger, interview by author, May 7, 1997.

205 "was a strange mixture of leftover Nixon people": Ron Nessen, interview by author, April 25, 1997.

205 Grand Rapids Rotarians: Thompson, ed., *The Ford Presidency*, p. 63.

206 "Everyone wanted a portion of my time": Ford, *A Time to Heal*, p. 186.

206 "For a time, after Haig departed, the White House was close to anarchy": Nessen, *It Sure Looks Different from the Inside*, p. 74.

206 "Eventually, we got away from that type of confusion": Thompson, *The Ford Presidency*, p. 64.

206 "He arrived as the instant president": Donald Rumsfeld, interview by author, April 23, 1997.

206 "the person who is drawn to a career": Robert Hartmann, interview by author, September 5, 1996.

206 "I have never seen anyone more immune": Casserly, *The Ford White House*, p. 37.

206 Approval rating plunged from 71 to 49 percent: *Gerald R. Ford: Presidential Prespectives from the National Archives*, GRFL, p. 6.

206 "I thought there would be greater forgiveness": ibid.

206 "It wasn't hard to convince him": Firestone and Ugrinsky, eds., *Gerald R. Ford and the Politics of Post-Watergate America*, p. 236.

207 "Ford had a great executive talent": Ron Nessen, interview by author, April 25, 1997.

207 "Of the eight men in George Bush's war council": Hugh Sidey, "Ford's Forgotten Legacy," *Time*, March 25, 1991, p. 20.

207 Ford restored the Cabinet system: Bradley D. Nash with Milton S. Eisen-

hower, R. Gordon Hoxie, and William C. Spragens, *Organizing and Staffing the Presidency* (New York: Center for the Study of the Presidency, 1980), p. 50.

207 "I've been criticized": Reeves, *A Ford, Not a Lincoln,* p. 75.

207 "With Nixon, you had to try to save him": Nessen, *It Sure Looks Different from the Inside,* p. 162.

207 "How can you get mad at a president": Nash et al., *Organizing and Staffing the Presidency,* p. 52.

207 "Don't push people around": Casserly, *The Ford White House,* p. 4.

207 "You write simply": ibid., p. 9.

207 "He worked quietly and patiently": Thompson, ed., *The Ford Presidency,* pp. 160, 161.

207 "What does UNESCO do?": ibid., p. 161.

207 "I am probably too easygoing": Nessen, *It Sure Looks Different from the Inside,* p. 162.

207 "I'm damn sick and tired"; "Goddamn it, I don't want any more of this": Nessen, *It Sure Looks Different from the Inside,* pp. 161, 162.

208 *Mayaguez* background: author interviews with Henry Kissinger, James Schlesinger, Brent Scowcroft, Donald Rumsfeld, Ron Nessen; Ford, *A Time to Heal,* pp. 275–83; Greene, *The Presidency of Gerald R. Ford,* pp. 143–51; Nessen, *It Sure Looks Different from the Inside,* pp. 122–30; Roy Rowan, *The Four Days of* Mayaguez (New York: W.W. Norton & Co., 1975), passim. The *Mayaguez* NSC minutes reprinted here are from the Kissinger–Scowcroft Parallel File, NSC Meeting Minutes Series, GRFL.

208 "Let's look ferocious": Greene, *The Presidency of Gerald R. Ford,* p. 150.

208 "I think we should just give it to them": ibid., p. 147.

208 "Evidence also suggests": ibid., p. 144.

208 "there wasn't a dove in the place": ibid.

214 "I believe I see Caucasian faces"; "They actually had the pilot": Brent Scowcroft, interview by author, November 12, 1996.

214 "Let the boat go. Do not fire": ibid. For a slightly different version, see Ford, *Time to Heal,* p. 278.

217 Ford ended the briefing: Nessen, *It Sure Looks Different from the Inside,* p. 124.

217 "We were lucky all of the marines": Greene, *The Presidency of Gerald R. Ford,* p. 140.

218 "The bombing of the Cambodian mainland": Greene, *The Presidency of Gerald R. Ford,* p. 150.

Even though the crew was safe, the bombing of Cambodia continued through midnight. Ford wanted it to go on longer, but the last air strike he ordered never occurred, and Ford believed that Schlesinger, who had argued strenuously against the strike, canceled it on his own authority. He was right. In a September 22, 1996 interview, Schlesinger explained, "There were four air strikes. The first was canceled mistakenly by the White House. Numbers two and three went forward. The fourth one was scheduled after we received the message that they were bringing the crew of the *Mayaguez* out to our ship. I did not see any purpose to be served in simply inflicting damage after we had achieved our objective."

218 "All of a sudden": Ford, *A Time to Heal*, p. 284.

218 "During my fifteen months at the White House": Casserly, *The Ford White House*, p. 297.

218 "I am appalled by the amount of time": Nessen, *It Sure Looks Different from the Inside*, p. 148.

219 "There was never, for all thirty months he was president": Hartmann, *Palace Politics*, p. 220.

219 "internal anarchy": ibid., p. 360.

219 "The nice guy approach doesn't always work": Ron Nessen, interview by author, April 25, 1997.

219 "President Ford's candidacy is threatened": Hartmann, *Palace Politics*, p. 396.

219 "Nothing in life is more important": Ford, *A Time to Heal*, p. 50.

219 "nice person, who worked at the job": *Gerald R. Ford: Presidential Perspectives from the National Archives*, GRFL, p. 10.

220 "He saved the country": Henry A. Kissinger, interview by author, May 7, 1997. Kissinger added: "You look at a whole bunch of things he did. On the European Security Conference, he got beaten to death. He was accused of selling out Eastern Europe. Everybody today recognizes that that was the first step toward the dissolution of the satellite orbit, and even toward the collapse of the Soviet Union. There is no dispute about this anymore. When we said majority rule for Rhodesia, today—so what else is new. For twenty years, nobody could get [white Rhodesian leader] Ian Smith to do it. We got it done in a Fordian manner. That is to say, we treated Smith with respect, but told him the facts of life."

220 "he wielded the veto more often": "Nostalgia Time," *WSJ*, January 17 1980, p. 17.

220 "President Ford came into office": Donald Rumsfeld, interview by author, May 7, 1997.

220 "By the end of his presidency": Thompson, ed., *The Ford Presidency*, p. 64.

220 "His first and foremost problem": Alexander Haig, interview by author, November 25, 1996.

CHAPTER 8
JIMMY CARTER: THE TECHNOCRAT EXECUTIVE

222 "I'm an engineer at heart": Erwin C. Hargrove, *Jimmy Carter as President: Leadership and the Politics of the Public Good* (Baton Rouge: Louisiana State University Press, 1988), p. 6.

222 Camp David background: Jimmy Carter, *Keeping Faith: Memoirs of a President* (New York: Bantam Books, 1982), pp. 391–402; William B. Quandt, *Camp David: Peacemaking and Politics* (Washington, DC: Brookings Institution, 1986), pp. 238–51; Peter G. Bourne, *Jimmy Carter: A Comprehensive Biography from Plains to Postpresidency* (New York: Scribner, 1997), pp. 408–9; Jody Powell and Jack Watson, interviews by author, May 4, 1997.

222 Carter thought Begin a "psycho": Zbigniew Brzezinski, *Power and Principle:*

Memoirs of the National Security Adviser, 1977–1981 (New York: Farrar, Straus & Giroux, 1983), p. 262.

222   Brzezinski proposed bugging Israelis and Egyptians: Zbigniew Brzezinski, interview by author, April 29, 1997.

223   Carter diary tape recordings: Carter, *Keeping Faith*, p. xiii; Bourne, *Jimmy Carter*, p. 475; Steven Hochman, Carter assistant, interview by author, April 30, 1997.

223   "I told him that peace": Carter, *Keeping Faith*, p. 311.

223   "It will mean first of all an end to the relationship": Quandt, *Camp David*, pp. 238, 239.

223   "If you give me this statement": Carter, *Keeping Faith*, p. 393.

223   Carter's feverish negotiating pace: Brzezinski, *Power and Principle*, p. 264.

223   "He is driving himself mercilessly": ibid., p. 269.

223   "You cannot find two personalities more different": interview with Jack Watson, May 4, 1997.

224   "the smile and the dagger": ABC, *A Day with President Carter*, April 4, 1977.

224   "The outcome was a triumph": Brzezinski, *Power and Principle*, p. 273.

224   "played the role of draftsman": Quandt, *Camp David*, p. 258.

224   Dispute over settlement freeze: ibid., p. 238.

224   Carter's first moments in the White House: Carter, *Keeping Faith*, pp. 23, 24; Bourne, *Jimmy Carter*, p. 365.

224   "I never saw the Oval Office": Betty Glad, *Jimmy Carter: In Search of the Great White House* (New York: Norton, 1980), p. 453.

225   "The newness of each detail": Carter, *Keeping Faith*, p. 47.

225   Carter historical background: Gary M. Fink and Hugh Davis Graham, eds., *The Carter Presidency: Policy Choices in the Post–New Deal Era* (Lawrence: University Press of Kansas, 1998), p. vii.

225   Carter installed Truman items: Hugh Sidey, "Impressions of Power and Poetry," *Time*, June 20, 1977, p. 31; Hedley Donovan, "The Enigmatic President," *Time*, May 6, 1985, p. 26.

225   Carter populist touches: Bourne, *Jimmy Carter*, p. 368.

225   Carter at his desk at 5:30 A.M.: Jack Watson, interview by author, May 4, 1997.

225   Worked late in the Oval Office in his blue jeans: ABC, *A Day with President Carter*, April 4, 1977.

225   "He worked a driven, disciplined": Kenneth W. Thompson, ed. *The Carter Presidency: Fourteen Intimate Perspectives of Jimmy Carter* (University of Virginia: The Miller Center, 1990), p. 240.

225   Carter Oval Office details: *Time*, June 20, 1977, p. 31; Stanley Cloud, "With Jimmy from Dawn to Midnight," *Time*, April 18, 1977, p. 14; ABC, *A Day with President Carter*, April 4, 1977; Carter, *Keeping Faith*, p. 24; Jack Watson, interview by author, May 4, 1997.

225   Carter biographical details 1946–1975: Bradley D. Nash et al., *Organizing and Staffing the Presidency*, p. 57; Glad, *In Search of the Great White House*, p. 493; James D. Barber, *The Presidential Character* (Englewood Cliffs, NJ: Prentice-Hall, 1972), pp. 497–534; *WSJ* editorial, July 18, 1988, p.18; "Jimmy Carter: Man of the Year," *Time*, January 3, 1977, pp. 15–19.

226 "I like to run things": *Time,* January 3, 1977, p. 17.

226 "is not easy to get close to": Barber, *The Presidential Character,* p. 533.

226 "At the core of Jimmy Carter's political personality": Hargrove, *Jimmy Carter as President,* p. 171.

226 "When it came to understanding the issues of the day": Thomas "Tip" O'Neill, with William Novak, *Man of the House: The Life and Political Memoirs of Speaker Tip O'Neill* (New York: Random House, 1987), pp. 297–303.

226 "I think of all the presidents I've worked with": Thompson, ed., *The Carter Presidency,* p. 139.

226 "He could master masses of material": Hedley Donovan, *Roosevelt to Reagan: A Reporter's Encounter with Nine Presidents* (New York: Harper & Row, 1985), p. 234.

227 "a very logical, methodological": Glad, *In Search of the Great White House,* p. 483.

227 Carter worked through an issues book: ibid., p. 483.

227 Fallows on Carter scheduling tennis courts, Carter denials: "President and Fallows: One Serve, One Return," *NYT,* May 1, 1979, p. 19.

227 "Carter did schedule the tennis courts": Professor Stanly Godbold, Mississippi State University, interview by author, March 19, 1997.

227 "a classic case of no good deed goes unpunished": Jody Powell, interview by author, May 4, 1997.

227 "You can overwhelm yourself": "Ford, Looking Back, Stresses the Importance of Experience," *Washington Star,* October 8, 1978, p. D3.

228 "it's just not within the bounds of human capability": Carter, *Keeping Faith,* p. 35.

228 Carter note on margin "Why so many?": Carter comment on memo from Hugh Carter, January 21, 1977, Office of the Staff Secretary's File, informally known as the President's Handwriting File, hereinafter referred to as SSF, JECL.

228 "There are about thirty people working at Blair House": handwritten note from Carter to Hugh Carter, February 5, 1977, SSF, JECL.

228 "Explain the barber shop staffing/pay to me": handwritten note from Carter to Richard Harden, February 7, 1977, SSF, JECL.

228 Carter signed off on travel requests: Carter margin comments on Memo from Hugh Carter to President Carter, February 14, 1977, SSF; Memo from Hugh Carter to President Carter, "Travel for the Month of February," March 1, 1977; Carter margin comments on Memo from Hugh Carter to President Carter, September 1, 1977, SSF, JECL.

228 Carter authorized only dry rolls and coffee: former Carter aide who requested anonymity, interview by author.

228 Summit meeting at Carter's pond house: ibid.

228 Carter charged officials $1.75 for breakfast: Brzezinski, *Power and Principle,* pp. 68, 69.

228 Carter and staff analysis of newspaper and magazine subscriptions: Carter margin notes on memos from Hugh Carter to President Carter, February 4 and February 8, 1977, SSF, JECL.

229 "At times, I thought he was like a sculptor": Brzezinski, *Power and Principle,* p. 522.

229 "Carter had a tremendous appetite for detail": Joseph Califano, interview by author, July 10, 1997.

229 "He was an intelligence briefer's delight": Frank Carlucci, interview by author, December 30, 1996.

229 "On the one hand it made you feel good": Robert Kimmitt, interview by author, December 9, 1996.

229 "My God, he was a leaf man!": *Time,* May 6, 1985, p. 29.

229 Carter ordered twenty-eight different reorganization studies, called in experts two and three levels down in the hierarchy: Donald A. Marchand, "Carter and the Bureaucracy," in M. Glenn Abernathy, Dilys M. Hill, and Phil Williams, eds., *The Carter Years: The President and Policy Making* (New York: St. Martin's Press, 1984), p. 201.

229 OMB officials stunned to find they were to brief the president, eight-hour meeting: Colin Campbell, *Managing the Presidency: Carter, Reagan, and the Search for Executive Harmony* (Pittsburgh: University of Pittsburgh Press, 1986), pp. 175–78; *Congressional Quarterly Guide to the Presidency* (Washington, DC: Congressional Quarterly, 1989), p. 10.

229 "Carter governed by memo": Stanly Godbold, interview by author, March 19, 1997.

229 Carter explained memos were time-savers: Carter, *Keeping Faith,* p. 56

230 "At times, Carter could also be extremely pedantic": Brzezinski, *Power and Principle,* p. 22.

230 "Do not use the sexist address": Carter margin note on memo from Bert Lance and Jim McIntyre, February 9, 1977, SSF, JECL.

230 "The president liked to have decision memoranda": Thompson, ed., *The Carter Presidency,* p. 121.

230 "President Carter called me up": ibid., p. 122.

230 "President Carter wanted to know every detail": ibid., p. 31.

230 Carter showing off in meetings: Hargrove, *Jimmy Carter as President,* p. 26.

230 "a very strange man": Pedro Sanjuan, interview by author, September 14, 1997, p. 1.

231 "had the pride an uneducated man": Hargrove, *Jimmy Carter as President,* p. 179.

231 "seemed to have that engineer's method": Thompson ed., *The Carter Presidency,* p. 244.

231 "I spent hour after hour": ibid., p. 25

231 Schlesinger on meeting with auto executives: James Schlesinger, interview by author, September 22, 1996.

231 "Carter's anti-political attitudes": Bourne, *Jimmy Carter,* p. 419.

232 "The president thought there was something tawdry": Steven V. Roberts, "Carter, at Midterm, Is Still 'Outsider' to Many in Congress," *NYT,* March 7, 1979, p. 1.

232 "to work ever harder": Bourne, *Jimmy Carter,* p. 422.

232 "He was a proud man": E. J. Dionne, Jr., "A Decade Afterward, Carter's

Record Is Defended," *WP*, November 19, 1990, p. A6.

232 "You know, after a couple of hours": Brzezinski, *Power and Principle*, p. 27.

232 "I was in the room when he fired": Thompson, ed., *The Carter Presidency*, p. 65.

232 "One of his strengths": Jody Powell, interview by author, May 4, 1997.

232 "Behavior Carter enthusiasts attribute to high integrity": *WP*, November 19, 1990, p. A6.

232 "like a movie set for a Marx Brothers picture": Frank Kessler, *The Dilemmas of Presidential Leadership: Of Caretakers and Kings* (Englewood Cliffs, NJ: Prentice-Hall, 1982), p. 67.

232 "By filling jobs with people": Bourne, *Jimmy Carter*, p. 364.

233 "That's the way I structured my warehouse": Abernathy et al., eds., *The Carter Years*, p. 151.

233 "Policy, politics, and strategy": Bourne, *Jimmy Carter*, p. 360.

233 "Carter did not like to have people": ibid.

233 "It was a mistake for all of us": Jody Powell, interview by author, May 4, 1997.

233 "Try as hard as he could": Thompson, ed., *The Carter Presidency* p. 240.

233 Jordan by his own admission: Abernathy et al., eds., *The Carter Years*, p. 153.

233 Cabinet meetings "were almost useless": Brzezinski, *Power and Principle*, p. 67.

234 "Zbig would sit at his side": Hamilton Jordan, *Crisis: The Last Year of the Carter Presidency* (New York: Putnam, 1982), pp. 46, 47.

234 "I deliberately chose advisers": Interview with Jimmy Carter, *Harvard Business Review*, March/April 1988, p. 62.

234 Vance and Brzezinski "were fighting all the time": Thompson ed., *The Carter Presidency* p. 242.

234 Vance "preferred to litigate issues endlessly": Brzezinski, *Power and Principle*, p. 42.

234 "It was an unsatisfactory relationship": Thompson ed., *The Carter Presidency*, p. 142.

235 "I thought it was important": ibid., 226.

235 "People thought that": ibid., p. 131.

235 Power in Congress suddenly fragmented: Garland A. Haas, *Jimmy Carter and the Politics of Frustration* (Jefferson, NC: McFarland & Co., 1992), pp. 64–65.

235 "There is no doubt I gave Congress": "The Man from Plains Sums It All Up," *Time*, October 11, 1982, p. 64.

235 "an unmitigated disaster": Thompson, *The Carter Presidency*, p. 121.

235 "I knew the Carter administration was finished": Bourne, *Jimmy Carter*, p. 361.

236 "We made a lot of mistakes": Jack Watson, interview by author, May 4, 1997.

236 "Hey, wait a minute": Glad, *In Search of the Great White House*, p. 420.

236 Inaugural episode; "Hannibal Jerkin"; Congressmen complaining: Glad, *In*

Search of the Great White House, p. 417.

236   "think we're just a pack of crooked whores": ibid., p. 426.

236   Water projects episode: ibid., p. 419.

236   B-1 bomber; O'Neill friend's firing episodes: ibid., pp. 422, 424.

236   "I was so mad," "All the finesse of an alcoholic hippopotamus": Terence Smith, "Carter Striving to Ease Strains with Congress," *NYT,* August 7, 1978, p. 1.

236   "Carter was not a buddy": Thompson, ed., *The Carter Presidency,* p. 240.

236   "Carter has an almost irresistible inclination": Jack Watson, interview by author, May 4, 1997.

237   "This was an important aspect of the Carter enigma": *Time,* May 6, 1985, p. 31.

237   "He felt morally superior to Congress": ibid.

237   "He viewed political problems as cube roots": Hargrove, *Jimmy Carter as President,* p. 16.

237   "Presidential power . . . is the power to persuade": Richard Tanner Johnson, *Managing the White House* (New York: Harper & Row, 1974), p. xxi.

237   "In close person-to-person contact": Thompson, *The Carter Presidency,* p. 167.

237   "He tended to speak to the public in the language of an engineer": ibid., p. 240.

237   Inter-administration confusion: Glad, *In Search of the Great White House,* pp. 440–42; Joseph A. Califano, Jr., *Governing America: An Insider's Report from the White House and the Cabinet* (New York: Simon & Schuster, 1981), p. 405.

237   Camp David retreat, purge, congressional reaction, loyalty questionairre: Glad, *In Search of the Great White House,* pp. 444, 445; "Carter's Great Purge," *Time,* July 30, 1979, p. 10–22.

238   "The more the president becomes a captive": James MacGregor Burns, *Presidential Government: The Crucible of Leadership* (Boston: Houghton Mifflin, 1966), p. 45.

239   "in the same manner": Thompson, *The Carter Presidency,* p. 165.

239   A "devastated" Carter: ibid., p. 127.

239   "He just never got his act together": Steven V. Roberts, "Analysts Give Carter Higher Marks in Foreign Affairs than in Domestic Policy," *NYT,* January 19, 1981, p. A22.

239   "The Carter administration was not a disaster": *Time,* May 6, 1985, p. 24.

239   "History will treat him more kindly": Terence Smith, "Experts See '76 Victory as Carter's Big Achievement," *NYT,* January 8, 1981, p. B14.

239   "effective executives focus on outward contribution": Peter Drucker, *The Effective Executive* (New York: Harper & Row, 1967), p. 24.

239   Henderson on "profound internal contradiction": Campbell, *Managing the Presidency,* p. 21.

240   *Wall Street Journal* editorial: "Jimmy, We Hardly Knew Ye," *WSJ,* July 18, 1988, p. 18.

240 "Every single strategic offensive weapon": Robert Gates, interview by author, July 15, 1997.

240 "Jimmy Carter in many respects laid the foundation": Robert Gates, speech at Tattered Cover bookstore, C-SPAN, June 22, 1996.

241 "The basic idea that the U.S. would rush to defend": Walter Mossberg, "High-Tech, Low-Casualty Success in War So Far Owes Much to Jimmy Carter's Defense Planning," *WSJ*, January 22, 1991, p. A16.

241 "When I hear commentators saying that the credit": ibid.

241 "When you look at the bottom line on Congress": Jack Watson, interview by author, May 4, 1997.

241 Carter domestic accomplishments: Stuart Eizenstat exit interview, January 10, 1981, JECL, p. 18–21.

241 "We deregulated oil and gas, airlines, railroads": *Harvard Business Review*, March/April 1988, p. 62.

242 "under Carter we always front-loaded pain": Thompson, *The Carter Presidency*, p. 245.

242 "could have been great": Abernathy et al., eds., *The Carter Years*, p. 76.

242 Last moments in Oval Office; "He was as near despair"; had to be physically helped: Ed Magnuson, "An End to the Long Ordeal," *Time*, February 2, 1981, p. 26.

CHAPTER 9

RONALD REAGAN: THE VISIONARY EXECUTIVE

243 In early 1996, I came across the remarkable collection of White House TV videotapes at the Ronald Reagan Library in Simi Valley, California, shot by the little-known White House Television unit of the White House Communications Agency. The videos showed President Reagan in a variety of public and ceremonial roles from the second year of his presidency until his last day in office. But the footage also included scenes of Reagan in action in the opening portions of meetings closed to the press as he conferred with congressmen, his staff, his Cabinet, and others. I learned that I was the first researcher to review these tapes, which had been filmed to document Reagan's activities for history.

According to RRL audiovisual archivist Steve Branch, 6,436 videotapes were created by White House TV during Reagan's term, at an average of fifteen minutes per tape, and the footage is split about evenly between public events and "closed" events to which the press and public were not admitted. Roughly 800 hours, then, are of Reagan in action in closed meetings. The footage was sealed the day it was recorded, shipped to the Reagan Library, then filed away and forgotten by history. The video of Reagan's closed meetings was unknown to outsiders from the opening of the library in 1992 until the author's first visit there in February 1996, during and after which logs and eventually hundreds of hours of tapes were reviewed.

The existence of a Reagan audiotaping system was revealed first in a page one, December 19, 1986, article by Bob Woodward in the *Washington Post* titled "NSC Tapes, Computers May Hold Data." Woodward cited "informed sources" describing a sophisticated Situation Room taping capability that could record meetings and presidential phone calls. The decision to install the system was made in the wake of Secretary of State Alexander Haig's statements and actions in the Situation Room after the March 1981 assassination attempt on Reagan, according to Woodward. "Senior members of the White House staff realized the need to have a verbatim record during a crisis," Woodward wrote. White House spokesman Daniel Howard said that phone calls with foreign heads of state were sometimes recorded, but the only audio system in the Situation Room was connected to a Defense Department video system that was turned on only for tests.

Also in 1986, White House spokesman Larry Speakes confirmed that some of Reagan's phone calls were taped, but the news generated little attention. In 1990, writing in the *New York Times,* Seymour Hersh reported that in 1987, during the Iran-Contra investigation, congressional staff attorney Pamela Naughton asked a White House lawyer whether there was an Oval Office taping system. "He wasn't upset," she said of the White House attorney. "His attitude was, 'Oh, gee, they finally asked.'" The White House told the investigators that there were some Situation Room tapes, but that they contained nothing relevant to their investigation. The matter was dropped. (Seymour M. Hersh, "The Iran-Contra Committees: Did they Protect Reagan?" *NYT Magazine,* April 29, 1990, p. 46.)

The surviving Reagan audiotapes were not identified until early 1996, during research for this book and a corresponding A&E special, when officials at the Ronald Reagan Library searched their vault of classified materials and found a container of twelve audiocassettes that were gathered up in the Situation Room in response to the 1987 congressional Iran-Contra inquiries, labeled, boxed, and eventually sent to the Library. According to labels on the audiocassette recordings, which are still classified, their contents include President Reagan communicating (presumably by phone) with heads of state including Israeli Prime Minister Menachem Begin (undated), President Hafez Assad of Syria (undated), President Zia of Pakistan (November 1984), a sympathy call to British Prime Minister Margaret Thatcher after she narrowly avoided being blown up by an IRA bomb in 1984, and a phone conversation with Thatcher on Grenada labeled 1:28 P.M., October 26, 1983.

One of the tapes is of a twenty-seven-minute conversation with Mexican President Miguel De La Madrid on the Contadora peace negotiations on Nicaragua on April 8, 1985. Other recordings include seemingly ceremonial greetings to or from heads of state such as Canadian Prime Minister Brian Mulroney, King Hassan of Morroco, Mohamed Nimeiri of Sudan, and Prime Minister Malcolm Fraser of Australia. According to a national security official, Reagan's tapes were usually reused or discarded after memoranda of conversation were prepared, so only a handful survive today.

Not all of the tapes are of Reagan conversing with heads of state: one is of Reagan speaking with U.S. Marine Colonel Timothy Geraghty, commander of U.S. forces in Lebanon. Five other recordings are labeled, sometimes cryptically, in a way that indicates that not only might Reagan have not been included in the conversation, but that the recordings were, contrary to White House descriptions of the system at the time, either room recordings of meetings or taped group conference calls, most connected to crises in the Mideast. The labels read: "Tape 1: (Moshe) Arens to Shultz and Weinberger"; "Tape 4: 2/6/84, Report of Rumsfeld mtg with (Amin) Gemayel (Lebanon), Rumsfeld-continuation Civil War in Lebanon"; "McFarlane & Bartholomew in Situation Room"; "Secure Conference, McFarlane/Shultz/Weinberger/ Casey/Vessey -Subj. TWA 847-MK response." The meaning of MK is thus far unknown.

243 "the saddest day of my presidency": Ronald Reagan, *An American Life* (New York: Simon & Schuster, 1992), p. 437.

243 Background to Grenada: Ed Magnuson, "D-Day in Grenada," *Time,* November 7, 1983, pp. 22–28; Caspar Weinberger, *Fighting For Peace: Seven Critical Years in the Pentagon* (New York: Warner Books, 1990), p. 124; George P. Shultz, *Turmoil and Triumph: My Years as Secretary of State* (New York: Charles Scribner's Sons, 1993), pp. 334, 335; Michael Deaver, A&E Fleisher interview; Caspar Weinberger, interview by author, July 23, 1997; Robert McFarlane, interview by author, June 30, 1997.

244 "You know, Jeane, a lot of people criticize me": Jeane Kirkpatrick, interview by author, April 1, 1997.

244 "always had the manner of an earnest gas-station attendant": Lance Morrow, "Yankee Doodle Magic," *Time,* July 7, 1986, p. 12.

244 Reagan hitting rock bottom in Las Vegas: Michael Deaver and Mickey Herskowitz, *Behind the Scenes* (New York: William Morrow, 1987), p. 40.

244 Reagan career highlights: Fred I. Greenstein, ed., *The Reagan Presidency: An Early Assessment* (Baltimore: Johns Hopkins University Press, 1983), p. 10; Reagan Presidential Library Documentation of Exhibition (Museum), Volume 1, RRL.

244 In Sacramento he developed a clean-desk, board-of-directors system: William Clark, interview by author, April 1, 1997.

244 "Let's roundtable it with the fellas": Edwin Meese, interview by author, February 10, 1997.

245 Fondness for tightly focused "mini-memos"; "If you can't reduce it to one page": William Clark, interview by author, April 1, 1997.

245 "But once he concluded the operation was necessary": Caspar Weinberger, interview by author, July 23, 1997.

245 "When he made a decision": Howard Baker, interview by author, March 25, 1997.

245 "I asked McFarlane"; "Do it": Reagan, *An American Life,* p. 450.

245 Reagan briefing legislators in Oval Room, Thatcher call: Robert McFarlane, interview by author, June 30, 1997; A&E Fleisher interview with Michael Deaver.

245 Reagan tape recordings: Richard Allen, interview by author, January 8, 1997; interviews with former national security officials involved with the taping; former congressional investigator Pamela Naughton, interview by author,

December 21, 1996; letter from RRL Supervisory Archivist Rod Soubers to author, August 26, 1996.

245 "Early on in the administration": A&E Fleisher interview with Michael Deaver.

246 "The only conversations that I can detect or find . . . We are not recording his private conversations": "White House Details Policy on Recordings," *NYT*, February 5, 1982, p. 12.

246 Details of surviving Reagan recordings: letter from RRL Supervisory Archivist Rod Soubers to author, August 26, 1996. When interviewed in 1996 and 1997, many of the key players in the Reagan administration, including top national security officials, Cabinet officers, and senior White House staff, expressed surprise that any taping occurred under Reagan. Given the compartmentalization of Reagan's national security apparatus and the rapid growth of autonomous fiefdoms in Reagan's White House, this is not surprising.

246 Thatcher-Reagan phone exchange: Robert McFarlane, interview by author, June 30, 1997.

246 "She doesn't agree with us": A&E Fleisher interview with Michael Deaver.

246 Details of White House TV Reagan coverage: Steve Branch, Reagan Library audiovisual archivist, interview by author, February 10, 1996.

247 "He was a man of extraordinary self-confidence": Jeane Kirkpatrick, interview by author, April 1, 1997.

250 "the Provincetown police force could have conquered Grenada": Alexander Haig remarks to Nikkei BP Business Forum, July 1996, New York City.

250 "caused people to see that the U.S. would use its military power": Jay Winik, *On the Brink: The Dramatic, Behind-the-Scenes Saga of the Reagan Era and the Men and Women Who Won the Cold War* (New York: Simon & Schuster, 1996), p. 287.

250 "I had an agenda I wanted to get done": Lou Cannon, *President Regan: The Role of a Lifetime* (New York: Simon & Schuster, 1991), p. 845.

250 "He had goals which were already articulated in his speeches in 1961": Jeane Kirkpatrick, interview by author, April 1, 1997.

250 "Ronald Reagan had a strategic vision": Robert Gates, speech at Tattered Cover Bookstore, Denver, C-SPAN broadcast, June 22, 1996.

250 "He established two top priorities": Martin Anderson, *Revolution* (New York: Harcourt Brace Jovanovich, 1988), p. 57.

250 "All he worried about from the time he got up": "Ronald and the Reagan Bashers," *Insight on the News,* July 22, 1991, p. 19.

250 "Harry Truman said the main job": Oval Office Exhibit, RRL.

250 "He created images on the movie screen": Elizabeth Drew, "Letter From Washington," *The New Yorker,* February 16, 1987, p. 96.

250 "Visitors to the Oval Office are coming to see": Geoffrey Kemp, interview by author, March 6, 1997.

251 In his first moments in the Oval Office, Reagan parked a sign on his desk: Richard Allen, interview by author, January 8, 1997.

251 IT CAN BE DONE; "LET US NEVER NEGOTIATE OUT OF FEAR" signs: Oval Office exhibit, RRL.

251 Jimmy Carter's nuclear codes sent to dry cleaners: Bruce Blair, *The Logic of Accidental Nuclear War* (Washington, DC: Brookings Institution, 1983), p. 294.

251 Reagan Oval Office furnishings: The Office of the Chief Usher, The White House, in cooperation with the White House Historical Association and the National Park Service, *The White House: The Ronald W. Reagan Administration, 1981–1989,* pp. 35 and 36, RRL.

251 Nancy Reagan claimed to have found beer cans and sandwiches in the drawer: Nancy Reagan with William Novak, *My Turn: The Memoirs of Nancy Reagan* (New York: Random House, 1989), pp. 23, 24.

252 Reagan Oval Office desk, "Out of respect for this office": Oval Office exhibit, RRL.

252 Cabinet Room detail: Walter Isaacson, "America's Incredible Day," *Time,* February 2, 1981, p. 15.

252 YES, NO, and MAYBE sign, jellybean facts: interviews with Reagan aides, WHTV footage.

252 "It's true hard work never killed anybody": "Will Reagan's Luck Outlast Reagan?" editorial, *NYT,* January 1, 1989, p. 11.

252 "He does not devote large chunks": Ann Reilly Dowd, "What Managers Can Learn From Manager Reagan," *Fortune,* September 15, 1986, p. 35.

252 "The problem with Carter": Anderson, *Revolution,* p. 56.

252 "There is no way you could do this job": "There Haven't Been Too Many Surprises," interview with editors, *USNWR,* July 7, 1981, p. 21.

252 Reagan schedule: James Baker, Donald Regan, Howard Baker, interviews by Jane Mayer and Doyle McManus, *Landslide: The Unmaking of the President, 1984–1988* (Boston: Houghton Mifflin, 1988), pp. 25–27.

253 "He hated to keep people waiting": Geoffrey Kemp, interview by author, March 6, 1997.

253 Reagan threw his glasses: William Clark, interview by author, April 1, 1997.

253 "She has always had more influence": Kurt Andersen, "Co-Starring at the White House," *Time,* January 14, 1985, p. 24.

253 Nancy's influence: Deaver, *Behind the Scenes,* p. 39. Nancy clashed most notoriously with the tough, acerbic Donald Regan, who later accused her of behaving "as if the office that had been bestowed on her husband by the people somehow fell into the category of worldly goods covered by the marriage vows." Regan retaliated for his humiliating forced exit in 1987 by charging that "virtually every major move and decision the Reagans made during my time as White House chief of staff was cleared in advance with a woman in San Francisco who drew up horoscopes to make certain that the planets were in a favorable alignment for the enterprise" (Donald Regan, *For the Record,* pp. 3, 288).

254 "Every afternoon he went home complete with material": Donald Regan, interview by author, January 9, 1997.

254 Reagan edits on 11/14/85 speech: White House Staff Member & Office Files, Dennis Thomas Files, Geneva Oversight Group, Reagan notes on 11/6/85, 2:15 A.M., and 11/9/85, 5:00 P.M. drafts, RRL.

254 "I don't think, at least when I was in the White House": Deaver in panel discussion, "The Reagan Legacy" forum presented by The Ronald Reagan Center for Public Affairs, May 20, 1996, transcript p. 52, RRL.

254 "amiable dunce": Cannon, *Role of a Lifetime*, p. 132. Clifford later asserted that this quote was taken out of context, but the phrase stuck.

254 "He was a hard worker and a quick study": William Clark, interview by author, April 1, 1997.

254 "Reagan never, never minded being underestimated": Richard Allen, interview by author, January 8, 1997.

254 "In my experience he was always prepared": Jeane Kirkpatrick, interview by author, April 1, 1997.

255 "Show me an executive": Cannon, *Role of a Lifetime*, p. 125.

255 "Listen, I want you folks to know I don't want any delays": Charles Wick in panel discussion, "The Reagan Legacy" forum presented by The Ronald Reagan Center for Public Affairs, May 20, 1996, transcript p. 7, RRL.

255 "You just tell the Soviets": Strobe Talbott, "Behind Closed Doors," *Time*, December 18, 1983, p. 18.

255 "He didn't hesitate to make the tough decisions": Jeane Kirkpatrick, interview by author, April 1, 1997.

255 Background and details of Reagan/Begin phone exchange over Beirut: Shultz, *Turmoil and Triumph*, pp. 69–73; Deaver, *Behind the Scenes*, p. 24; Robert C. McFarlane and Zofia Smardz, *Special Trust* (New York: Cadell & Davies, 1994), p. 209; Cannon, *Role of a Lifetime*, pp. 400, 401; William E. Smith, "Menachem, Shalom," *Time*, August 16, 1982, pp. 28–30; A&E Fleisher interview with Michael Deaver; Robert McFarlane, interview by author, June 30, 1997, and Geoffrey Kemp, interview by author, March 6, 1997.

257 "He was indefatigable when it came to working at some of those bills": A&E Fleisher interview with Michael Deaver.

257 Reagan charm offensive on Congress, congressional reactions: Kenneth Duberstein tape-recorded White House Exit Interview, December 15, 1983, RRL.

257 "We had barely got seated and Carter started lecturing us": Greenstein, ed., *The Reagan Presidency*, p. 10.

257 Congressional talking points: Reagan margin notes on memos in WHORM Subject File: Public Relations, Presidential Telephone Calls, 1982–1984, RRL.

258 Reagan's 1981 success rate with Congress of 82.4 percent was the seventh highest ever measured in 41 years by *Congressional Quarterly* from 1953–1992, but by 1987 it plunged to 43.5, the second lowest ever recorded: *Congressional Quarterly* weekly reports, December 19, 1992, p. 3896.

258 "Do what is necessary to get the program adopted": Edwin Meese, *With Reagan: The Inside Story* (Washington, DC: Regnery, 1992), p. 130.

264 "we were able to present the president with all viewpoints": James Baker, interview by author, April 1, 1997. The troika was expanded to a quadumvirate in 1982–83 with the addition of National Security Adviser William Clark (Reagan's first national security adviser, Richard Allen, reported to Reagan

through Meese). The national security adviser's job under Reagan was a revolving door; six men held the position from 1981 to 1989 (seven, counting one acting adviser).

265   Baker/Regan job switch: Cannon, *Role of a Lifetime,* pp. 553-88.

265   "He's a lot like Reagan's friends": Eleanor Clift and Thomas deFrank, "Reagan's White House," *Newsweek,* April 8, 1985, p. 23.

265   "It's clear that Regan's calling the shots": Barrett Seaman, "The 'De Facto President,'" *Time,* December 1, 1986, p. 22.

265   "grown to rely on a small group of people": A&E Fleisher interview with Michael Deaver.

265   "Reagan's management style is unique": Anderson, *Revolution,* p. 293.

265   "He was a highly intelligent man": Cannon, *Role of a Lifetime,* p. 139.

265   "Reagan is like a great racehorse": Mayer and McManus, *Landslide,* p. 32.

265   "His decisions were more visceral than cerebral": Alexander Haig, interview by author, November 25, 1996.

266   "He was flat-out not a detail man": Howard Baker, interview by author, March 25, 1997.

266   "When the staff were all organized": Geoffrey Kemp, interview by author, March 6, 1997.

266   "Everybody leaked on everybody": Robert Gates, interview by author, July 15, 1997.

266   "I use a system in which I want to hear": *Fortune,* September 15, 1986, p. 36.

266   "More than anybody it's ever been my experience to know": James Baker, interview by author, April 1, 1997.

266   "Reagan not only was aware of the contentions": Robert Gates, interview by author, July 15, 1997.

266   Reagan administration feuding: Cannon, *Role of a Lifetime,* p. 373.

267   "It's terrible": *The New Yorker,* February 16, 1987, p. 95.

267   Arms control meeting in the Situation Room: Robert Gates, interview by author, July 15, 1997.

267   Meeting of Economic Policy Council: Lance Morrow, "Yankee Doodle Magic," *Time,* July 7, 1986, p. 12.

267   "He doesn't function well if there are tensions": George J. Church, "How Reagan Decides," *Time,* December 13, 1982, p. 15.

267   "He really disliked personal confrontation": Robert McFarlane, interview by author, June 30, 1997.

267   "In this respect he was a classic": Cannon, *Role of a Lifetime,* p. 401.

267   "Reagan liked that fine": Jeane Kirkpatrick, interview by author, April 1, 1997.

267   But the missing ingredient was follow-up: Cannon, *Role of a Lifetime,* p. 373.

267   "I sat through many meetings": Geoffrey Kemp, interview by author, March 6, 1997.

267   Reagan watched *The Sound of Music:* Steven R. Weisman, "Can the Magic Prevail?" *NYT Magazine,* April 29, 1984, p. 39.

268   Reagan "seemed so serene and passive"; "Okay, you fellas work it out":
David A. Stockman, *The Triumph of Politics: Why the Reagan Revolution
Failed* (New York: Harper & Row, 1986), pp. 76, 109.

268   "He does not know in any specific way": *Time*, December 13, 1982, p. 15.

268   "Reagan seldom criticized, seldom complained": Regan, *For the Record*,
p. 268.

268   "Gee, Colin, I didn't think we signed on to run the country": Frank Carlucci,
interview by author, December 30, 1996.

268   "There's never been any discipline": *The New Yorker*, February 16, 1987,
p. 95.

268   "Nobody ever feared the old man": Phil Gailey, "Reagan's Final Days," *St.
Petersburg* (FL) *Times*, March 22, 1988, p. 4A.

268   "He could not bring himself to look somebody in the eye": Donald Regan,
interview by author, January 9, 1997.

268   Iran-Contra background: Cannon, *Role of a Lifetime*, pp. 589–737. The
Iran-Contra debacle also triggered the end of Reagan's tape recordings. After
congressional inquiries identified a handful of head-of-state phone tapings
(none related to Iran-Contra, according to Reagan officials), White House
lawyers advised that the practice of electronically recording conversations
should be discontinued, and the taping was stopped.

269   "Reagan had a total incapacity to manage": James Schlesinger, interview by
author, September 22, 1996.

269   "I'm a firm believer": interview with former Reagan aide who requested
anonymity.

269   "He does not have an inquiring style": Steven V. Roberts, "Did the Reagan
Style of Management Fail Him?" *NYT*, March 6, 1987, p. B6.

270   "with Ronald Reagan, no one is there": Cannon, *Role of a Lifetime*, p. 714.
An opposing view: Howard Baker, who took over as chief of staff earlier that
year, recalled, "The most gratifying thing was after I got there, finding out he
was fully functional and alert. There were all sorts of rumors running around
at that time." Howard Baker, interview by author, March 25, 1997.

270   "The president loved seeing the raw intelligence": Peter Schweizer, *Victory:
The Reagan Administration's Secret Strategy that Hastened the Collapse of the
Soviet Union* (New York: The Atlantic Monthly Press, 1994), p. 5.

270   Casey and NSC staff hand delivered data to Oval Office: ibid., p. 5, 6.

270   "sometimes the easiest way": Reagan, *An American Life*, p. 637.

271   Background of April 1, 1985, Buckley meeting: James Buckley, interview by
author, September 18, 1997.

273   Reykjavík summit background: Shultz, *Turmoil and Triumph*, pp. 772–76;
Cannon, *Role of a Lifetime*, pp. 78–80.

273   Reagan and Gorbachev quotes: Cannon, *Role of a Lifetime*, pp. 78–80.

275   "I was absolutely awestruck": Paul Stevens, interview by author, January 2,
1997.

276   "He knows so little and accomplishes so much": Shultz, *Turmoil and Triumph*, p. 1134.

276 "Jimmy Carter just by default left him this legacy": Daniel Wattenberg, "Ronald and the Reagan Bashers," *Insight on the News,* July 22, 1991, p. 17.

276 "You couldn't figure him out": Shultz, *Turmoil and Triumph,* p. 1136.

276 Reagan economic figures: Cannon, *Role of a Lifetime,* pp. 20, 21, 275.

276 "Every budget that I submitted to the Congress": *Insight on the News,* July 22, 1991, p. 13.

276 "We won the Cold War": Trude B. Feldman, "Ronald Reagan at 85," *WSJ,* February 5, 1996, p. A14.

276 "The democratization of the world": Richard Allen, interview by author, January 8, 1997.

276 "It was Ronald Reagan who made the critical strategic decisions": Robert Gates, speech at Tattered Cover bookstore, C-SPAN broadcast, June 22, 1996.

276 Historian Stephen Ambrose speculated that "history will remember Reagan as the first Cold War president to preside over eight years of unbroken peace, the first to reach an arms reduction accord with the Soviets, and the American president who helped make it possible for Mikhail Gorbachev to begin the process of restructuring Soviet society. Historians will also stress the gap between Reagan's domestic goals and his accomplishments. Most obvious is the deficit; what he promised to eliminate he has allowed to swell beyond comprehension." Alvin S. Felzenberg, "There You Go Again," *Policy Review,* Fall 1988, p. 30.

276 "He won the Cold War": Meese, *With Reagan,* p. 173.

277 "I believe that you surround yourself with the best people you can find": *Fortune,* September 15, 1986, p. 36.

277 Reagan's last moments in White House: Marlin Fitzwater, *Call the Briefing!: Bush and Reagan, Sam and Helen, a Decade with Presidents and the Press* (New York: Times Books, 1995) p. 364; Colin Powell with Joseph E. Persico, *My American Journey* (New York: Ballantine Books, 1996), pp. 381–82; and WHTV videotape, January 19, 1991.

CHAPTER 10

GEORGE BUSH: THE DIPLOMATIC EXECUTIVE

278 "You know, every day, many important papers": remarks to Disabled American Veterans, Washington D.C., September 12, 1991, Editors of the *New Republic, Bushisms* (New York: Workman, 1992), p. 65.

278 Gulf War introduction: "War in the Gulf," *Time,* January 28, 1991, pp. 14–70; *USNWR, Triumph Without Victory: The History of the Persian Gulf War* (New York: Times Books, 1993), pp. 212–26; David Lauter, "Bush 'Calm' as War Clock Ticks Down," *Los Angeles Times,* January 17, 1991, p. 25.

279 White House TV video crew was shooting the scene, Bush letting them into less substantive White House activity: interview with former White House TV employee who requested anonymity.

279 No other recordings under Bush: Brent Scowcroft and John Sununu, inter-

views by author, November 12, 1996, and December 7, 1996. Near-verbatim minutes of Bush's Gulf War Council meetings were taken by deputy national security adviser Robert Gates, but they are not yet declassified. Also, National Security Council note-takers were often on the line during Bush's multitudinous head-of-state telephone calls, manually taking down the conversation. Robert Gates, interview by author, July 15, 1997. These Bush records are also still classified.

279 "Anyone who taped would have been shot": Jim Cicconi, interview by author, April 13, 1997.

280 Details of Bush's tape-recorded diary: Herbert Parmet, interview by author, April 15, 1997.

280 "You work your ass off"; "The single most important job of the President": Michael Kramer, "Read My Lips," *Time,* August 20, 1990, p. 20.

280 "I've resolved all the moral issues": Colin Campbell and Bert Rockman, *The Bush Presidency: First Appraisals* (Chatham, NJ: Chatham House Publishers, 1991), p. 98.

280 "Bush's decision to commit U.S. troops": John Sununu, interview with author, December 7, 1996.

280 "You have to remember that people like George Bush": Michael Duffy and Dan Goodgame, *Marching in Place* (New York: Simon & Schuster, 1992), p. 135.

280 Bush biographical details: Jacob V. Lamar, "The Man Who Would Be President," *Time,* March 21, 1988, p. 18; *The Los Angeles Times,* September 11, 1988, p. 1; Gary Wills, "The Ultimate Loyalist," *Time,* August 22, 1988, p. 23; Ann Reilly Dowd, "Bush and Dukakis and Managers," *Fortune,* September 12, 1988, p. 111; David S. Broder, "The Team Player," *WP,* March 30, 1981, p. A8; Ronald E. Riel, "Bush's Ultimate Management Test," *Newsday,* January 15, 1989, p. 80.

281 "Bush's company did not exactly boom"; "One would think that Bush's broad-based experience": *Fortune,* September 12, 1988, p. 111.

281 "The vice president's office": *Newsday,* January 15, 1989, p. 80.

281 "Bush wasn't intellectually penetrating": ibid.

281 Frosty relations between Barbara Bush and Nancy Reagan: Ann McDaniel, "Reagan and Bush: Call It a Snub," *Newsweek,* March 9, 1992, p. 34.

282 "Jimmy Carter got credit for knowing": Ann Devroy, "Commander in Chief Leaves Military Details to the Pentagon," *WP,* January 19, 1991, p. 26.

282 "I think you have to delegate": Jack Nelson, "Tranquil Presidency Cited," *The Los Angeles Times,* September 11, 1988, p. 1.

282 "Hey, I'm gonna have to": Douglas Harbrecht et. al., "Managing the War," *Business Week,* February 4, 1991, p. 34.

282 "I think we were blessed with a group of political leaders": *USNWR, Triumph Without Victory,* p. 95.

282 "This is so different": ibid., p. 116.

282 Bush "was a hero to all of us": ibid., p. 95.

282 Bush shunned rushing to the West Wing, instead stayed in the White House: *WP,* January 19, 1991, p. 26.

283 "a sponge for detail": John Sununu quoted in Thomas M. Defrank and Ann McDaniel, "Bush: The Secret Presidency," *Newsweek,* January 1, 1990, p. 26.

283 Bush grabbed intelligence cables, stayed glued to his television for war news: Rita Beamish, "Bush Takes Hands-on Approach, but Leaves Details to the Pros," *Associated Press,* January 21, 1991.

283 Spent 80 percent of day huddled with War Council: Maureen Dowd, "War in the Gulf," *NYT,* January 23, 1991, p. 8.

283 "We were all friends": James Baker, interview by author, April 1, 1997.

283 "The Mad Dialer": Kenneth W. Thompson, ed., *The Bush Presidency: Ten Intimate Perspectives of George Bush* (University of Virginia: The Miller Center, 1997), pp. 118, 119.

283 Bush had 190 phone conferences, met with world leaders 135 times in first year: David Hoffman and Don Oberdorfer, "Bush Makes Personal Contact Hallmark of His Diplomacy," *WP,* April 13, 1990, p. 1.

283 Bush calls on Cicippio: Michael Duffy, "The Consensus," *Time,* August 21, 1989, p. 18.

283 Fake Rafsanjani call, Tiananmen Square call: *WP,* April 13, 1990, p. 1.

283 "He would turn to the phone at any opportunity": Brent Scowcroft, interview with author, November 12, 1996.

284 "speed-dial mode"; "knew twenty-four hours after the invasion": Ann Devroy and Dan Balz, "For Bush, Moment of Decision Came Saturday at Camp David," *WP,* August 9, 1990, p. 31.

284 Bush's list of calls: Campbell and Rockman, *The Bush Presidency,* pp. 204, 205.

284 Call to Mitterand: Thompson, ed., *The Bush Presidency,* p. 119.

284 "No memos were required": *Time,* August 20, 1990, pp. 20, 21.

285 "an incredibly hands-on president"; "Baker would hold the phone away from his ear": Thompson, ed., *The Bush Presidency,* p. 118.

285 "where he's coming from"; "where they're coming from": *NYT,* January 23, 1991, p. 8.

285 "I was very careful in being sure": *USNWR, Triumph Without Victory,* p. 400.

285 "We had done the right thing": Colin Powell with Joseph E. Persico, *My American Journey* (New York: Random House, 1995), pp. 524, 527, 528.

286 Bush's first moments in the White House, Reagan note, "What a sweet man": Marline Fitzwater, *Call the Briefing!: Bush and Reagan, Sam and Helen, a Decade with Presidents and the Press* (New York: Times Books, 1995), p. 366.

286 Desk drawers crammed with paraphernalia: Maureen Dowd, "The 'New' Oval Office," *NYT,* September 3, 1993, p. A15.

286 Bush routine: Ann Reilly Dowd, "How Bush Manages the Presidency," *Fortune,* August 27, 1990, p. 68; *Los Angeles Times,* January 21, 1989, p. 1; Duffy and Goodgame, *Marching in Place,* pp. 49–80; John Sununu, Brent Scowcroft, Dan Quayle, Robert Gates, interviews by the author.

286 "He reads and scans a lot of news stories": Duffy and Goodgame, *Marching in Place,* p. 77.

286   "How are the overnights, Marlin?": ibid.

286   "the catalyzing meeting, on a daily basis"; "Bush managed the presidency through a very onion-layered structure": John Sununu, interview by author, December 7, 1996.

287   Bush morning meeting: John Sununu, Brent Scowcroft, Dan Quayle, interviews by author.

287   "Bush had a knack for putting people at ease": Powell, *My American Journey*, p. 504.

287   "He always wanted people to be comfortable": Dan Quayle, *Standing Firm* (New York: HarperCollins, 1994), p. 93.

287   "This is coffee, this is tea": *Newsweek*, January 20, 1990, p. 26.

287   Bush would fiddle with Swiss Army knife: *NYT*, September 3, 1993, p. A15.

287   "If you're so damned smart": Michael Duffy, "Mr. Consensus," *Time*, August 21, 1989, p. 16.

287   "He is just as likely to pick up the telephone": *Los Angeles Times*, January 21, 1989, p. 1.

287   "Bush came up through the system": James Baker, interview by author, April 1, 1997.

287   "his own chief of staff"; "his own best intelligence agent": Dan Goodgame, "Rude Awakening," *Time*, March 20, 1989, p. 22.

287   attempted coup against Noriega: *Fortune*, August 27, 1990, p. 68.

288   Bush cleaned out in-box several times a day: Thompson, ed., *The Bush Presidency*, p. 92.

288   "Reagan was comfortable": *Fortune*, August 27, 1990, p. 68.

288   "His instinct is to return as many phone calls as possible": Duffy and Goodgame, *Marching in Place*, p.75.

288   "And yes, he likes to check": *Fortune*, August 27, 1990, p. 68.

288   Bush Oval Office detail: John Aloysius Farrell, "George Bush, War, and the Spirit of American Exceptionalism," *Boston Globe Magazine*, March 31, 1991, p. 12.

288   Bush afternoon and evening routine, thank-you notes: Duffy and Goodgame, *Marching in Place*, p. 54; *Time*, August 21, 1989, p. 16.

288   "a throwback to the patrician 'wise men'": David Hoffman, "Zip My Lips: Bush's Secret Conduct of U.S. Policy," *WP*, January 7, 1990, p. B1.

289   Scowcroft secret visit with Chinese leaders, didn't tell Sununu: *WP*, January 7, 1990, p. 1.

289   "If we cannot maintain proper secrecy": *Newsweek*, January 7, 1990, p. 26.

289   "intellectually very curious": Dan Quayle, interview by author, May 20, 1997.

289   "I've been to Cabinet meetings": *Time*, August 21, 1989, p. 16.

289   Aides organized policy debates, multiple advocacy; "I've known pretty well how I want to reach decisions"; "He doesn't want filters": ibid.

289   "There are no ideologues around George Bush": *Time*, March 21, 1988, p. 18.

289   "George Bush is very loyal to people": *Time*, August 21, 1989, p. 16.

289   "bland, upper-class, middlebrow": David Brock, "Foxy Roger," *New York* magazine, November 17, 1997, p. 33.

289 "very small, very clubby": *Fortune*, August 27, 1990, p. 68.

289 "Bush wants twins around him": *NYT*, May 6, 1990, p. 3.

290 Quayle traced troubles: Dan Quayle, interview by author, May 20, 1997.

290 Bush "didn't mind varying viewpoints": Dan Quayle, ibid.

290 "George Bush always was willing to listen": John Sununu, interview by author, December 7, 1996.

290 "I thank my lucky stars": *Fortune*, August 27, 1990, p. 68.

290 "Loyalty is not a character flaw": *WP*, January 7, 1990, p. B1.

290 Marching orders: *Time*, August 21, 1989, p. 16.

290 "the absence of creative tension": *NYT Magazine*, March 25, 1990, p. 30.

291 "Baker dots every *i* and crosses every *t*"; "This office intimidates people": Maureen Dowd and Thomas L. Friedman, "The Fabulous Bush and Baker Boys," *NYT Magazine*, May 6, 1990, p. 34.

291 "President Bush, like President Reagan": James Baker, interview by author, April 1, 1997.

291 "Fuck you, Kemp!" story: Fitzwater, *Call the Briefing*, pp. 350, 351.

291 "He dosen't seem to stand for anything": *Newsweek*, March 9, 1992 p. 34.

291 "I am a practical man": John G. Yang, "An Enigmatic President Is a Study in Contrasts," *WP*, February 12, 1992, p. 1.

291 "I am no mystic": Ann Reilly Dowd, "Bush and Business," *Fortune*, December 5, 1988, p. 40.

291 "He refuses to be managed": Duffy and Goodgame, *Marching in Place*, p. 70.

291 "Some see leadership as high drama": Inaugural address.

292 "Fluency in English": Editors of the *New Republic, Bushisms*, p. 43.

292 "I'm not good at expressing": Campbell and Rockman, *The Bush Presidency*, p. 145.

292 "The camera shrinks him": Michael Kramer, "A New Breeze Is Blowing," *Time*, January 30, 1989, p. 18.

292 "Hey, listen": Michael Duffy, "Mr. Consensus," *Time*, August 21, 1989, p. 22.

292 "Look, if an American marine is killed": Editors of the *New Republic, Bushisms*, p. 65.

292 "What his administration never had": Quayle, *Standing Firm*, p. 94.

292 "This is a White House": "Chief of Staff Sununu: Bush's Fiery Enforcer," *WP*, January 10, 1990, p. 4.

292 "I enjoy trying to put the coalition together": Jean Edward Smith, *George Bush's War* (New York: Holt, 1992), p. 163.

292 "On a scale of one to ten": Ann Reilly Dowd, "Will George Bush Really Change?" *Fortune*, June 29, 1992, p. 63.

293 "All stop and no go": Ann Devroy, "From Promise to Performance," *WP*, January 17, 1993, p. 1.

293 "finds it hard to get emotionally": Maureen Dowd, "Biography of a Candidate," *NYT*, August 20, 1992, p. 1.

293 "After Desert Storm": Thompson, ed., *The Bush Presidency*, p. 39.

293 "midway through what we still thought": Quayle, *Standing Firm*, p. 244.

293 "I don't want to do anything dumb": Duffy and Goodgame, *Marching in Place*, pp. 70, 71.

293 "In many areas": Quayle, *Standing Firm*, p. 245.

294 "failed governor of a small state": *WP*, January 17, 1993, p. 1.

294 "There was a lot of staff chaos": Dan Quayle, interview by author, May 20, 1997.

294 "No one could make a decision": Fitzwater, *Call the Briefing*, p. 322.

294 "When Bush and others in the administration began speaking": Thompson, ed., *The Bush Presidency*, p. 48.

294 "Reductions in the deficit": Nicholas F. Brady, "George Bush Was Right," *WSJ*, March 9, 1998, p. 18.

294 "I lost in '92 because": Kathy Lewis, "Let History Be My Judge, Bush Says of Library," *Dallas Morning News*, November 2, 1997, p. 1.

295 "This is a legacy": *WP*, January 17, 1993, p. 1.

295 "I would submit to you that the national security apparatus": James Baker, interview by author, April 1, 1997.

295 "It was always Bush": Robert Gates, interview by author, July 15, 1997.

295 "Was he a man of vision?": Clifford Krauss, "Bush Is a Self-Effacing Figure at Meeting on His Leadership," *NYT*, April 20, 1997, p. 24.

295 "My mother told me": remarks at 1997 Hofstra conference on the Bush presidency.

296 "I think I will be remembered": *Dallas Morning News*, November 2, 1997, p. 1.

CHAPTER 11

BILL CLINTON: THE CHAOTIC EXECUTIVE

297 "Wait a minute!"; Clinton and staff quotes and Oval Office activity: White House TV tape of Clinton in Oval Office, December 15, 1994, 7:50–8:15 P.M., consulted at National Archives Office of Presidential Libraries, Washington, DC. This White House TV videotape, transferred by the Clinton White House to the National Archives files and identified during research for this book in 1996, replicates the network TV feed, but includes footage of the Oval Office before and after the speech was made.

298 Dan Rather and Tom Brokaw comments: Tom Shales, "Bill Clinton, Hitting His Stride," *WP*, December 16, 1994, p. F1.

298 December 1, 1994 meeting, Clinton and Panetta and quotes: Evan Thomas, "On Target," *Newsweek*, November 18, 1996, pp. 36, 37.

298 "On a scale of one to ten": *Nightline*, ABC, October 7, 1997.

298 "You don't want to be in the room": Elizabeth Drew, *On the Edge: The Clinton Presidency* (New York: Simon & Schuster, 1994), p. 96.

298 Clinton Oval office detail: Jula Koncius, "The Courage to Change Curtains," *WP*, April 8, 1993, p. 9; Jula Koncius, "The Trappings of Power," *WP*, September 9, 1993, p. T11; Maureen Dowd, "The New Oval Office," *NYT*,

September 3, 1993, p. G1; Hugh Sidey, "Home Sweet White House," *Time*, October 11, 1993, p. 23.

299 February 1993 State of the Union; "he's riffing": Dan Balz and Ruth Marcus, "The Windup for the Pitch," *WP*, March 7, 1993, p. A1.

299 1995 State of the Union: Ann Devroy, "Still Emitting Mixed Messages," *WP*, February 12, 1995, p. A16.

300 Clinton studied videotapes of Reagan, chucked short pants: ibid, p. 48.

301 "Buy it": *Newsweek*, November 18, 1996, p. 72.

301 "The president controlled all of this": ibid.

301 "If you want this budget signed": ibid., p. 54.

301 "Hell, you work for Bill Clinton": ibid., p. 71.

301 "Energy in the executive": Alexander Hamilton, *The Federalist Papers*, Number 70.

302 "If you have energy": Sidney Blumenthal, "The Education of a President," *The New Yorker*, January 24, 1994, p. 33.

302 Clinton meeting JFK: Jason Vest, "Bill Clinton's Handshake with History," *WP*, July 26, 1993, p. B1.

302 "we want you to feel very much at home": Michael R. Beschloss, "Camelot (Not)," *WP*, November 15, 1992, p. C1.

302 "Someday I'm gonna have that job": *WP*, July 26, 1993, p. B1.

302 Clinton biographical details: Burt Solomon, "Clinton's Hands-on Management Might Not Work in Washington," *National Journal*, September 19, 1992, p. 2136.

302 "The principal strategist": David Maraniss, "Bill Clinton: Born to Run," *WP*, July 13, 1992, p. 1.

303 "instinct to try to make you feel good": *National Journal*, September 19, 1992, p. 2136.

303 "It's almost impossible not to be charmed": Todd S. Purdum, "Facets of Clinton," *NYT*, May 16, 1996, p. 36.

303 "The guy will pat you on the back": David Maraniss, "The Comeback Kid Is Back—Again," *WP*, August 27, 1996, p. 1.

303 "everything from policy to strategy": *National Journal*, September 19, 1992, p. 2136.

304 "I felt like the dog": Dan Balz, "From Promise to Performance," *WP*, January 17, 1993, p. 1.

304 "His management style": Michael Duffy, "That Sinking Feeling," *Time*, June 7, 1993, p. 22.

304 In 1992 he became enamored with the book *Lincoln on Leadership*: Michael Kramer, "What He Will Do," *Time*, November 16, 1992, p. 31.

304 "The key to being an effective political leader": ibid.

305 "What I'll never understand is how a man with such genius": John Brummett, *Highwire: From the Backroads to the Beltway—The Education of Bill Clinton* (New York: Hyperion, 1994), p. 44.

305 "There is no system there": Ann Devroy, "How the White House Runs and Stumbles," *WP*, November 9, 1993, p. 1.

305 "They are good at takeoffs": ibid.

305 "The fundamental problem was": Christopher Ogden, "How I Coped with Chaos at the White House," *Fortune,* March 17, 1997, p. 146.

305 "The president is into everything": *WP*, November 9, 1993, p. 1.

305 "He wants to hear various aspects": Ron Fournier, "Clinton: A Hands-on Manager with a Concept of Teamwork," *Associated Press*, March 27, 1993.

305 "The fundamental problem is": Burt Solomon, "Clinton's New Taskmaster Takes Charge," *National Journal*, August 6, 1994, p. 1872.

305 "A lot of decisions are put on his desk": ibid.

305 "President Clinton is inclusive": *WP*, November 9, 1993, p. 1.

305 "He's like a kid": Susan Page, "Clinton's First Year," *Newsday,* December 19, 1993, sec. 7, p. 70.

305 "He doesn't want to do everything": *National Journal,* September 19, 1992, p. 2136.

305 Clinton spent days huddled with budget director Panetta; "That was fun!"; "He's the great synthesizer": *The New Yorker,* January 24, 1994, p. 37.

305 "If I have brought anything": "The Clinton Record: Interview with Clinton," *NYT,* July 28, 1996, p. 1.

306 "He has a subtle mind": *WP,* January 17, 1993, p. 1.

306 "Clinton is not sequential": Drew, *On the Edge,* p. 67.

306 "If you go to him and say": George J. Church, "The Learning Curve," *Time,* September 2, 1996, p. 33.

306 "You do not stick a twenty-page memo on his desk": Ann Devroy and Ruth Marcus, "Clinton's First 100 Days," *WP,* April 29, 1993, p. 1.

306 "Clinton never stops thinking": Drew, *On the Edge,*, p. 67.

306 "They've got to get somebody to manage": *Time,* June 7, 1993, p. 22.

306 "He doesn't want hierarchy": Drew, *On the Edge,* p. 99.

306 "B doesn't give a fig": Robert B. Reich, *Locked in the Cabinet* (New York: Knopf, 1997), p. 221.

306 "Everybody goes down the court": *WP,* November 9, 1993, p. 1.

306 "the meetingest fellow I know": Garry Wills, "The Clinton Principle," *NYT,* January 19, 1997, p. 28.

306 Meetings could have been "held in Yankee Stadium": Ann Devroy, "Loops of Power Snarl in Clinton White House," *WP,* April 3, 1994, p. 1.

306 By 8:00 or 9:00 P.M., staffers would groan as Clinton said "let's continue," and the sessions droned on for hours more: Drew, *On the Edge*, pp. 67, 68.

307 Clinton didn't want debates settled: *WP,* April 29, 1993, p. 1.

307 An aide called Clinton "the staffer-in-chief": ibid.

307 "He really loves the intellectual give-and-take": *Time,* June 7, 1993, p. 22.

307 "I may have overextended myself": *WP,* April 29, 1993, p. 1.

307 "you wouldn't consider giving him a job anywhere": Dan Balz, "Perot Slams the President," *WP,* May 27, 1993, p. A1.

307 "One of the things that you risk": Gwen Ifill, "Clinton Sees Need to Focus His Goals and Sharpen Staff," *NYT,* May 5, 1993, p. 1.

307 Legislator asked Clinton to "stop the policy-a-day nonsense," congressmen applauded: *Time,* June 7, 1993, p. 22.

307 "If Mack or Mark were really angry at you": ibid.

307 "What the president needs is an enforcer": R. W. Apple, Jr., "An Offering to the Wolves," *NYT,* May 3, 1993, p. 1.

307 McLarty took the president by the arm, "Get to the point, Haiti": Brummett, *Highwire,* p. 44.

308 "help me interpret Washington"; "the fucking Washington crowd": *Newsweek,* November 18, 1996, p. 37.

308 "He'd like more order": *The New Yorker,* January 24, 1994, pp. 36, 37.

308 "I think in a way it may be my fault": *WP,* November 9, 1993, p. 1.

308 "Give me that 'no' list": *The New Yorker,* January 24, 1994, p. 40.

308 "He knew which buttons to push": ibid.

308 "We've had too many near-death experiences in here": *WP,* November 9, 1993, p. 1.

309 Mrs. Clinton helped supervise office assignments: Margaret Carlson, "At the Center of Power," *Time,* May 10, 1993, p. 28.

309 Mrs. Clinton signed off on senior White House appointments, reportedly blocked the hiring of white male candidates: Kenneth T. Walsh et al., "Taking Their Measure," *USNWR,* January 31, 1994, p. 46.

309 Mrs. Clinton helped choose federal judges: David Maraniss, "First Lady of Paradox," *WP,* January 15, 1995, p. A1.

309 "the most complicated relationship I have ever seen": *NYT Magazine,* May 16, 1996, p. 62.

309 "I want to see a plan": Bob Woodward, *The Agenda: Inside the Clinton White House* (New York: Simon & Schuster, 1994), p. 255.

309 An expression that said "I've already thought about that"; "kind of Nazi-ish feeling" of "get on the program or get off the train": *WP,* January 15, 1995, p. 1.

309 "The president sits in the middle of the table": *Time,* May 10, 1993, p. 28.

310 "A speech that needs a rewrite, get Hillary": ibid.

310 Residents of "Hillaryland" were loyal, staff closed ranks and refused to leak, endeared herself, necklace of Christmas lights, goofy phrases: *Newsweek,* November 18, 1996, pp. 74, 77.

310 "an asset to women eighteen to thirty-four ": *WP,* January 15, 1995, p. 1.

310 Details of Mrs. Clinton's health care planning: *Time,* May 10, 1993, p. 28; Abigail Trafford, "Mistakes Sank Health Reform, Clinton Admits," *WP,* April 21, 1996, p. 1; Michael Winer and Robert Pear, "President Finds Benefits in Defeat of Health Care," *NYT,* July 30, 1996, p. B8; *NYT Magazine,* May 16, 1996, pp. 33, 34.

310 "The person who's in charge shouldn't sleep with the president": *WP,* April 21, 1996, p. 1.

310 "I knew that she could manage"; "The reaction was more negative"; "In retrospect, I think that was a mistake": *WP,* April 21, 1996, p. 1.

311 Mrs. Clinton retreated from public policy arena, helped recruit Dick Morris, helped author the campaign strategy, in 1997 reemerged with a new cause: Karen Tumulty, "Turning Fifty," *Time,* October 20, 1997, p. 38.

311 Clinton regularly offered the floor to Gore; put Gore on speakerphone; "His voice is heard on every policy decision"; "He does more to make this

place work"; partnerships with Chernomyrdin, Mubarak, and Mandela: *WP*, August 26, 1996, p. 1.

311 "What the president needs": Ann Devroy, "Clinton Names Panetta Chief of Staff," *WP*, June 28, 1994, p. 1.

311 "Clinton recognizes his own mistakes": Ann Reilly Dowd, "Can Clinton Learn How to Manage?" *Fortune*, October 3, 1994, p. 16.

311 "The one thing he wants is tough management": Ann Devroy, "Still Emitting Mixed Messages," *WP*, February 12, 1995, p. 16.

312 Panetta's first move was to ask for an organizational chart: John F. Harris, "The Man Who Squared the Oval Office," *WP*, January 4, 1997, p. A1.

312 "As far as I know, anybody who walked down the hall"; Panetta seized control of the President's schedule and appointments: ibid.; see also *Fortune*, March 17, 1997, p. 147.

312 "Look at the past week and weep": *WP*, February 12, 1995, p.16.

312 "One of President Clinton's main problems": ibid.

312 "no deep thought was given": ibid.

312 "Ask yourself, two years into an administration": ibid.

313 "Clinton is very bright and capable": Bruce W. Nelan, "The No Guts, No Glory Presidency," *Time*, November 22, 1993, p. 48.

313 Woolsey boycotted briefings: Walter Pincus, "PDB, The Only News Not Fit for Anyone Else to Read," *WP*, August 27, 1994, p. 7.

313 "First of all, it's a more disciplined": "Blending Force with Diplomacy," *Time*, October 31, 1994, p. 35.

313 "Certainly I would have to rate Bill Clinton": Jeffrey H. Birnbaum, "A Week in the Life," *WSJ*, March 9, 1993, p. 1.

313 "He has had them jogging": *The New Yorker*, January 24, 1994, p. 38.

313 "He asks a lot of questions": ibid.

313 "You know I love this stuff": *WSJ*, March 9, 1993, p. 1.

313 "The president was far more successful": *The New Yorker*, January 24, 1994, p. 38.

314 "most powerful setter of mood": *WP*, August 27, 1996, p. 1.

314 "I need two hours to detoxify": *Newsweek*, November 18, 1996, p. 54.

314 "Gingrich found himself caught in a trance": ibid.

314 "There is this residual belief": ibid.

314 "The White House didn't have a clue"; "They were pushing all the wrong buttons": John M. Broder and Lizette Alvarez, "Democrats Sound Like a Couple in Need of Therapy," *NYT*, November 15, 1997, p. 11.

314 "It reminds me of how I got my term papers done": John M. Broder, "The Trade Bill," *NYT*, November 11, 1997, p. 1.

314 Discovery of "Coffee Tapes": On July 26, 1996, I was in the White House mansion using a press pass granted by the White House for research on this book, following President Clinton around as he conducted events open to the press, when I asked a young White House aide whether White House Television (WHTV) was still filming presidential events. The aide said that White House TV was indeed still in action, and pointed to an audiovisual

crew in the back of the East Room. Within days, I learned that the White House had made available a limited amount of this footage, mostly of events open to the press during Clinton's first term, for research at the National Archives in Washington, DC, where I soon reviewed the footage.

Later in the summer of 1996, I began asking the Clinton White House press office for White House TV footage of Clinton at work in open or closed White House meetings, and for copies of videotapes of Clinton Oval Office speeches. Despite the fact that some of the requested footage was of public events, and that the 111-member, $122 million-a-year White House Communications Agency unit was a taxpayer-funded operation, the Clinton press office turned down my requests, saying they were under no legal obligation to let me view the footage.

In July 1997, during the congressional investigation into campaign finance abuse, it occurred to me that the White House TV unit might have covered some of the infamous Clinton coffees with political contributors. I contacted *Washington Post* reporter George Lardner, Jr., who had been covering White House recordings since the days of Watergate, and who in March 1997 had published a story on the discovery (triggered by research for this book) of secret Eisenhower Oval Office recordings at the Eisenhower Library in Kansas. I told Lardner about White House TV, and suggested that since the crew seemed to cover all presidential events, footage may have been shot of Clinton with people such as Democratic fundraisers John Huang and Johnny Chung, which would shed some light on the fundraising story. I suggested he inform congressional investigators of the tapes, which he soon did, and that they might have better luck than I was having. Did they ever.

On Monday, October 6, 1997, Lardner reported in the *Post*'s lead story that the White House was turning over to congressional investigators White House Television footage of forty-four coffee events with wealthy political supporters shot between August 3, 1995, and August 23, 1996. The footage included clips of Clinton meeting and greeting contributors in the Oval Office, Map Room, and Roosevelt Room of the White House. Congress had subpoenaed all materials connected to political fundraising in April 1997, including videos, but Lardner's tip to Senate Committee official Paul Clark to suggest pressing the White House specifically for WHCA coffee tapes spurred another subpoena in August, and the belated discovery of the tapes in October. Ever since April 1997, congressional investigators had been asking for all relevant documents and materials on White House fundraising, including any tapes, but the White House said there weren't any. It wasn't until they were pressed specifically for coffee tapes that the tapes were found. On October 1, White House associate counsel Michael X. Imbroscio discovered the forty-four coffee tapes and another 100 additional video- and audiotapes of "DNC finance-related events." George Lardner and Senate Committee official Paul Clark, interviews by the author, October 1997.

315 "They thwarted our subpoenas": CNN, October 8, 1997.

315 Clinton had a fondness for the White House television crews: interview

with former White House Television staff member who requested anonymity.

315 "They're not incriminating": Richard Lacayo, "It's Groundhog Day," *Time,* October 27, 1997, p. 43.

316 "One of the biggest, most talented": *NYT Magazine,* May 16, 1996, p. 36.

317 Oval Office peepholes, tracking, tunnel: Kenneth T. Walsh, "Through the White House Peepholes," *USNWR,* February 23, 1998, p. 34.

320 "I'm a lot like Baby Huey"; "I'm fat, I'm ugly": Nancy Gibbs and Michael Duffy, "Fall of the House of Newt," *Time,* November 16, 1998, p. 39.

320 "I'm not perfect, but I work hard": Richard Reeves, *Running in Place: How Bill Clinton Disappointed America* (Kansas City: Andrews & McMeel, 1996), p. 26.

320 Sources for possibility of Clinton taping system: Vincent Morris, Brian Blomquist, and Deborah Orin, "Lott: Probe Reports White House Taped Bill's Sexgate Calls," *The New York Post,* February 9, 1999, p. 4; "Senate Resumes Impeachment Deliberations; White House Again Denies Existence of Secret Tapes," *The White House Bulletin,* February 10, 1999; Chris Moeser and David Wagner, "Kyl: Feds Taped Intern, Clinton Calls," *The Arizona Republic,* February 10, 1999, p. 1; Elaine S. Povich, Knut Royce, and William Douglas, "The Impeachment Trial: Senate Won't Pause for Tape Tip, White House Denies Recording Phone Calls," *Newsday,* February 10, 1999, p. 25.

EPILOGUE

324 Federal and state taping consent laws: Jim Dempsey, Center for Democracy and Technology official, interview by author, September 10, 1998; Reporters Committee for Freedom of the Press Web site, "Can We Tape?" section, October 1998 (http://www.rcfp.org/taping).

324 "The worst thing in our society": Hugh Sidey, "LBJ, Hoover and Domestic Spying," *Time,* February 10, 1975, p. 16.

325 FBI requesting expansion of wiretapping ability: John Schwartz, "FBI Lists Technical Needs for Wiretaps in Digital Age," *WP,* January 15, 1997, p. 2.

325 Court-authorized wiretaps reach 2 million private conversations: Vivienne Walt, "Shelves of Snooping Aids Make Privacy Hard to Come By," *NYT,* May 21, 1998, p. G8.

325 FISA wiretaps: see Suzanne Crowell, Holly Syrrakos, "The Government's 'Right' to Snoop" (letter), *WP,* May 11, 1998, p. 22; Fran Fragos Townsend, "Limits on Counterespionage" (Op-Ed), *WP,* May 27, 1998, p. 17. See also: Richard Willing, "With Secret Court's OK, Wiretapping on the Rise," *USA Today,* September 30, 1998, p. 1; Benjamin Wittes, "The Catch-22 Law" (Op-Ed), *WP,* April 21, 1998, p. 21; "Intelligence on the FISA Court," *Legal Times,* April 14, 1997, p. 18; Daniel J. Malooly, "Physical Searches Under FISA: A Constitutional Analysis," *American Criminal Law Review,* January 1998.

325 "We're on the precipice"; "That's not a metaphor but a reality": Stephen C. Fehr, "Spying Eyes," *WP,* August 28, 1997, p. B1.

325 Electronic surveillance in sixty cities and New York: Mark Boal, "Spycam

City," *Village Voice*, October 6, 1998, pp. 40, 43.

325 Legal to place cameras in locker rooms and bathrooms: *Village Voice*, October 6, 1998, p. 43.

325 Rise in security device sales, increase of surveillance in society: Margaret Webb Pressler, "Listening Is In," *WP*, January 23, 1998, p. D2.

325 Palm-sized and credit card–sized recorders: Joann S. Lublin, "Secret Taping Goes on Outside the Beltway, Too," *WSJ*, February 2, 1998, p. B1.

325 Shutdown of the Spy Factory: Sharon Walsh, "Owner of Spy Shop Chain, 2 Executives Plead Guilty," *WP*, March 11, 1997, p. C1.

326 FBI busting largest price-fixing conspiracy; Archer Daniels Midland bust: Kurt Eichenwald, "The Tale of the Secret Tapes," *NYT*, November 16, 1997, Section 3, p. 1.

326 Sales of security cameras approaching $6 billion: *Village Voice*, October 6, 1998, p. 40.

326 "random and periodic silent monitoring": ibid.

326 Use of recordings against and by companies: *WSJ*, February 2, 1998, p. 1.

326 APEC story: Timothy W. Maier, "APEC-Espionage" series, *Insight on the News*, September 15, September 29, and October 20, 1997.

327 Bugging of Japan/U.S. talks; "It was a remarkable performance": David E. Sanger and Tim Weiner, "Emerging Role for the C.I.A.," *NYT*, October 15, 1995, p. 1.

327 French expulsion of U.S. agents: Tim Weiner, "C.I.A. Faces Issue of Economic Spying," *NYT*, February 23, 1995, p. 12.

327 The story of ECHELON was broken by New Zealand activist Nicky Hager in his book *Secret Power: New Zealand's Role in the International Spy Network*, published in New Zealand in 1996. Details from Andrew Wood, *BBC Business*, December 18, 1997; Jason Vest, "Listening In," *Village Voice*, August 18, 1998, pp. 33–35; Claudio Gatti, "Eavesdropping on the Whole World," *Il Mondo* (Italy), March 20 and March 27, 1998, feature story on ECHELON reprinted in *World Press Review*, July 1998.

327 "routine and indiscriminate": *BBC Business*, December 18, 1997.

328 "Information collected": *World Press Review*, July 1998, p. 21.

328 See also: Neal Thompson, "NSA Listening Practices Called European 'Threat,'" *Baltimore Sun*, September 19, 1998, p. 9; Simon Davies, "Connected," *London Daily Telegraph*, July 16, 1998, p. 6; Jamie Dettmer, "Report Spotlights Anglo-U.S. Big Brotherhood," *Insight on the News*, August 17, 1998, p. 6; Duncan Campbell, "Computing and the Net," *Guardian* (London), September 10, 1998; Miu Oikawa Dieter, "EU Urges Debate on U.S. Wiretapping of Foreign Firms," *Japan Economic Newswire*, October 10, 1998.

328 Senator Frank Church quotes: NBC *Meet the Press*, August 17, 1975, cited in V. James Bamford, *The Puzzle Palace: A Report on America's Most Secret Agency* (New York: Penguin Books, 1983), p. 379.

328 "unrelenting intensity of decision making": Margaret Carlson, "Where's Al?" *Time*, September 13, 1993, p. 29.

330 Truman on presidency: CBS Television broadcast, *Five Presidents on the Presidency*, 1973.

Index

About the Author

In 1998 William Doyle won the Writers Guild of America Award for Best Documentary for the A&E Investigative Reports special, *The Secret White House Tapes,* which he co-wrote and co-produced.

The *Washington Post* wrote that the program was "fascinating" and "brings us as close to the presidency as we are likely to get."

He lives in New York and can be reached via e-mail at billdoyleusa@yahoo.com.